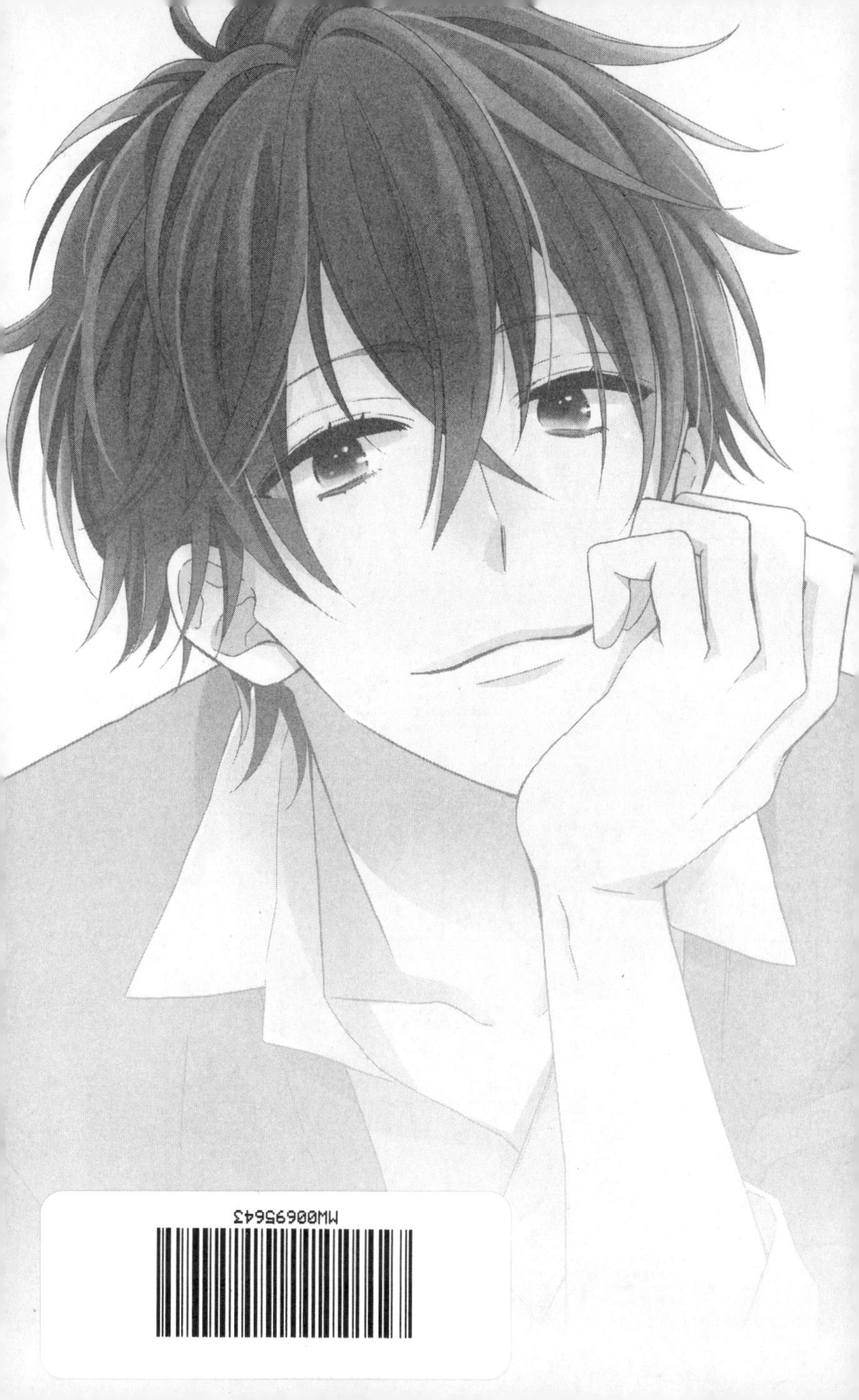

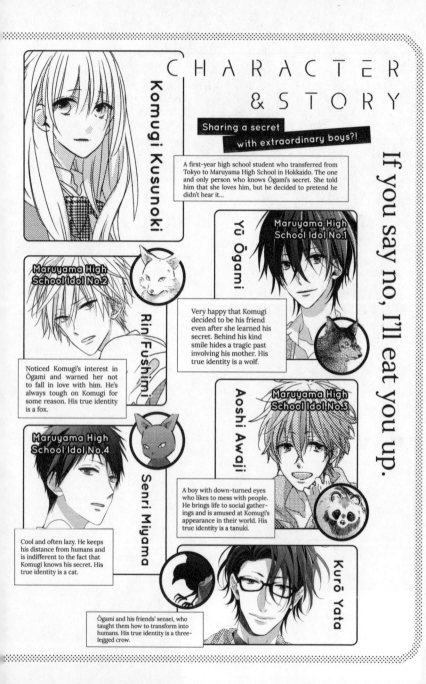

CHARACTER & STORY

Sharing a secret with extraordinary boys?!

If you say no, I'll eat you up.

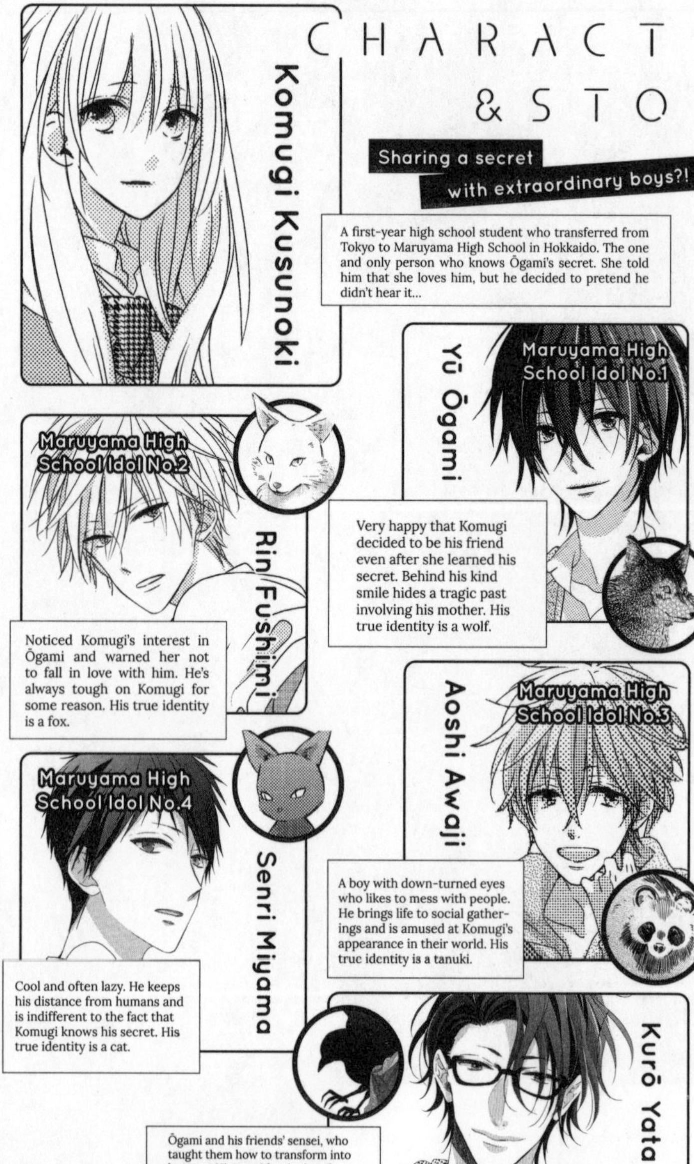
Komugi Kusunoki
Maruyama High School Idol No.1
Yū Ōgami
Maruyama High School Idol No.2
Rin Fushimi
Maruyama High School Idol No.3
Aoshi Awaji
Maruyama High School Idol No.4
Senri Miyama
Kurō Yata

Komugi Kusunoki

A first-year high school student who transferred from Tokyo to Maruyama High School in Hokkaido. The one and only person who knows Ōgami's secret. She told him that she loves him, but he decided to pretend he didn't hear it...

Yū Ōgami — Maruyama High School Idol No.1

Very happy that Komugi decided to be his friend even after she learned his secret. Behind his kind smile hides a tragic past involving his mother. His true identity is a wolf.

Rin Fushimi — Maruyama High School Idol No.2

Noticed Komugi's interest in Ōgami and warned her not to fall in love with him. He's always tough on Komugi for some reason. His true identity is a fox.

Aoshi Awaji — Maruyama High School Idol No.3

A boy with down-turned eyes who likes to mess with people. He brings life to social gatherings and is amused at Komugi's appearance in their world. His truc identity is a tanuki.

Senri Miyama — Maruyama High School Idol No.4

Cool and often lazy. He keeps his distance from humans and is indifferent to the fact that Komugi knows his secret. His true identity is a cat.

Kurō Yata

Ōgami and his friends' sensei, who taught them how to transform into humans. His true identity is a three-legged crow.

The boy Komugi meets at her new school...is actually a wolf! Despite knowing his true identity, she can't help but feel close to him. When she confesses her love to him, he flat-out rejects her.

Then, out of the blue, Yata appears. He's the man who taught Yū Rin, Aoshi, and Senri how to transform into their human forms. Yata expresses an interest in Komugi, the girl who can't be hypnotized. But her heart is preoccupied with her longing to be by Yū's side.

When Yū starts to fear that Komugi is becoming distant, the way he reaches out to her ends up hurting her even more. She runs away in tears, straight into the arms of...?!

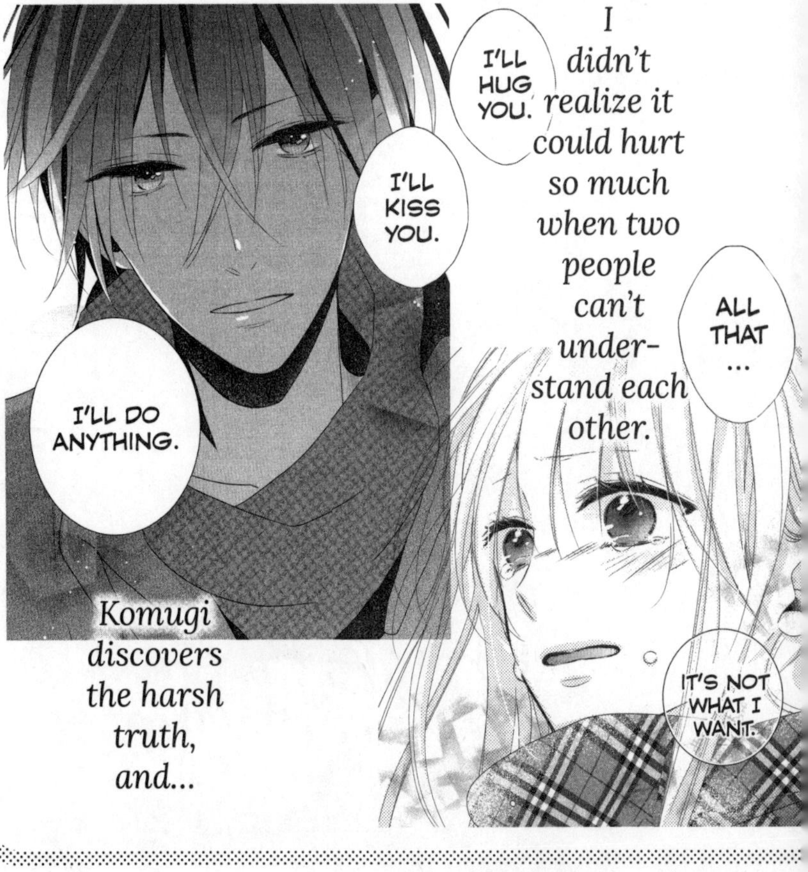
I didn't realize it could hurt so much when two people can't under-stand each other.
ALL THAT ...
I'LL HUG YOU.
I'LL KISS YOU.
I'LL DO ANYTHING.
IT'S NOT WHAT I WANT.
Komugi discovers the harsh truth, and...

That Wolf-Boy is Mine!

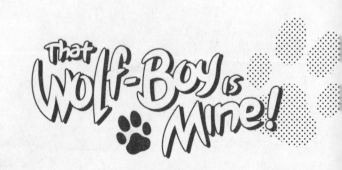

Chapter 9

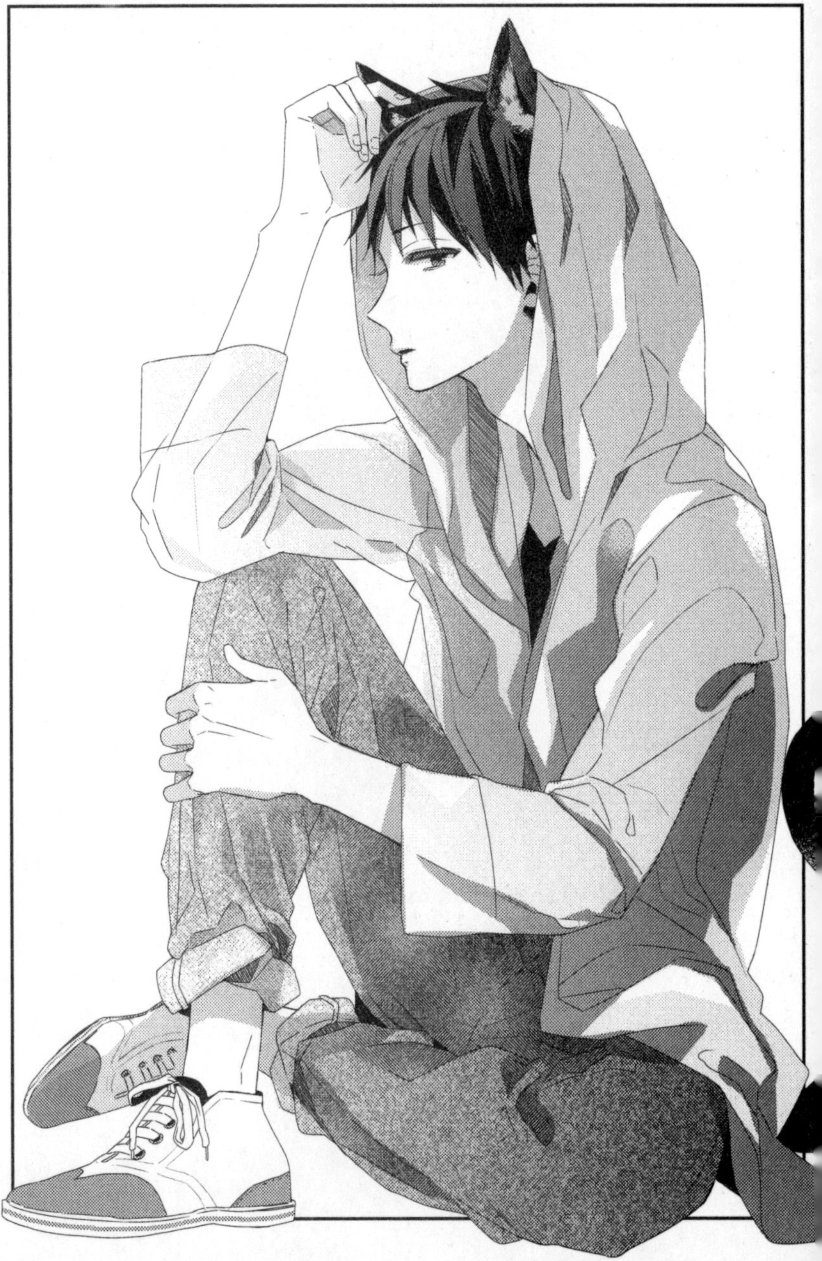

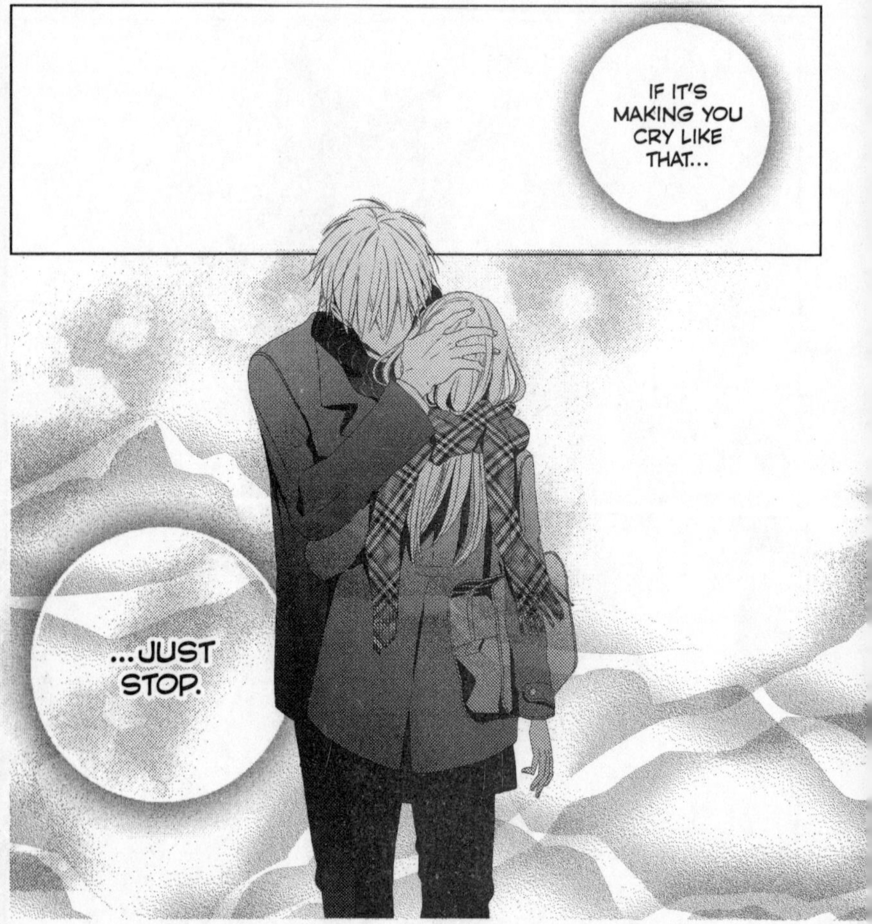
IF IT'S MAKING YOU CRY LIKE THAT...
...JUST STOP.

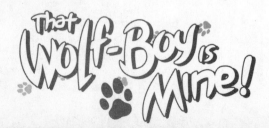

That Wolf-Boy is Mine!

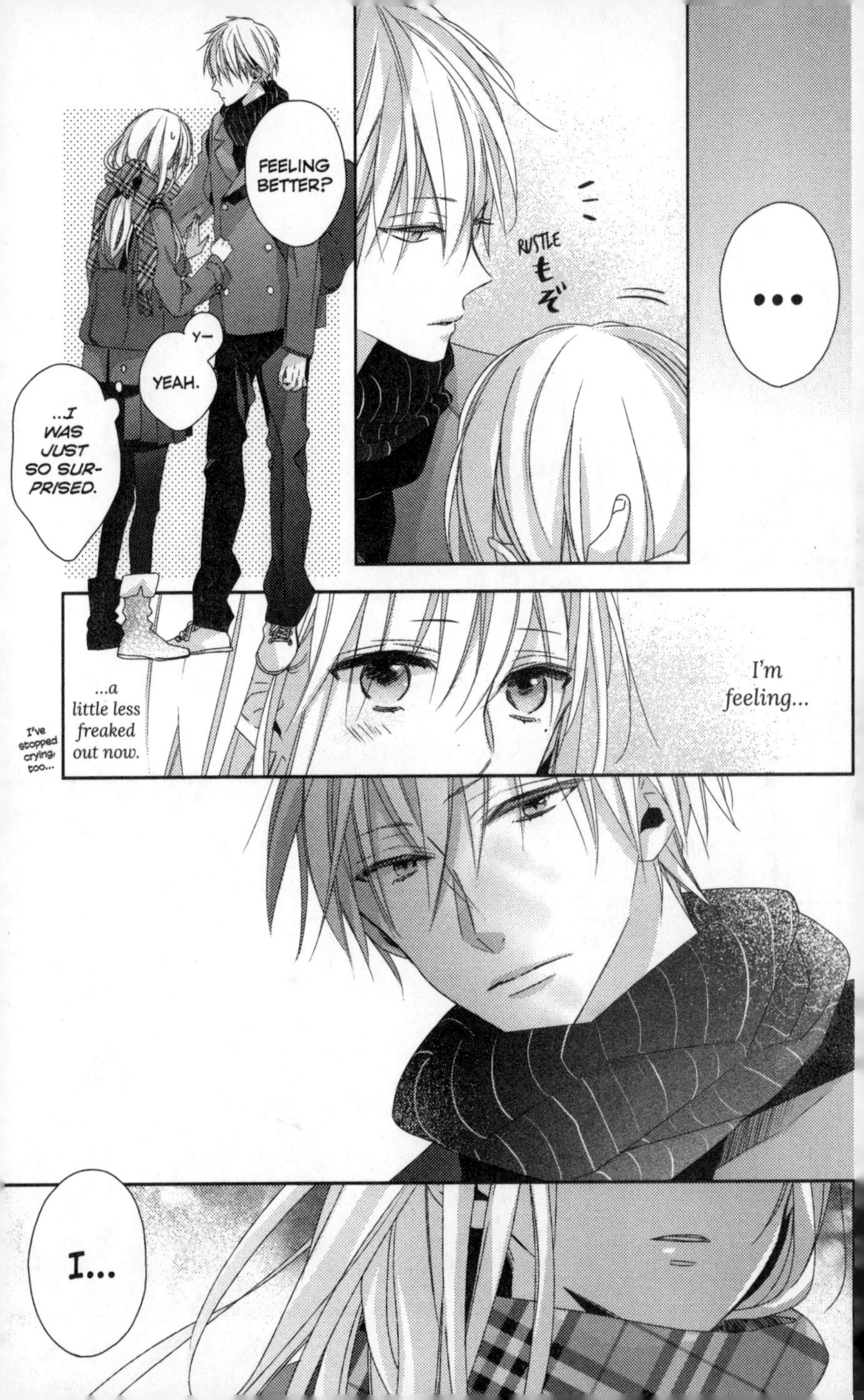
...
RUSTLE
もぞ
FEELING BETTER?
Y— YEAH.
...I WAS JUST SO SURPRISED.
I'm feeling...
...a little less freaked out now.
I've stopped crying, too...
I...

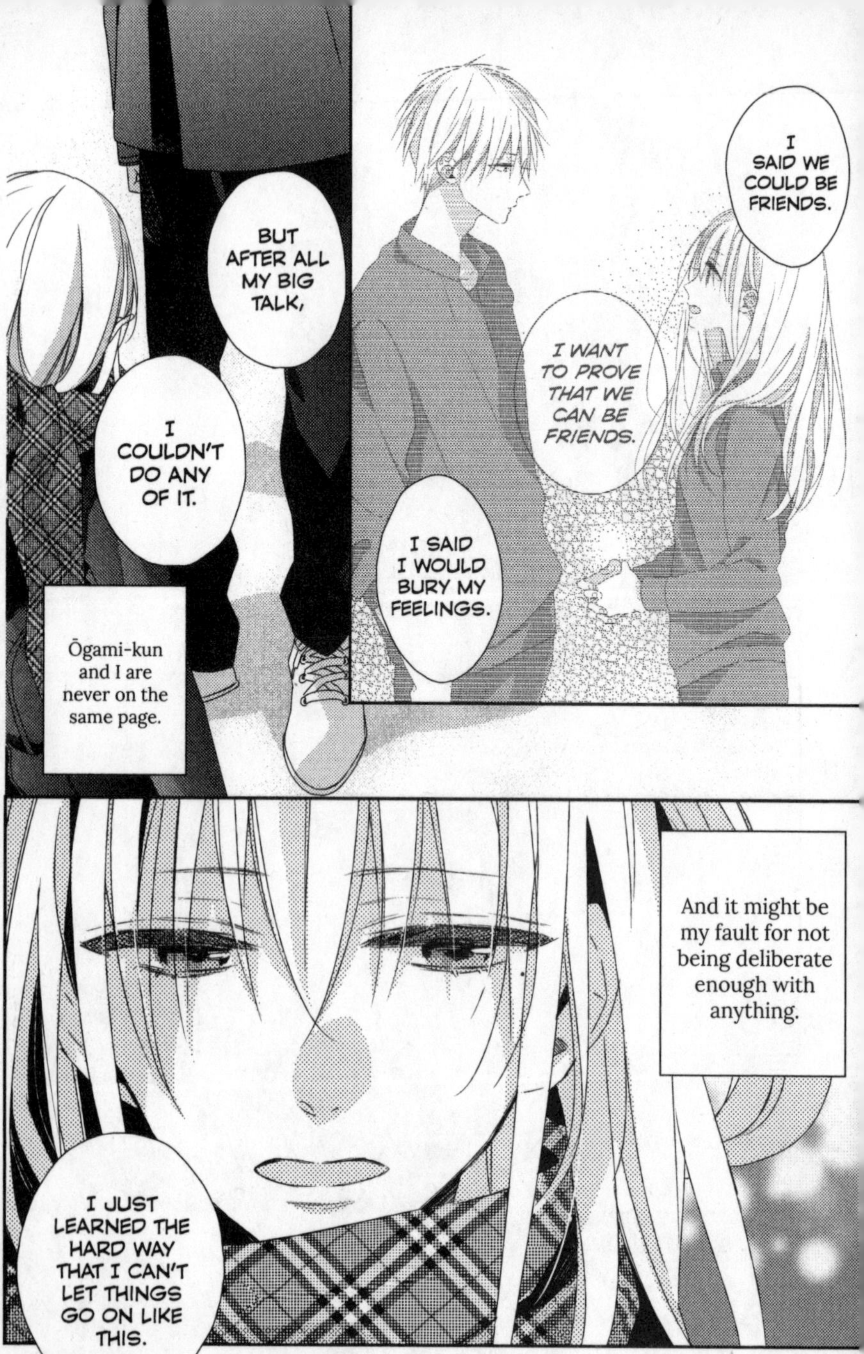
I SAID WE COULD BE FRIENDS.
I WANT TO PROVE THAT WE CAN BE FRIENDS.
I SAID I WOULD BURY MY FEELINGS.
BUT AFTER ALL MY BIG TALK,
I COULDN'T DO ANY OF IT.
Ōgami-kun and I are never on the same page.
And it might be my fault for not being deliberate enough with anything.
I JUST LEARNED THE HARD WAY THAT I CAN'T LET THINGS GO ON LIKE THIS.

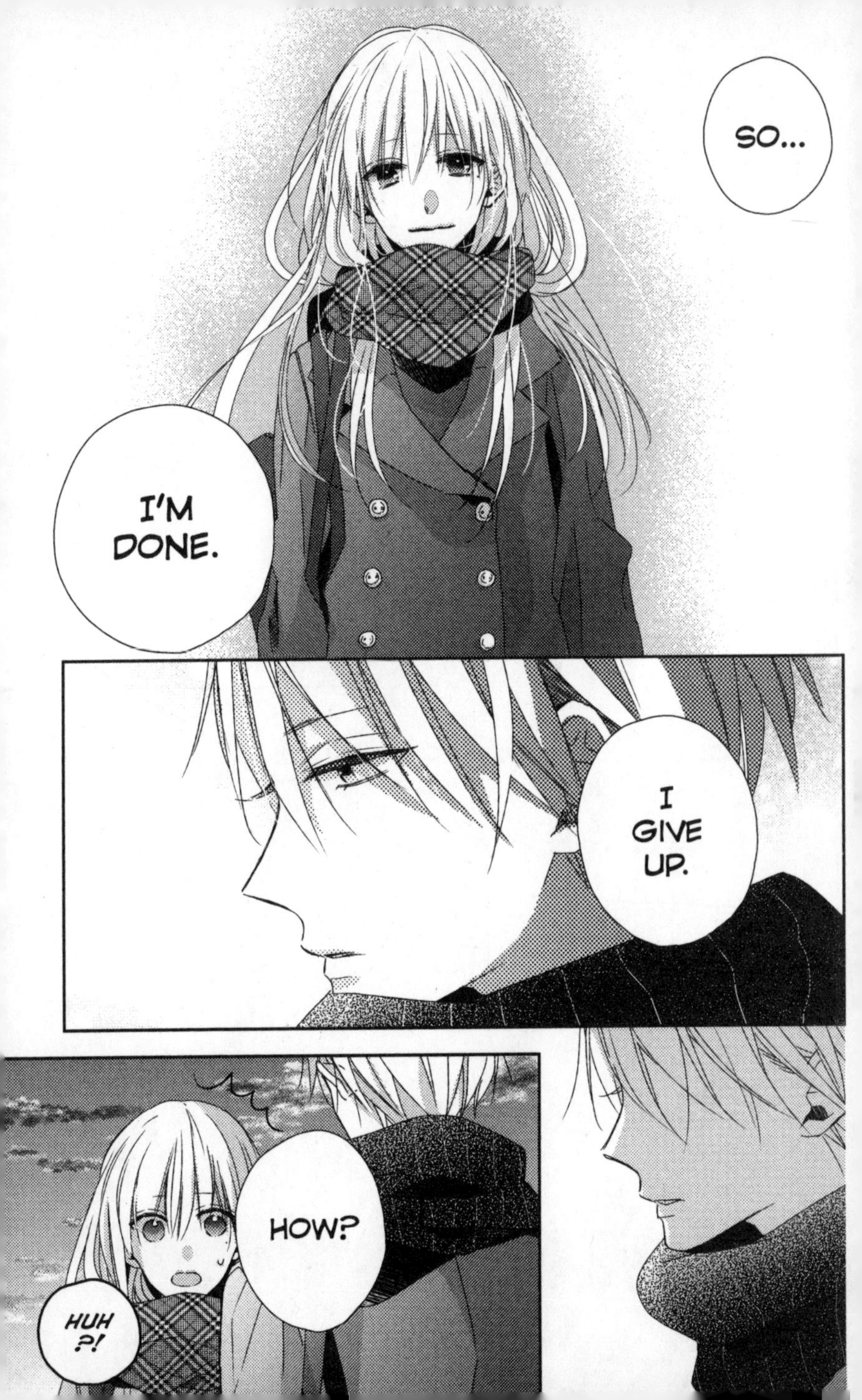
SO...
I'M DONE.
I GIVE UP.
HOW?
HUH?!

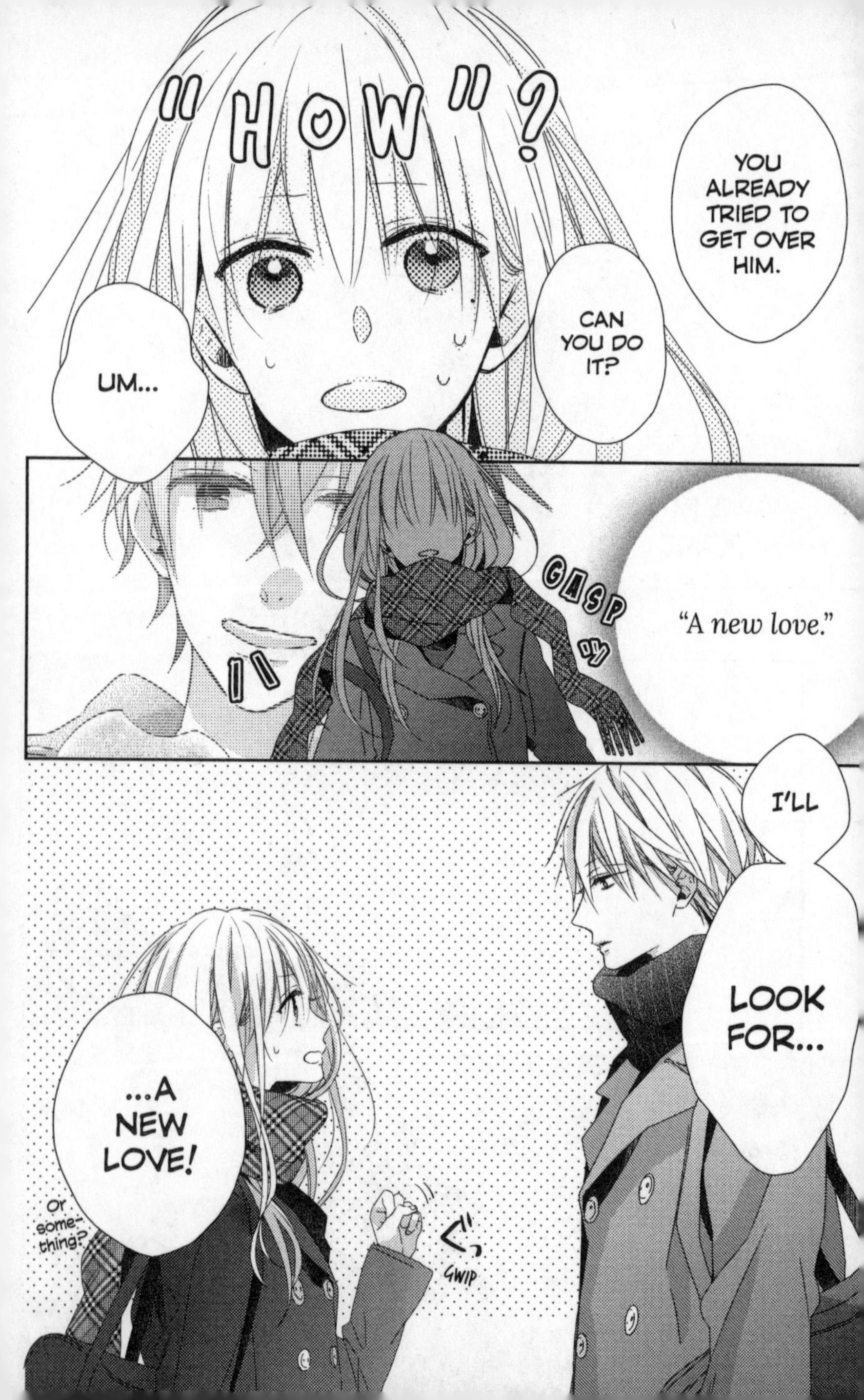
YOU ALREADY TRIED TO GET OVER HIM.
CAN YOU DO IT?
"HOW"?
UM...
"A new love."
GASP
I'LL
LOOK FOR...
...A NEW LOVE!
Or some-thing?
ぐっ
GWIP

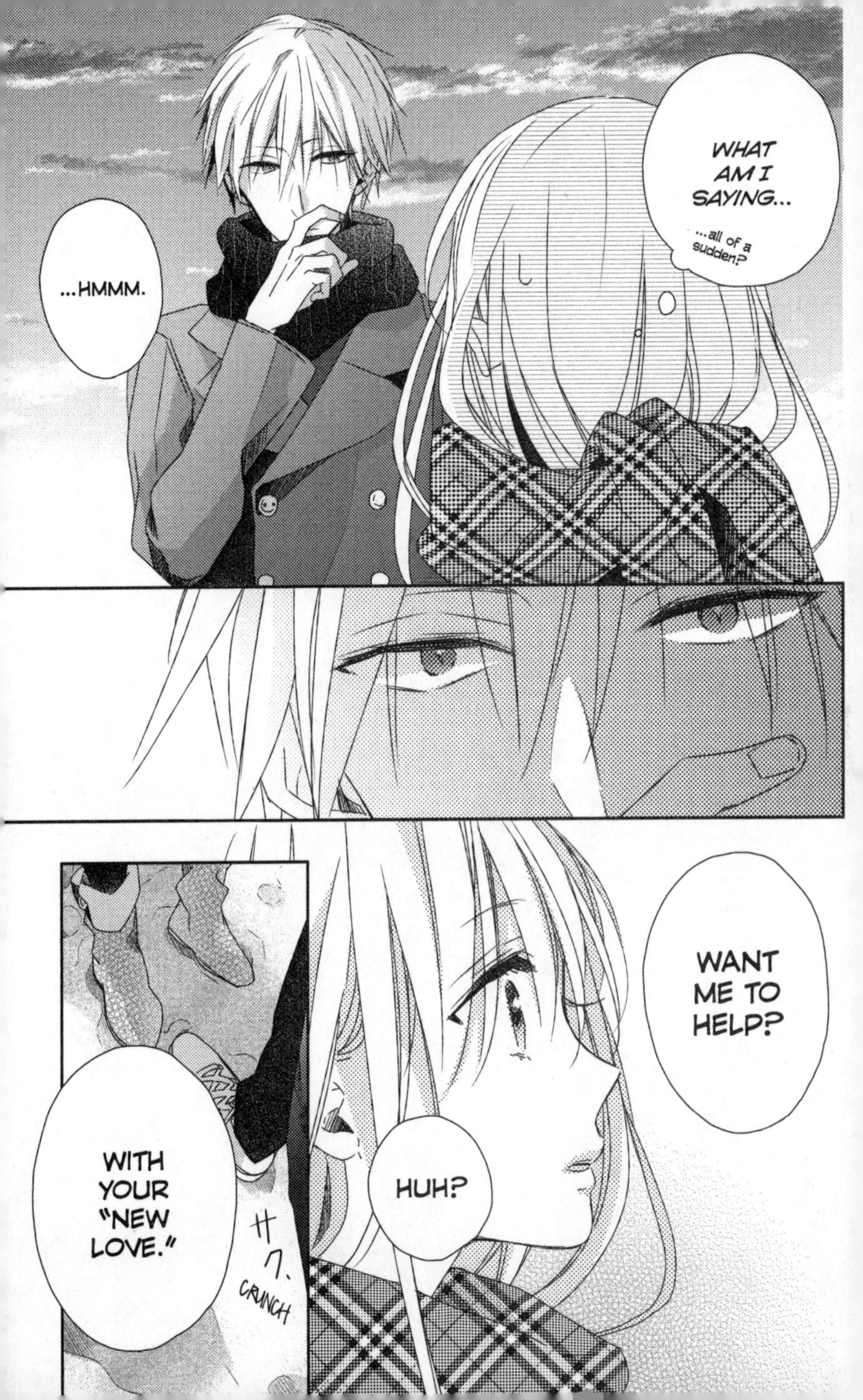
WHAT AM I SAYING...
...all of a sudden?
...HMMM.
WANT ME TO HELP?
HUH?
WITH YOUR "NEW LOVE."
CRUNCH

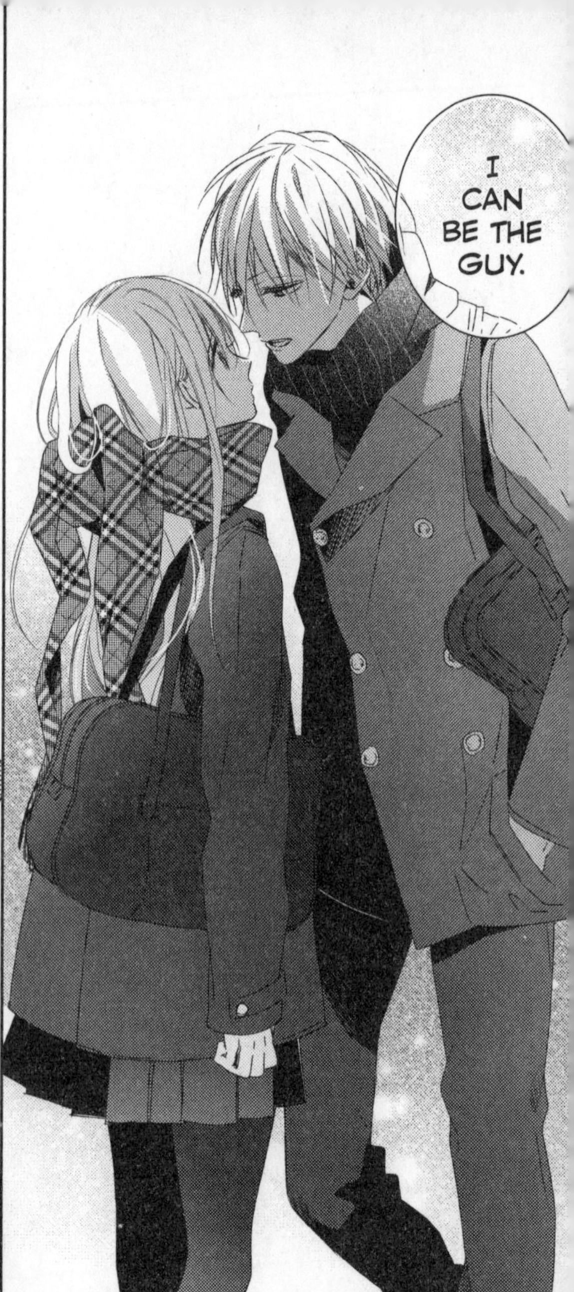
I CAN BE THE GUY.
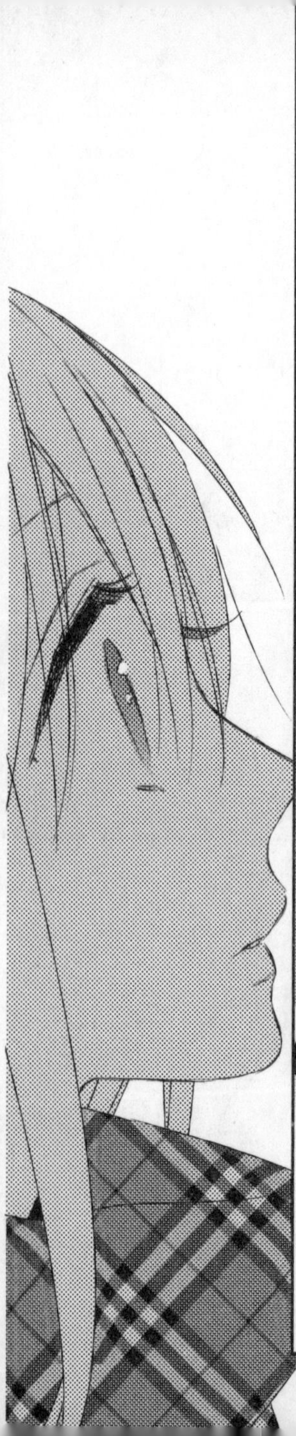

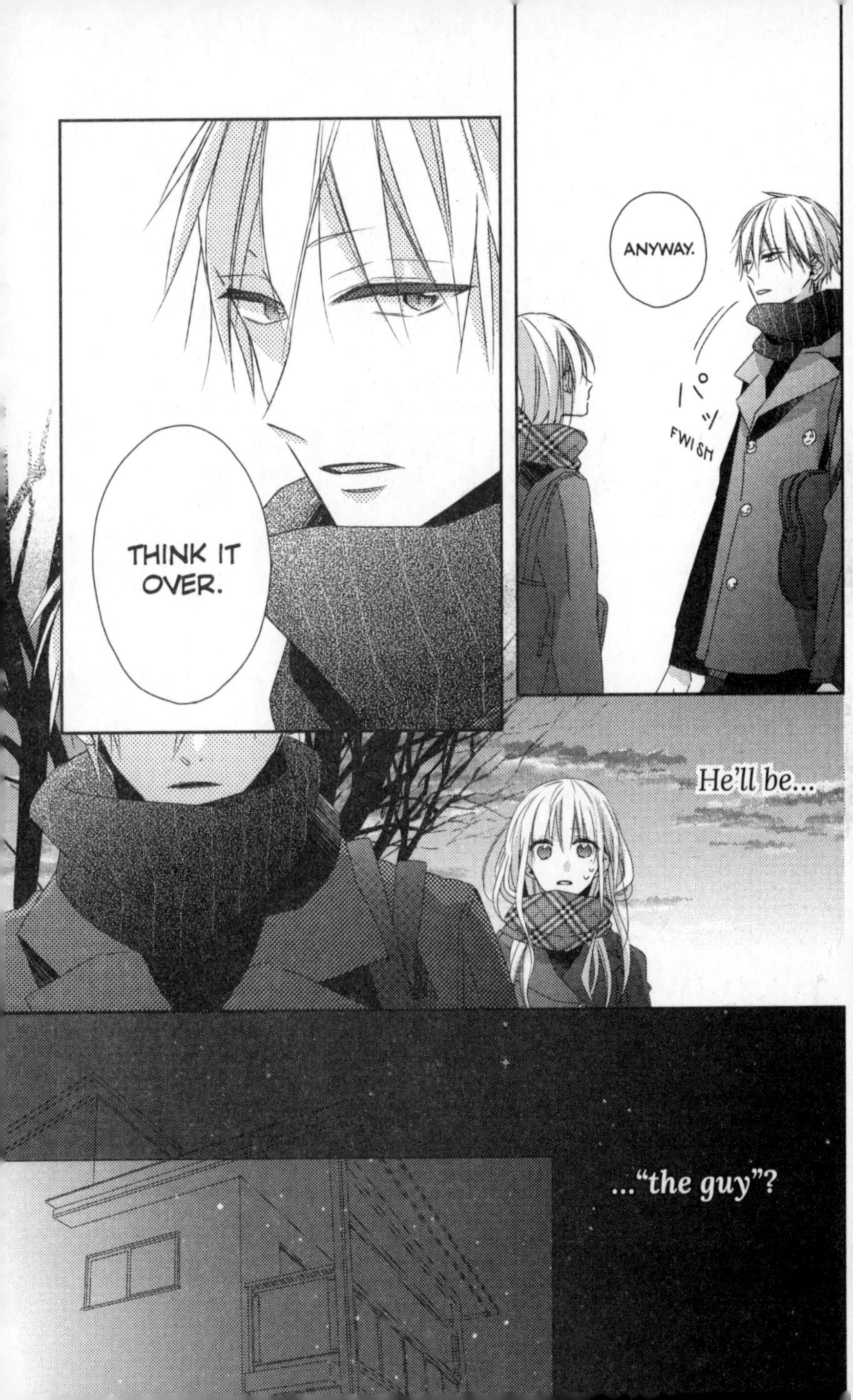
ANYWAY.
パッ
FWISH
THINK IT OVER.
He'll be...
..."the guy"?

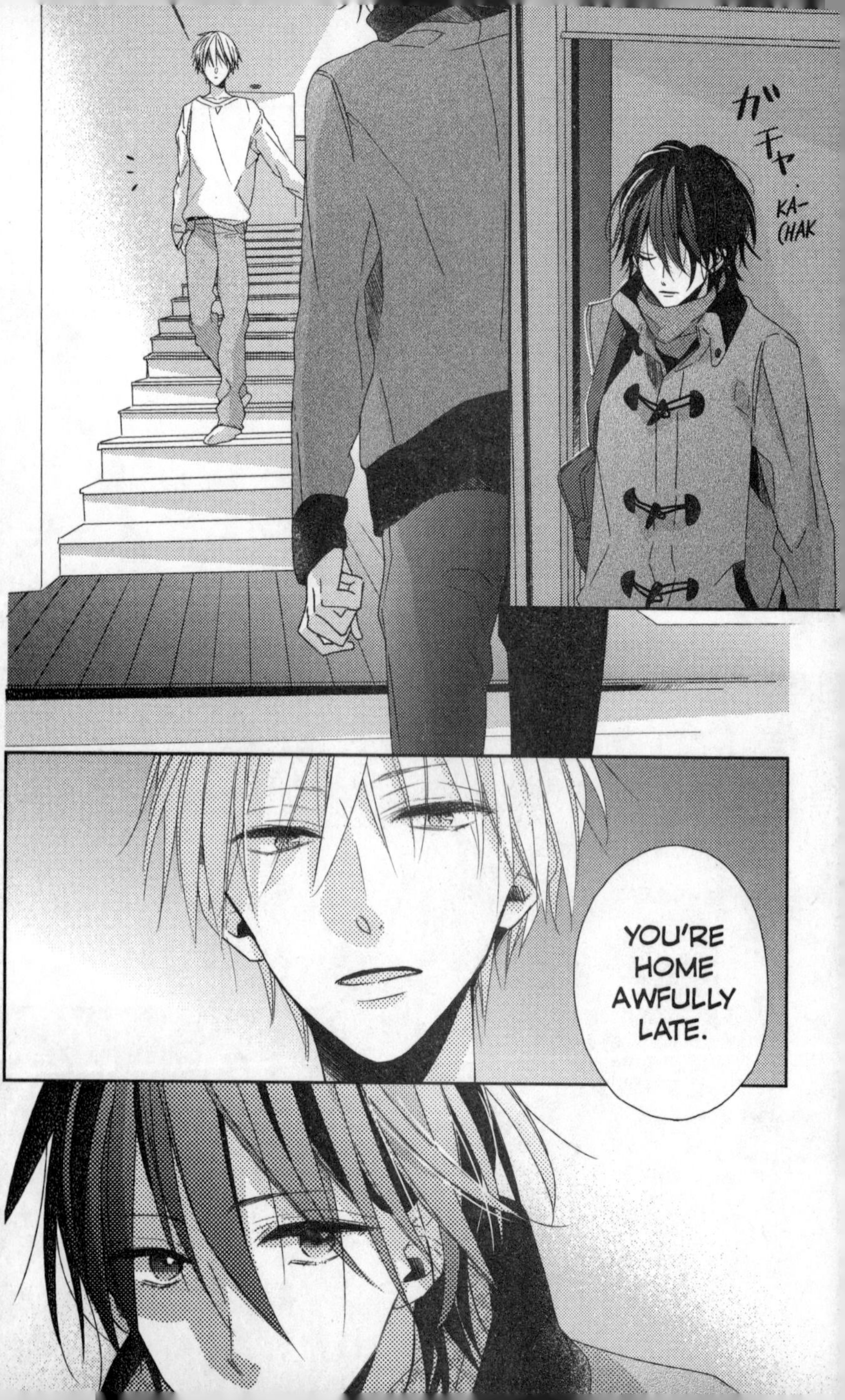
ガチャ
KA-CHAK
YOU'RE HOME AWFULLY LATE.

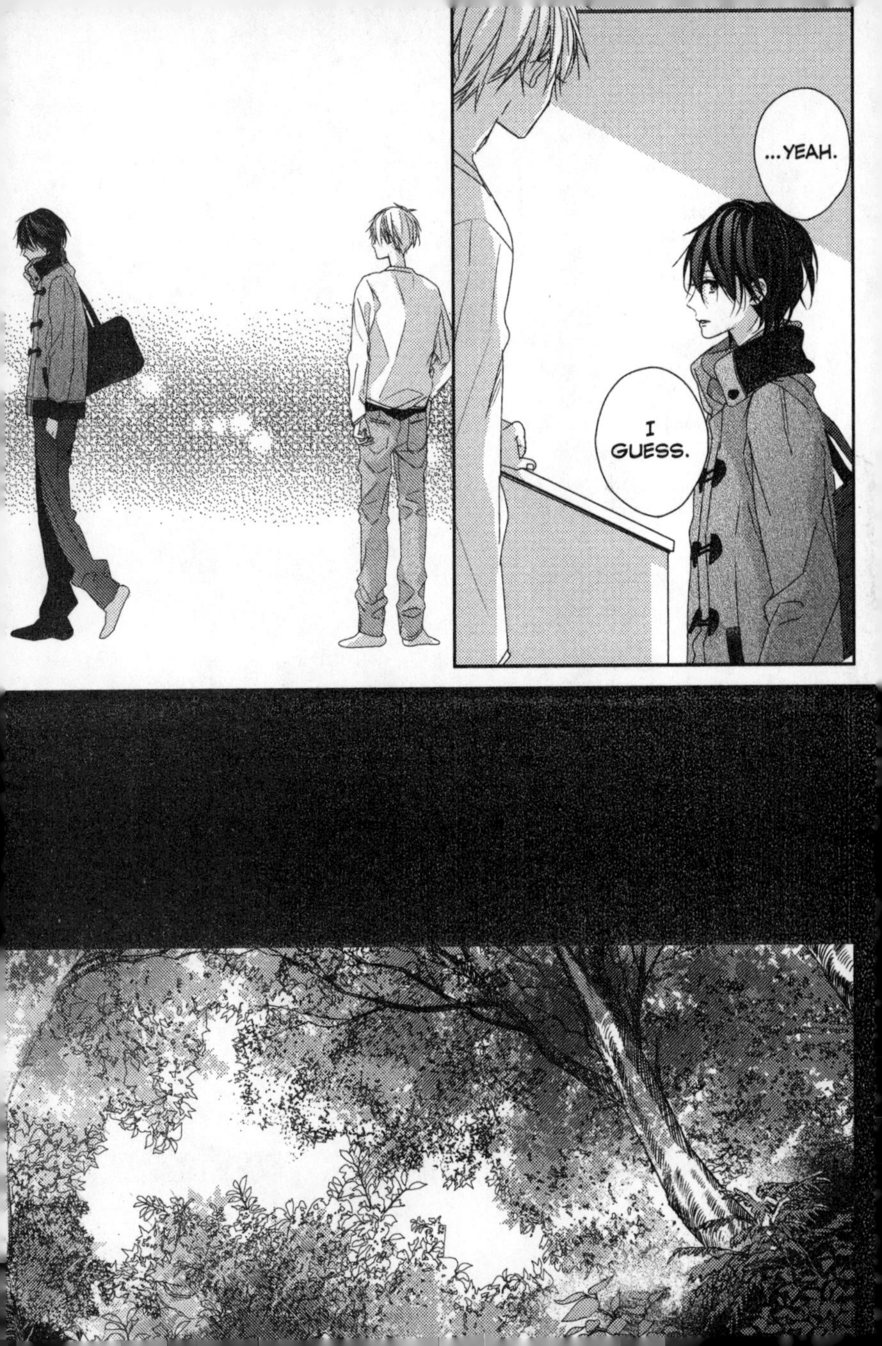
...YEAH.
I GUESS.

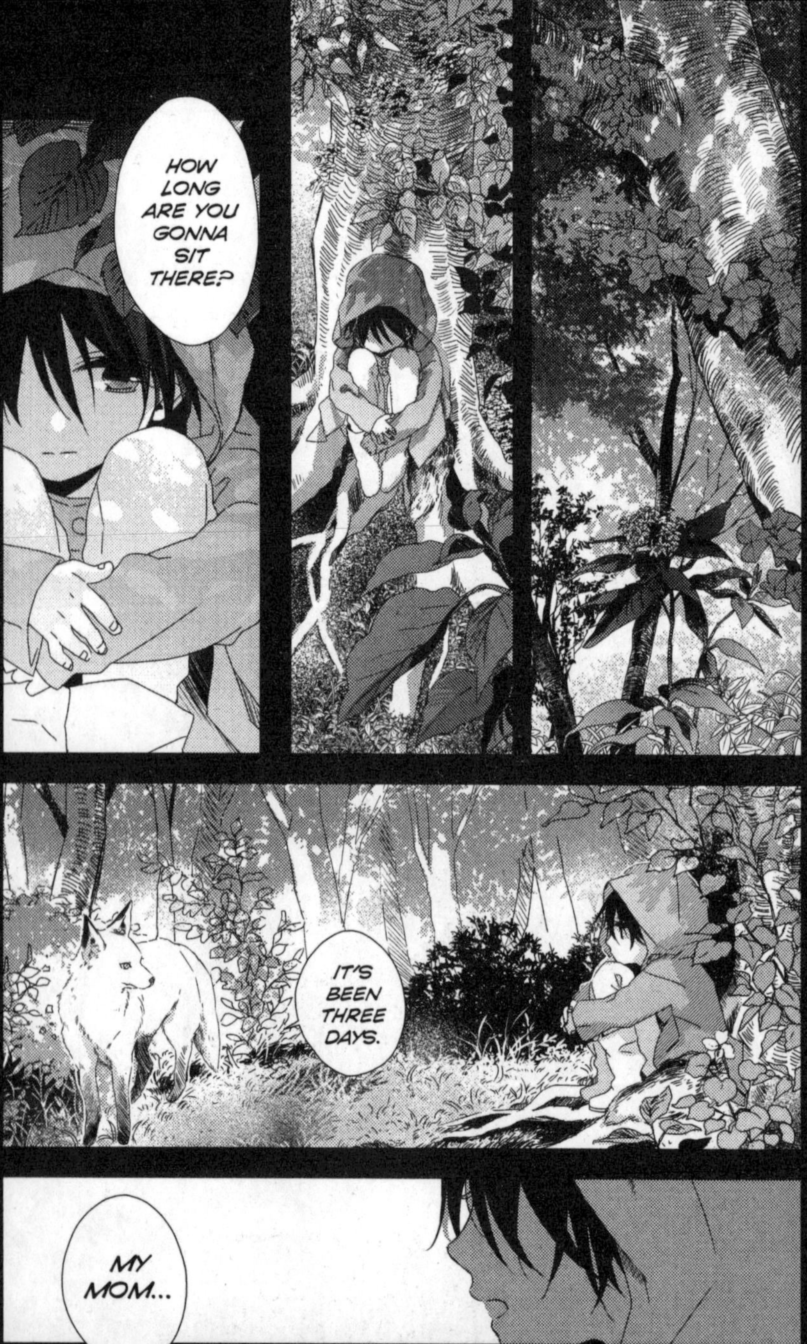
HOW LONG ARE YOU GONNA SIT THERE?
IT'S BEEN THREE DAYS.
MY MOM...

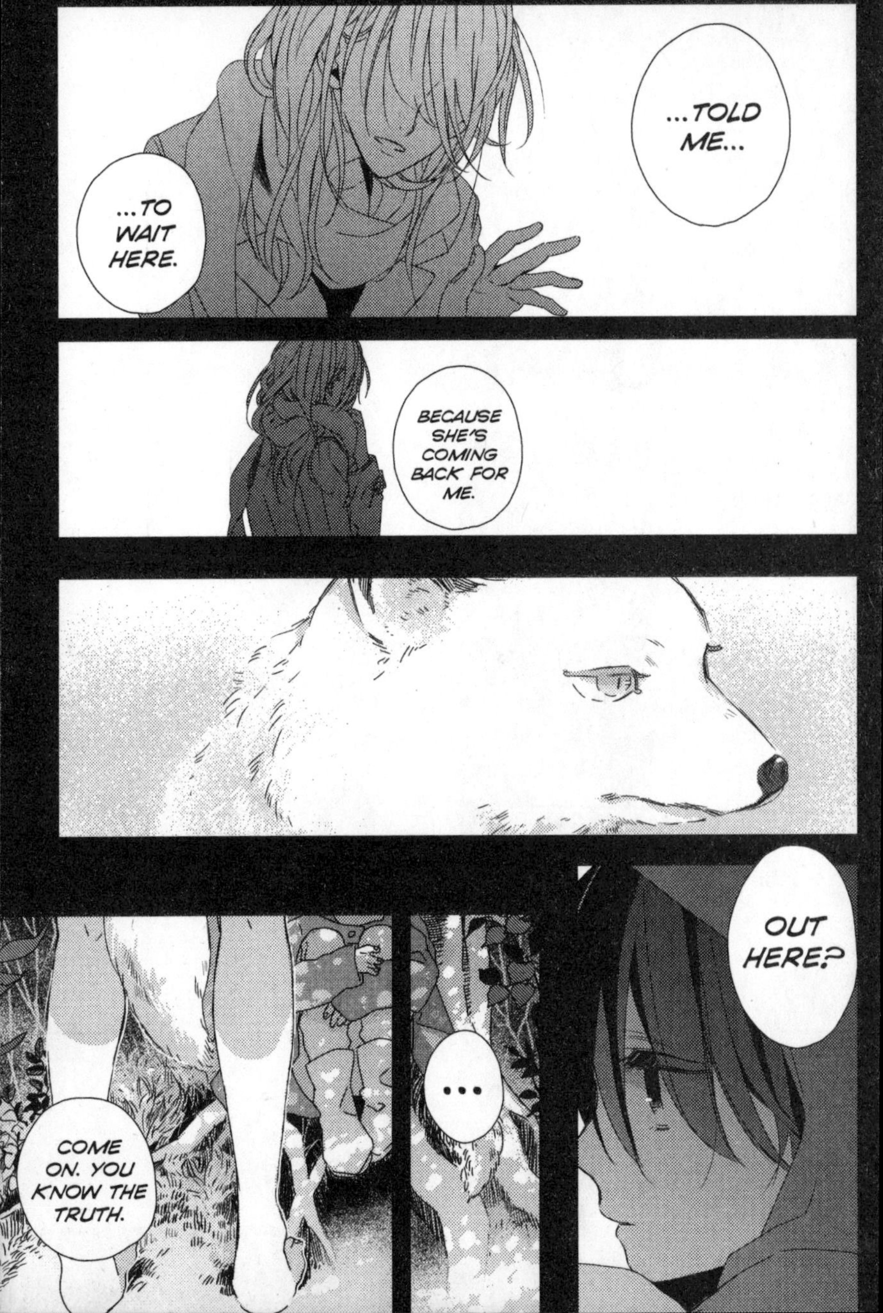
...TOLD ME...
...TO WAIT HERE.
BECAUSE SHE'S COMING BACK FOR ME.
OUT HERE?
...
COME ON. YOU KNOW THE TRUTH.

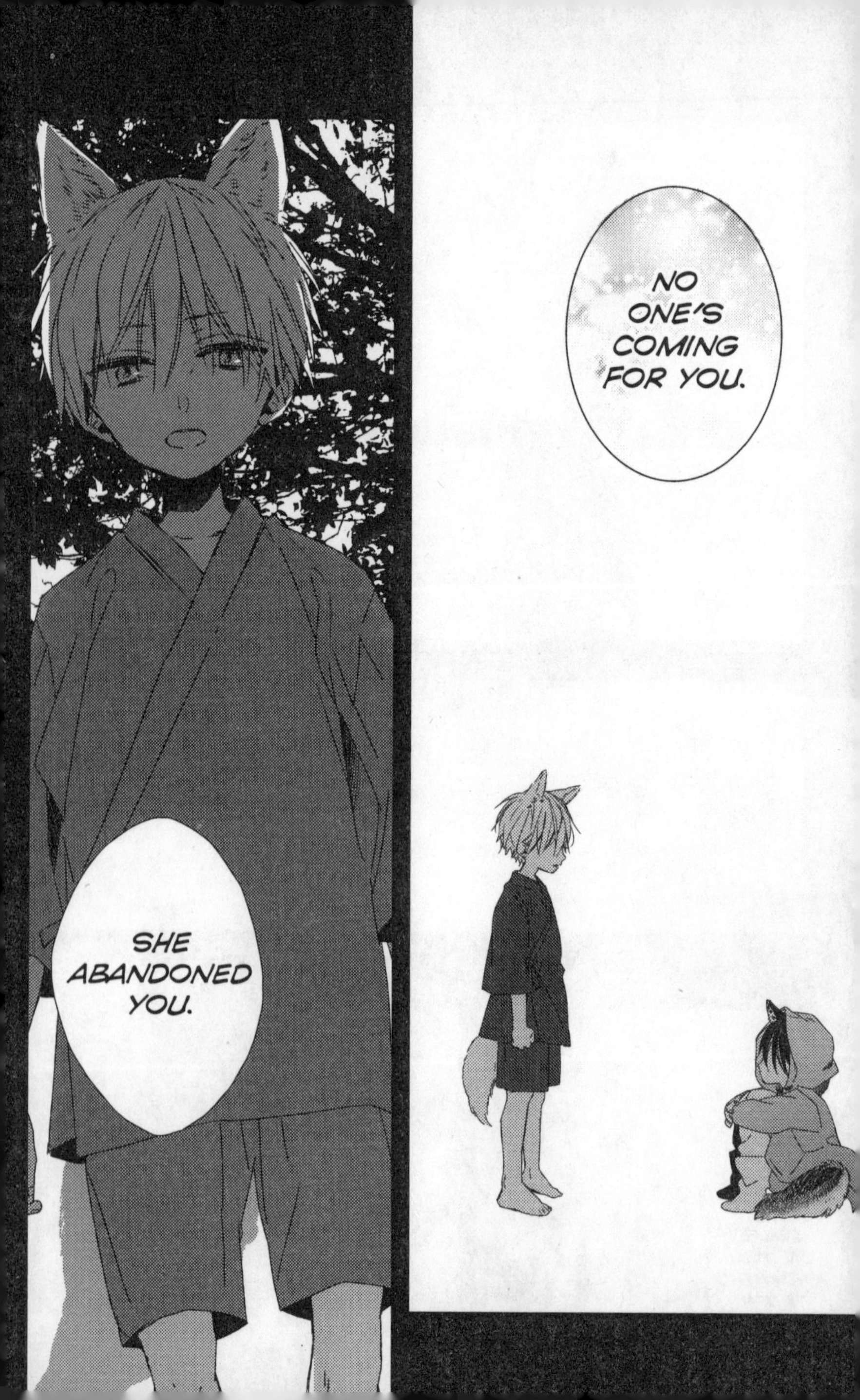
NO ONE'S COMING FOR YOU.
SHE ABANDONED YOU.

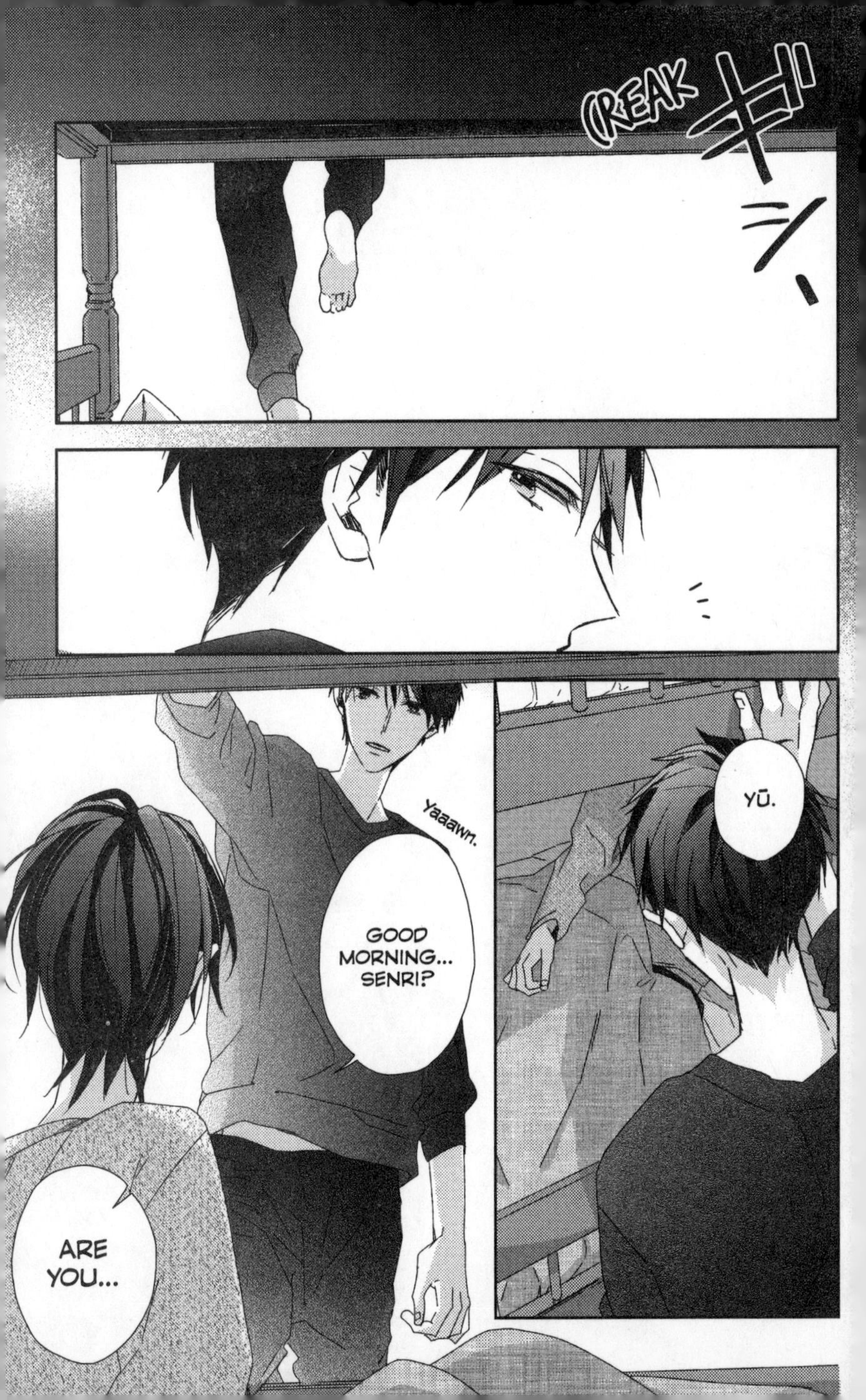
CREAK
YŪ.
Yaaawn.
GOOD MORNING... SENRI?
ARE YOU...

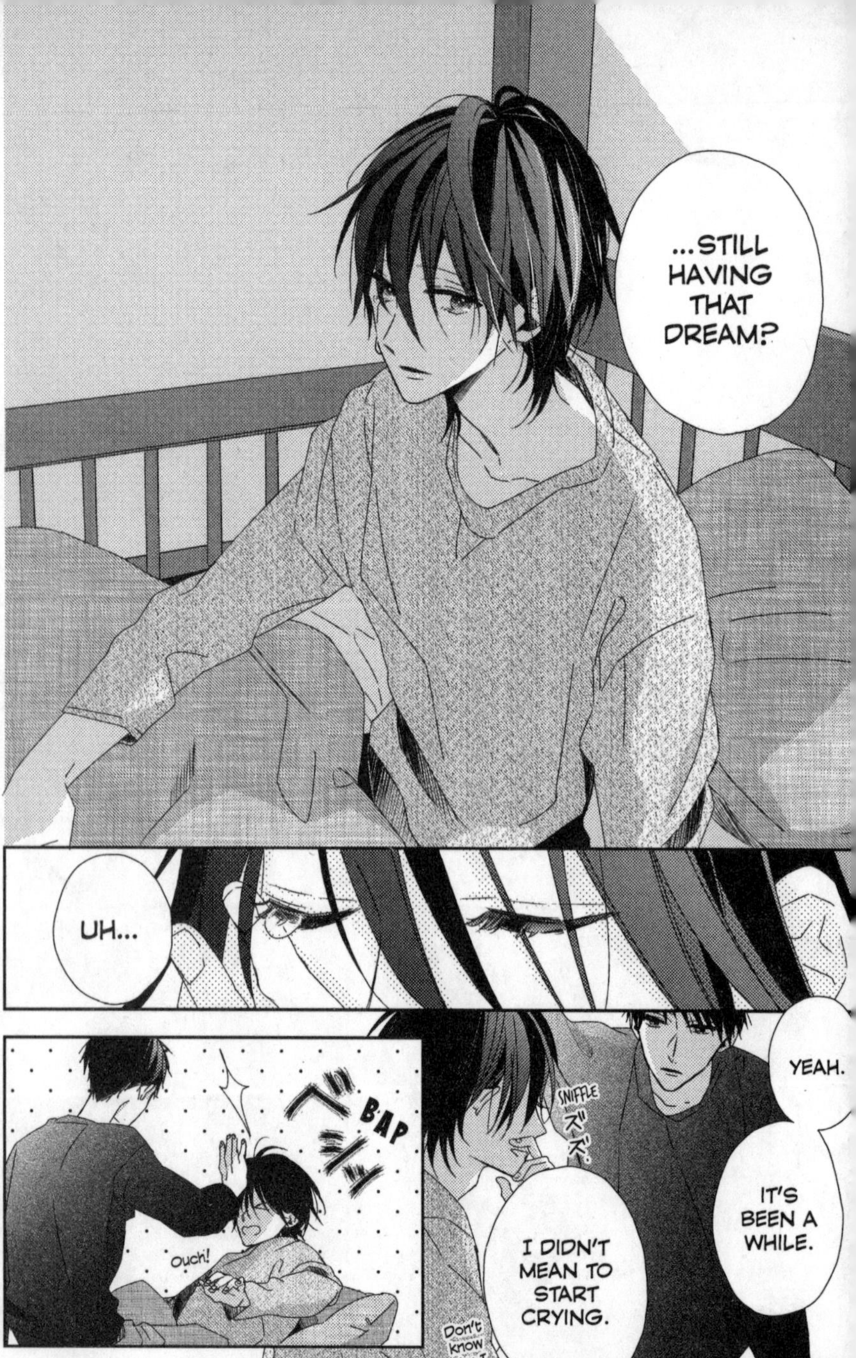
...STILL HAVING THAT DREAM?
UH...
YEAH.
IT'S BEEN A WHILE.
SNIFFLE
ズズ
I DIDN'T MEAN TO START CRYING.
Don't know why I am.
ベシッ
BAP
Ouch!

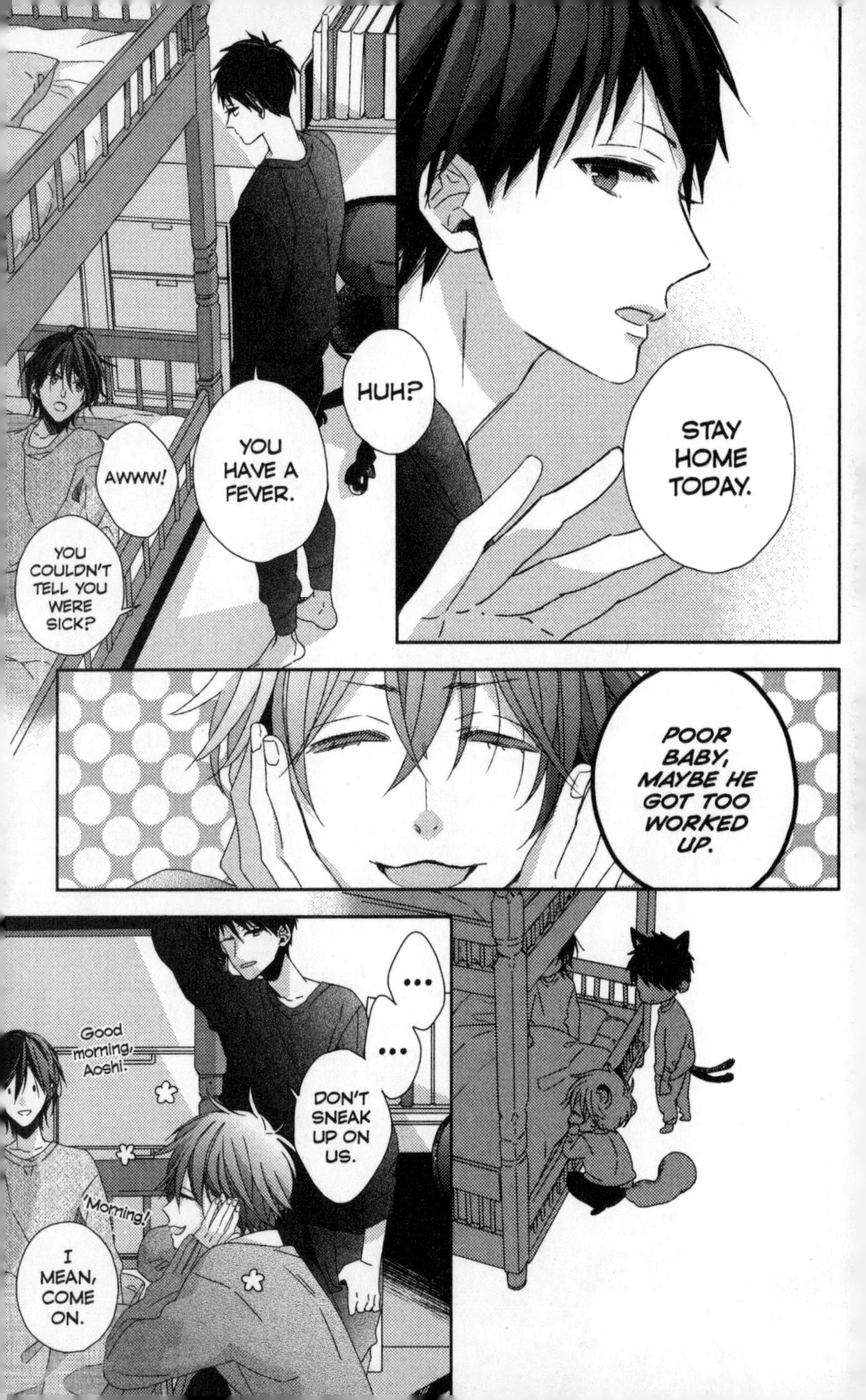
STAY HOME TODAY.
HUH?
YOU HAVE A FEVER.
AWWW!
YOU COULDN'T TELL YOU WERE SICK?
POOR BABY, MAYBE HE GOT TOO WORKED UP.
...
...
DON'T SNEAK UP ON US.
Good morning, Aoshi.
'Morning!
I MEAN, COME ON.

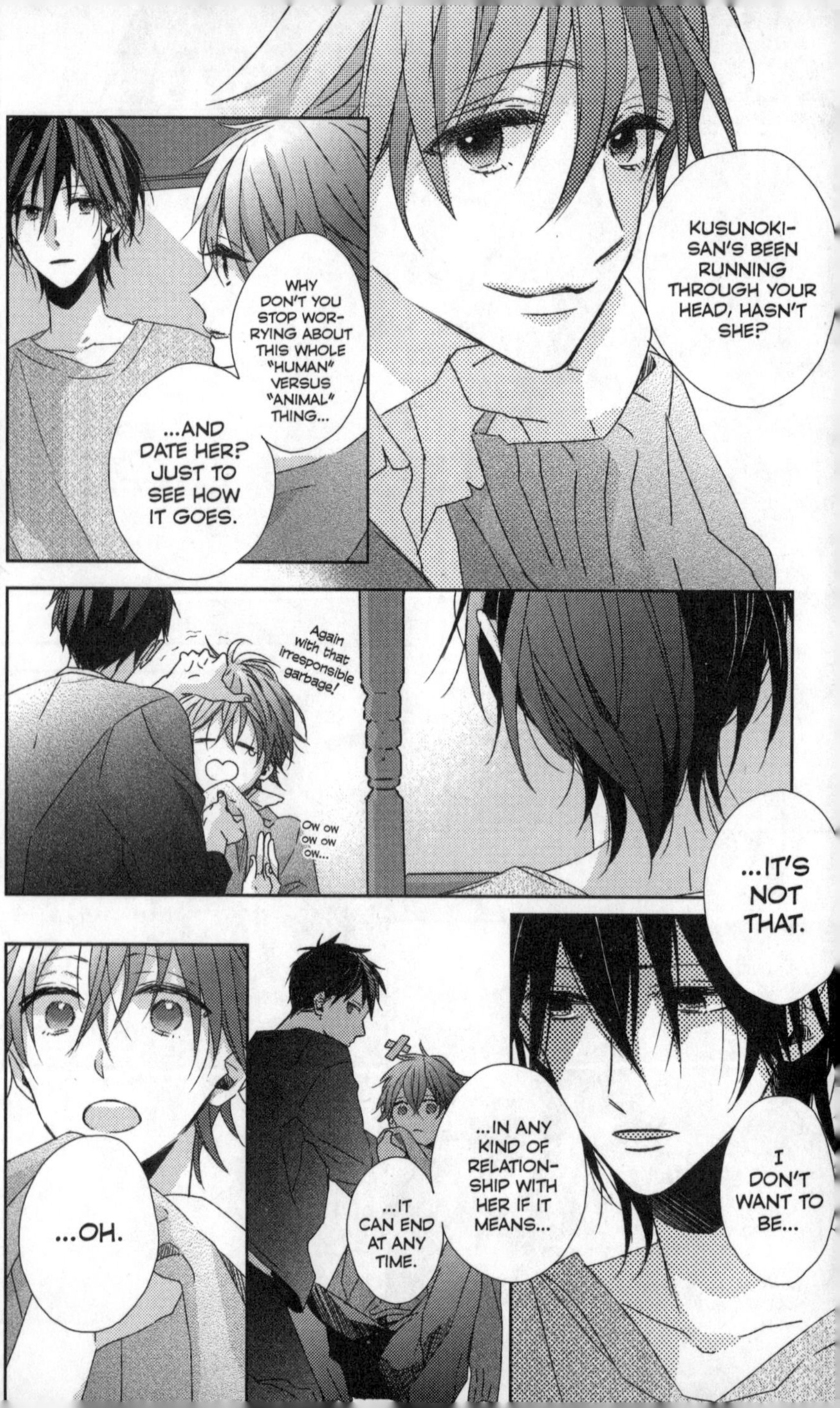
KUSUNOKI-SAN'S BEEN RUNNING THROUGH YOUR HEAD, HASN'T SHE?
WHY DON'T YOU STOP WOR-RYING ABOUT THIS WHOLE "HUMAN" VERSUS "ANIMAL" THING...
...AND DATE HER? JUST TO SEE HOW IT GOES.
...IT'S NOT THAT.
Again with that irresponsible garbage!
Ow ow ow ow ow...
I DON'T WANT TO BE...
...IN ANY KIND OF RELATION-SHIP WITH HER IF IT MEANS...
...IT CAN END AT ANY TIME.
...OH.

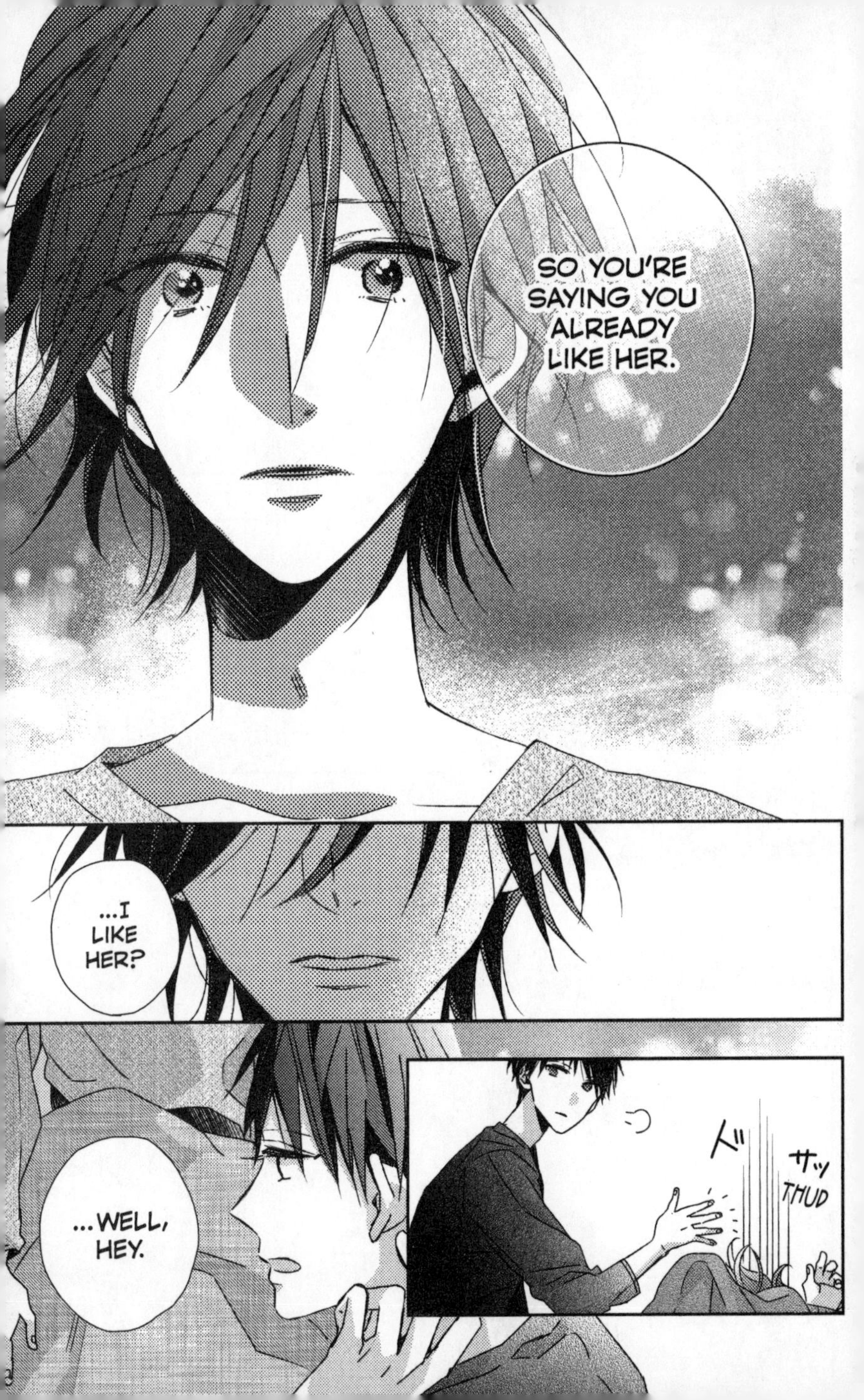
SO YOU'RE SAYING YOU ALREADY LIKE HER.
...I LIKE HER?
ド
サッ
THUD
...WELL, HEY.

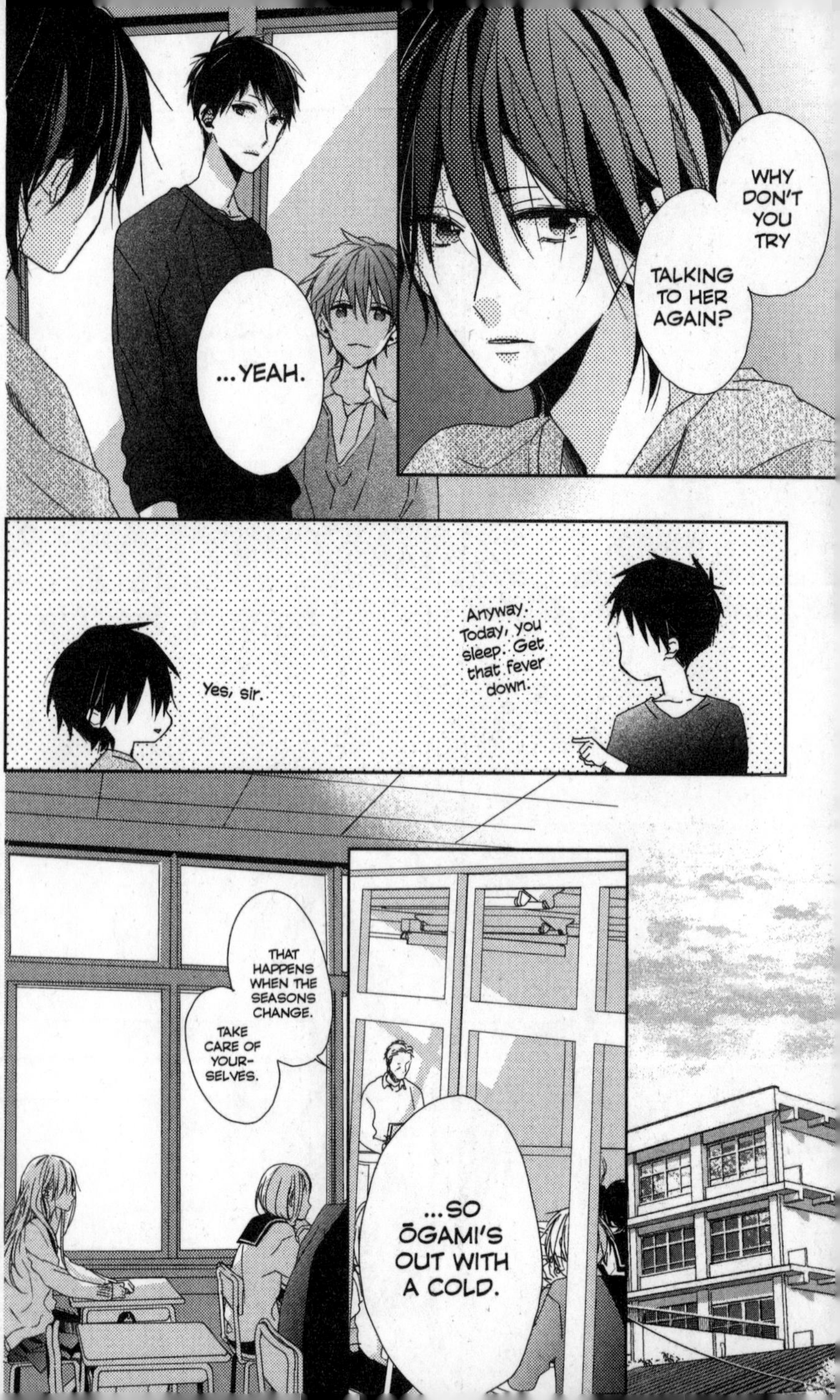
WHY DON'T YOU TRY TALKING TO HER AGAIN?
...YEAH.
Anyway. Today, you sleep. Get that fever down.
Yes, sir.
...SO ŌGAMI'S OUT WITH A COLD.
THAT HAPPENS WHEN THE SEASONS CHANGE.
TAKE CARE OF YOUR-SELVES.

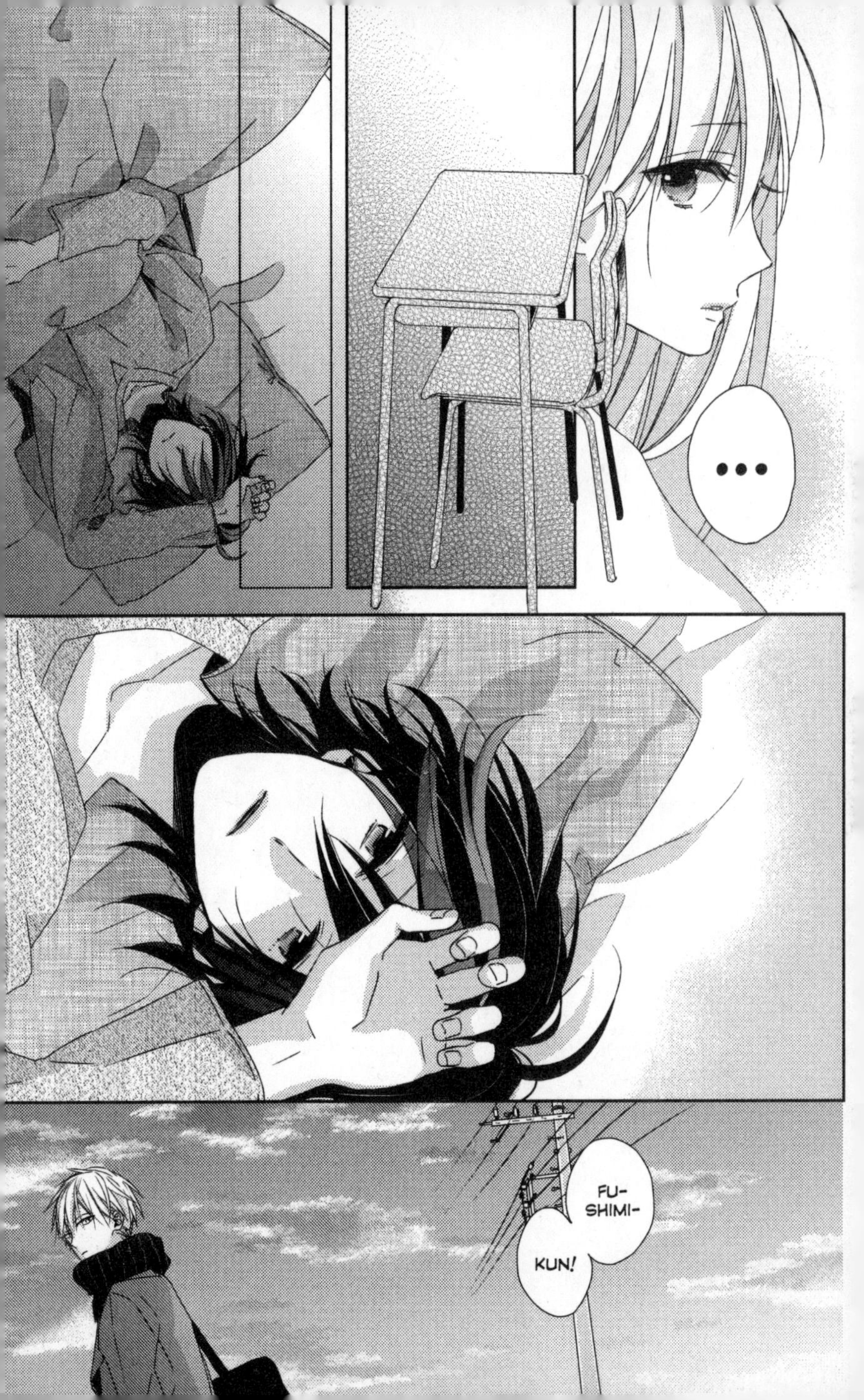
...
FU-SHIMI-
KUN!

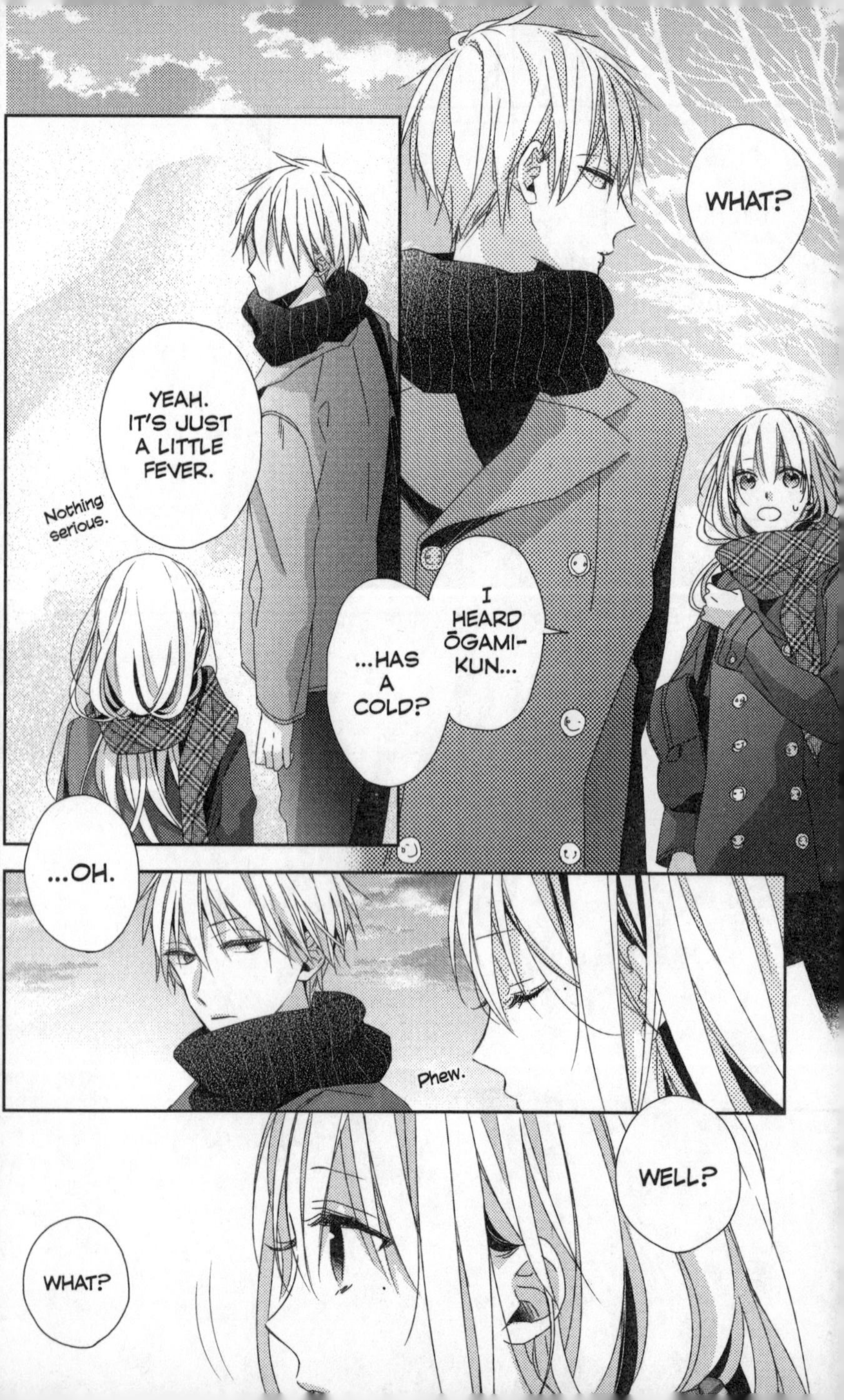
WHAT?
I HEARD ŌGAMI-KUN...
...HAS A COLD?
YEAH. IT'S JUST A LITTLE FEVER.
Nothing serious.
...OH.
Phew.
WELL?
WHAT?

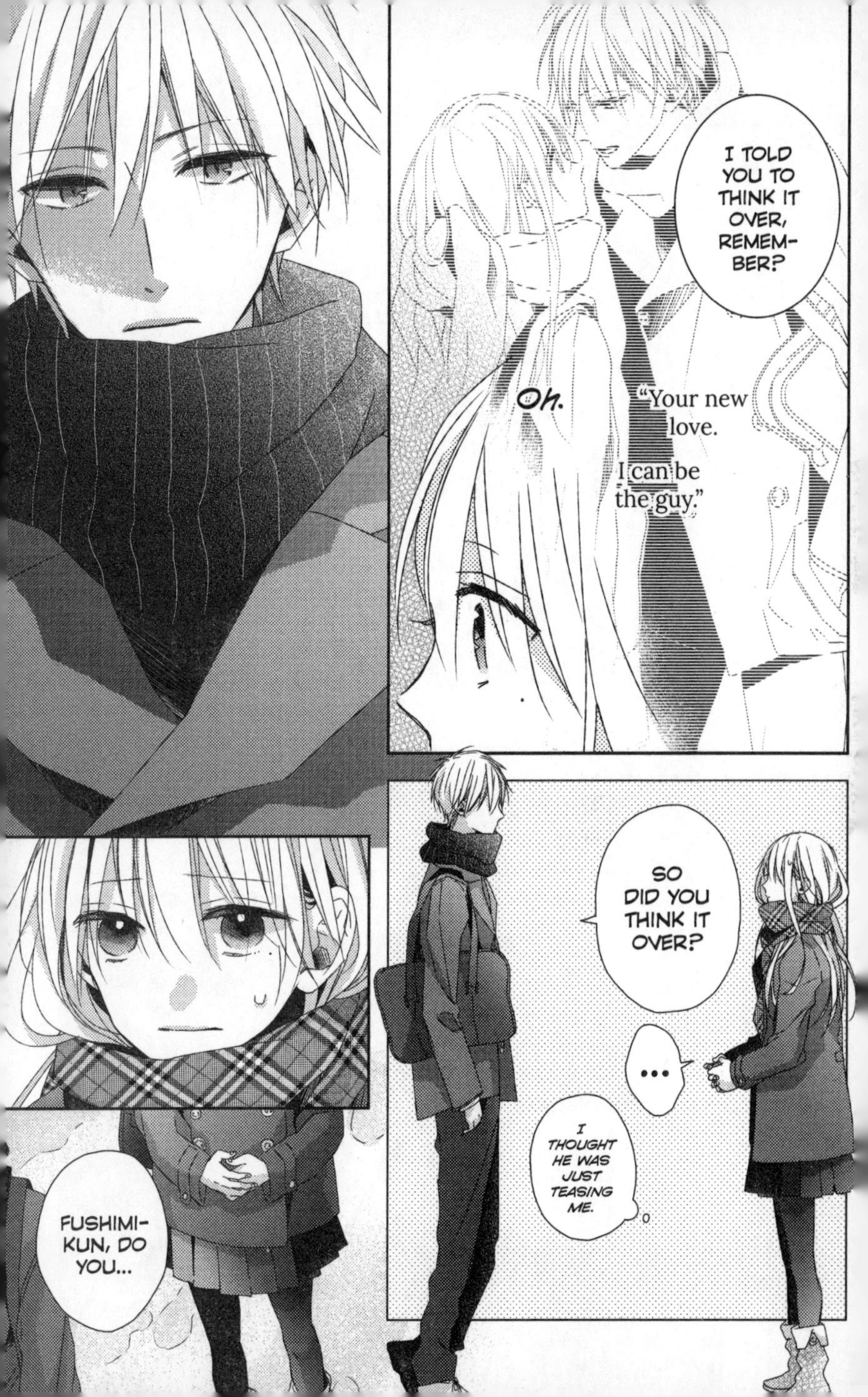
I TOLD YOU TO THINK IT OVER, REMEMBER?
“Your new love. I can be the guy.”
Oh.
SO DID YOU THINK IT OVER?
...
I THOUGHT HE WAS JUST TEASING ME.
FUSHIMI-KUN, DO YOU...

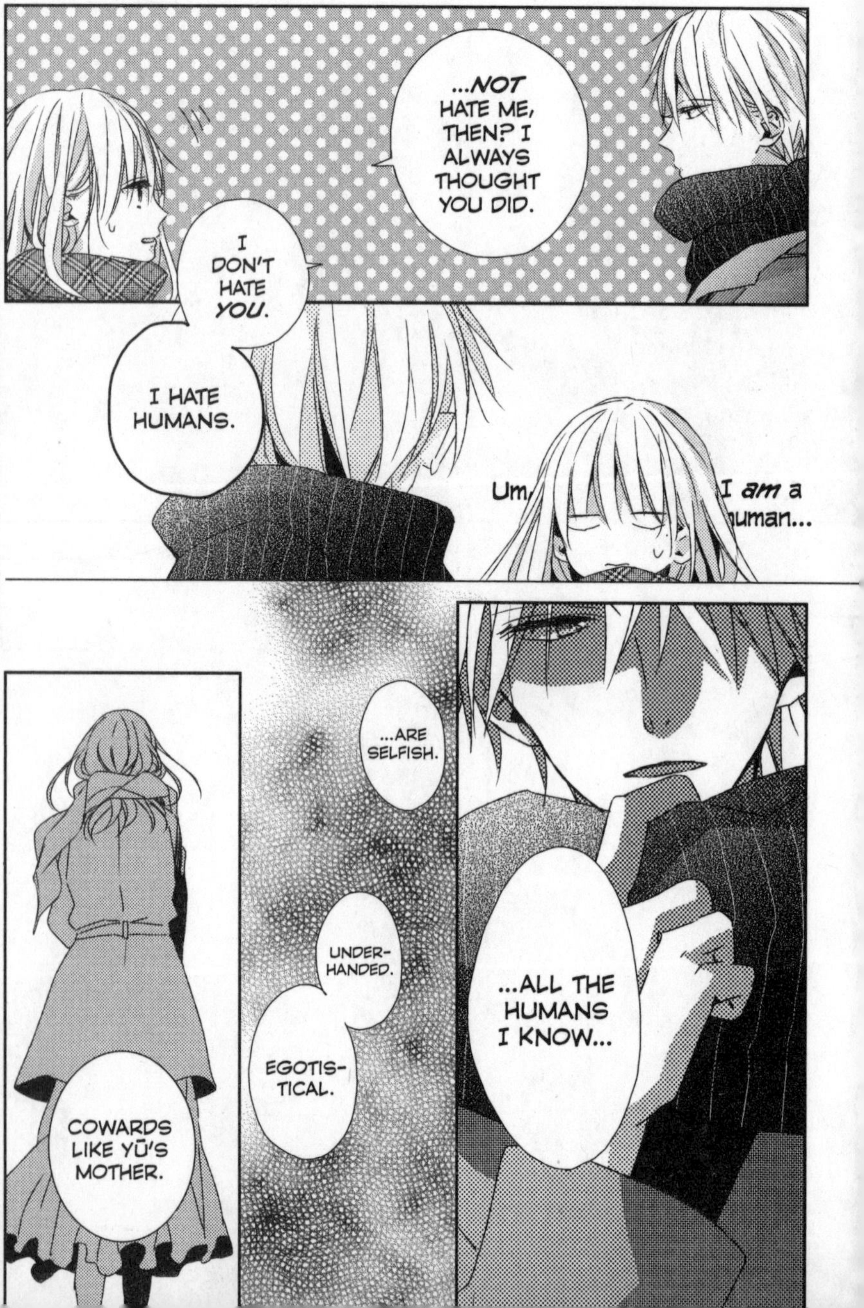
...NOT HATE ME, THEN? I ALWAYS THOUGHT YOU DID.
I DON'T HATE YOU.
I HATE HUMANS.
Um,
I am a
...ALL THE HUMANS I KNOW...
...ARE SELFISH.
UNDER-HANDED.
EGOTIS-TICAL.
COWARDS LIKE YŪ'S MOTHER.

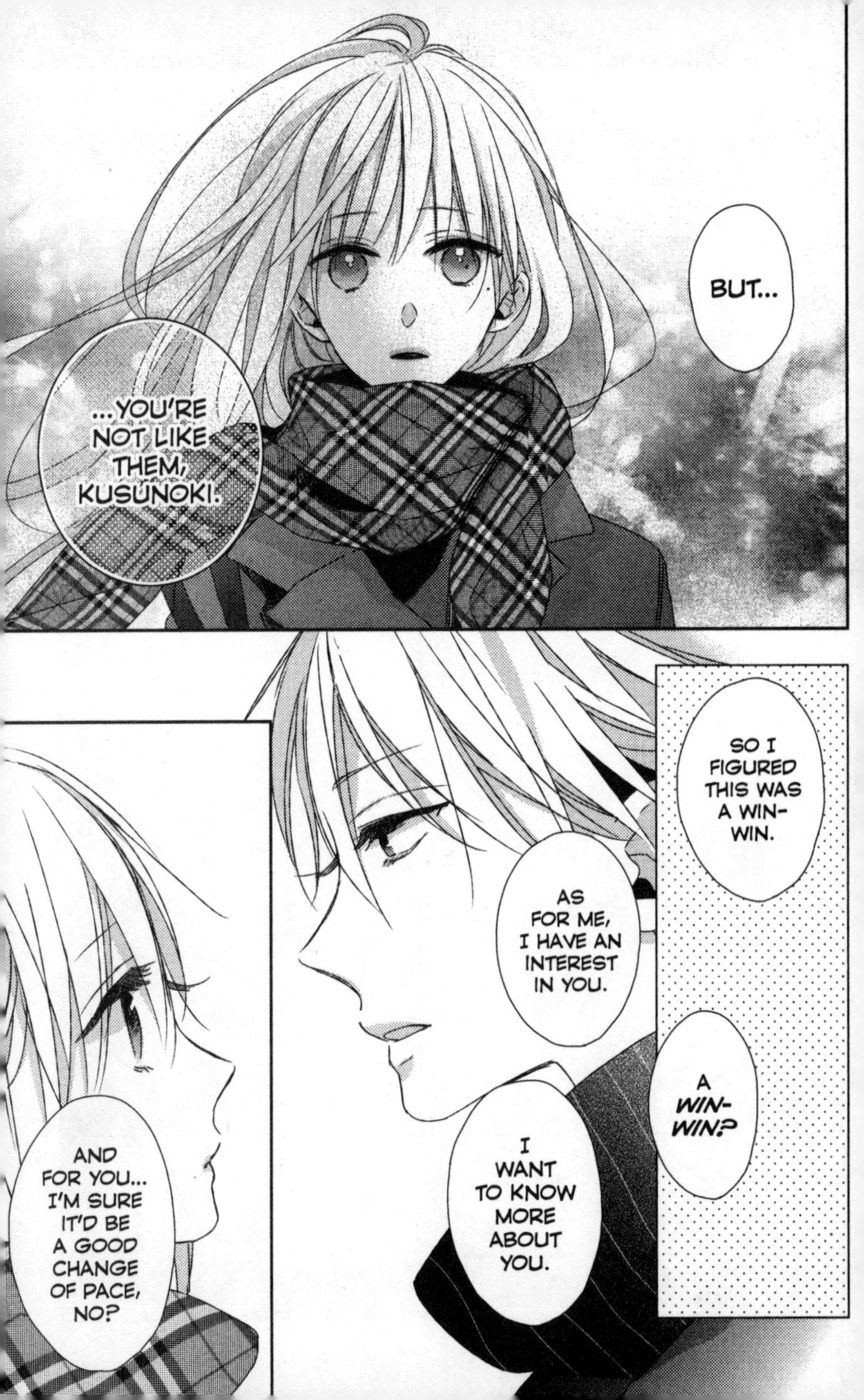
BUT...
...YOU'RE NOT LIKE THEM, KUSUNOKI.
SO I FIGURED THIS WAS A WIN-WIN.
AS FOR ME, I HAVE AN INTEREST IN YOU.
A *WIN-WIN?*
I WANT TO KNOW MORE ABOUT YOU.
AND FOR YOU... I'M SURE IT'D BE A GOOD CHANGE OF PACE, NO?

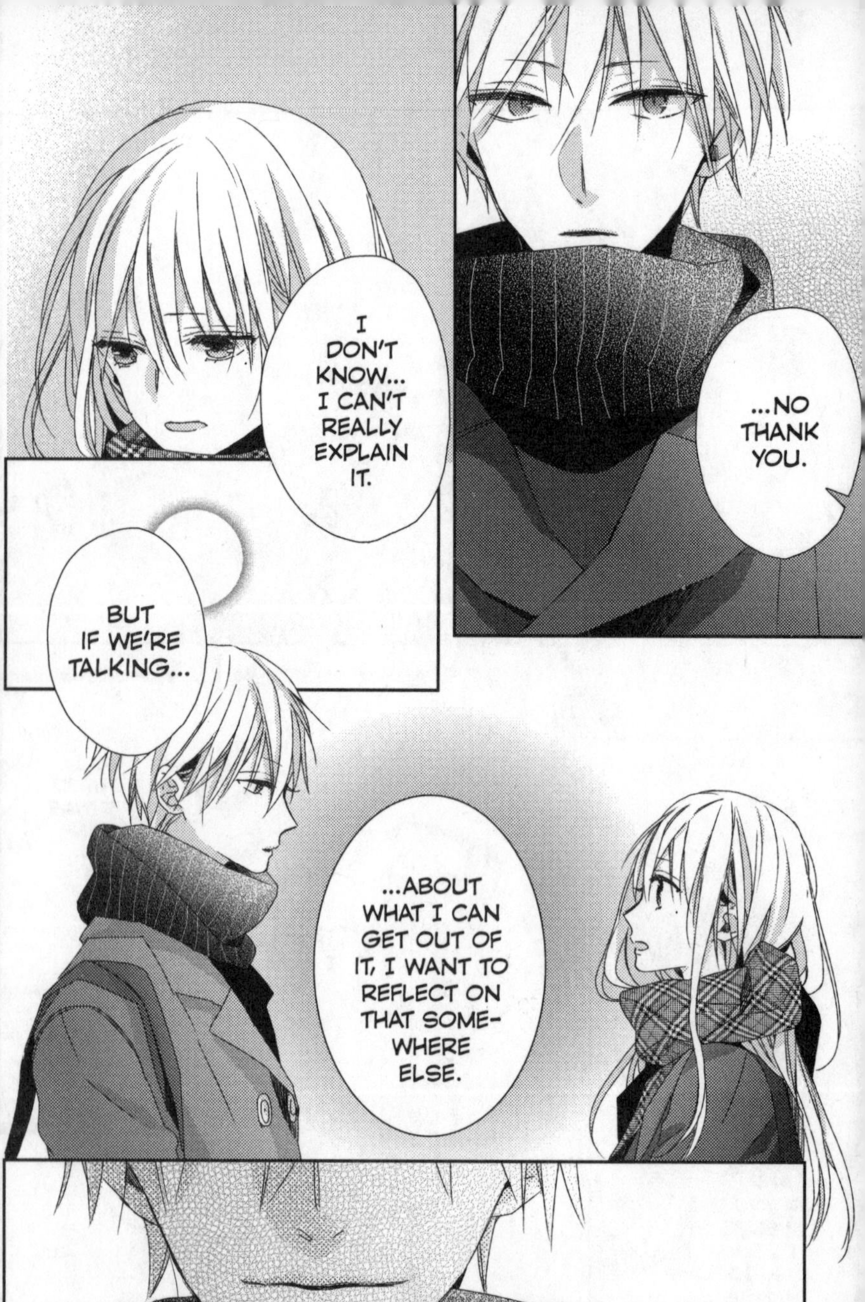
...NO THANK YOU.
I DON'T KNOW... I CAN'T REALLY EXPLAIN IT.
BUT IF WE'RE TALKING...
...ABOUT WHAT I CAN GET OUT OF IT, I WANT TO REFLECT ON THAT SOME-WHERE ELSE.

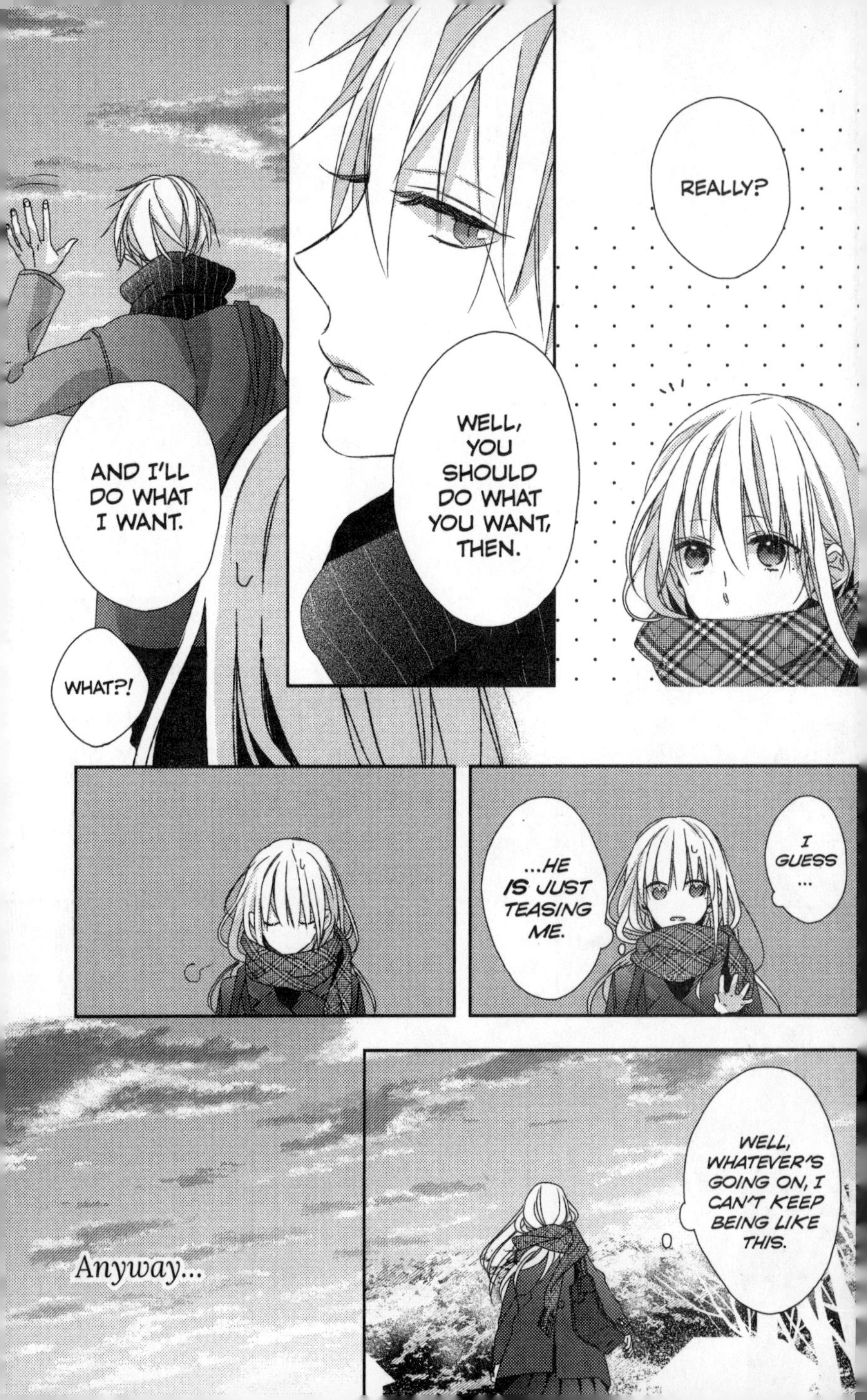
REALLY?
WELL, YOU SHOULD DO WHAT YOU WANT, THEN.
AND I'LL DO WHAT I WANT.
WHAT?!
I GUESS ...
...HE IS JUST TEASING ME.
WELL, WHATEVER'S GOING ON, I CAN'T KEEP BEING LIKE THIS.
Anyway...

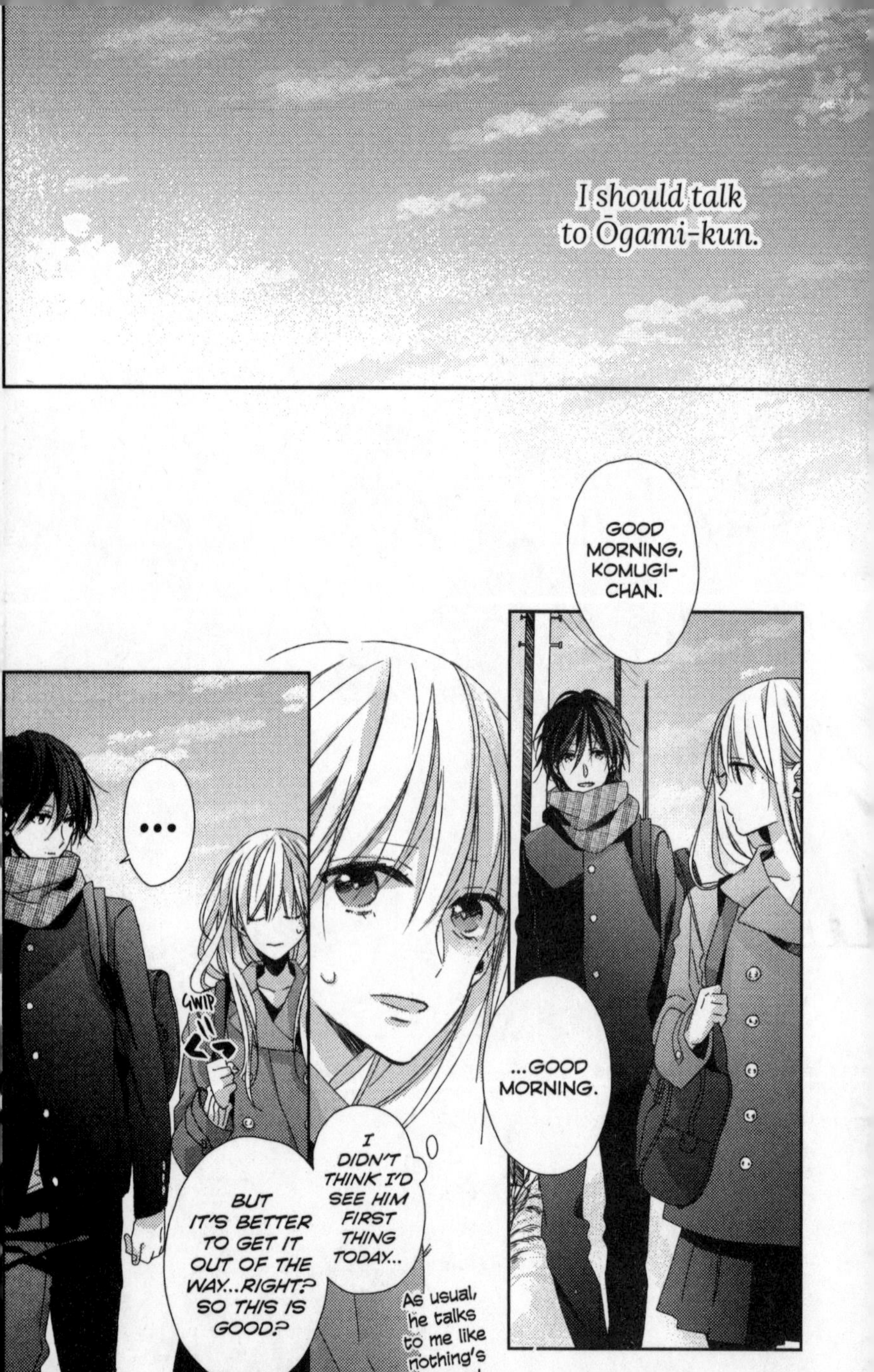
I should talk to Ōgami-kun.
GOOD MORNING, KOMUGI-CHAN.
...GOOD MORNING.
I DIDN'T THINK I'D SEE HIM FIRST THING TODAY...
As usual, he talks to me like nothing's changed.
...
GWIP
BUT IT'S BETTER TO GET IT OUT OF THE WAY...RIGHT? SO THIS IS GOOD?

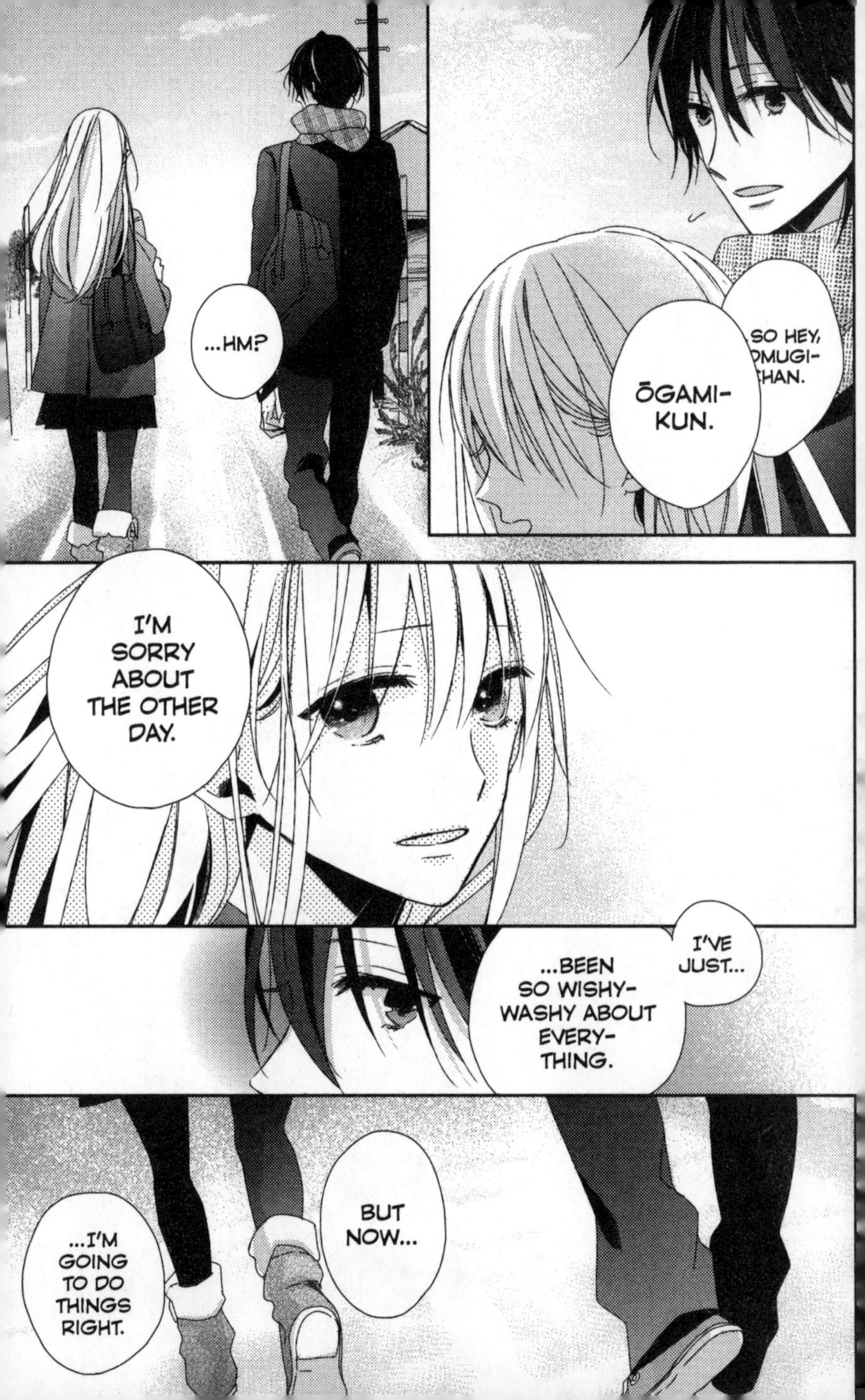
SO HEY, OMUGI-CHAN.
ŌGAMI-KUN.
...HM?
I'M SORRY ABOUT THE OTHER DAY.
I'VE JUST...
...BEEN SO WISHY-WASHY ABOUT EVERY-THING.
BUT NOW...
...I'M GOING TO DO THINGS RIGHT.

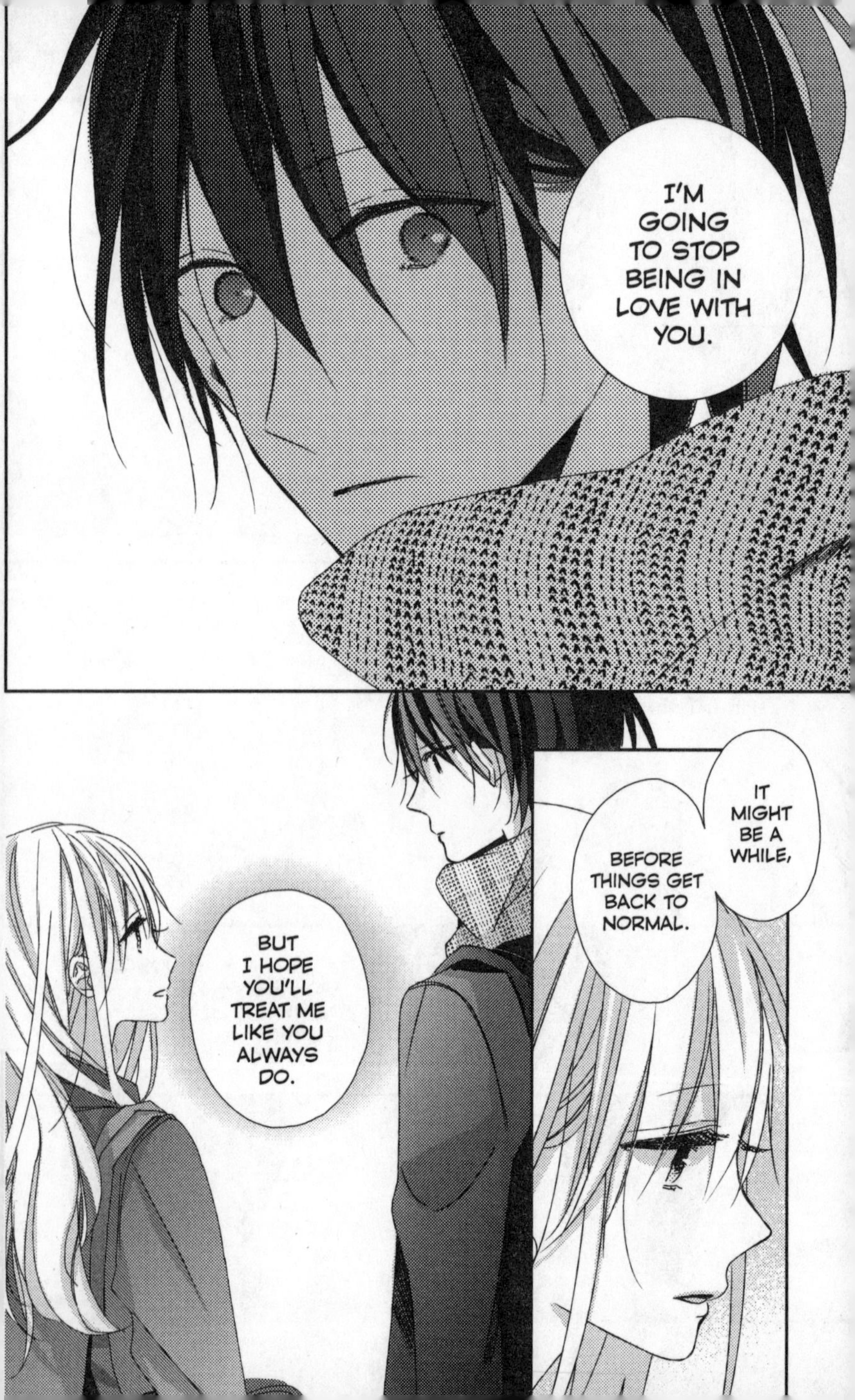
I'M GOING TO STOP BEING IN LOVE WITH YOU.
IT MIGHT BE A WHILE,
BEFORE THINGS GET BACK TO NORMAL.
BUT I HOPE YOU'LL TREAT ME LIKE YOU ALWAYS DO.

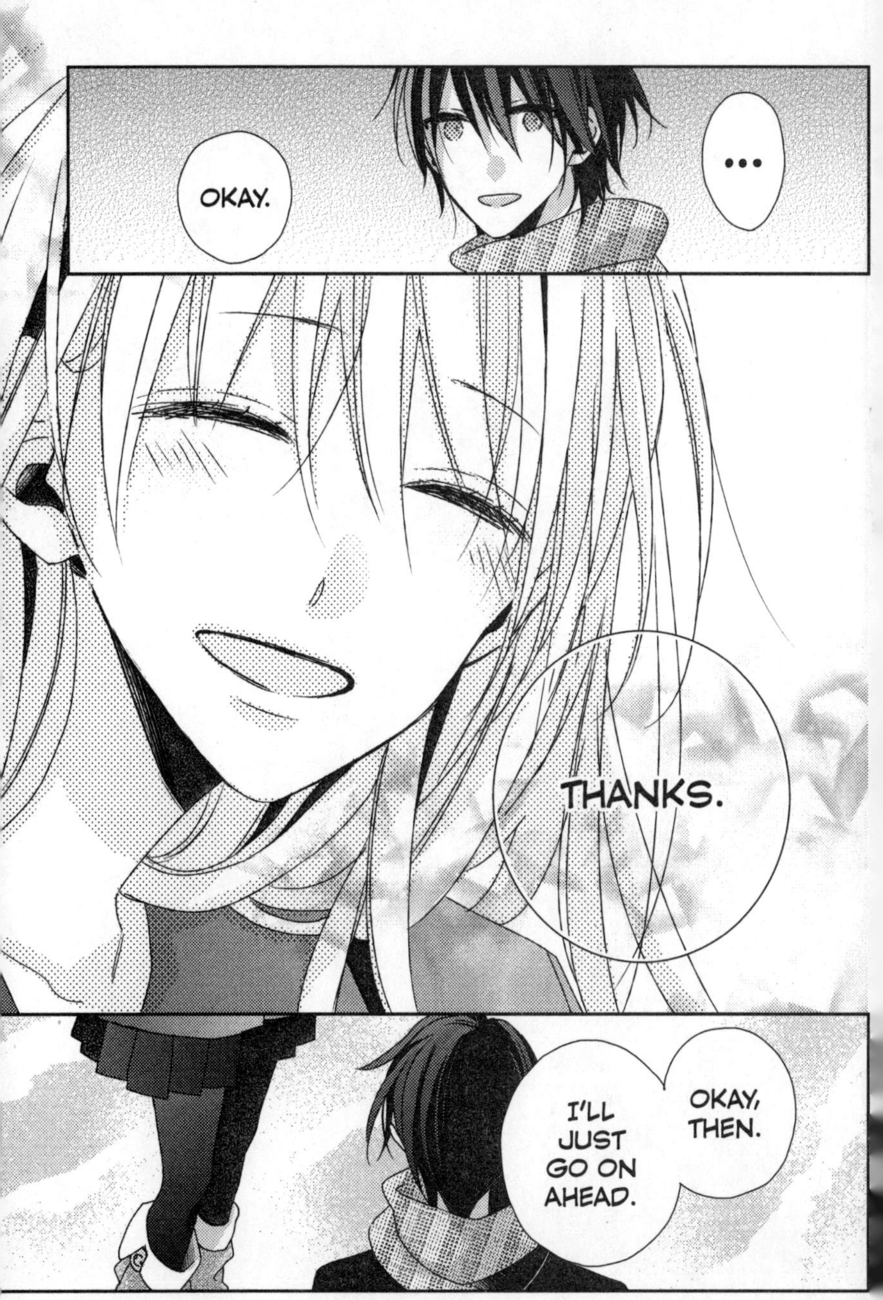
...
OKAY.
THANKS.
OKAY, THEN.
I'LL JUST GO ON AHEAD.

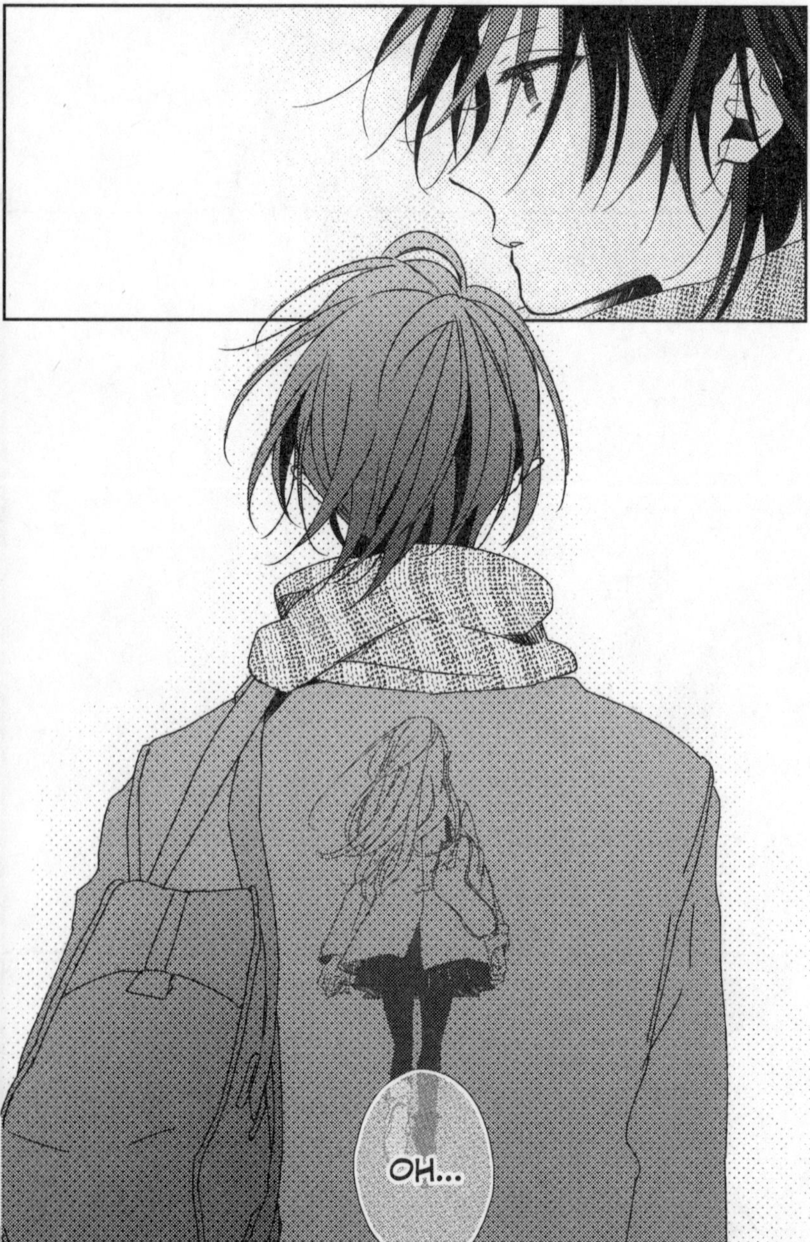
OH...

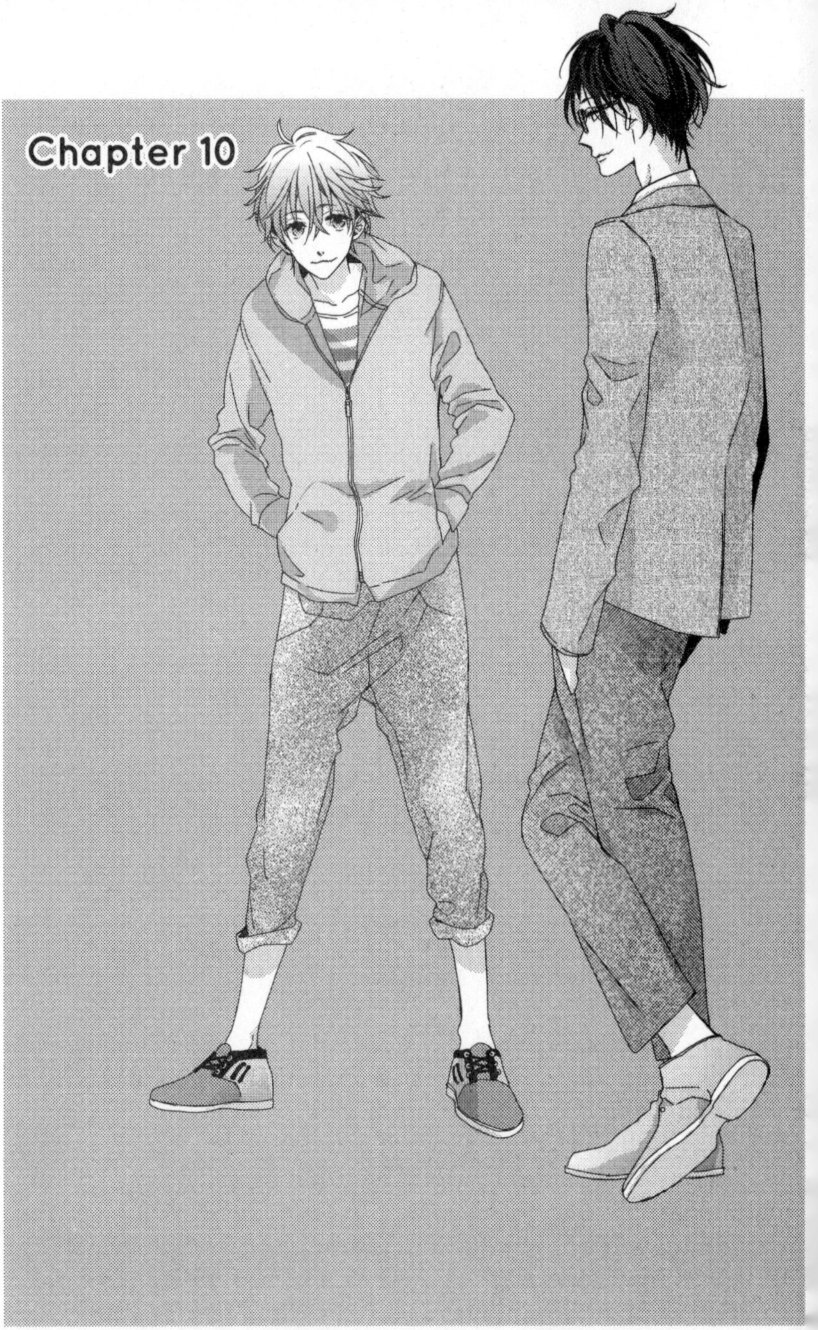
Chapter 10

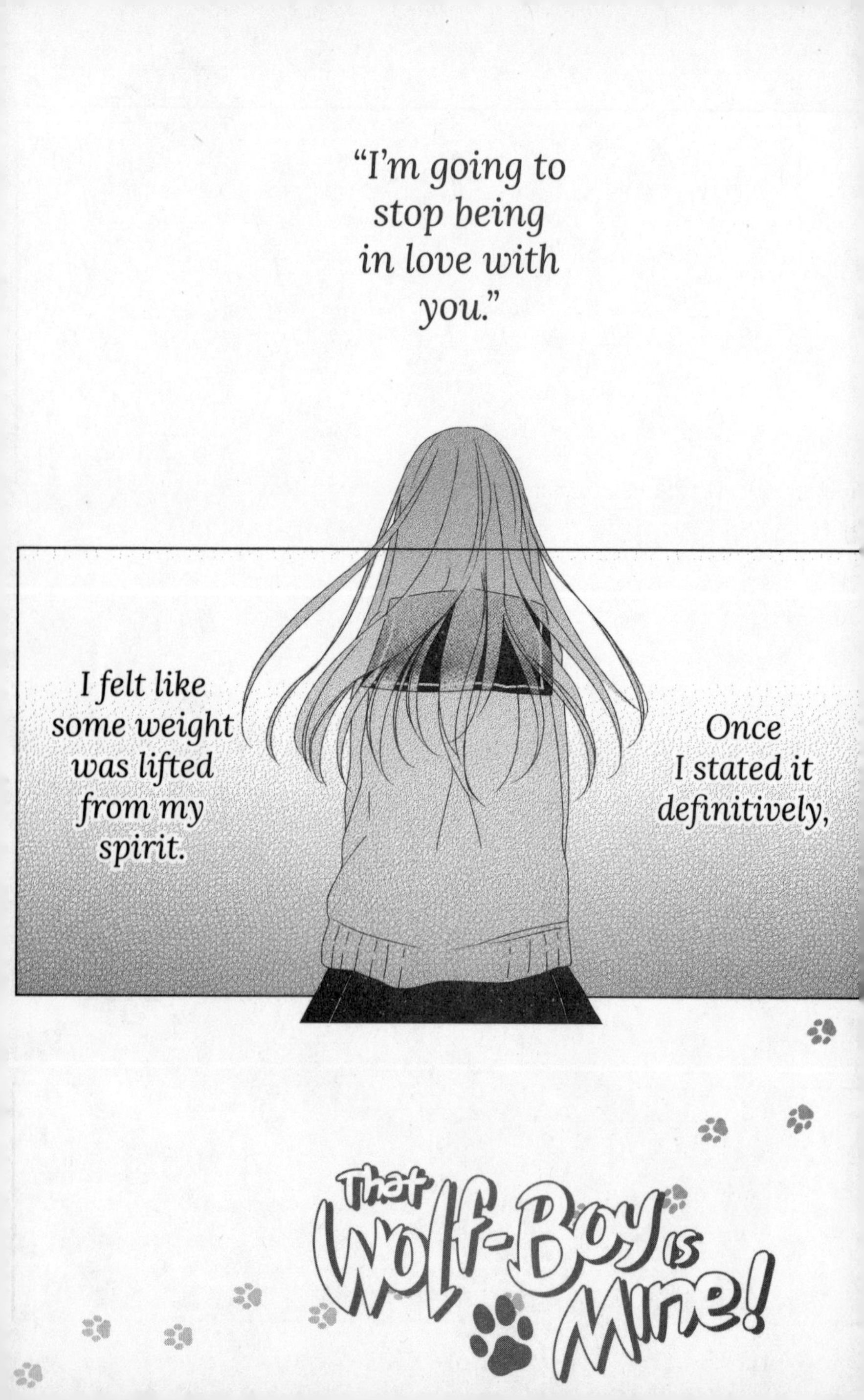
"I'm going to stop being in love with you."
Once I stated it definitively,
I felt like some weight was lifted from my spirit.
That Wolf-Boy is Mine!

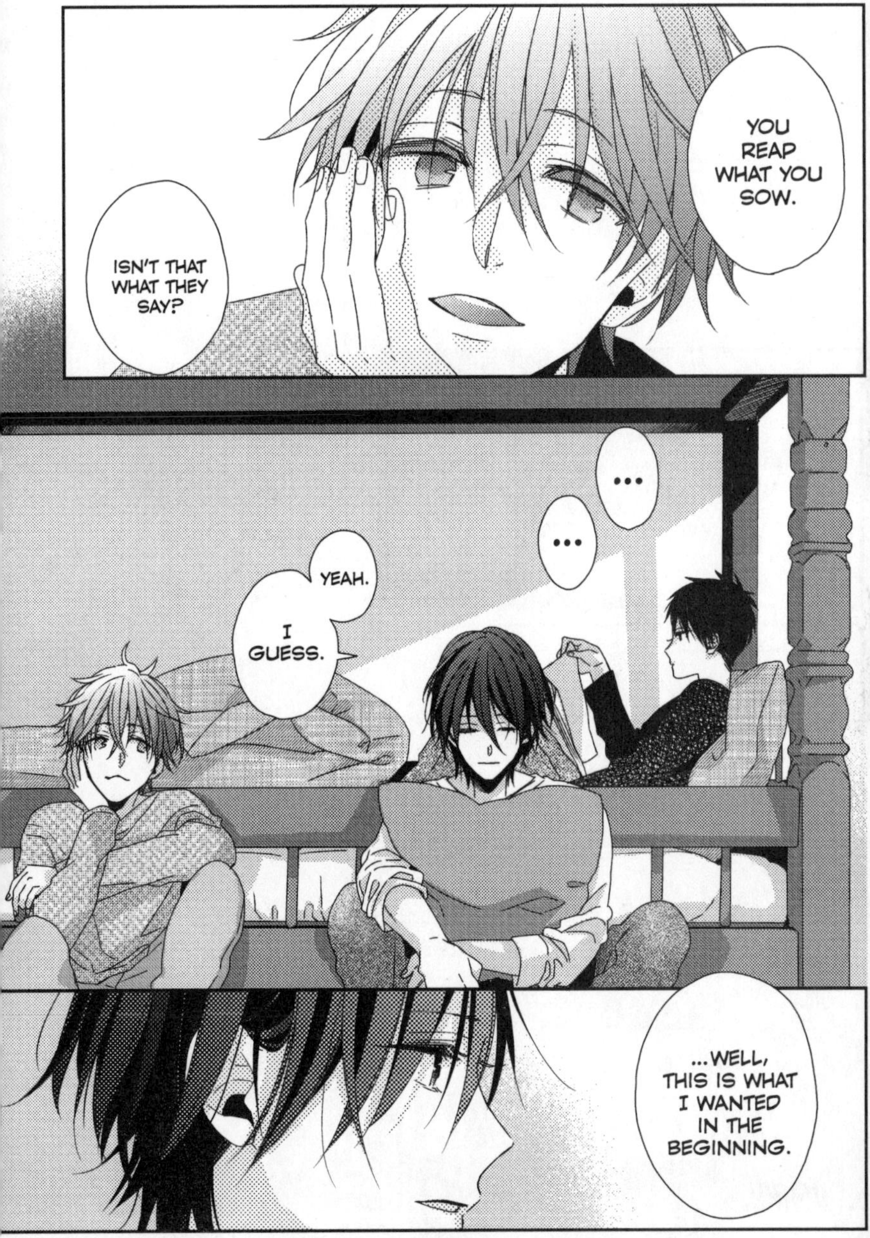
YOU REAP WHAT YOU SOW.
ISN'T THAT WHAT THEY SAY?
...
...
YEAH.
I GUESS.
...WELL, THIS IS WHAT I WANTED IN THE BEGINNING.

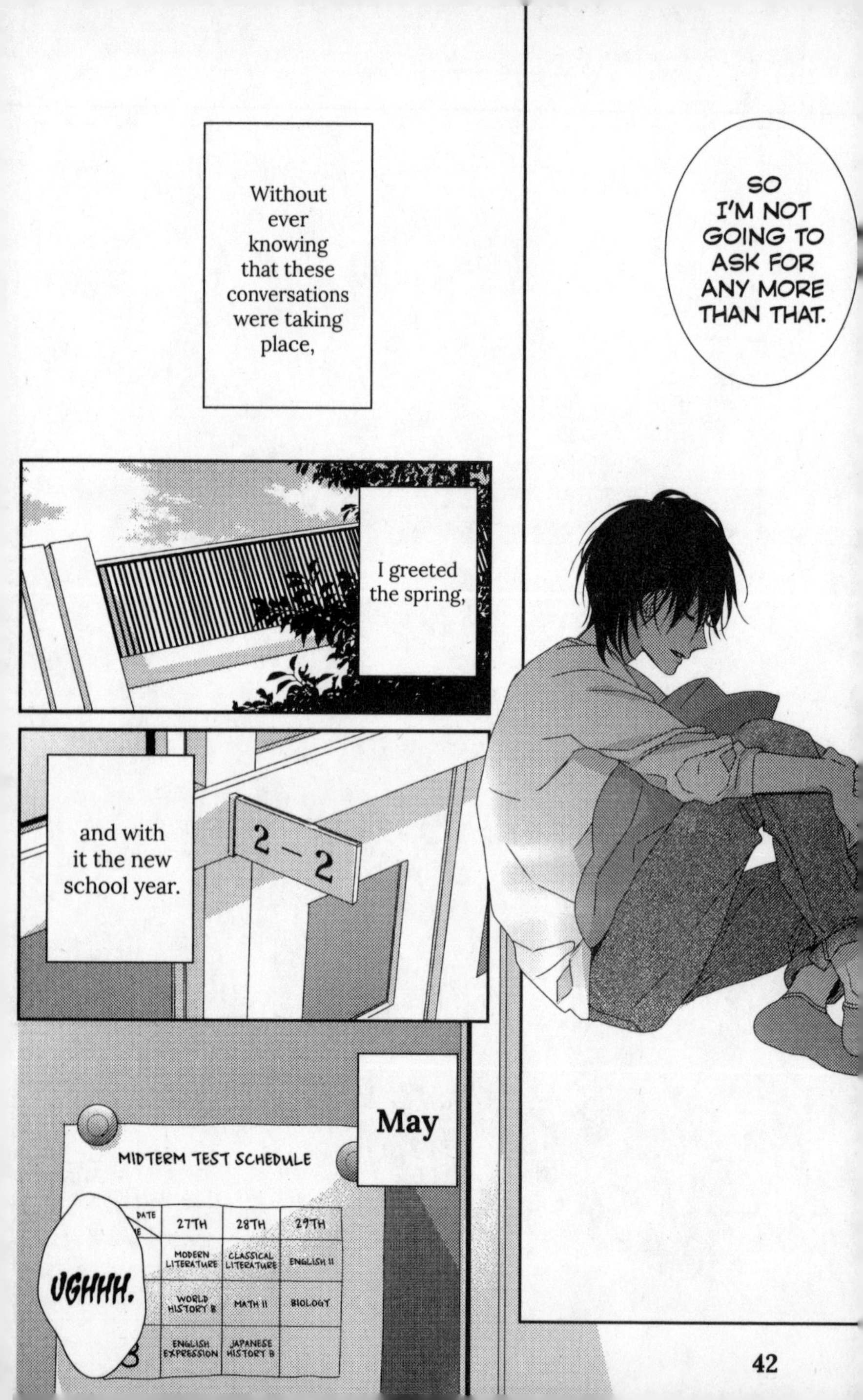
SO I'M NOT GOING TO ASK FOR ANY MORE THAN THAT.
Without ever knowing that these conversations were taking place,
I greeted the spring,
and with it the new school year.
2-2
May
MIDTERM TEST SCHEDULE
DATE
27TH
28TH
29TH
MODERN LITERATURE
CLASSICAL LITERATURE
ENGLISH II
WORLD HISTORY B
MATH II
BIOLOGY
ENGLISH EXPRESSION
JAPANESE HISTORY B
UGHHH.

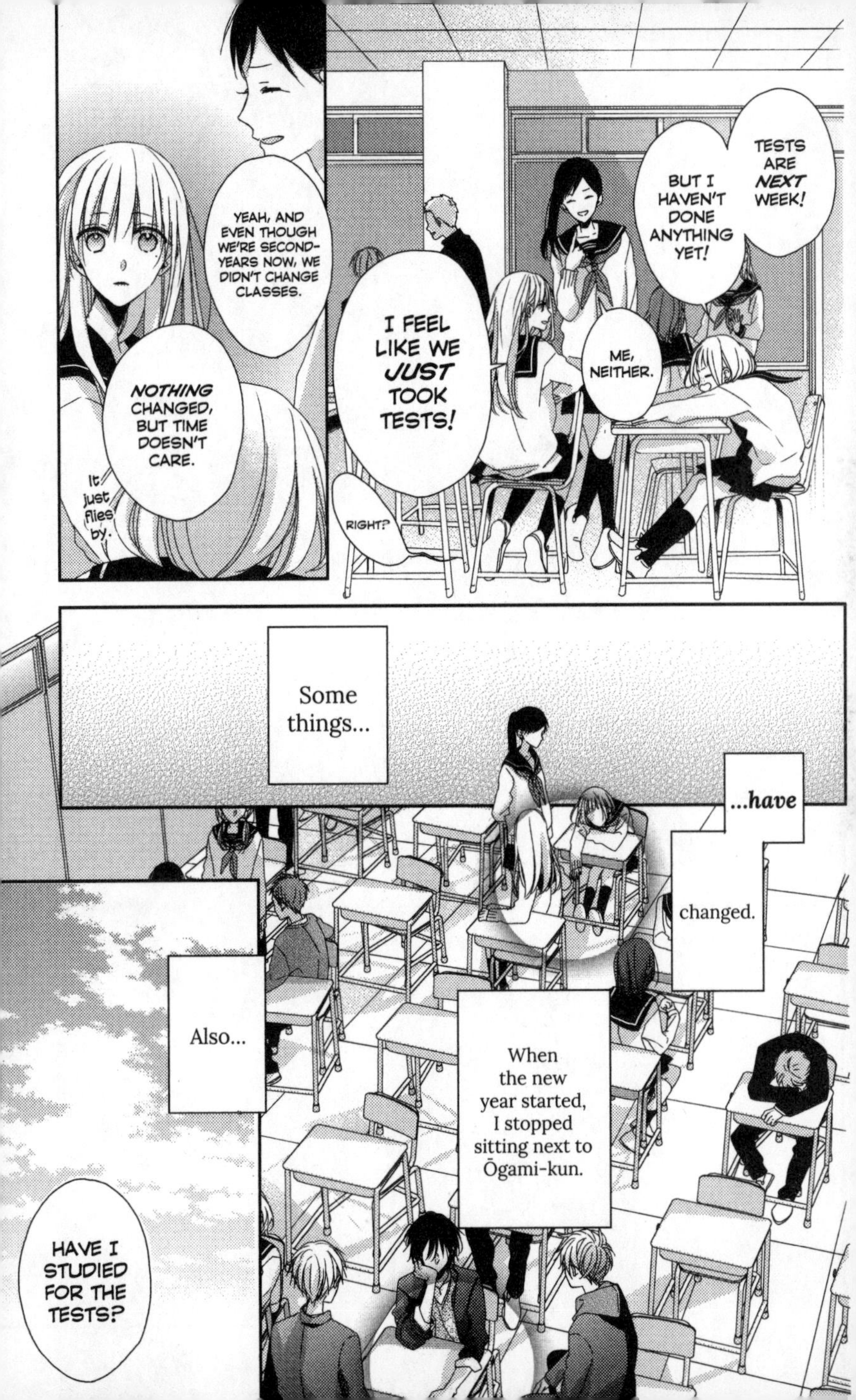
TESTS ARE NEXT WEEK!
BUT I HAVEN'T DONE ANYTHING YET!
ME, NEITHER.
I FEEL LIKE WE JUST TOOK TESTS!
RIGHT?
YEAH, AND EVEN THOUGH WE'RE SECOND-YEARS NOW, WE DIDN'T CHANGE CLASSES.
NOTHING CHANGED, BUT TIME DOESN'T CARE.
It just flies by.
Some things...
...have
changed.
Also...
When the new year started, I stopped sitting next to Ōgami-kun.
HAVE I STUDIED FOR THE TESTS?

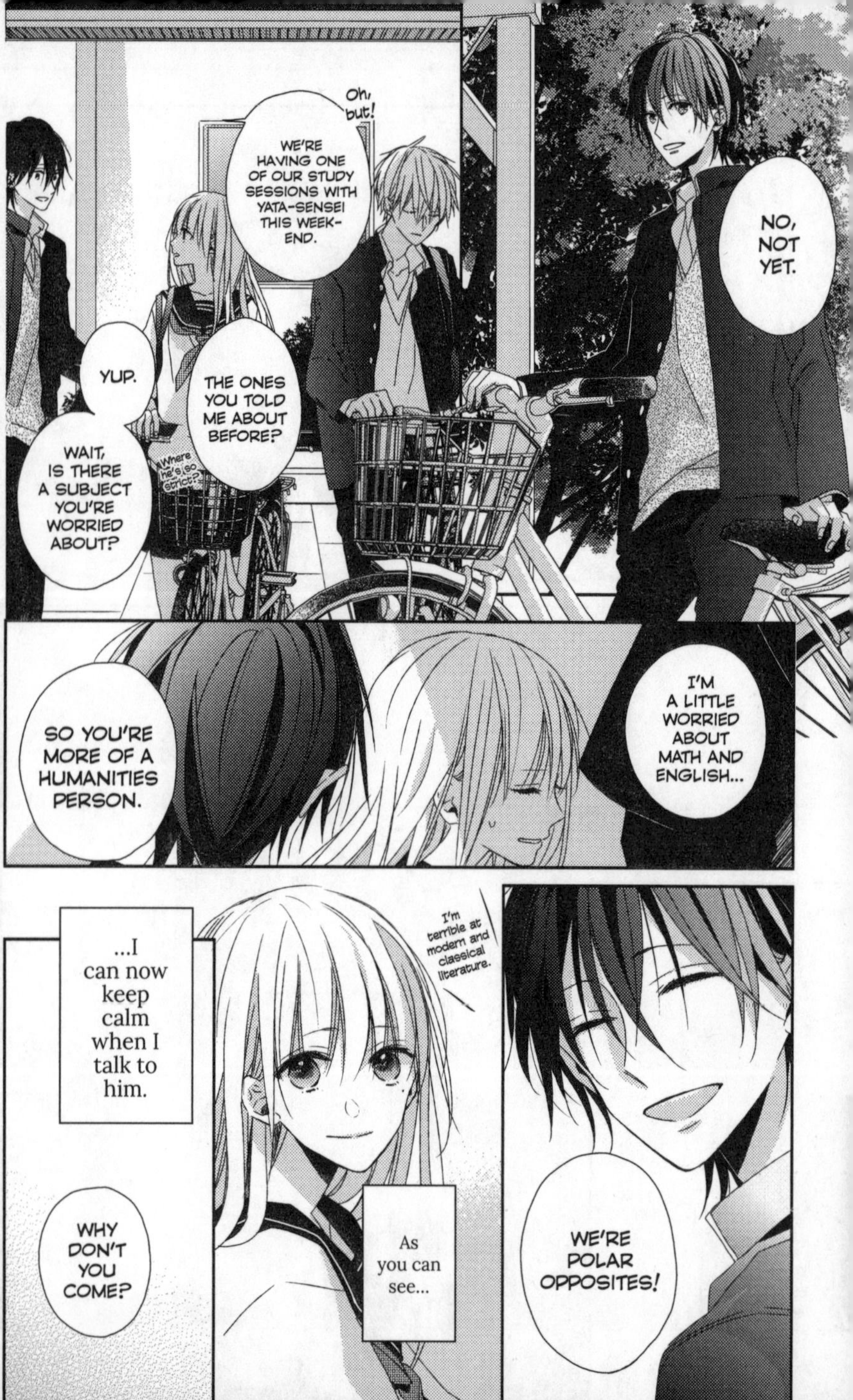
NO, NOT YET.
Oh, but!
WE'RE HAVING ONE OF OUR STUDY SESSIONS WITH YATA-SENSEI THIS WEEK-END.
THE ONES YOU TOLD ME ABOUT BEFORE?
YUP.
Where he's so strict?
WAIT, IS THERE A SUBJECT YOU'RE WORRIED ABOUT?
I'M A LITTLE WORRIED ABOUT MATH AND ENGLISH...
SO YOU'RE MORE OF A HUMANITIES PERSON.
WE'RE POLAR OPPOSITES!
I'm terrible at modern and classical literature.
...I can now keep calm when I talk to him.
As you can see...
WHY DON'T YOU COME?

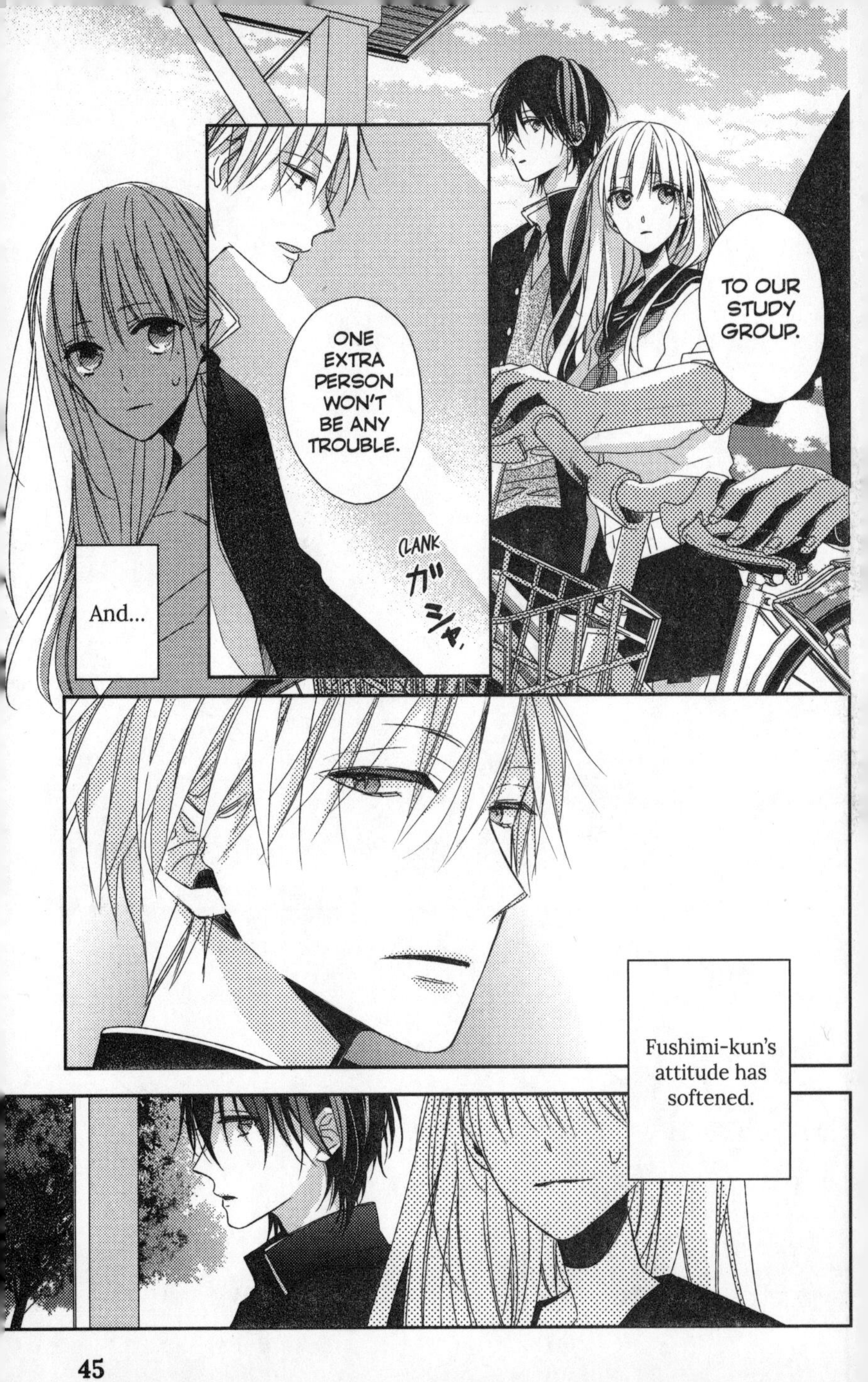
TO OUR STUDY GROUP.
ONE EXTRA PERSON WON'T BE ANY TROUBLE.
CLANK
ガシャ
And...
Fushimi-kun's attitude has softened.

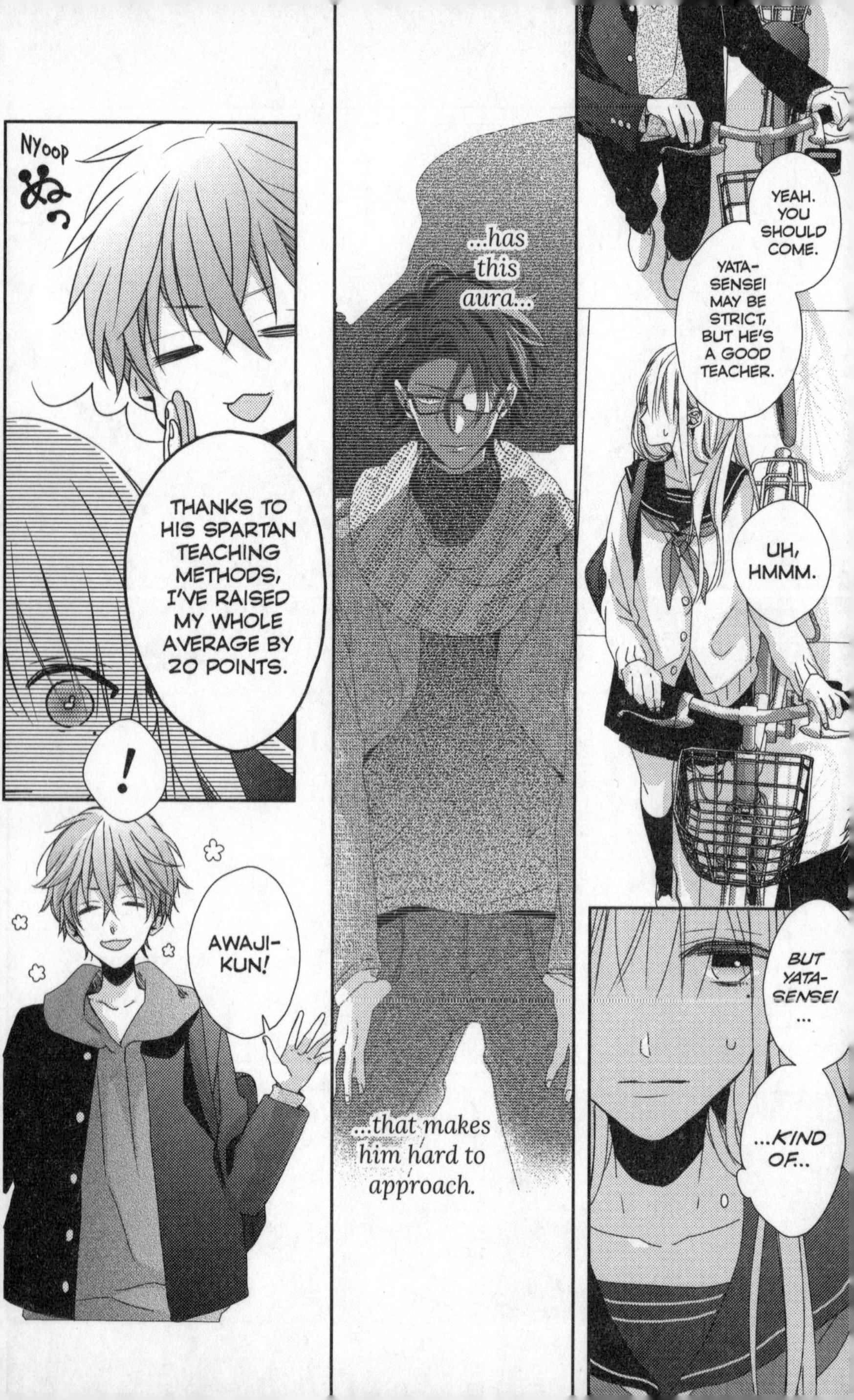
YEAH. YOU SHOULD COME.
YATA-SENSEI MAY BE STRICT, BUT HE'S A GOOD TEACHER.
UH, HMMM.
BUT YATA-SENSEI ...
...KIND OF...
...has this aura...
...that makes him hard to approach.
NYOOP
ぬっ
THANKS TO HIS SPARTAN TEACHING METHODS, I'VE RAISED MY WHOLE AVERAGE BY 20 POINTS.
!
AWAJI-KUN!

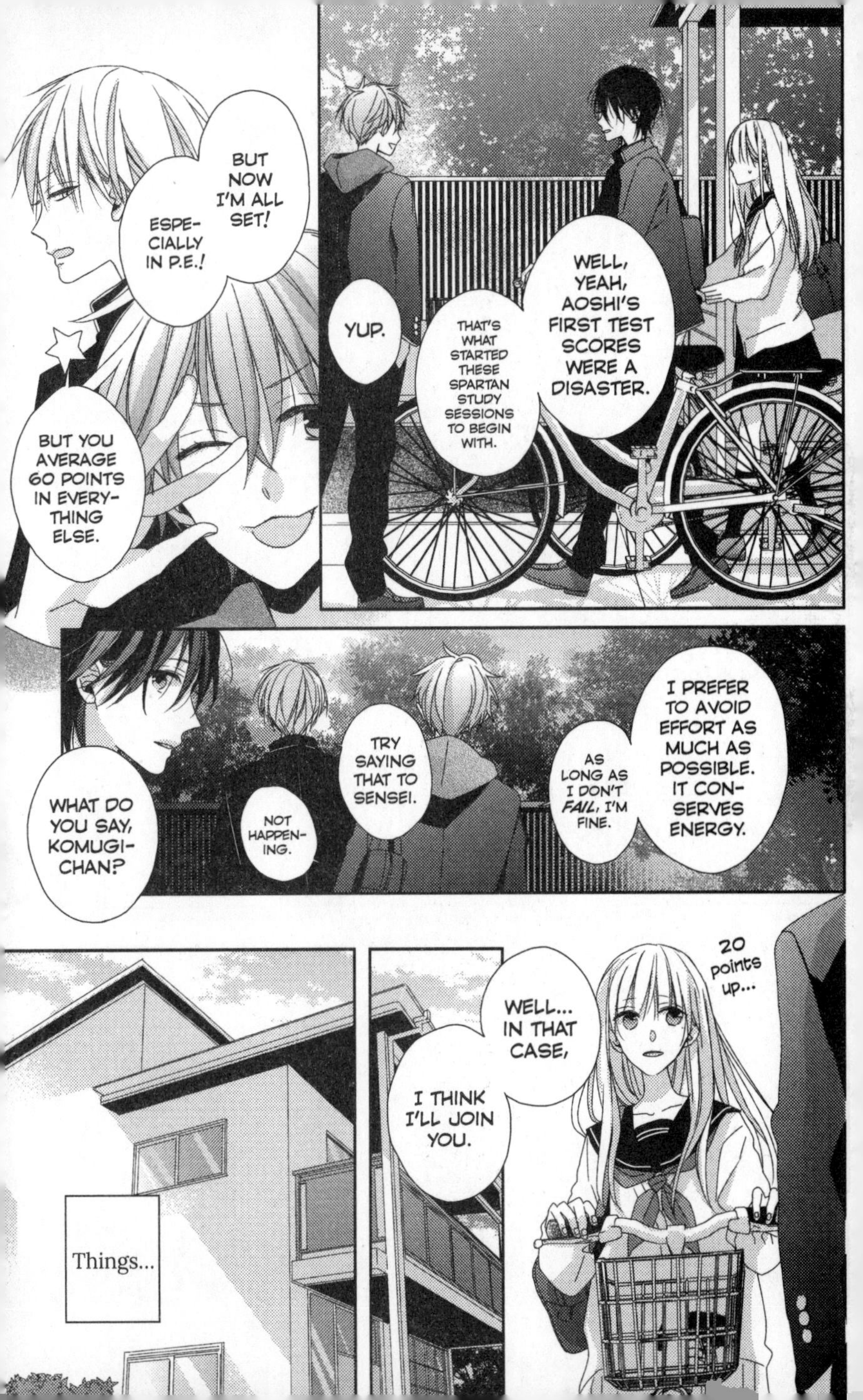
WELL, YEAH, AOSHI'S FIRST TEST SCORES WERE A DISASTER.
THAT'S WHAT STARTED THESE SPARTAN STUDY SESSIONS TO BEGIN WITH.
YUP.
BUT NOW I'M ALL SET!
ESPE-CIALLY IN P.E.!
BUT YOU AVERAGE 60 POINTS IN EVERY-THING ELSE.
I PREFER TO AVOID EFFORT AS MUCH AS POSSIBLE. IT CON-SERVES ENERGY.
AS LONG AS I DON'T *FAIL*, I'M FINE.
TRY SAYING THAT TO SENSEI.
NOT HAPPEN-ING.
WHAT DO YOU SAY, KOMUGI-CHAN?
20 points up...
WELL... IN THAT CASE,
I THINK I'LL JOIN YOU.
Things...

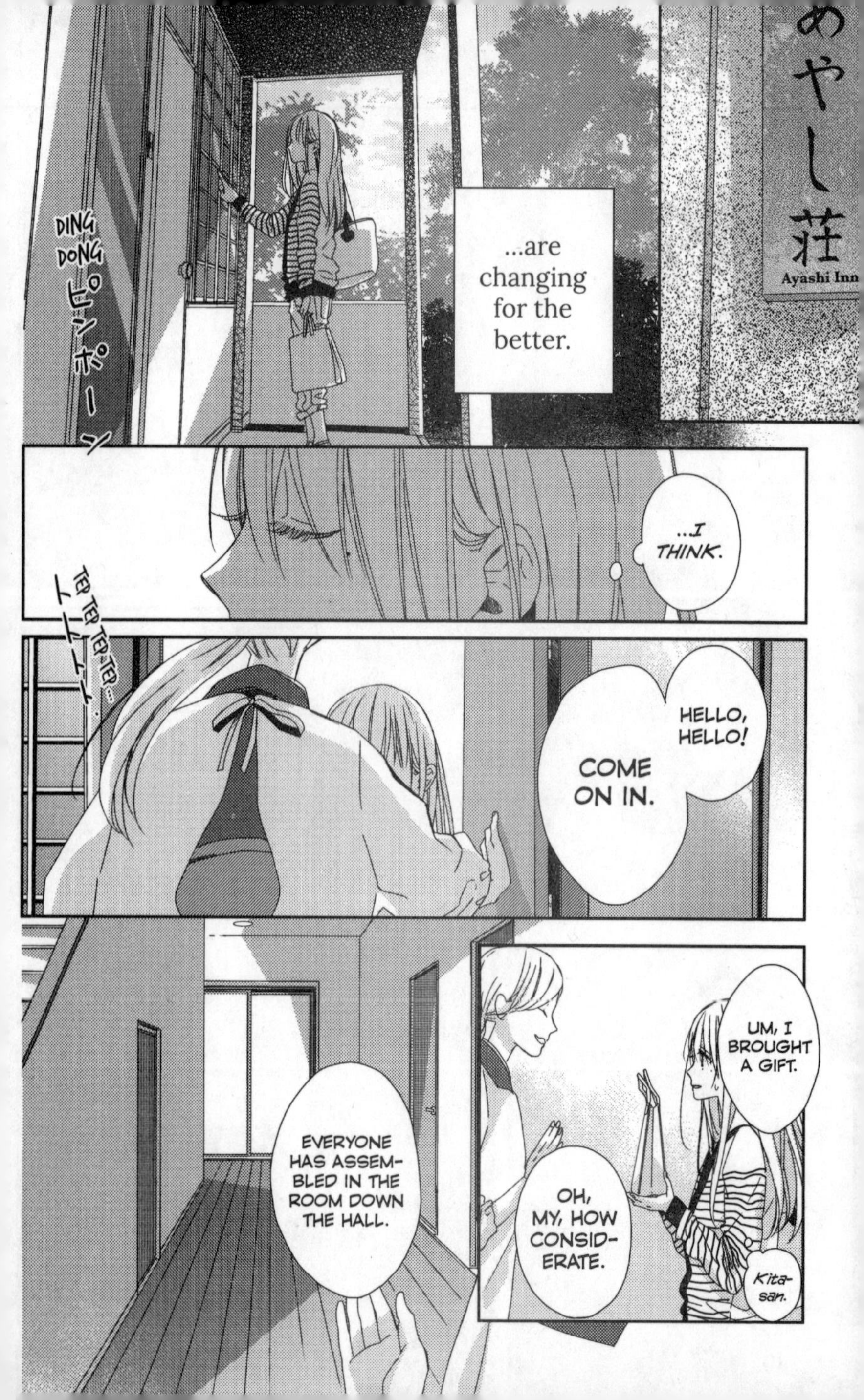
めやし荘
Ayashi Inn
...are changing for the better.
DING DONG ピンポーン
...I THINK.
TEP TEP TEP TEP...
HELLO, HELLO!
COME ON IN.
UM, I BROUGHT A GIFT.
Kita-san.
OH, MY, HOW CONSIDERATE.
EVERYONE HAS ASSEMBLED IN THE ROOM DOWN THE HALL.

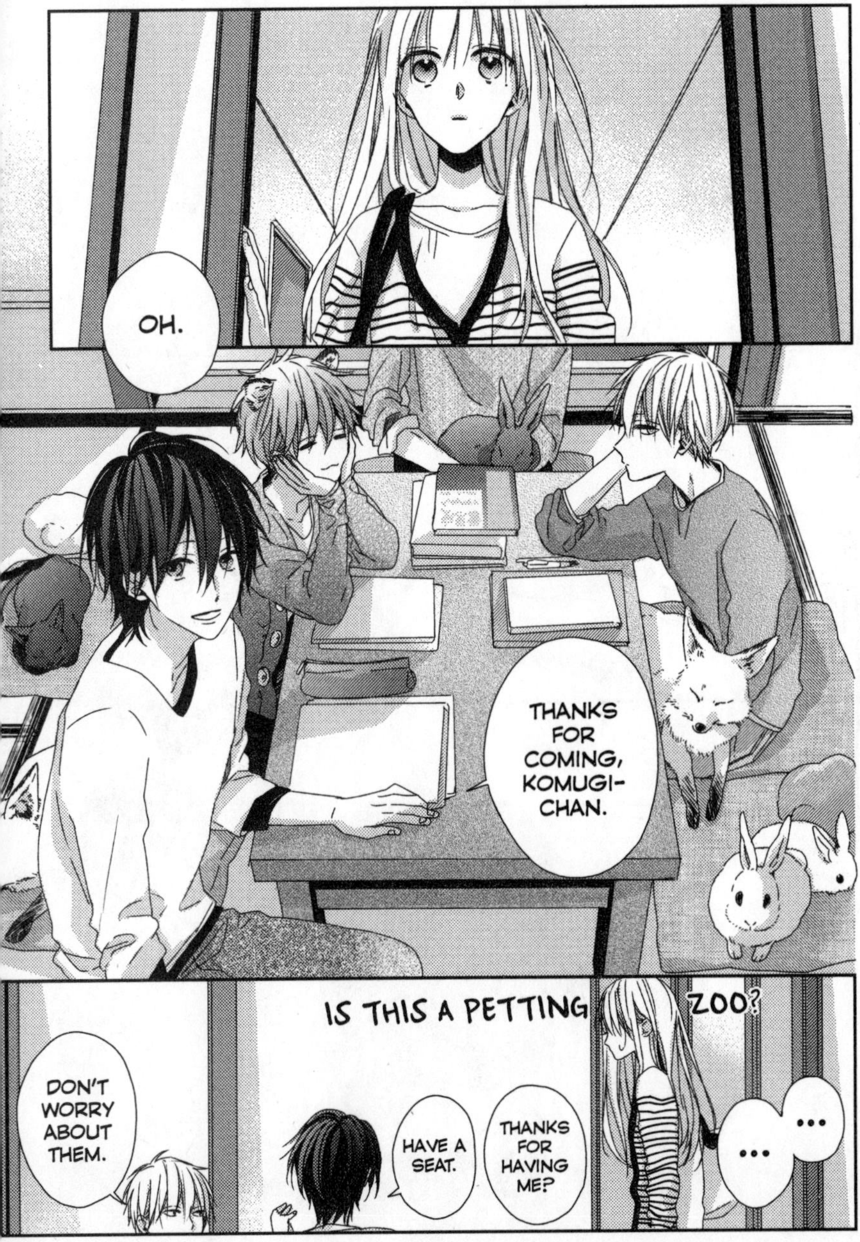
OH.
THANKS FOR COMING, KOMUGI-CHAN.
...
...
IS THIS A PETTING ZOO?
THANKS FOR HAVING ME?
HAVE A SEAT.
DON'T WORRY ABOUT THEM.

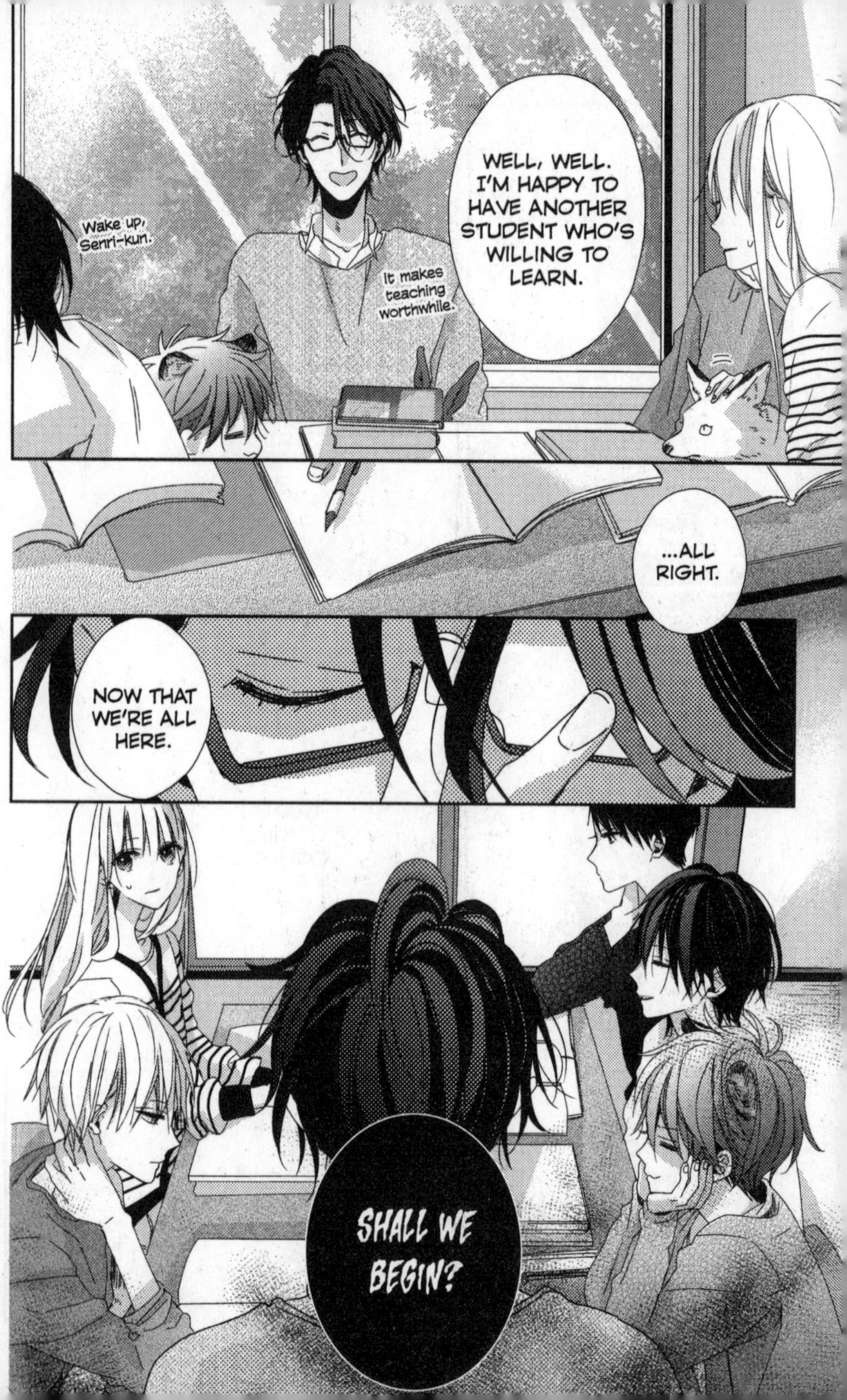
WELL, WELL. I'M HAPPY TO HAVE ANOTHER STUDENT WHO'S WILLING TO LEARN.
It makes teaching worthwhile.
Wake up, Senri-kun.
...ALL RIGHT.
NOW THAT WE'RE ALL HERE.
SHALL WE BEGIN?

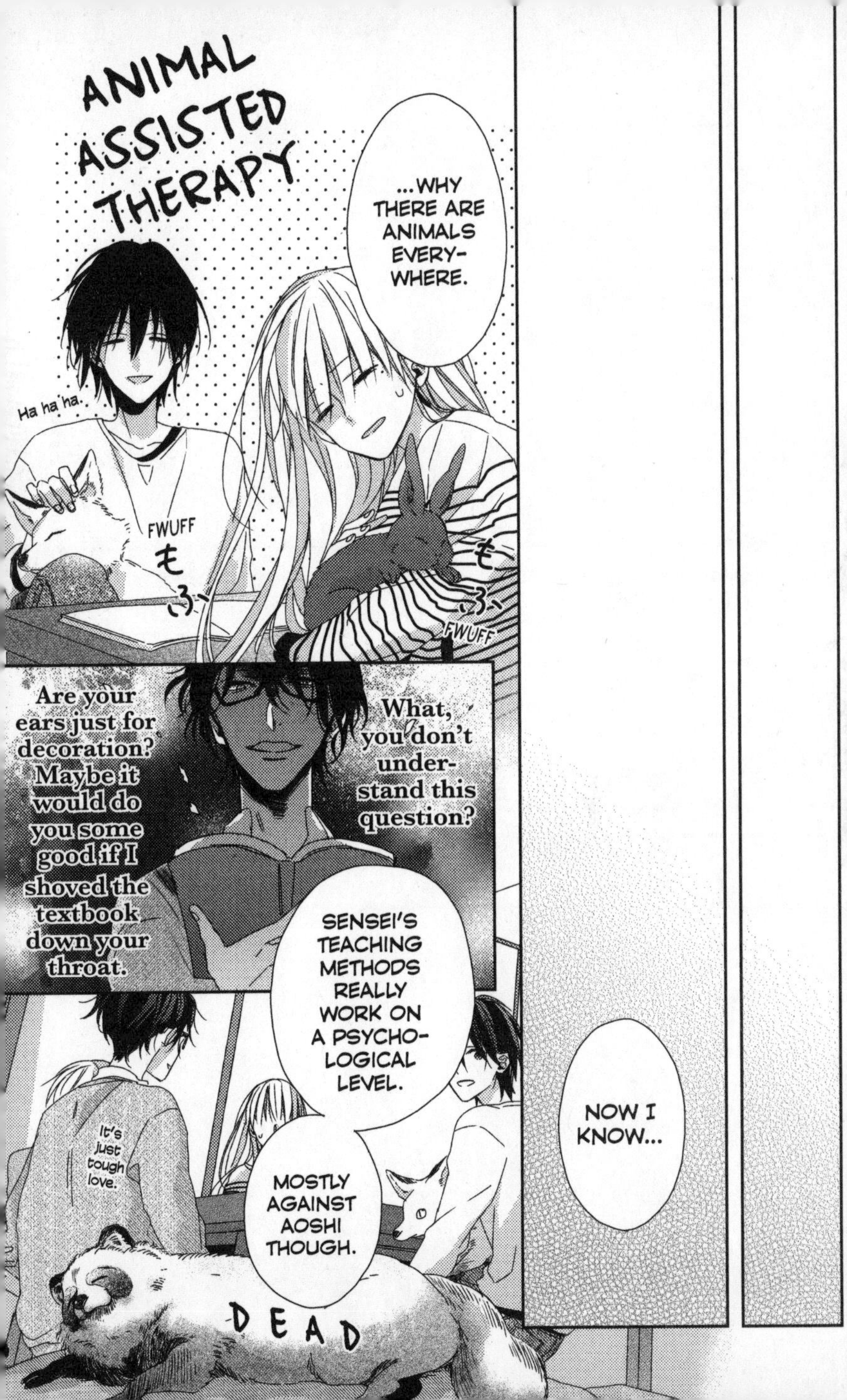
NOW I KNOW...
...WHY THERE ARE ANIMALS EVERY-WHERE.
ANIMAL ASSISTED THERAPY
Ha ha ha.
もふ
FWUFF
もふ
FWUFF
What, you don't under-stand this question?
Are your ears just for decoration? Maybe it would do you some good if I shoved the textbook down your throat.
SENSEI'S TEACHING METHODS REALLY WORK ON A PSYCHO-LOGICAL LEVEL.
MOSTLY AGAINST AOSHI THOUGH.
It's just tough love.
DEAD

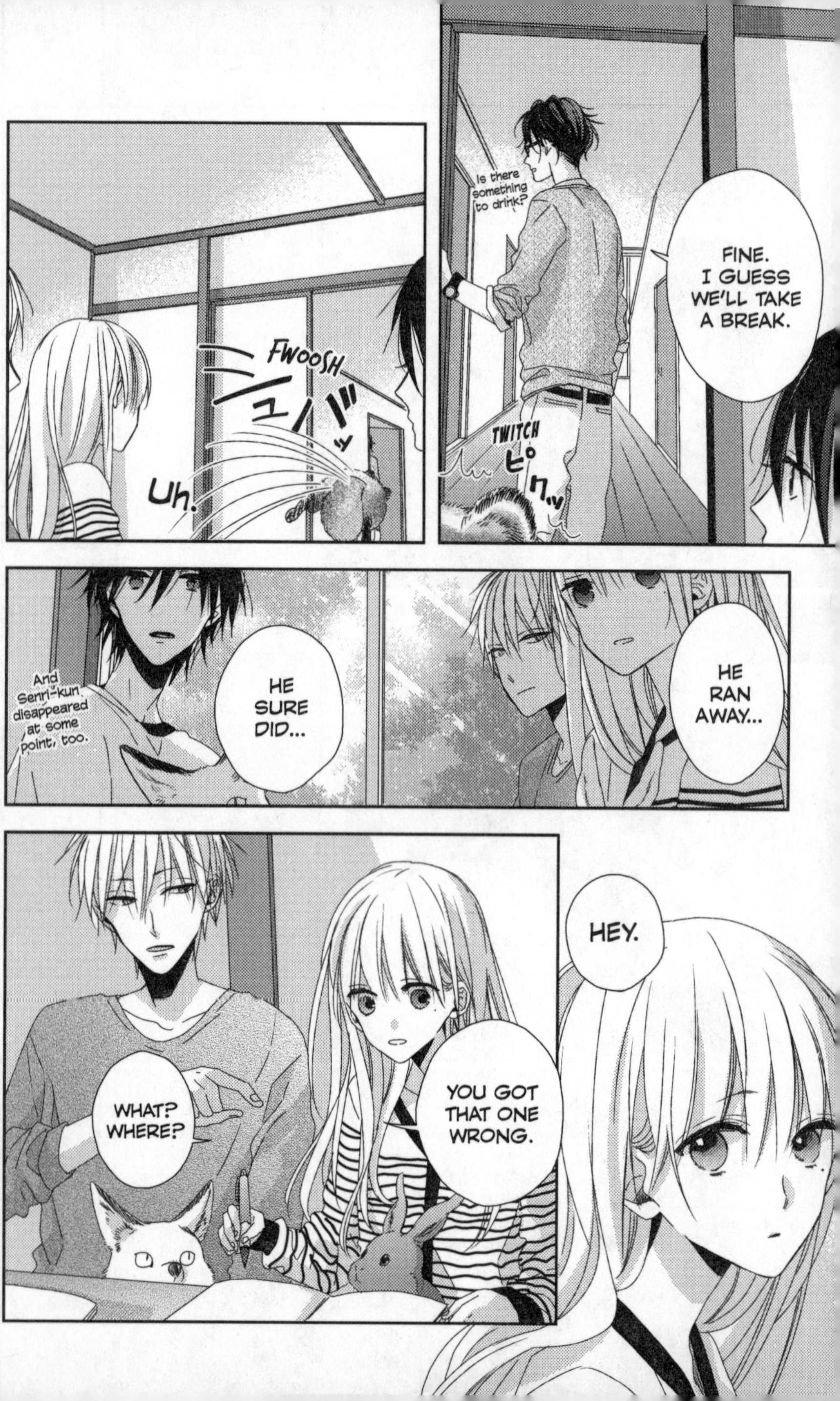
FINE. I GUESS WE'LL TAKE A BREAK.
Is there something to drink?
TWITCH
ピクッ
FWOOSH
シュバッ
Uh.
HE RAN AWAY...
HE SURE DID...
And Senri-kun disappeared at some point, too.
HEY.
YOU GOT THAT ONE WRONG.
WHAT? WHERE?

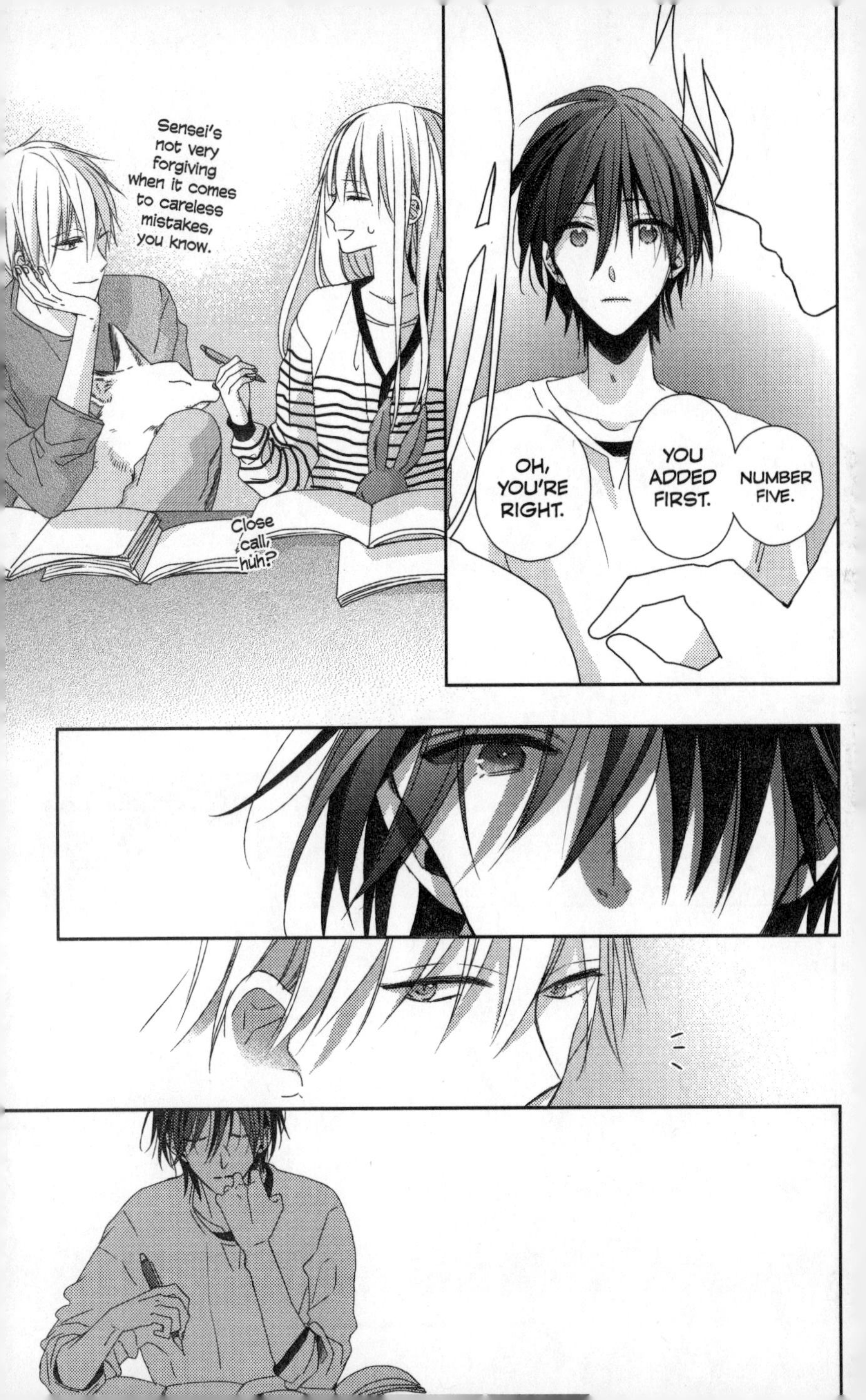
NUMBER FIVE.
YOU ADDED FIRST.
OH, YOU'RE RIGHT.
Sensei's not very forgiving when it comes to careless mistakes, you know.
Close call, huh?

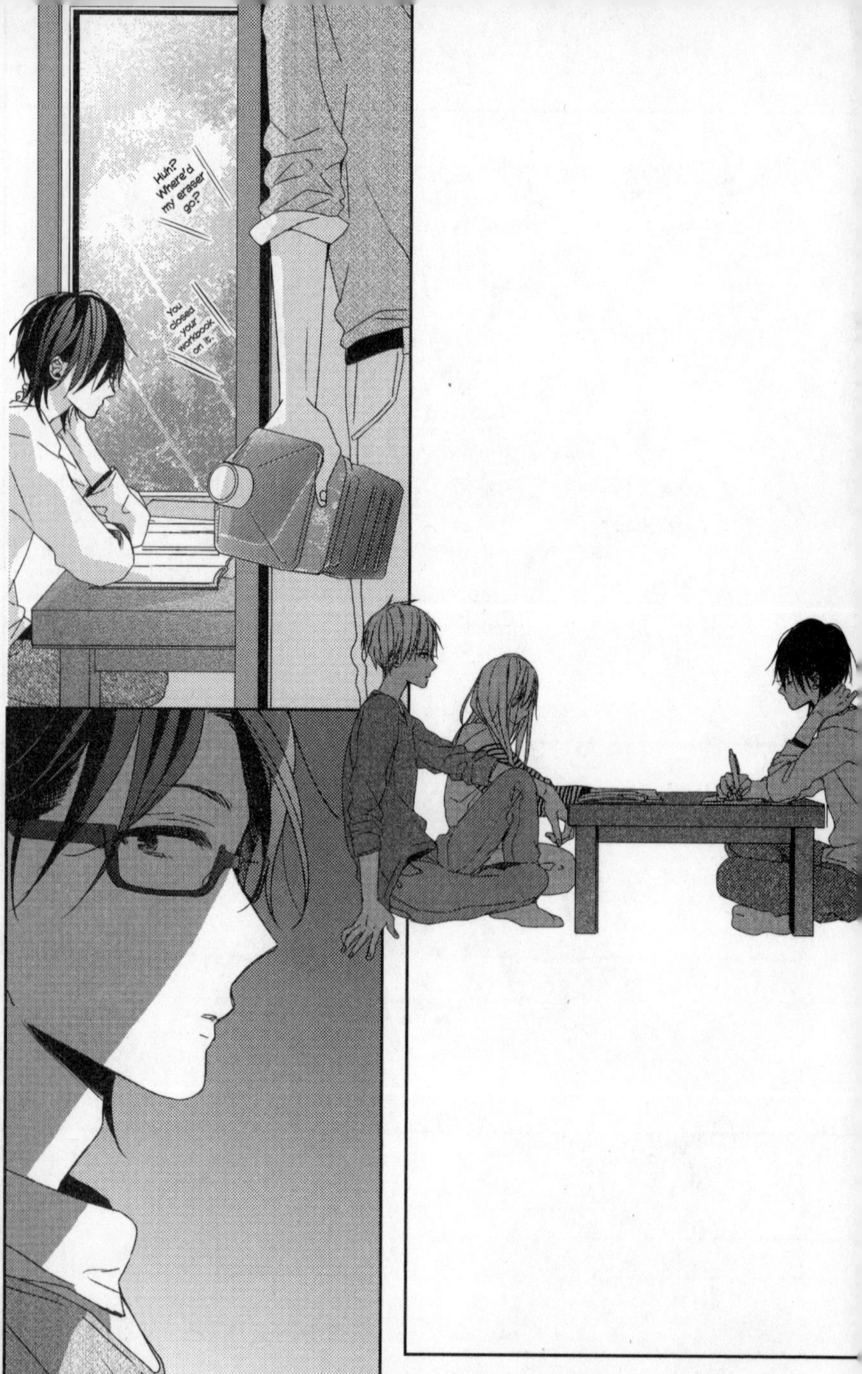
Huh? Where'd my eraser go?
You closed your workbook on it.

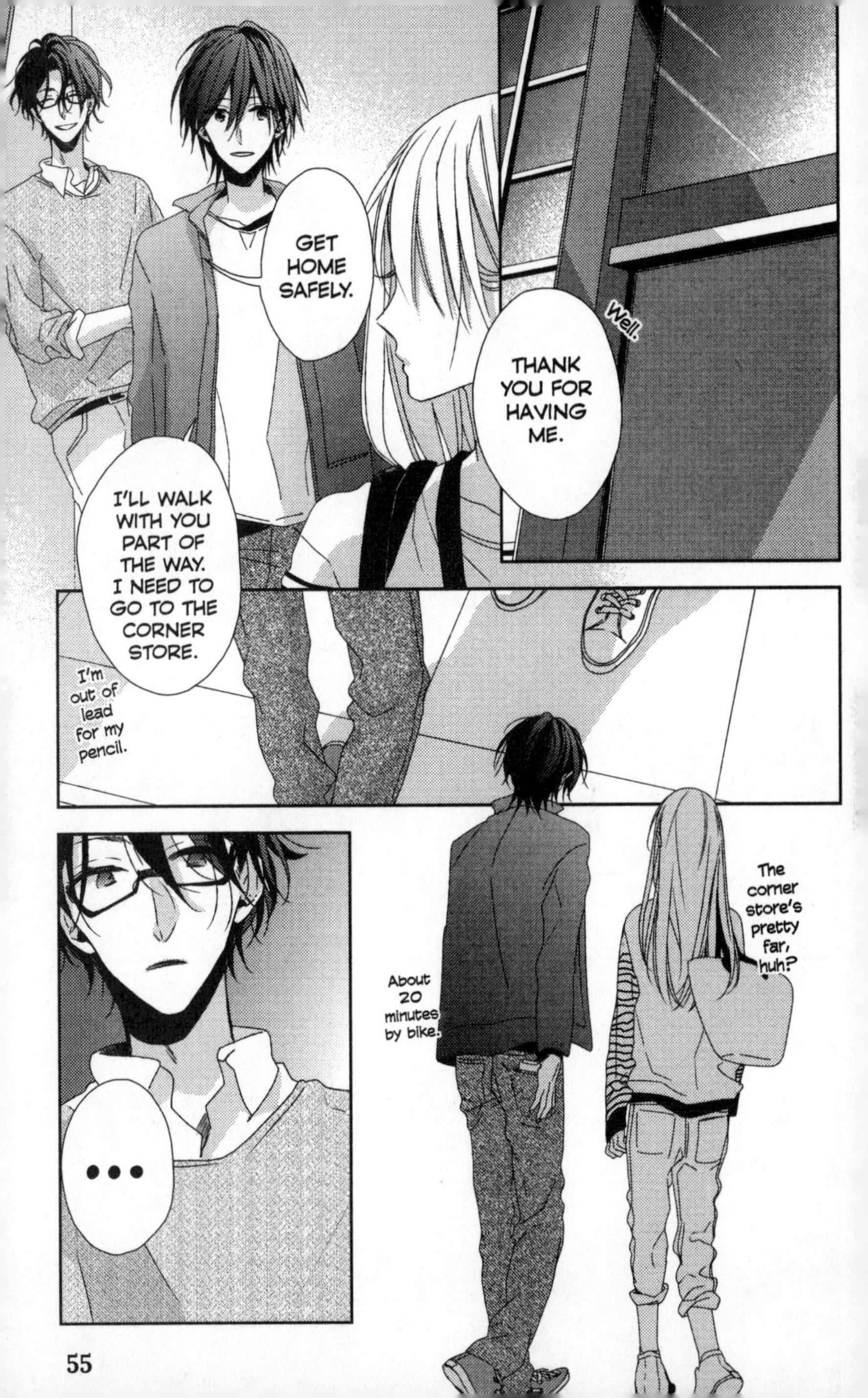
Well.
THANK YOU FOR HAVING ME.
GET HOME SAFELY.
I'LL WALK WITH YOU PART OF THE WAY. I NEED TO GO TO THE CORNER STORE.
I'm out of lead for my pencil.
The corner store's pretty far, huh?
About 20 minutes by bike.
...

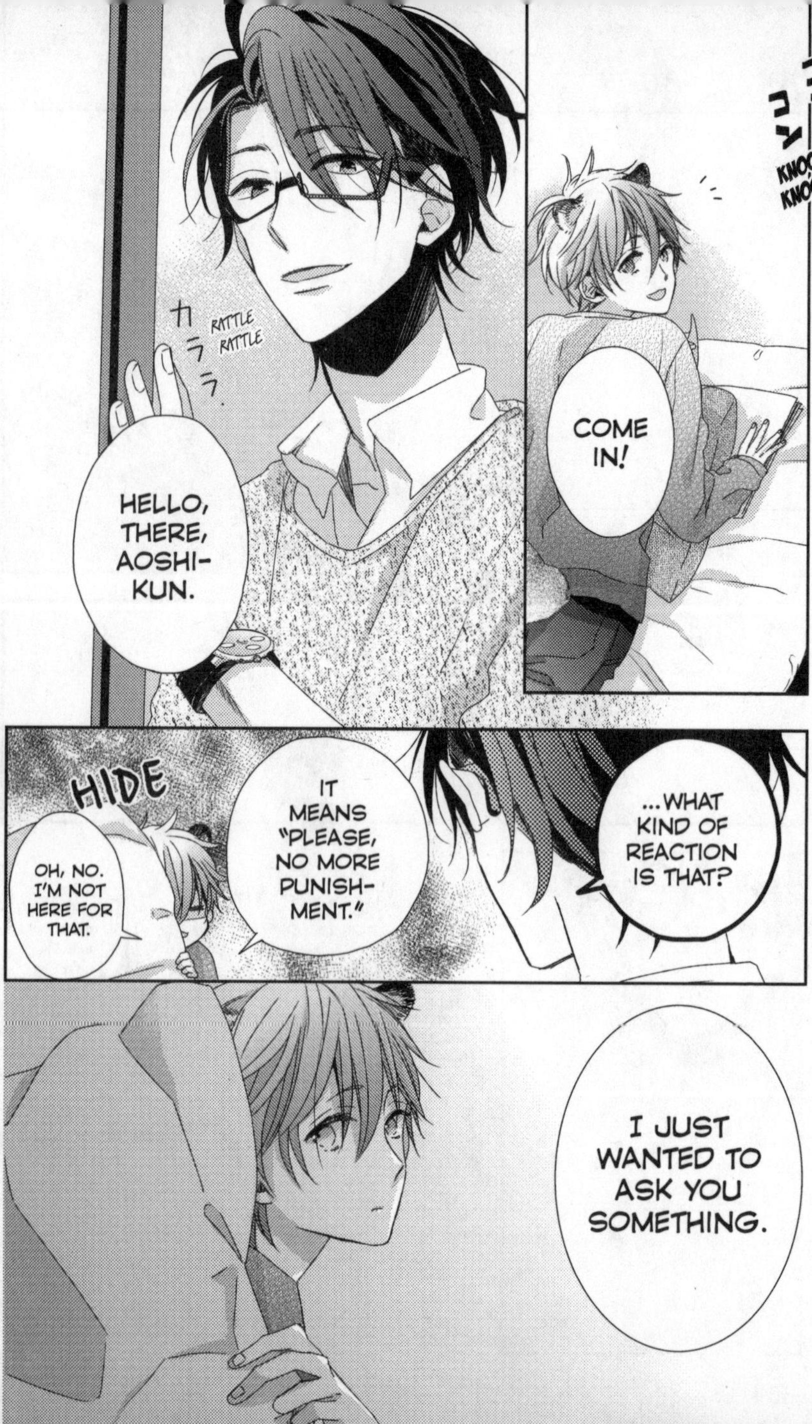

コンコン
KNOCK KNOCK
COME IN!
カララ
RATTLE RATTLE
HELLO, THERE, AOSHI-KUN.
...WHAT KIND OF REACTION IS THAT?
HIDE
IT MEANS "PLEASE, NO MORE PUNISH-MENT."
OH, NO. I'M NOT HERE FOR THAT.
I JUST WANTED TO ASK YOU SOMETHING.

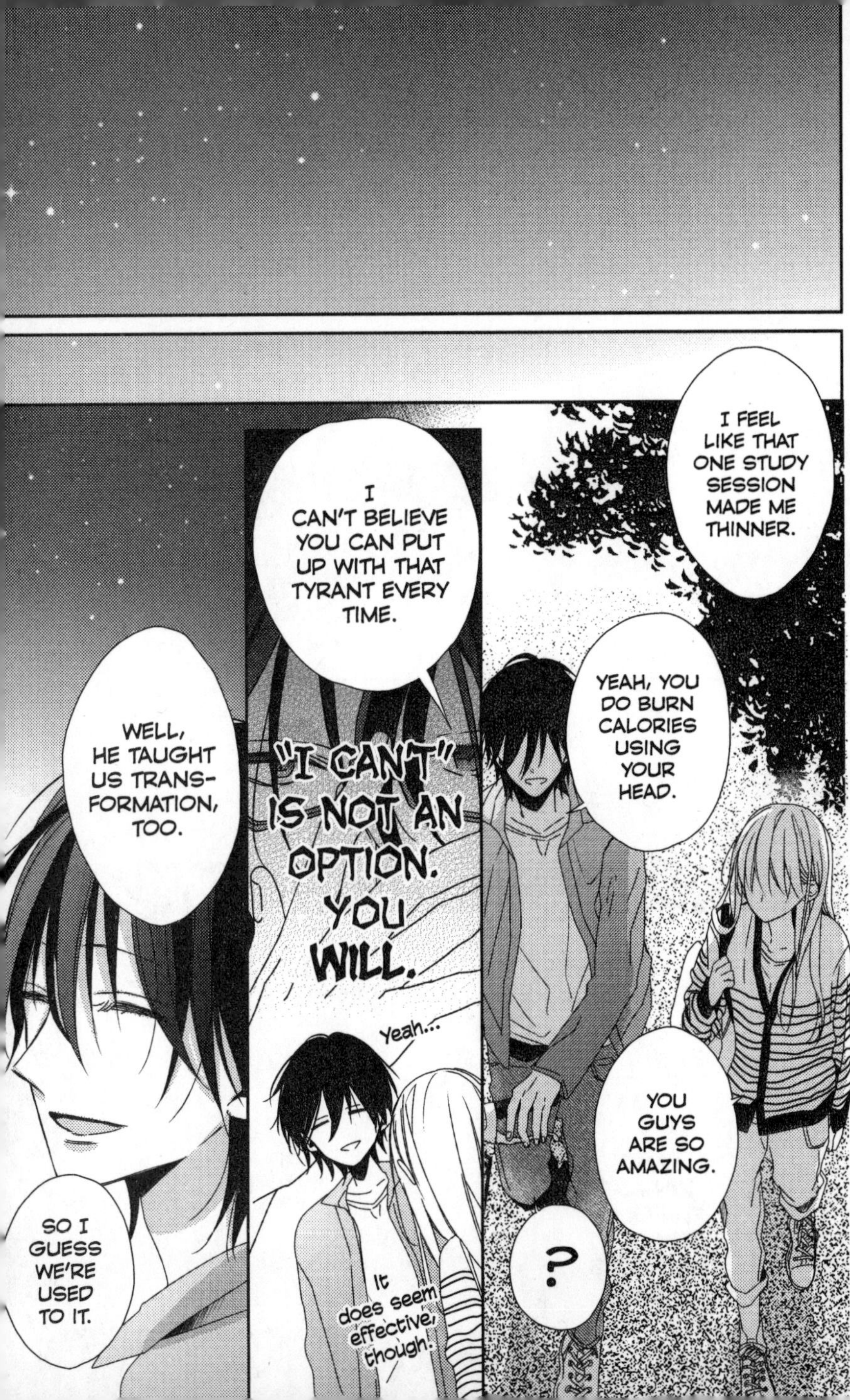
I FEEL LIKE THAT ONE STUDY SESSION MADE ME THINNER.
YEAH, YOU DO BURN CALORIES USING YOUR HEAD.
YOU GUYS ARE SO AMAZING.
?
I CAN'T BELIEVE YOU CAN PUT UP WITH THAT TYRANT EVERY TIME.
"I CAN'T" IS NOT AN OPTION. YOU WILL.
Yeah...
It does seem effective, though.
WELL, HE TAUGHT US TRANS-FORMATION, TOO.
SO I GUESS WE'RE USED TO IT.

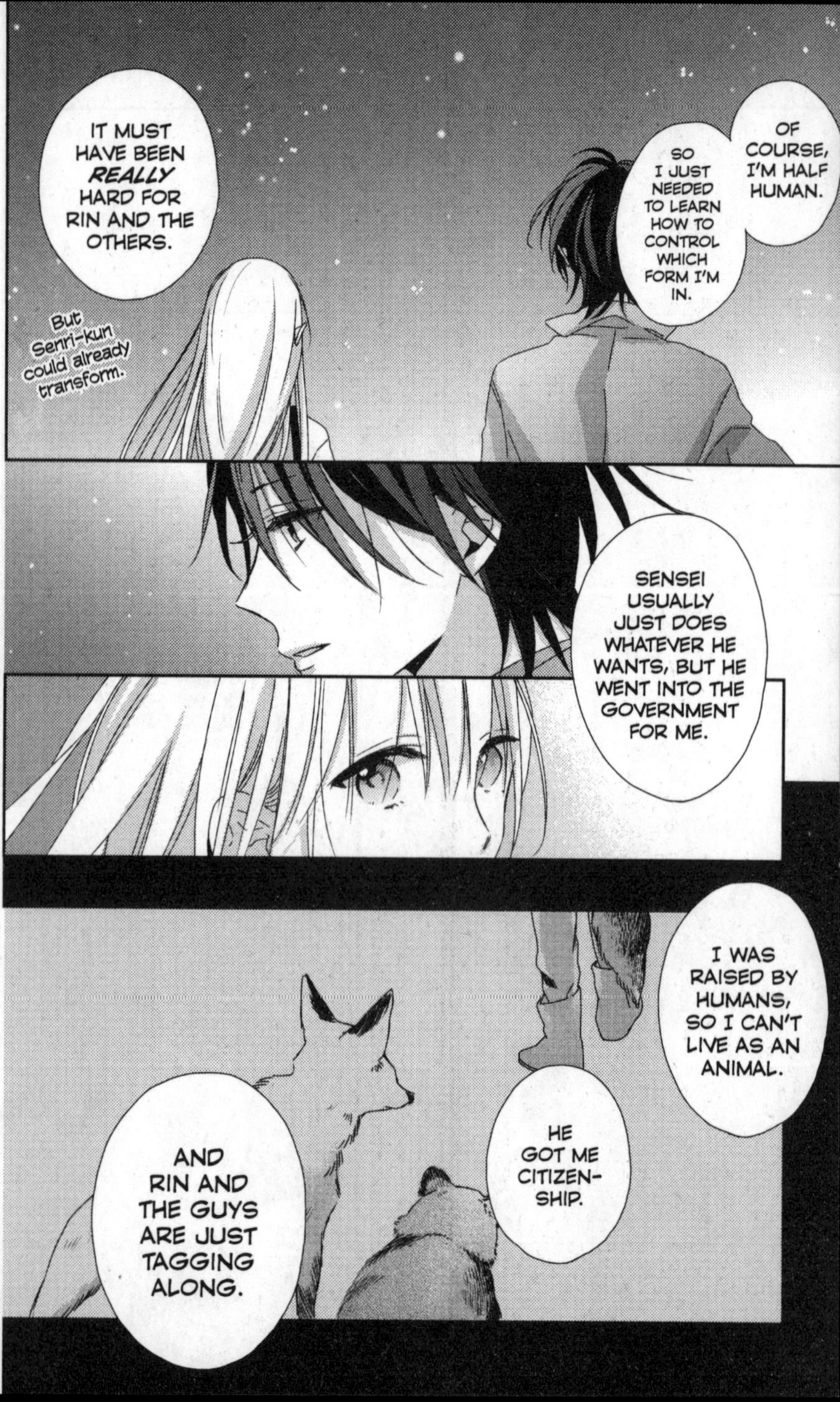
OF COURSE, I'M HALF HUMAN.
SO I JUST NEEDED TO LEARN HOW TO CONTROL WHICH FORM I'M IN.
IT MUST HAVE BEEN *REALLY* HARD FOR RIN AND THE OTHERS.
But Senri-kun could already transform.
SENSEI USUALLY JUST DOES WHATEVER HE WANTS, BUT HE WENT INTO THE GOVERNMENT FOR ME.
I WAS RAISED BY HUMANS, SO I CAN'T LIVE AS AN ANIMAL.
HE GOT ME CITIZEN-SHIP.
AND RIN AND THE GUYS ARE JUST TAGGING ALONG.

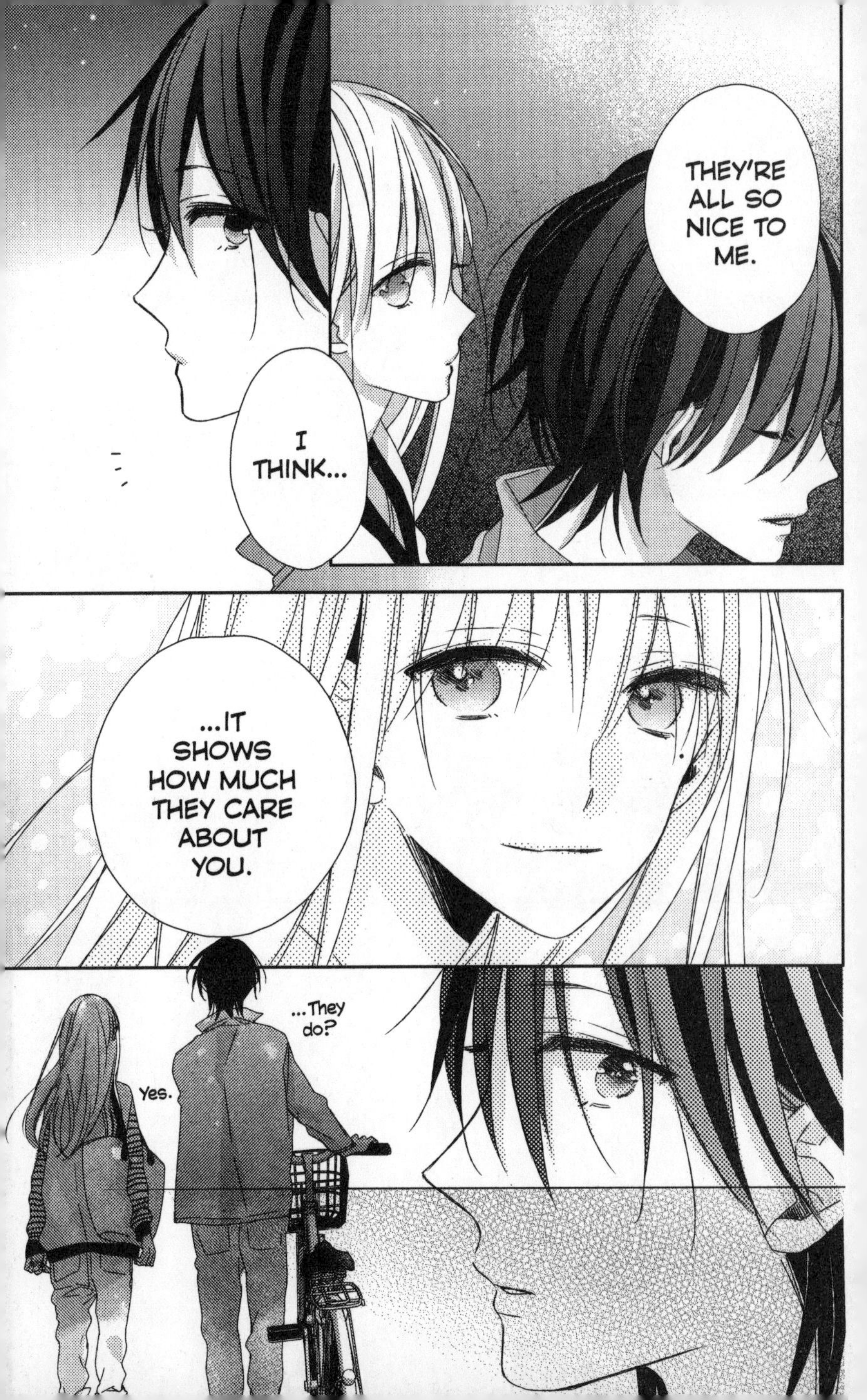
THEY'RE ALL SO NICE TO ME.
I THINK...
...IT SHOWS HOW MUCH THEY CARE ABOUT YOU.
...They do?
Yes.

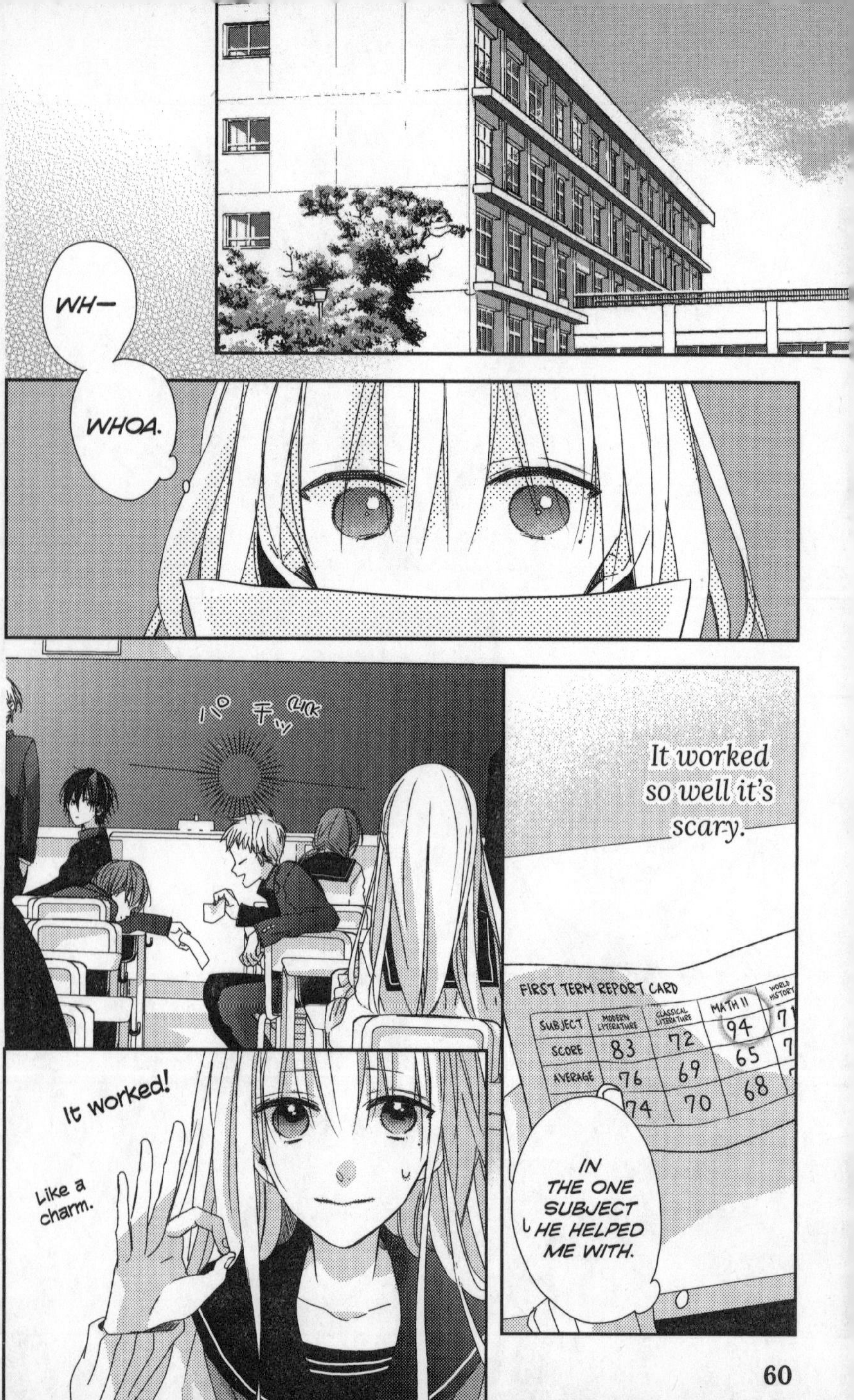

WH—
WHOA.
It worked so well it's scary.
FIRST TERM REPORT CARD
SUBJECT MODERN LITERATURE CLASSICAL LITERATURE MATH II WORLD HISTORY
SCORE 83 72 94
AVERAGE 76 69 65
74 70 68
IN THE ONE SUBJECT HE HELPED ME WITH.
パチッ CLICK
It worked!
Like a charm.

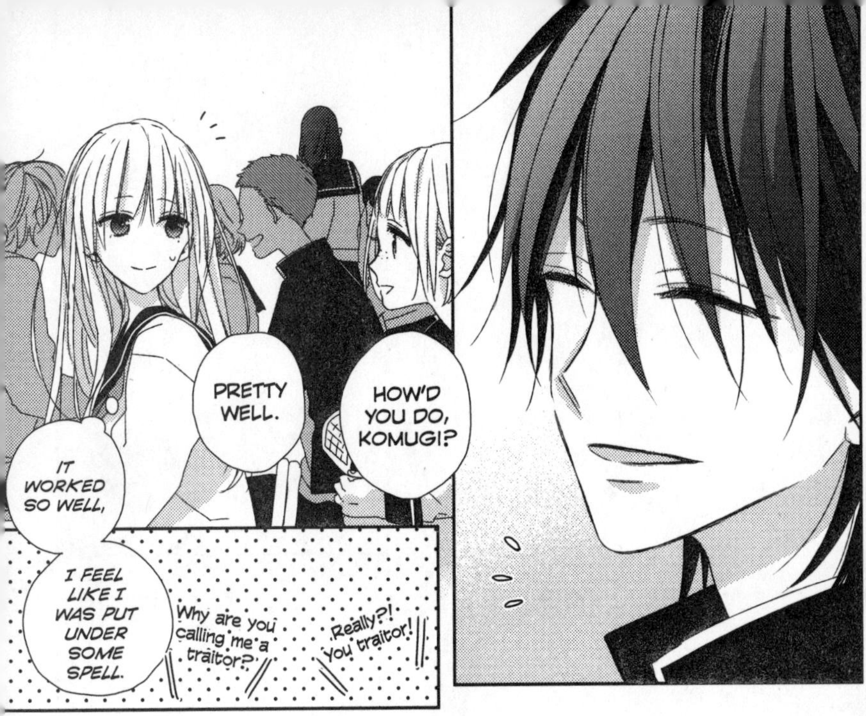
HOW'D YOU DO, KOMUGI?
PRETTY WELL.
IT WORKED SO WELL,
I FEEL LIKE I WAS PUT UNDER SOME SPELL.
Really?! You traitor!
Why are you calling me a traitor?

It's all moving in a good direction.

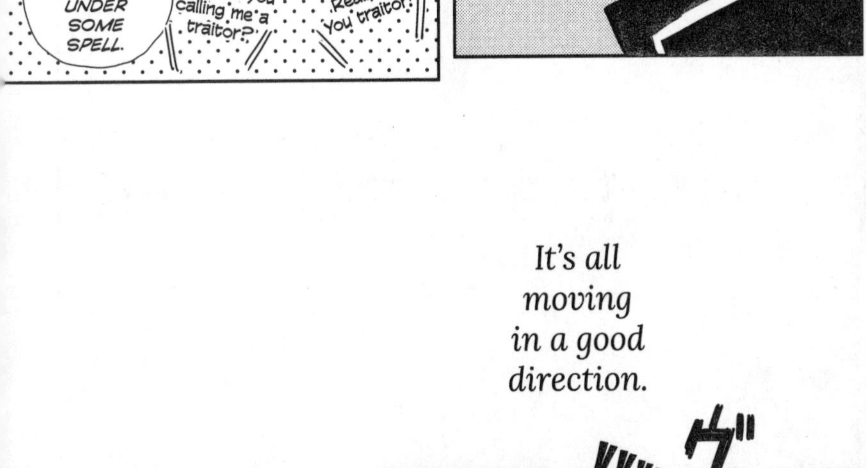
VVVR VVVR

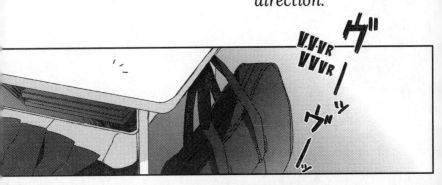

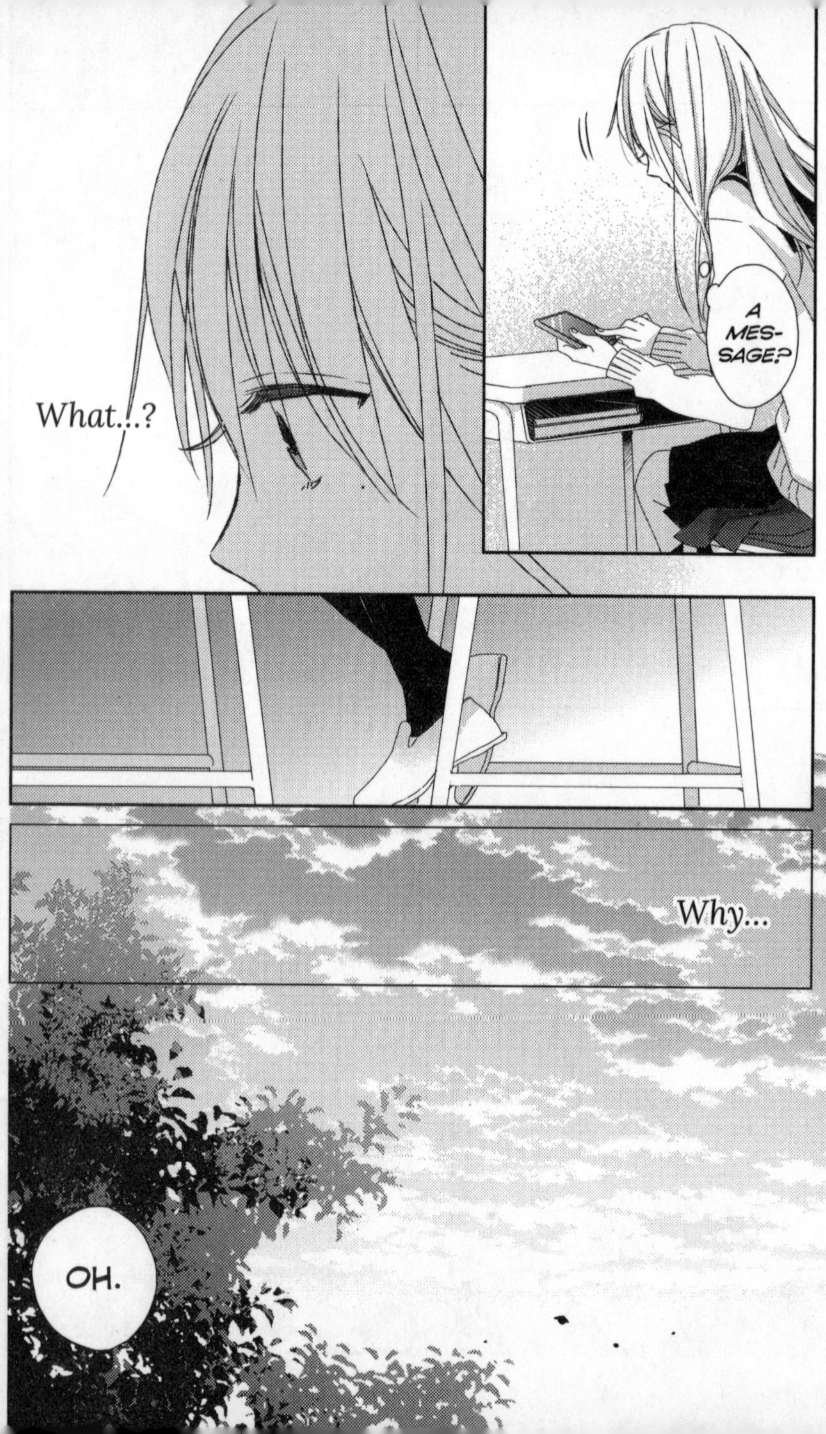
A MES-SAGE?
What...?
Why...
OH.

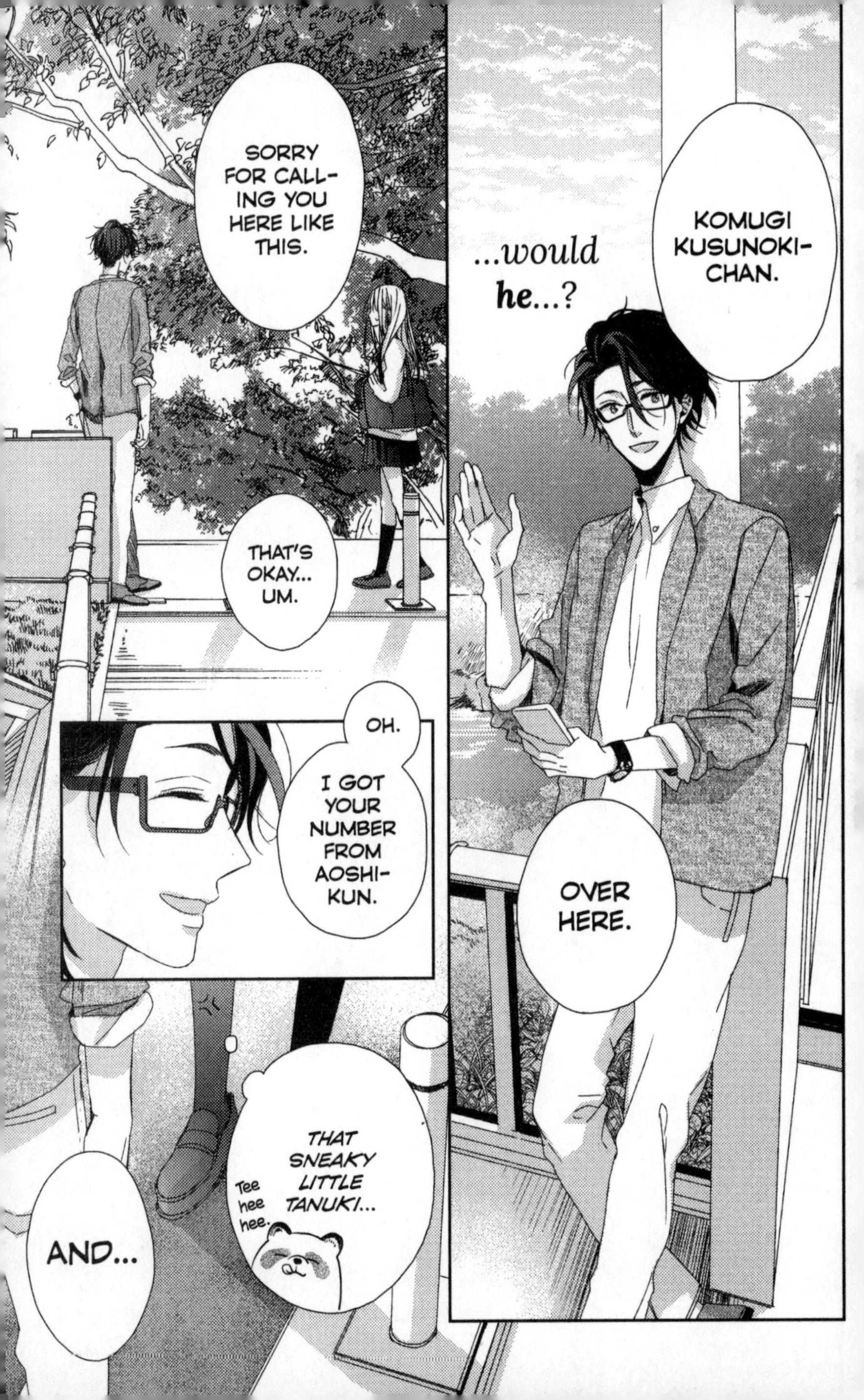
KOMUGI KUSUNOKI-CHAN.
...would he...?
OVER HERE.
SORRY FOR CALLING YOU HERE LIKE THIS.
THAT'S OKAY... UM.
OH.
I GOT YOUR NUMBER FROM AOSHI-KUN.
THAT SNEAKY LITTLE TANUKI...
Tee hee hee.
AND...

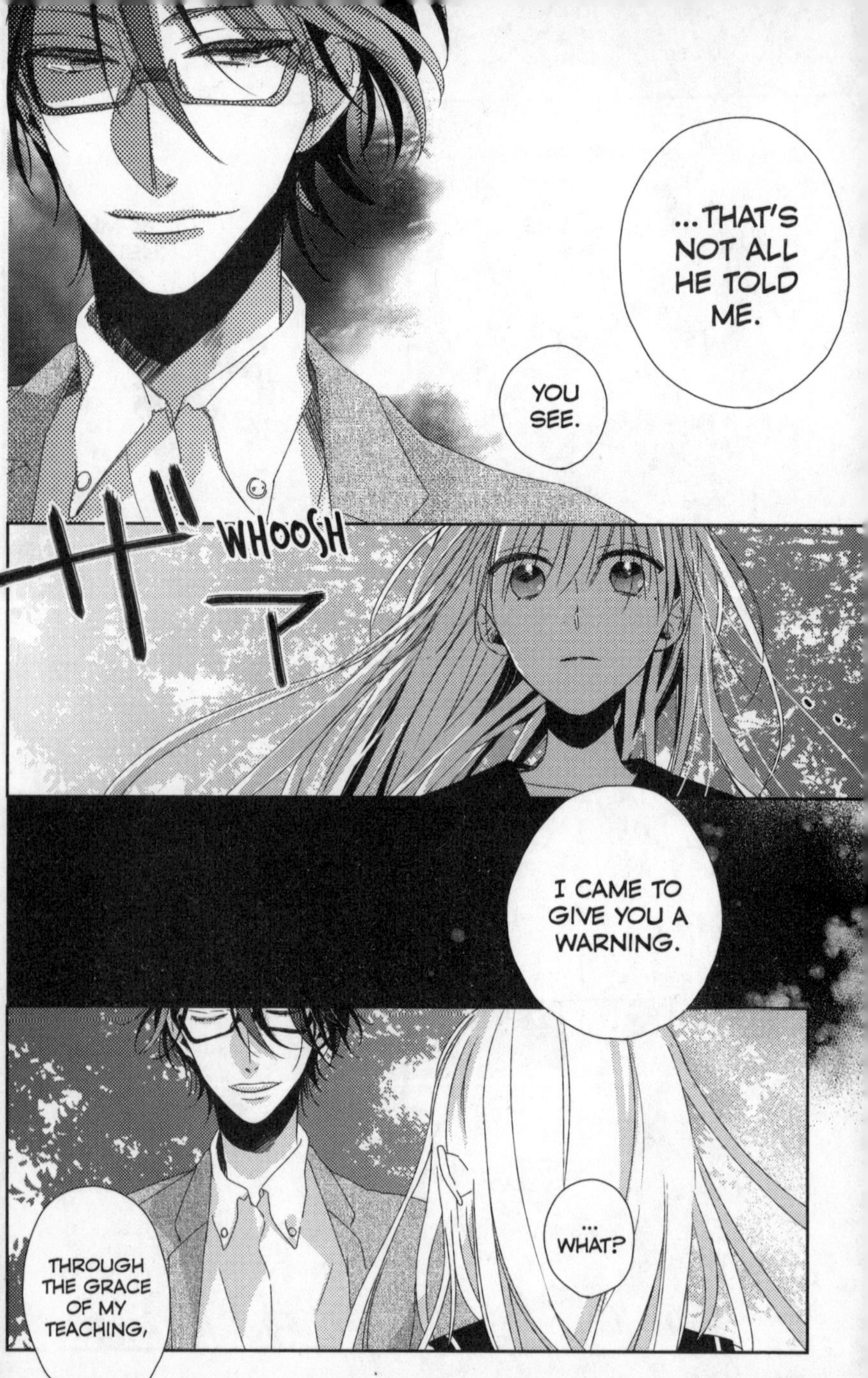
...THAT'S NOT ALL HE TOLD ME.
YOU SEE.
ザァ
WHOOSH
I CAME TO GIVE YOU A WARNING.
... WHAT?
THROUGH THE GRACE OF MY TEACHING,

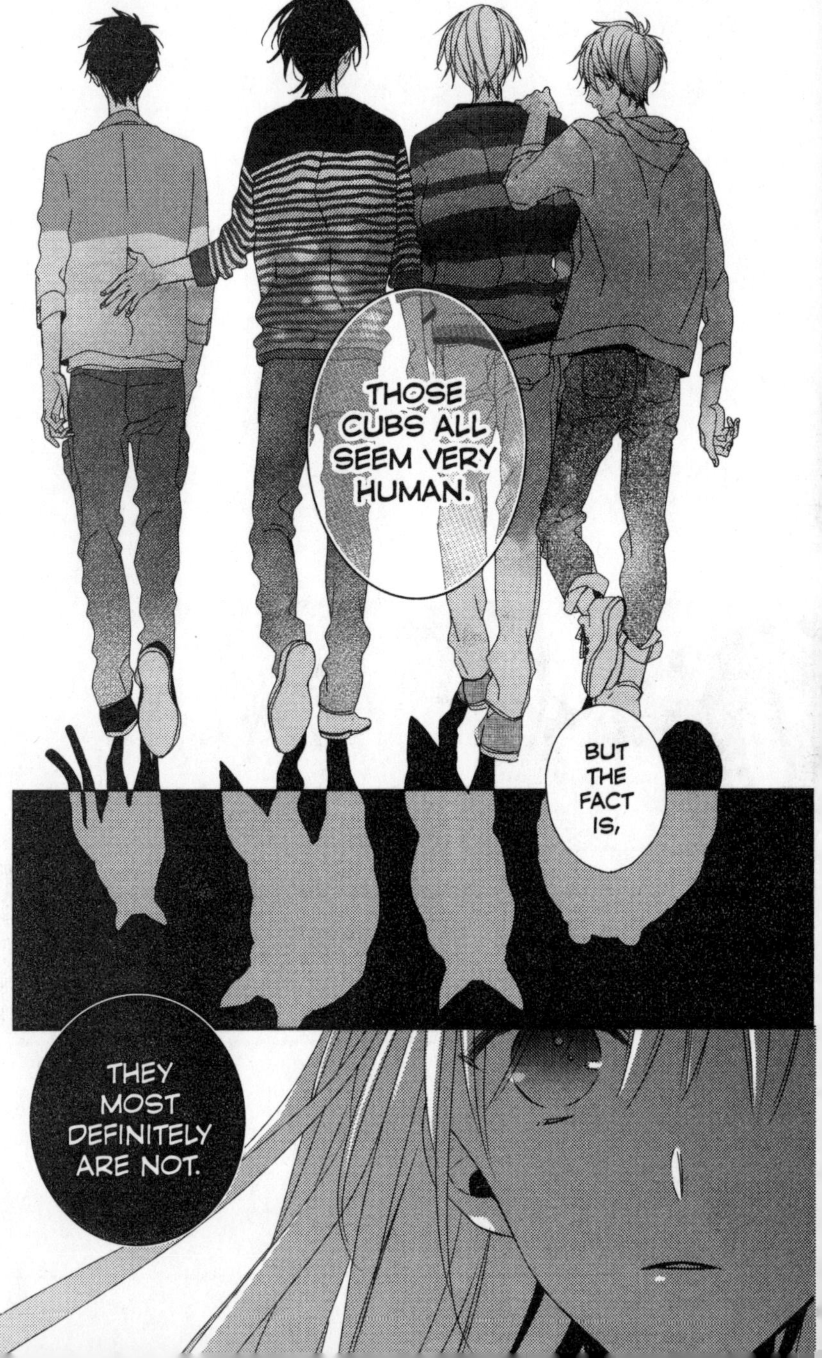
THOSE CUBS ALL SEEM VERY HUMAN.
BUT THE FACT IS,
THEY MOST DEFINITELY ARE NOT.

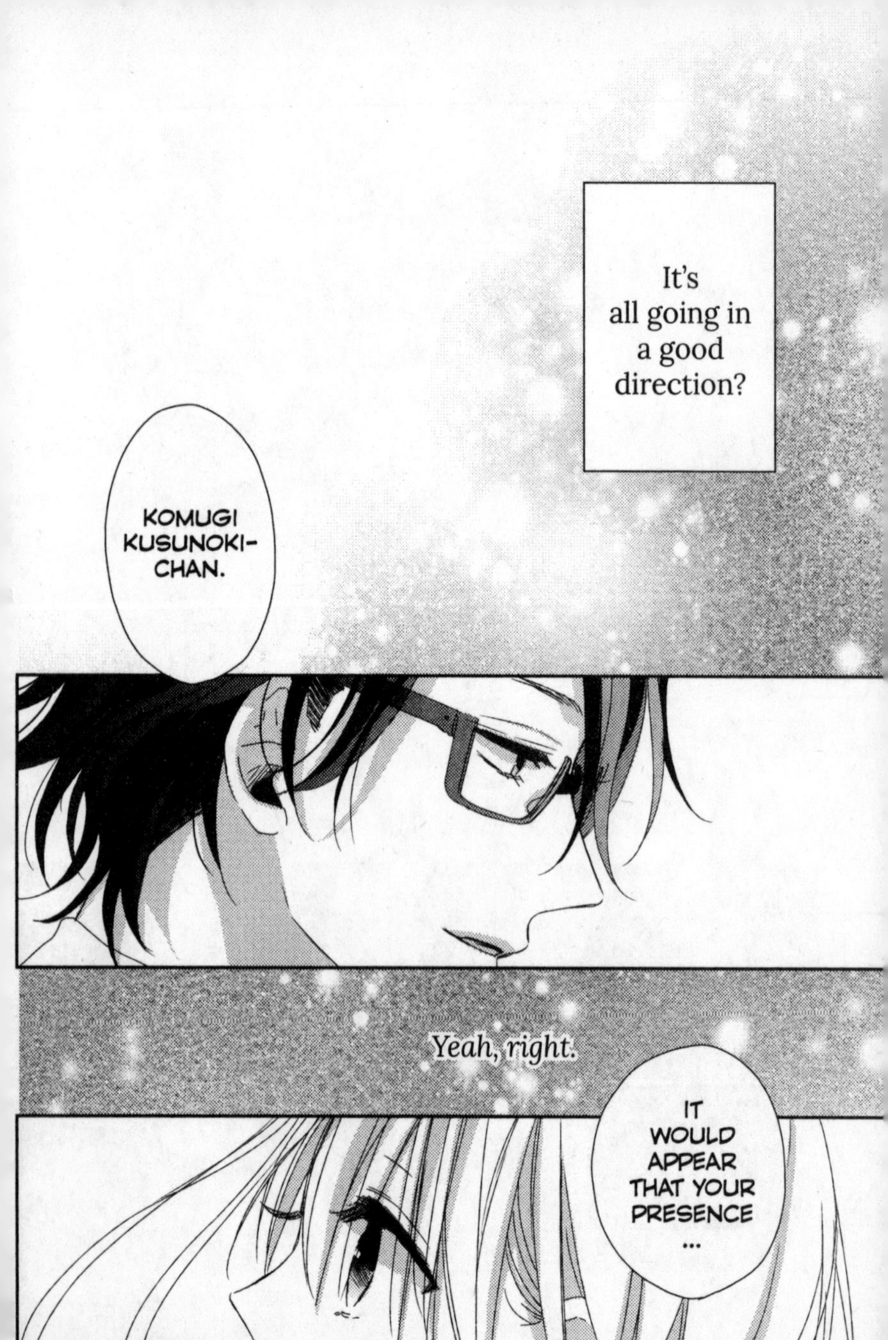
It's all going in a good direction?
KOMUGI KUSUNOKI-CHAN.
Yeah, right.
IT WOULD APPEAR THAT YOUR PRESENCE ...

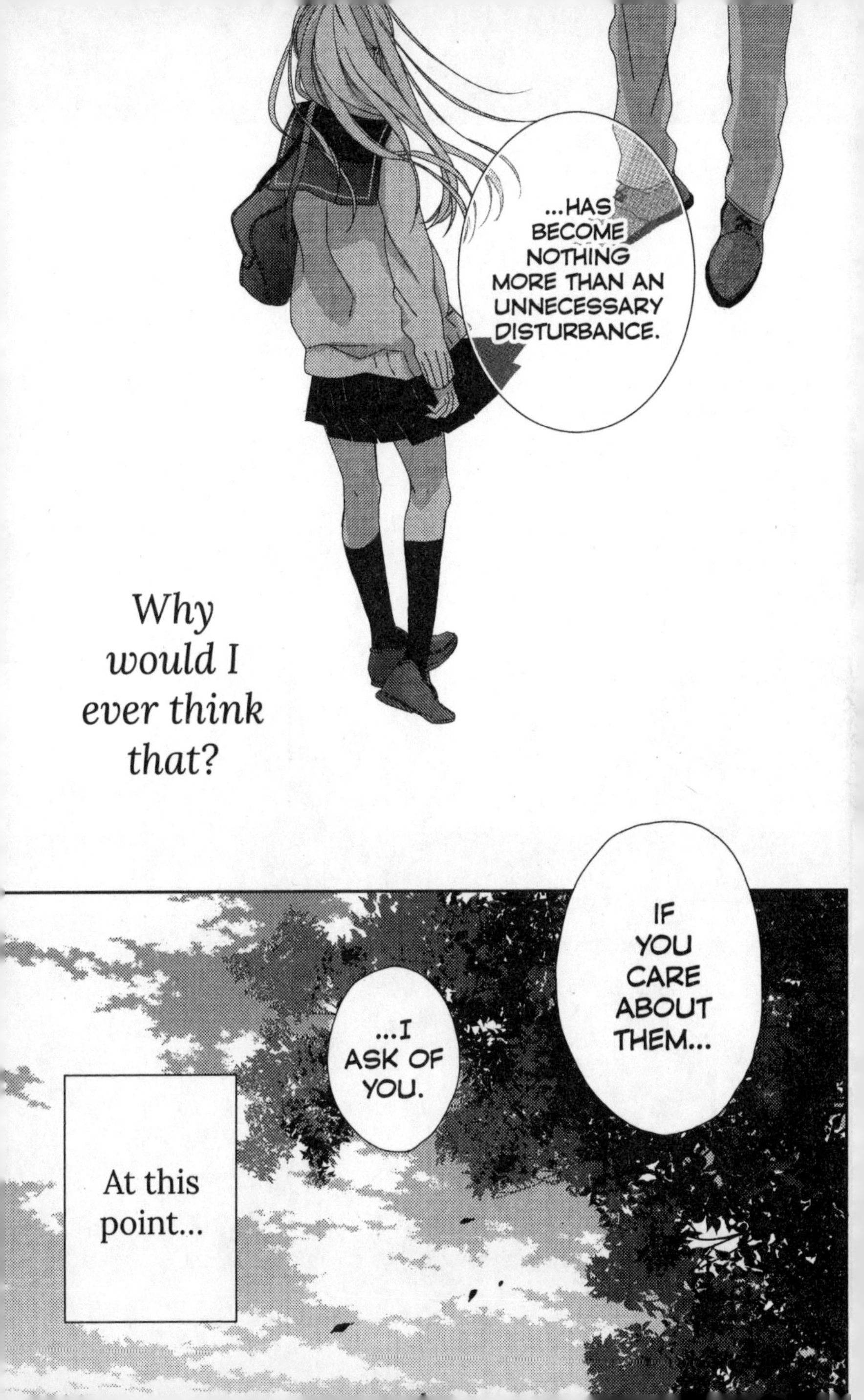
...HAS BECOME NOTHING MORE THAN AN UNNECESSARY DISTURBANCE.
Why would I ever think that?
IF YOU CARE ABOUT THEM...
...I ASK OF YOU.
At this point...

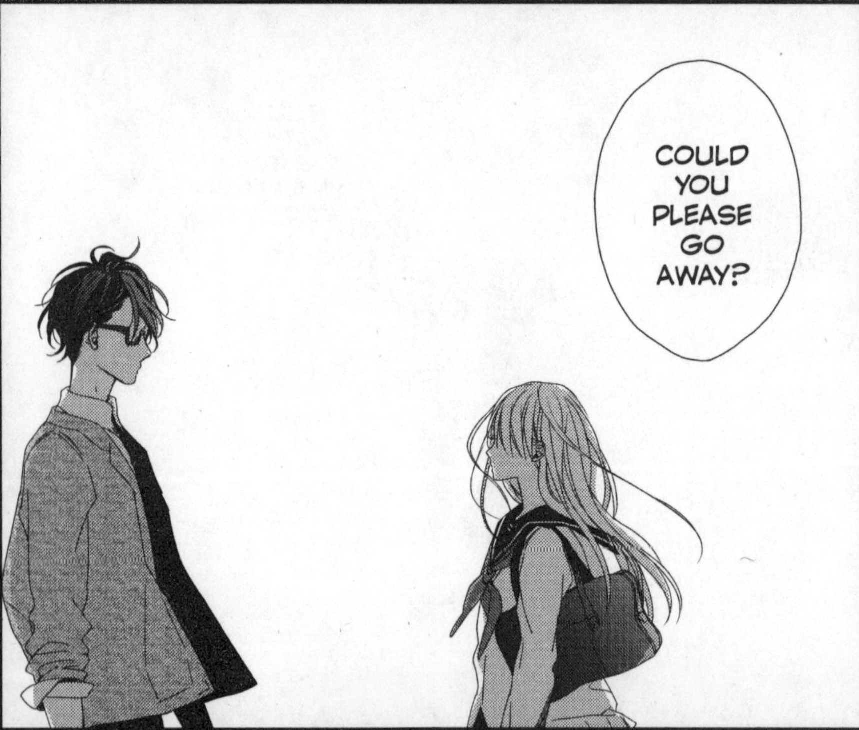
COULD YOU PLEASE GO AWAY?

...I knew nothing.

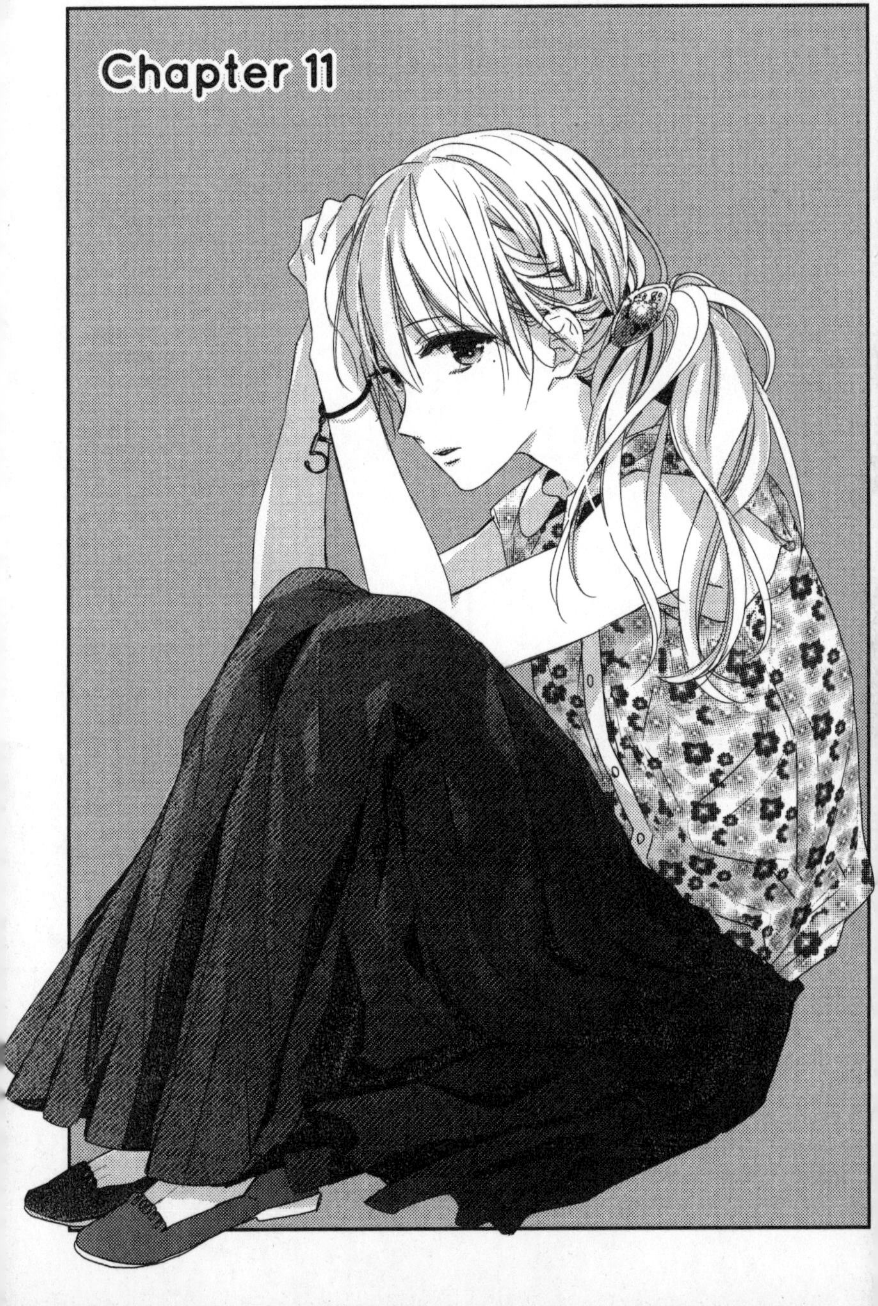
Chapter 11

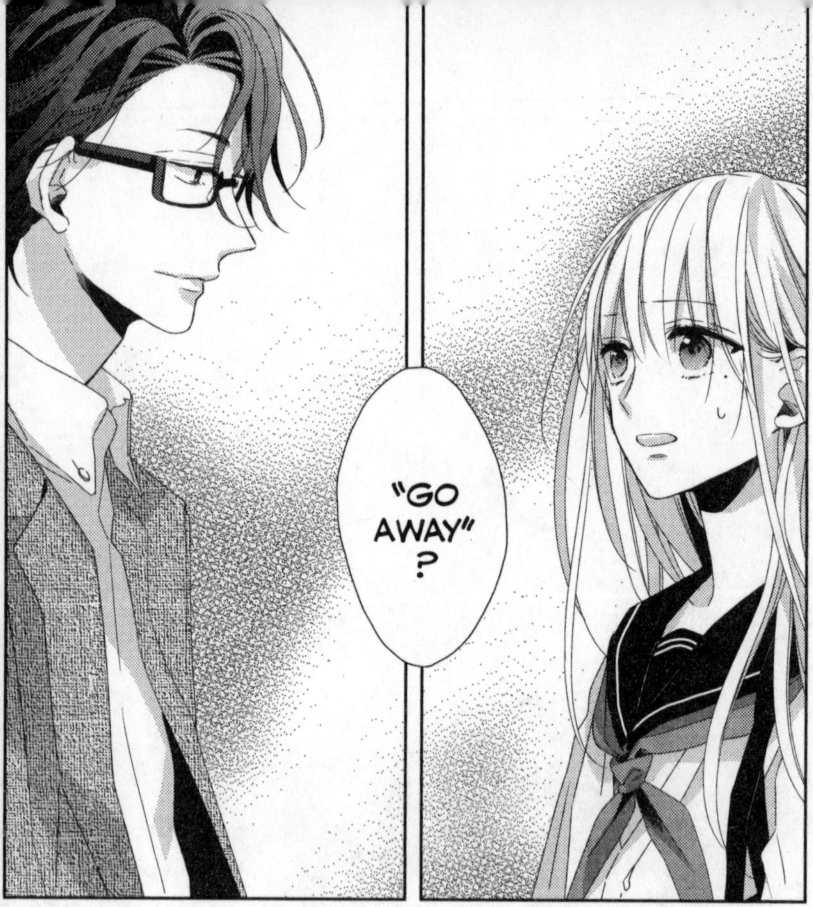
"GO AWAY" ?

That Wolf-Boy is Mine!

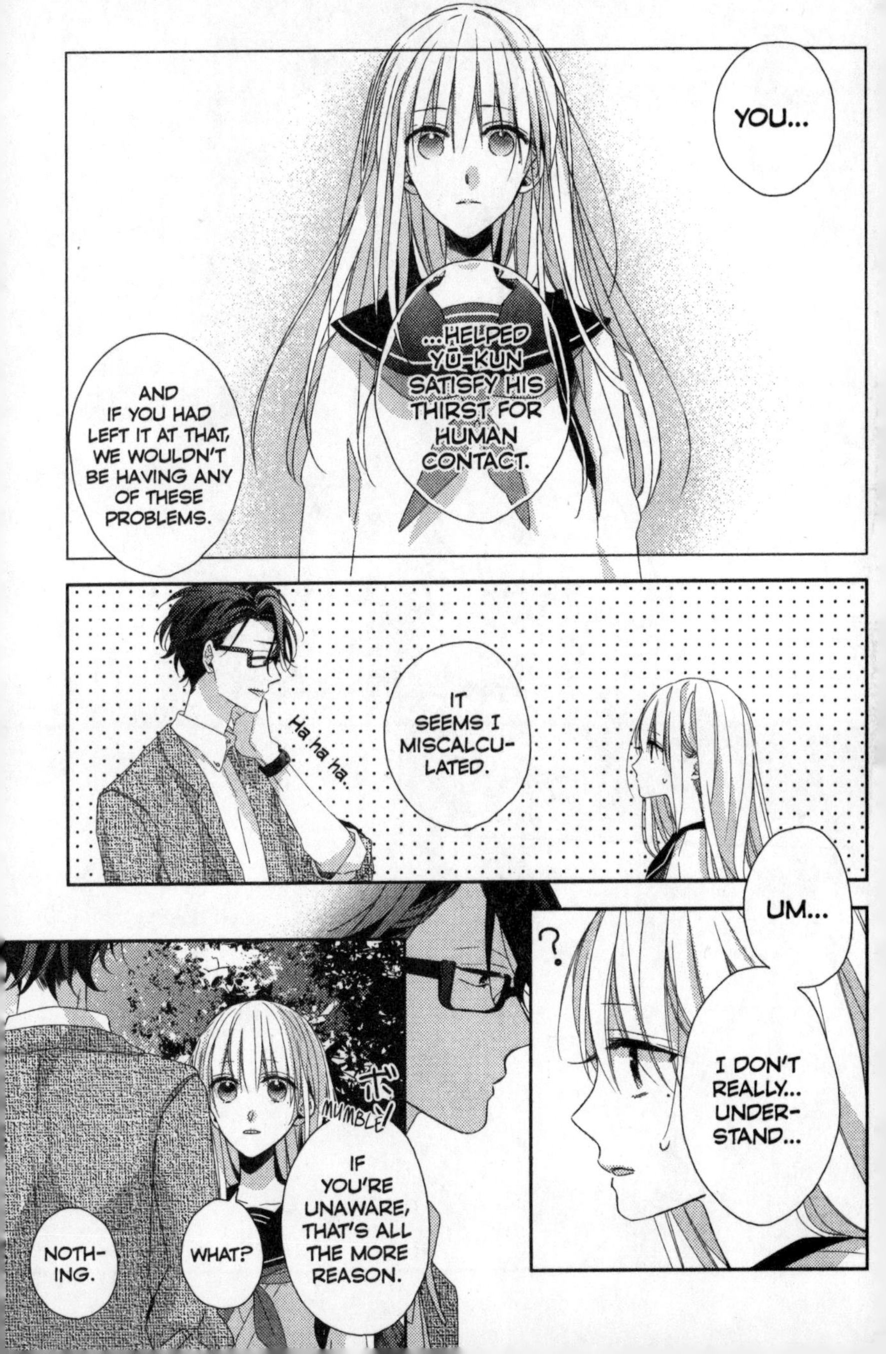
YOU...
...HELPED YŪ-KUN SATISFY HIS THIRST FOR HUMAN CONTACT.
AND IF YOU HAD LEFT IT AT THAT, WE WOULDN'T BE HAVING ANY OF THESE PROBLEMS.
IT SEEMS I MISCALCULATED.
Ha ha ha.
?
UM...
I DON'T REALLY... UNDERSTAND...
MUMBLE
IF YOU'RE UNAWARE, THAT'S ALL THE MORE REASON.
WHAT?
NOTH-ING.

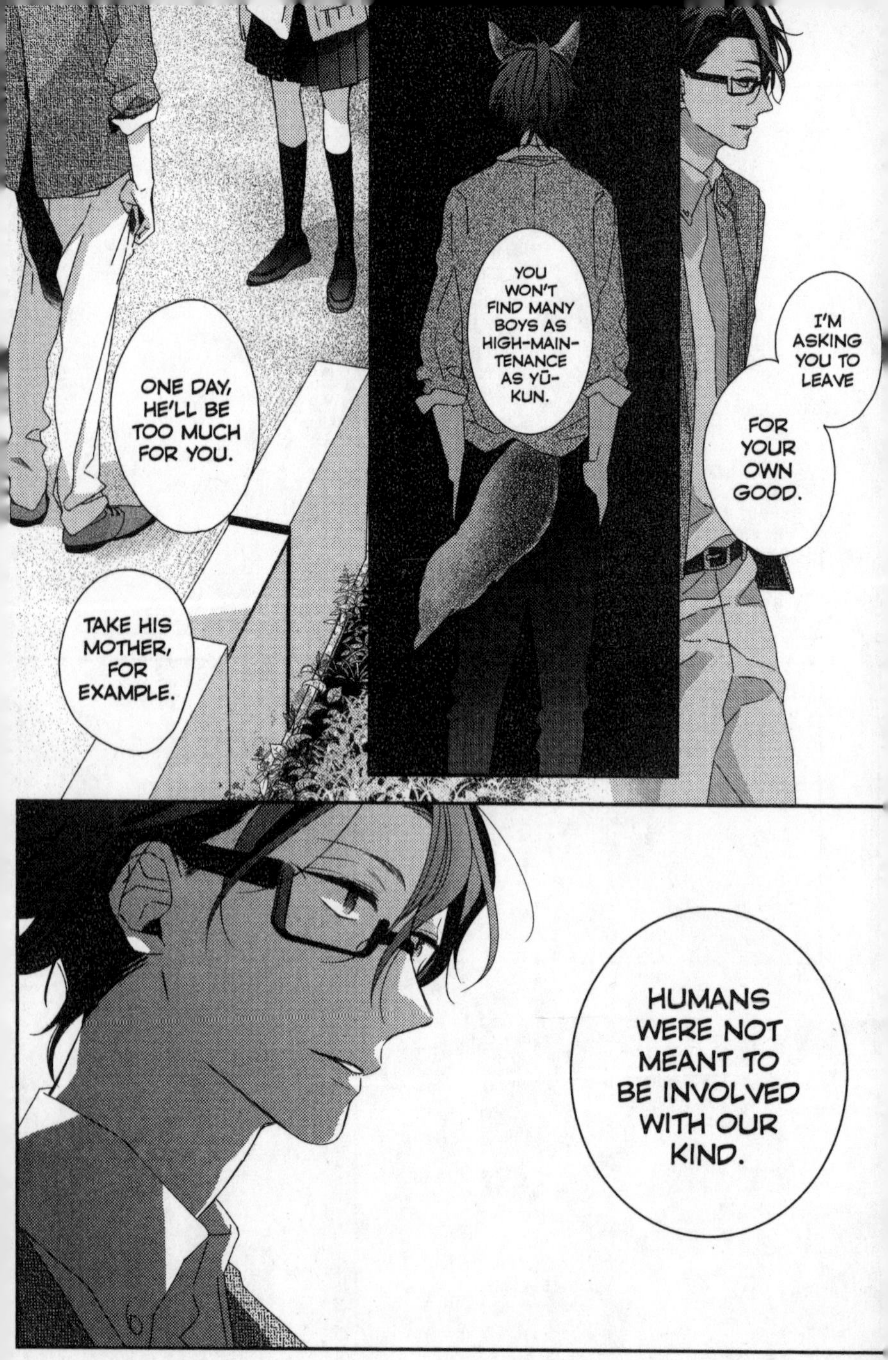
I'M ASKING YOU TO LEAVE
FOR YOUR OWN GOOD.
YOU WON'T FIND MANY BOYS AS HIGH-MAINTENANCE AS YŪ-KUN.
ONE DAY, HE'LL BE TOO MUCH FOR YOU.
TAKE HIS MOTHER, FOR EXAMPLE.
HUMANS WERE NOT MEANT TO BE INVOLVED WITH OUR KIND.

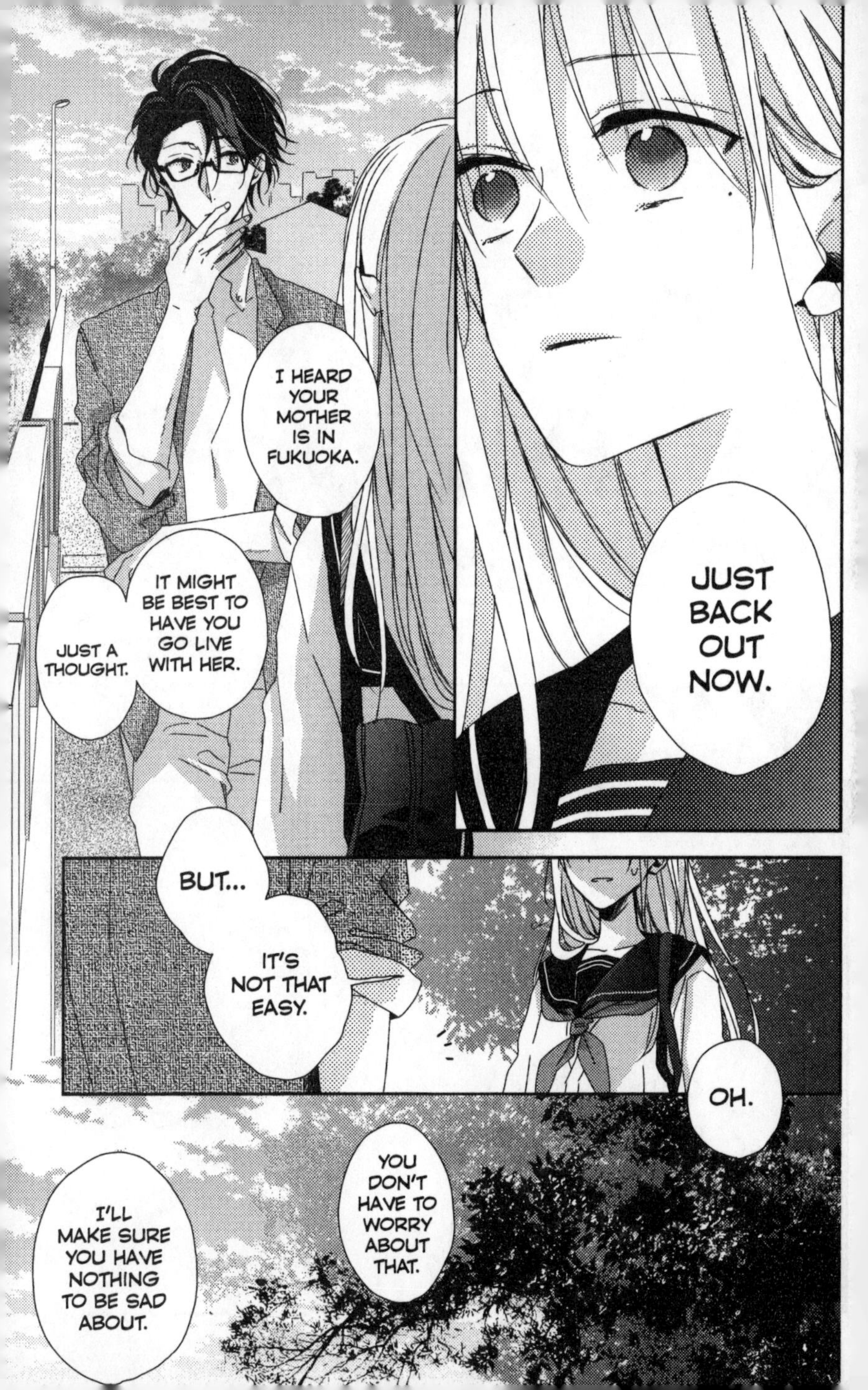
JUST BACK OUT NOW.
I HEARD YOUR MOTHER IS IN FUKUOKA.
IT MIGHT BE BEST TO HAVE YOU GO LIVE WITH HER.
JUST A THOUGHT.
BUT...
IT'S NOT THAT EASY.
OH.
YOU DON'T HAVE TO WORRY ABOUT THAT.
I'LL MAKE SURE YOU HAVE NOTHING TO BE SAD ABOUT.

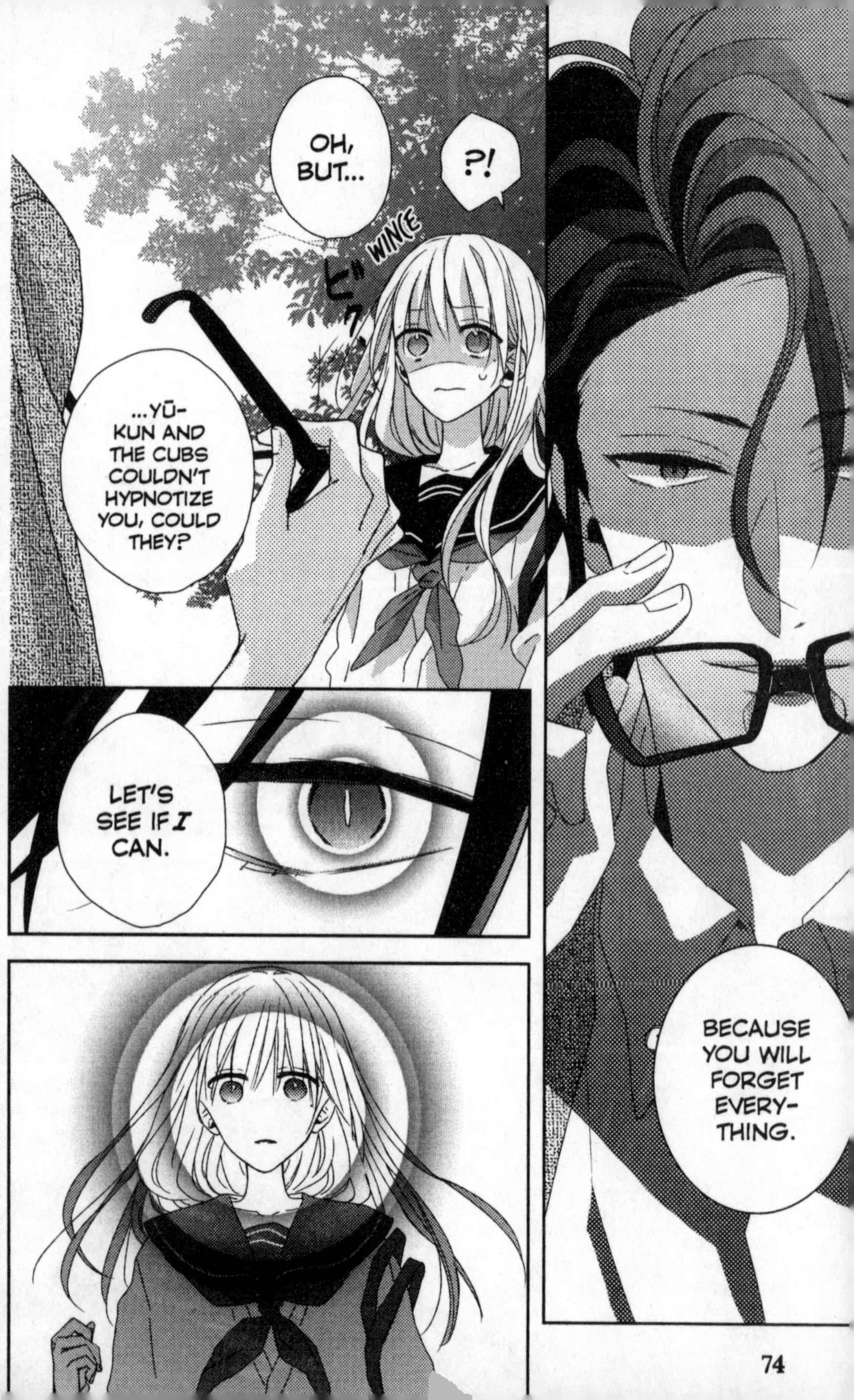
BECAUSE YOU WILL FORGET EVERY-THING.
?!
OH, BUT...
WINCE
...YŪ-KUN AND THE CUBS COULDN'T HYPNOTIZE YOU, COULD THEY?
LET'S SEE IF *I* CAN.

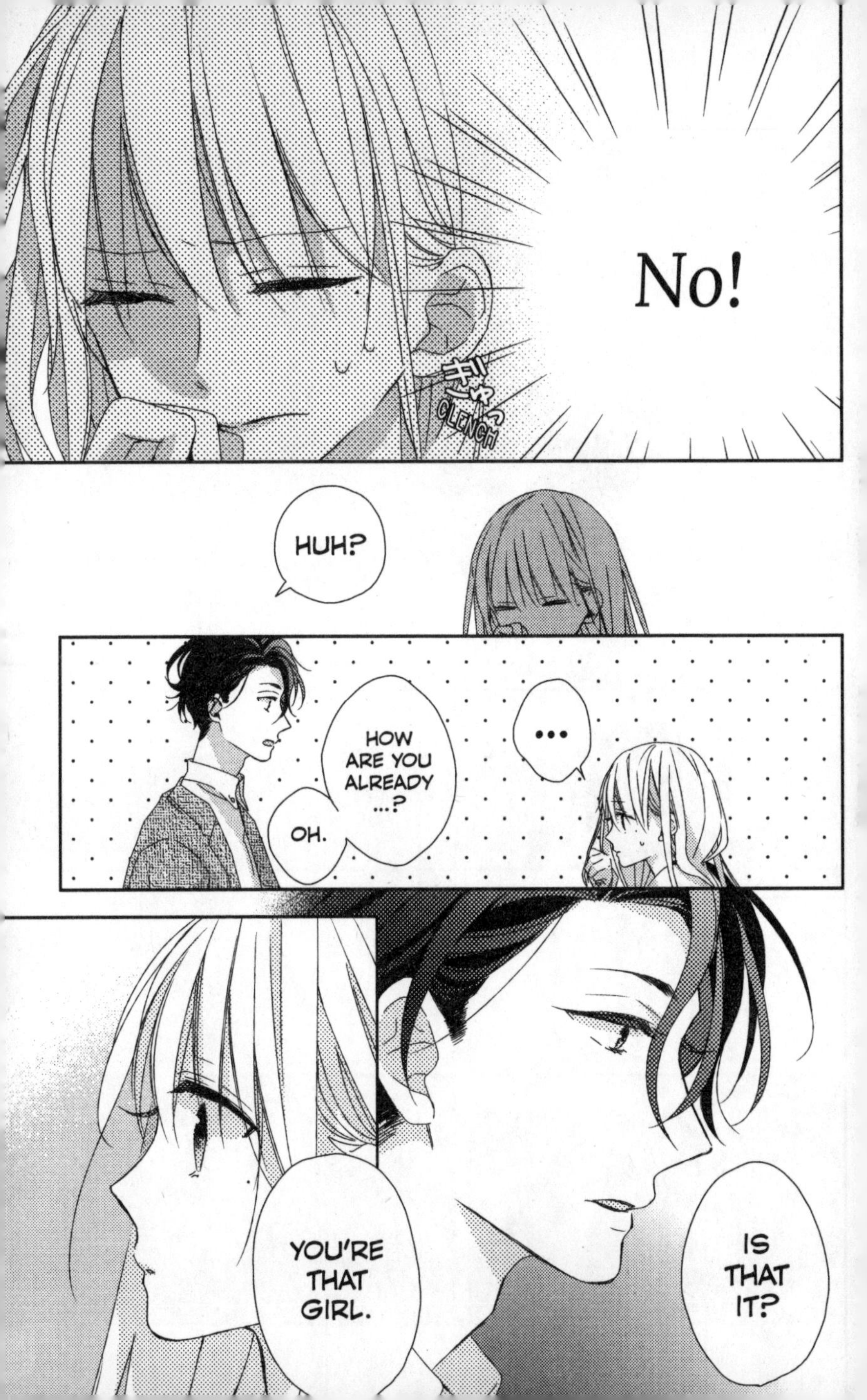
No!
ギュッ
CLENCH
HUH?
...
HOW ARE YOU ALREADY ...?
OH.
IS THAT IT?
YOU'RE THAT GIRL.

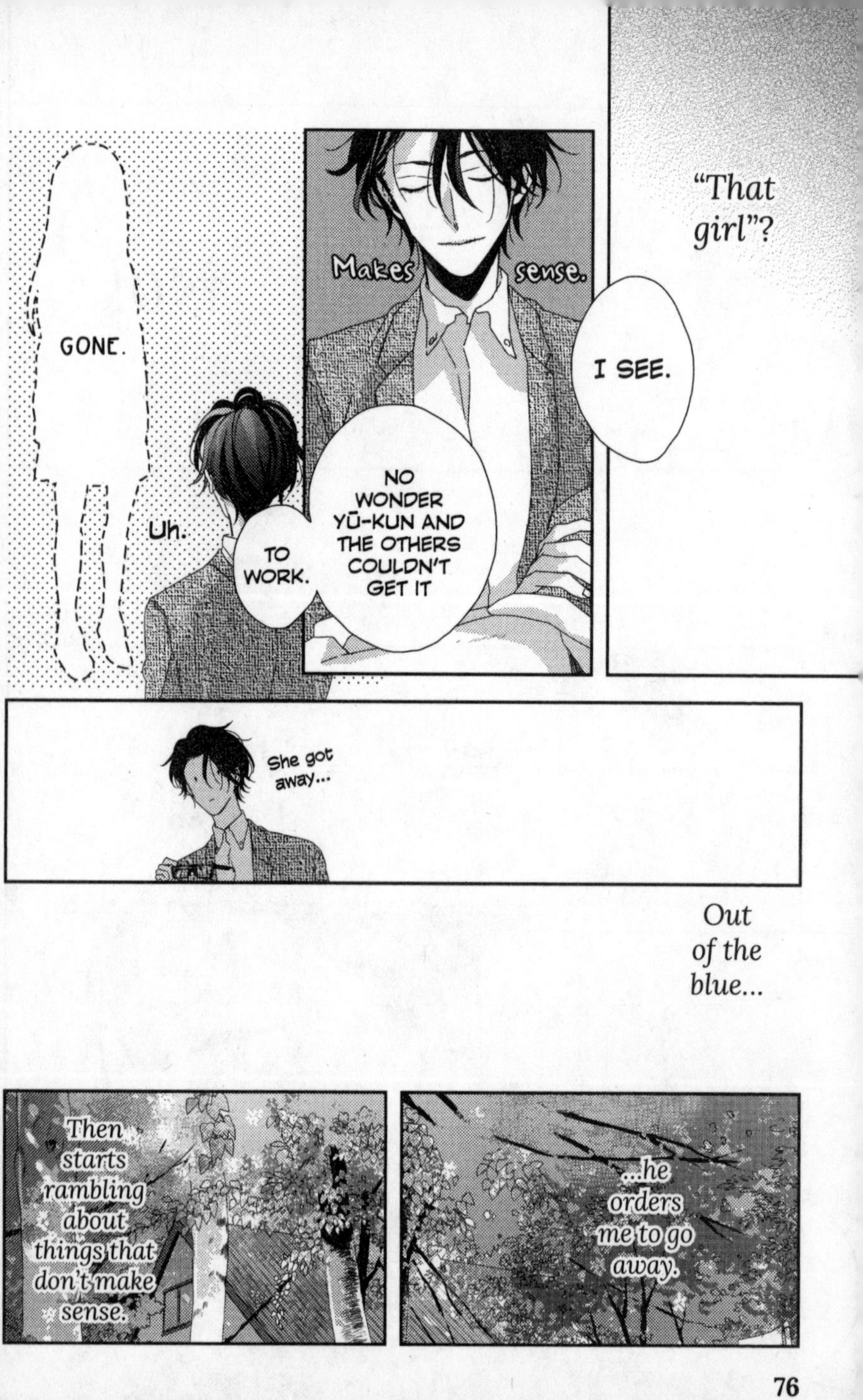
"That girl"?
I SEE.
Makes sense.
NO WONDER YŪ-KUN AND THE OTHERS COULDN'T GET IT
TO WORK.
Uh.
GONE.
She got away...
Out of the blue...
...he orders me to go away.
Then starts rambling about things that don't make sense.

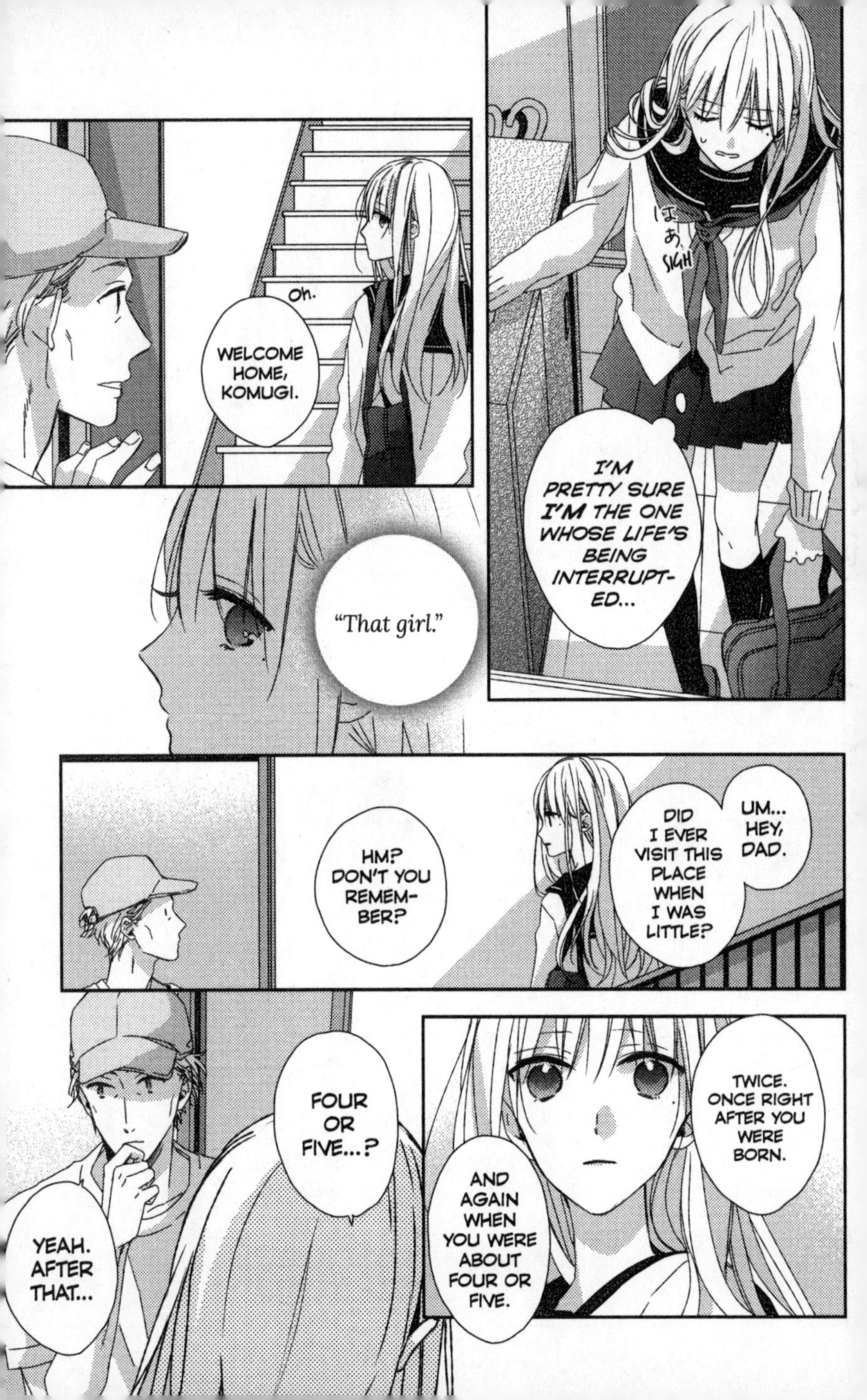
はぁ SIGH
I'M PRETTY SURE I'M THE ONE WHOSE LIFE'S BEING INTERRUPTED...
Oh.
WELCOME HOME, KOMUGI.
"That girl."
UM... HEY, DAD.
DID I EVER VISIT THIS PLACE WHEN I WAS LITTLE?
HM? DON'T YOU REMEMBER?
TWICE. ONCE RIGHT AFTER YOU WERE BORN.
AND AGAIN WHEN YOU WERE ABOUT FOUR OR FIVE.
FOUR OR FIVE...?
YEAH. AFTER THAT...

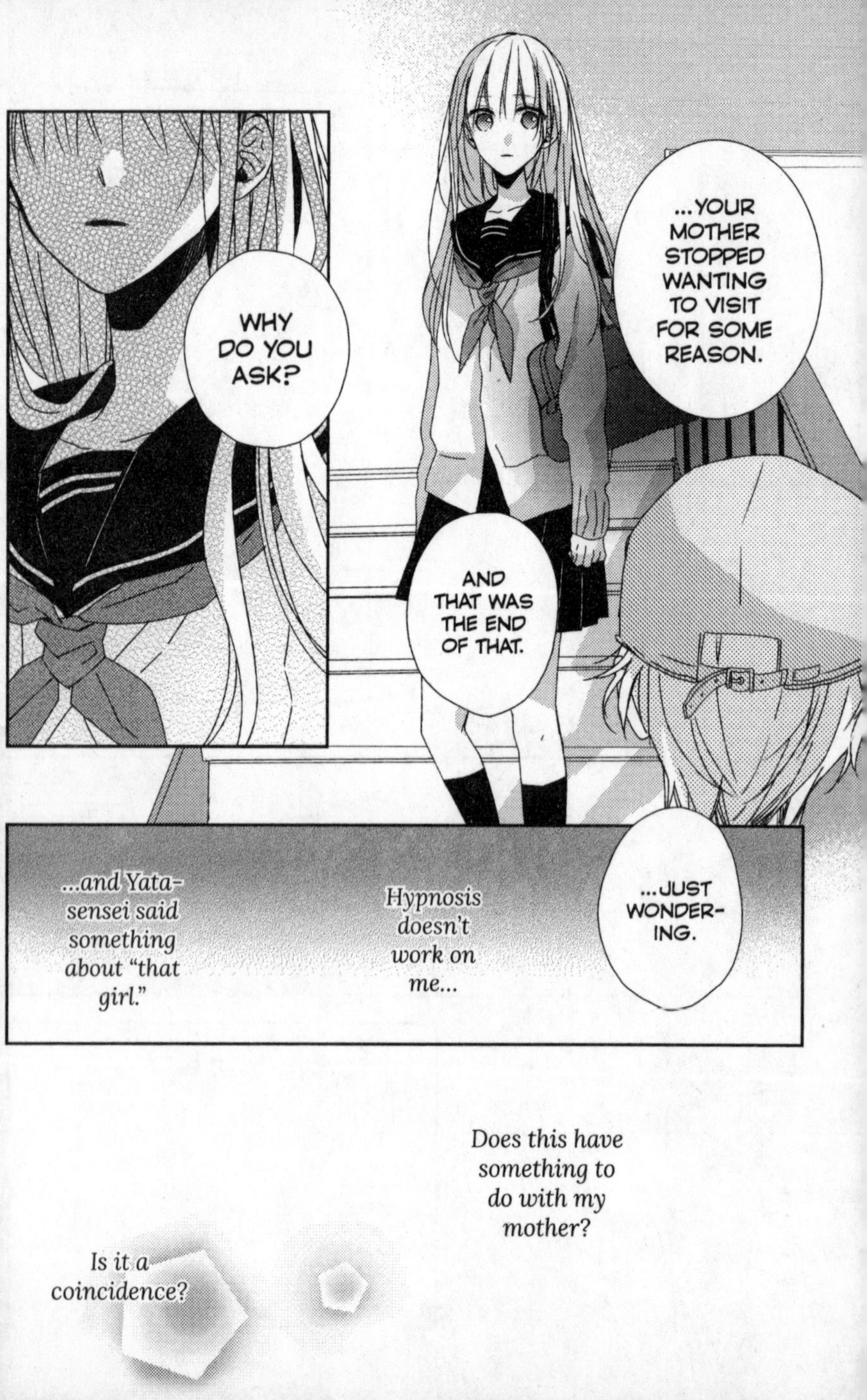
...YOUR MOTHER STOPPED WANTING TO VISIT FOR SOME REASON.
AND THAT WAS THE END OF THAT.
WHY DO YOU ASK?
...JUST WONDER-ING.
Hypnosis doesn't work on me...
...and Yata-sensei said something about "that girl."
Does this have something to do with my mother?
Is it a coincidence?

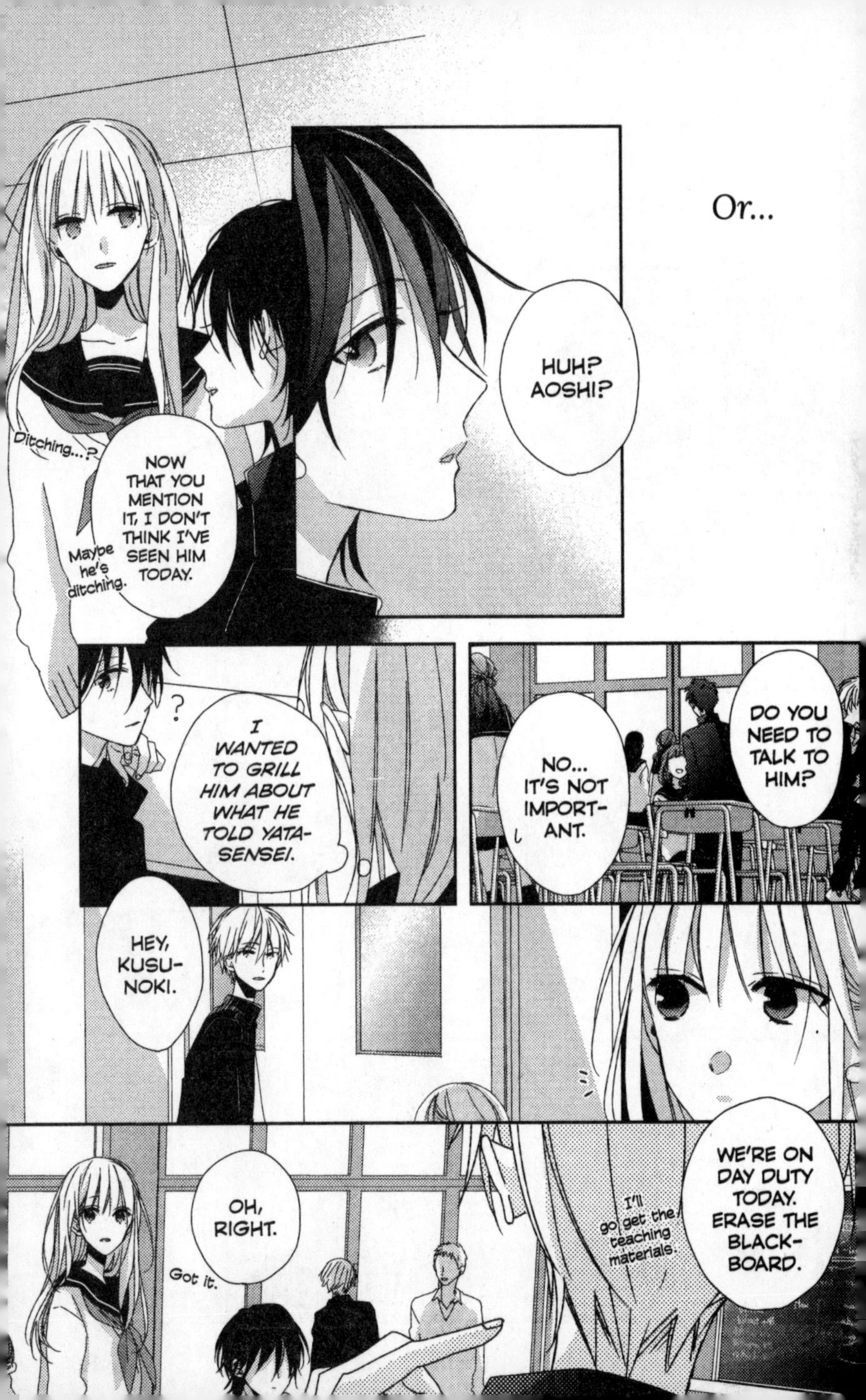
Or...
HUH? AOSHI?
NOW THAT YOU MENTION IT, I DON'T THINK I'VE SEEN HIM TODAY.
Maybe he's ditching.
Ditching...?
DO YOU NEED TO TALK TO HIM?
NO... IT'S NOT IMPORT-ANT.
I WANTED TO GRILL HIM ABOUT WHAT HE TOLD YATA-SENSEI.
HEY, KUSU-NOKI.
WE'RE ON DAY DUTY TODAY. ERASE THE BLACK-BOARD.
I'll go get the teaching materials.
OH, RIGHT.
Got it.

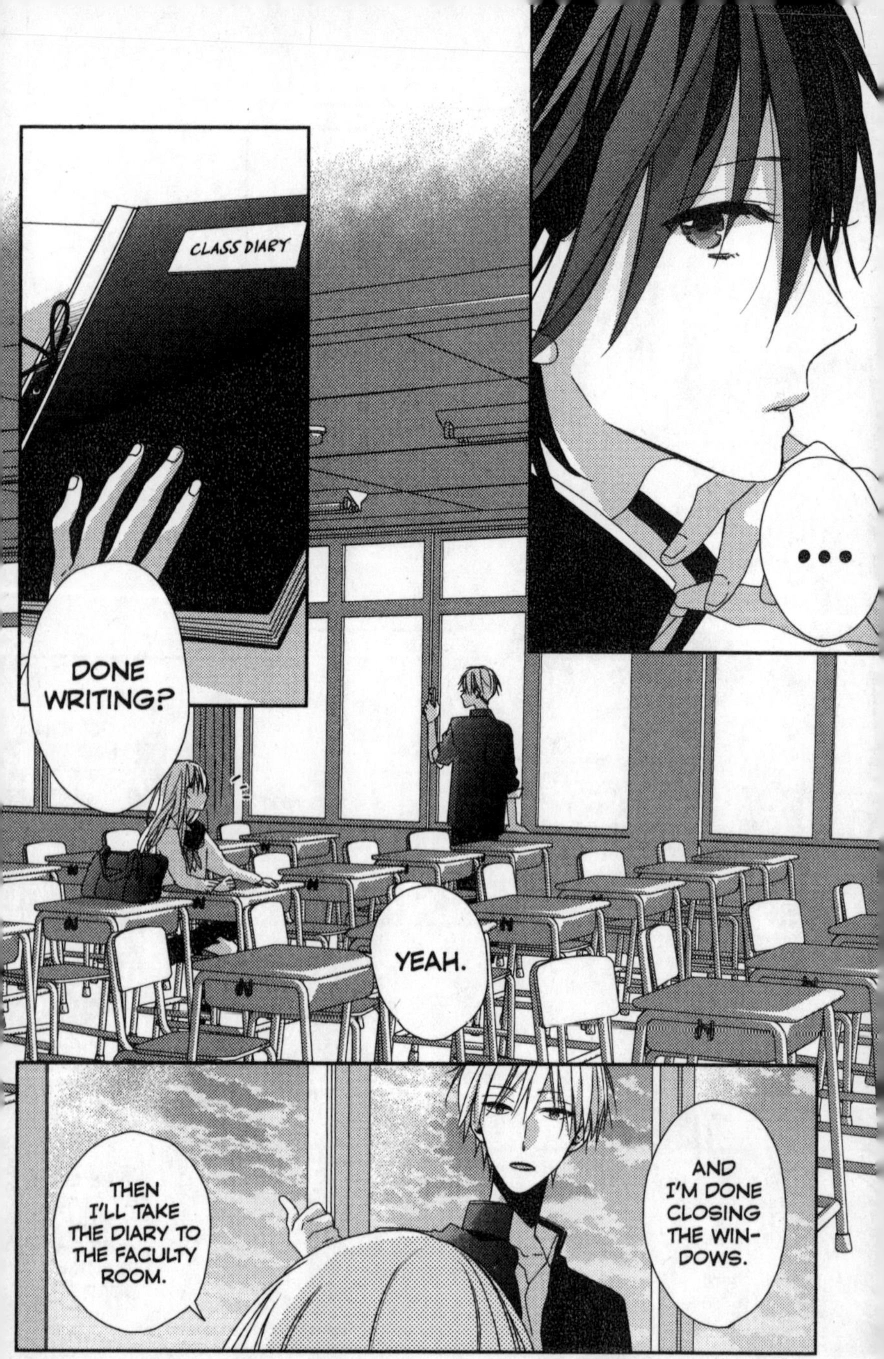
...
CLASS DIARY
DONE WRITING?
YEAH.
AND I'M DONE CLOSING THE WIN-DOWS.
THEN I'LL TAKE THE DIARY TO THE FACULTY ROOM.

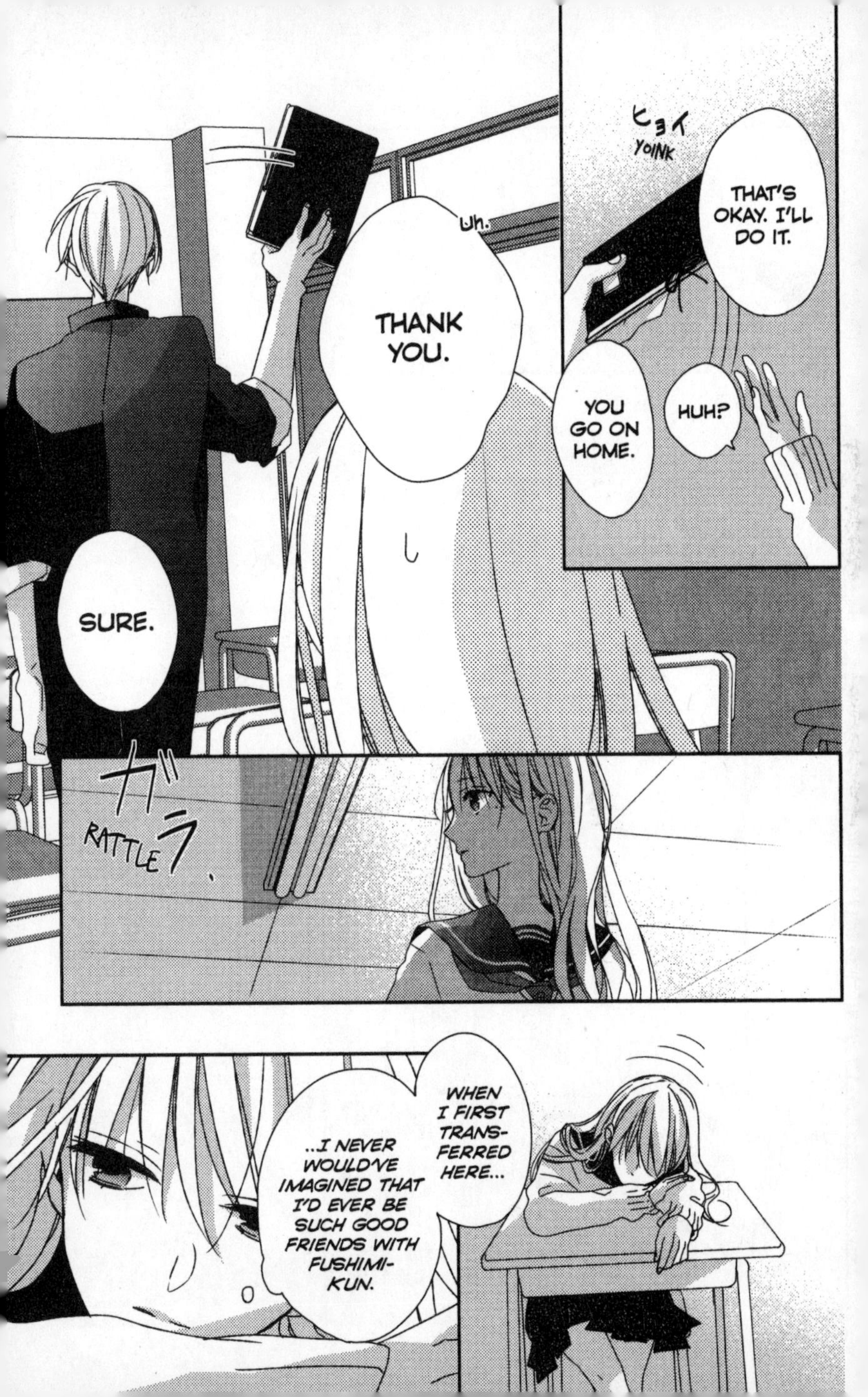
ヒョイ
YOINK
THAT'S OKAY. I'LL DO IT.
HUH?
YOU GO ON HOME.
Uh.
THANK YOU.
SURE.
ガラ
RATTLE
WHEN I FIRST TRANS-FERRED HERE...
...I NEVER WOULD'VE IMAGINED THAT I'D EVER BE SUCH GOOD FRIENDS WITH FUSHIMI-KUN.

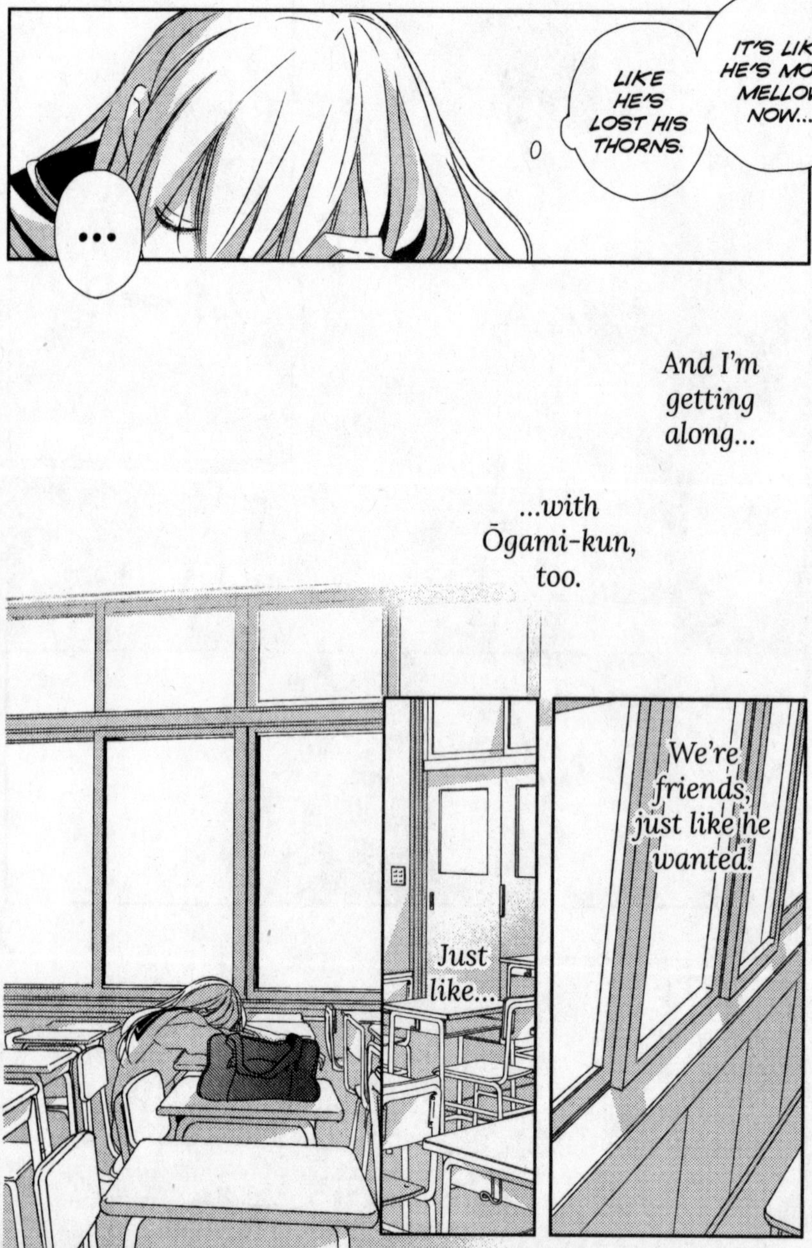
IT'S LIKE HE'S MORE MELLOW NOW...
LIKE HE'S LOST HIS THORNS.
...
And I'm getting along...
...with Ōgami-kun, too.
We're friends, just like he wanted.
Just like...

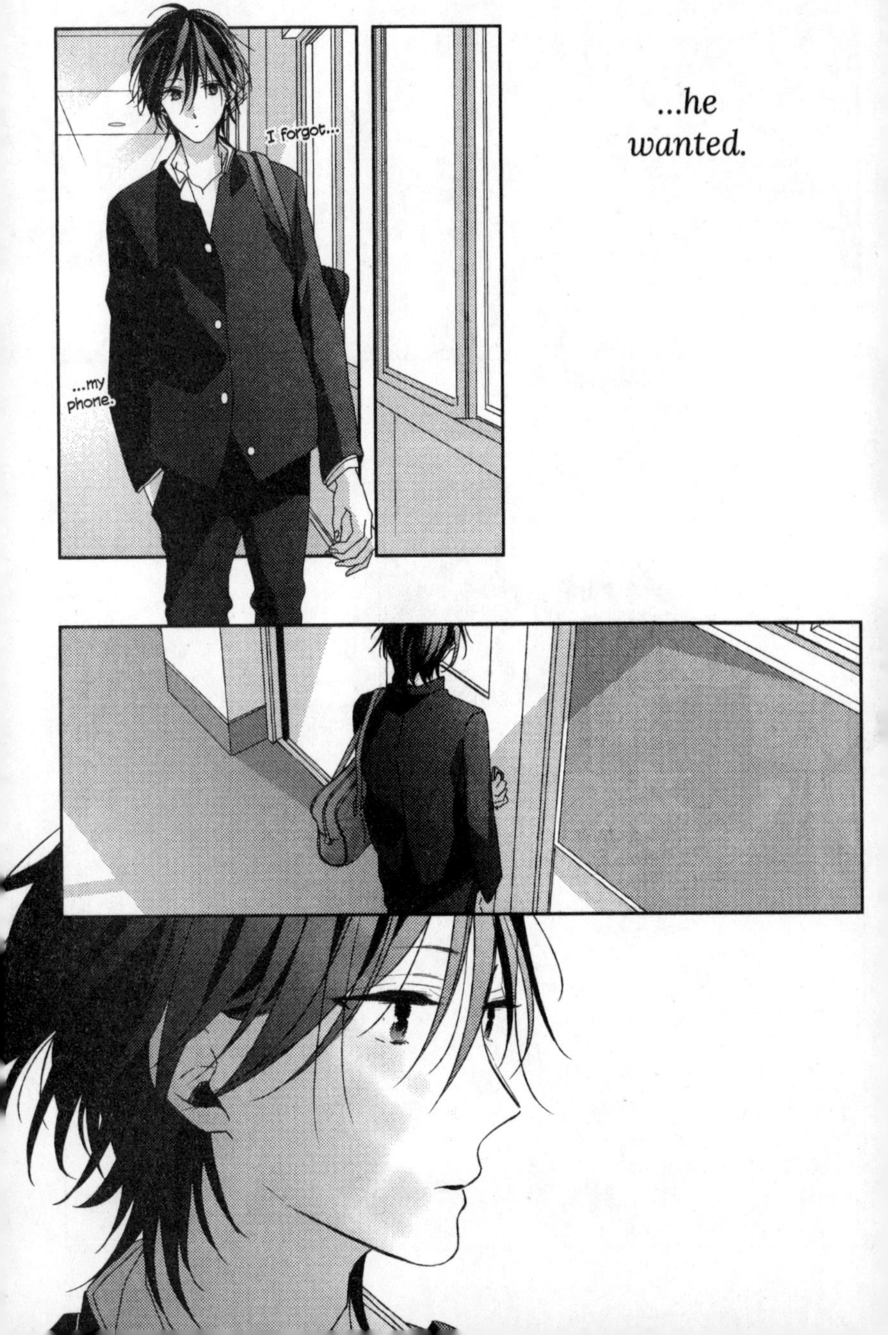
...he wanted.
I forgot...
...my phone.

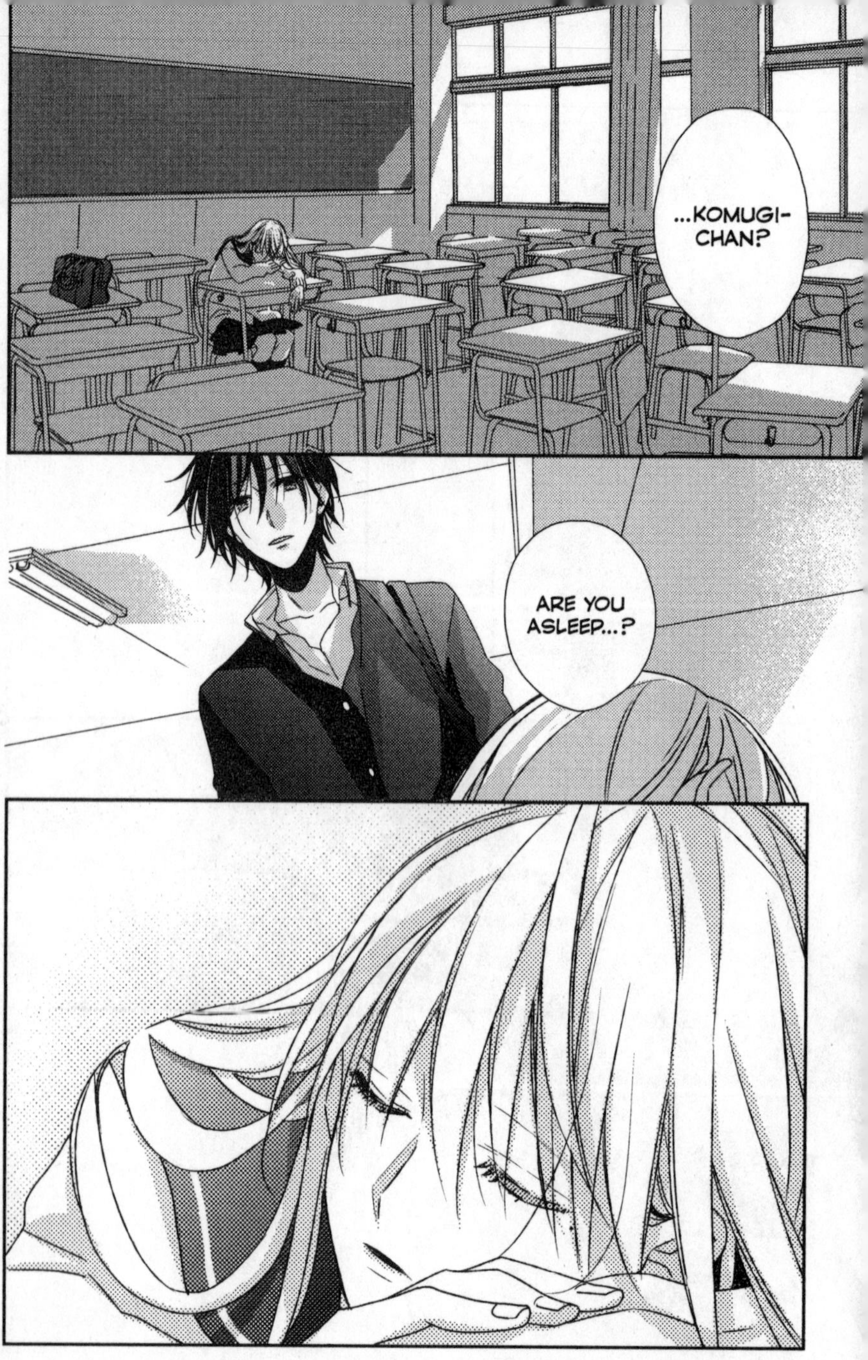
...KOMUGI-CHAN?
ARE YOU ASLEEP...?

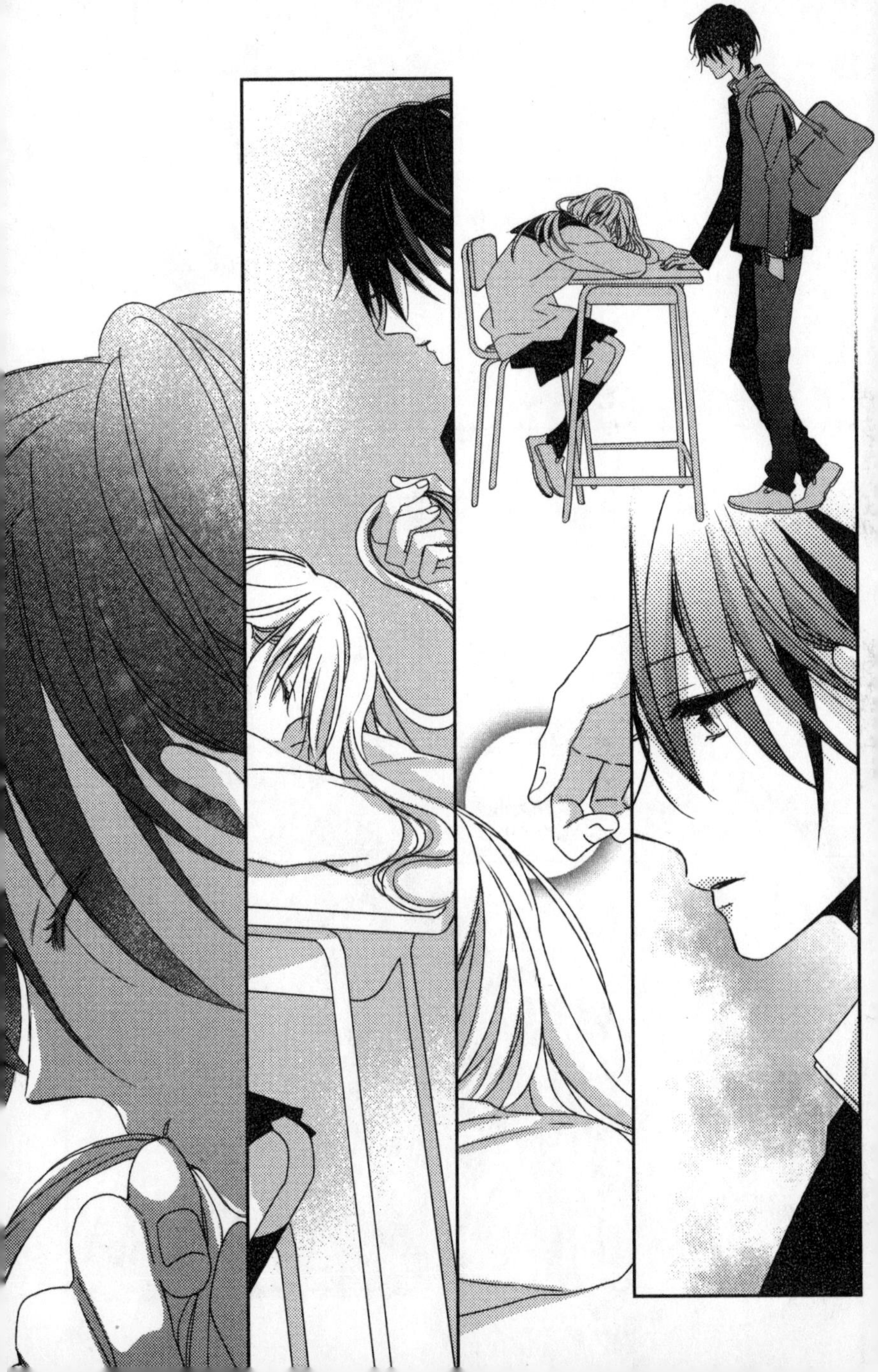

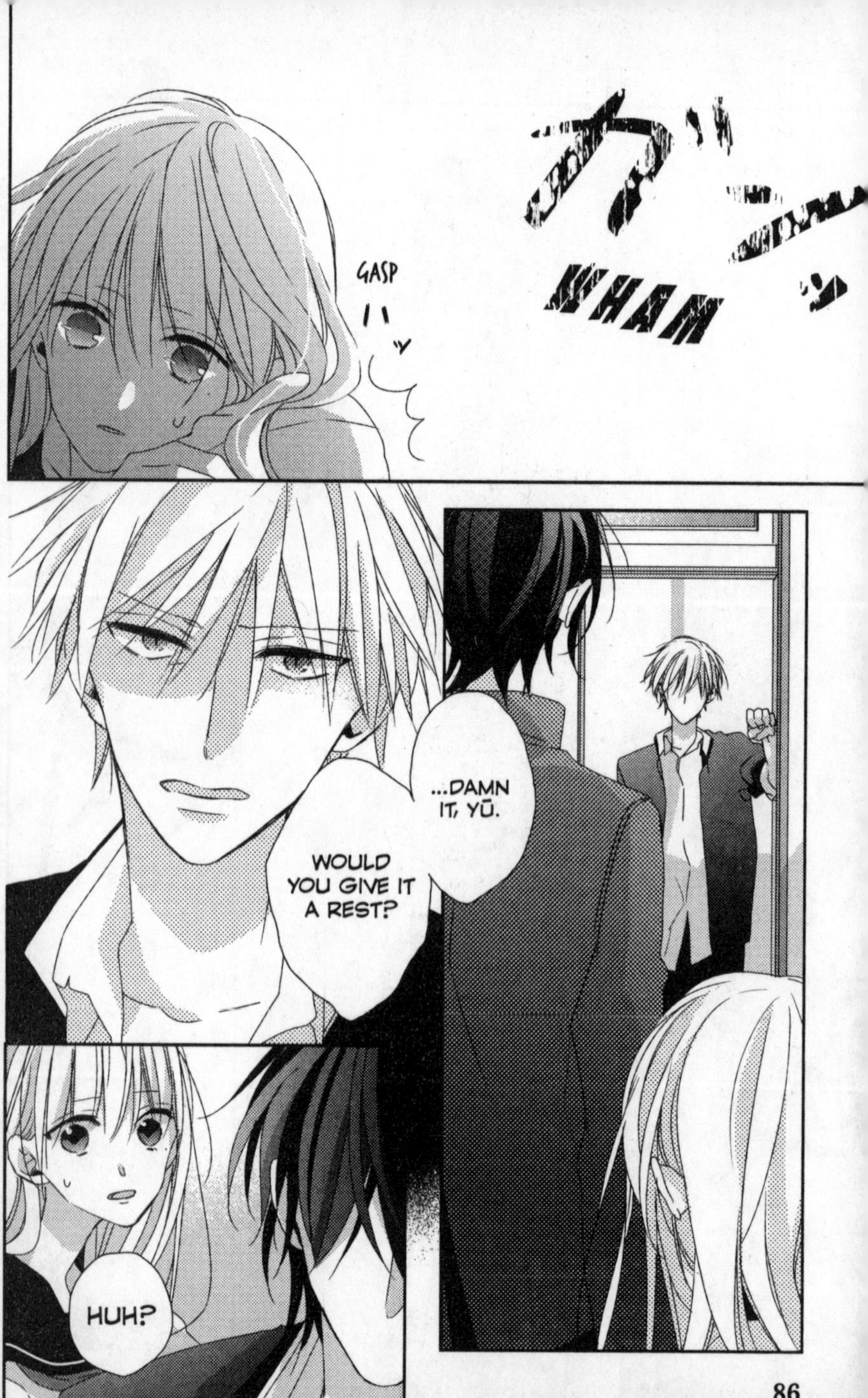
WHAM
GASP
...DAMN IT, YŪ.
WOULD YOU GIVE IT A REST?
HUH?

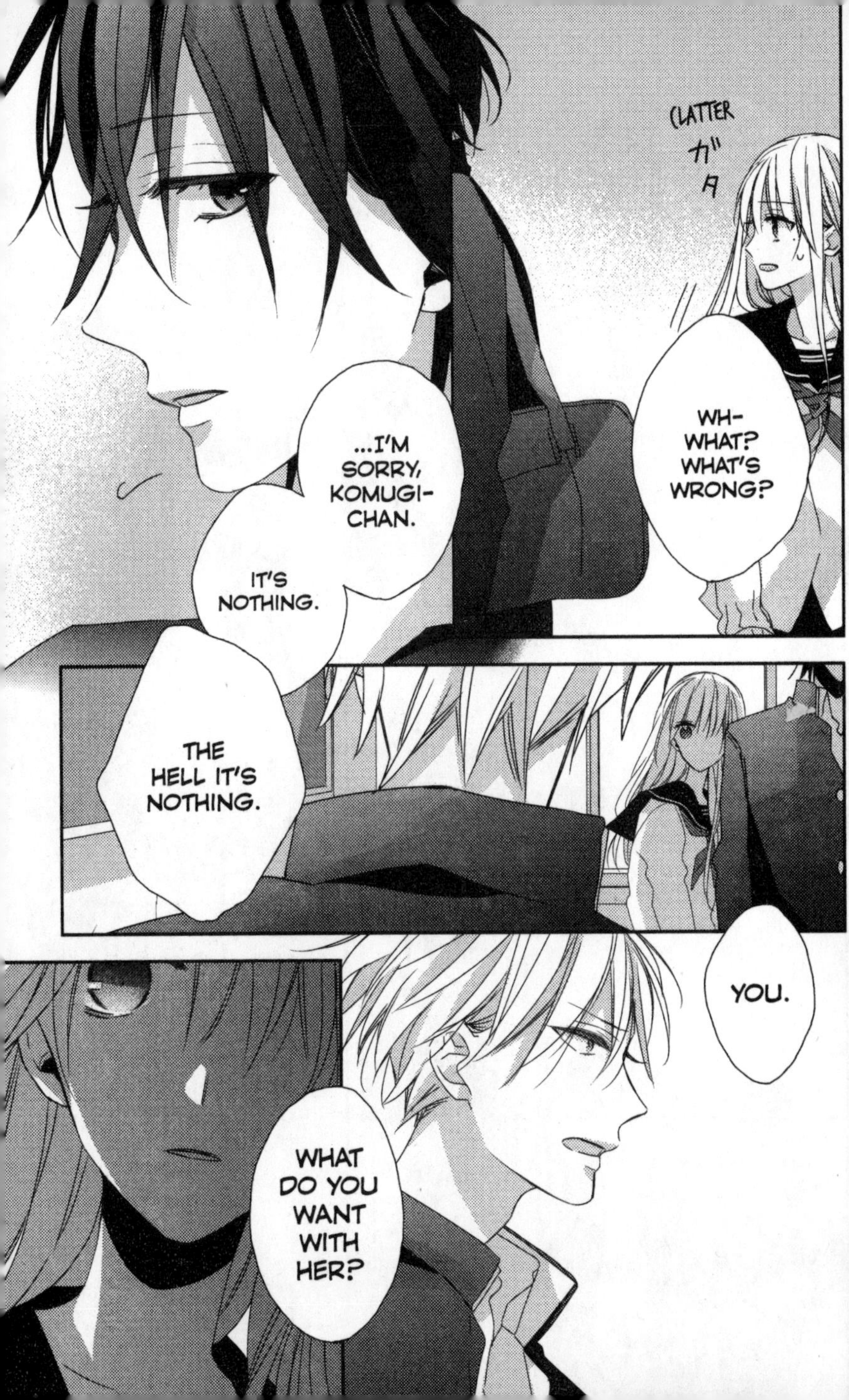
CLATTER
ガタ
WH-WHAT? WHAT'S WRONG?
...I'M SORRY, KOMUGI-CHAN.
IT'S NOTHING.
THE HELL IT'S NOTHING.
YOU.
WHAT DO YOU WANT WITH HER?

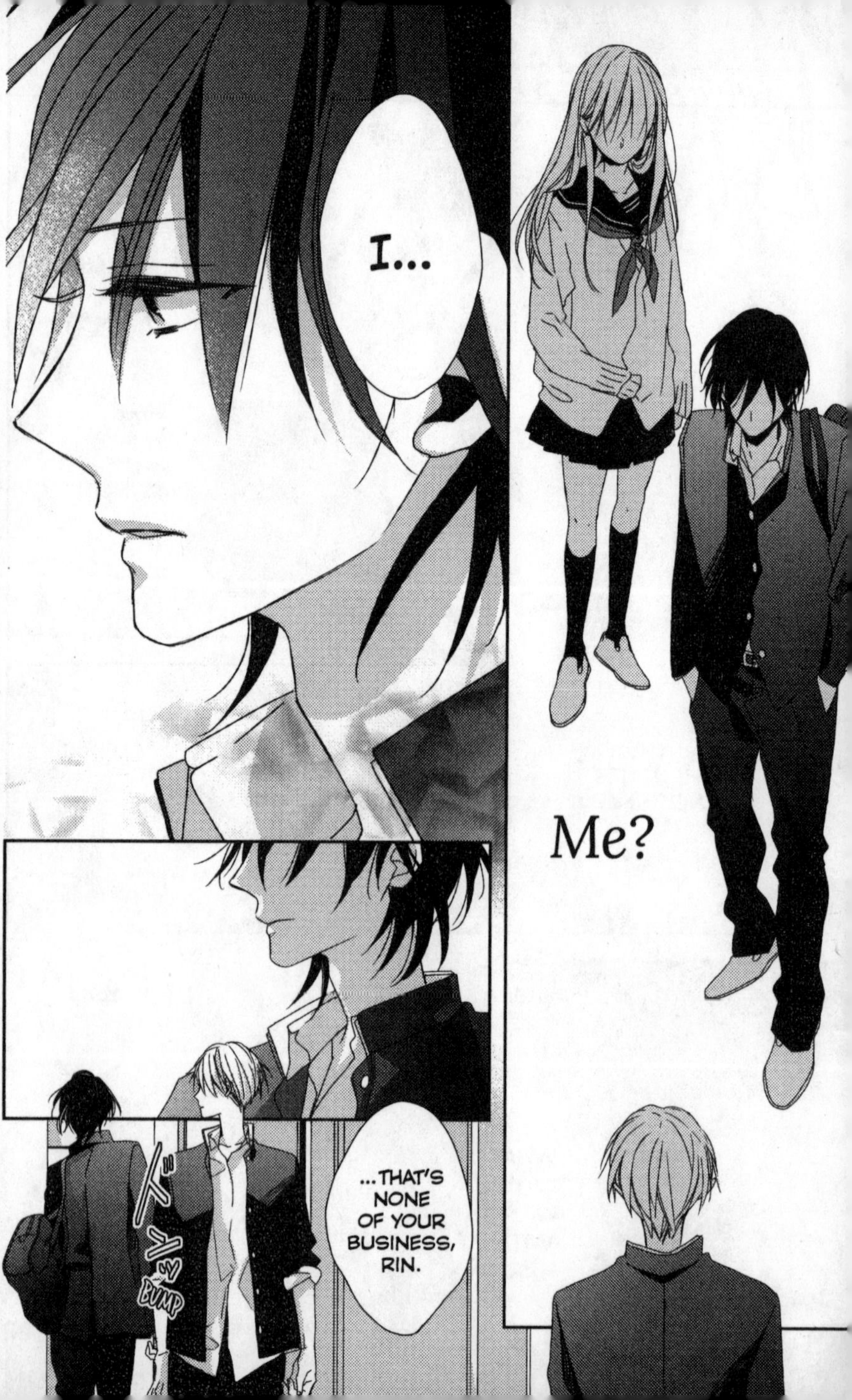
Me?
I...
...THAT'S NONE OF YOUR BUSINESS, RIN.
BUMP

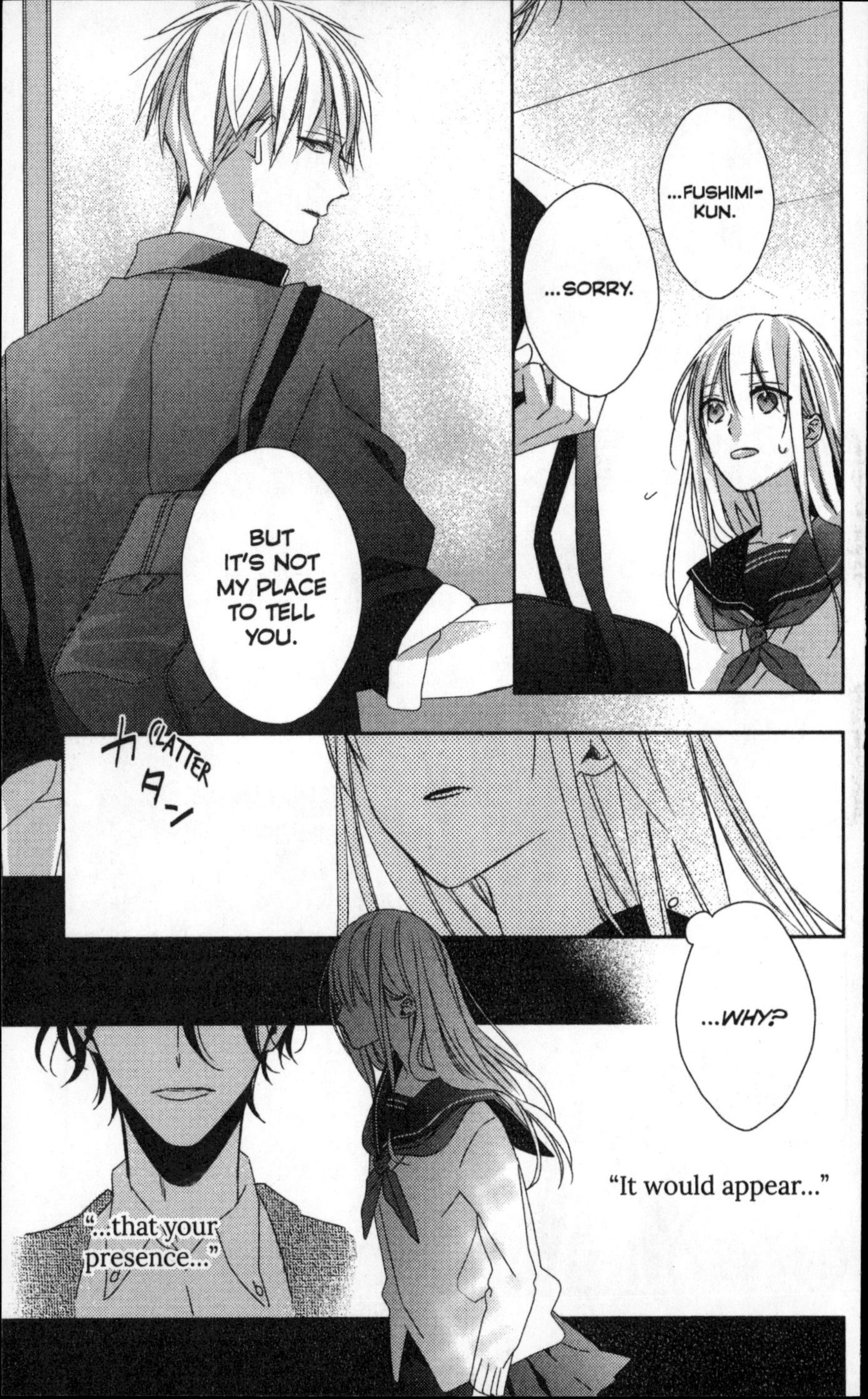
...FUSHIMI-KUN.
...SORRY.
BUT IT'S NOT MY PLACE TO TELL YOU.
カターン
CLATTER
...WHY?
"It would appear..."
"...that your presence..."

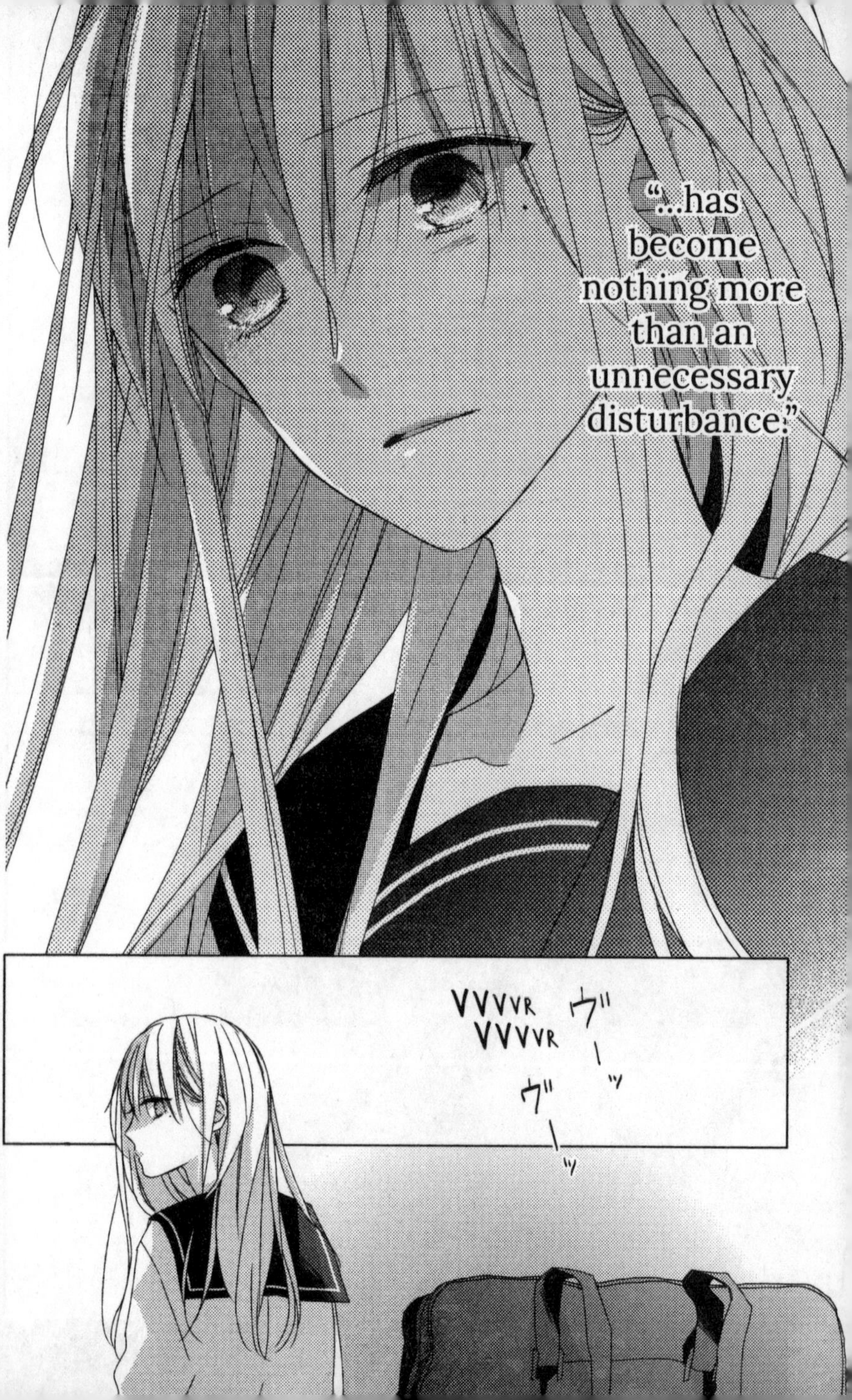
"...has become nothing more than an unnecessary disturbance."
VVVVR VVVVR
ヴーッ
ヴーッ

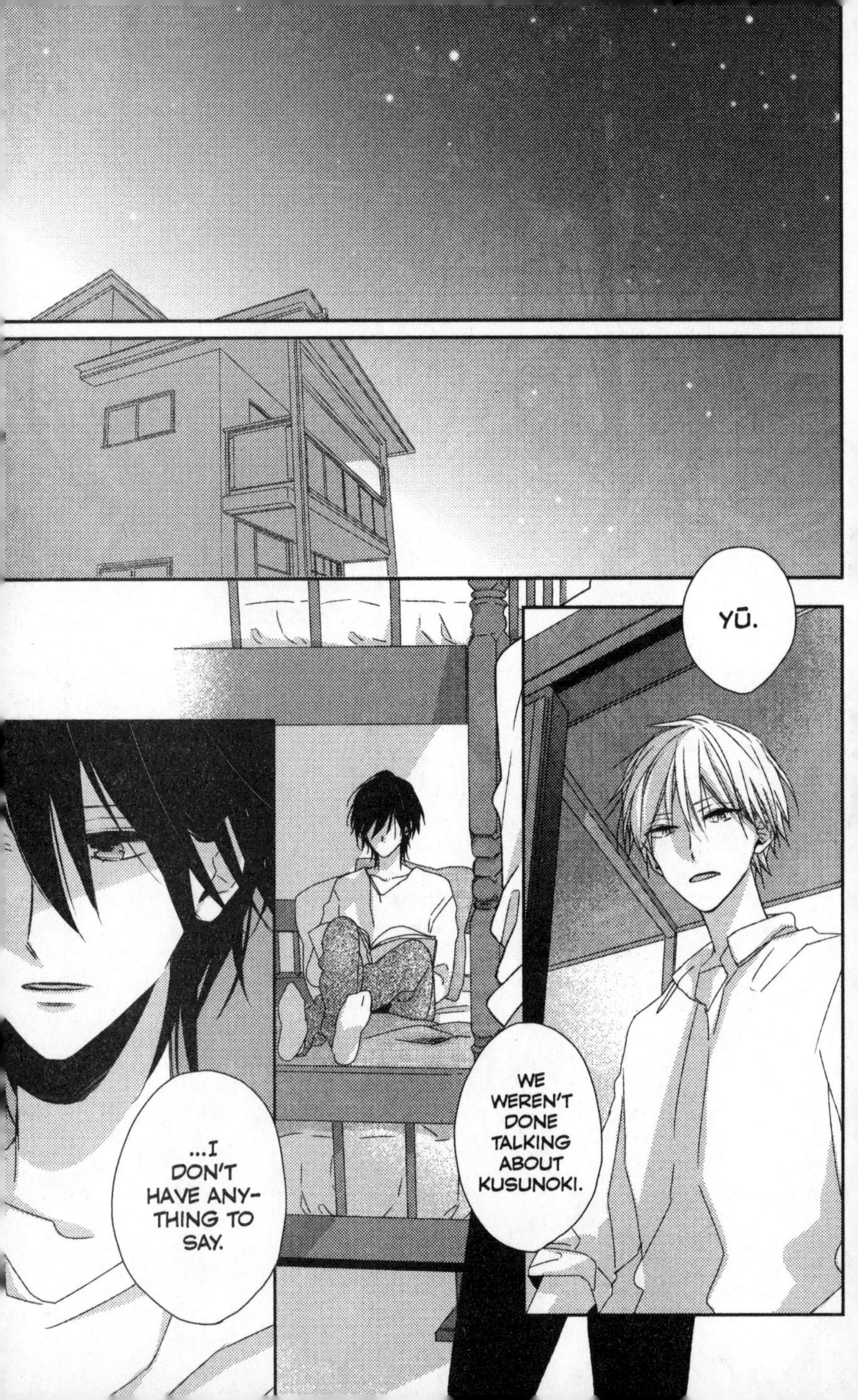
YŪ.
WE WEREN'T DONE TALKING ABOUT KUSUNOKI.
...I DON'T HAVE ANY-THING TO SAY.

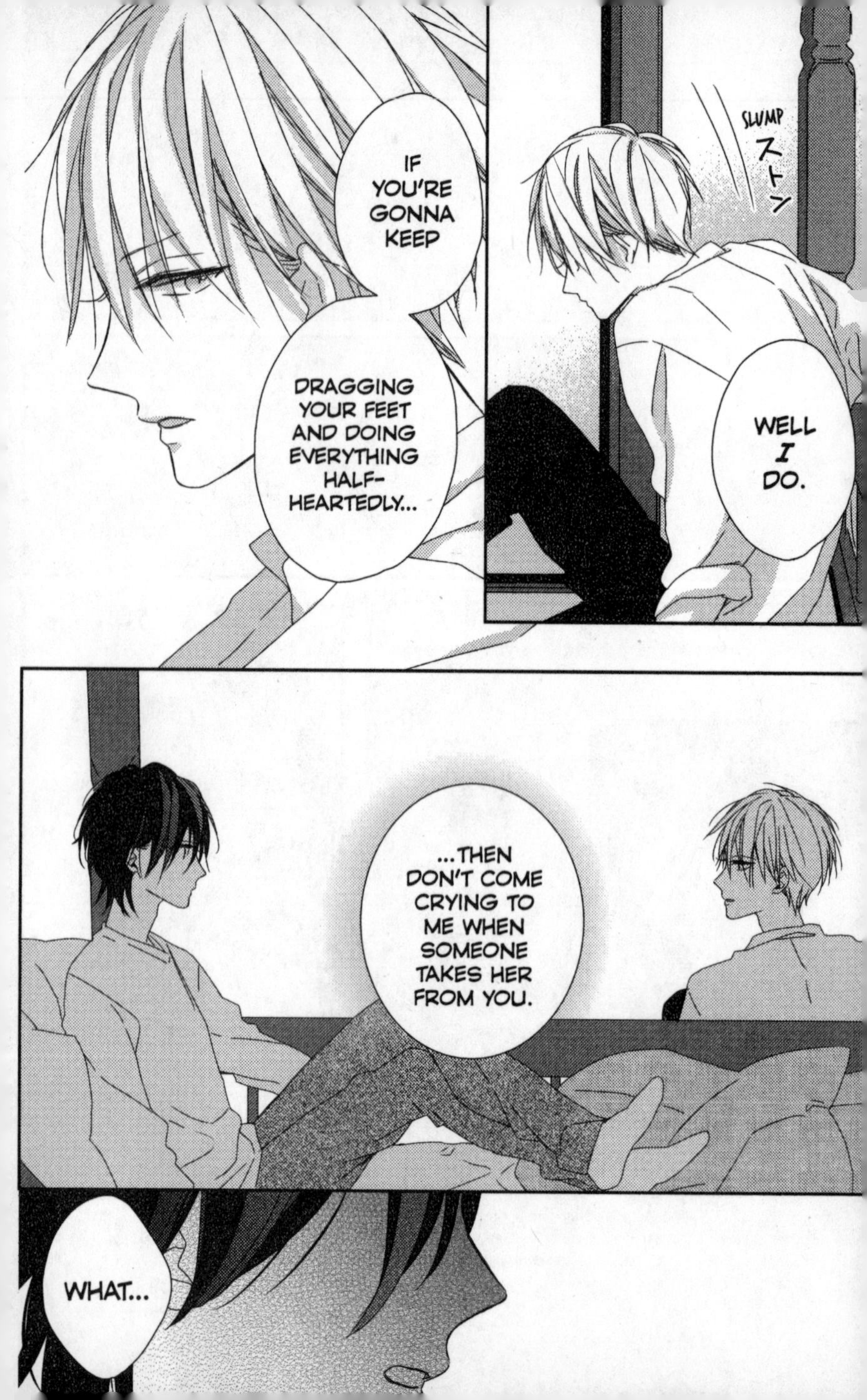
SLUMP
ストン
WELL I DO.
IF YOU'RE GONNA KEEP
DRAGGING YOUR FEET AND DOING EVERYTHING HALF-HEARTEDLY...
...THEN DON'T COME CRYING TO ME WHEN SOMEONE TAKES HER FROM YOU.
WHAT...

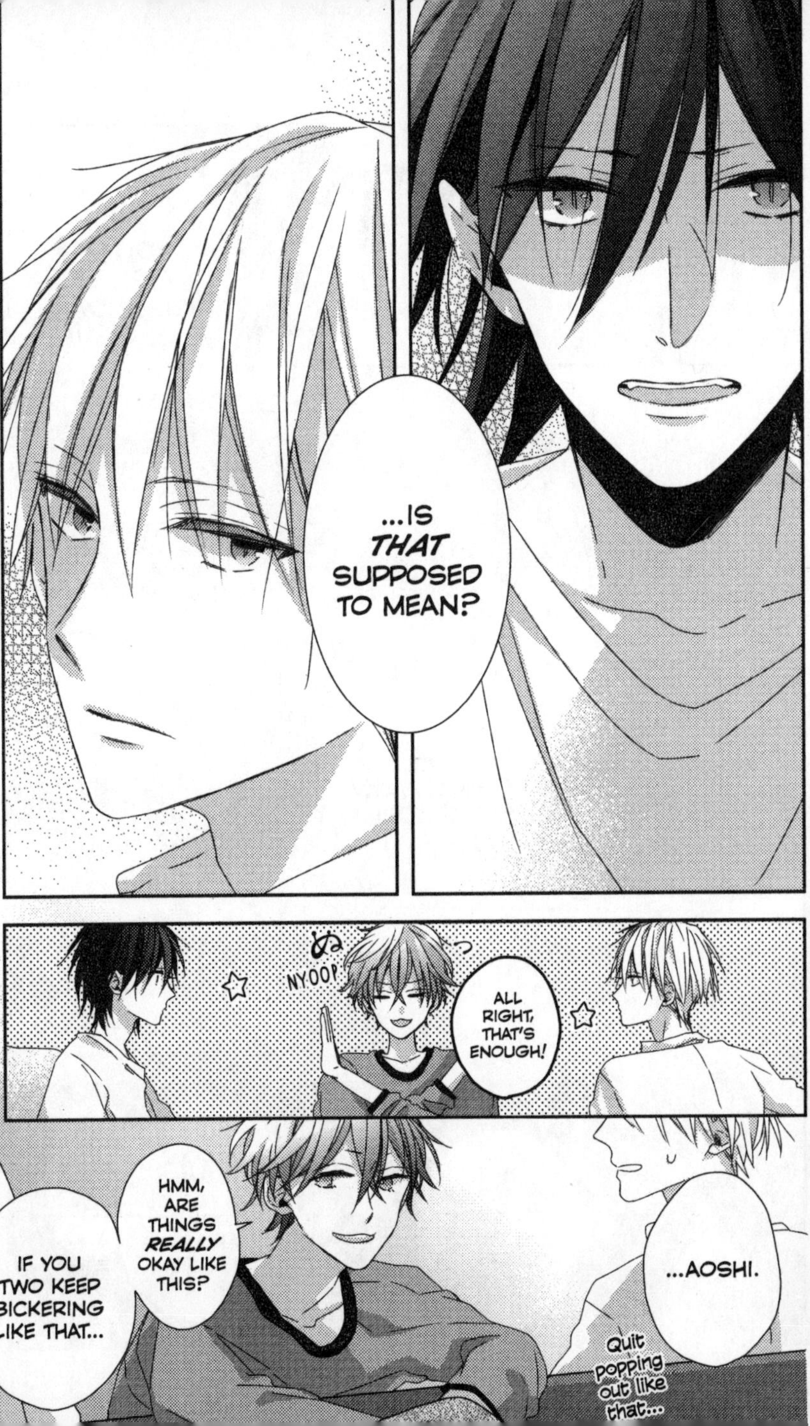
...IS *THAT* SUPPOSED TO MEAN?
ALL RIGHT, THAT'S ENOUGH!
ぬ
NYOOP
...AOSHI.
Quit popping out like that...
HMM, ARE THINGS *REALLY* OKAY LIKE THIS?
IF YOU TWO KEEP BICKERING LIKE THAT...

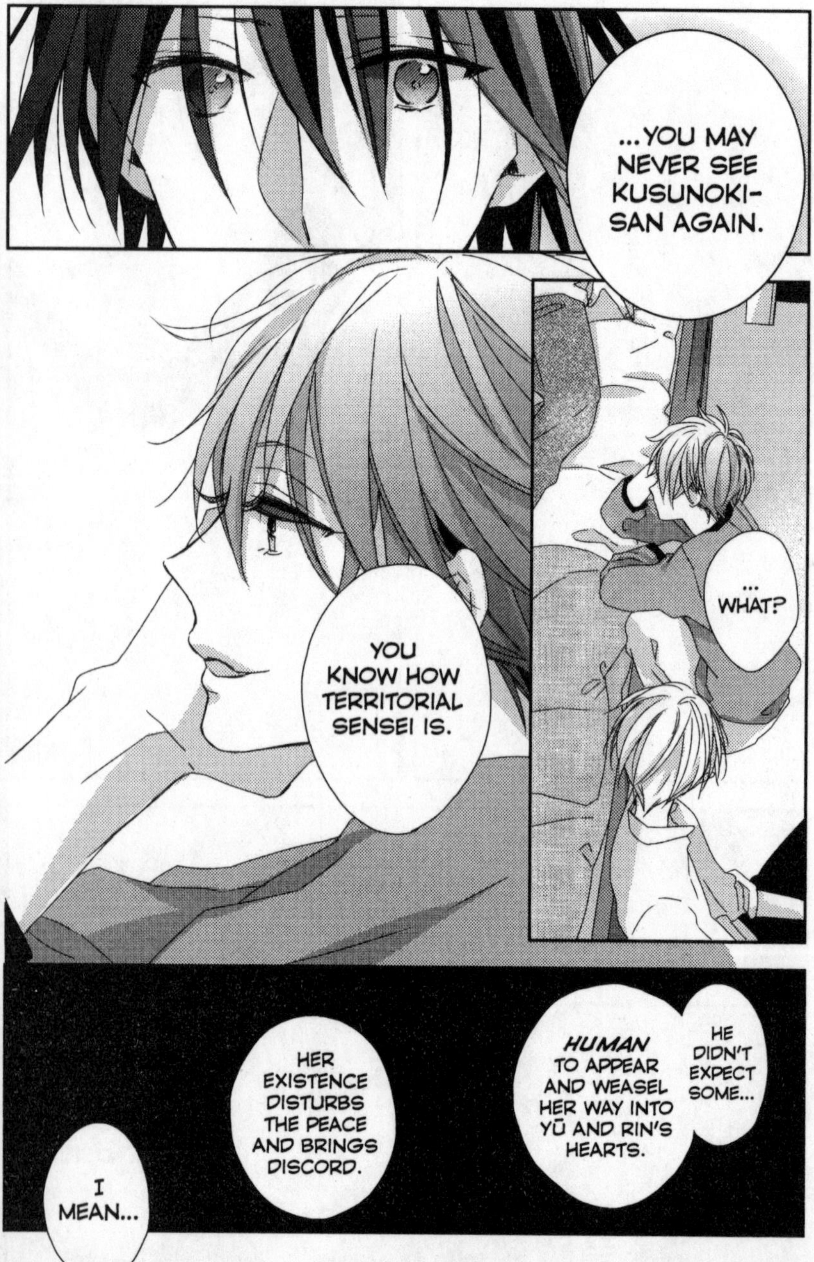
...YOU MAY NEVER SEE KUSUNOKI-SAN AGAIN.
... WHAT?
YOU KNOW HOW TERRITORIAL SENSEI IS.
HE DIDN'T EXPECT SOME...
HUMAN TO APPEAR AND WEASEL HER WAY INTO YŪ AND RIN'S HEARTS.
HER EXISTENCE DISTURBS THE PEACE AND BRINGS DISCORD.
I MEAN...

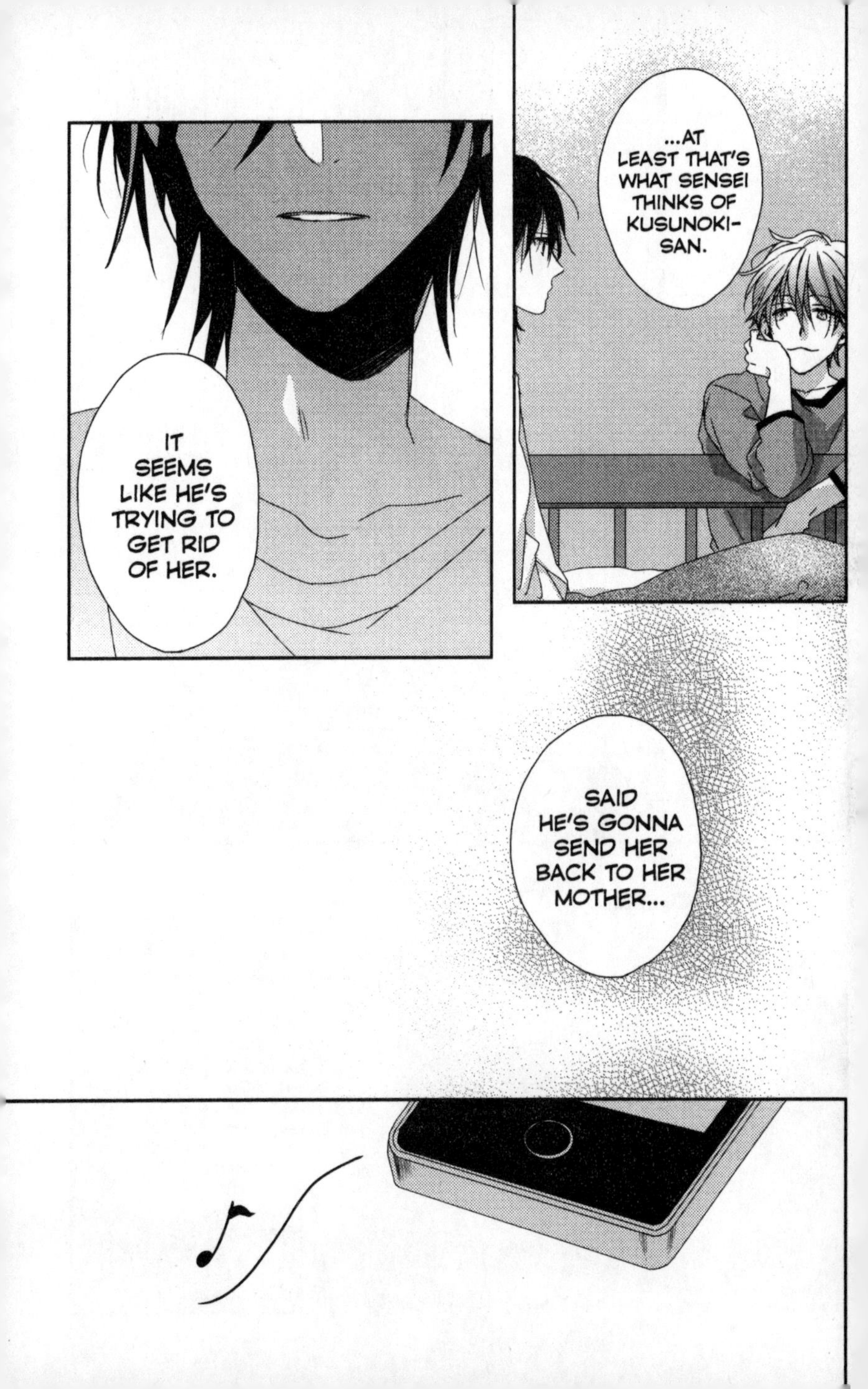
...AT LEAST THAT'S WHAT SENSEI THINKS OF KUSUNOKI-SAN.
IT SEEMS LIKE HE'S TRYING TO GET RID OF HER.
SAID HE'S GONNA SEND HER BACK TO HER MOTHER...

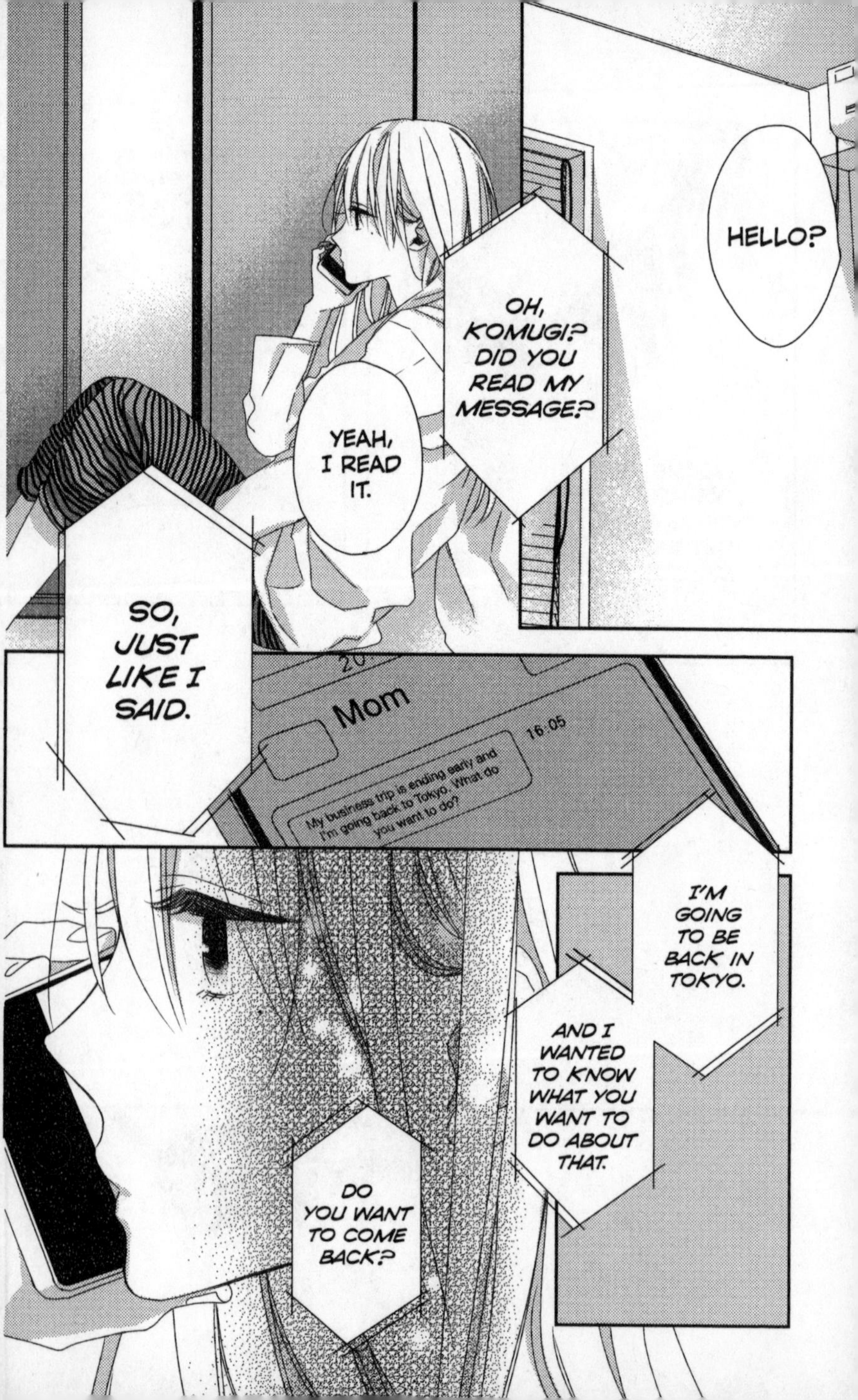
HELLO?
OH, KOMUGI? DID YOU READ MY MESSAGE?
YEAH, I READ IT.
SO, JUST LIKE I SAID.
20
Mom
16:05
My business trip is ending early and I'm going back to Tokyo. What do you want to do?
I'M GOING TO BE BACK IN TOKYO.
AND I WANTED TO KNOW WHAT YOU WANT TO DO ABOUT THAT.
DO YOU WANT TO COME BACK?

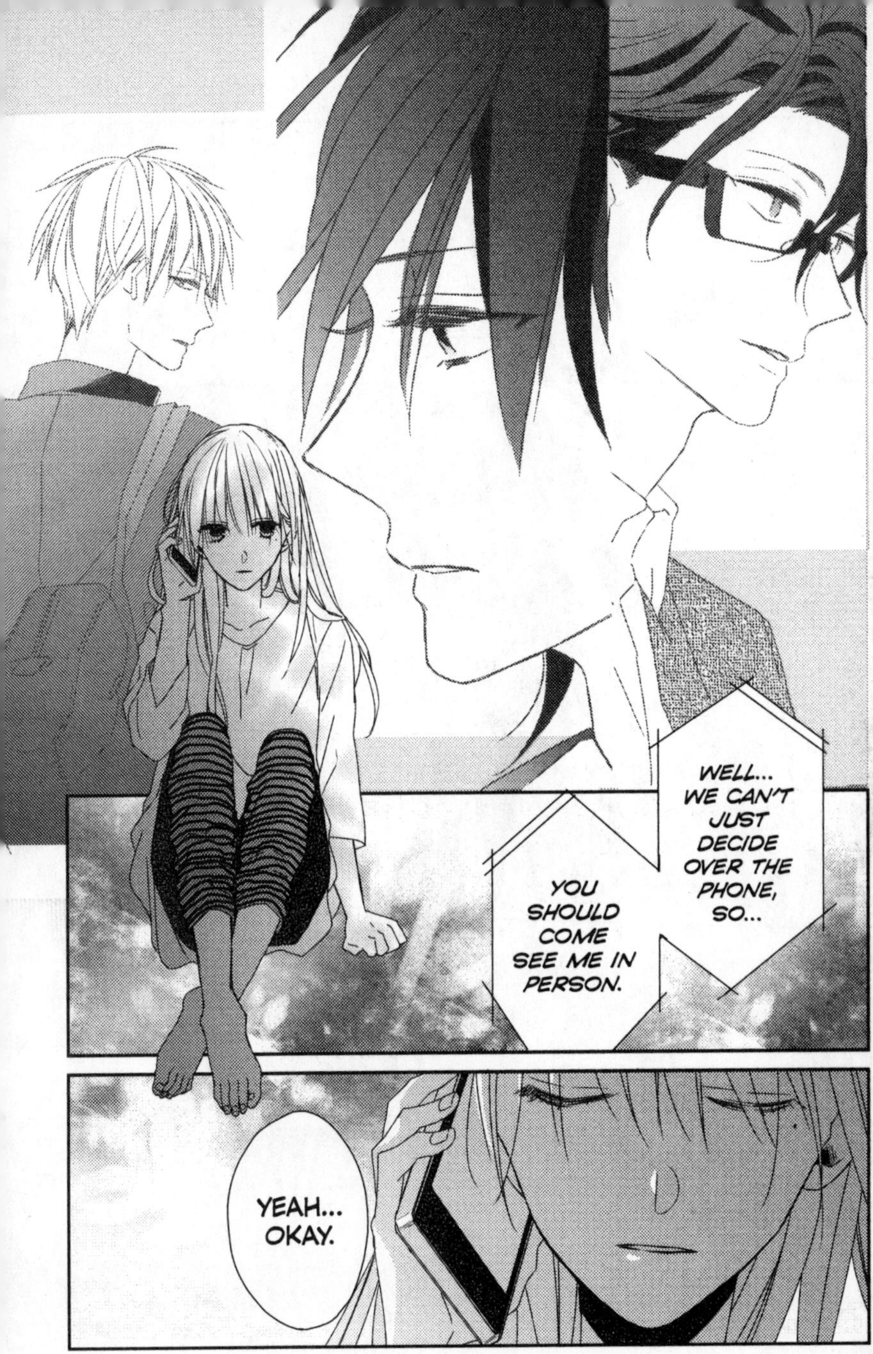
WELL... WE CAN'T JUST DECIDE OVER THE PHONE, SO...
YOU SHOULD COME SEE ME IN PERSON.
YEAH... OKAY.

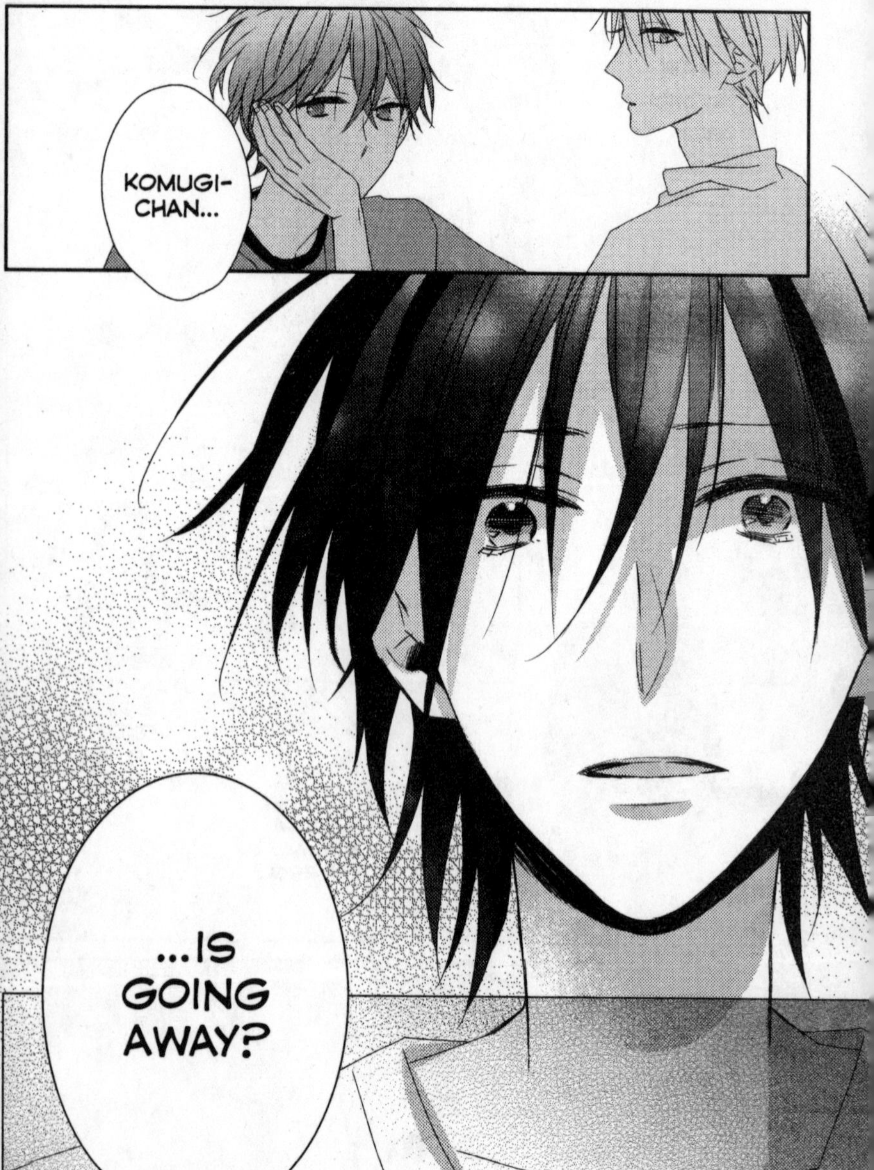
KOMUGI-CHAN...
...IS GOING AWAY?

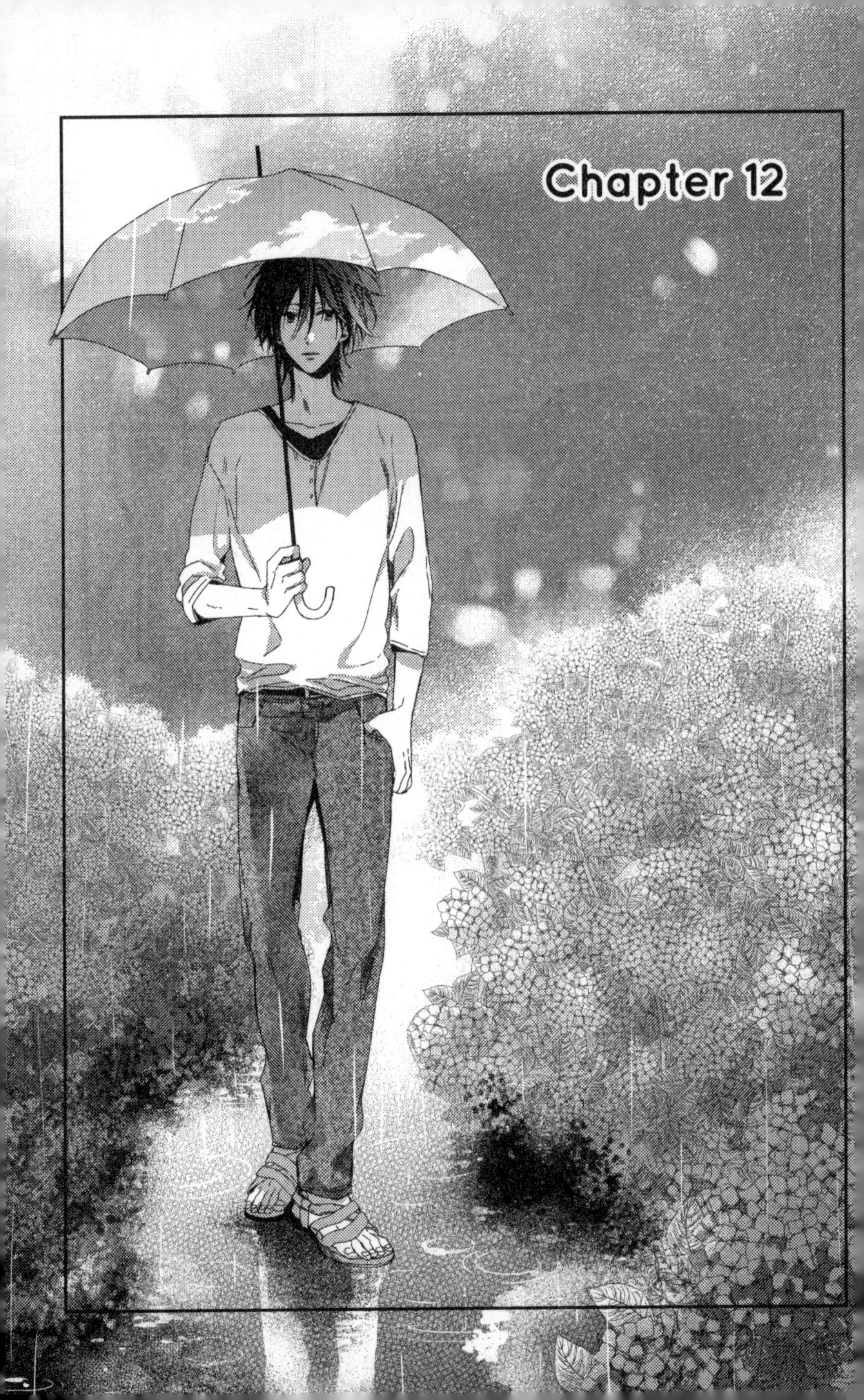
Chapter 12

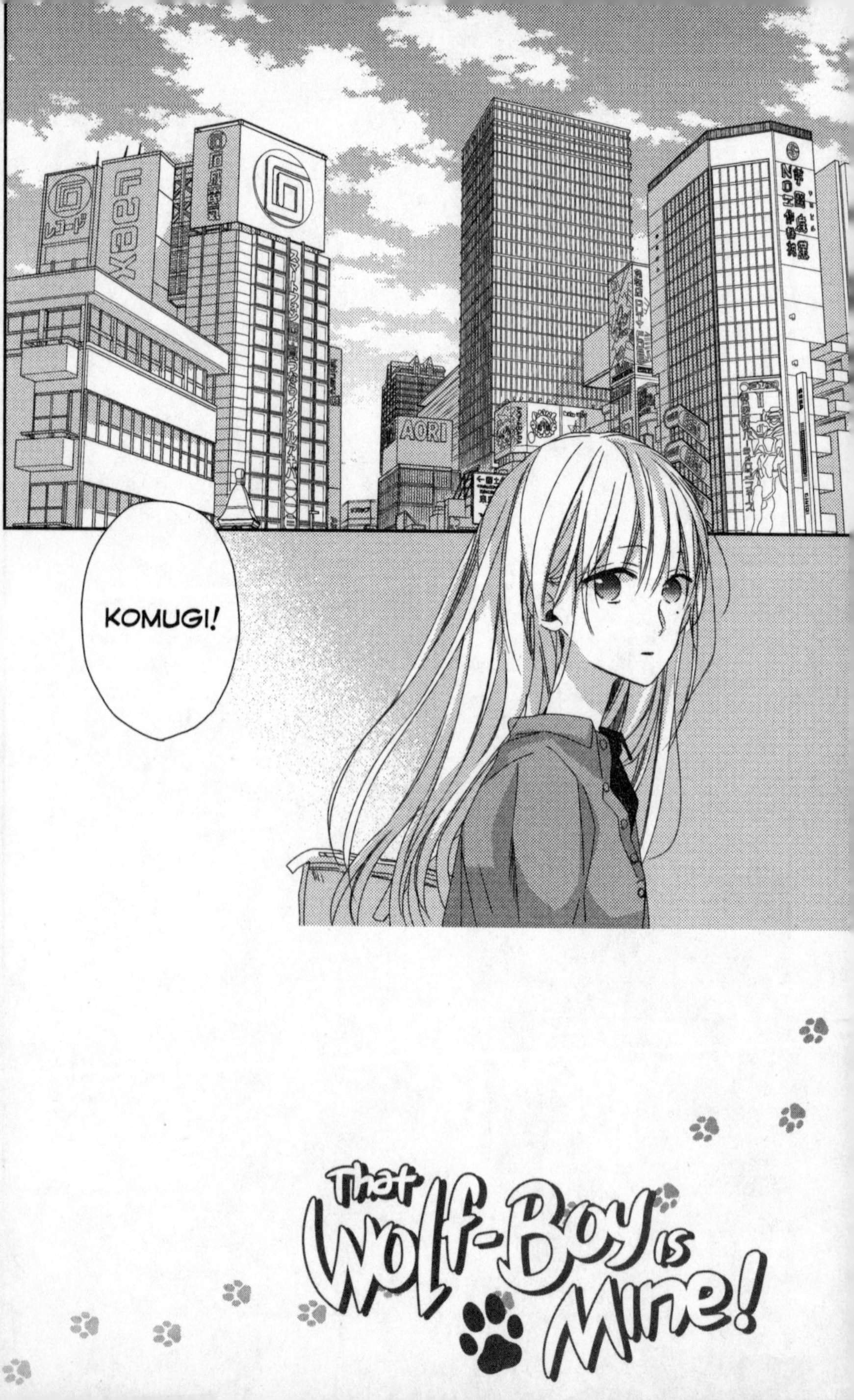
KOMUGI!
That Wolf-Boy is Mine!

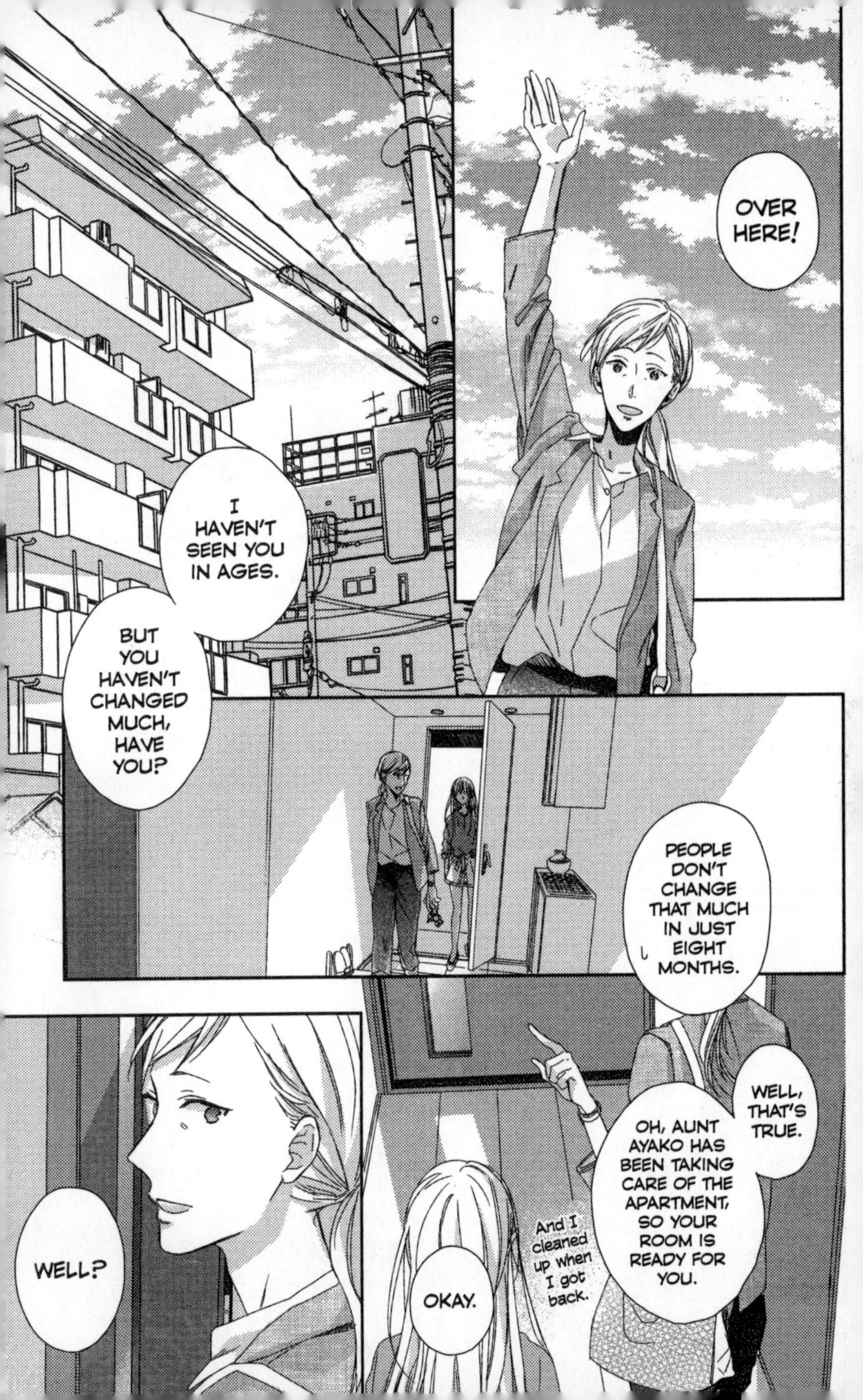
OVER HERE!
I HAVEN'T SEEN YOU IN AGES.
BUT YOU HAVEN'T CHANGED MUCH, HAVE YOU?
PEOPLE DON'T CHANGE THAT MUCH IN JUST EIGHT MONTHS.
WELL, THAT'S TRUE.
OH, AUNT AYAKO HAS BEEN TAKING CARE OF THE APARTMENT, SO YOUR ROOM IS READY FOR YOU.
And I cleaned up when I got back.
OKAY.
WELL?

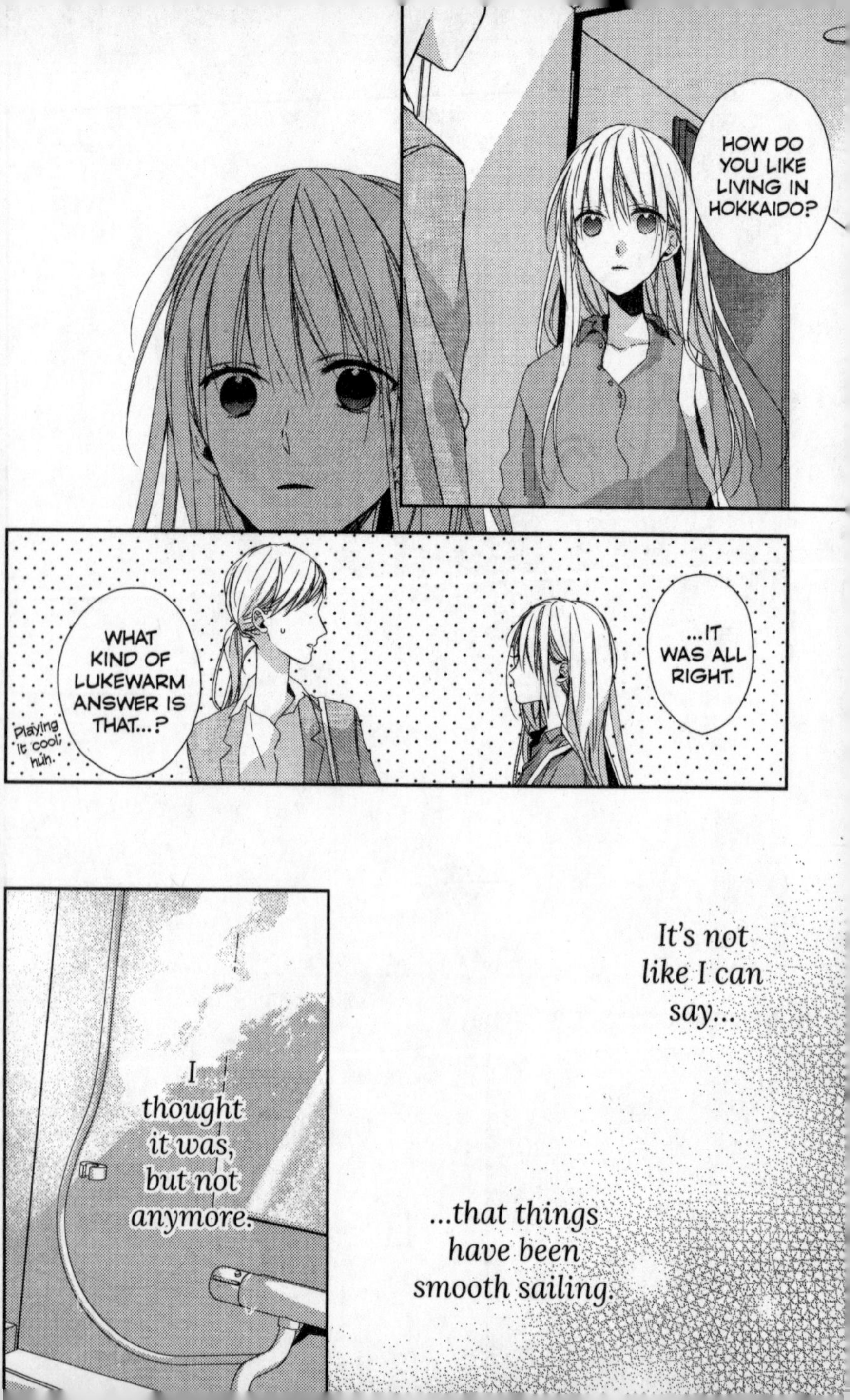
HOW DO YOU LIKE LIVING IN HOKKAIDO?
...IT WAS ALL RIGHT.
WHAT KIND OF LUKEWARM ANSWER IS THAT...?
Playing it cool, huh.
It's not like I can say...
...that things have been smooth sailing.
I thought it was, but not anymore.

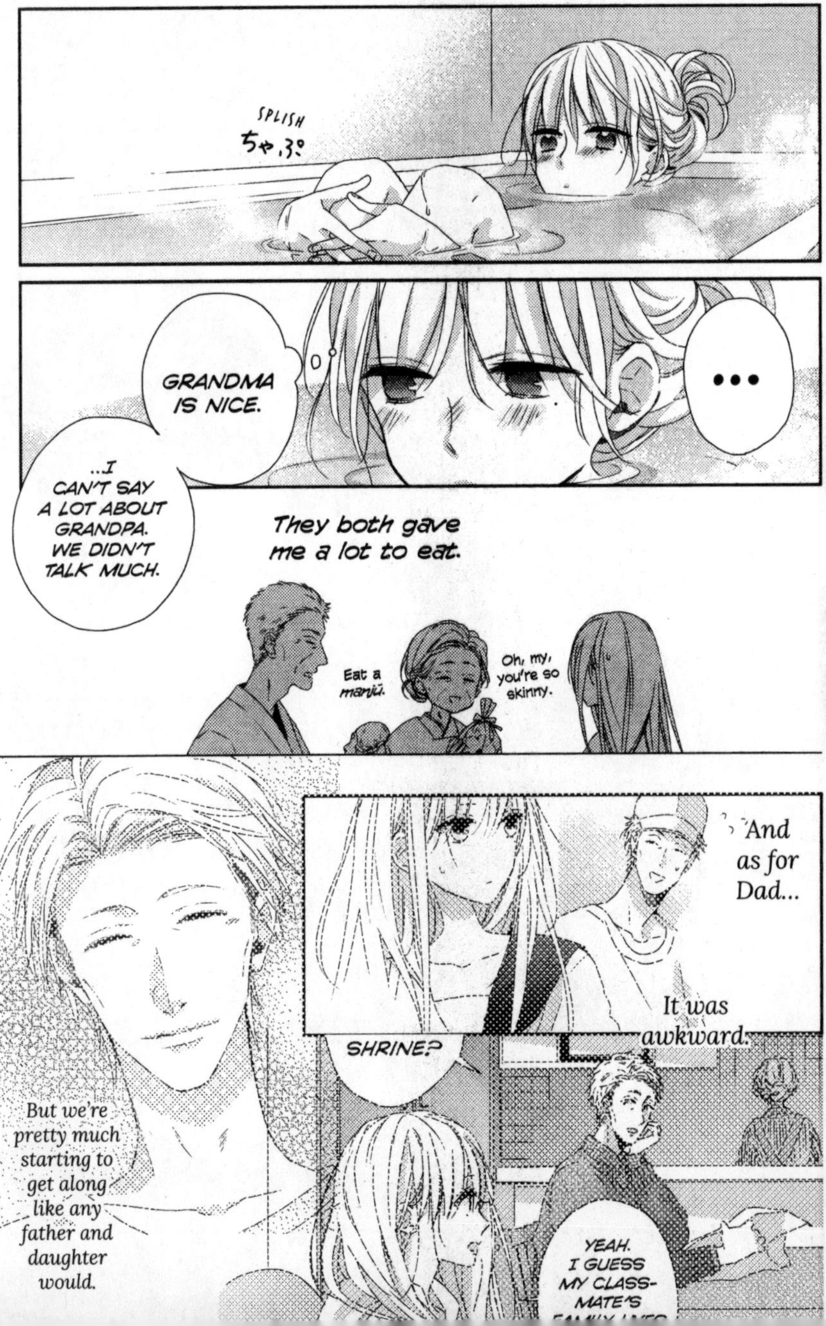

SPLISH
ちゃぷ
...
GRANDMA IS NICE.
...I CAN'T SAY A LOT ABOUT GRANDPA. WE DIDN'T TALK MUCH.
They both gave me a lot to eat.
Oh, my, you're so skinny.
Eat a manjū.
And as for Dad...
It was awkward.
SHRINE?
YEAH. I GUESS MY CLASS-MATE'S
But we're pretty much starting to get along like any father and daughter would.

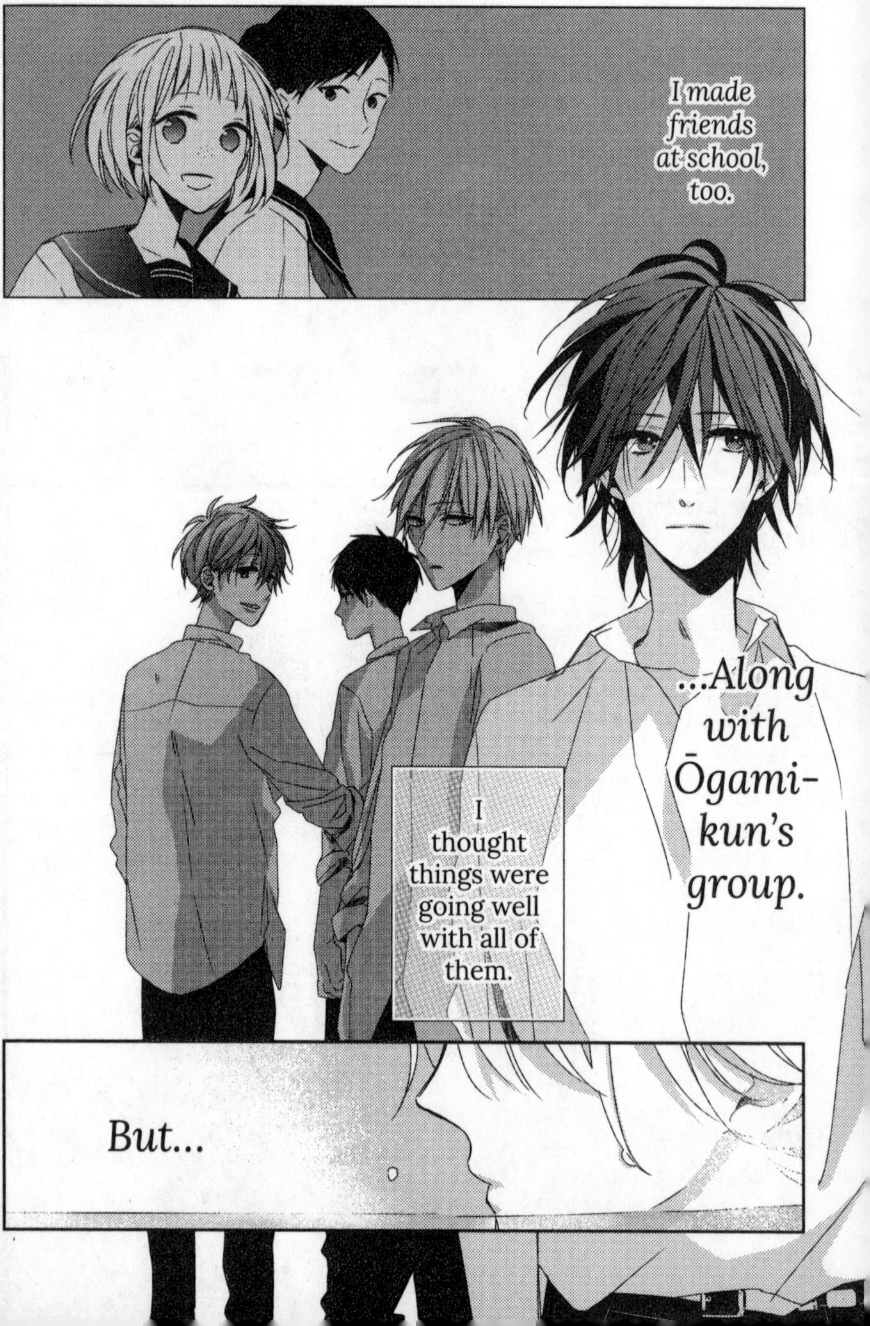
I made friends at school, too.
...Along with Ōgami-kun's group.
I thought things were going well with all of them.
But...

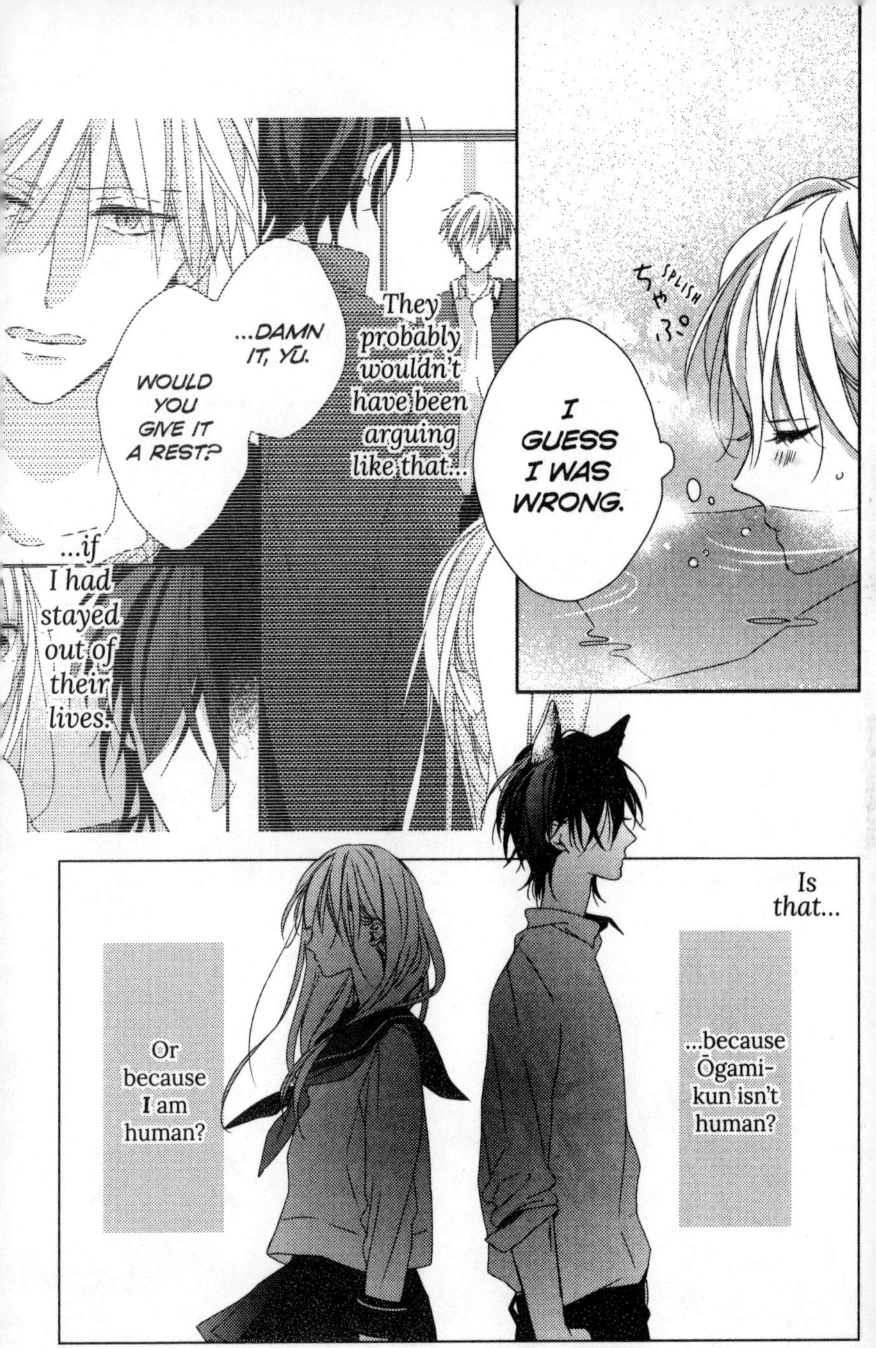
ちゃぷ SPLISH
I GUESS I WAS WRONG.
They probably wouldn't have been arguing like that...
...DAMN IT, YU.
WOULD YOU GIVE IT A REST?
...if I had stayed out of their lives.
Is that...
...because Ōgami-kun isn't human?
Or because I am human?

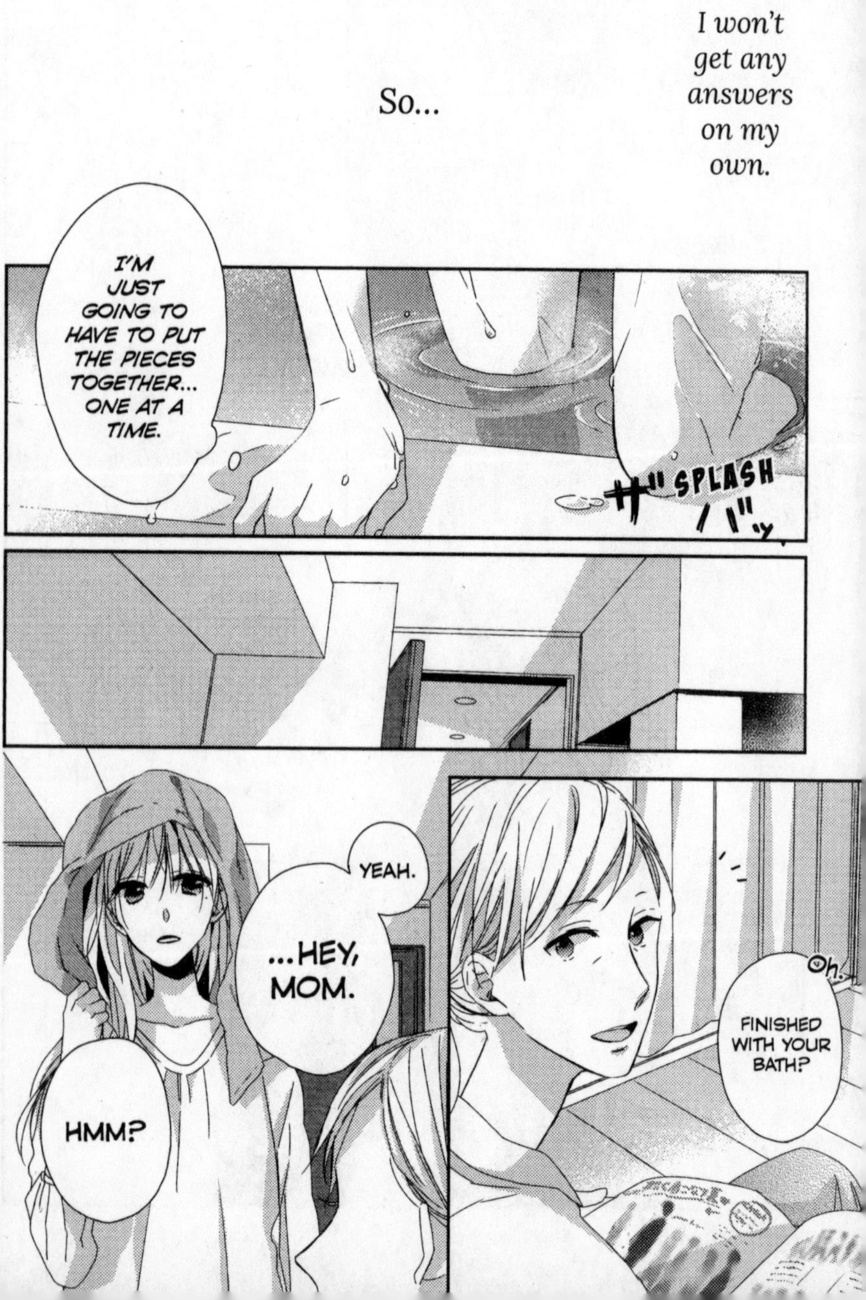
I won't get any answers on my own.
So...
I'M JUST GOING TO HAVE TO PUT THE PIECES TOGETHER... ONE AT A TIME.
SPLASH
Oh.
FINISHED WITH YOUR BATH?
YEAH.
...HEY, MOM.
HMM?

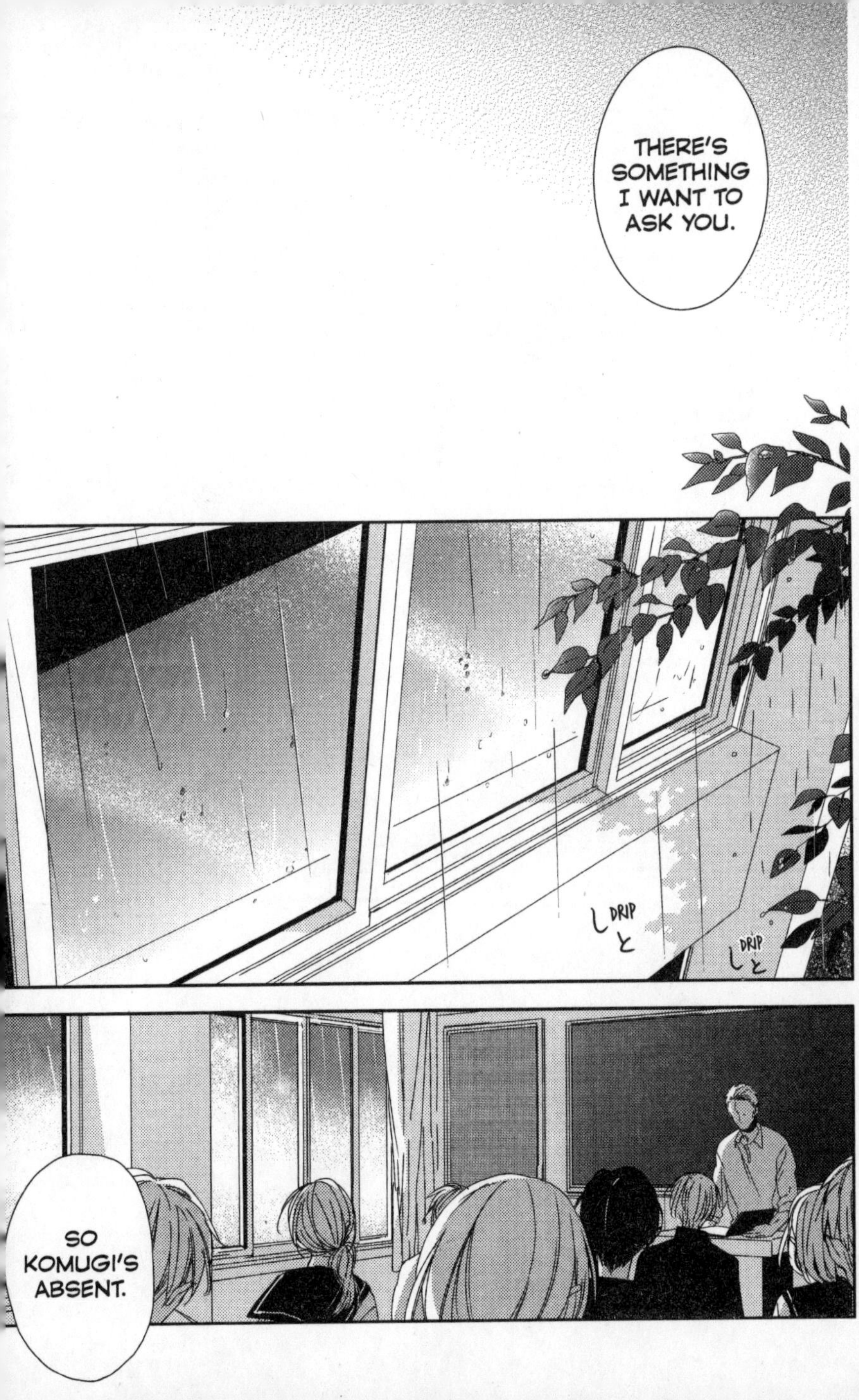
THERE'S SOMETHING I WANT TO ASK YOU.
DRIP
しと
DRIP
しと
SO KOMUGI'S ABSENT.

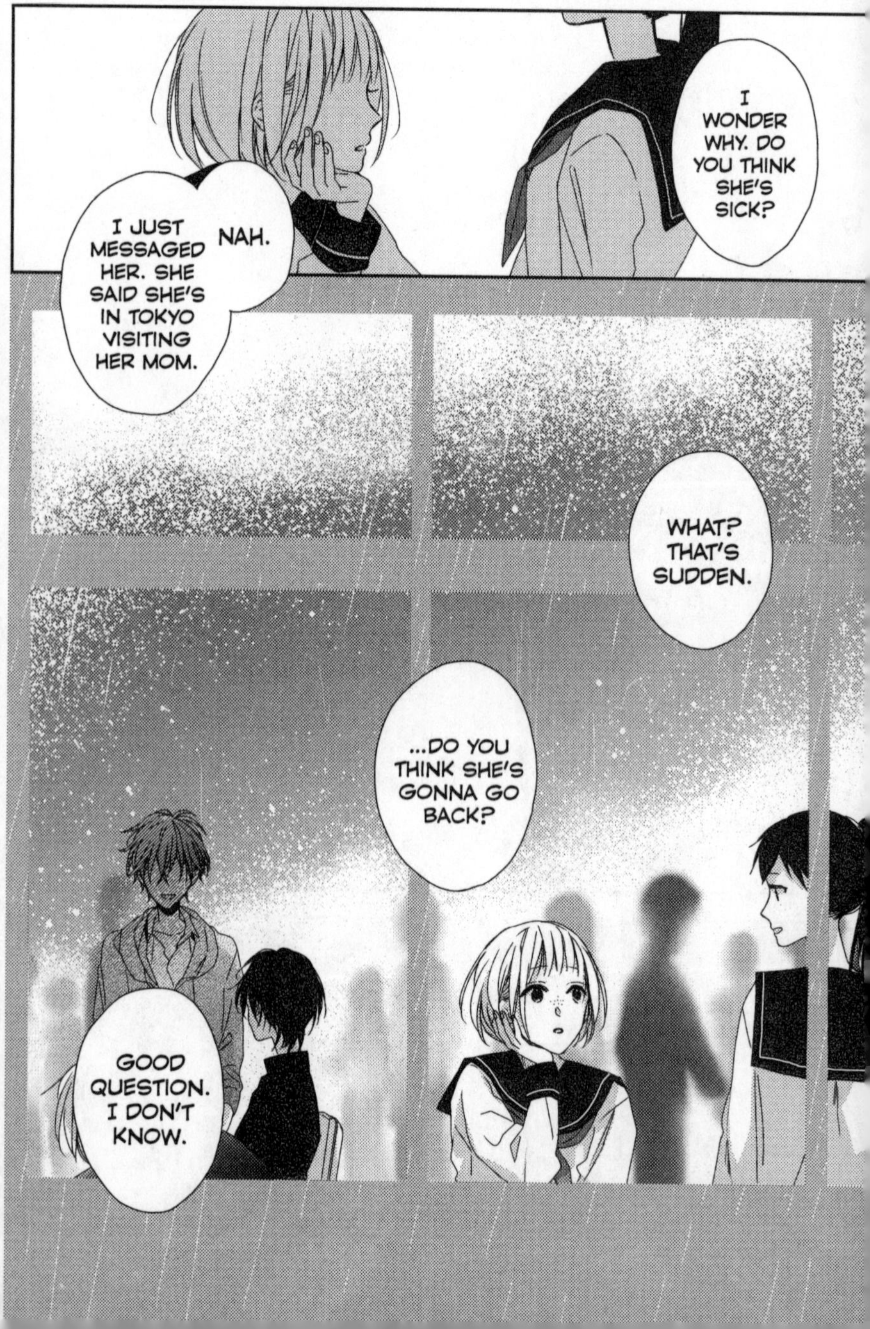
I WONDER WHY. DO YOU THINK SHE'S SICK?
NAH.
I JUST MESSAGED HER. SHE SAID SHE'S IN TOKYO VISITING HER MOM.
WHAT? THAT'S SUDDEN.
...DO YOU THINK SHE'S GONNA GO BACK?
GOOD QUESTION. I DON'T KNOW.

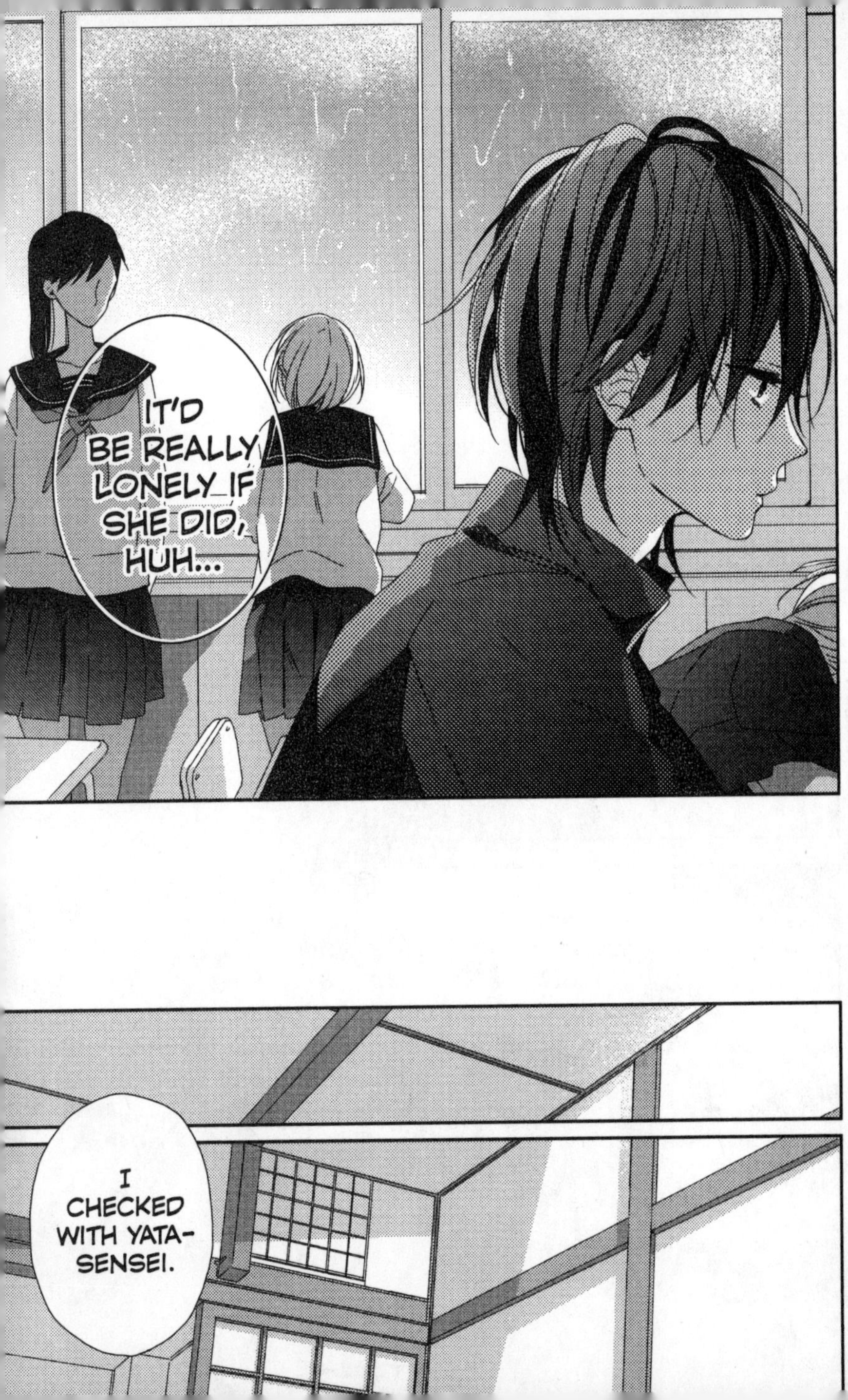
IT'D BE REALLY LONELY IF SHE DID, HUH...
I CHECKED WITH YATA-SENSEI.

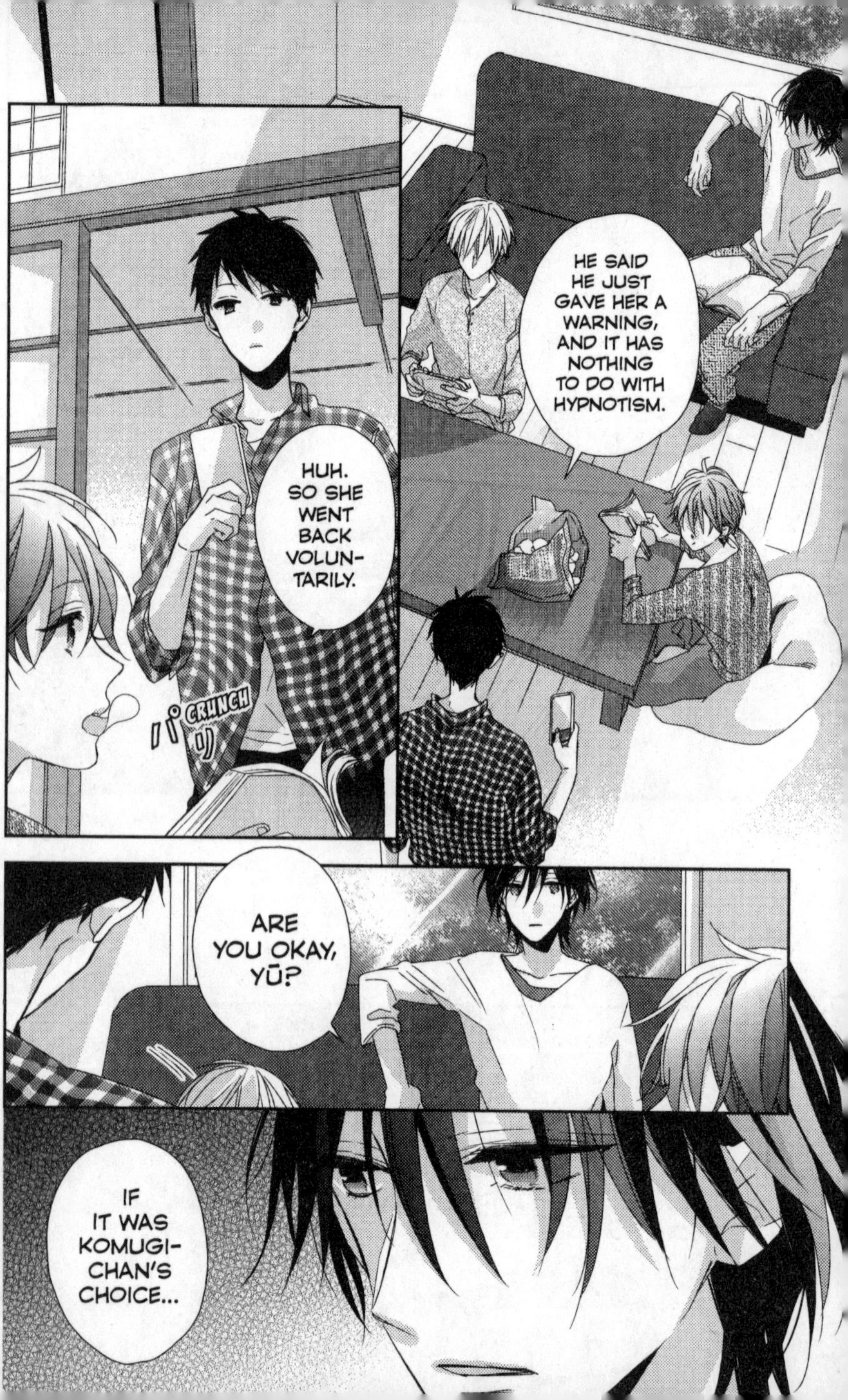
HE SAID HE JUST GAVE HER A WARNING, AND IT HAS NOTHING TO DO WITH HYPNOTISM.
HUH. SO SHE WENT BACK VOLUN-TARILY.
CRUNCH
ARE YOU OKAY, YŪ?
IF IT WAS KOMUGI-CHAN'S CHOICE...

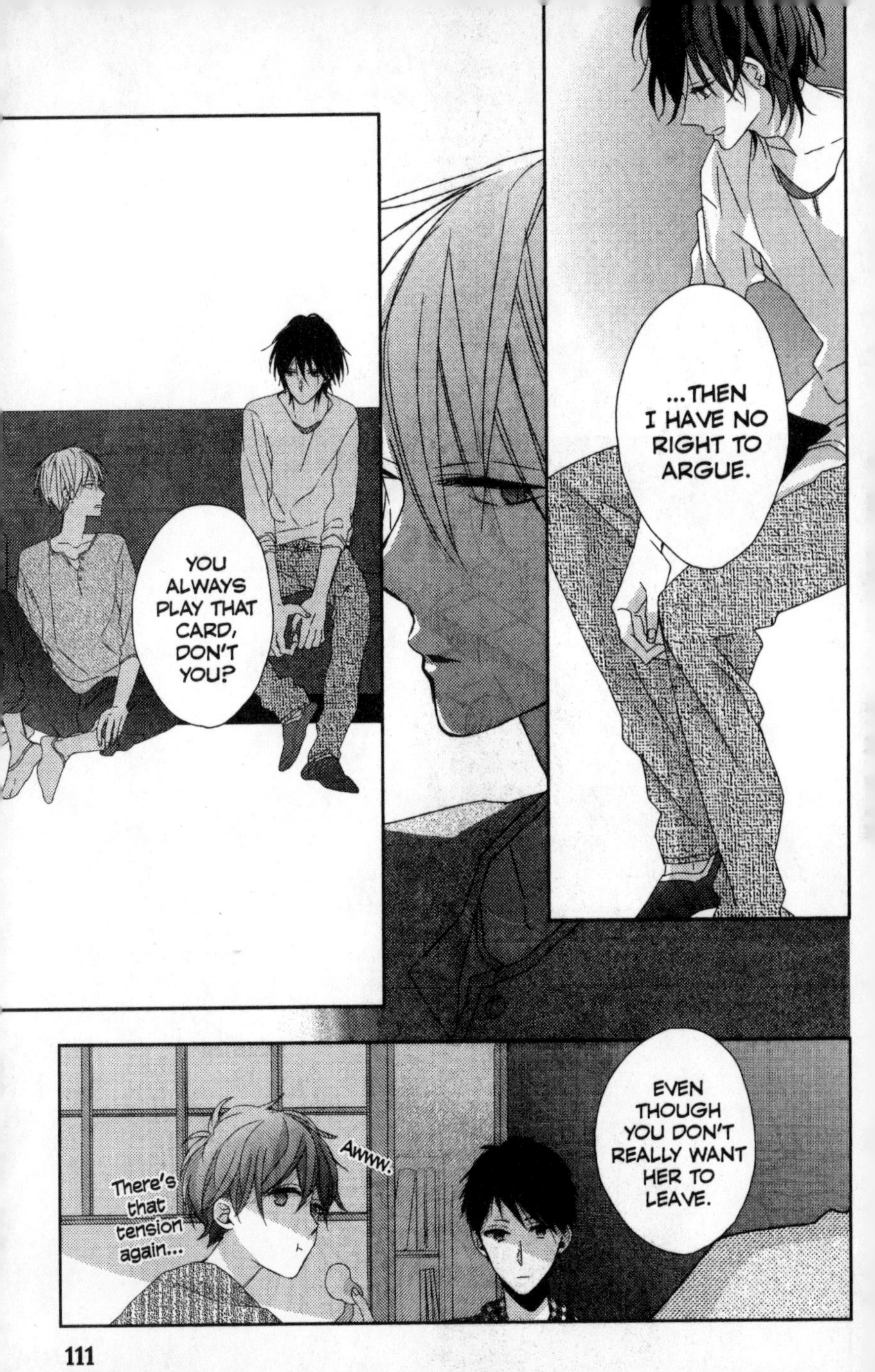
...THEN I HAVE NO RIGHT TO ARGUE.
YOU ALWAYS PLAY THAT CARD, DON'T YOU?
EVEN THOUGH YOU DON'T REALLY WANT HER TO LEAVE.
Awww.
There's that tension again...

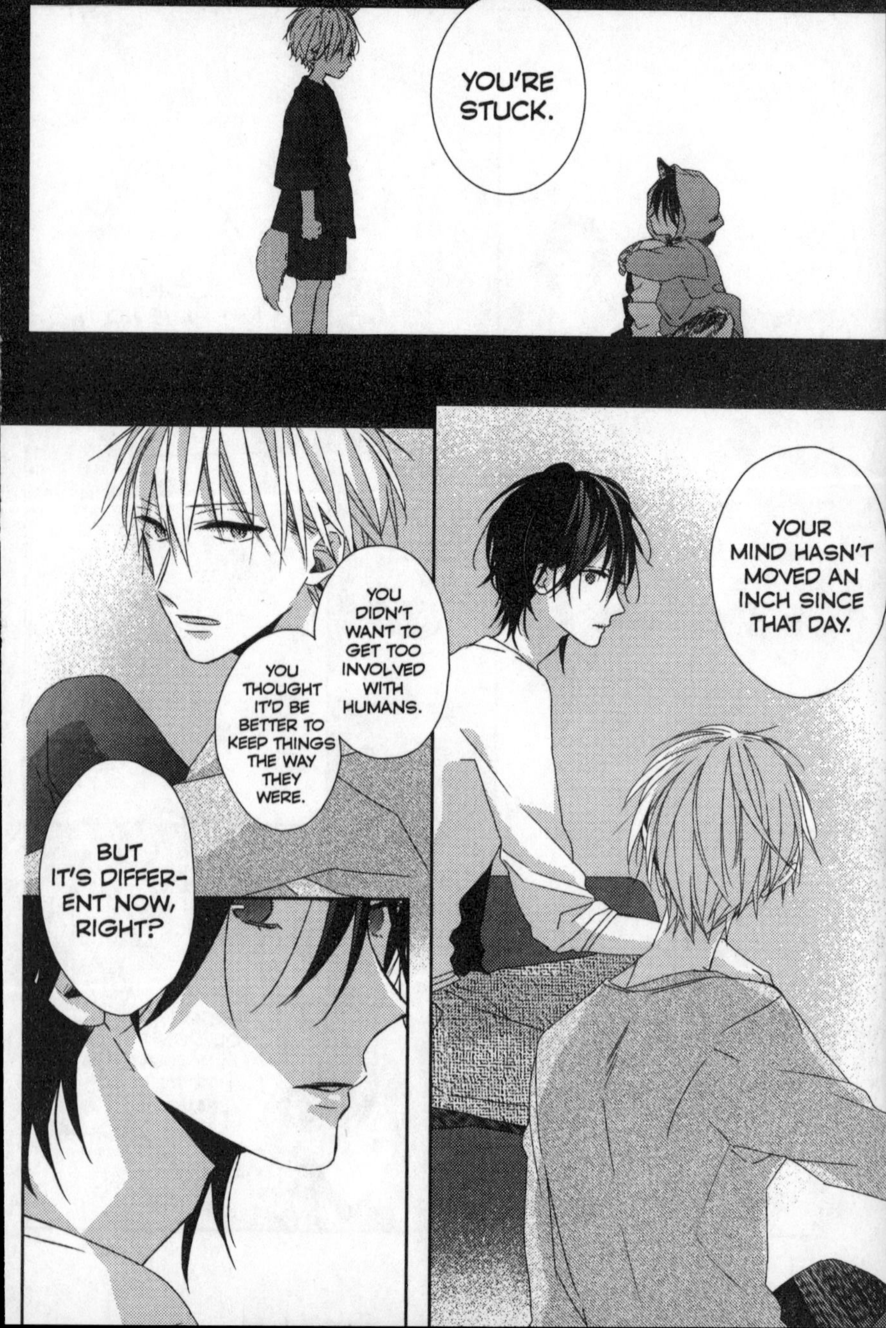
YOU'RE STUCK.
YOUR MIND HASN'T MOVED AN INCH SINCE THAT DAY.
YOU DIDN'T WANT TO GET TOO INVOLVED WITH HUMANS.
YOU THOUGHT IT'D BE BETTER TO KEEP THINGS THE WAY THEY WERE.
BUT IT'S DIFFERENT NOW, RIGHT?

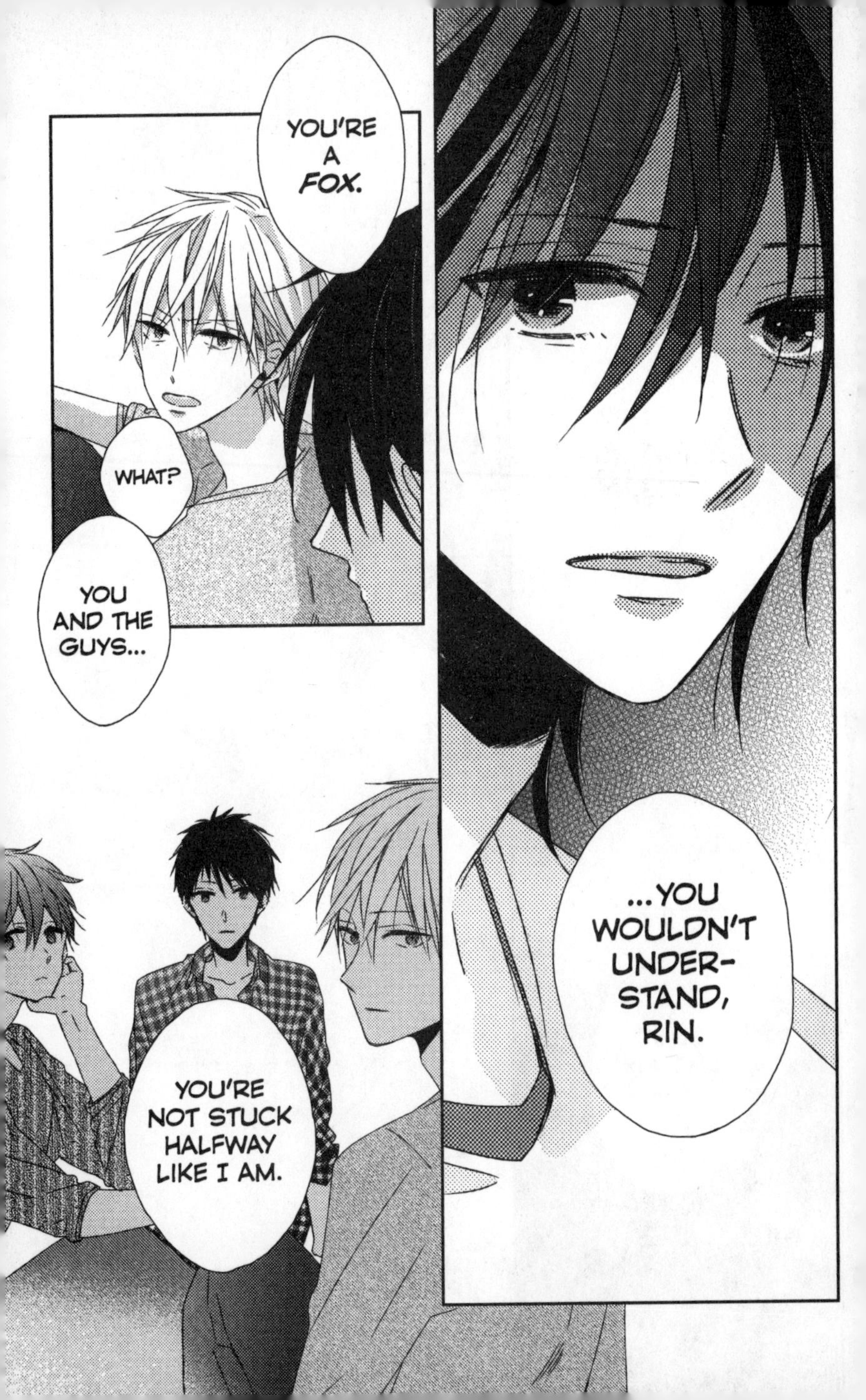
...YOU WOULDN'T UNDER-STAND, RIN.
YOU'RE A *FOX.*
WHAT?
YOU AND THE GUYS...
YOU'RE NOT STUCK HALFWAY LIKE I AM.

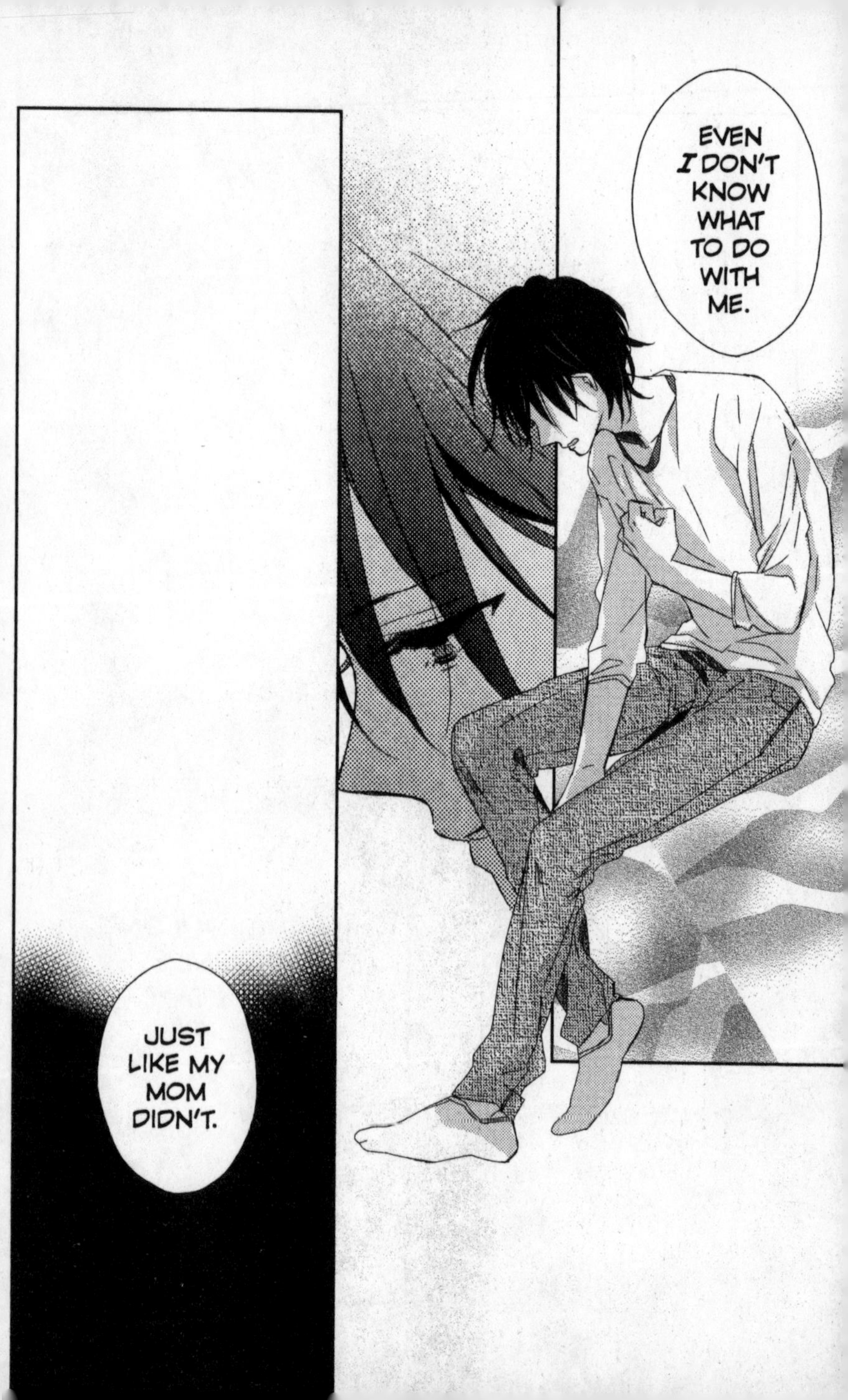
EVEN *I* DON'T KNOW WHAT TO DO WITH ME.
JUST LIKE MY MOM DIDN'T.

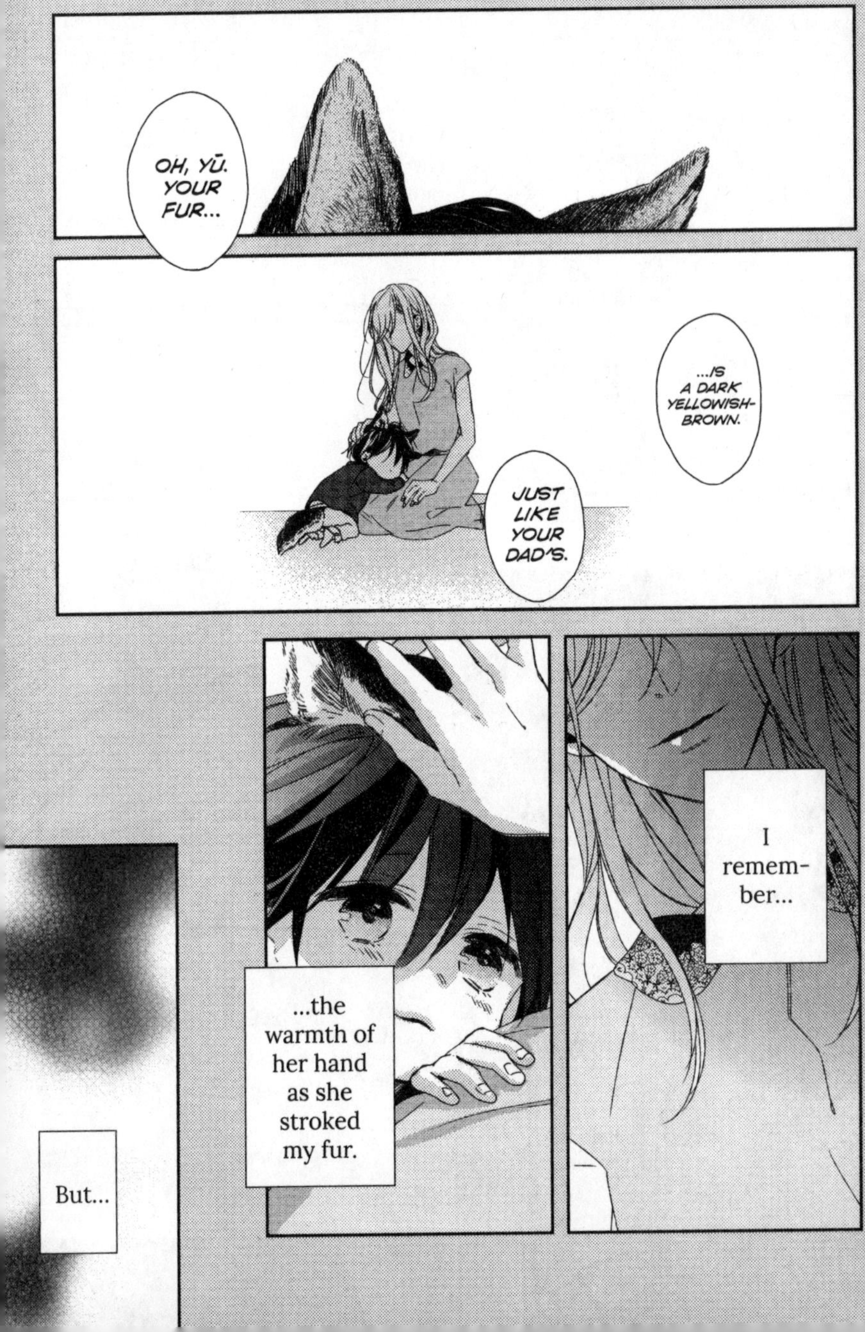
OH, YŪ. YOUR FUR...
...IS A DARK YELLOWISH-BROWN.
JUST LIKE YOUR DAD'S.
I remember...
...the warmth of her hand as she stroked my fur.
But...

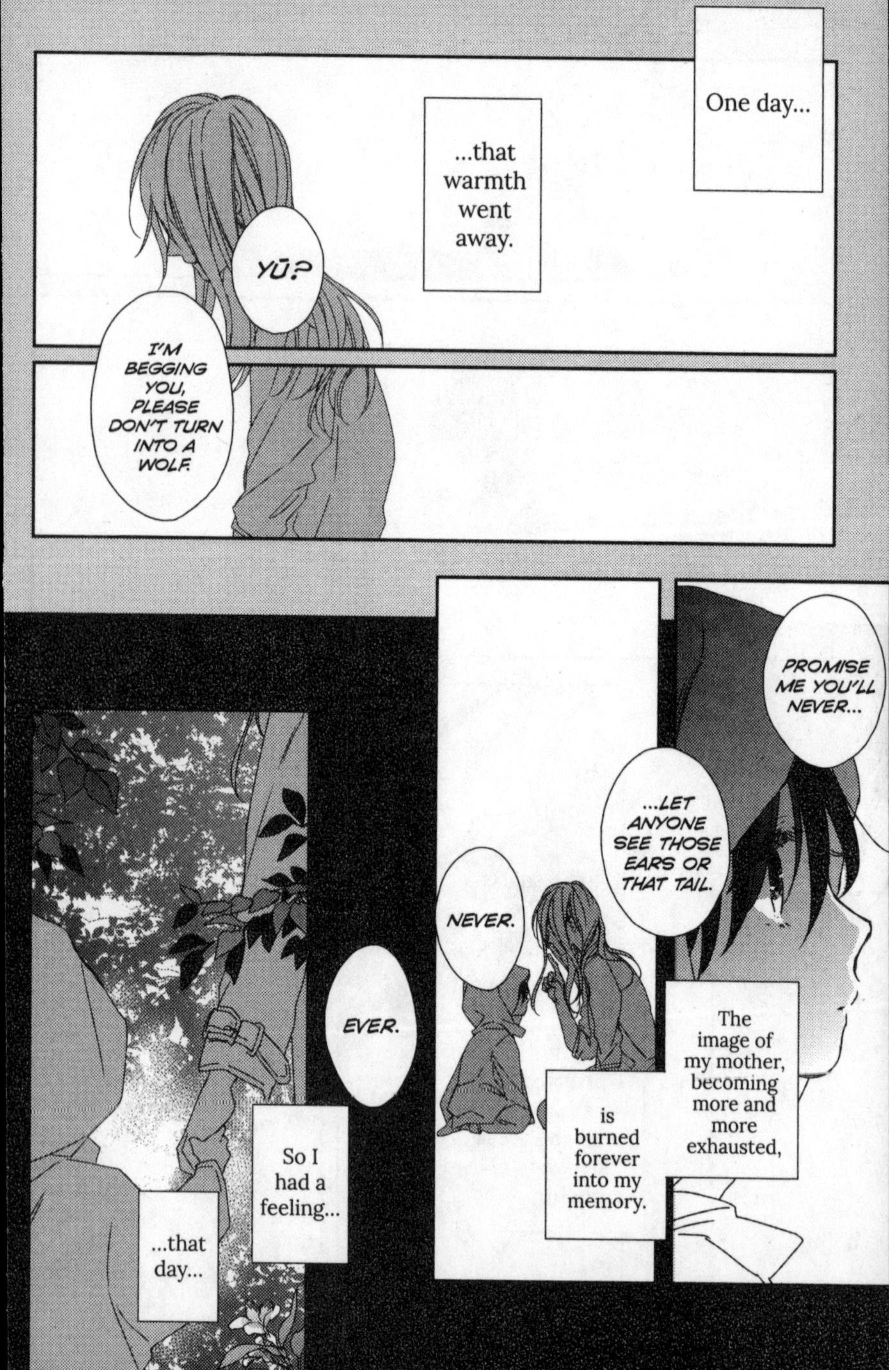
One day...
...that warmth went away.
YŪ?
I'M BEGGING YOU, PLEASE DON'T TURN INTO A WOLF.
PROMISE ME YOU'LL NEVER...
...LET ANYONE SEE THOSE EARS OR THAT TAIL.
NEVER.
The image of my mother, becoming more and more exhausted,
is burned forever into my memory.
EVER.
So I had a feeling...
...that day...

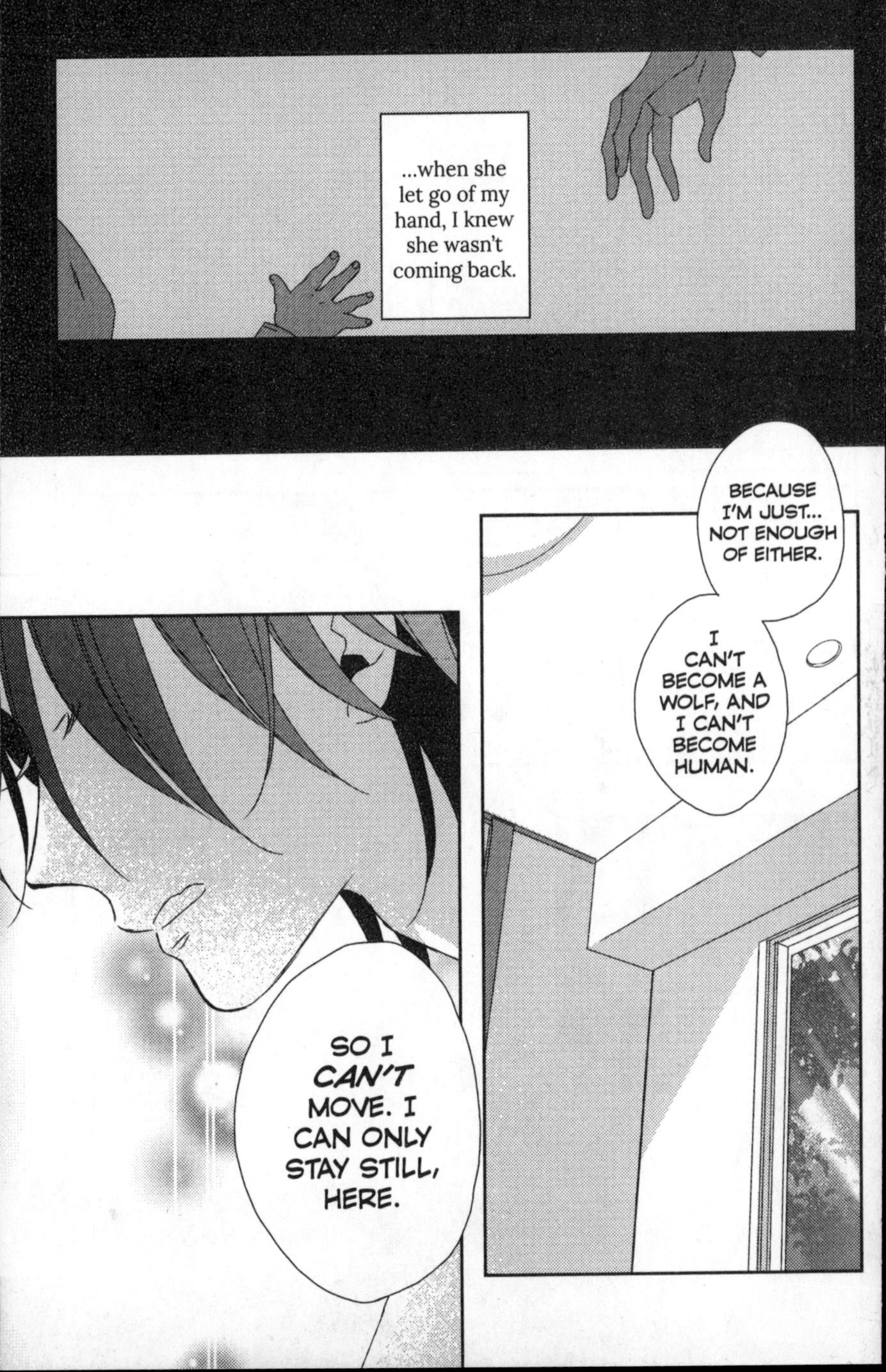
...when she let go of my hand, I knew she wasn't coming back.
BECAUSE I'M JUST... NOT ENOUGH OF EITHER.
I CAN'T BECOME A WOLF, AND I CAN'T BECOME HUMAN.
SO I *CAN'T* MOVE. I CAN ONLY STAY STILL, HERE.

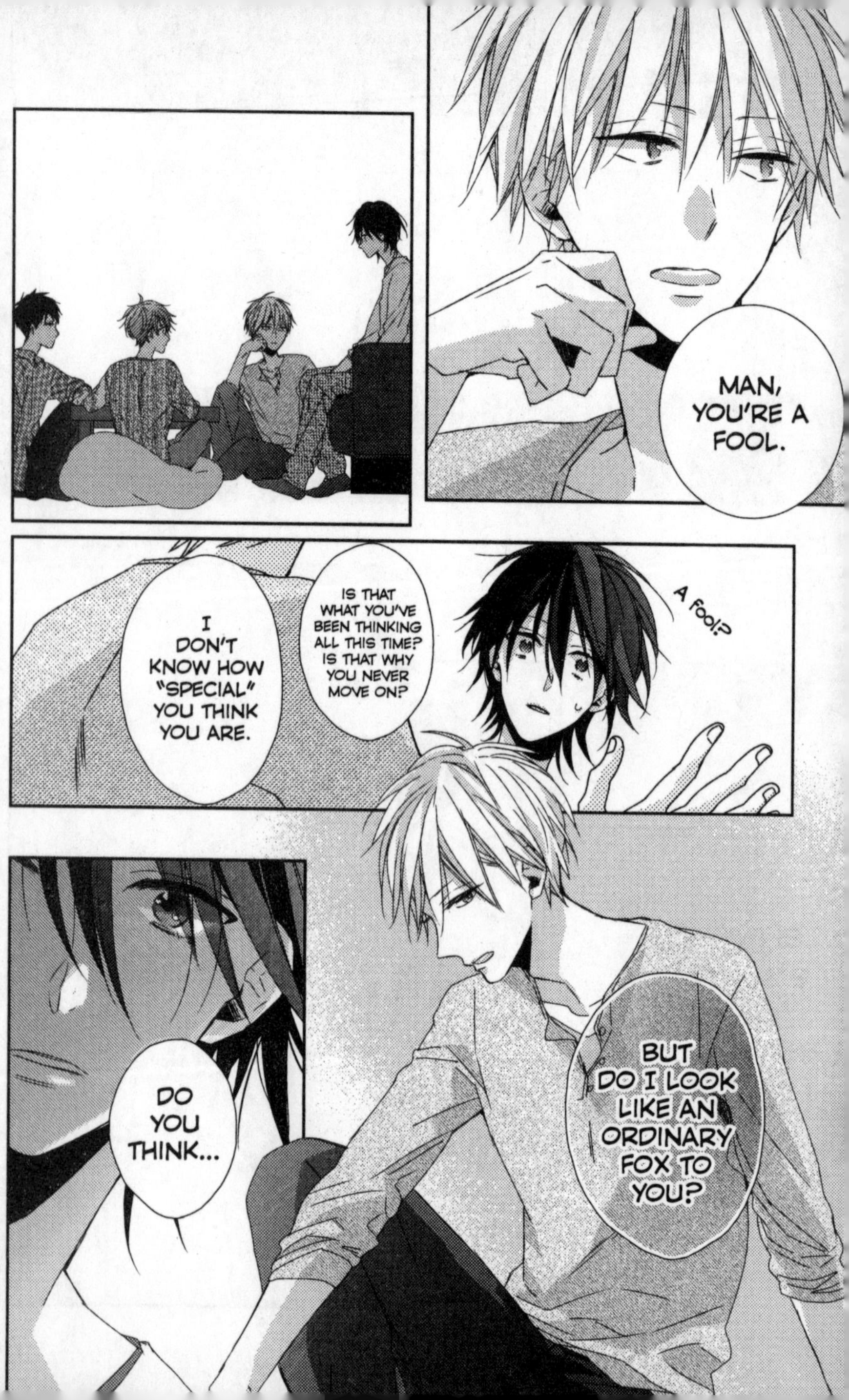
MAN, YOU'RE A FOOL.
A FOOL?
IS THAT WHAT YOU'VE BEEN THINKING ALL THIS TIME? IS THAT WHY YOU NEVER MOVE ON?
I DON'T KNOW HOW "SPECIAL" YOU THINK YOU ARE.
BUT DO I LOOK LIKE AN ORDINARY FOX TO YOU?
DO YOU THINK...

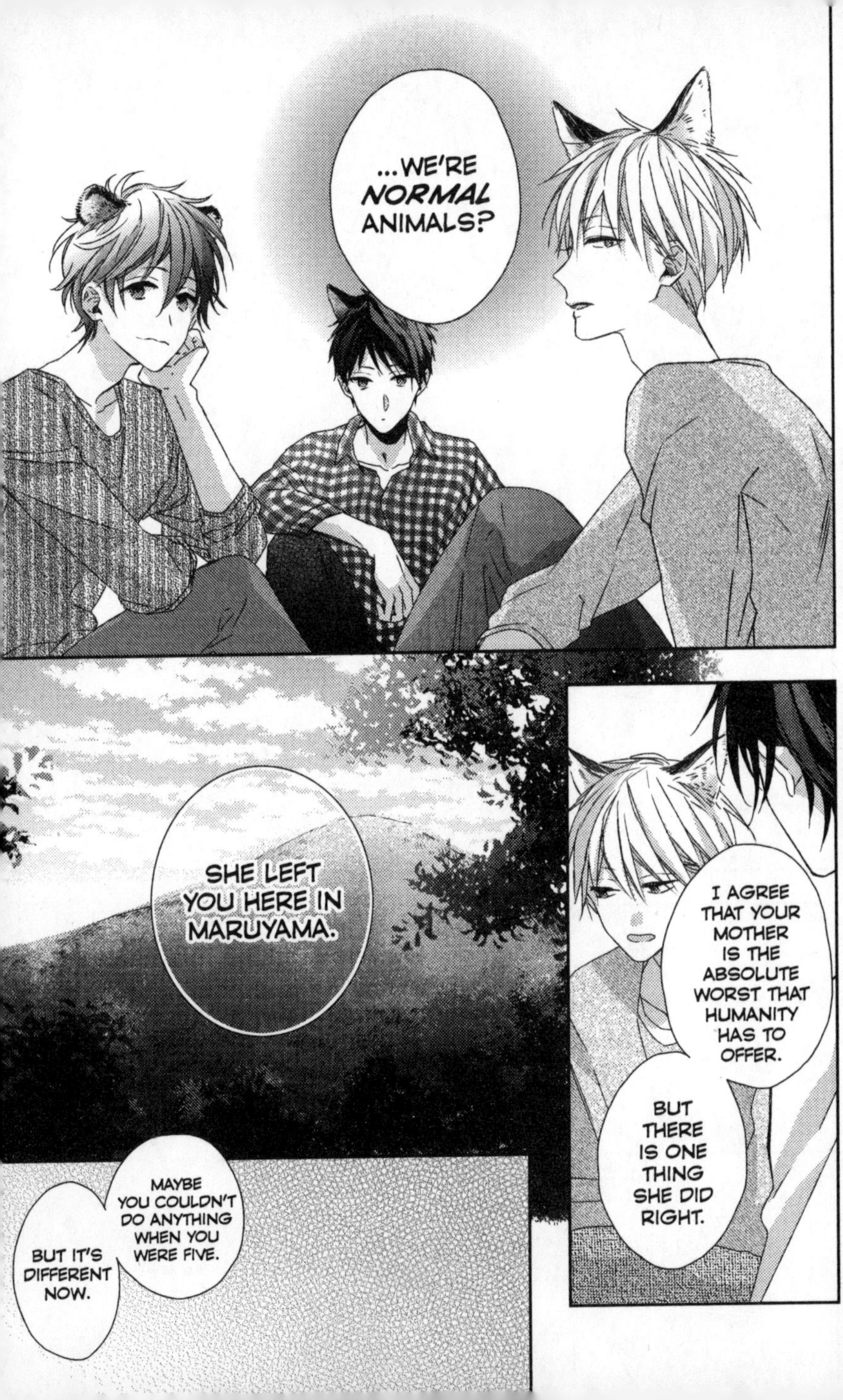
...WE'RE *NORMAL* ANIMALS?
I AGREE THAT YOUR MOTHER IS THE ABSOLUTE WORST THAT HUMANITY HAS TO OFFER.
BUT THERE IS ONE THING SHE DID RIGHT.
SHE LEFT YOU HERE IN MARUYAMA.
MAYBE YOU COULDN'T DO ANYTHING WHEN YOU WERE FIVE.
BUT IT'S DIFFERENT NOW.

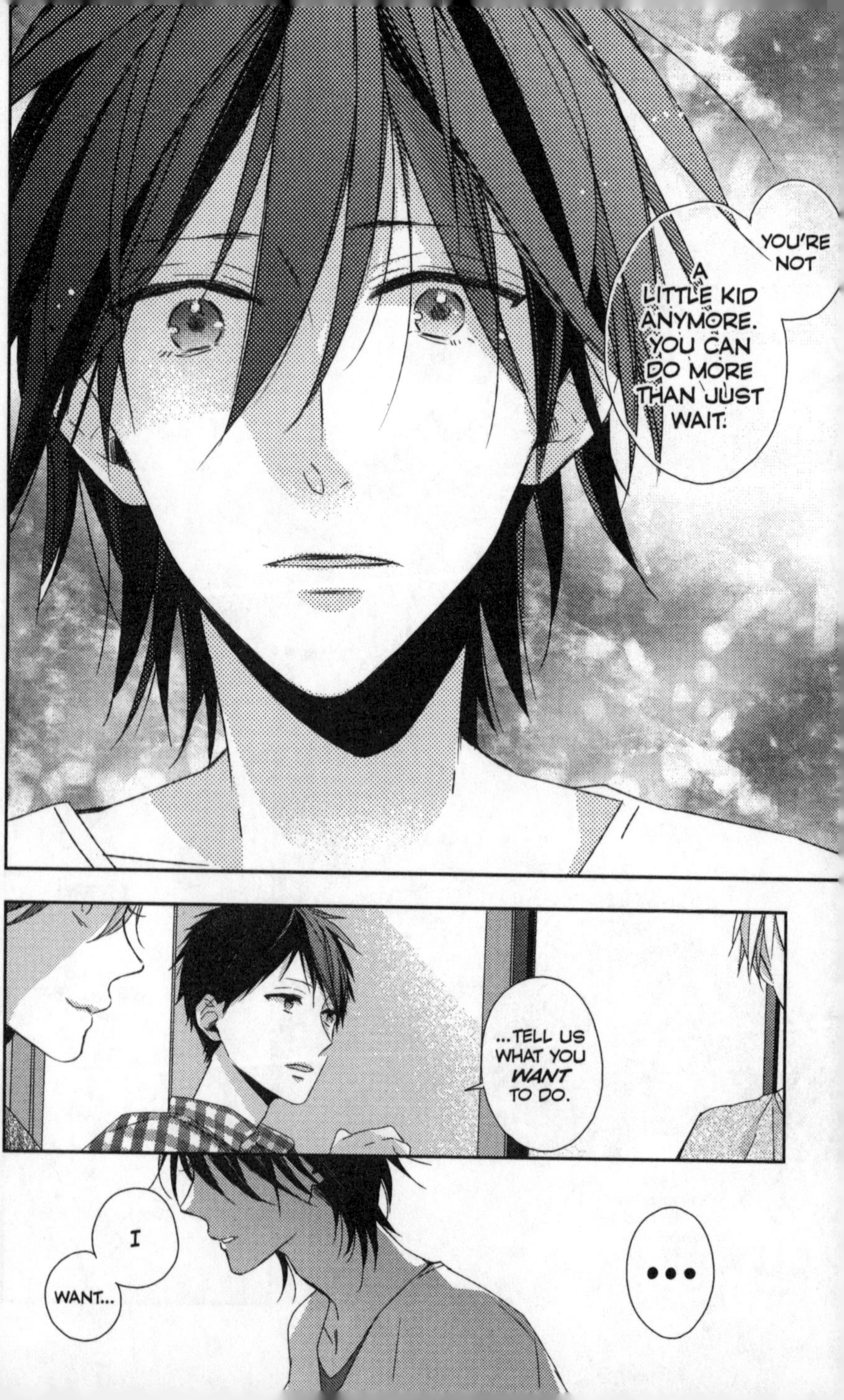
YOU'RE NOT A LITTLE KID ANYMORE. YOU CAN DO MORE THAN JUST WAIT.
...TELL US WHAT YOU *WANT* TO DO.
...
I WANT...

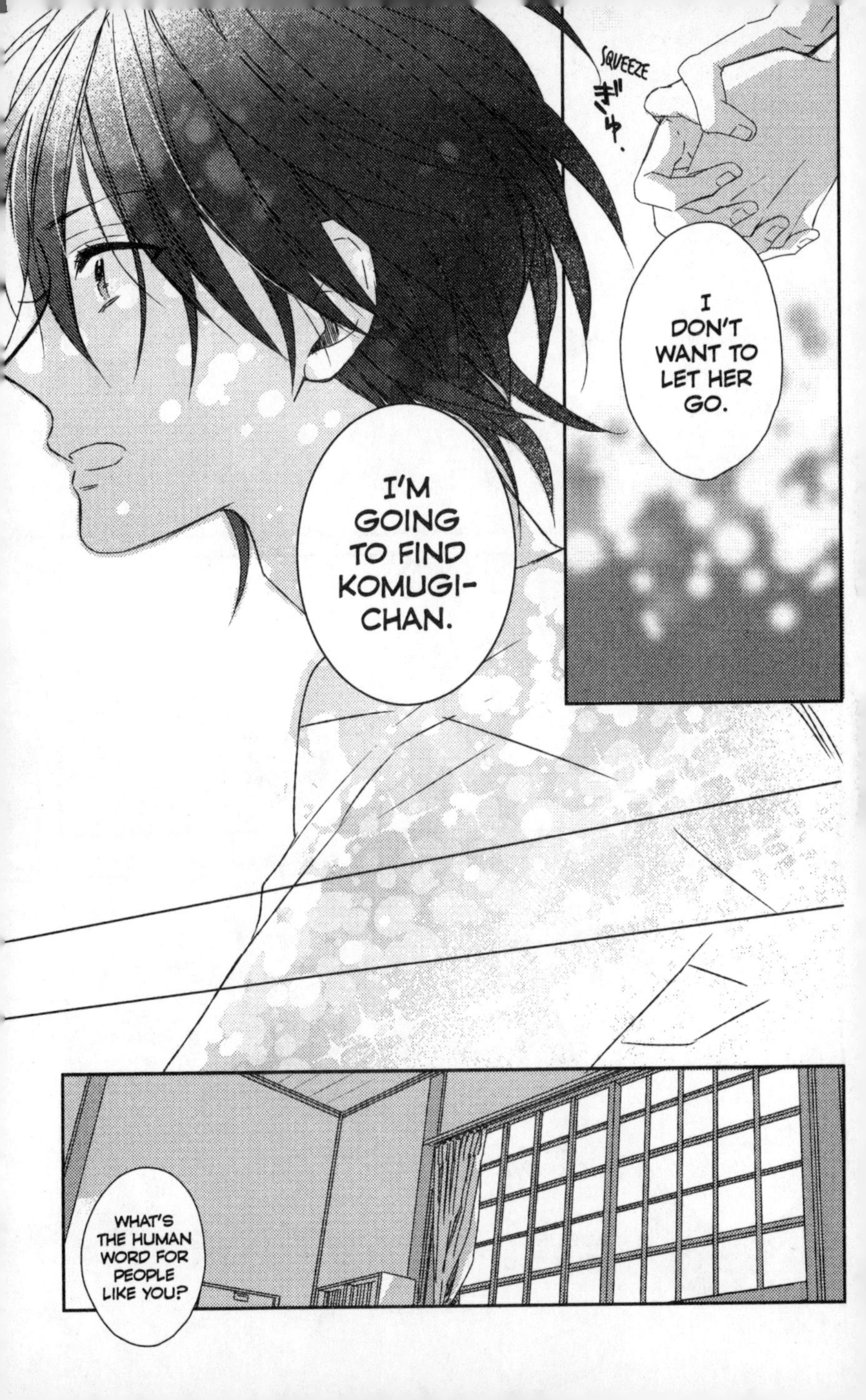
SQUEEZE
ぎゅ.
I DON'T WANT TO LET HER GO.
I'M GOING TO FIND KOMUGI-CHAN.
WHAT'S THE HUMAN WORD FOR PEOPLE LIKE YOU?

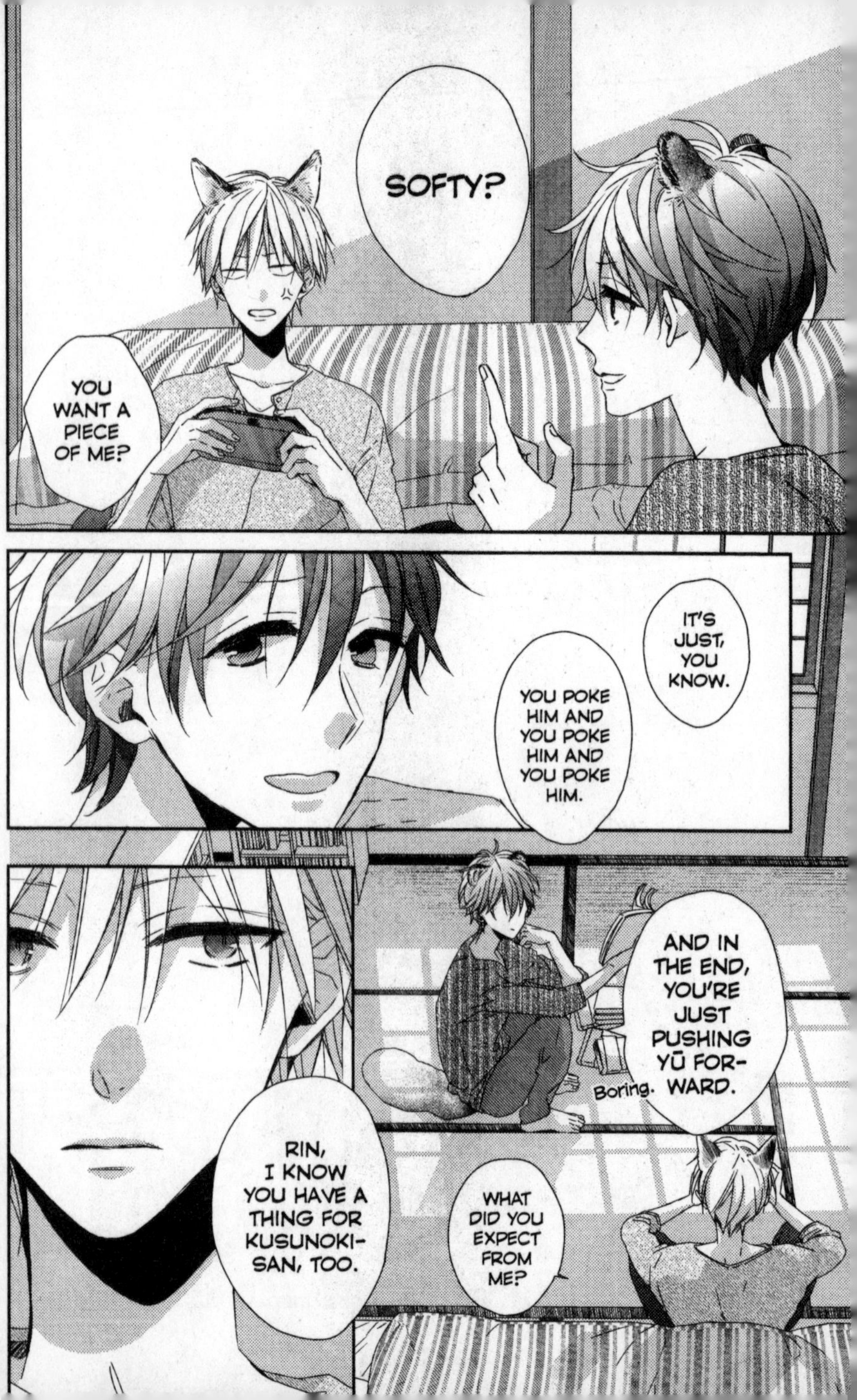
SOFTY?
YOU WANT A PIECE OF ME?
IT'S JUST, YOU KNOW.
YOU POKE HIM AND YOU POKE HIM AND YOU POKE HIM.
AND IN THE END, YOU'RE JUST PUSHING YŪ FOR-WARD.
Boring.
WHAT DID YOU EXPECT FROM ME?
RIN, I KNOW YOU HAVE A THING FOR KUSUNOKI-SAN, TOO.

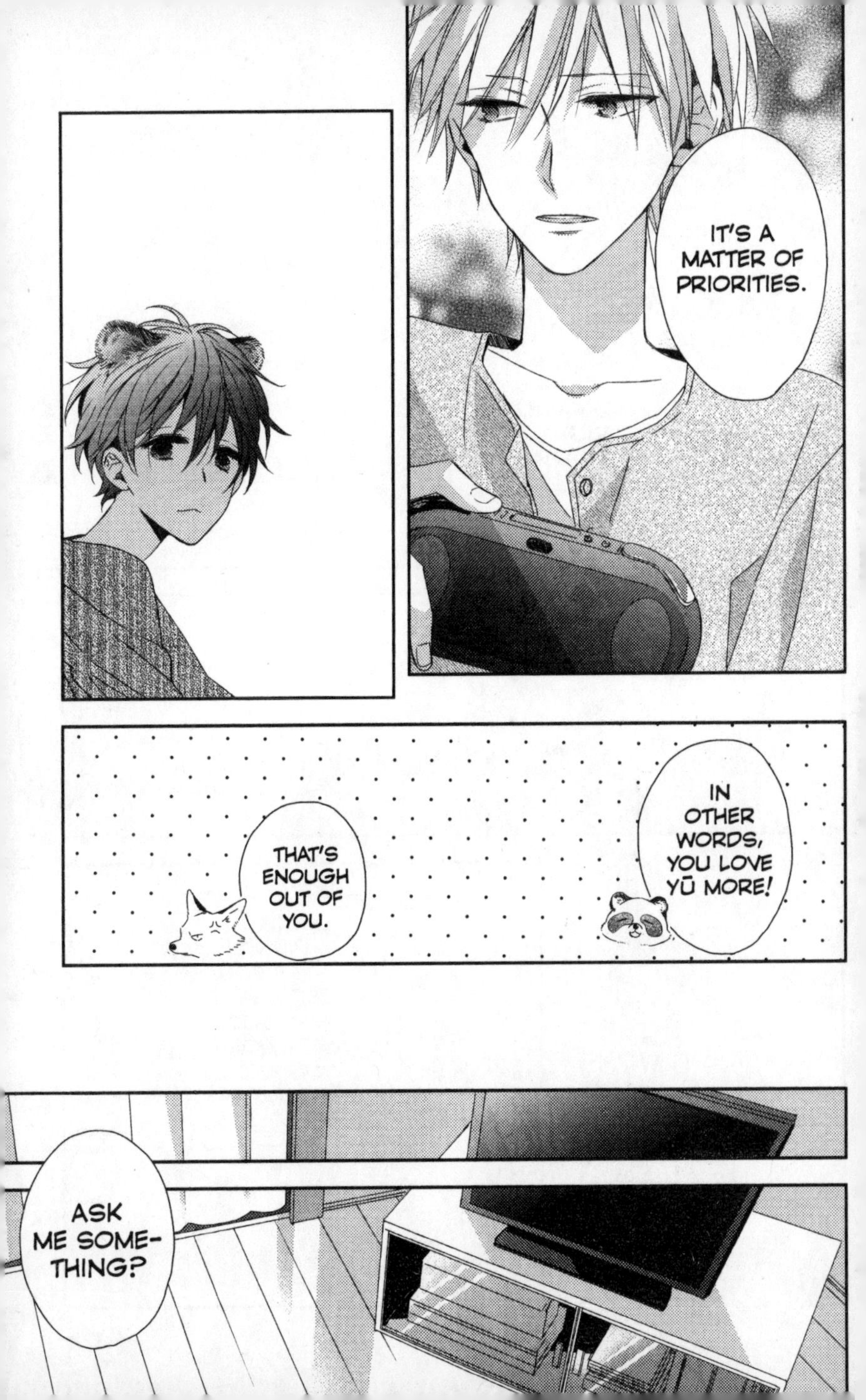
IT'S A MATTER OF PRIORITIES.
IN OTHER WORDS, YOU LOVE YŪ MORE!
THAT'S ENOUGH OUT OF YOU.
ASK ME SOME-THING?

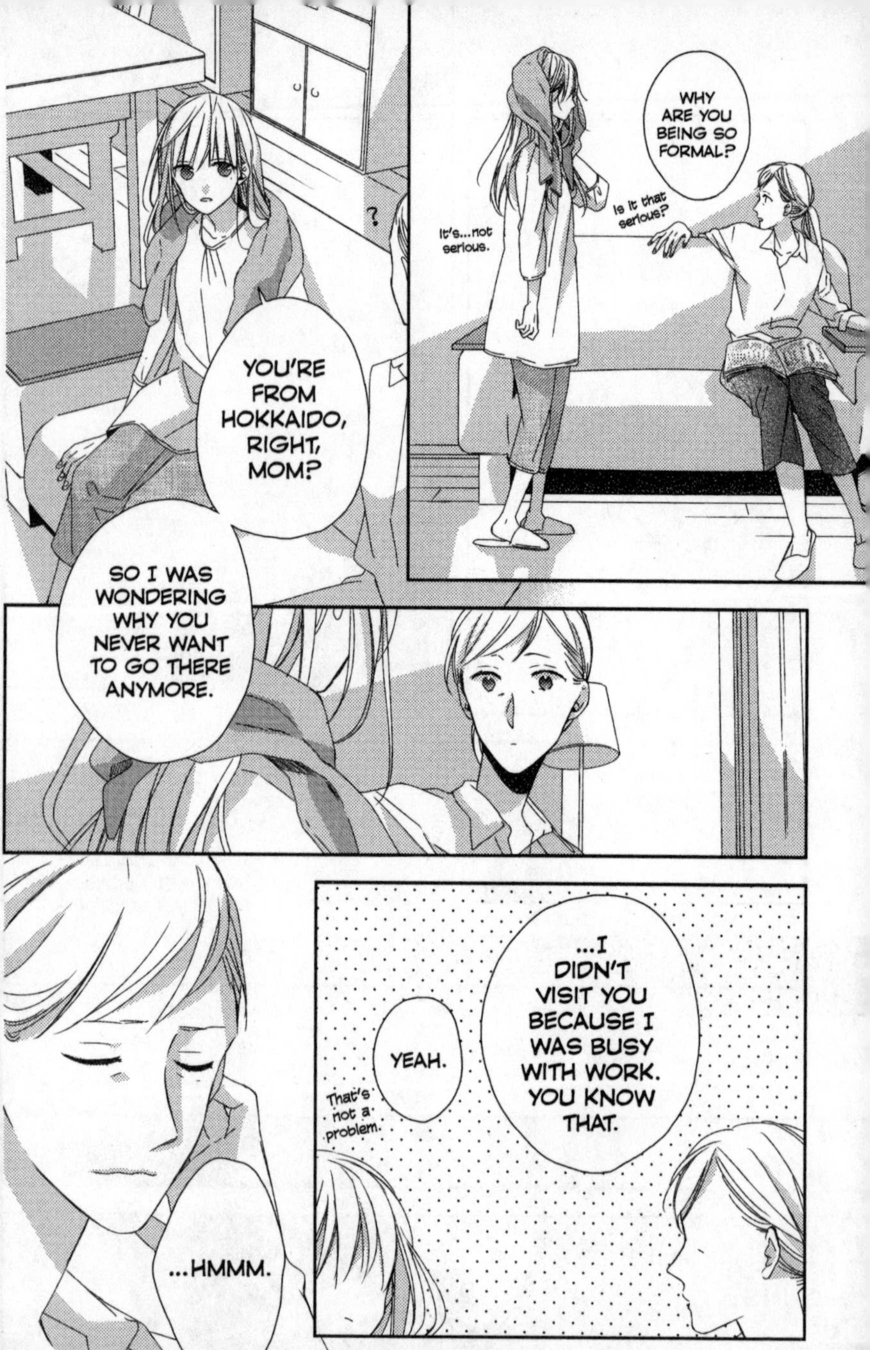
WHY ARE YOU BEING SO FORMAL?
Is it that serious?
It's...not serious.
?
YOU'RE FROM HOKKAIDO, RIGHT, MOM?
SO I WAS WONDERING WHY YOU NEVER WANT TO GO THERE ANYMORE.
...I DIDN'T VISIT YOU BECAUSE I WAS BUSY WITH WORK. YOU KNOW THAT.
YEAH.
That's not a problem.
...HMMM.

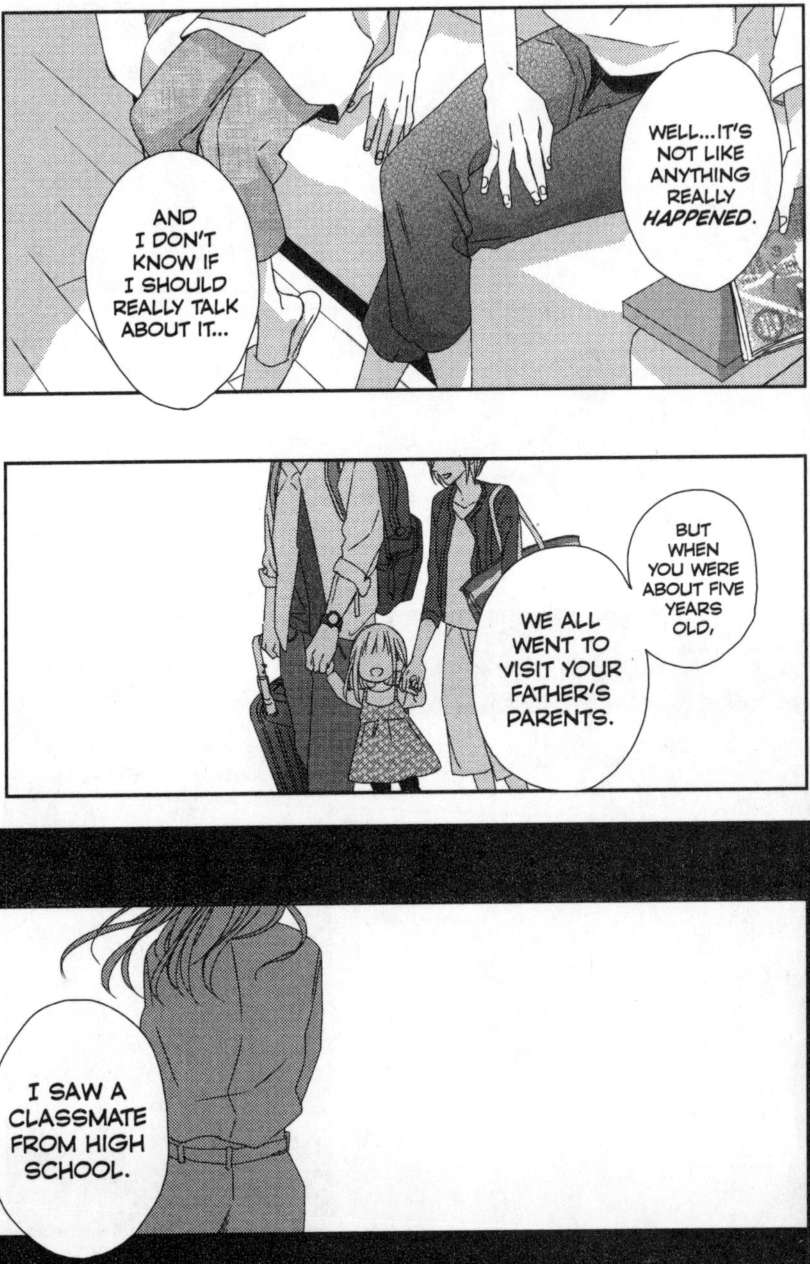
WELL...IT'S NOT LIKE ANYTHING REALLY *HAPPENED*.
AND I DON'T KNOW IF I SHOULD REALLY TALK ABOUT IT...
BUT WHEN YOU WERE ABOUT FIVE YEARS OLD,
WE ALL WENT TO VISIT YOUR FATHER'S PARENTS.
I SAW A CLASSMATE FROM HIGH SCHOOL.

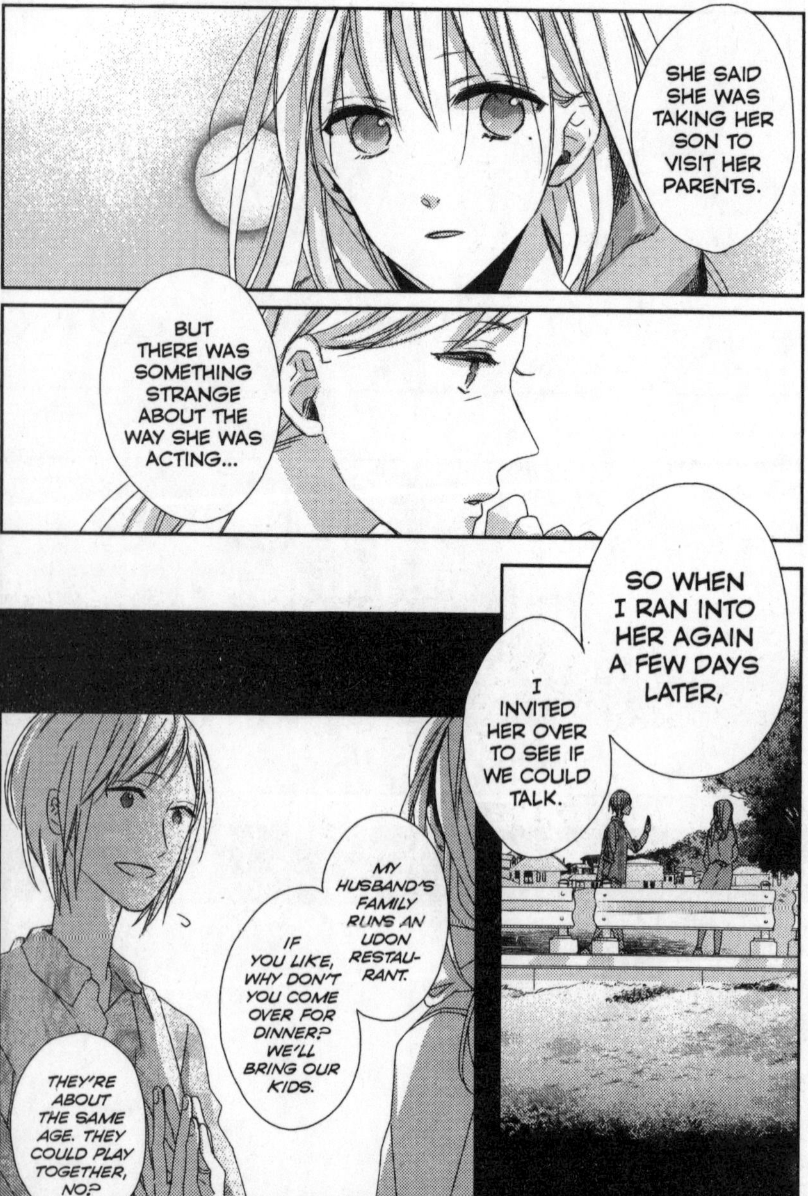
SHE SAID SHE WAS TAKING HER SON TO VISIT HER PARENTS.
BUT THERE WAS SOMETHING STRANGE ABOUT THE WAY SHE WAS ACTING...
SO WHEN I RAN INTO HER AGAIN A FEW DAYS LATER,
I INVITED HER OVER TO SEE IF WE COULD TALK.
MY HUSBAND'S FAMILY RUNS AN UDON RESTAU-RANT.
IF YOU LIKE, WHY DON'T YOU COME OVER FOR DINNER? WE'LL BRING OUR KIDS.
THEY'RE ABOUT THE SAME AGE. THEY COULD PLAY TOGETHER, NO?

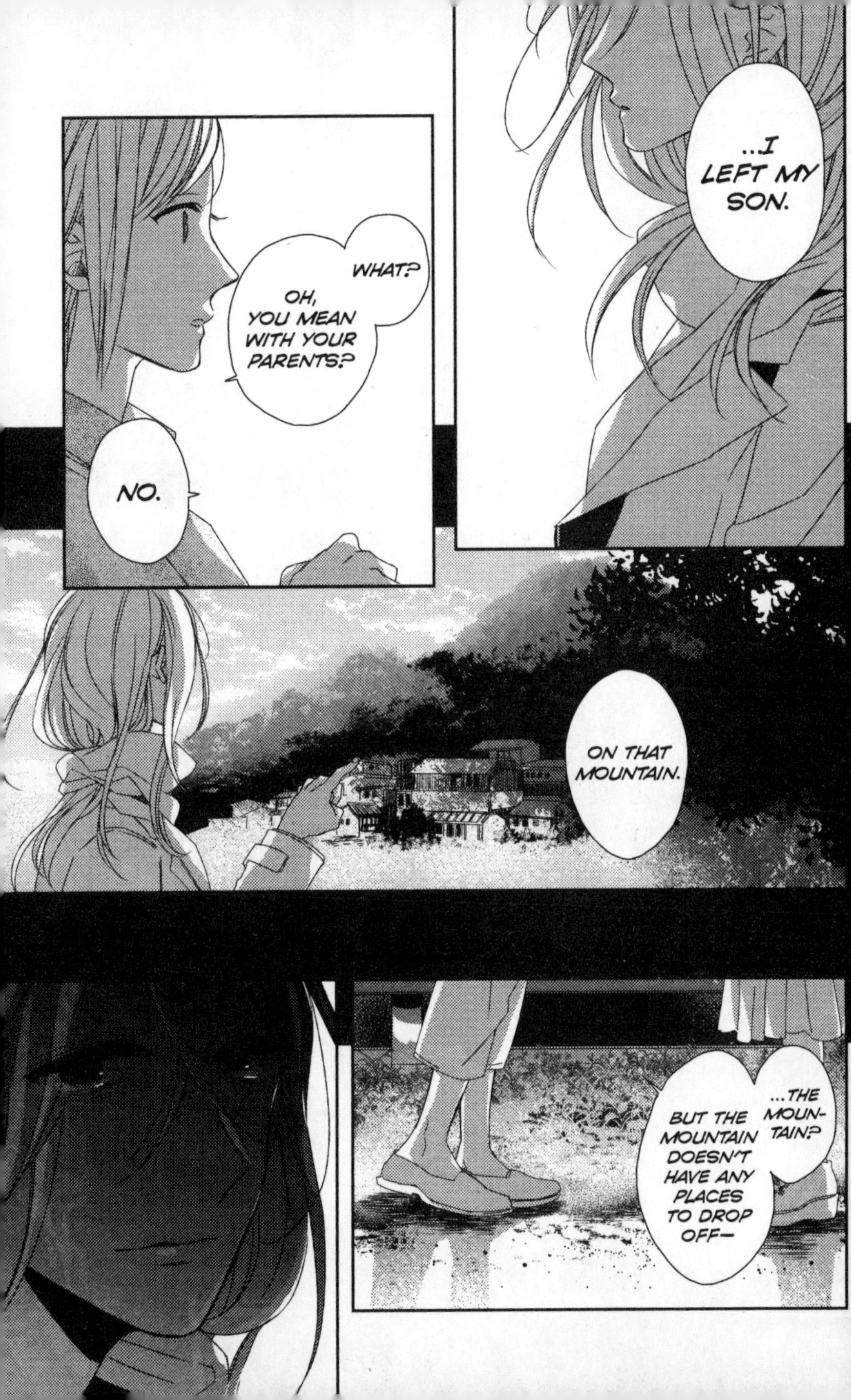
...I LEFT MY SON.
WHAT?
OH, YOU MEAN WITH YOUR PARENTS?
NO.
ON THAT MOUNTAIN.
...THE MOUN-TAIN?
BUT THE MOUNTAIN DOESN'T HAVE ANY PLACES TO DROP OFF—

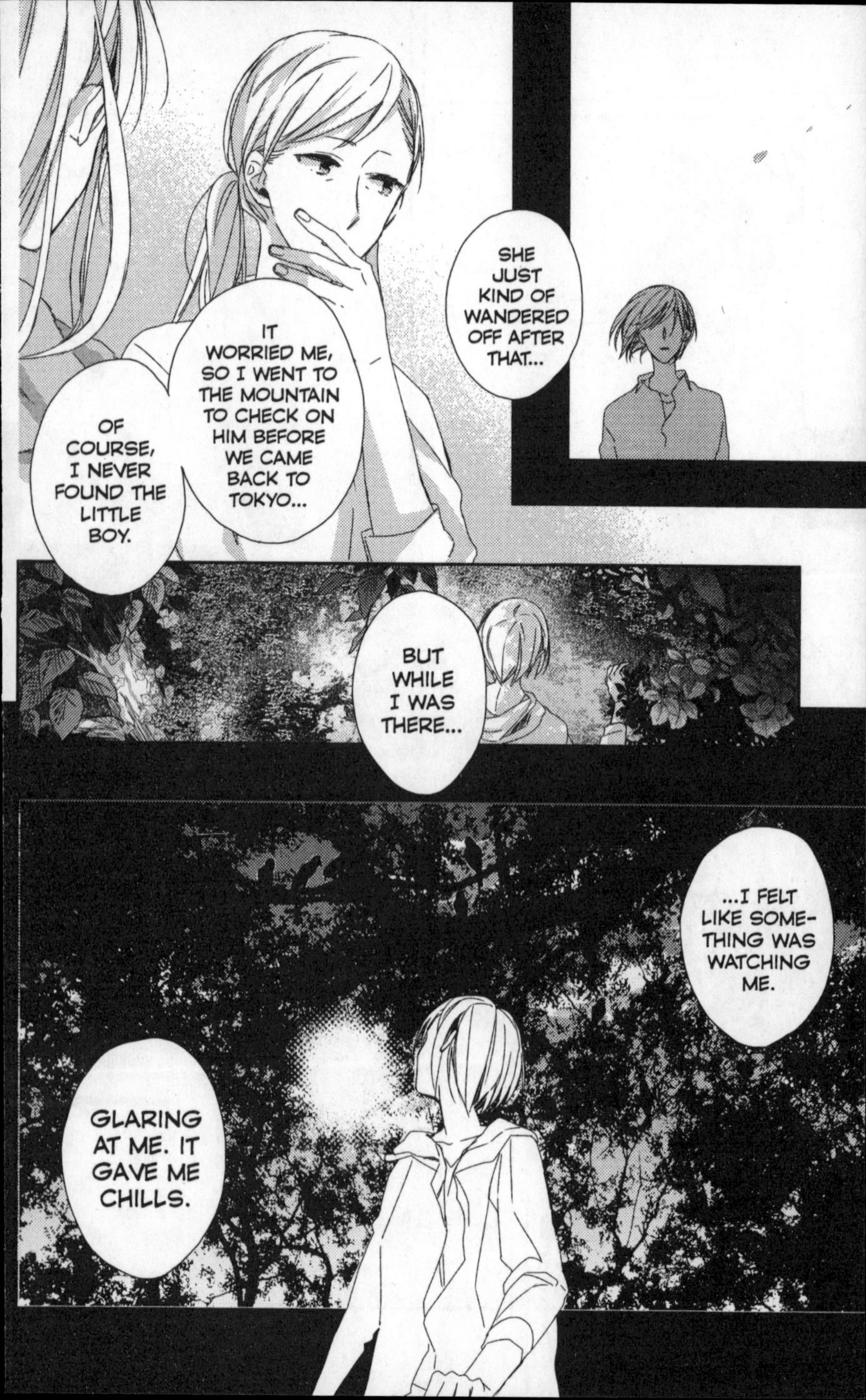
SHE JUST KIND OF WANDERED OFF AFTER THAT...
IT WORRIED ME, SO I WENT TO THE MOUNTAIN TO CHECK ON HIM BEFORE WE CAME BACK TO TOKYO...
OF COURSE, I NEVER FOUND THE LITTLE BOY.
BUT WHILE I WAS THERE...
...I FELT LIKE SOME-THING WAS WATCHING ME.
GLARING AT ME. IT GAVE ME CHILLS.

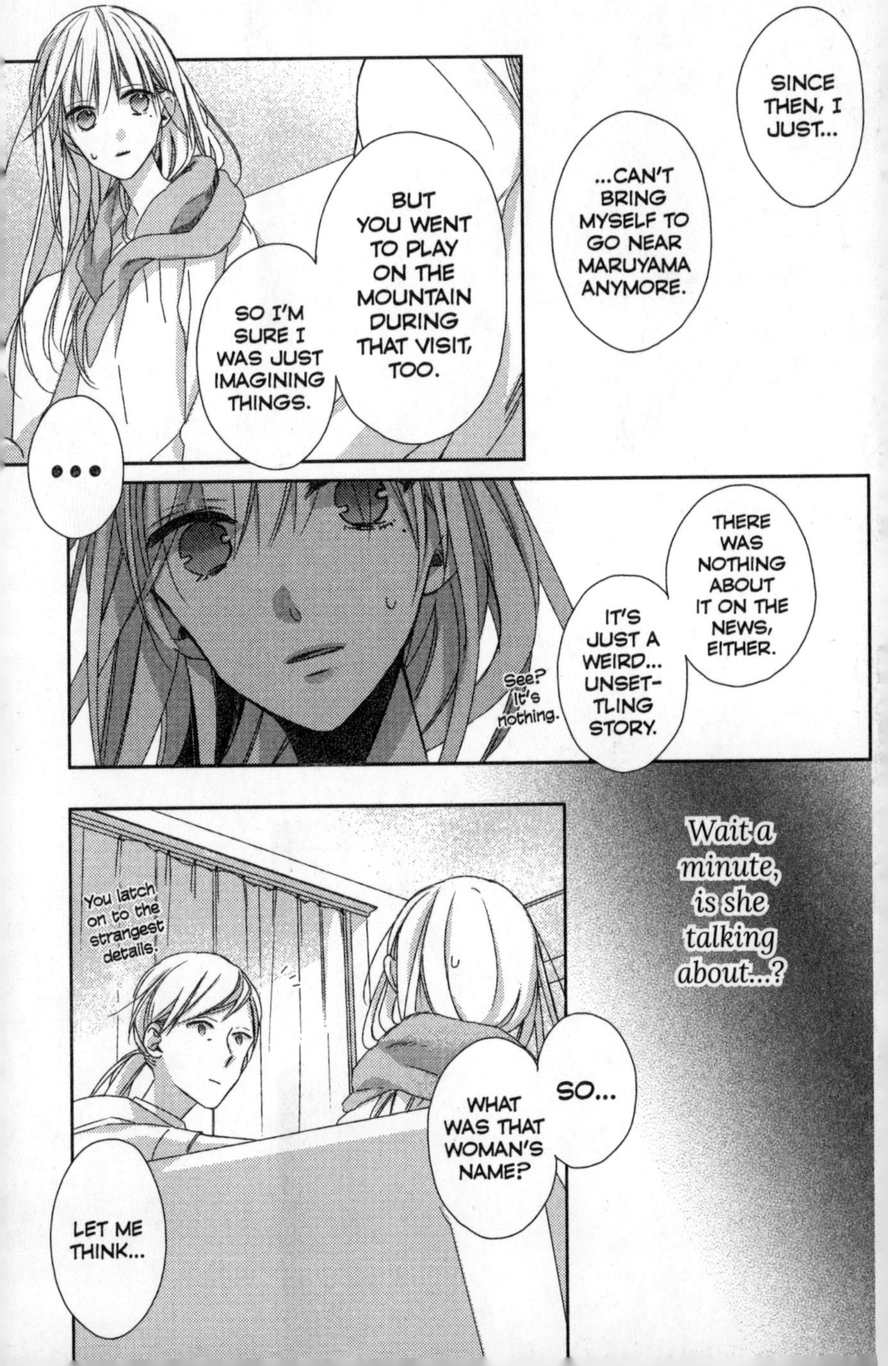
SINCE THEN, I JUST...
...CAN'T BRING MYSELF TO GO NEAR MARUYAMA ANYMORE.
BUT YOU WENT TO PLAY ON THE MOUNTAIN DURING THAT VISIT, TOO.
SO I'M SURE I WAS JUST IMAGINING THINGS.
...
THERE WAS NOTHING ABOUT IT ON THE NEWS, EITHER.
IT'S JUST A WEIRD... UNSET-TLING STORY.
See? It's nothing.
Wait a minute, is she talking about...?
SO...
WHAT WAS THAT WOMAN'S NAME?
You latch on to the strangest details.
LET ME THINK...

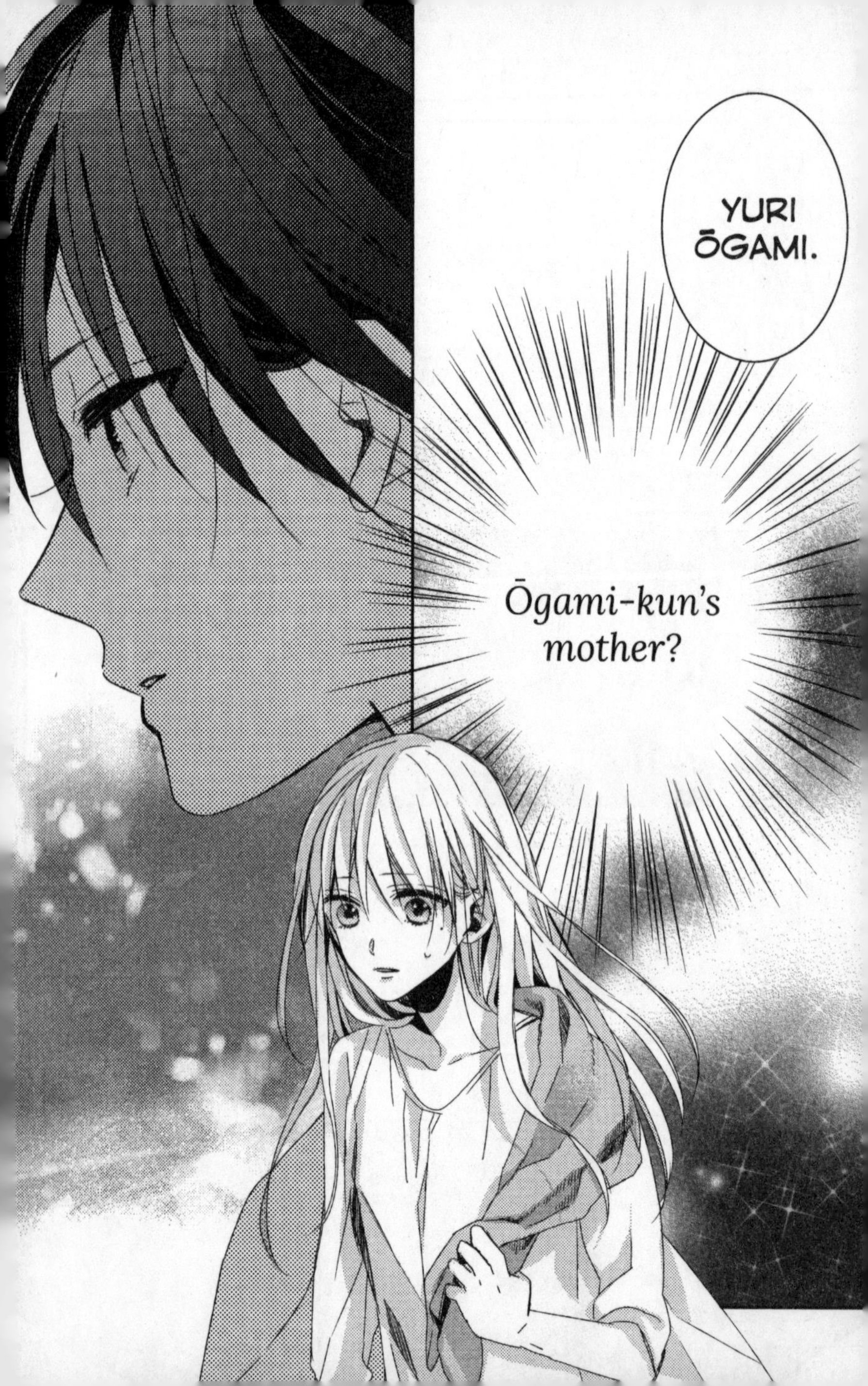
YURI ŌGAMI.
Ōgami-kun's mother?

Chapter 13

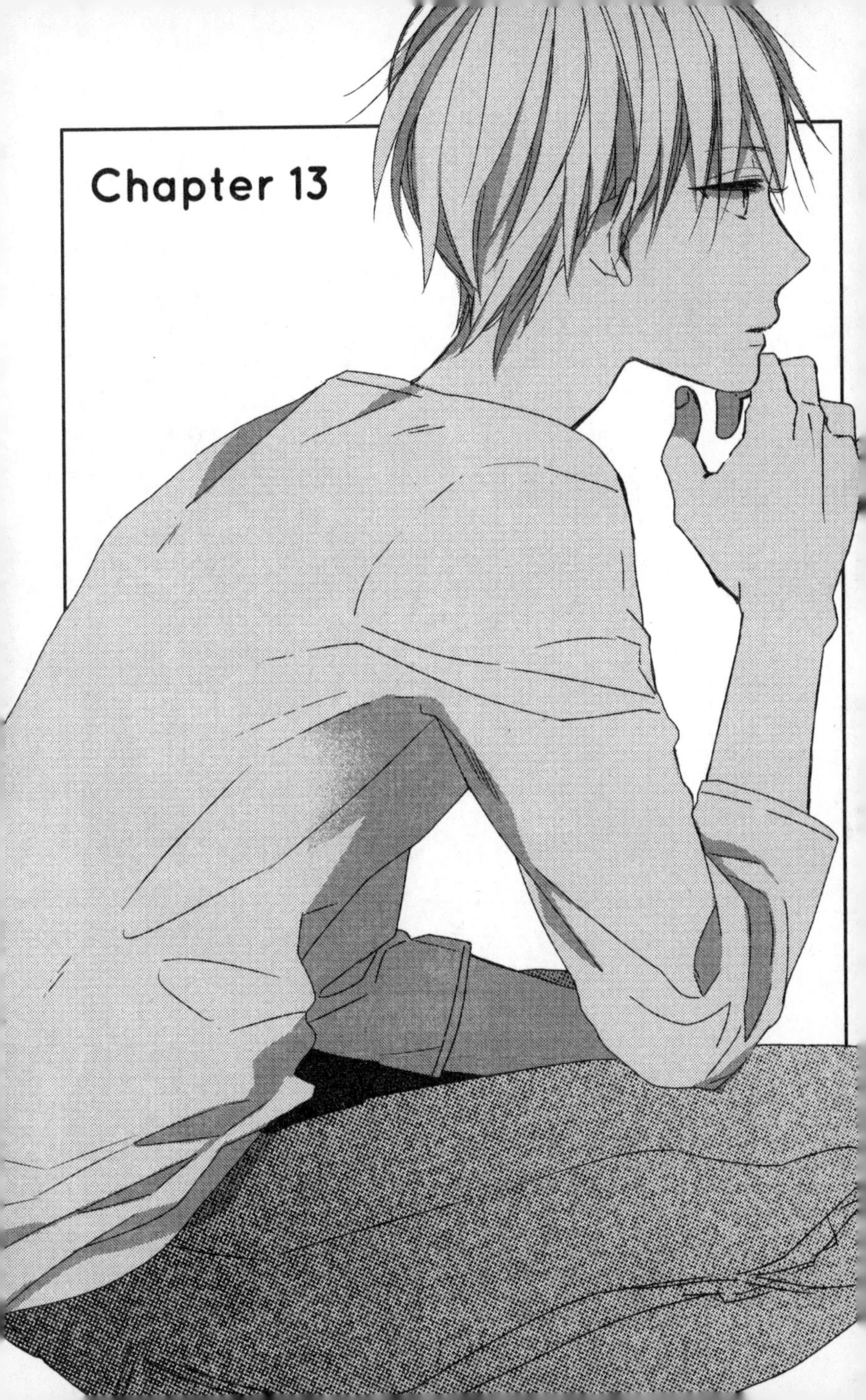

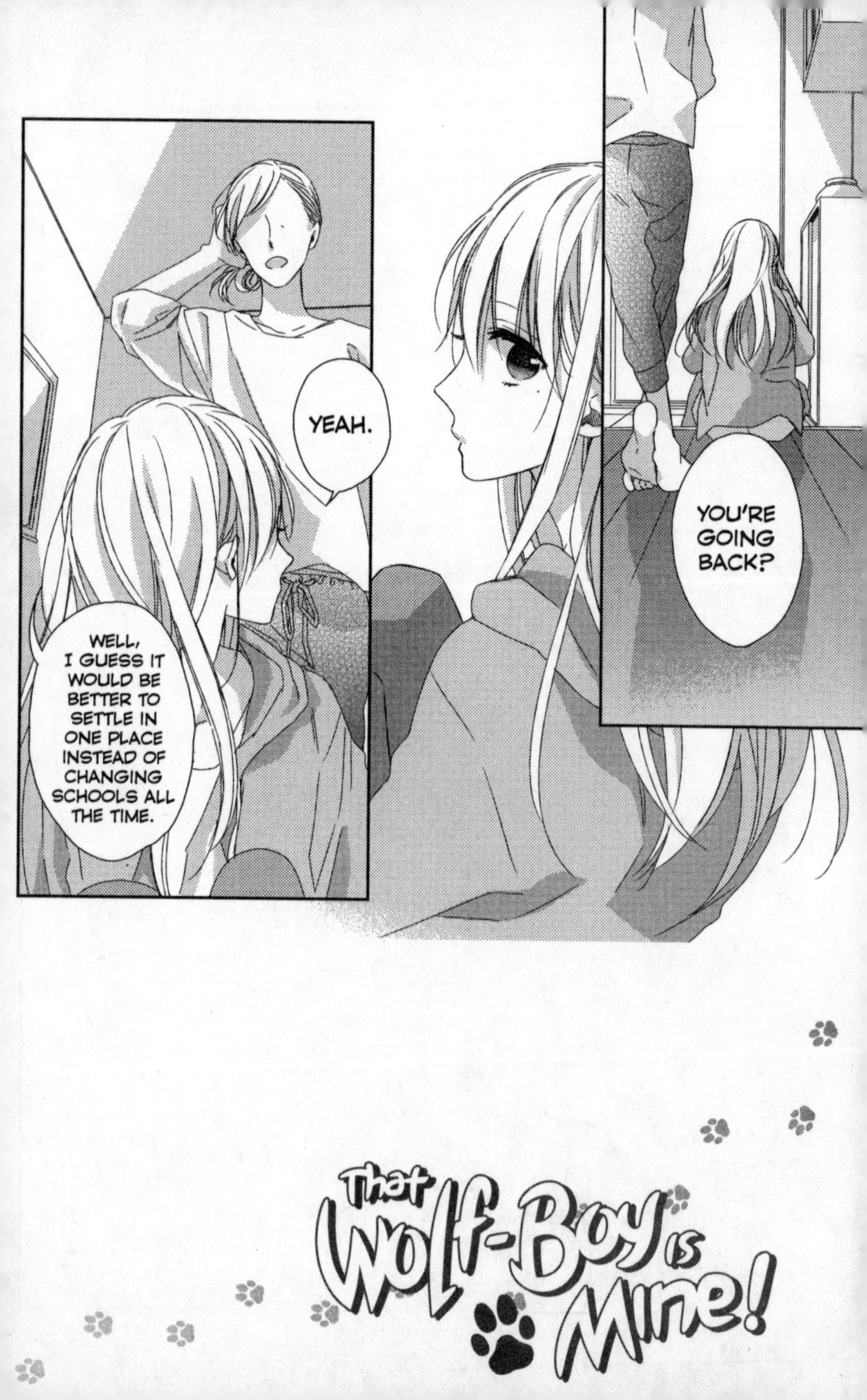
YOU'RE GOING BACK?
YEAH.
WELL, I GUESS IT WOULD BE BETTER TO SETTLE IN ONE PLACE INSTEAD OF CHANGING SCHOOLS ALL THE TIME.

That Wolf-Boy is Mine!

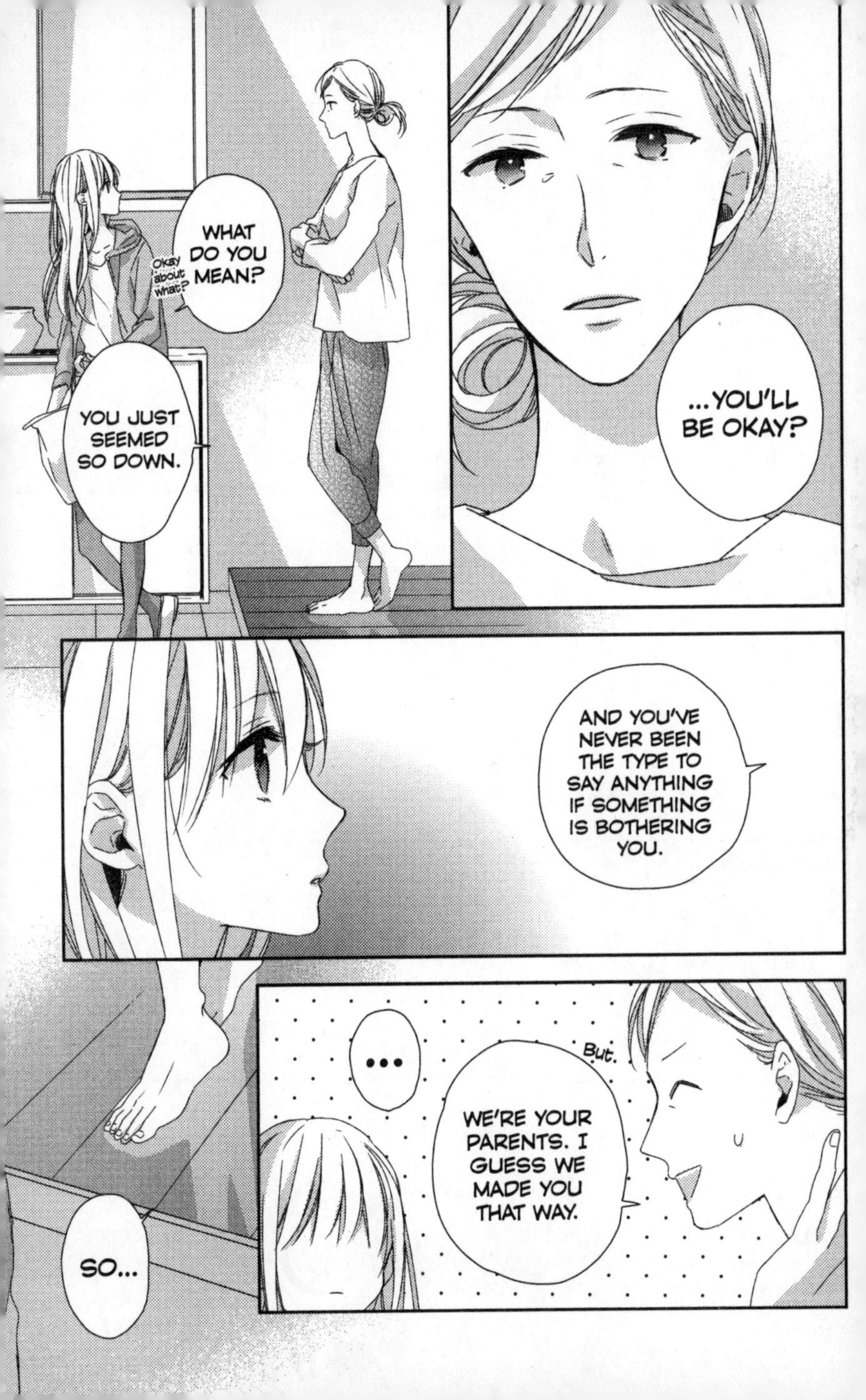
...YOU'LL BE OKAY?
WHAT DO YOU MEAN?
Okay about what?
YOU JUST SEEMED SO DOWN.
AND YOU'VE NEVER BEEN THE TYPE TO SAY ANYTHING IF SOMETHING IS BOTHERING YOU.
But.
WE'RE YOUR PARENTS. I GUESS WE MADE YOU THAT WAY.
...
SO...

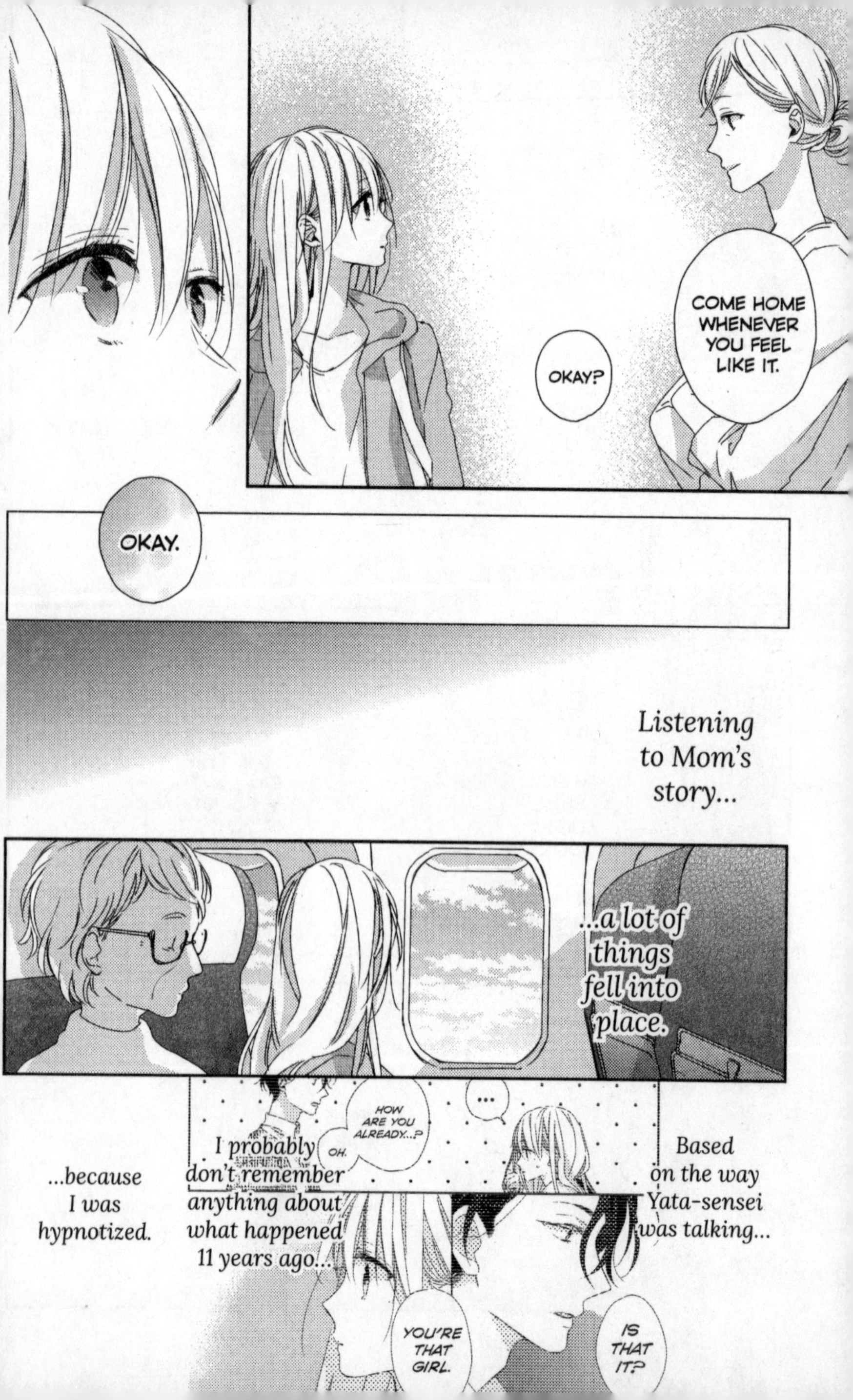
COME HOME WHENEVER YOU FEEL LIKE IT.
OKAY?
OKAY.
Listening to Mom's story...
...a lot of things fell into place.
Based on the way Yata-sensei was talking...
...
HOW ARE YOU ALREADY...?
OH.
IS THAT IT?
YOU'RE THAT GIRL.
I probably don't remember anything about what happened 11 years ago...
...because I was hypnotized.

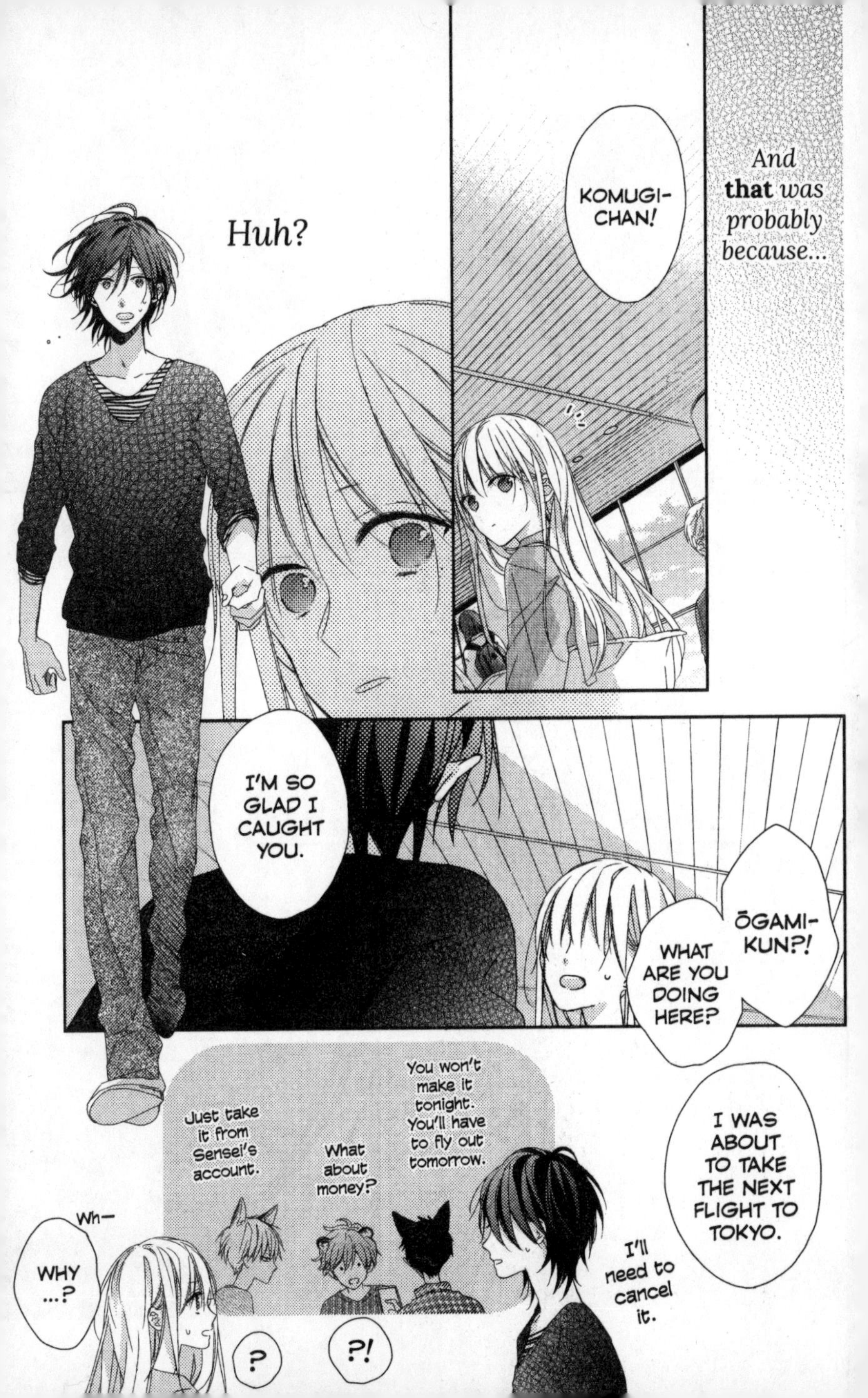
And **that** was probably because...
KOMUGI-CHAN!
Huh?
ŌGAMI-KUN?!
WHAT ARE YOU DOING HERE?
I'M SO GLAD I CAUGHT YOU.
I WAS ABOUT TO TAKE THE NEXT FLIGHT TO TOKYO.
I'll need to cancel it.
You won't make it tonight. You'll have to fly out tomorrow.
What about money?
Just take it from Sensei's account.
?!
?
Wh—
WHY ...?

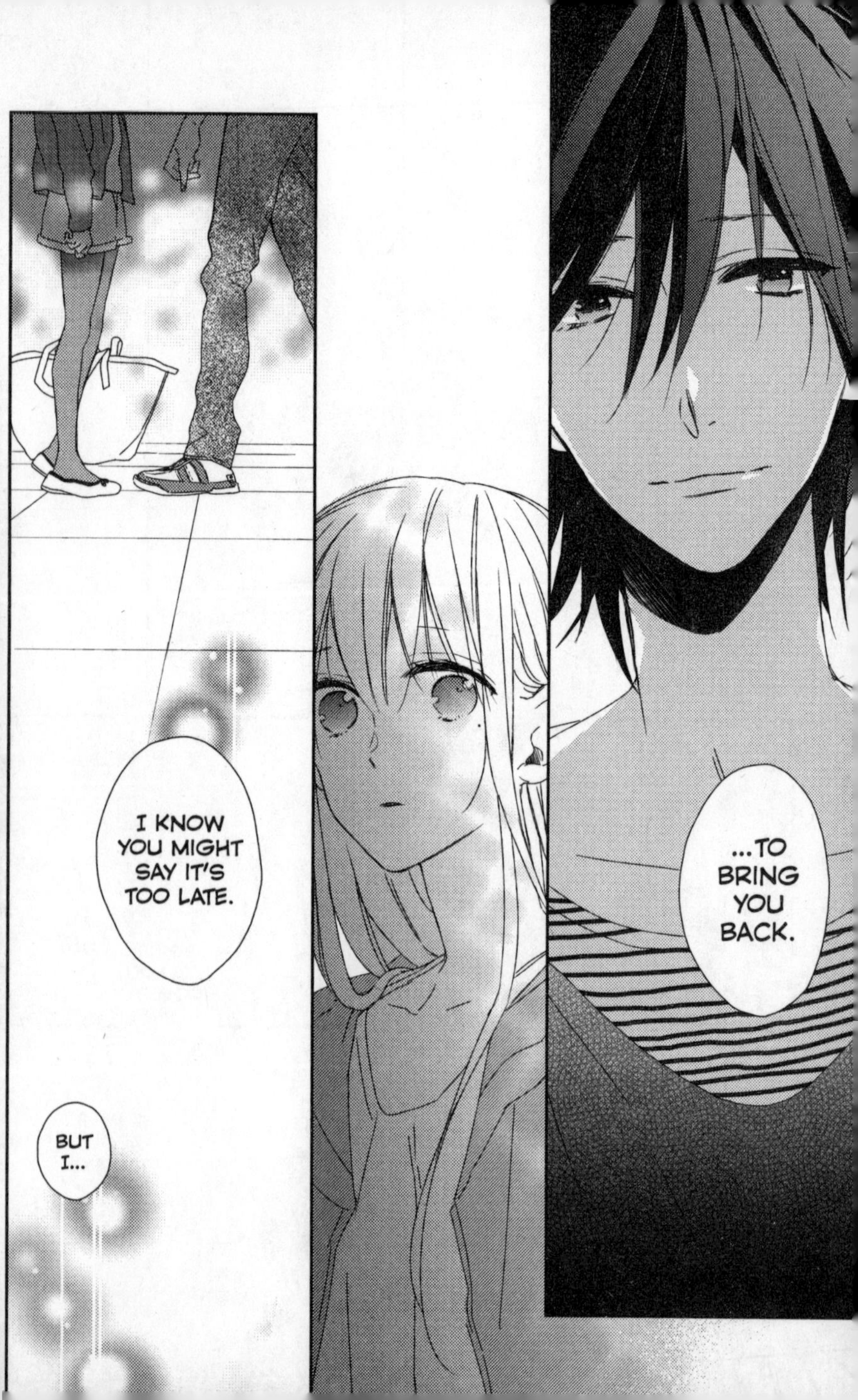
...TO BRING YOU BACK.
I KNOW YOU MIGHT SAY IT'S TOO LATE.
BUT I...

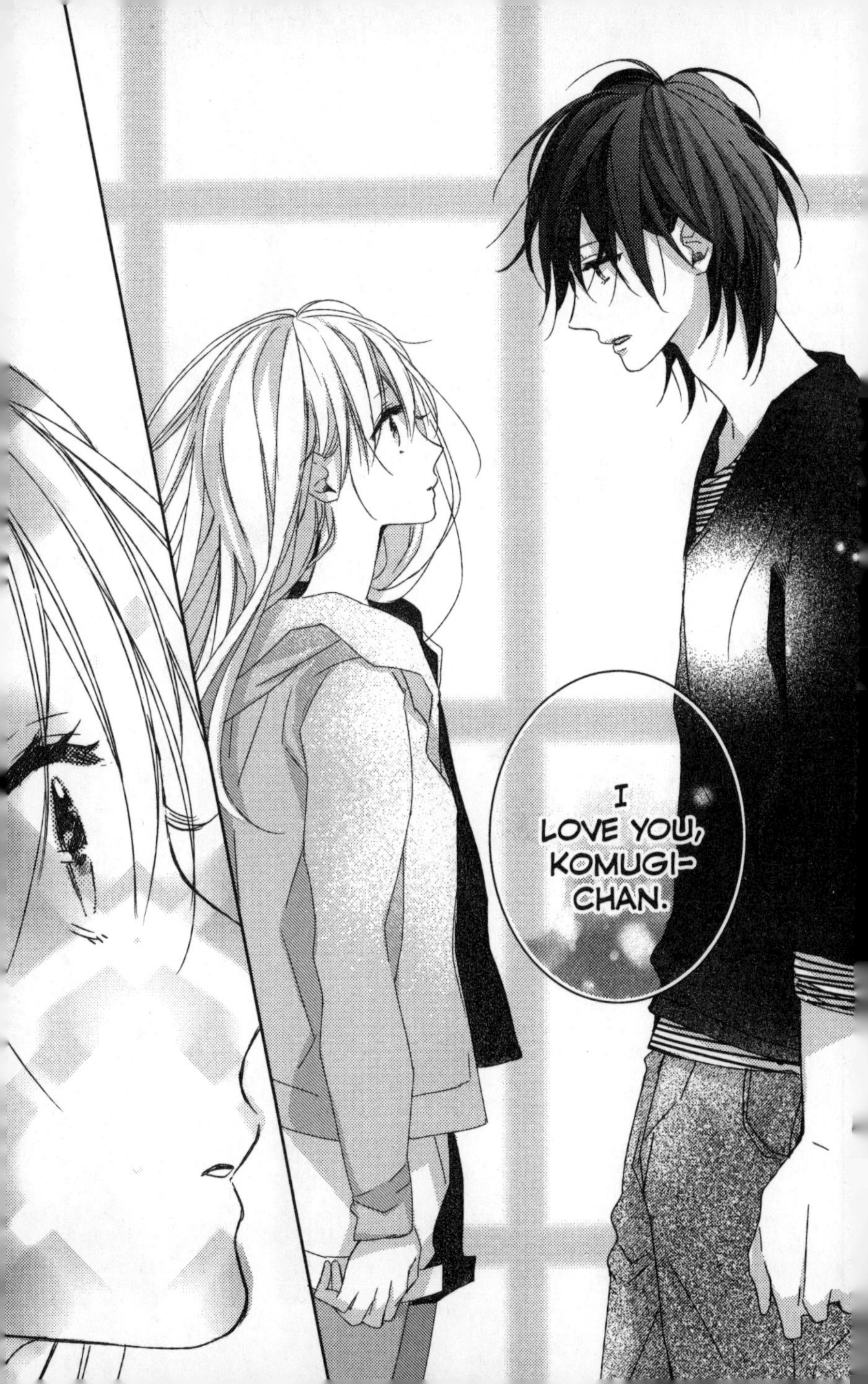
I LOVE YOU, KOMUGI-CHAN.

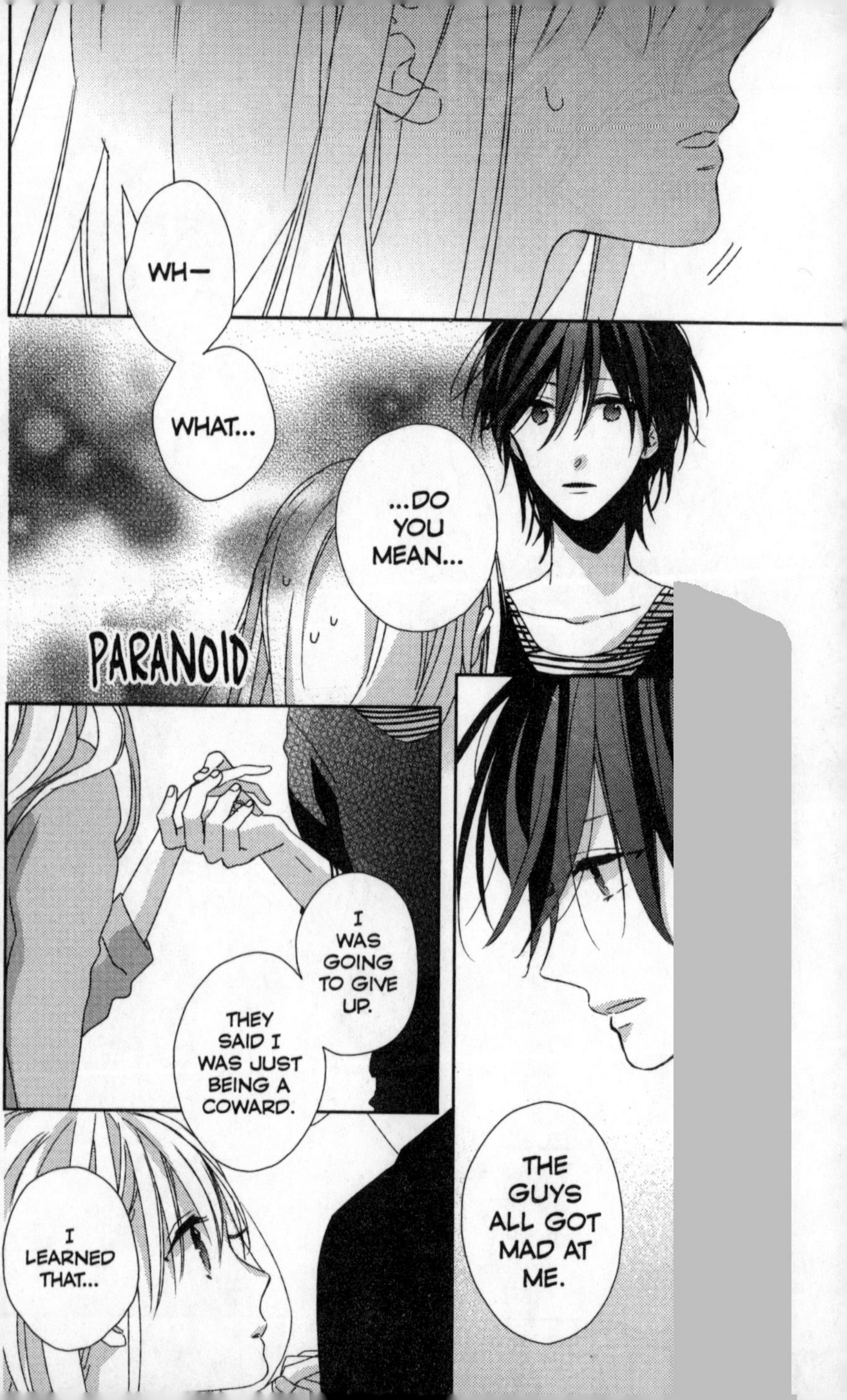
WH—
WHAT...
...DO YOU MEAN...
PARANOID
THE GUYS ALL GOT MAD AT ME.
I WAS GOING TO GIVE UP.
THEY SAID I WAS JUST BEING A COWARD.
I LEARNED THAT...

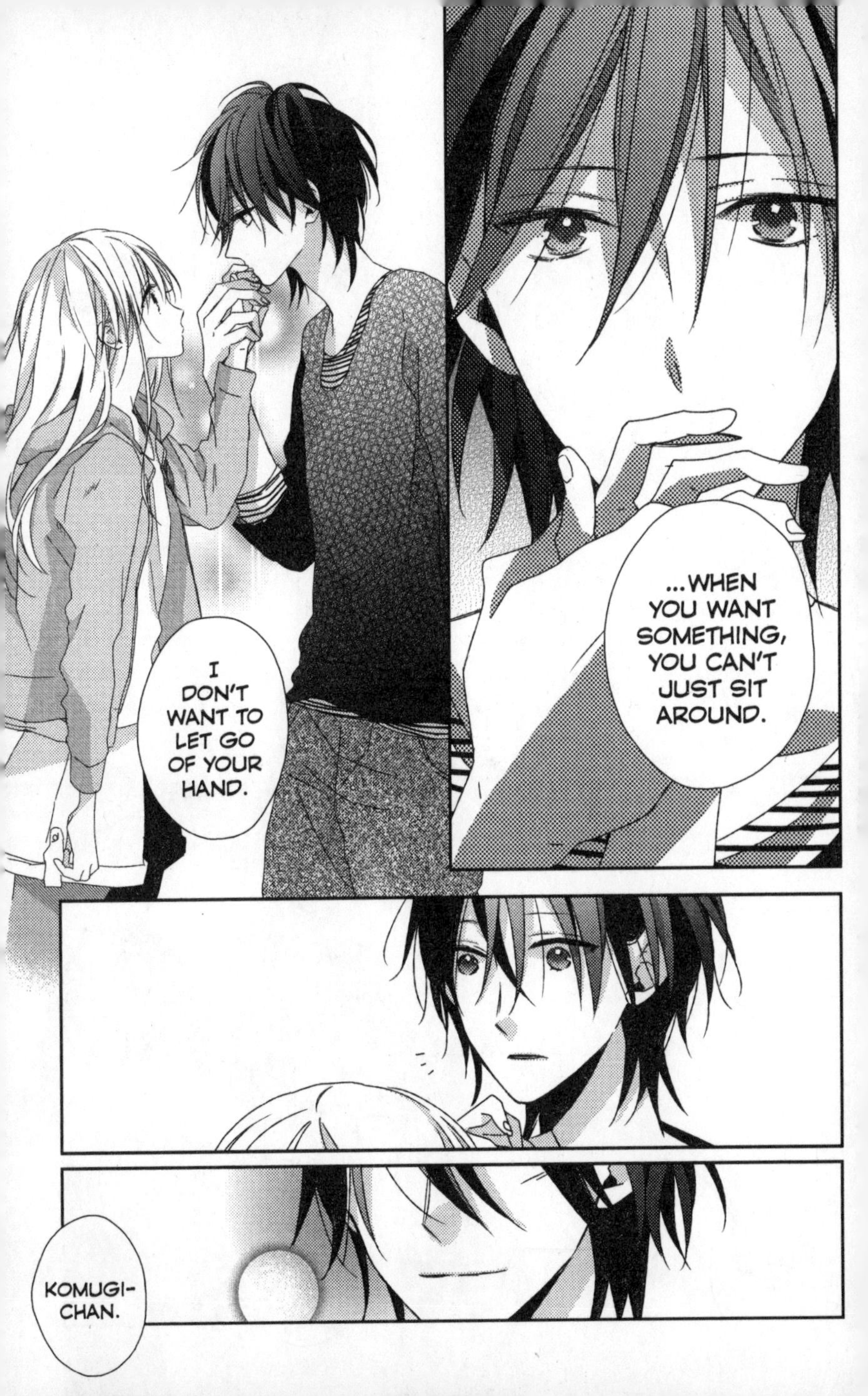
...WHEN YOU WANT SOMETHING, YOU CAN'T JUST SIT AROUND.
I DON'T WANT TO LET GO OF YOUR HAND.
KOMUGI-CHAN.

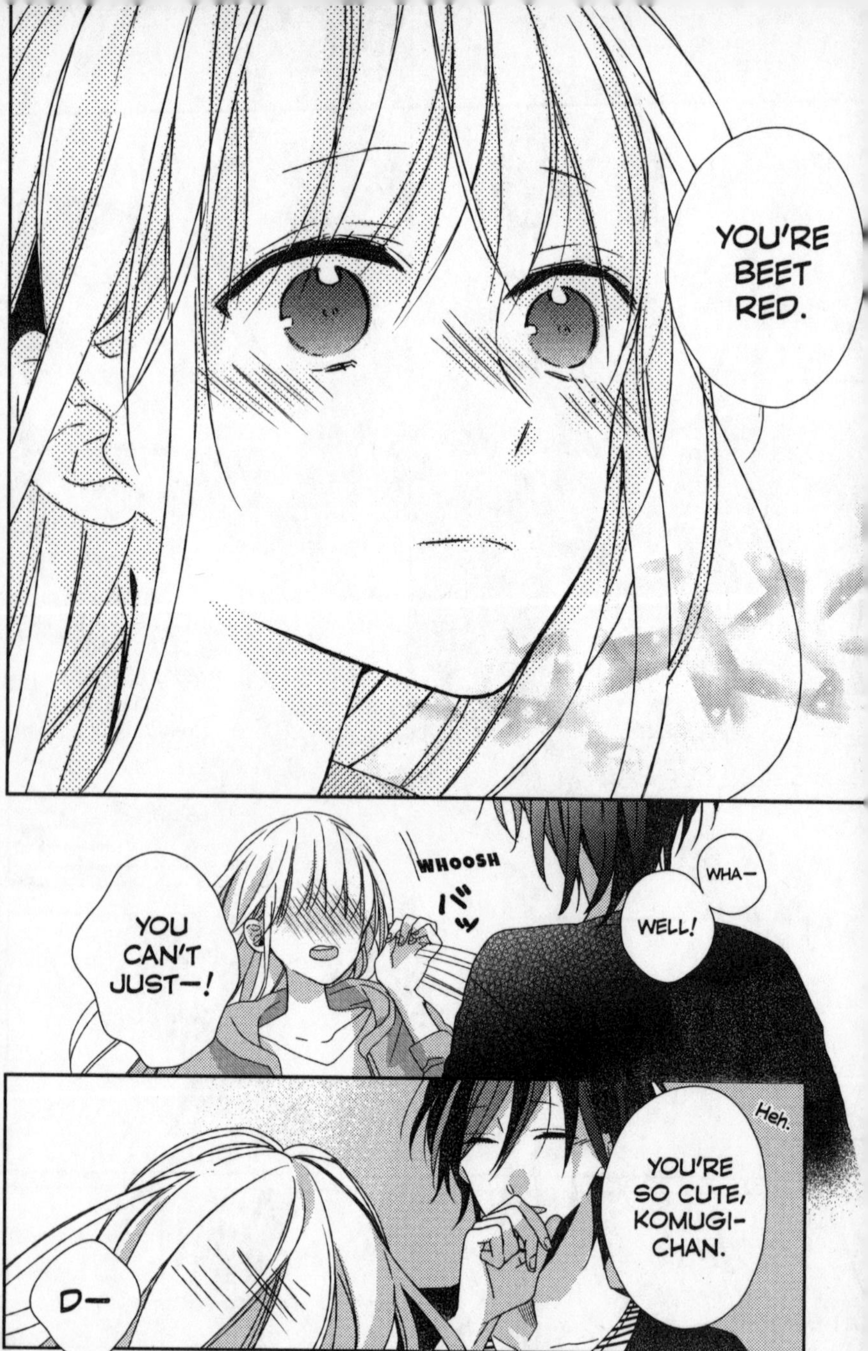
YOU'RE BEET RED.
WHA—
WELL!
WHOOSH
バッ
YOU CAN'T JUST—!
Heh.
YOU'RE SO CUTE, KOMUGI-CHAN.
D—

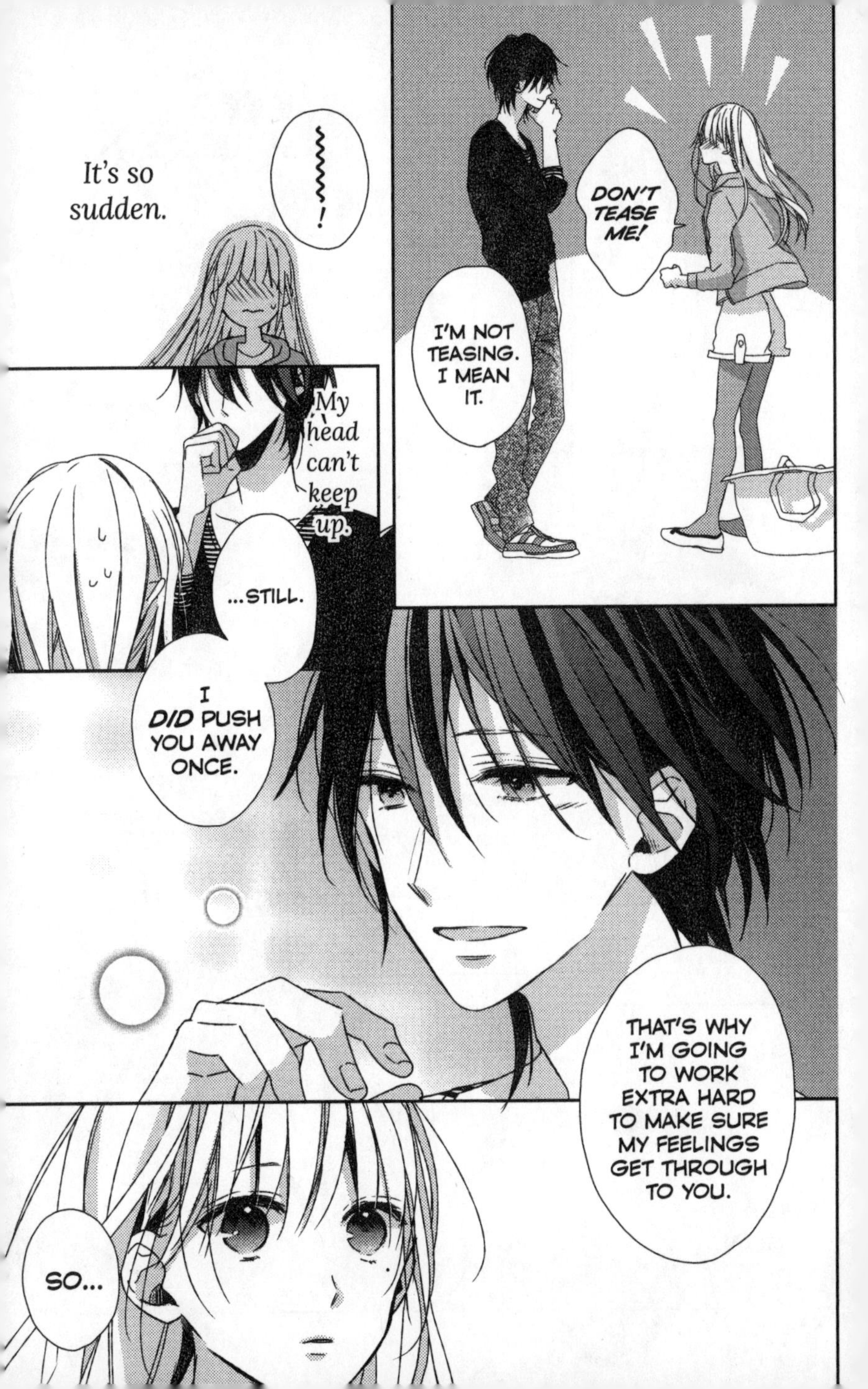
DON'T TEASE ME!
I'M NOT TEASING. I MEAN IT.
It's so sudden.
~~~!
My head can't keep up.
...STILL.
I *DID* PUSH YOU AWAY ONCE.
THAT'S WHY I'M GOING TO WORK EXTRA HARD TO MAKE SURE MY FEELINGS GET THROUGH TO YOU.
SO...
~~~

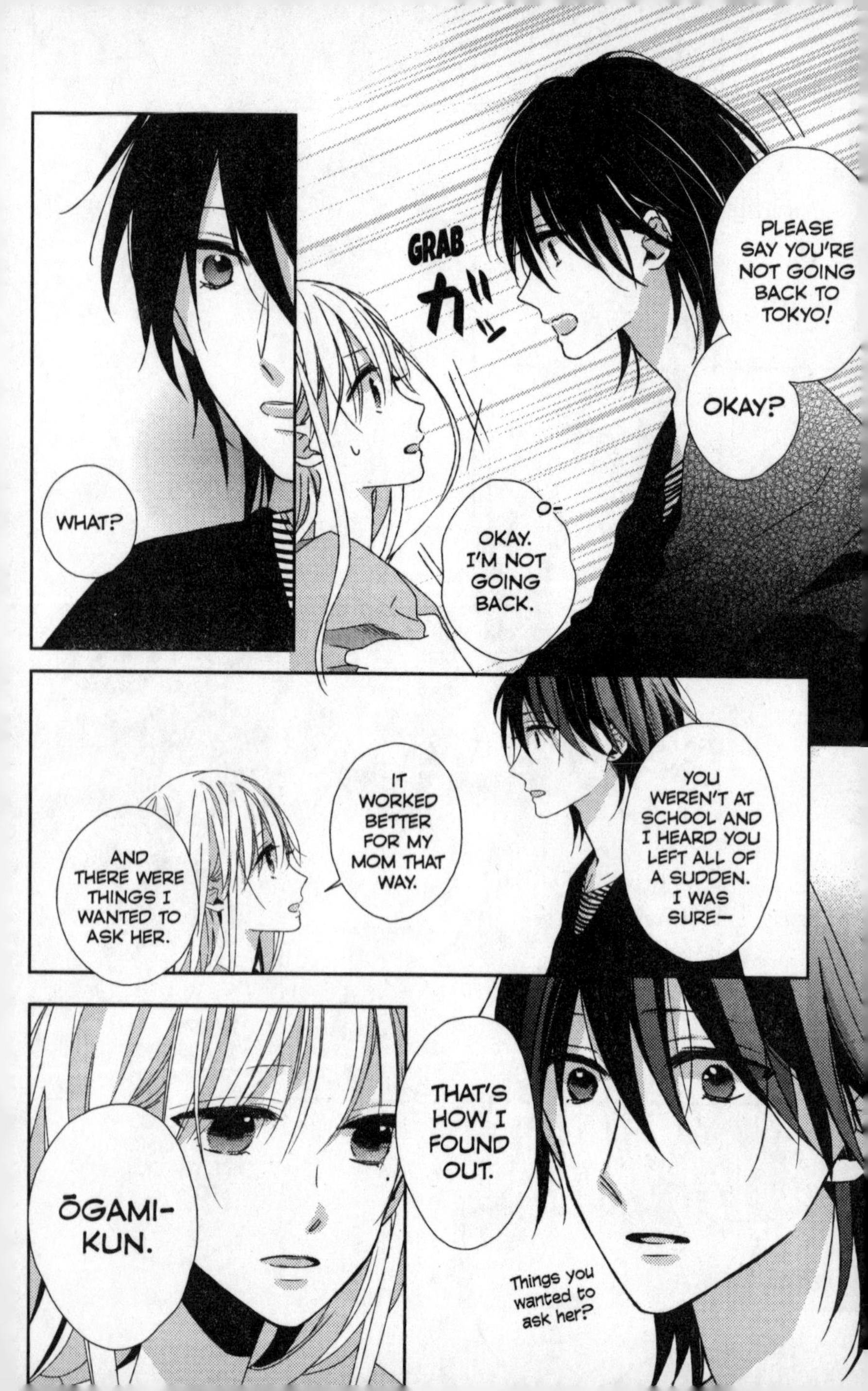
GRAB
カッ
PLEASE SAY YOU'RE NOT GOING BACK TO TOKYO!
OKAY?
O- OKAY. I'M NOT GOING BACK.
WHAT?
YOU WEREN'T AT SCHOOL AND I HEARD YOU LEFT ALL OF A SUDDEN. I WAS SURE—
IT WORKED BETTER FOR MY MOM THAT WAY.
AND THERE WERE THINGS I WANTED TO ASK HER.
THAT'S HOW I FOUND OUT.
Things you wanted to ask her?
ŌGAMI-KUN.

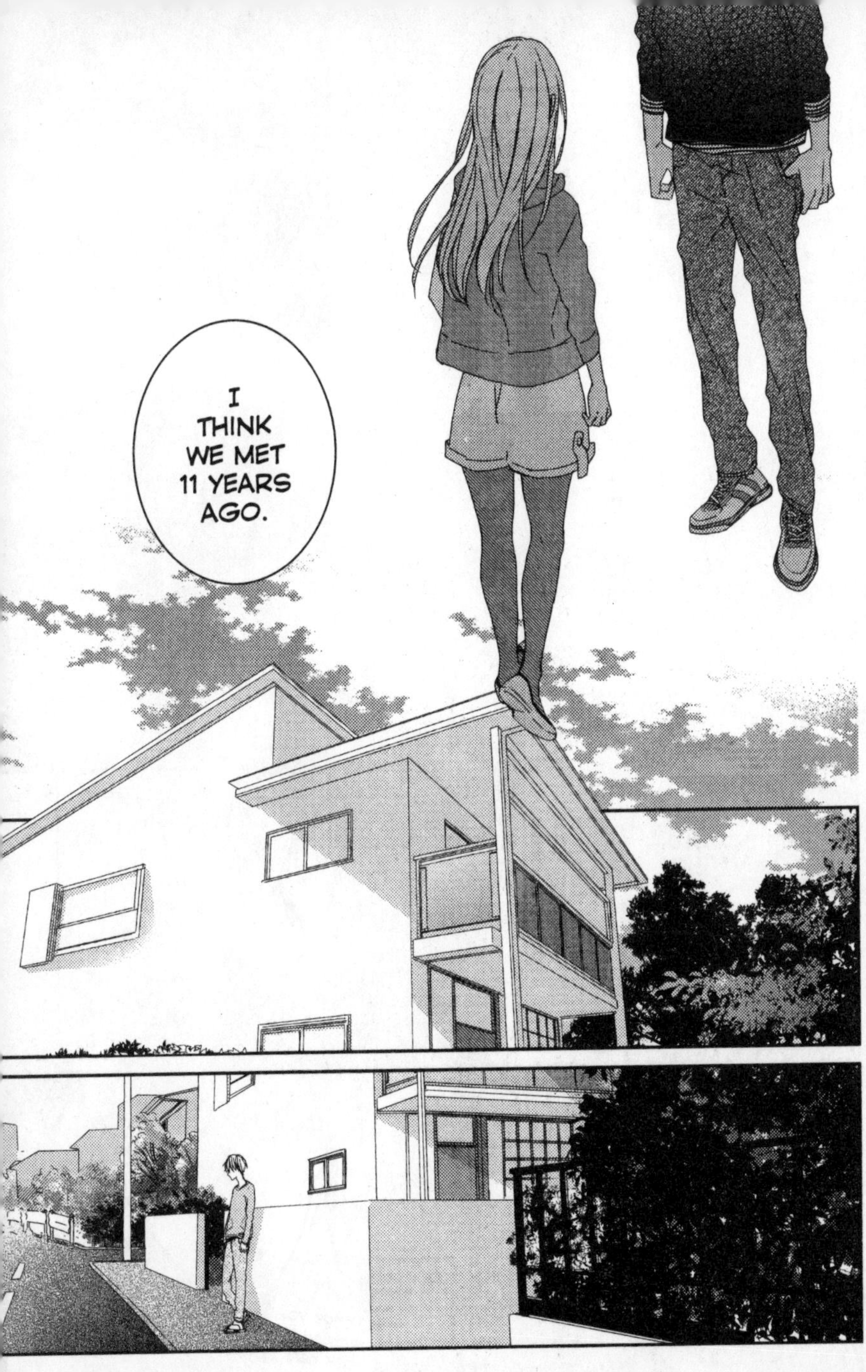
I THINK WE MET 11 YEARS AGO.

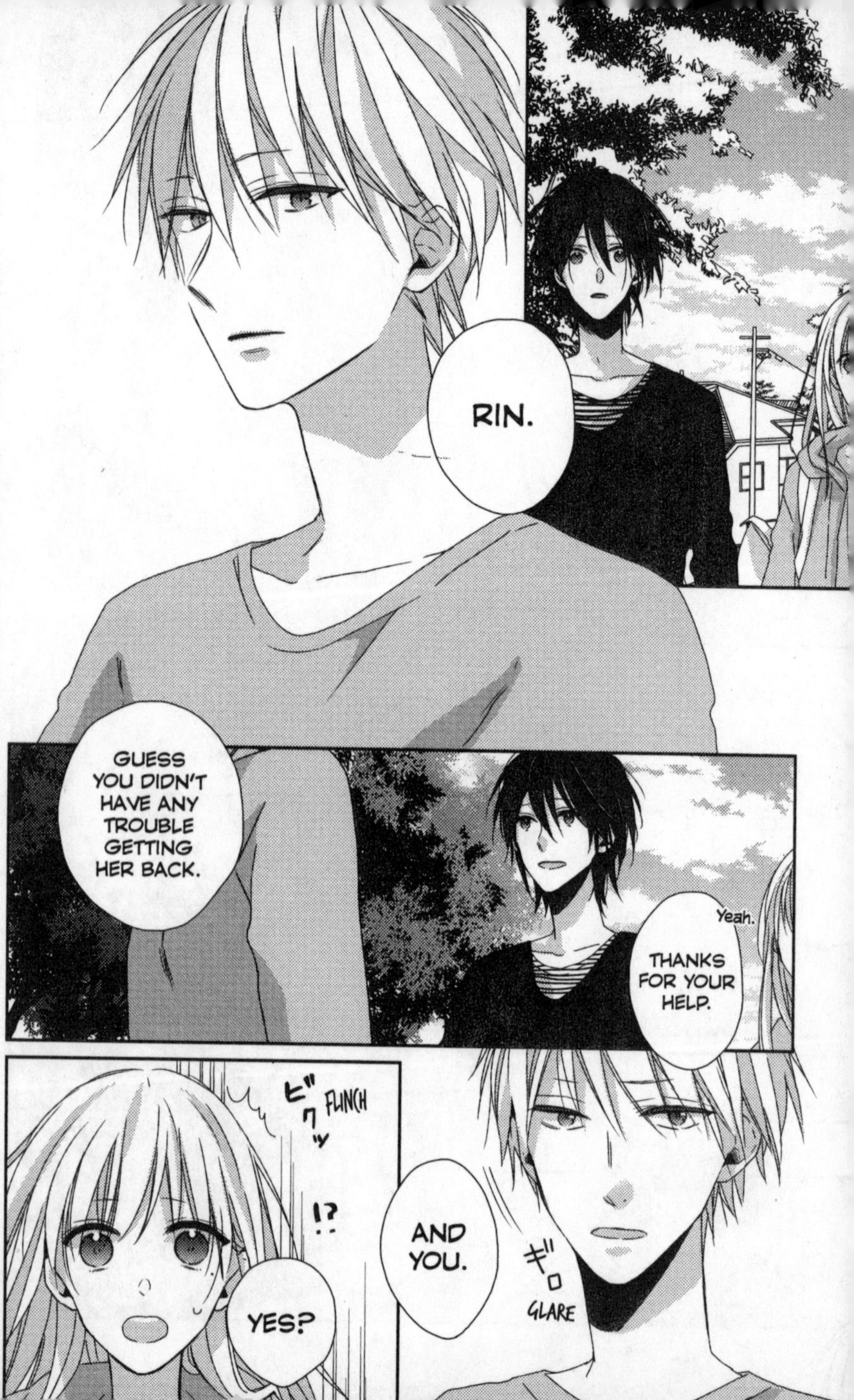
RIN.
GUESS YOU DIDN'T HAVE ANY TROUBLE GETTING HER BACK.
Yeah.
THANKS FOR YOUR HELP.
AND YOU.
ギロ
GLARE
ビクッ
FLINCH
!?
YES?

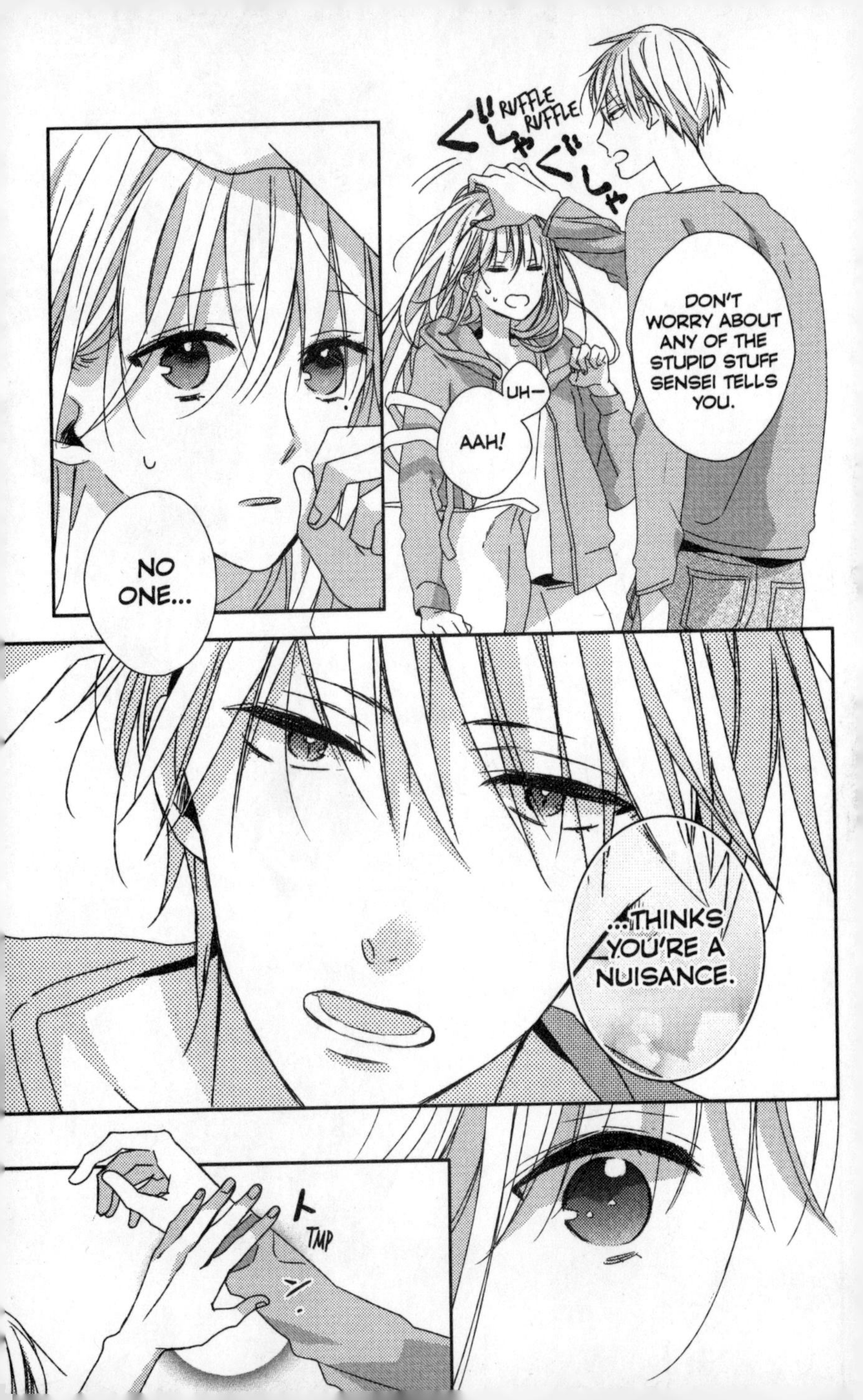
ぐしゃぐしゃ
RUFFLE RUFFLE
DON'T WORRY ABOUT ANY OF THE STUPID STUFF SENSEI TELLS YOU.
UH— AAH!
NO ONE...
...THINKS YOU'RE A NUISANCE.
ト
TMP

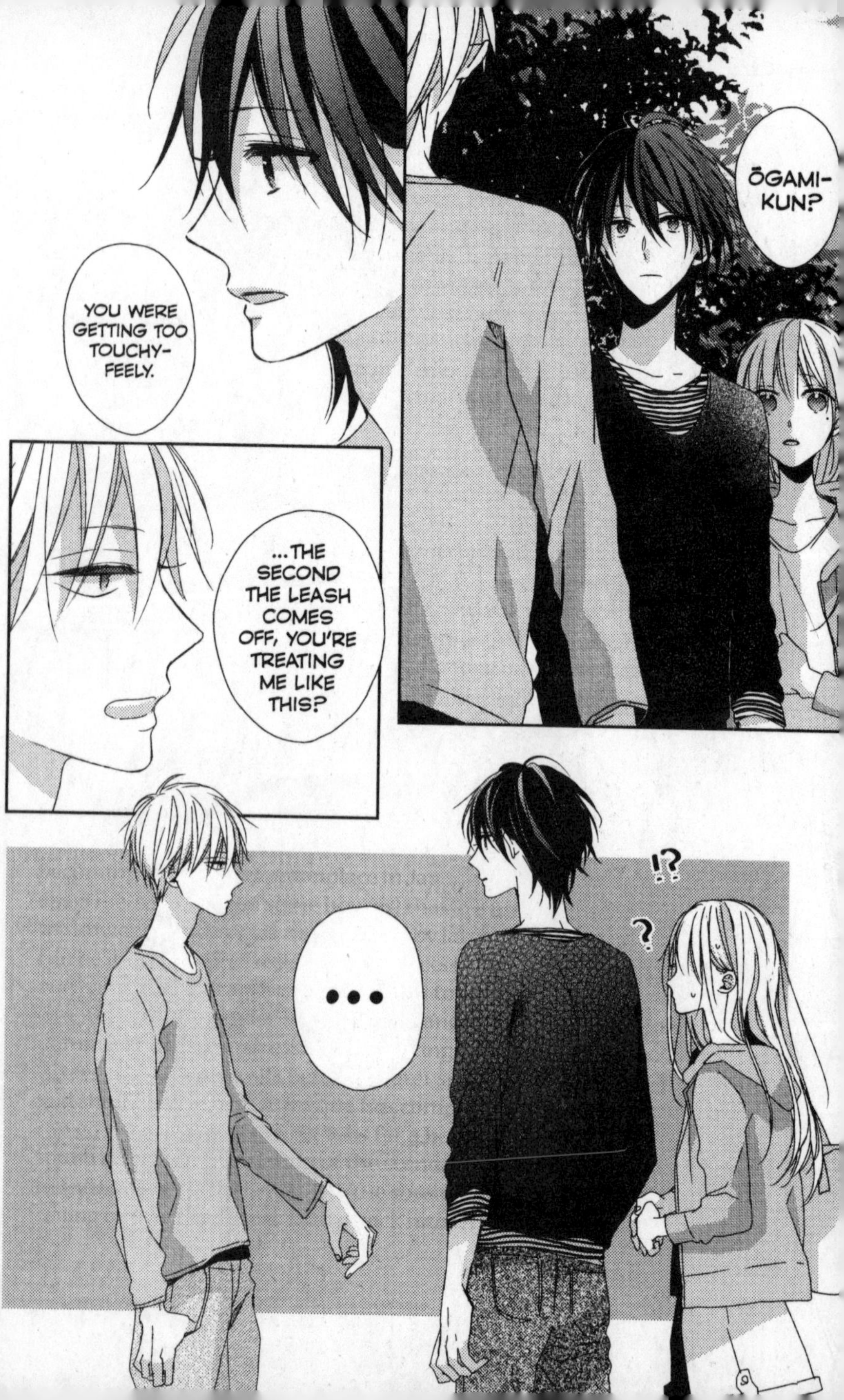
ŌGAMI-KUN?
YOU WERE GETTING TOO TOUCHY-FEELY.
...THE SECOND THE LEASH COMES OFF, YOU'RE TREATING ME LIKE THIS?
!?
?
...

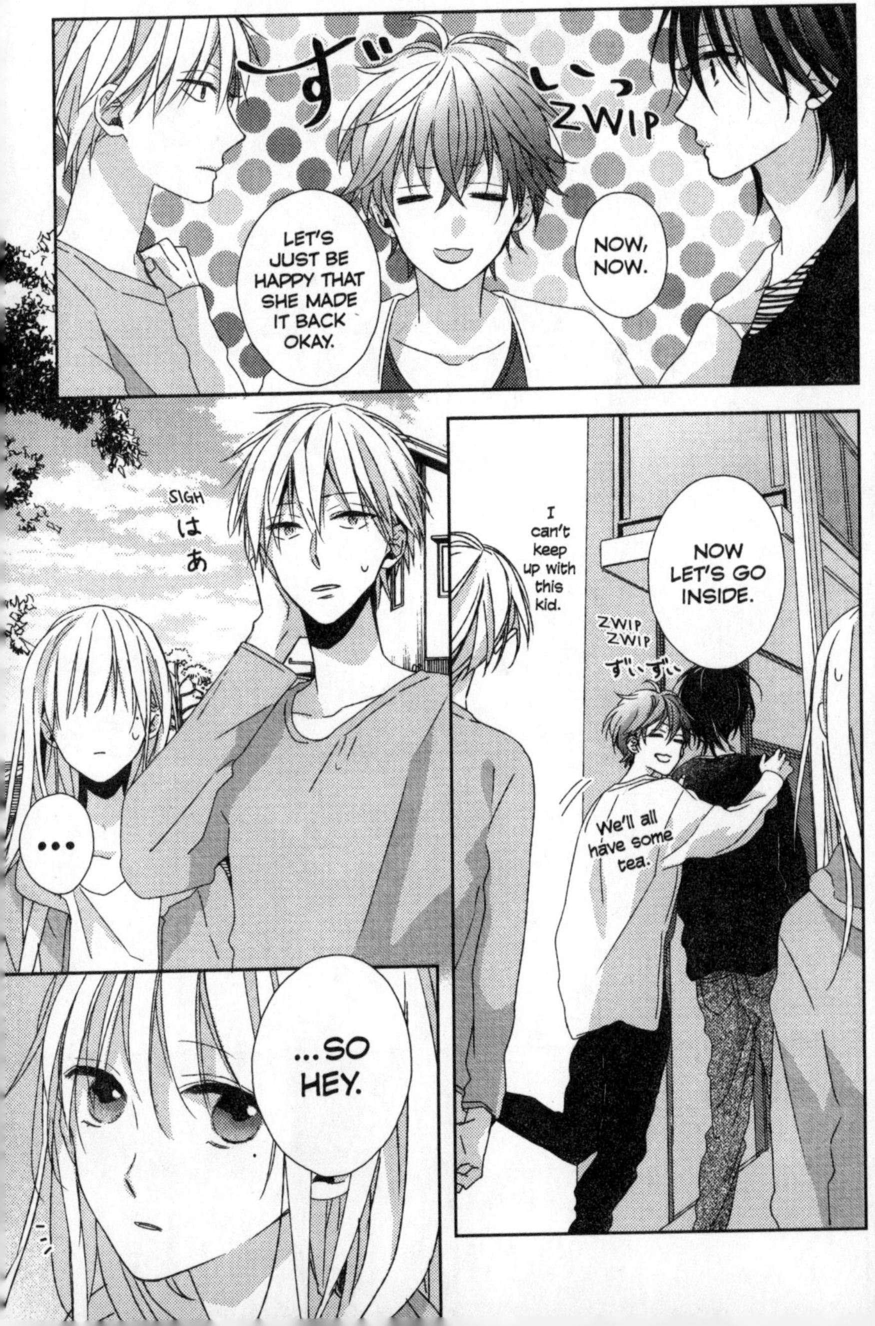
ずいっ
ZWIP
NOW, NOW.
LET'S JUST BE HAPPY THAT SHE MADE IT BACK OKAY.
NOW LET'S GO INSIDE.
I can't keep up with this kid.
ZWIP ZWIP
ずいずい
We'll all have some tea.
SIGH
はあ
...
...SO HEY.

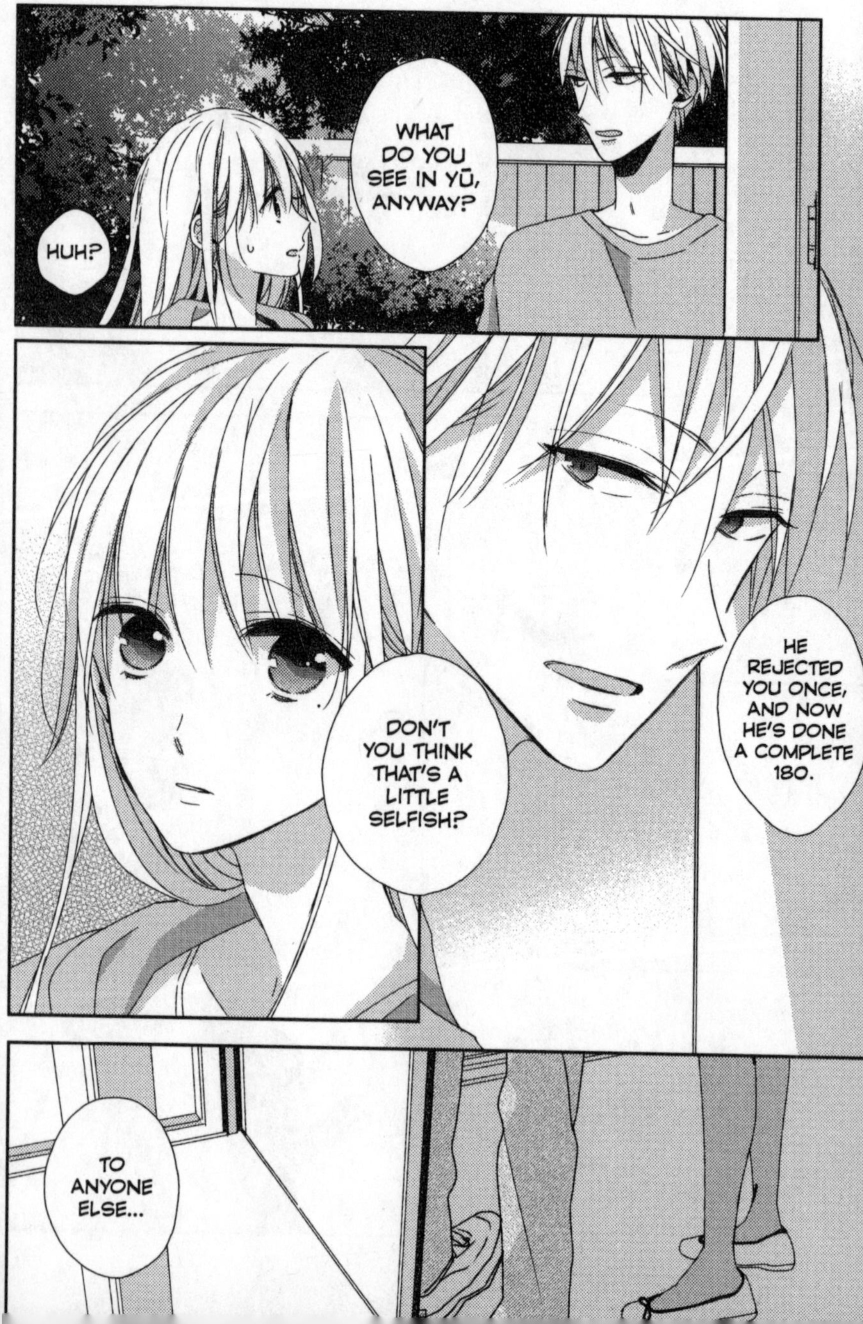
WHAT DO YOU SEE IN YŪ, ANYWAY?
HUH?
HE REJECTED YOU ONCE, AND NOW HE'S DONE A COMPLETE 180.
DON'T YOU THINK THAT'S A LITTLE SELFISH?
TO ANYONE ELSE...

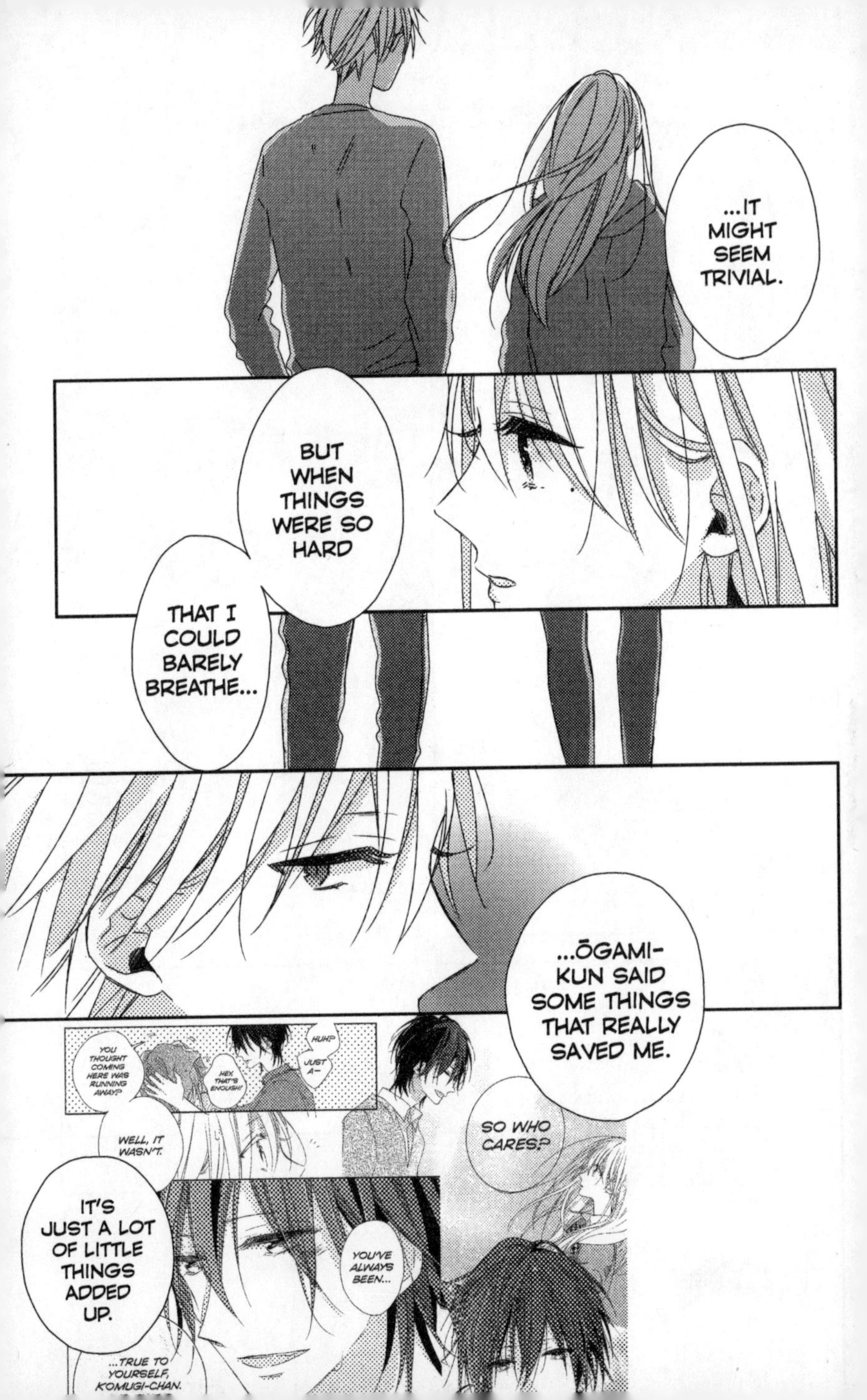
...IT MIGHT SEEM TRIVIAL.
BUT WHEN THINGS WERE SO HARD
THAT I COULD BARELY BREATHE...
...ŌGAMI-KUN SAID SOME THINGS THAT REALLY SAVED ME.
SO WHO CARES?
HUH? JUST A–
HEY, THAT'S ENOUGH!
YOU THOUGHT COMING HERE WAS RUNNING AWAY?
WELL, IT WASN'T.
YOU'VE ALWAYS BEEN...
...TRUE TO YOURSELF, KOMUGI-CHAN.
IT'S JUST A LOT OF LITTLE THINGS ADDED UP.

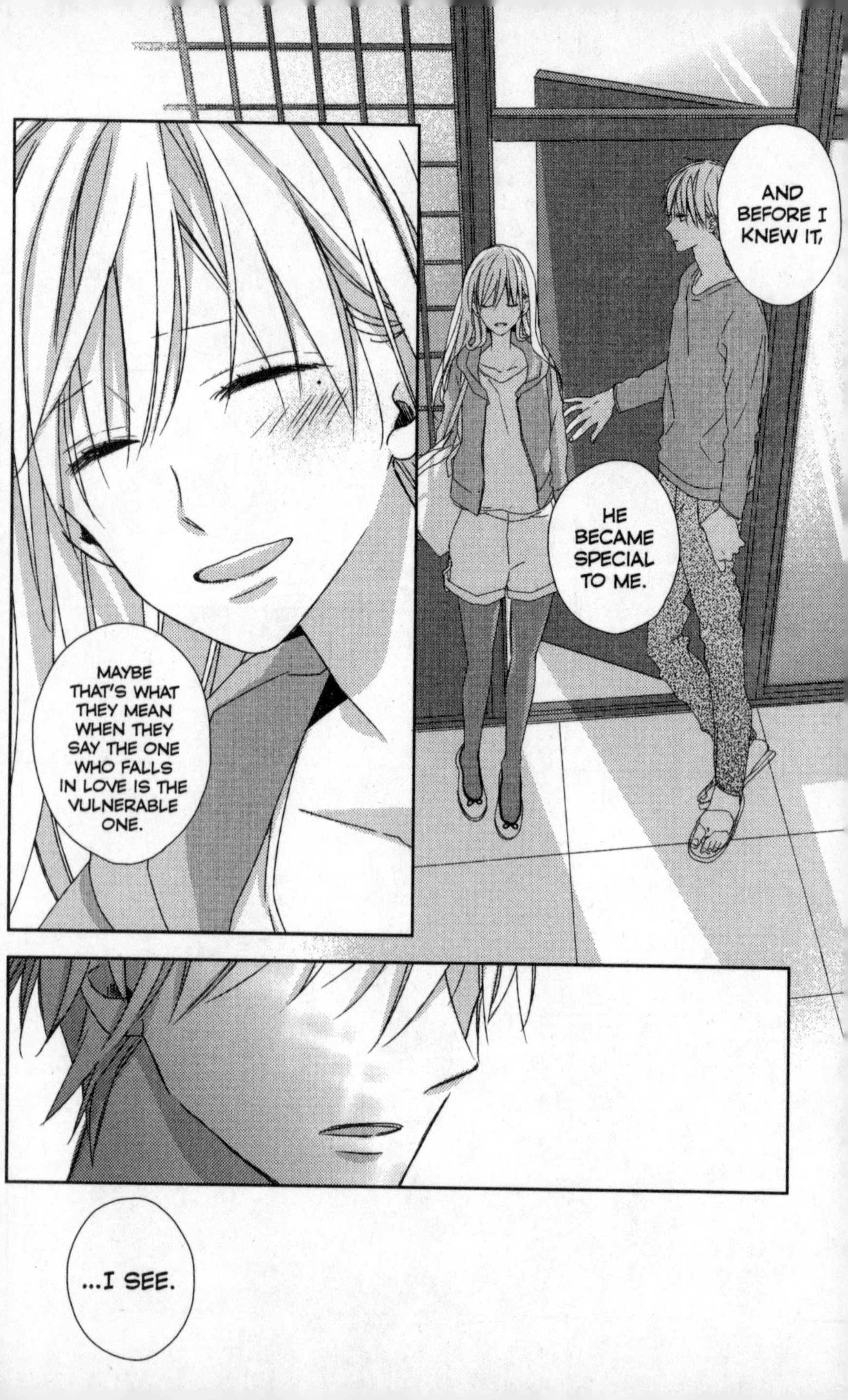
AND BEFORE I KNEW IT,
HE BECAME SPECIAL TO ME.
MAYBE THAT'S WHAT THEY MEAN WHEN THEY SAY THE ONE WHO FALLS IN LOVE IS THE VULNERABLE ONE.
...I SEE.

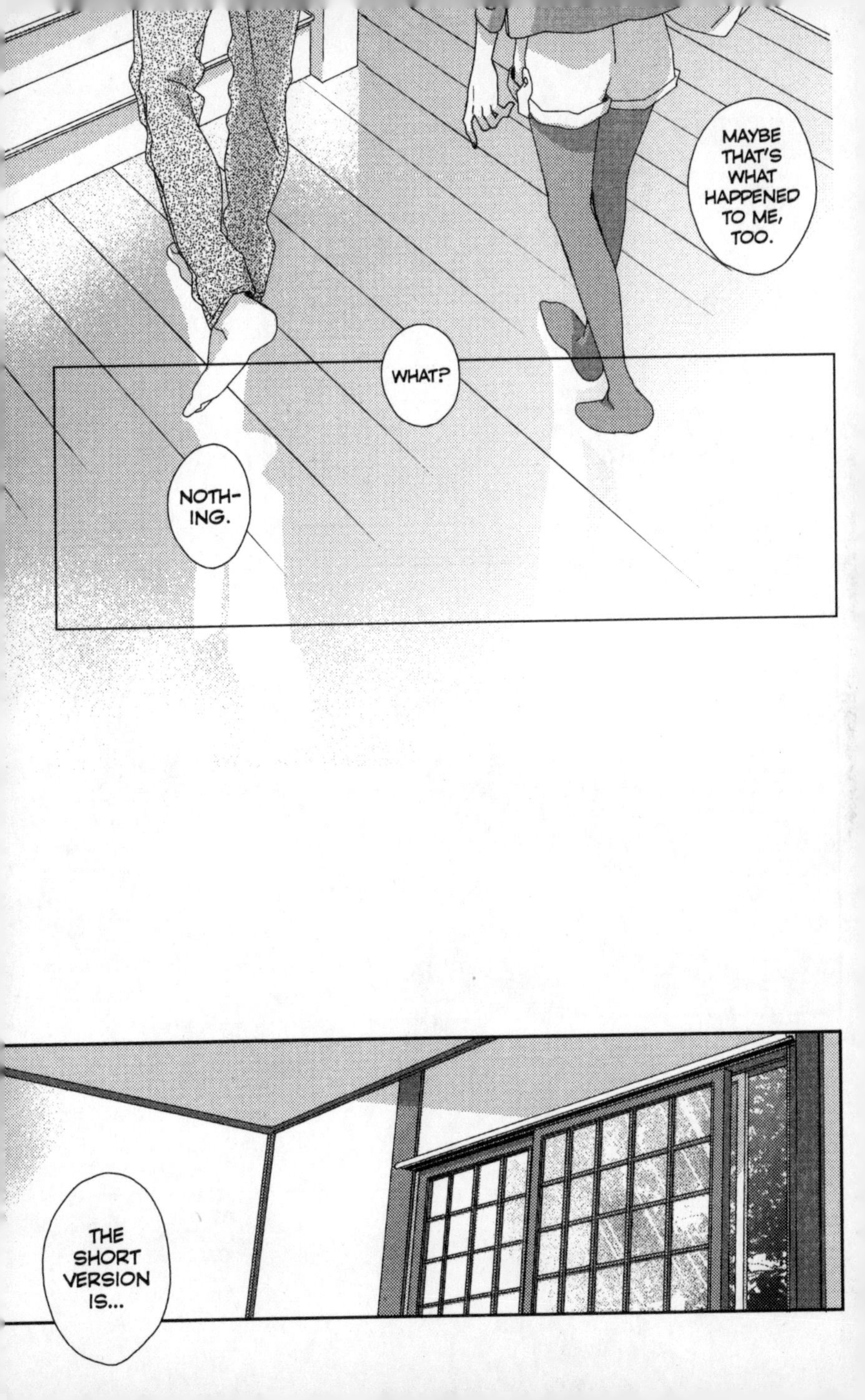
MAYBE THAT'S WHAT HAPPENED TO ME, TOO.
WHAT?
NOTH-ING.
THE SHORT VERSION IS...

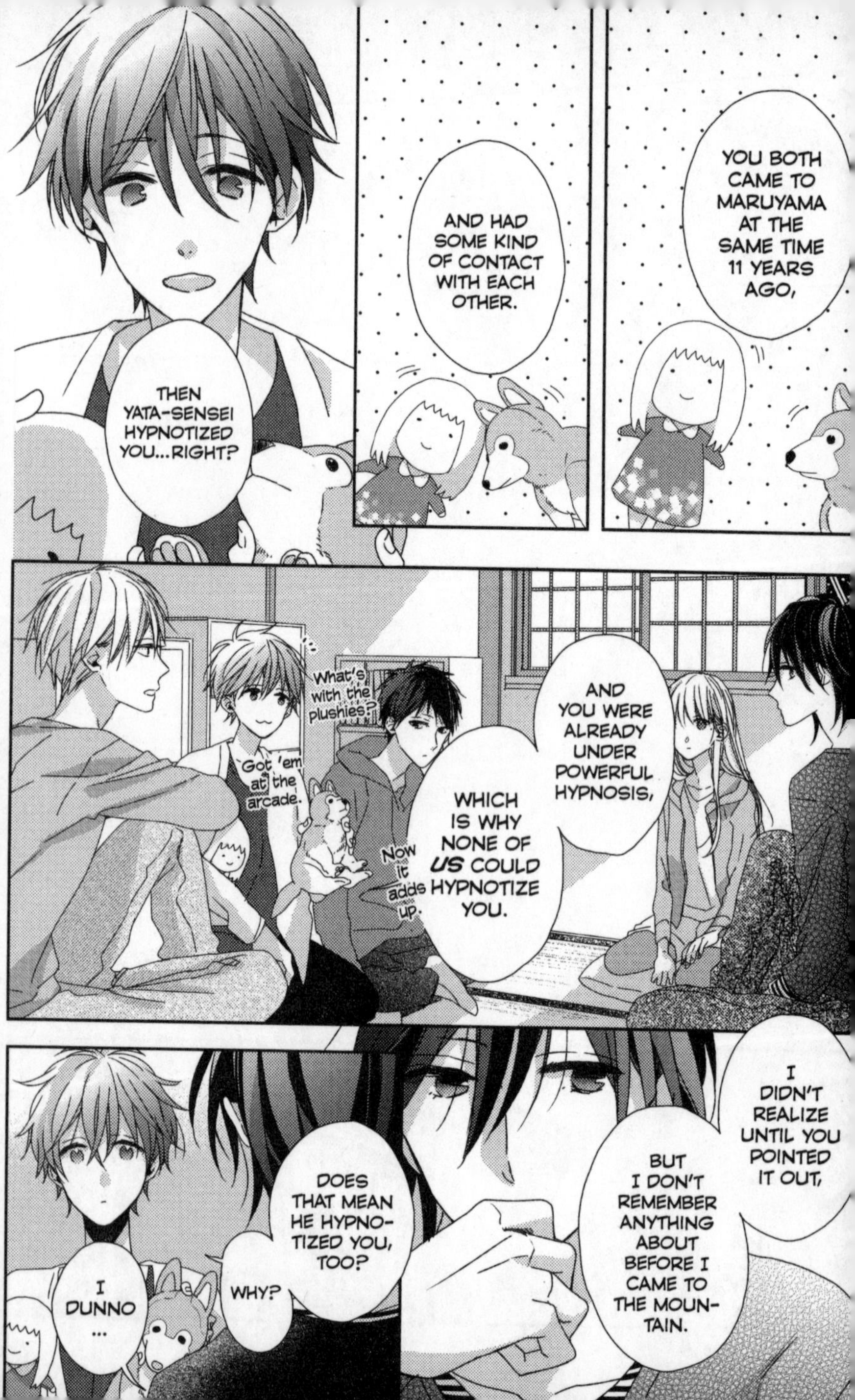
YOU BOTH CAME TO MARUYAMA AT THE SAME TIME 11 YEARS AGO,
AND HAD SOME KIND OF CONTACT WITH EACH OTHER.
THEN YATA-SENSEI HYPNOTIZED YOU...RIGHT?
AND YOU WERE ALREADY UNDER POWERFUL HYPNOSIS,
WHICH IS WHY NONE OF *US* COULD HYPNOTIZE YOU.
Now it adds up.
What's with the plushies?
Got 'em at the arcade.
I DIDN'T REALIZE UNTIL YOU POINTED IT OUT,
BUT I DON'T REMEMBER ANYTHING ABOUT BEFORE I CAME TO THE MOUNTAIN.
DOES THAT MEAN HE HYPNOTIZED YOU, TOO?
WHY?
I DUNNO...

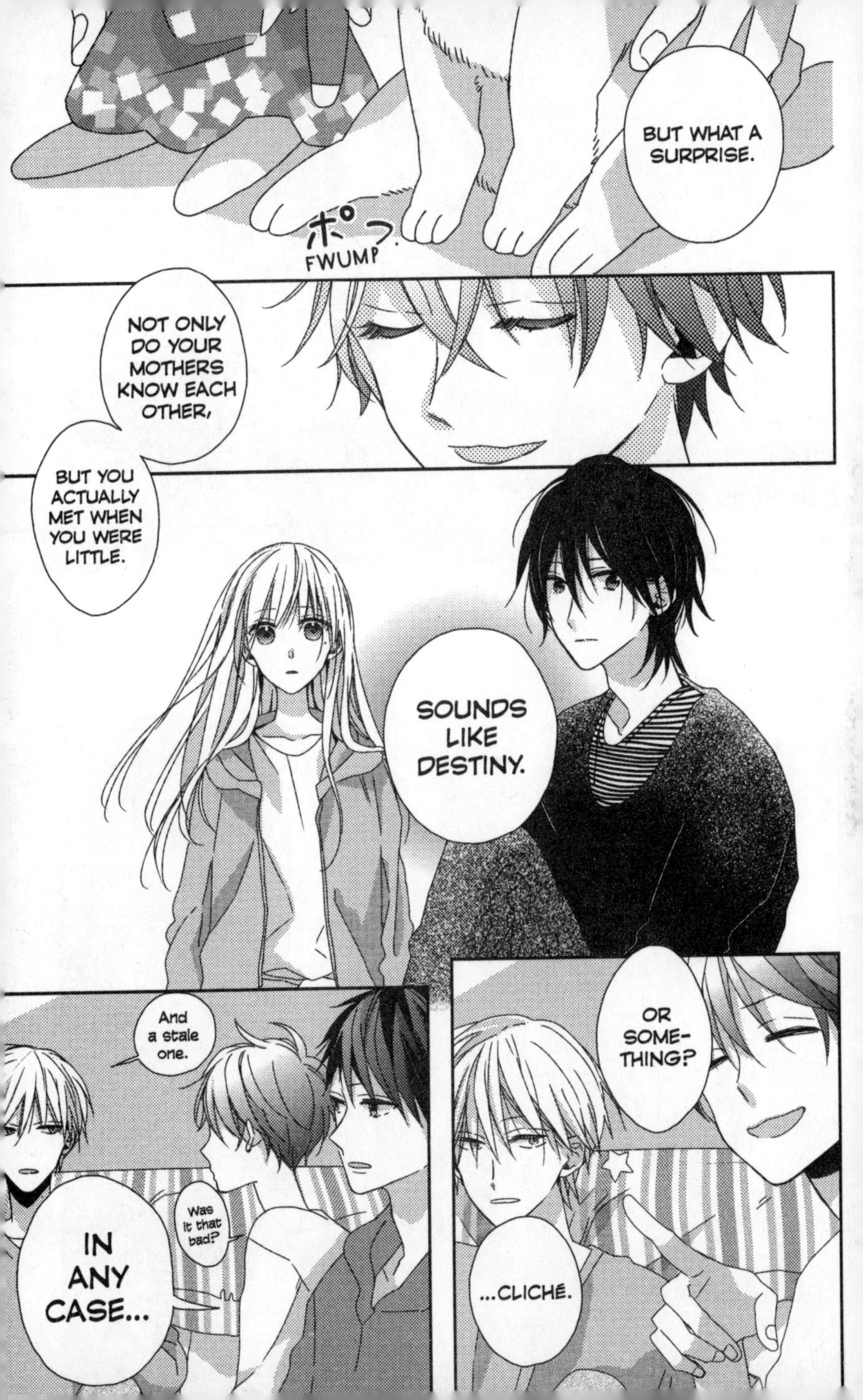
BUT WHAT A SURPRISE.
ポっ
FWUMP
NOT ONLY DO YOUR MOTHERS KNOW EACH OTHER,
BUT YOU ACTUALLY MET WHEN YOU WERE LITTLE.
SOUNDS LIKE DESTINY.
OR SOME-THING?
...CLICHÉ.
And a stale one.
Was it that bad?
IN ANY CASE...

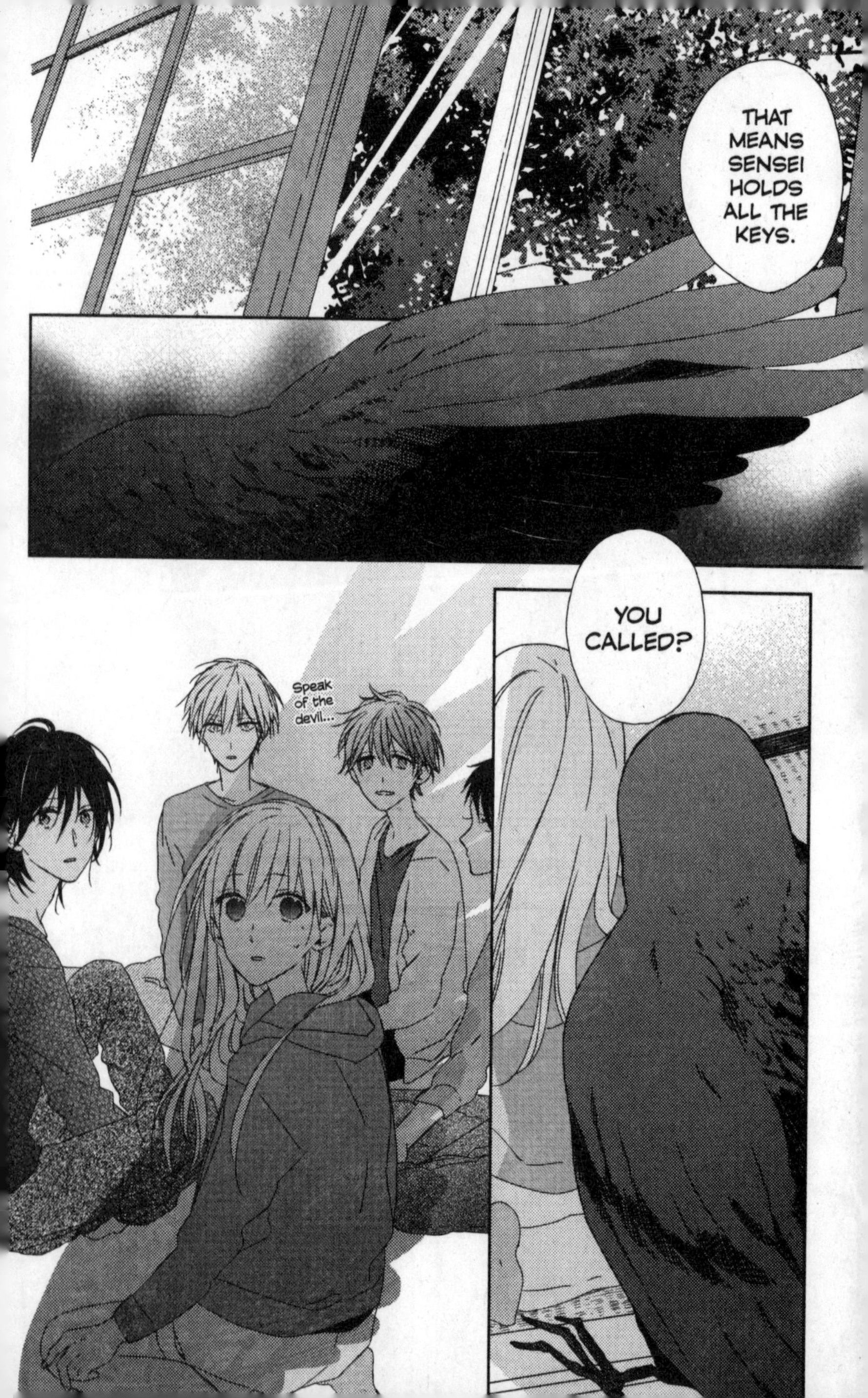
THAT MEANS SENSEI HOLDS ALL THE KEYS.
YOU CALLED?
Speak of the devil...

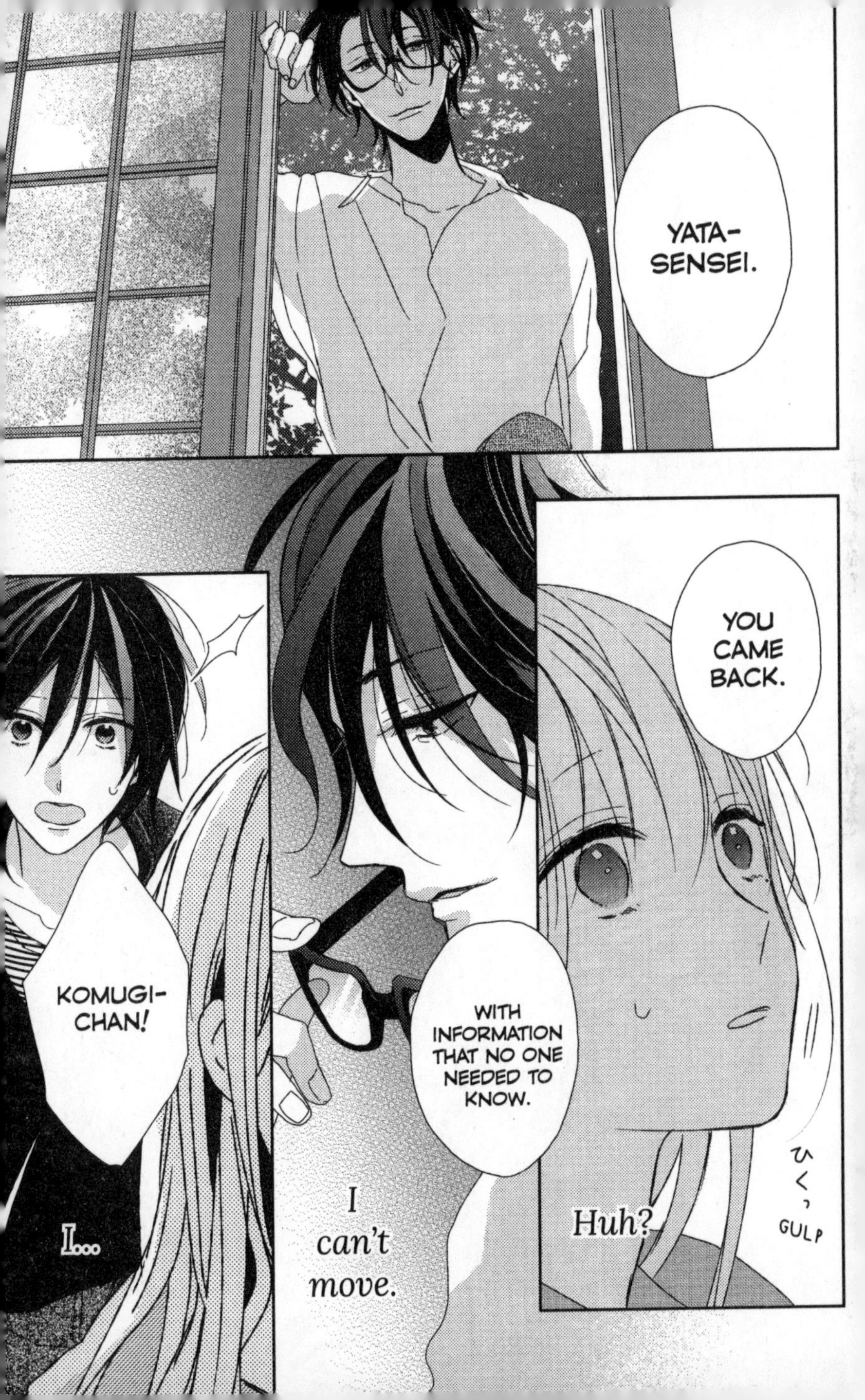
YATA-SENSEI.
YOU CAME BACK.
ひくっ
GULP
Huh?
WITH INFORMATION THAT NO ONE NEEDED TO KNOW.
I can't move.
KOMUGI-CHAN!
I...

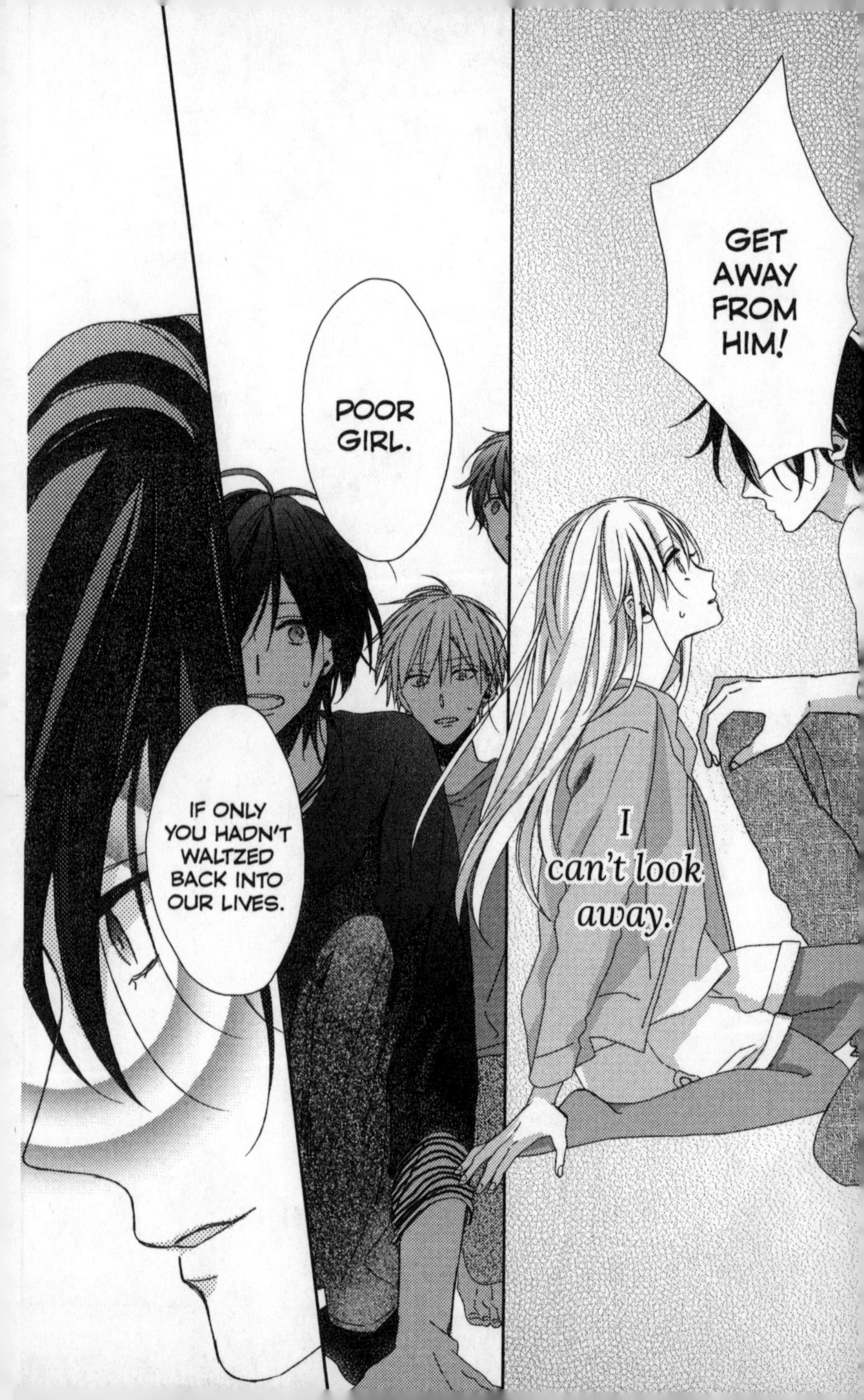
GET AWAY FROM HIM!
I can't look away.
POOR GIRL.
IF ONLY YOU HADN'T WALTZED BACK INTO OUR LIVES.

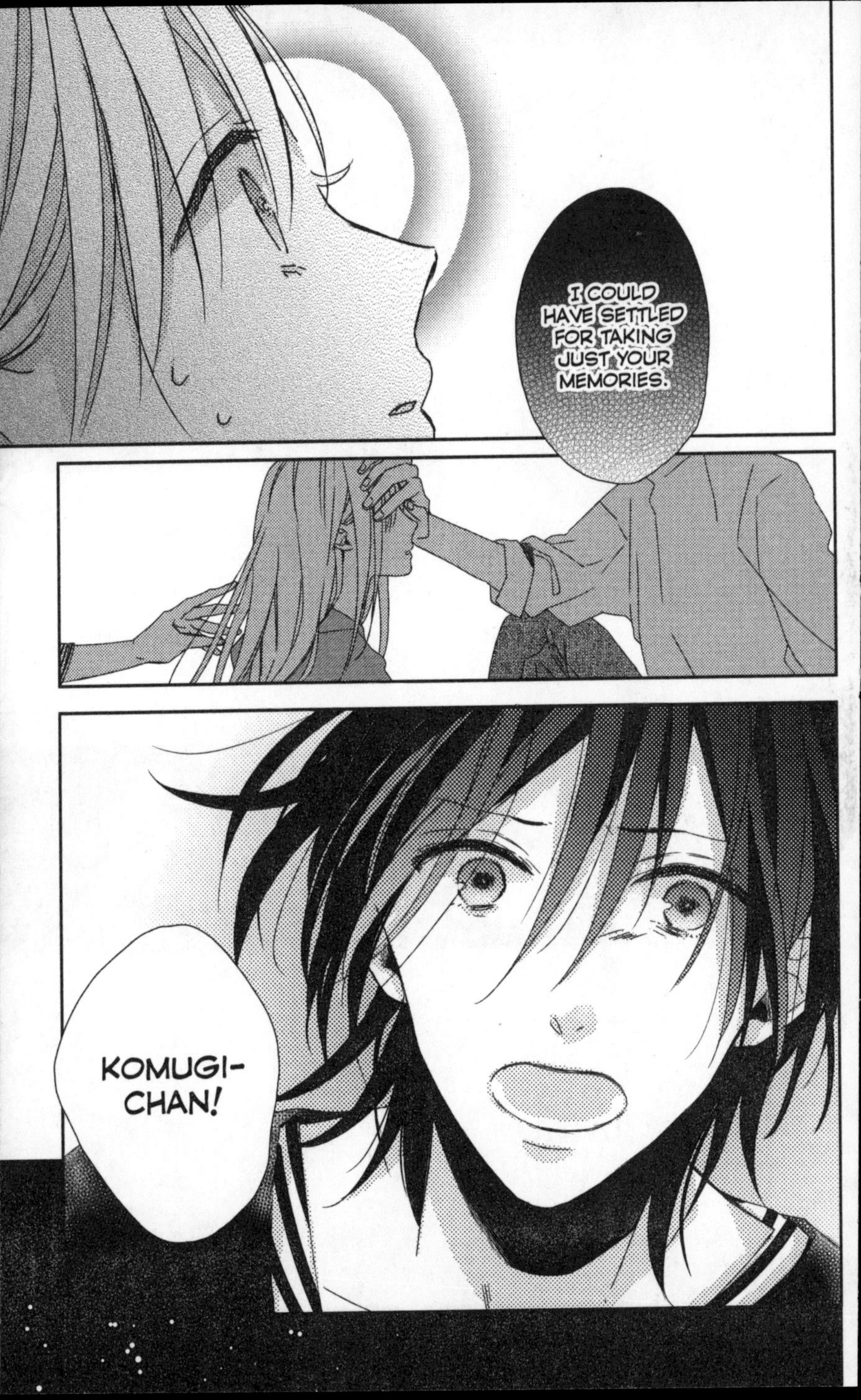
I COULD HAVE SETTLED FOR TAKING JUST YOUR MEMORIES.
KOMUGI-CHAN!

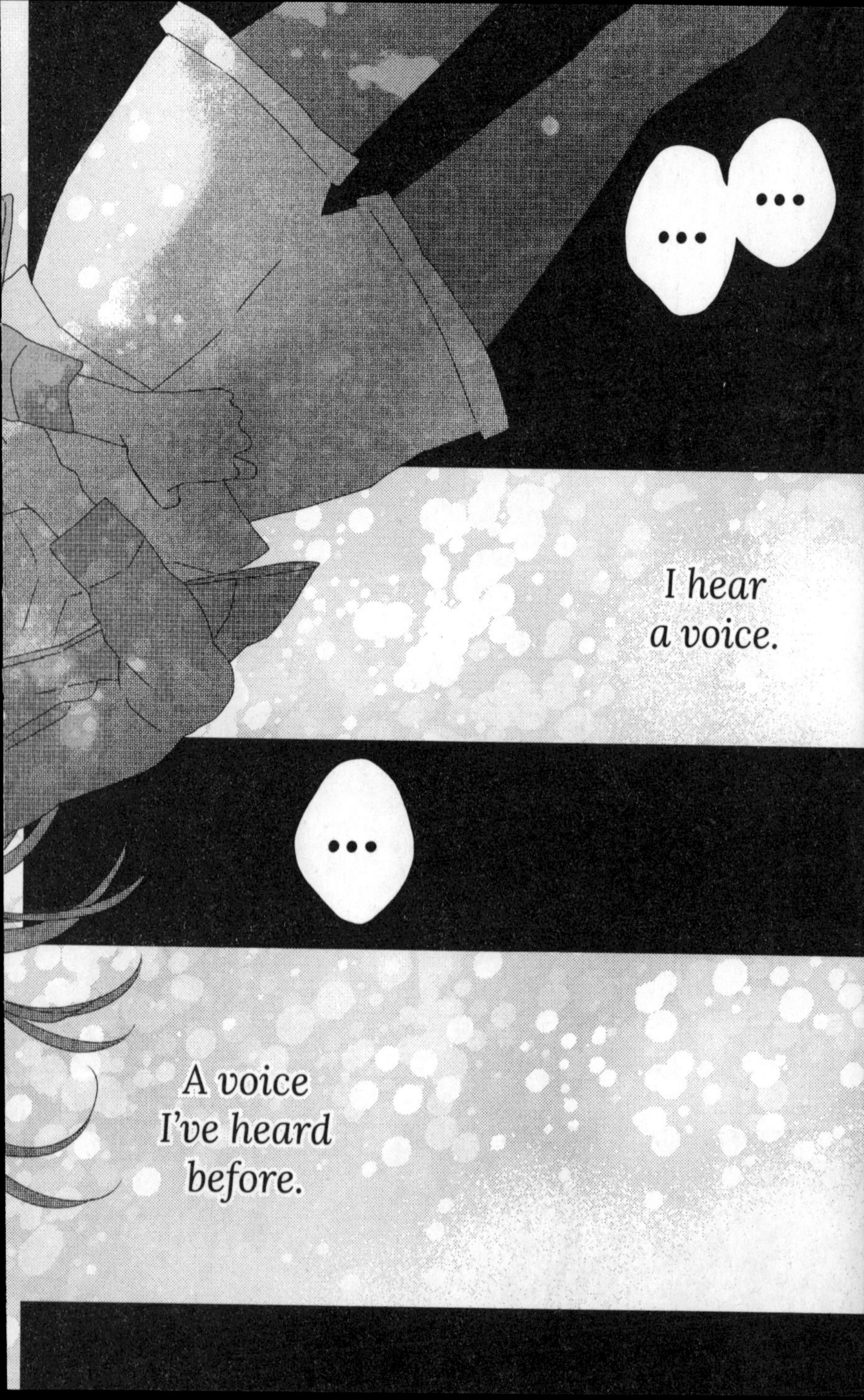
...
...
I hear a voice.
...
A voice I've heard before.

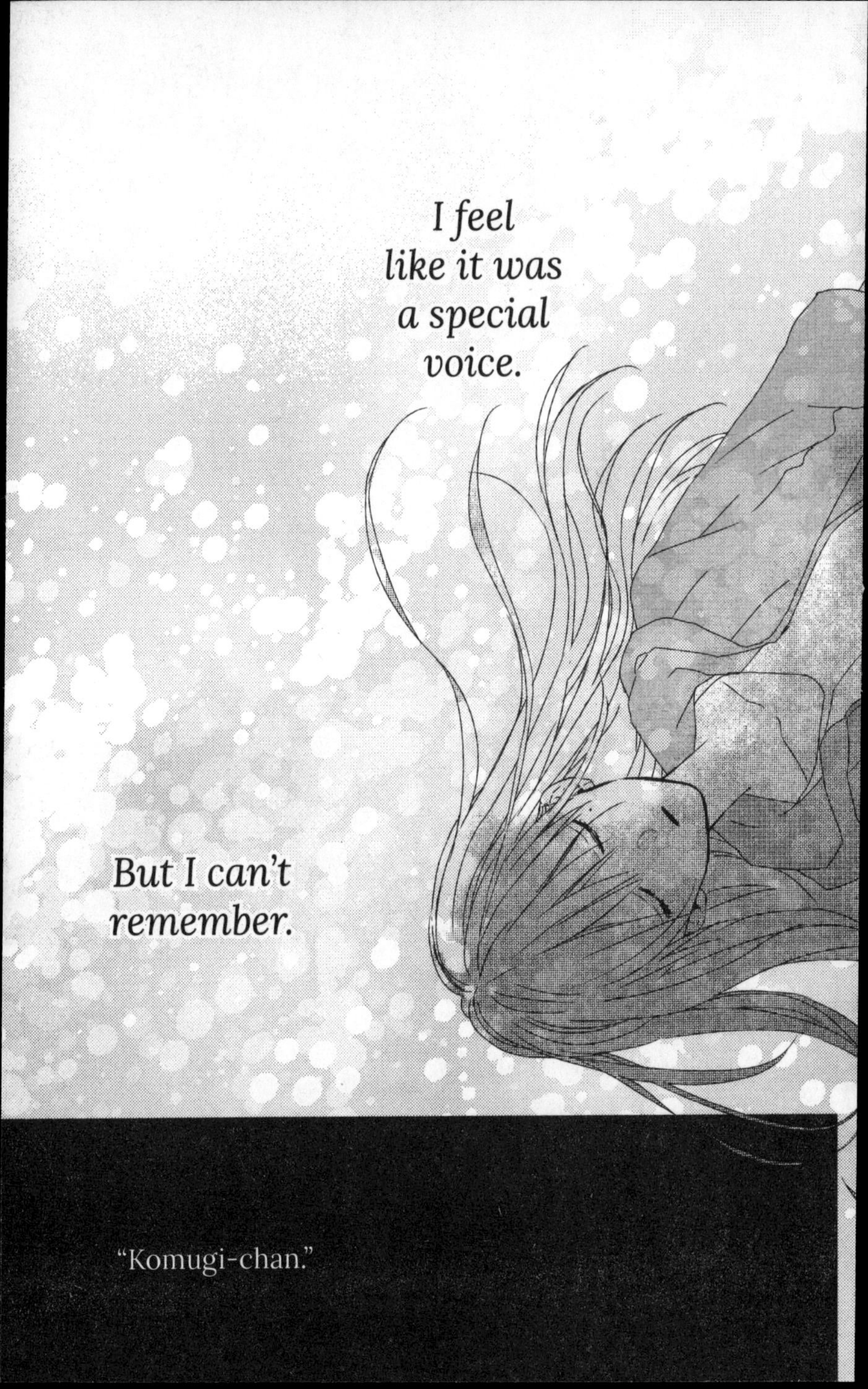
I feel like it was a special voice.
But I can't remember.
"Komugi-chan."

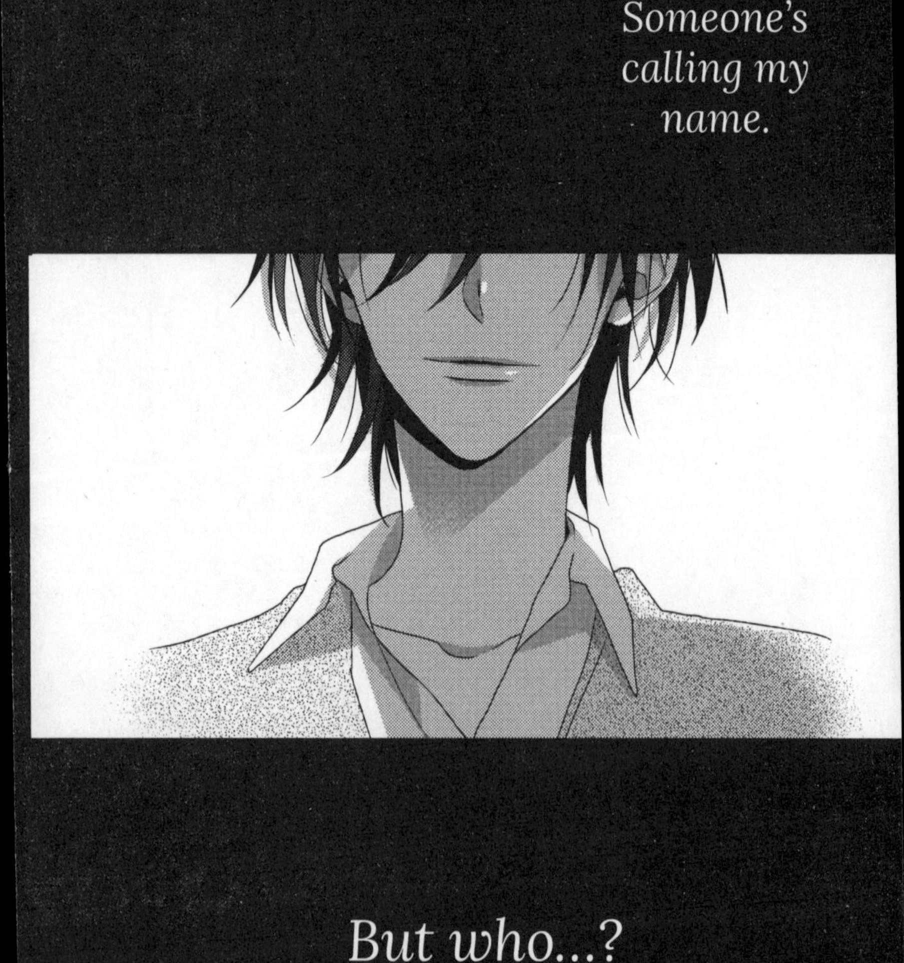
Someone's calling my name.
But who...?

That Wolf-Boy is Mine!

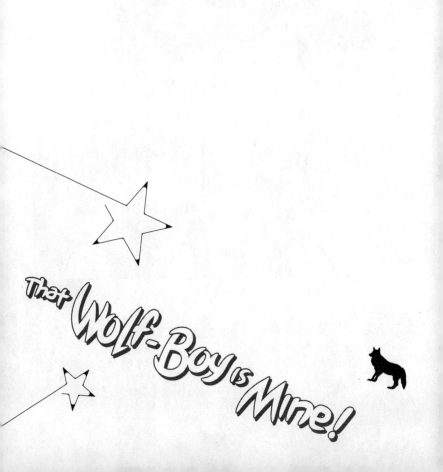

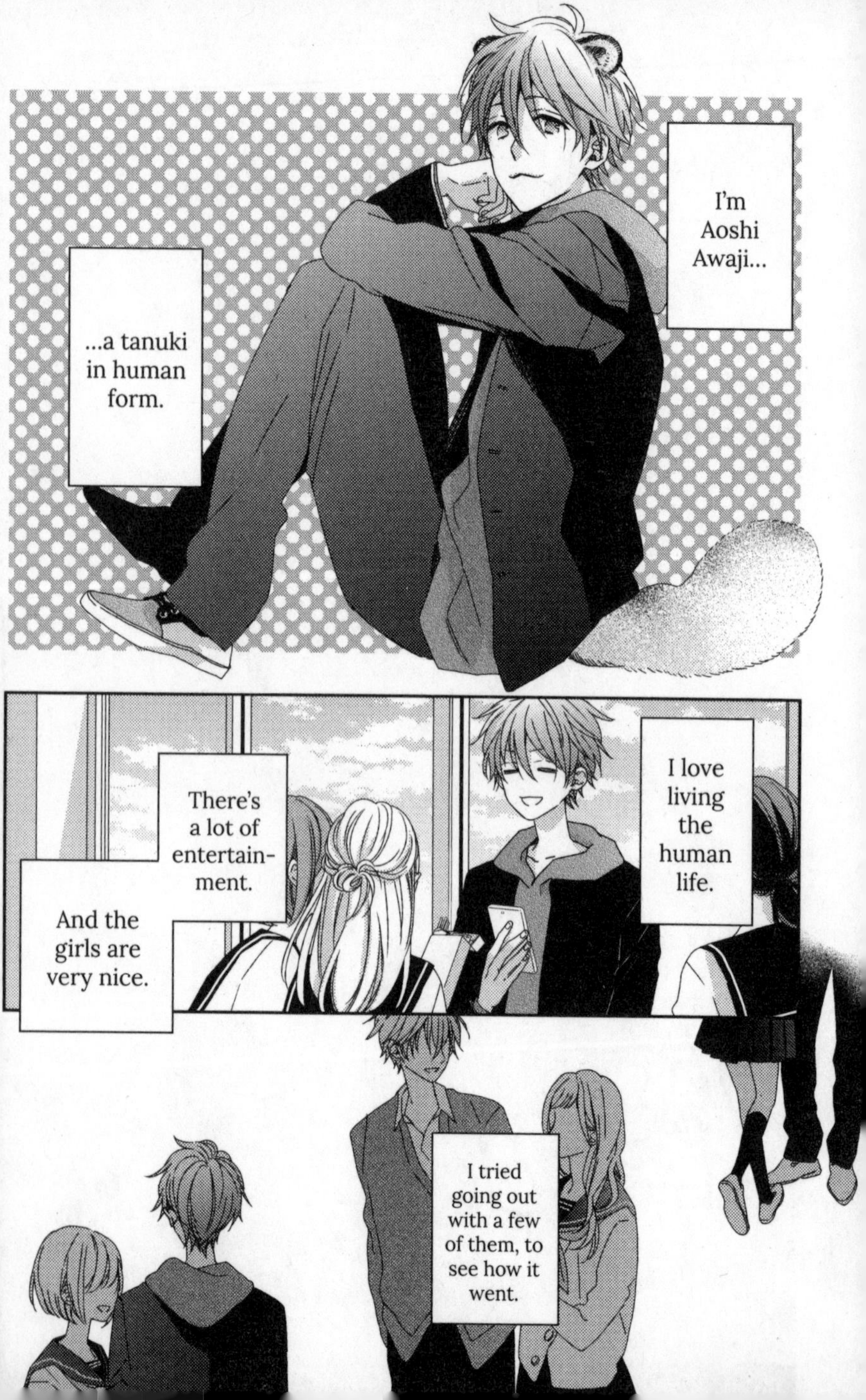
I'm Aoshi Awaji...
...a tanuki in human form.
I love living the human life.
There's a lot of entertain-ment.
And the girls are very nice.
I tried going out with a few of them, to see how it went.

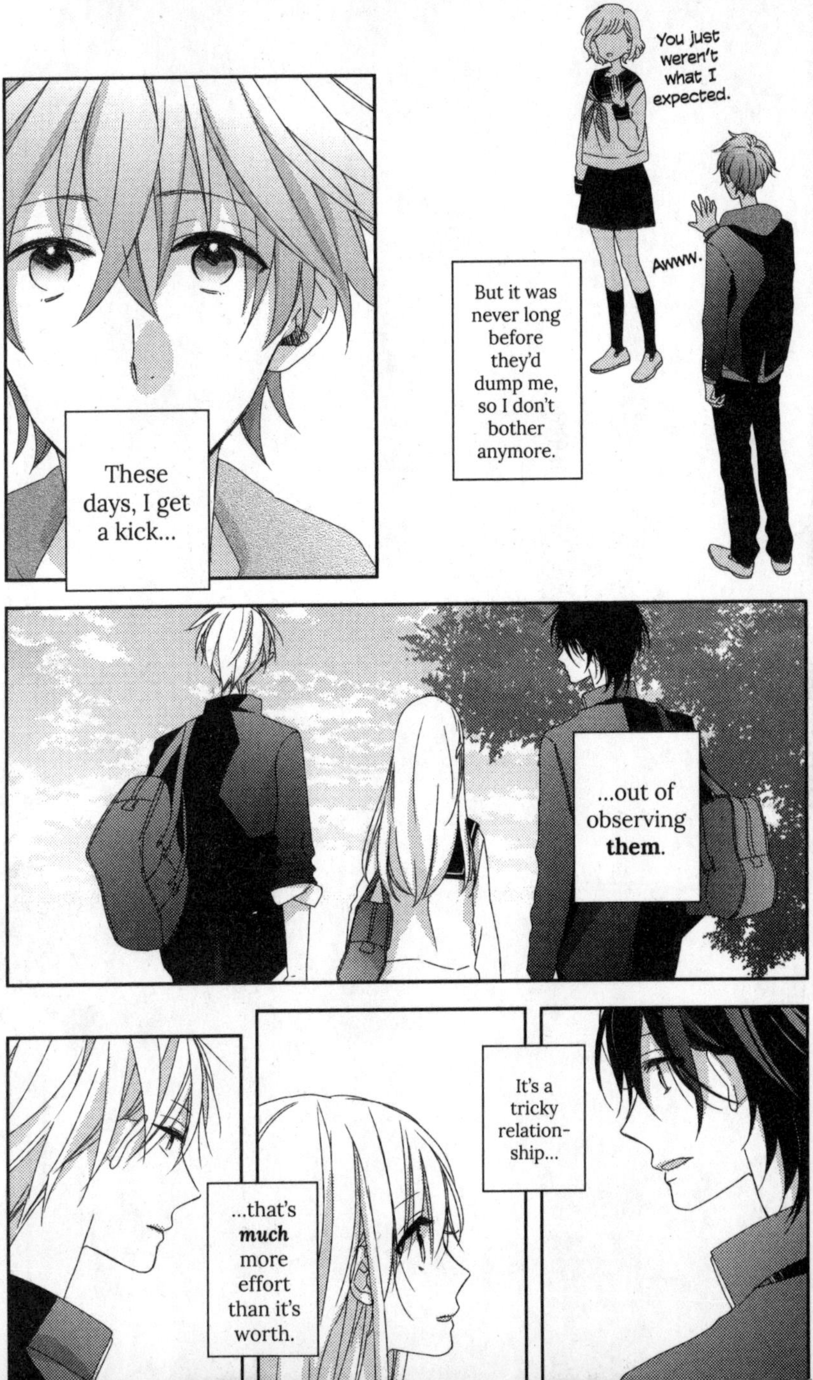
You just weren't what I expected.
Awww.
But it was never long before they'd dump me, so I don't bother anymore.
These days, I get a kick...
...out of observing **them**.
It's a tricky relation-ship...
...that's **much** more effort than it's worth.

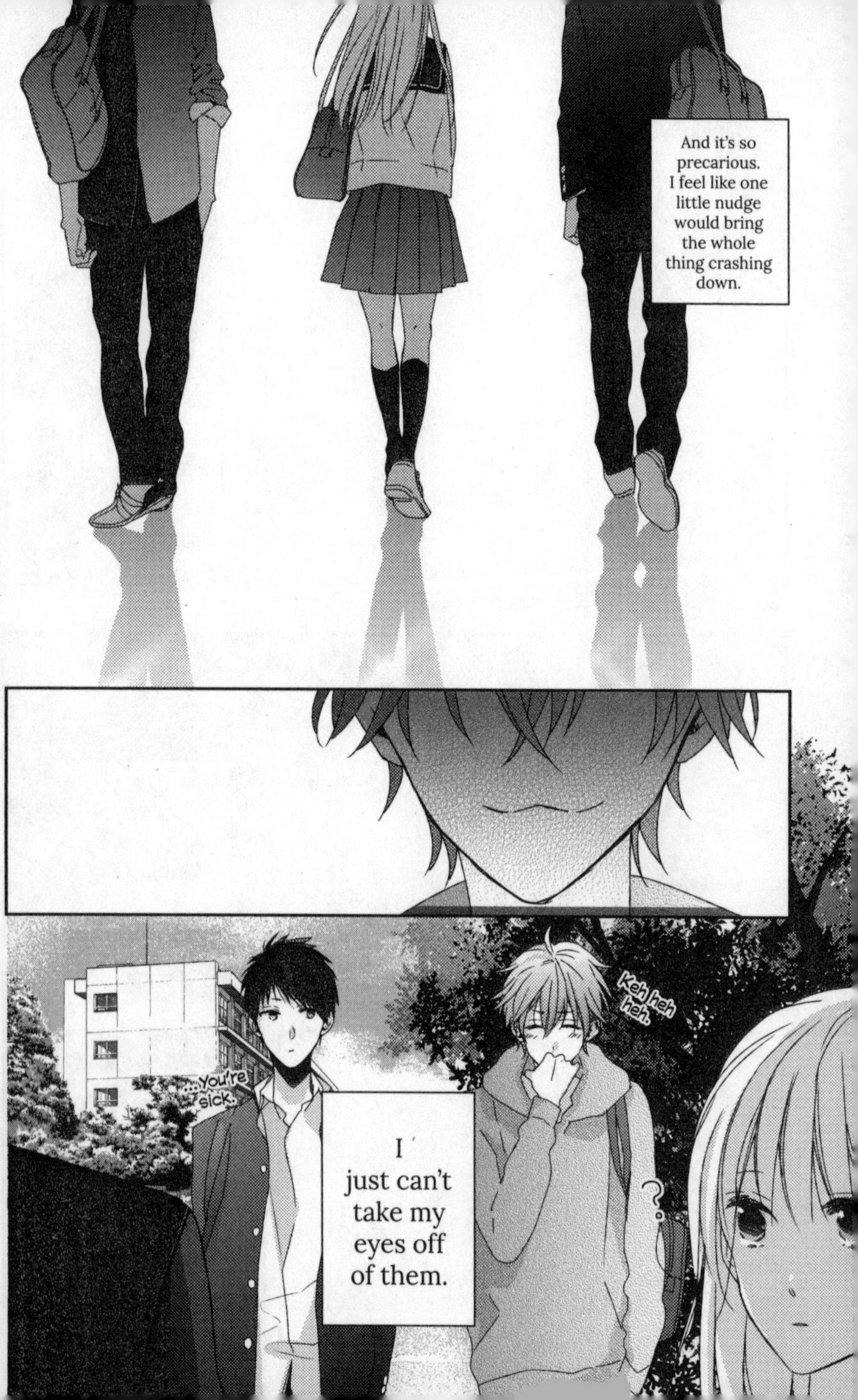

And it's so precarious. I feel like one little nudge would bring the whole thing crashing down.
Keh heh heh.
?
I just can't take my eyes off of them.
...You're sick.

Afterword

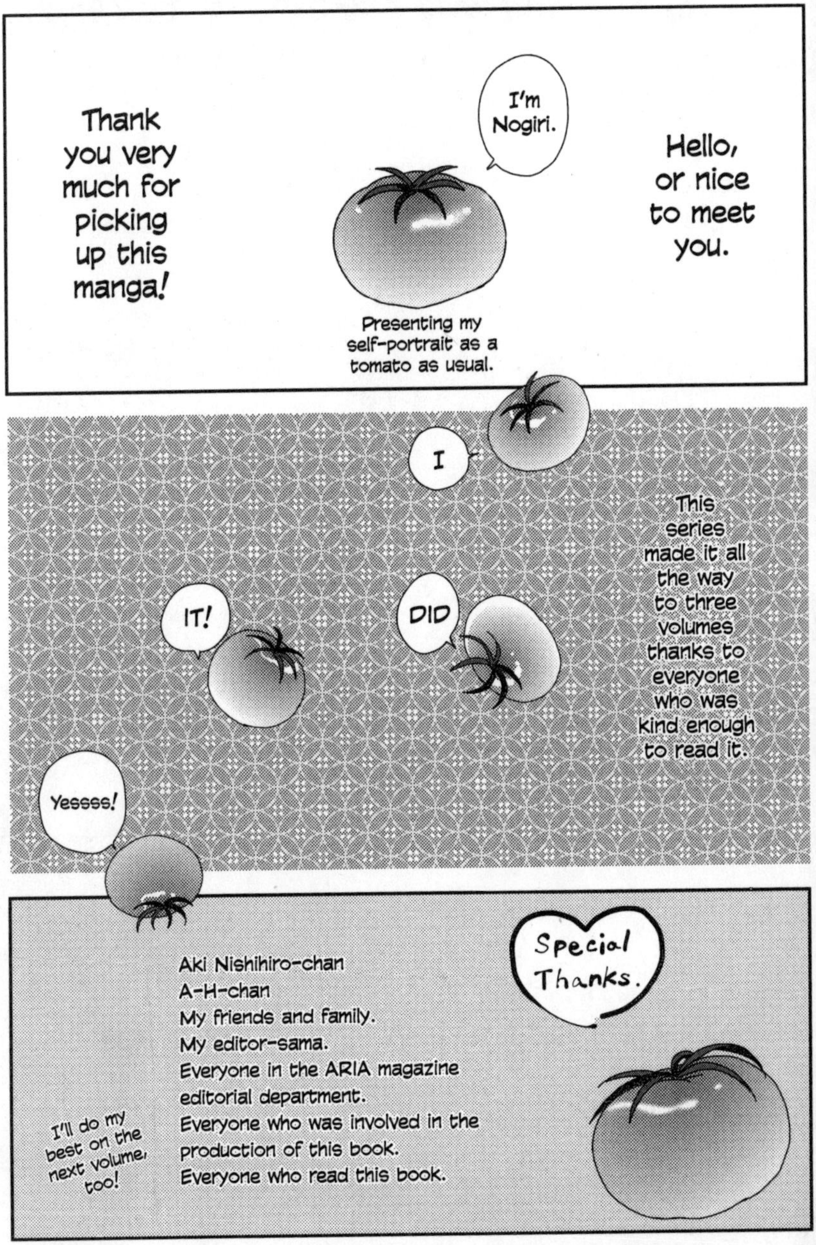
Hello, or nice to meet you.
I'm Nogiri.
Thank you very much for picking up this manga!
Presenting my self-portrait as a tomato as usual.
This series made it all the way to three volumes thanks to everyone who was kind enough to read it.
I
DID
IT!
Yessss!
Special Thanks.
Aki Nishihiro-chan
A-H-chan
My friends and family.
My editor-sama.
Everyone in the ARIA magazine editorial department.
Everyone who was involved in the production of this book.
Everyone who read this book.
I'll do my best on the next volume, too!

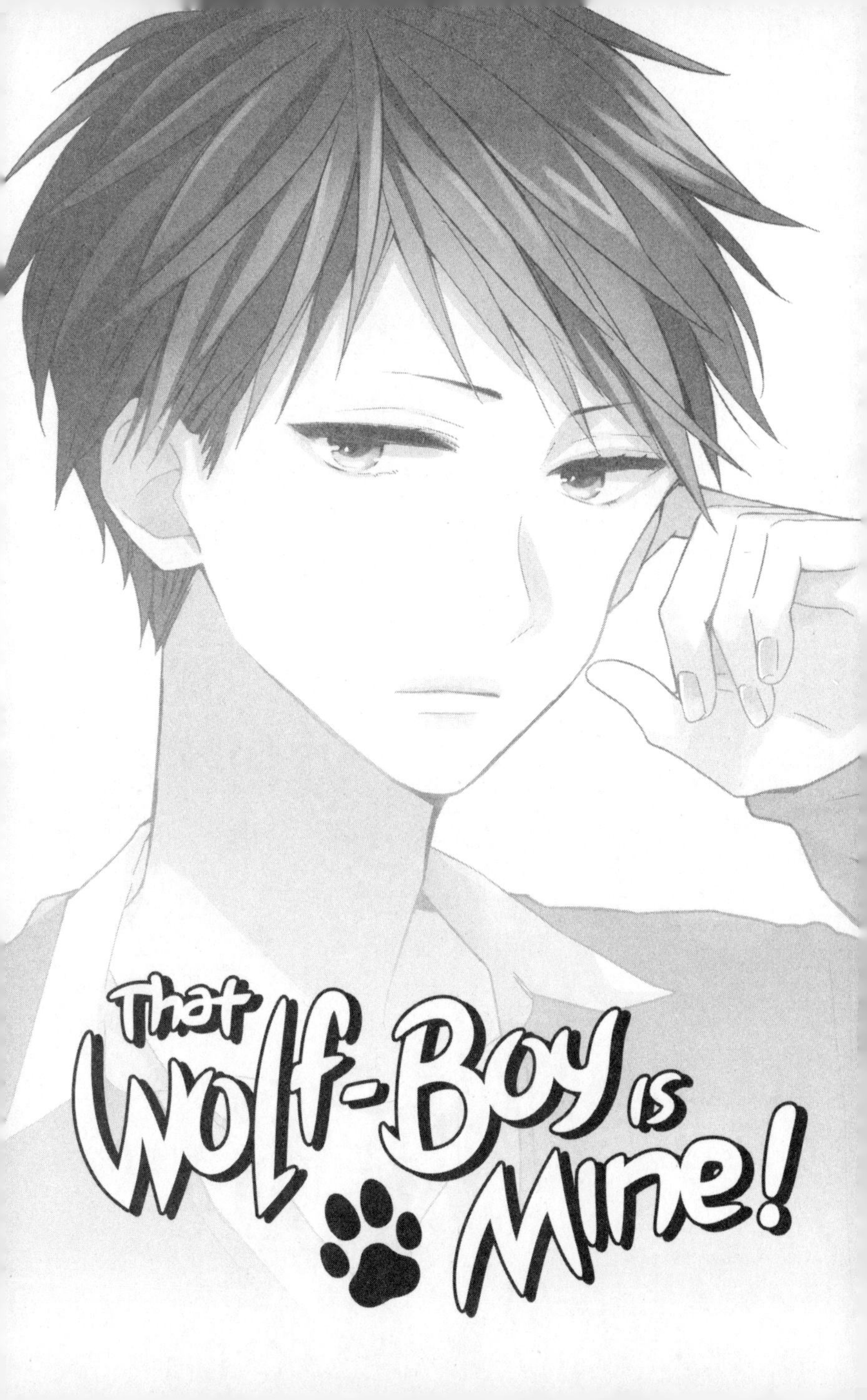
That Wolf-Boy is Mine!

That Wolf-Boy is Mine!

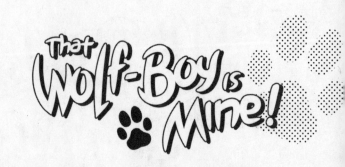

Chapter 14

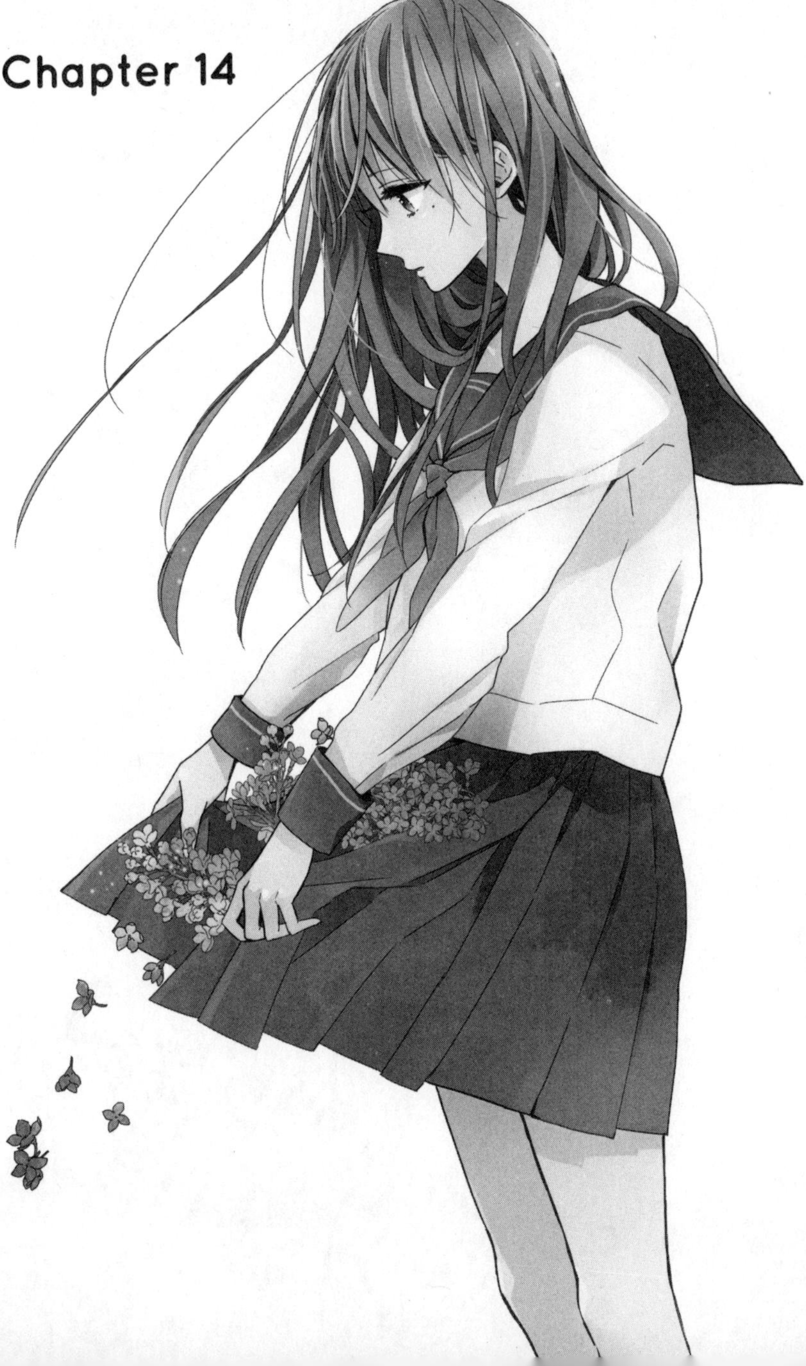

That Wolf-Boy is Mine!

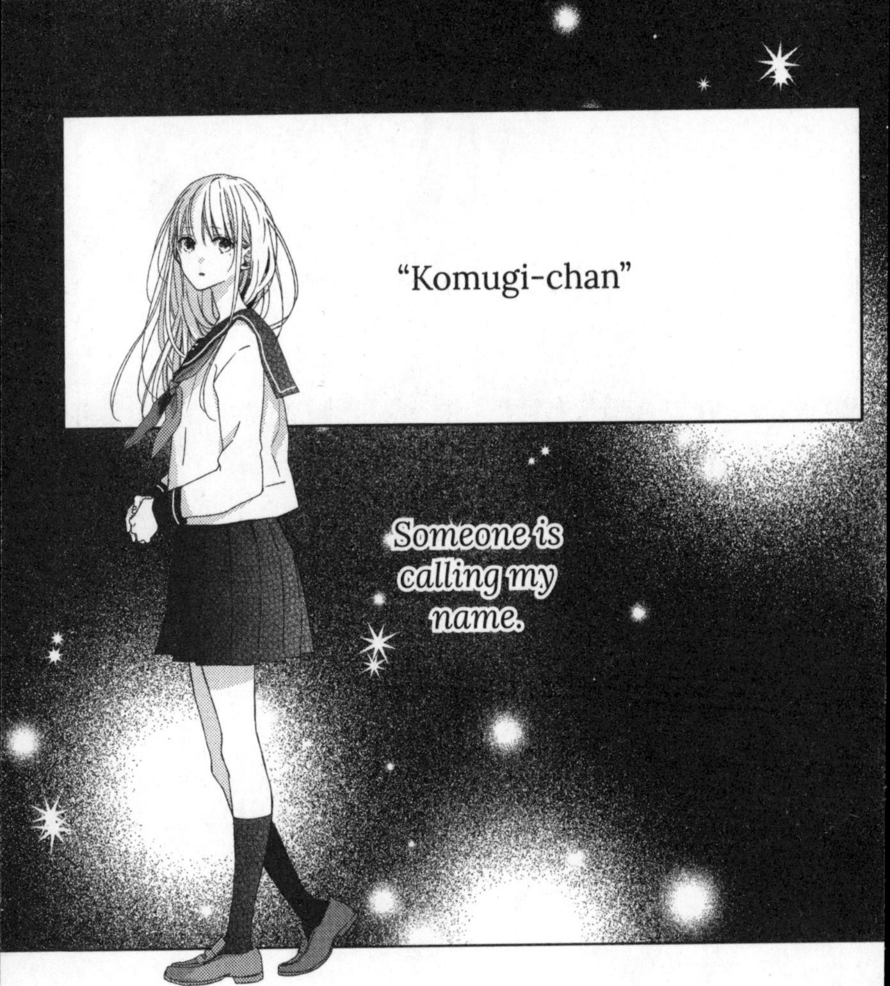
"Komugi-chan"
Someone is calling my name.

That Wolf-Boy is Mine!

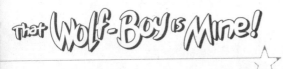

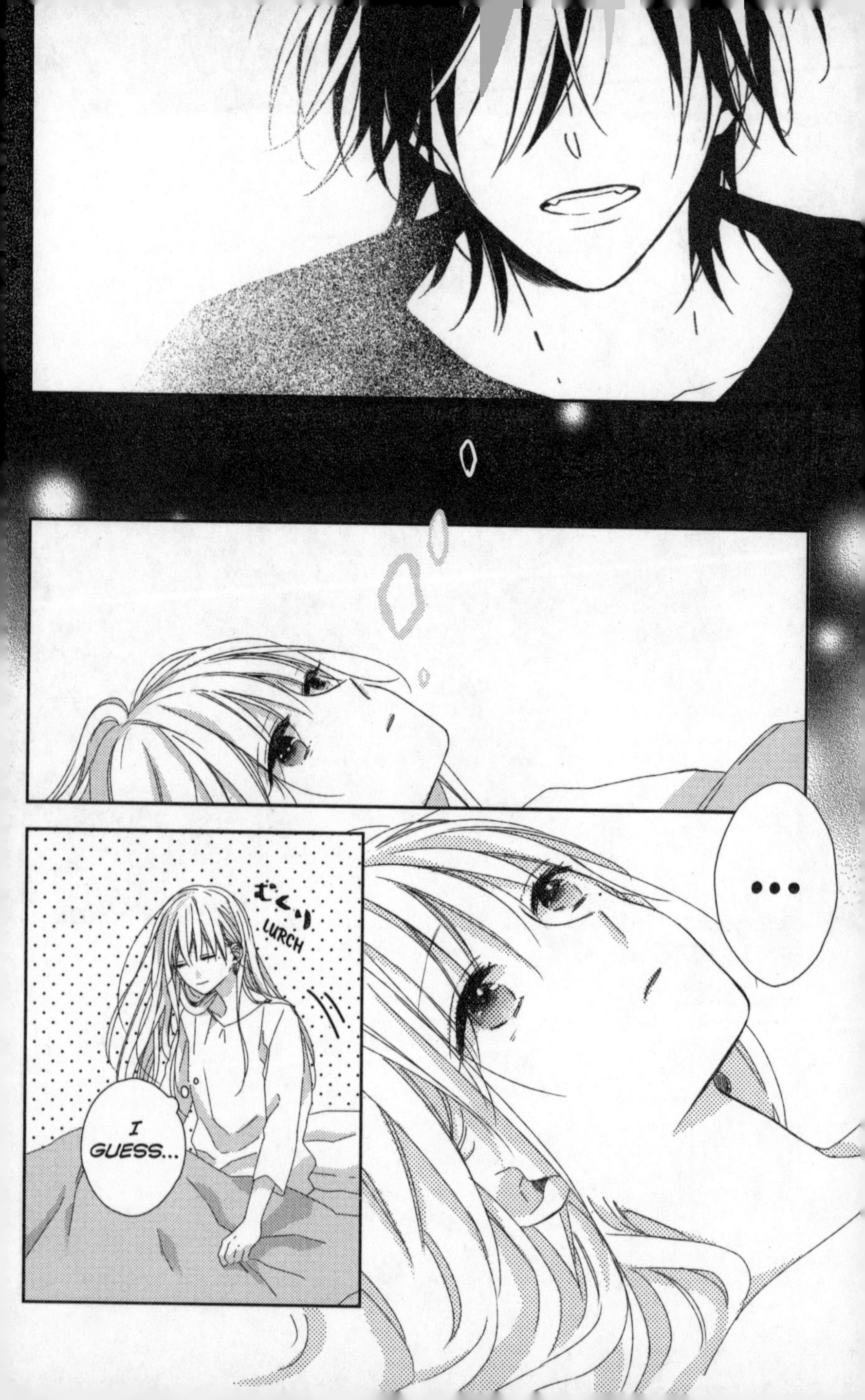
...
むくり
LURCH
I GUESS...

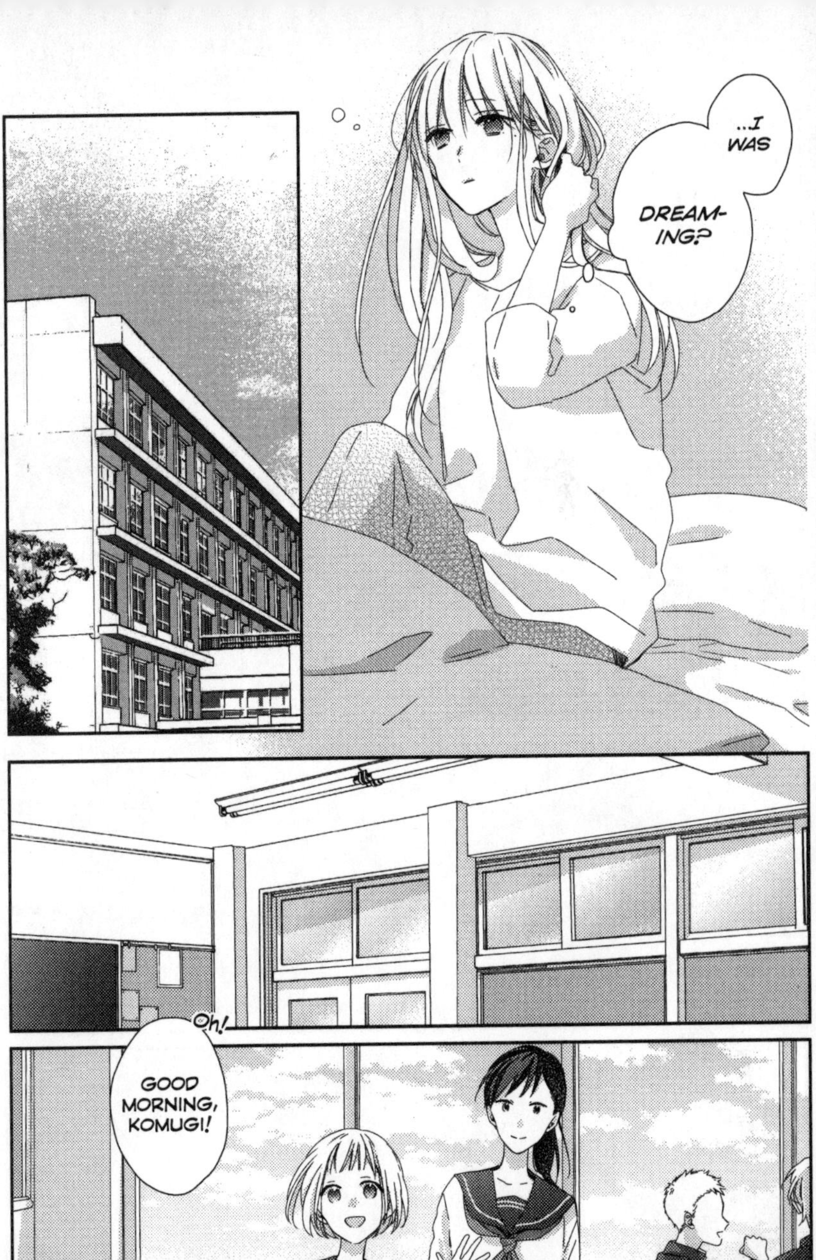
...I WAS DREAMING?
Oh!
GOOD MORNING, KOMUGI!

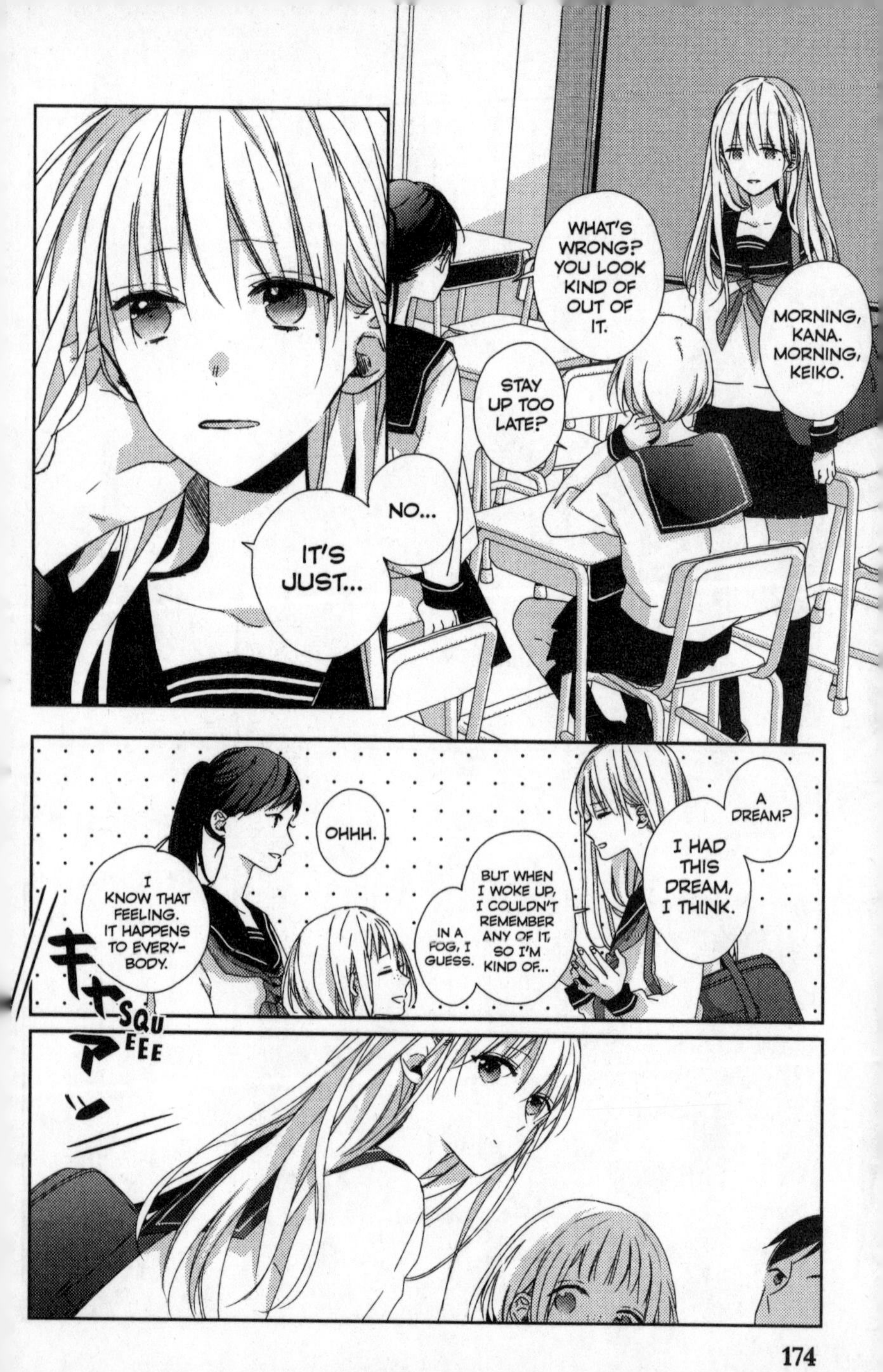
MORNING, KANA. MORNING, KEIKO.
WHAT'S WRONG? YOU LOOK KIND OF OUT OF IT.
STAY UP TOO LATE?
NO...
IT'S JUST...
A DREAM?
I HAD THIS DREAM, I THINK.
BUT WHEN I WOKE UP, I COULDN'T REMEMBER ANY OF IT, SO I'M KIND OF...
IN A FOG, I GUESS.
OHHH.
I KNOW THAT FEELING. IT HAPPENS TO EVERY-BODY.
キャ SQUEEEE
ア
ッ

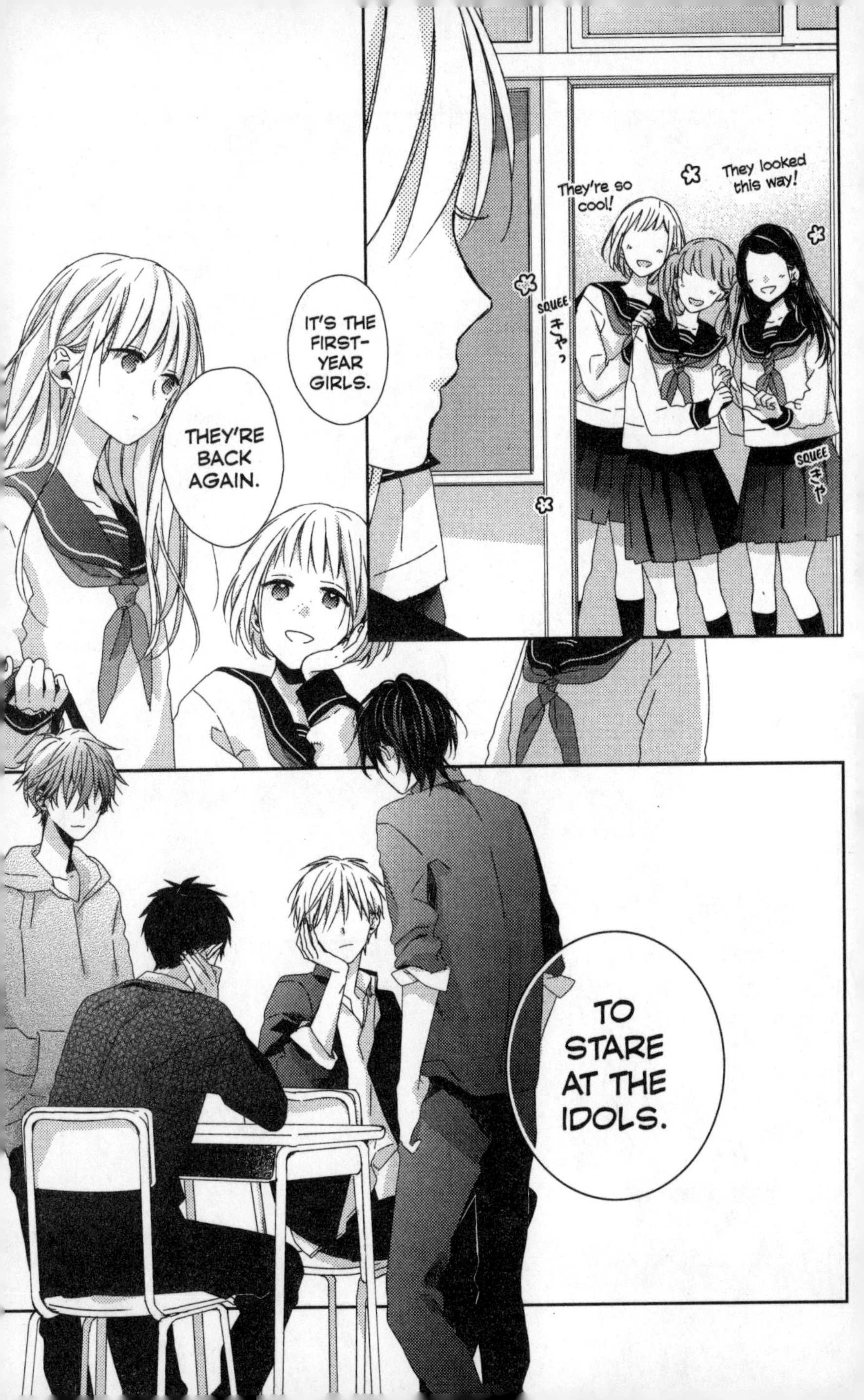

They looked this way!
They're so cool!
SQUEE キャッ
SQUEE キャ
IT'S THE FIRST-YEAR GIRLS.
THEY'RE BACK AGAIN.
TO STARE AT THE IDOLS.

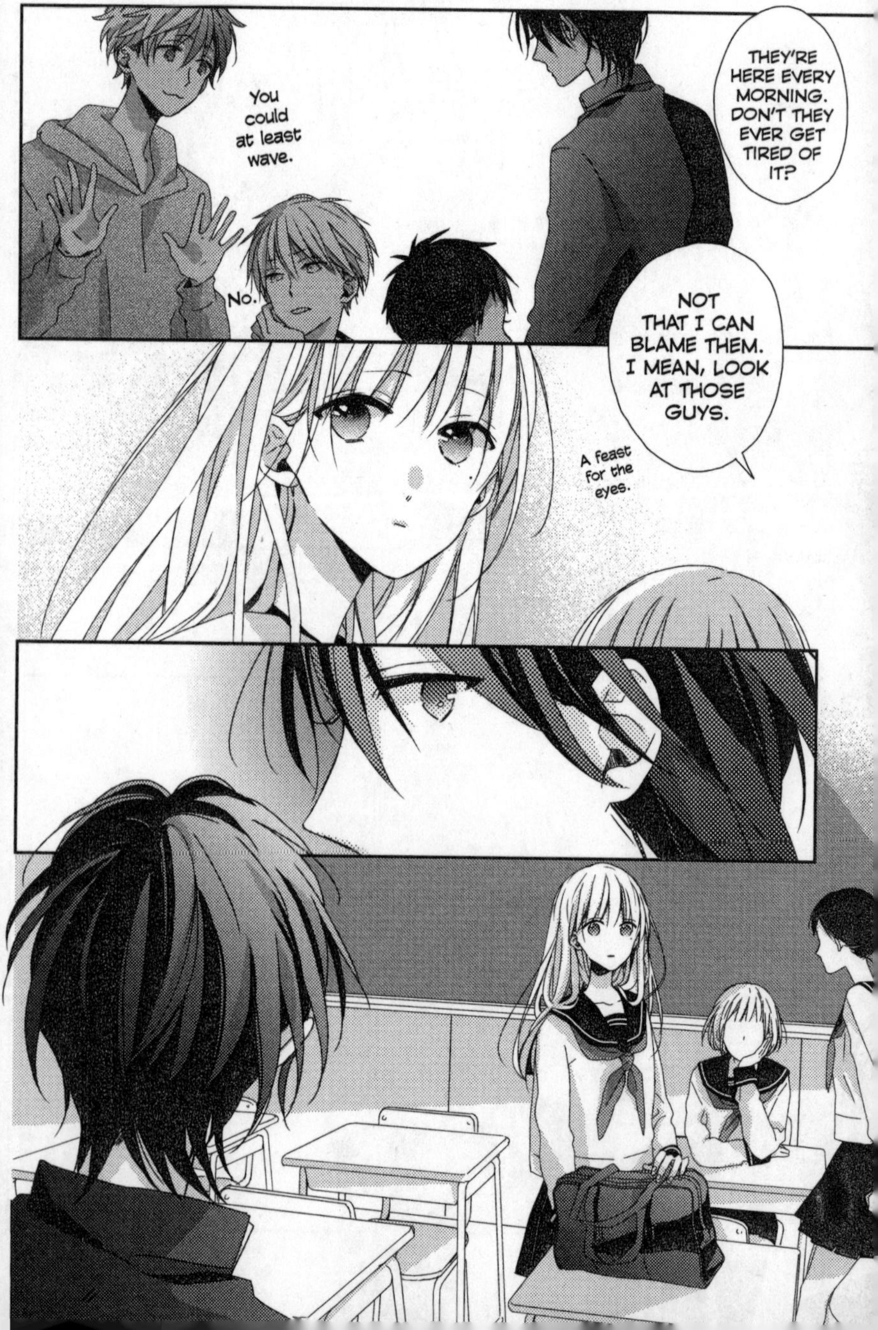
THEY'RE HERE EVERY MORNING. DON'T THEY EVER GET TIRED OF IT?
You could at least wave.
No.
NOT THAT I CAN BLAME THEM. I MEAN, LOOK AT THOSE GUYS.
A feast for the eyes.

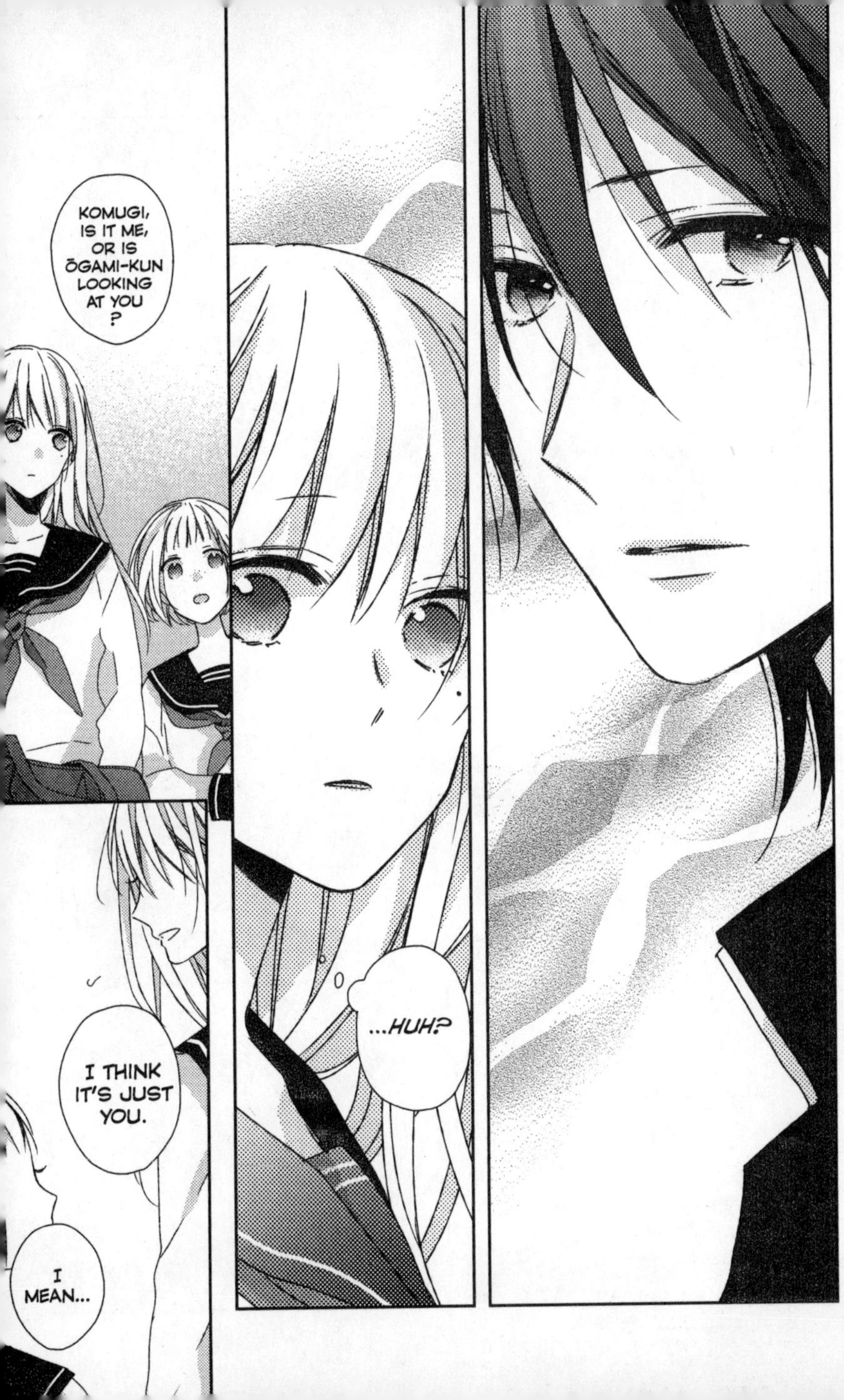
...HUH?
KOMUGI, IS IT ME, OR IS ŌGAMI-KUN LOOKING AT YOU?
I THINK IT'S JUST YOU.
I MEAN...

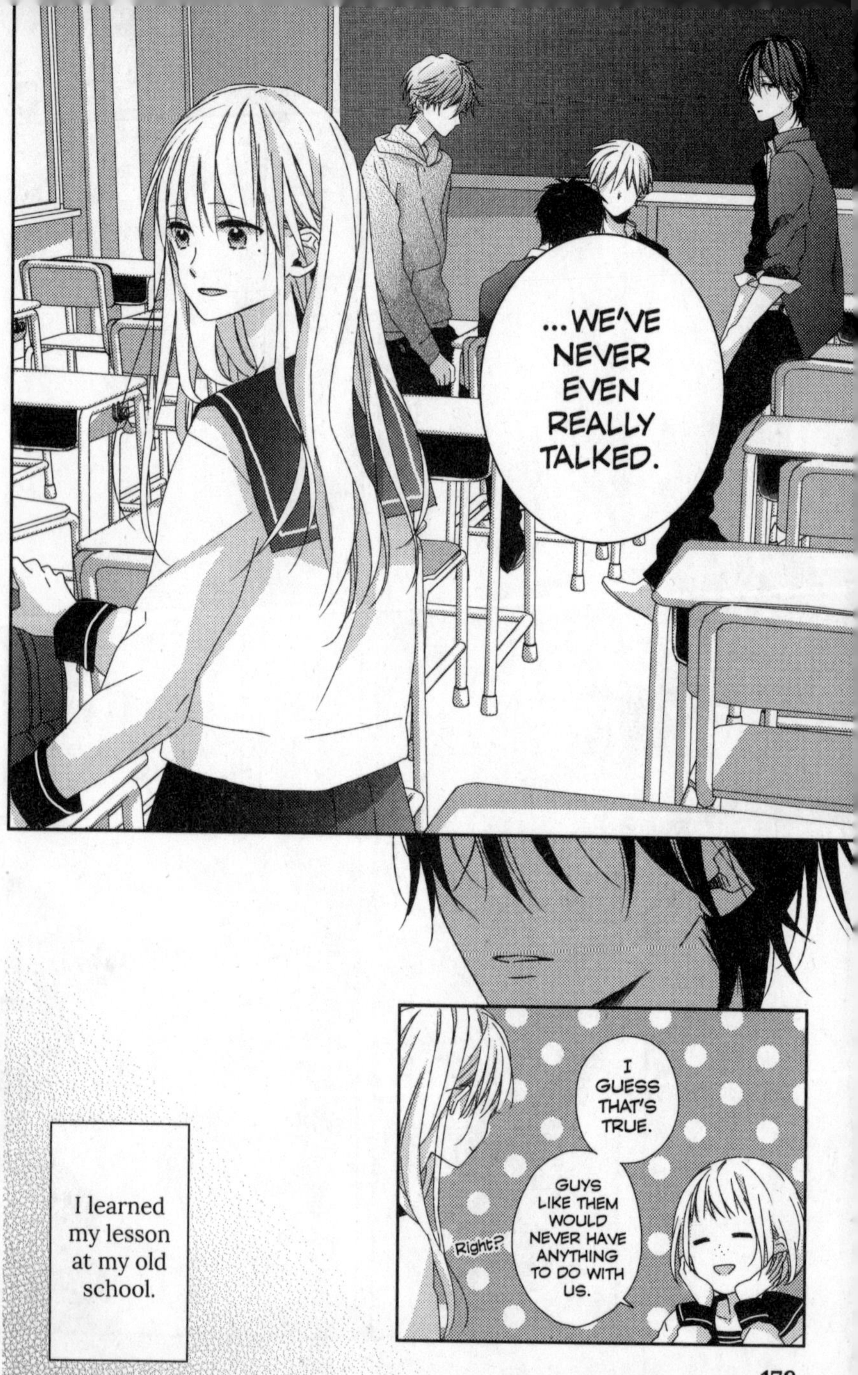
...WE'VE NEVER EVEN REALLY TALKED.
I GUESS THAT'S TRUE.
GUYS LIKE THEM WOULD NEVER HAVE ANYTHING TO DO WITH US.
Right?
I learned my lesson at my old school.

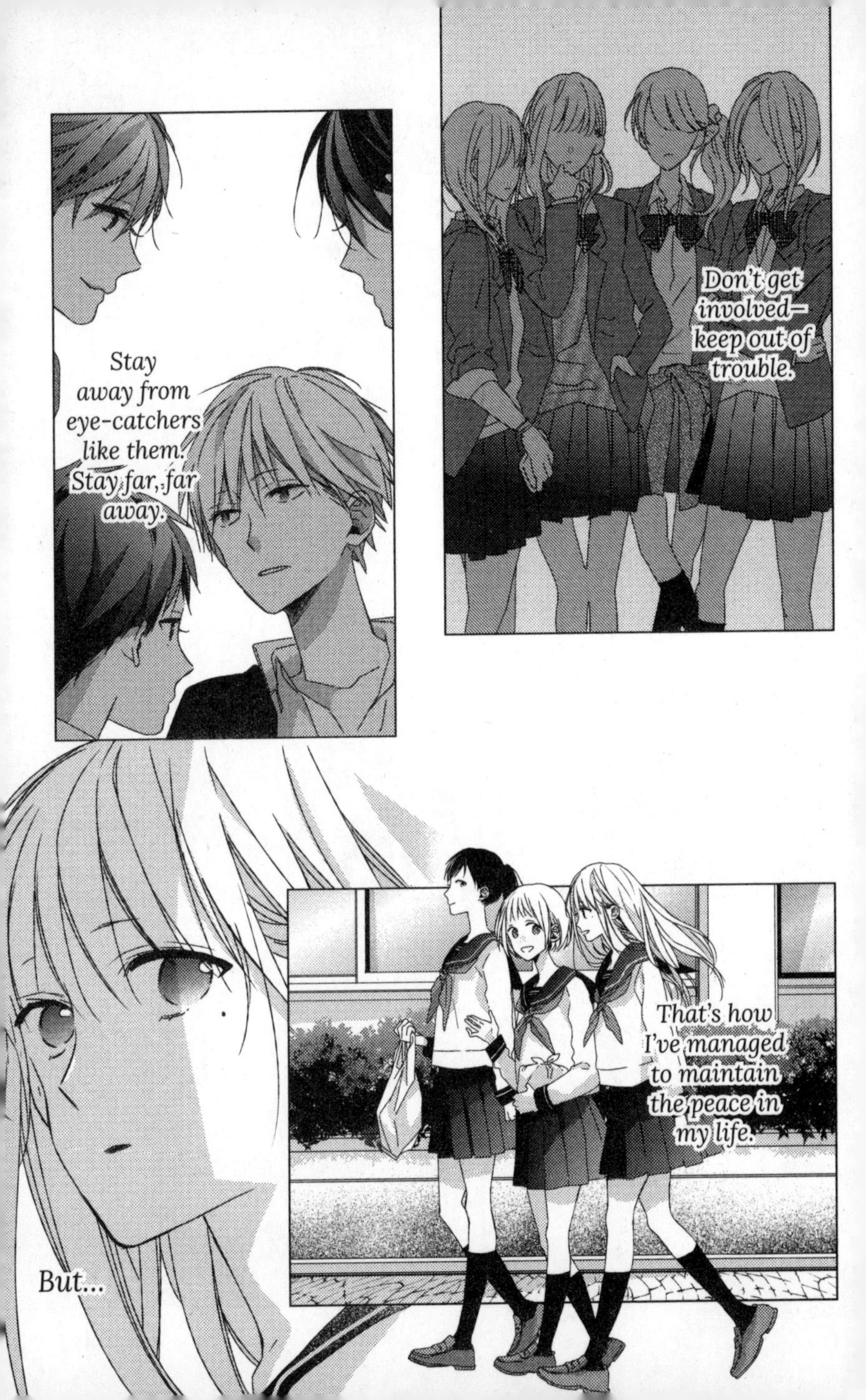
Don't get involved—keep out of trouble.
Stay away from eye-catchers like them. Stay far, far away.
That's how I've managed to maintain the peace in my life.
But...

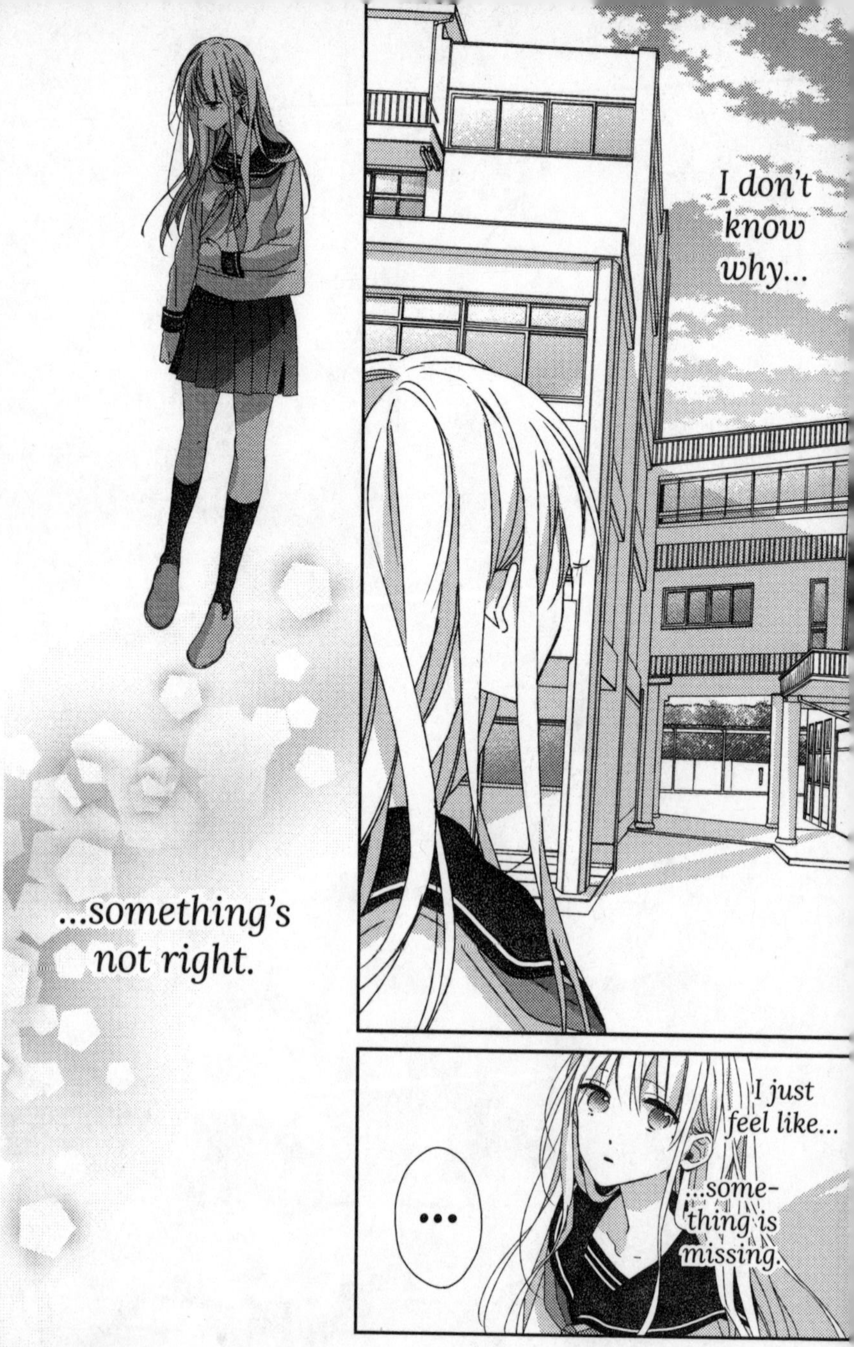
I don't know why...
I just feel like...
...some-thing is missing.
...
...something's not right.

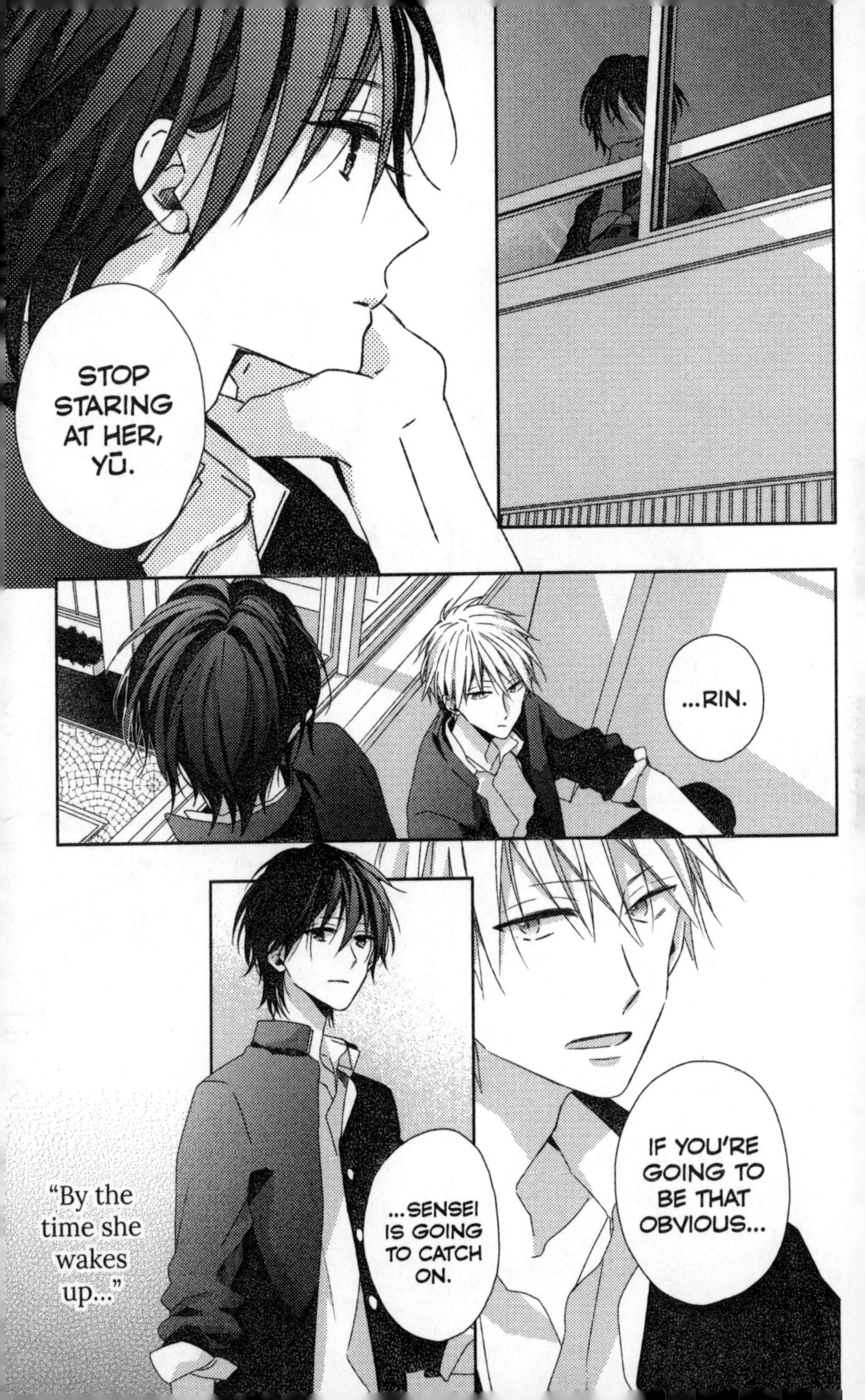
STOP STARING AT HER, YŪ.
...RIN.
IF YOU'RE GOING TO BE THAT OBVIOUS...
...SENSEI IS GOING TO CATCH ON.
"By the time she wakes up..."

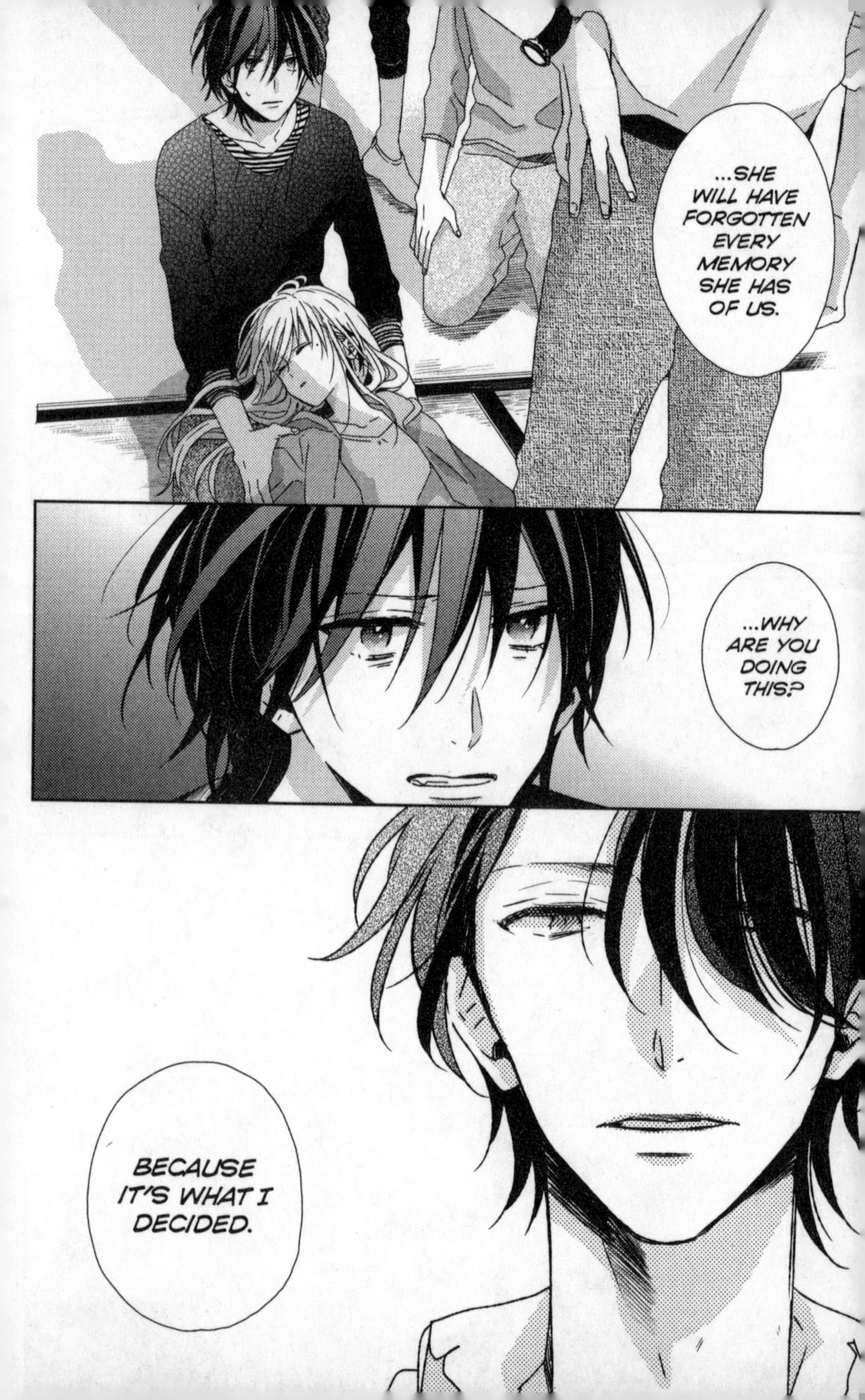
...SHE WILL HAVE FORGOTTEN EVERY MEMORY SHE HAS OF US.
...WHY ARE YOU DOING THIS?
BECAUSE IT'S WHAT I DECIDED.

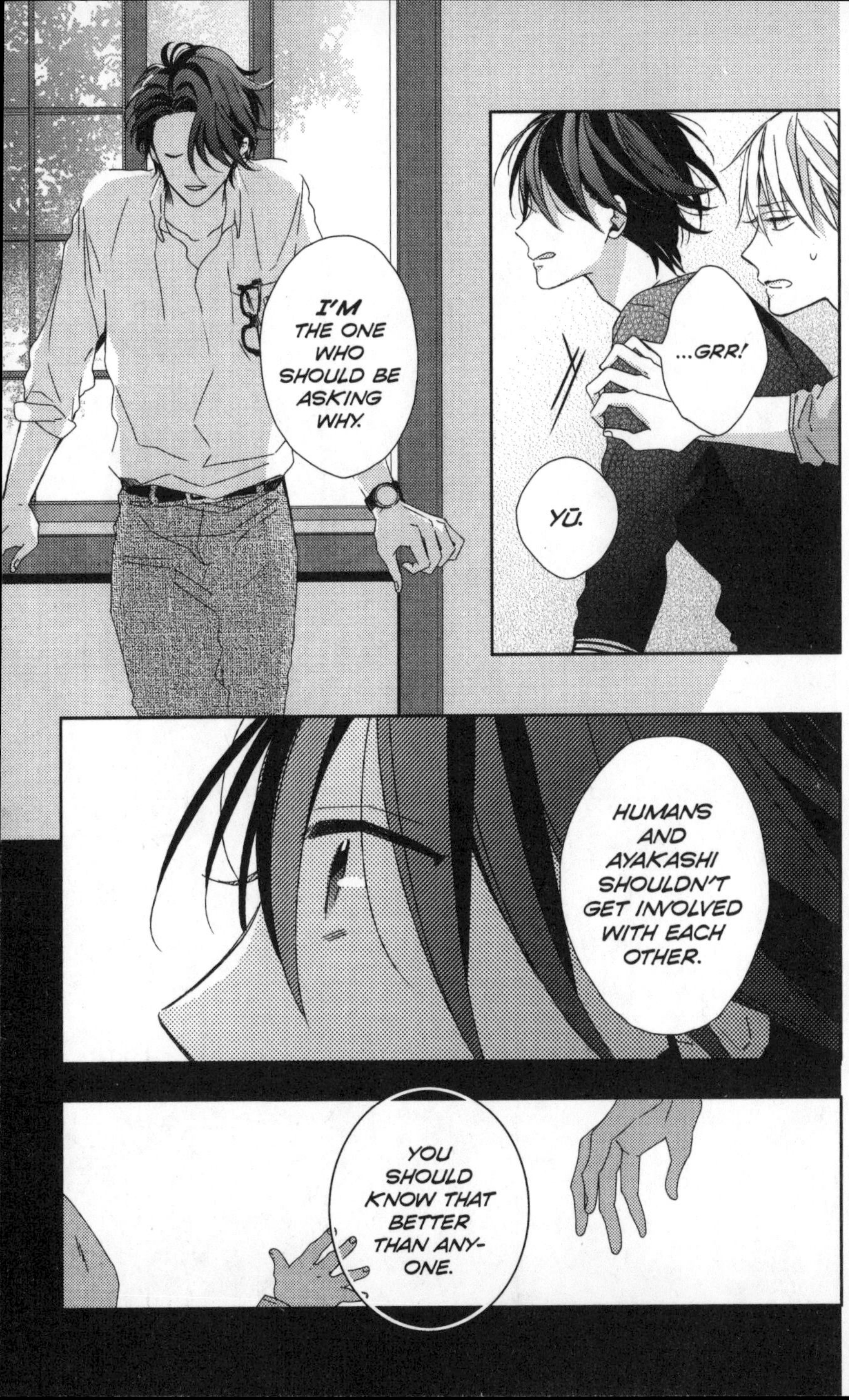
...GRR!
YŪ.
I'M THE ONE WHO SHOULD BE ASKING WHY.
HUMANS AND AYAKASHI SHOULDN'T GET INVOLVED WITH EACH OTHER.
YOU SHOULD KNOW THAT BETTER THAN ANY-ONE.

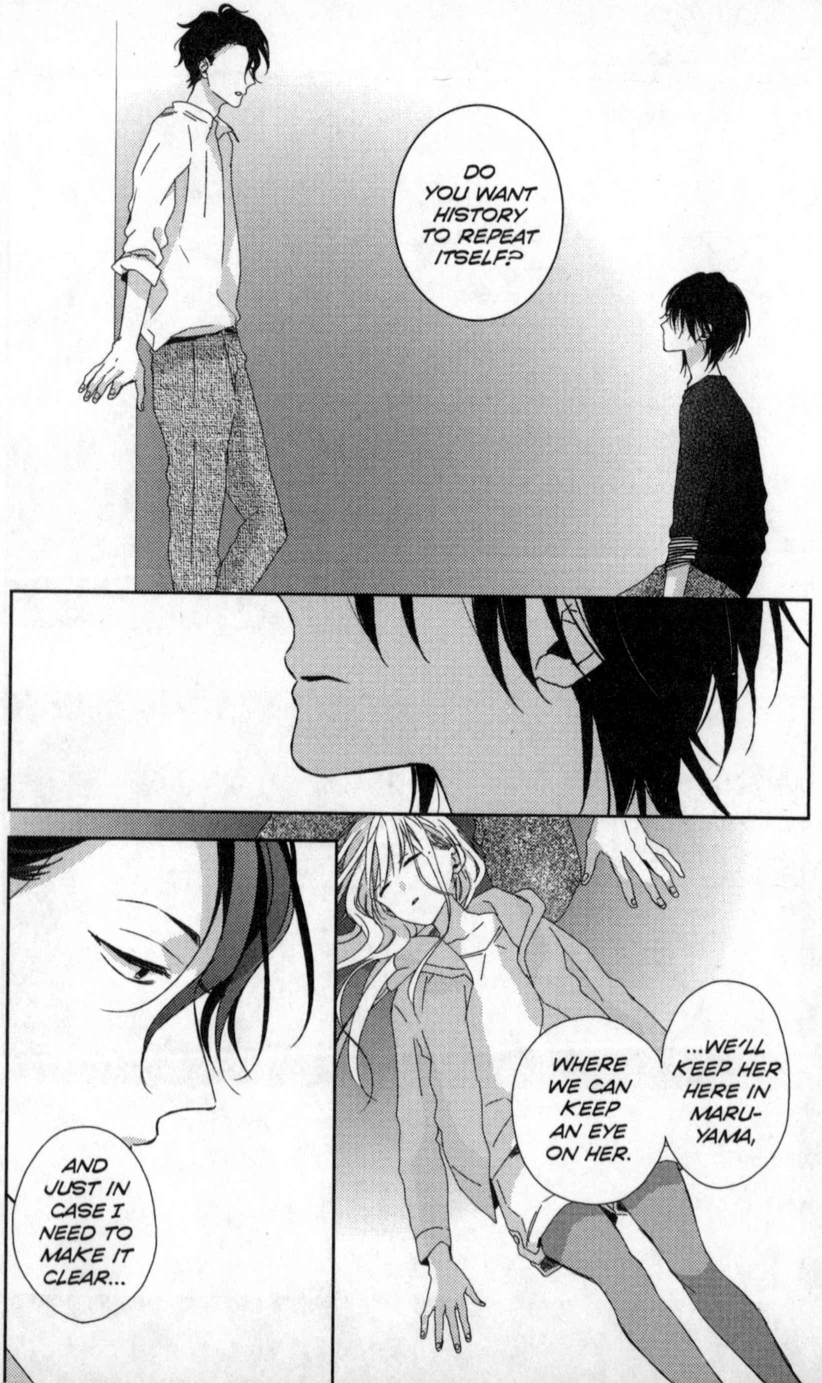
DO YOU WANT HISTORY TO REPEAT ITSELF?
...WE'LL KEEP HER HERE IN MARU-YAMA,
WHERE WE CAN KEEP AN EYE ON HER.
AND JUST IN CASE I NEED TO MAKE IT CLEAR...

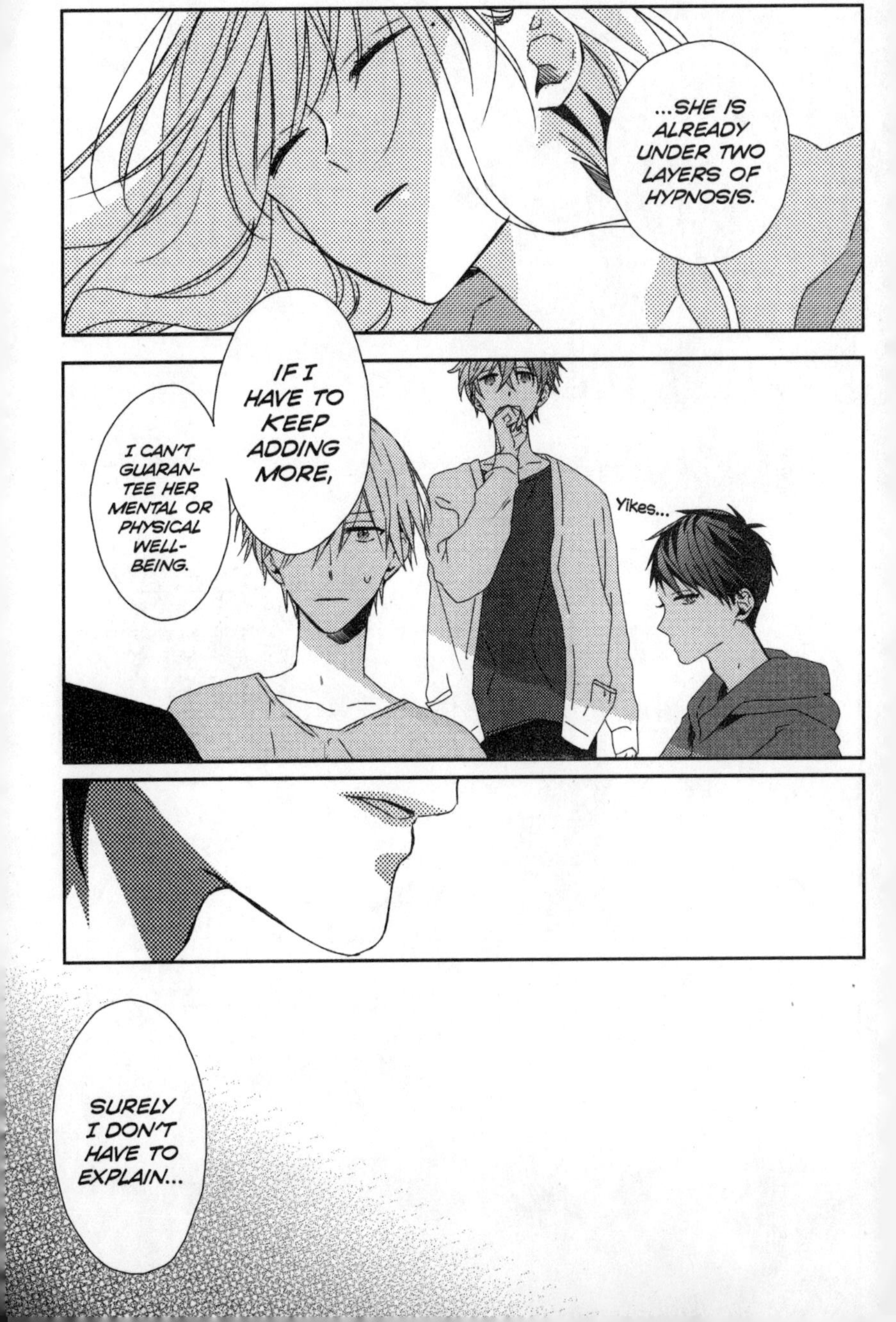
...SHE IS ALREADY UNDER TWO LAYERS OF HYPNOSIS.
IF I HAVE TO KEEP ADDING MORE,
I CAN'T GUARANTEE HER MENTAL OR PHYSICAL WELL-BEING.
Yikes...
SURELY I DON'T HAVE TO EXPLAIN...

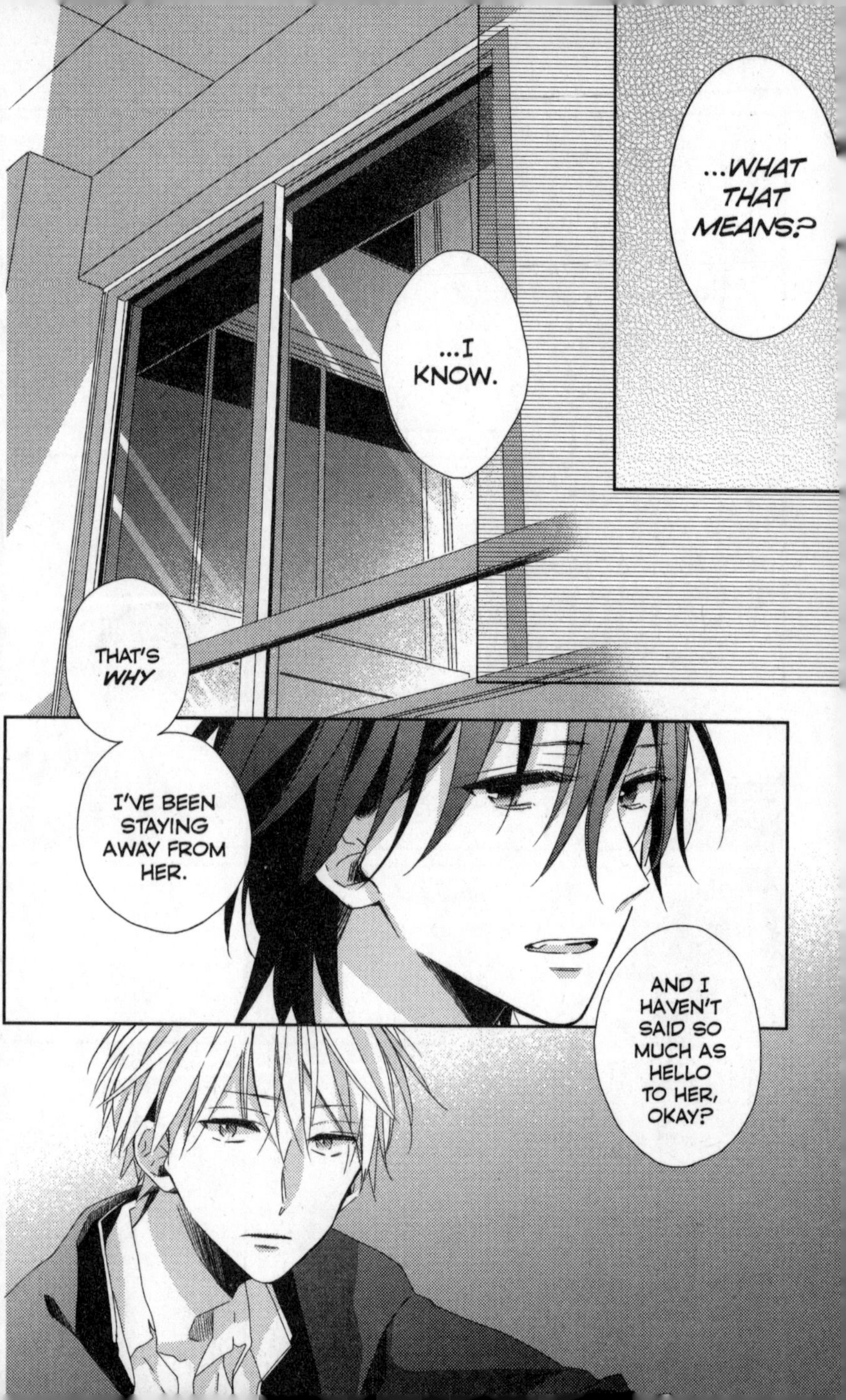
...WHAT THAT MEANS?
...I KNOW.
THAT'S *WHY*
I'VE BEEN STAYING AWAY FROM HER.
AND I HAVEN'T SAID SO MUCH AS HELLO TO HER, OKAY?

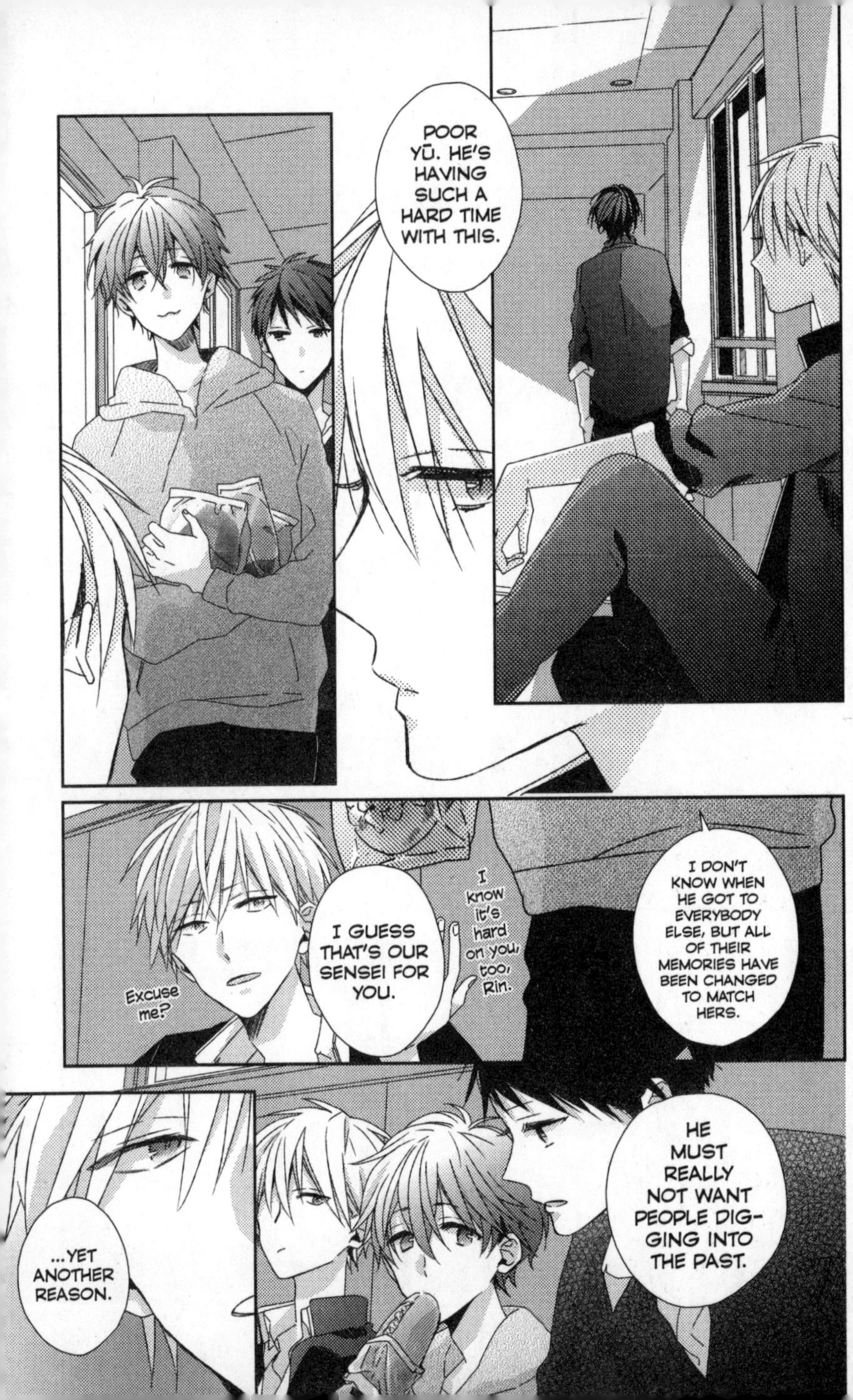
POOR YŪ. HE'S HAVING SUCH A HARD TIME WITH THIS.
I DON'T KNOW WHEN HE GOT TO EVERYBODY ELSE, BUT ALL OF THEIR MEMORIES HAVE BEEN CHANGED TO MATCH HERS.
I know it's hard on you, too, Rin.
I GUESS THAT'S OUR SENSEI FOR YOU.
Excuse me?
HE MUST REALLY NOT WANT PEOPLE DIG-GING INTO THE PAST.
...YET ANOTHER REASON.

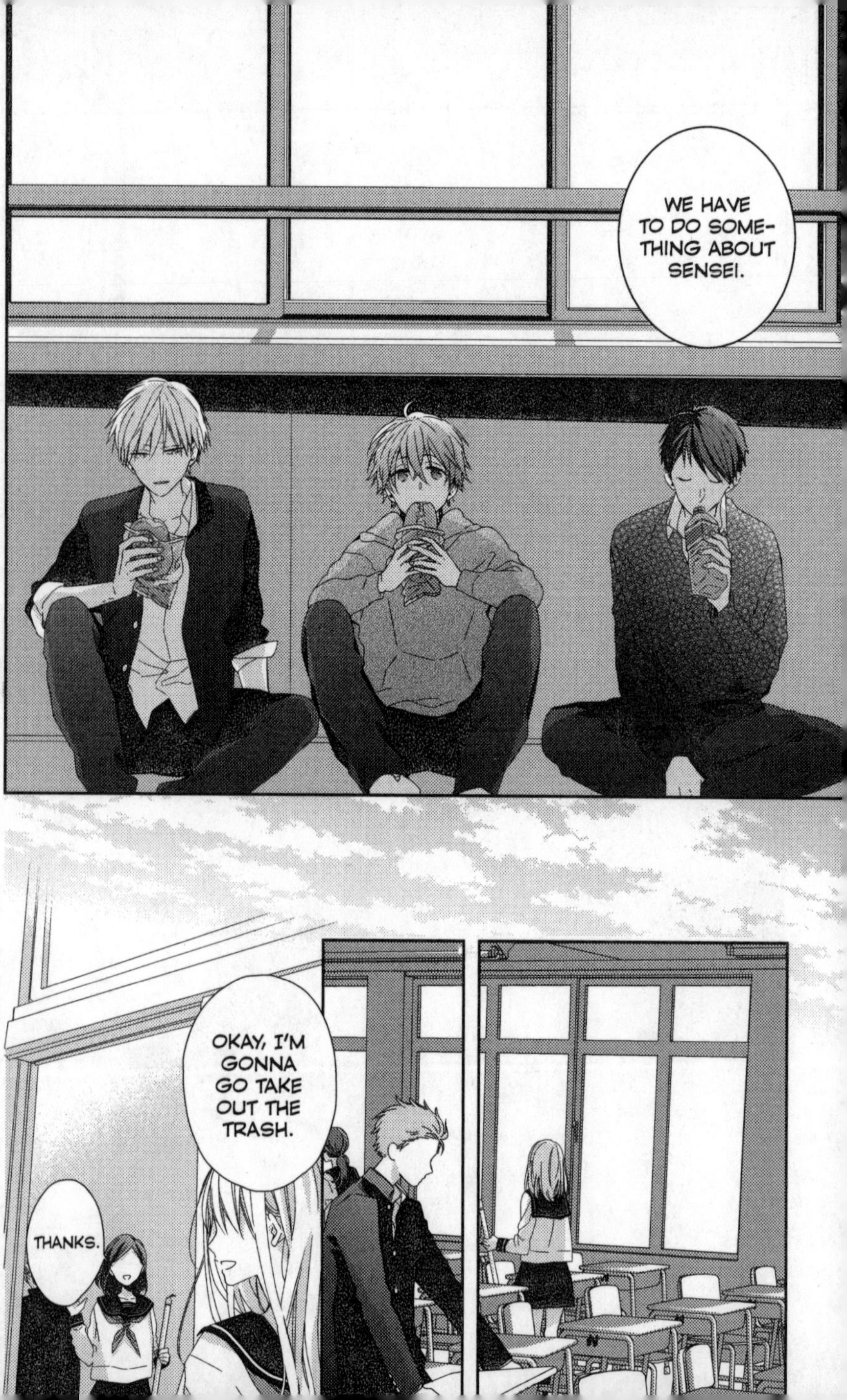
WE HAVE TO DO SOME-THING ABOUT SENSEI.
OKAY, I'M GONNA GO TAKE OUT THE TRASH.
THANKS.

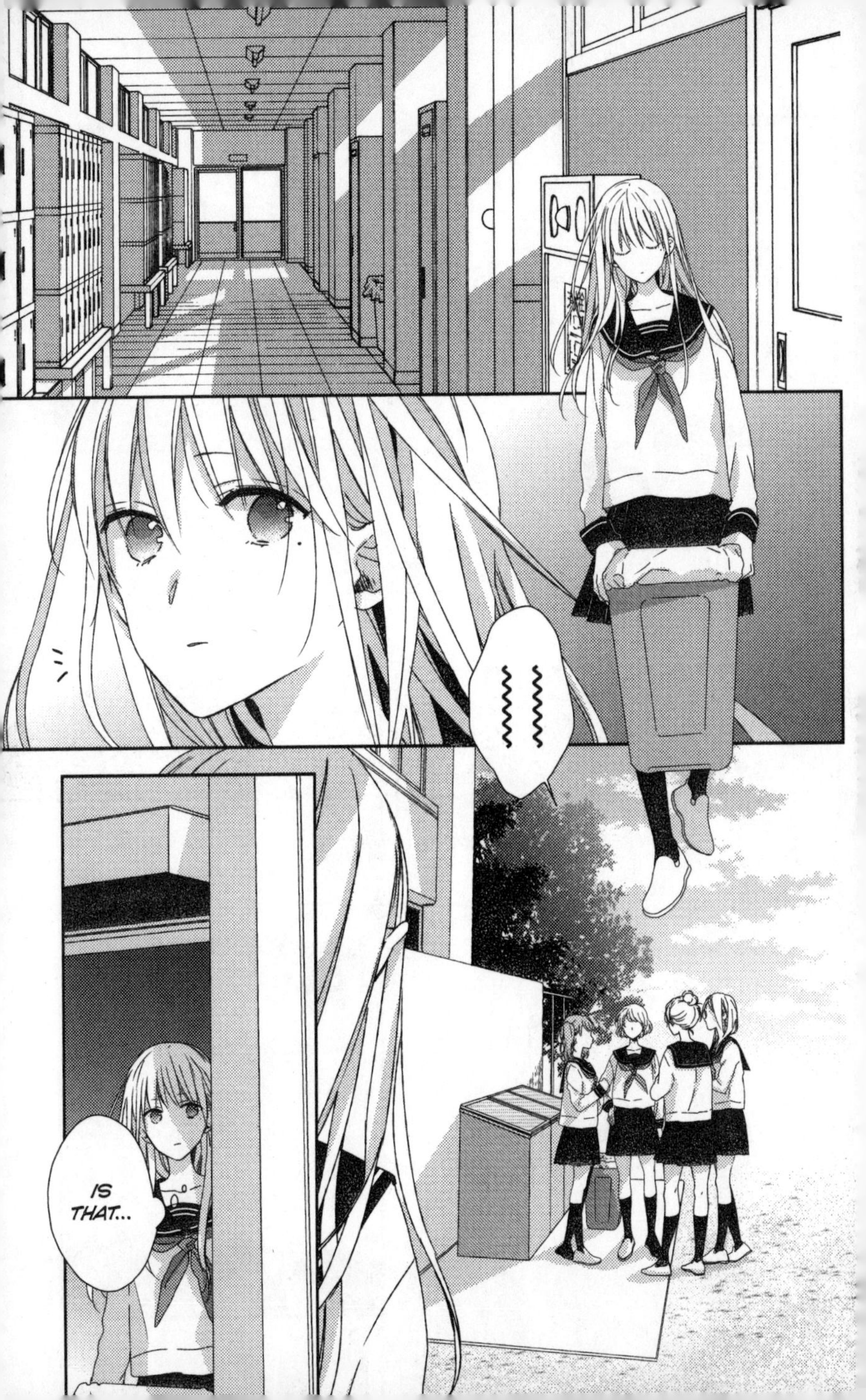
IS THAT...

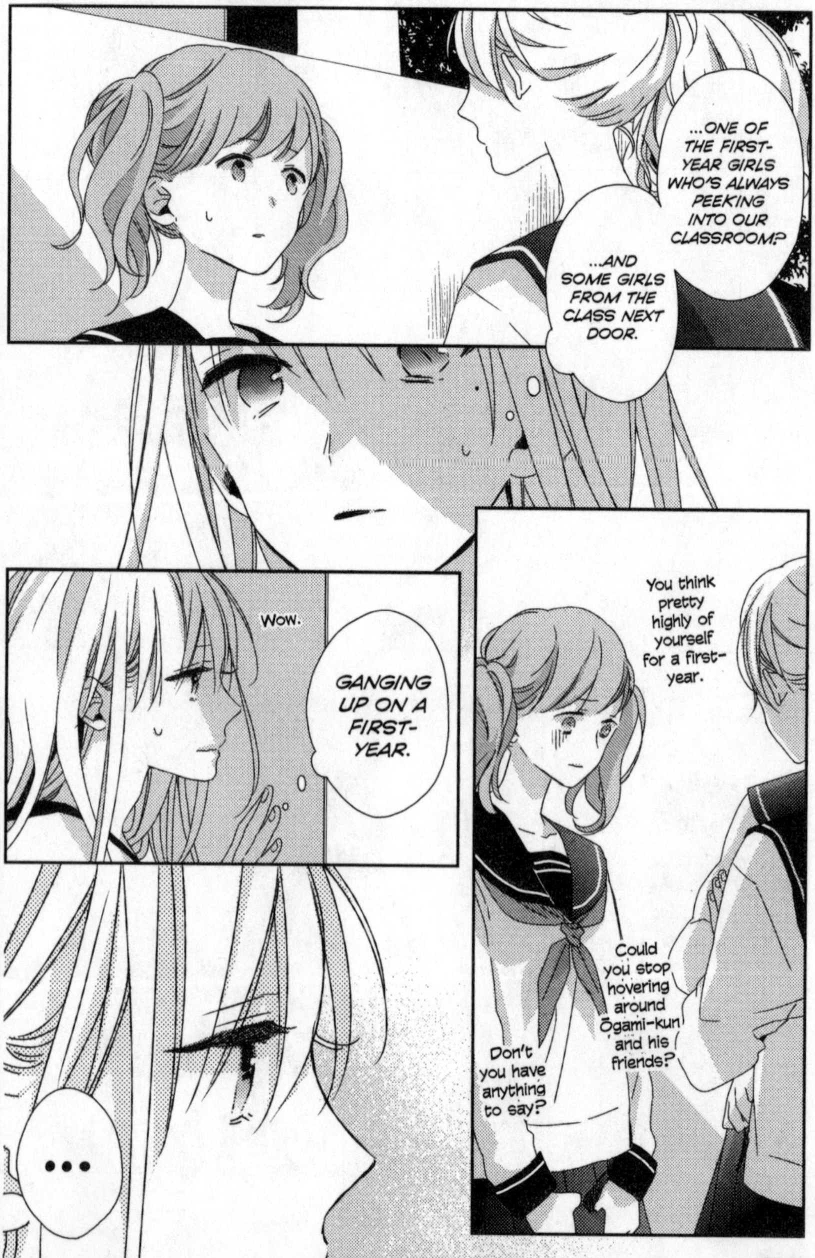
...ONE OF THE FIRST-YEAR GIRLS WHO'S ALWAYS PEEKING INTO OUR CLASSROOM?
...AND SOME GIRLS FROM THE CLASS NEXT DOOR.
You think pretty highly of yourself for a first-year.
Could you stop hovering around Ōgami-kun and his friends?
Don't you have anything to say?
Wow.
GANGING UP ON A FIRST-YEAR.
...

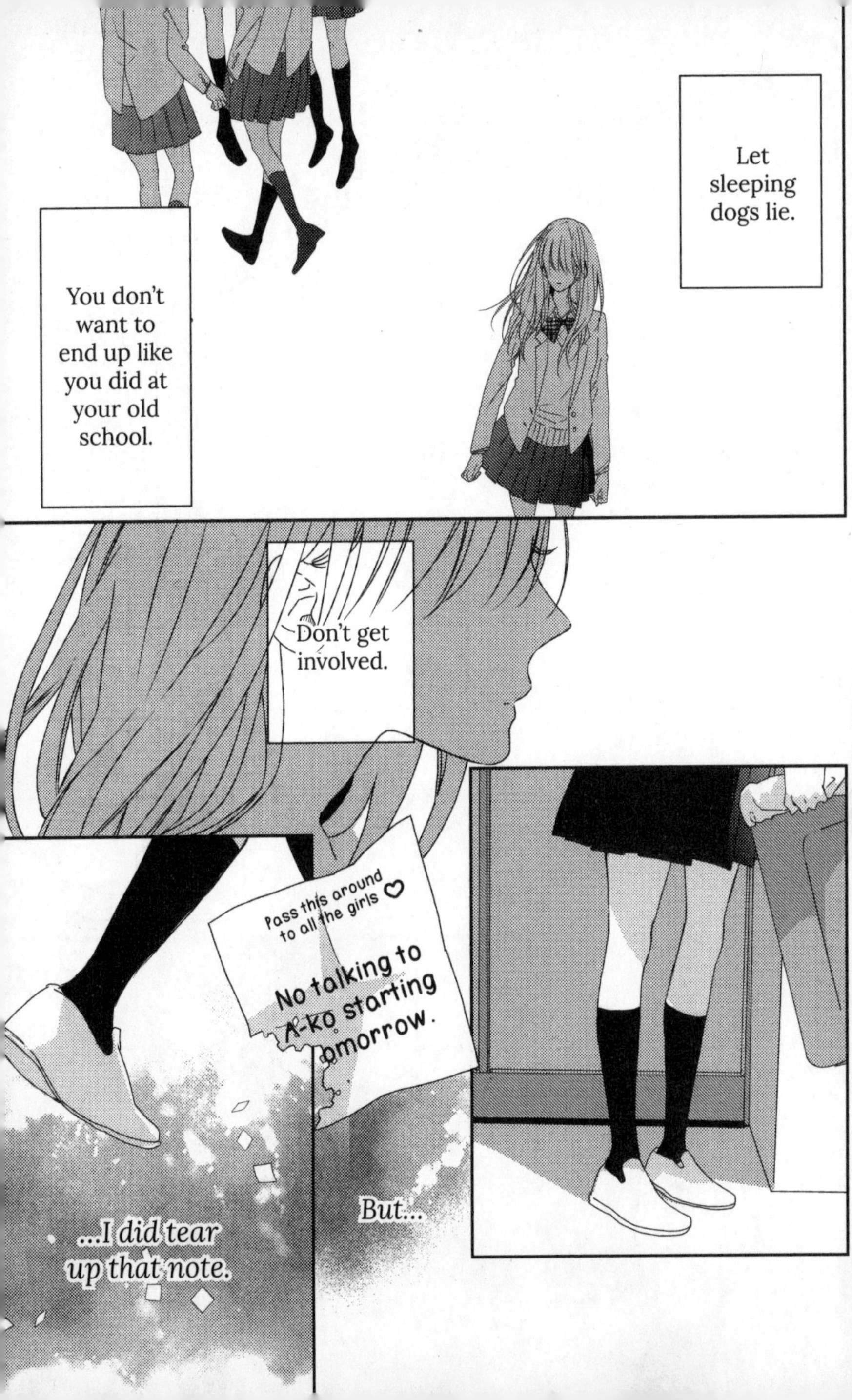

Let sleeping dogs lie.
You don't want to end up like you did at your old school.
Don't get involved.
Pass this around to all the girls ♡
No talking to A-ko starting tomorrow.
But...
...I did tear up that note.

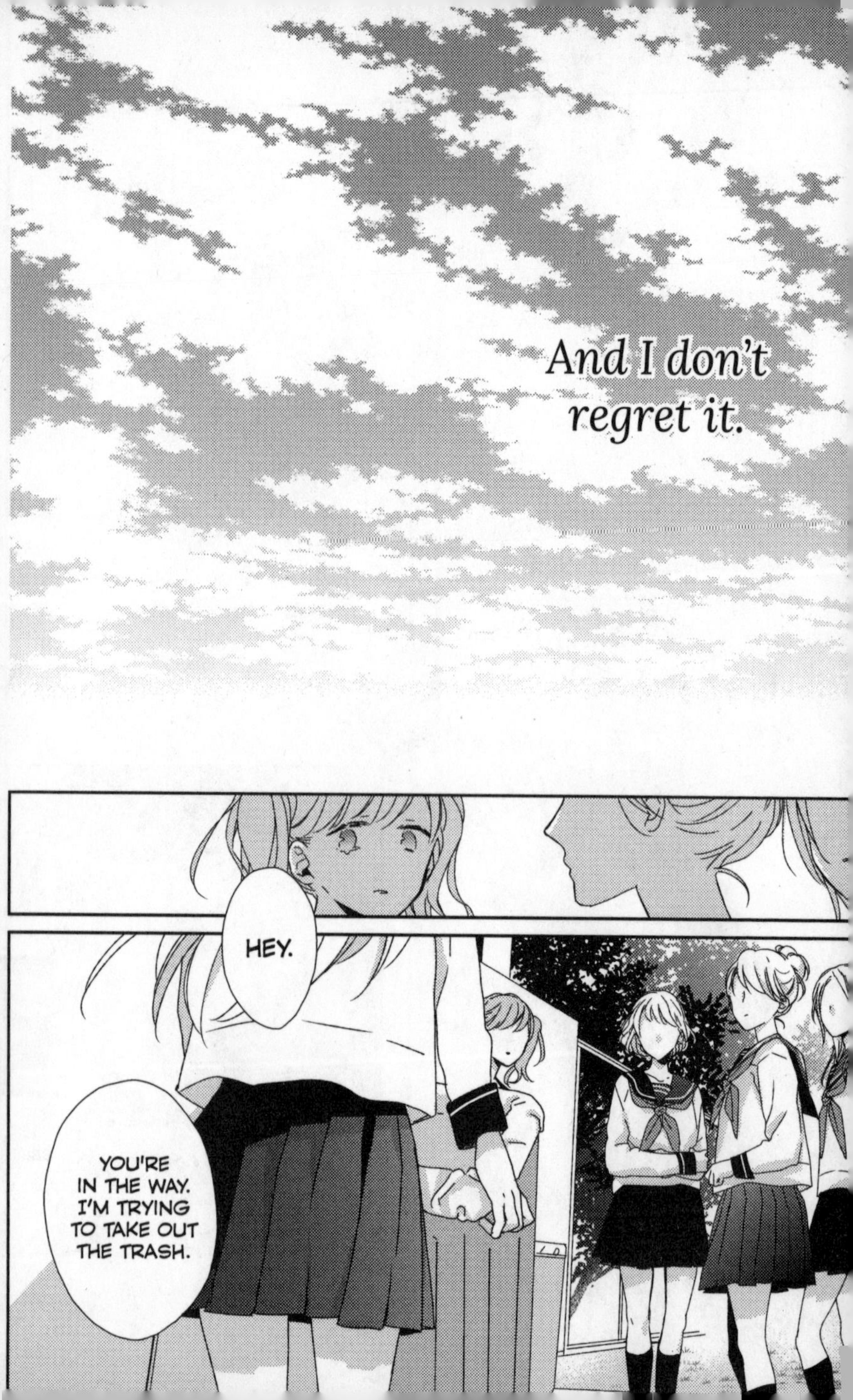
And I don't regret it.
HEY.
YOU'RE IN THE WAY. I'M TRYING TO TAKE OUT THE TRASH.

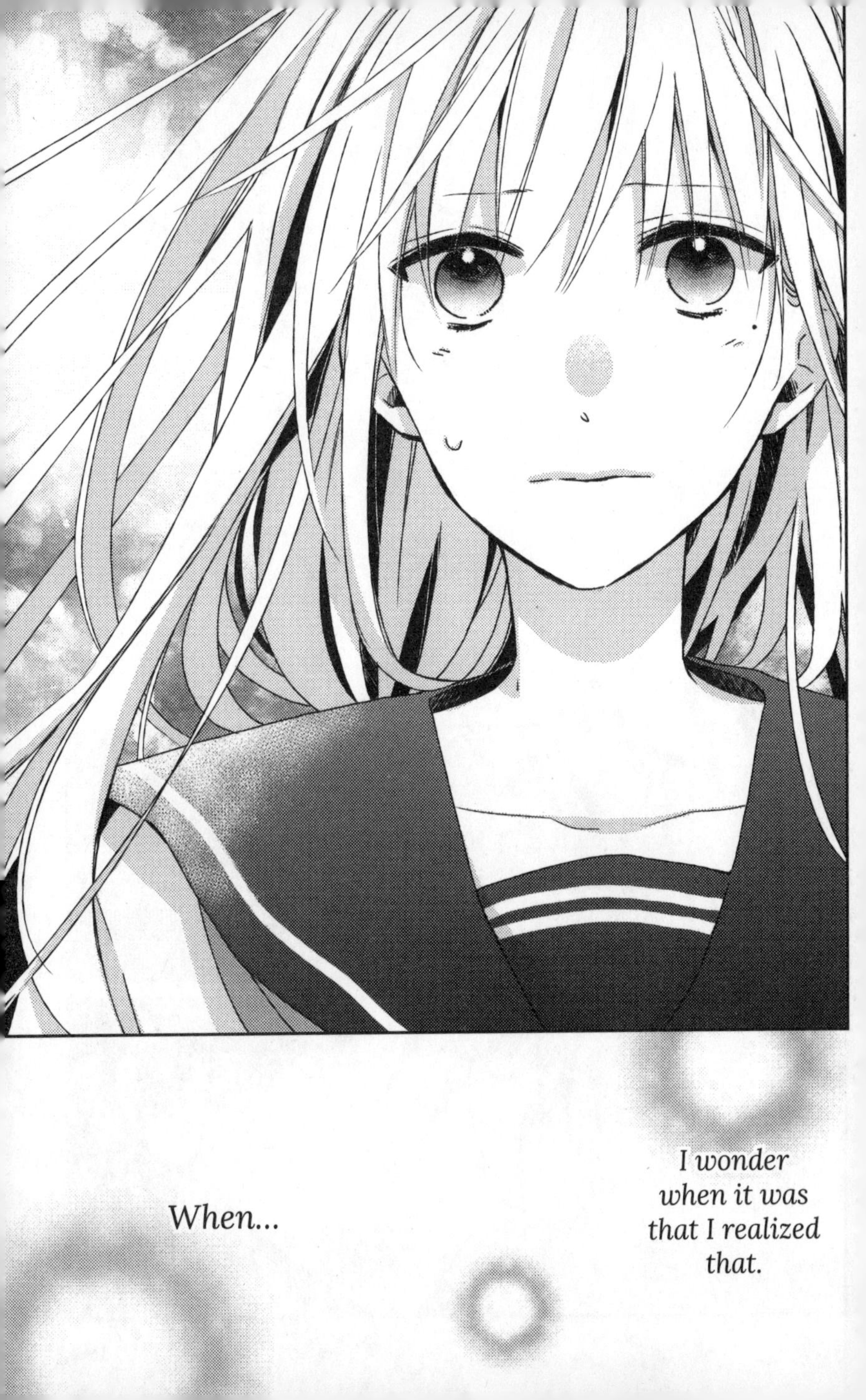
I wonder when it was that I realized that.
When...

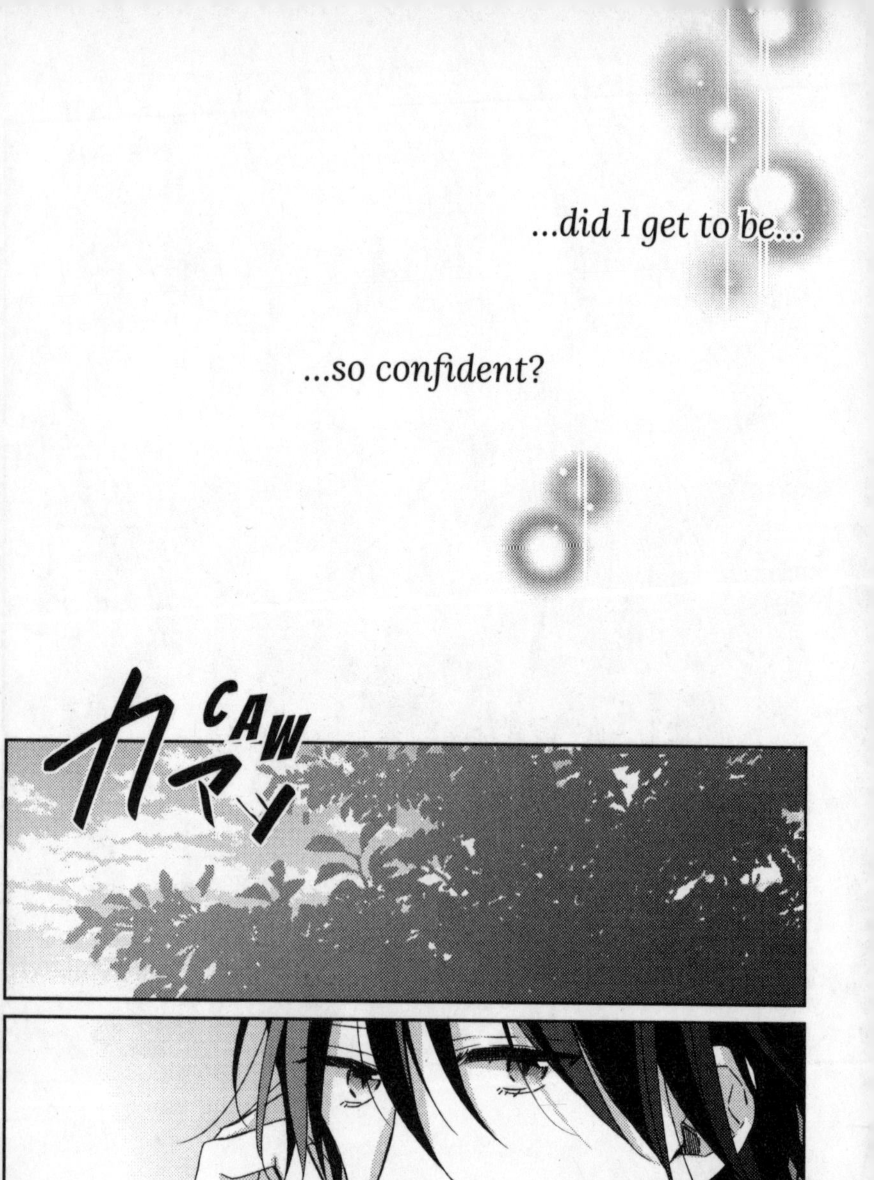
...did I get to be...
...so confident?
CAW
カァッ

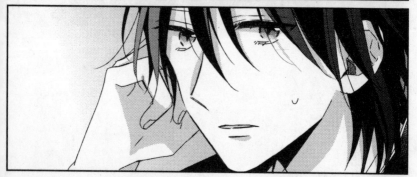

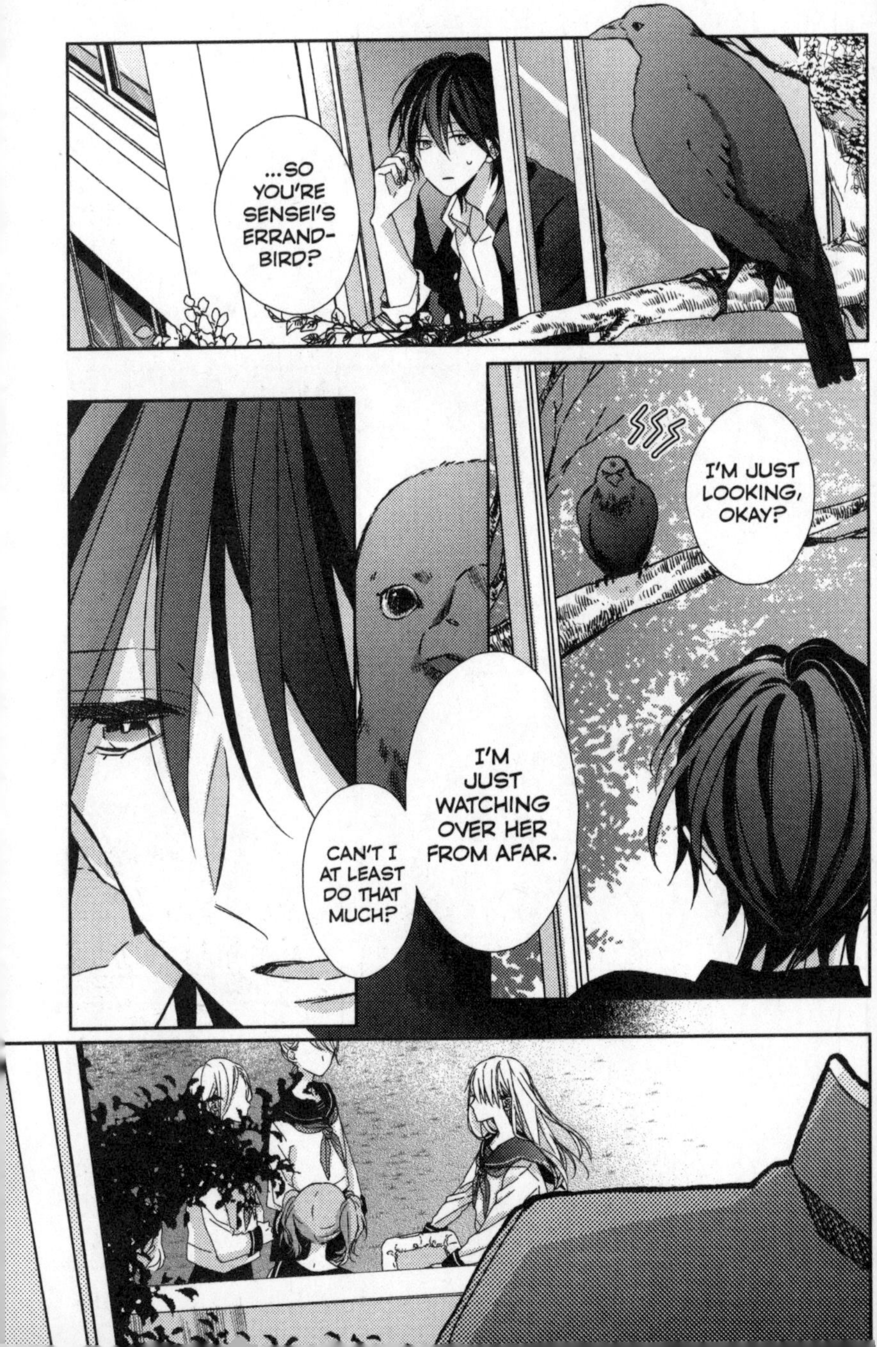
...SO YOU'RE SENSEI'S ERRAND-BIRD?
I'M JUST LOOKING, OKAY?
I'M JUST WATCHING OVER HER FROM AFAR.
CAN'T I AT LEAST DO THAT MUCH?

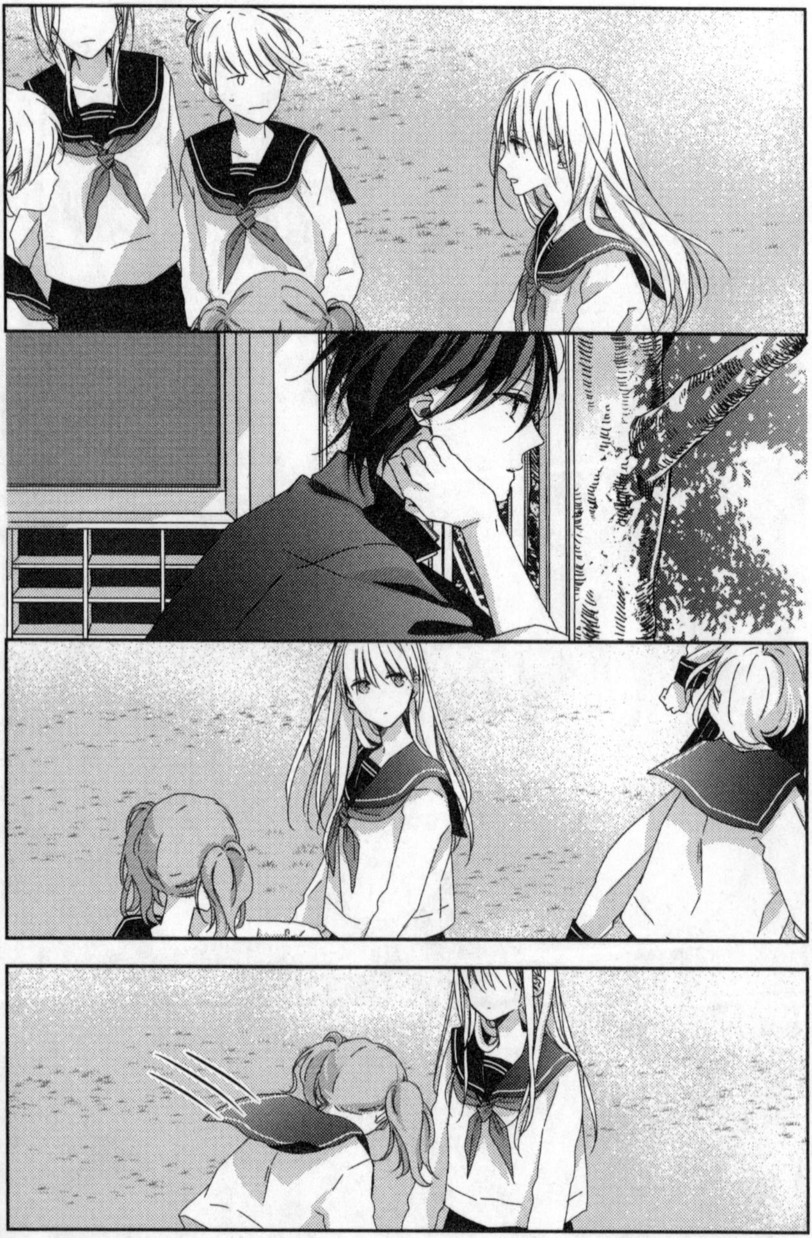

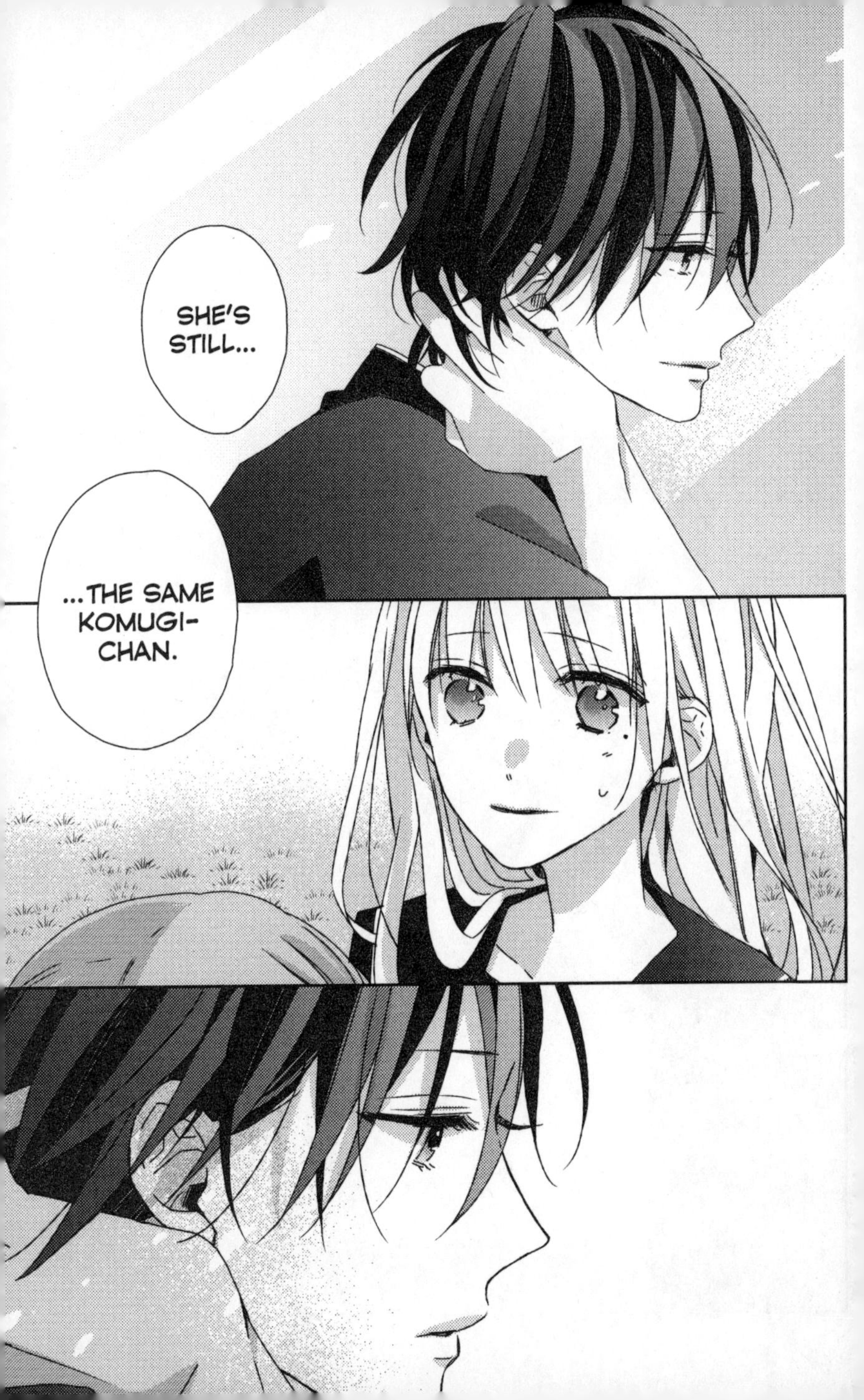
SHE'S STILL...
...THE SAME KOMUGI-CHAN.

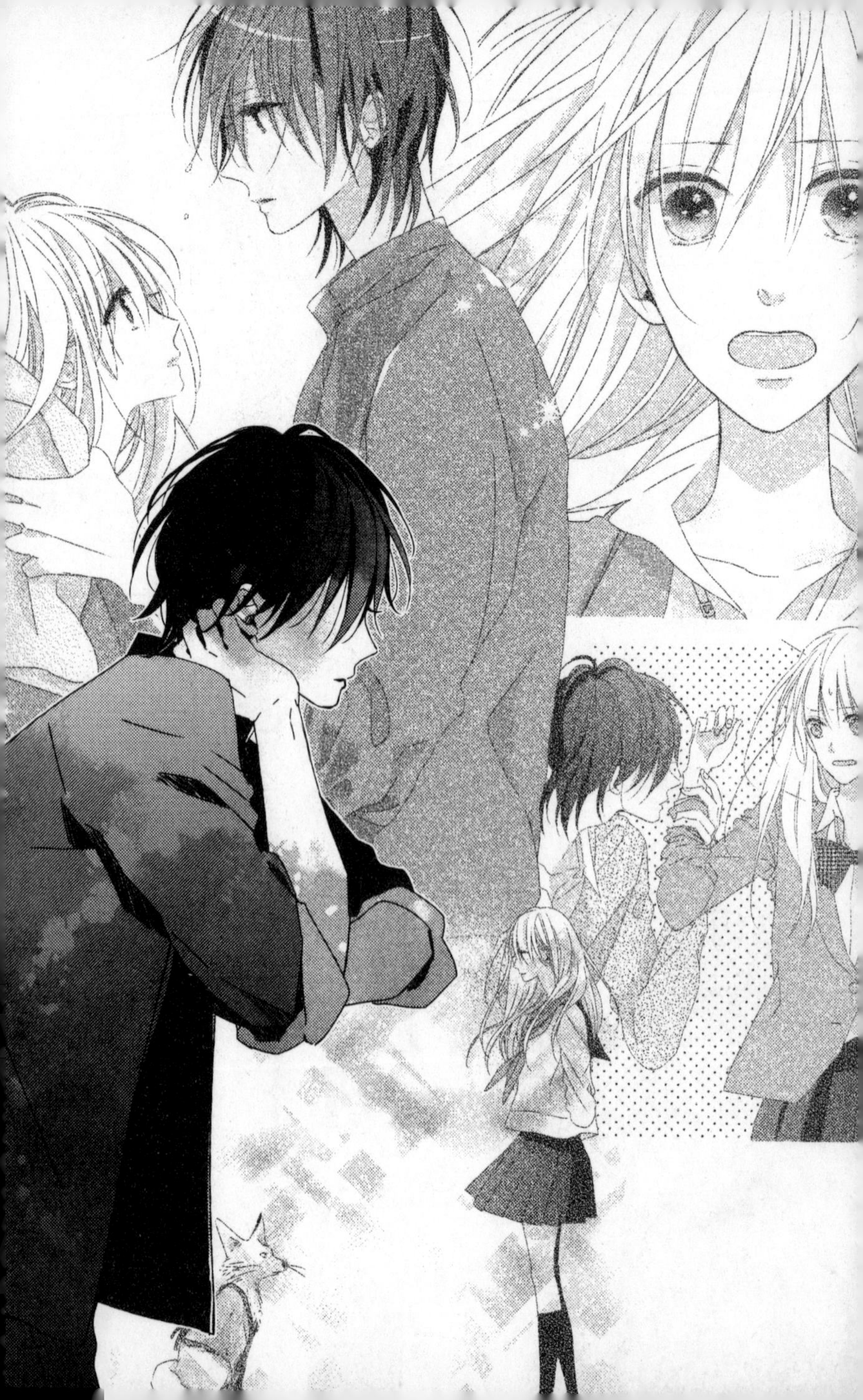

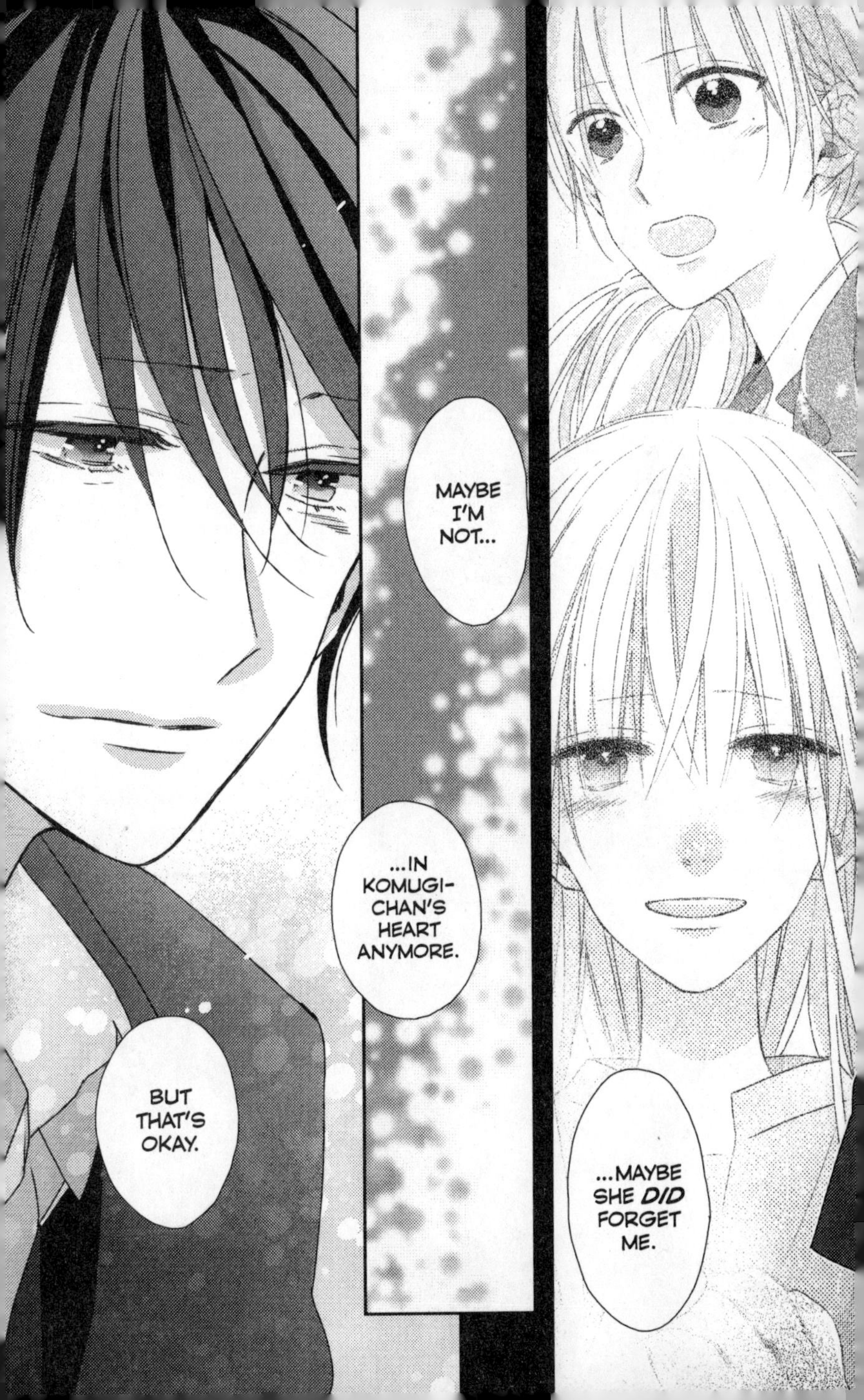
...MAYBE SHE *DID* FORGET ME.
MAYBE I'M NOT...
...IN KOMUGI-CHAN'S HEART ANYMORE.
BUT THAT'S OKAY.

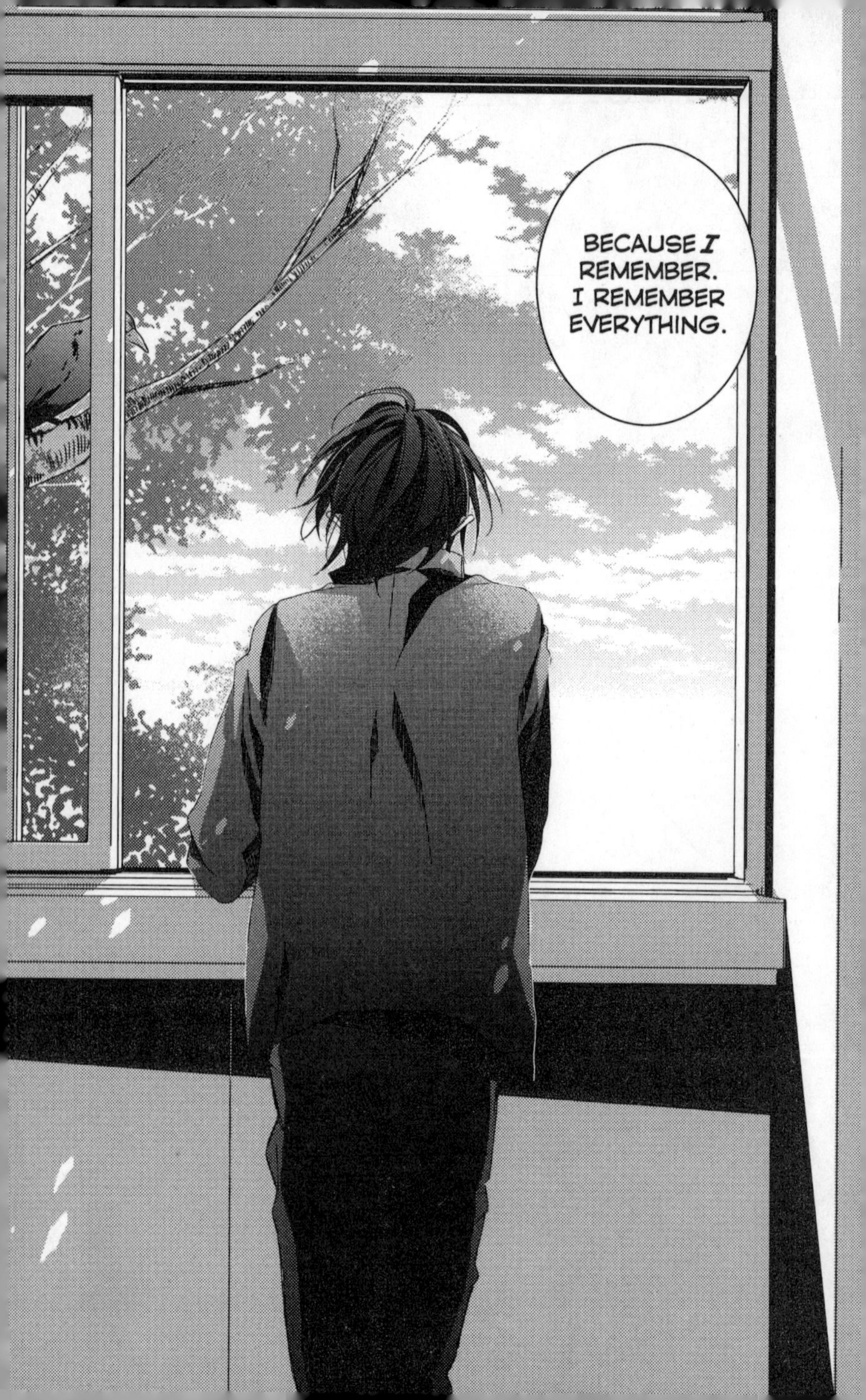
BECAUSE I REMEMBER. I REMEMBER EVERYTHING.

Chapter 15

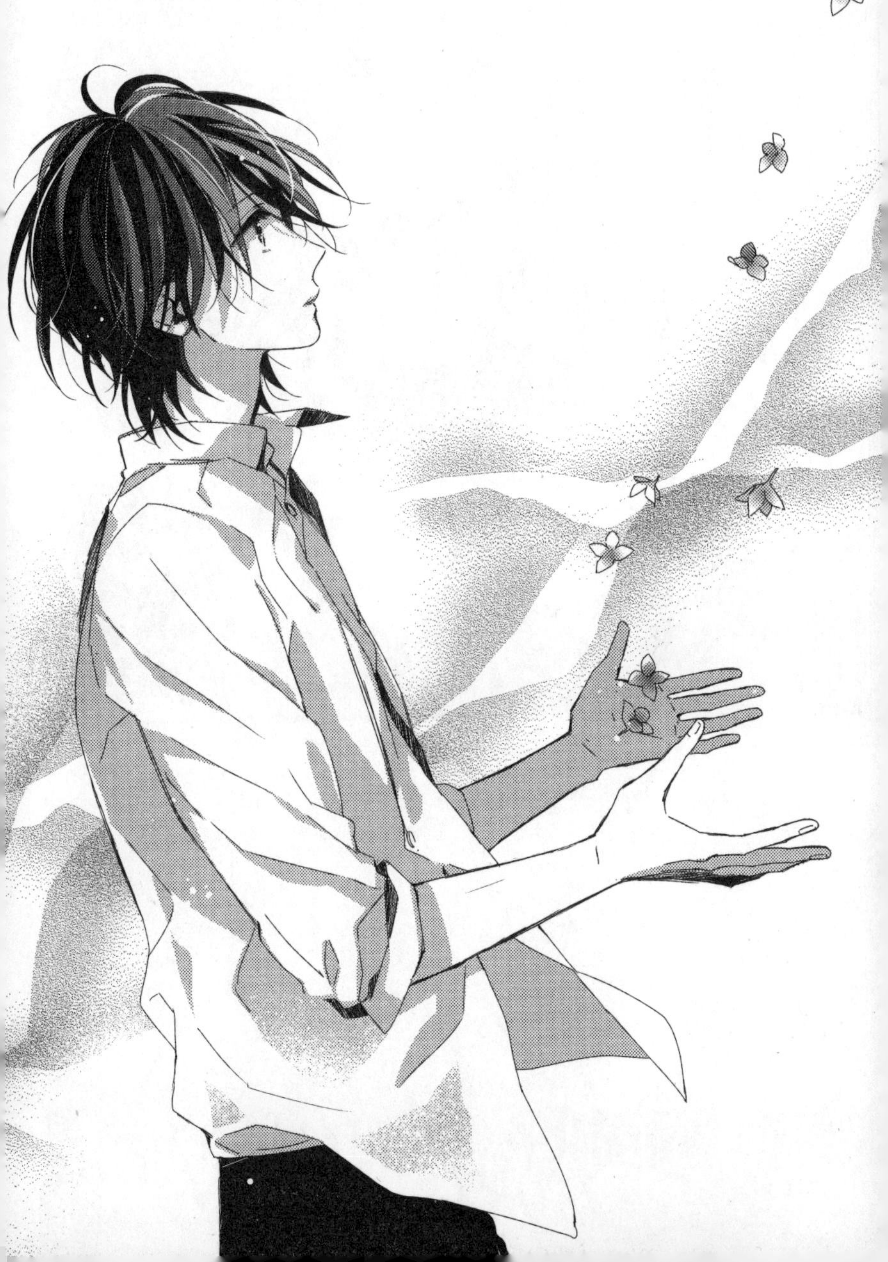

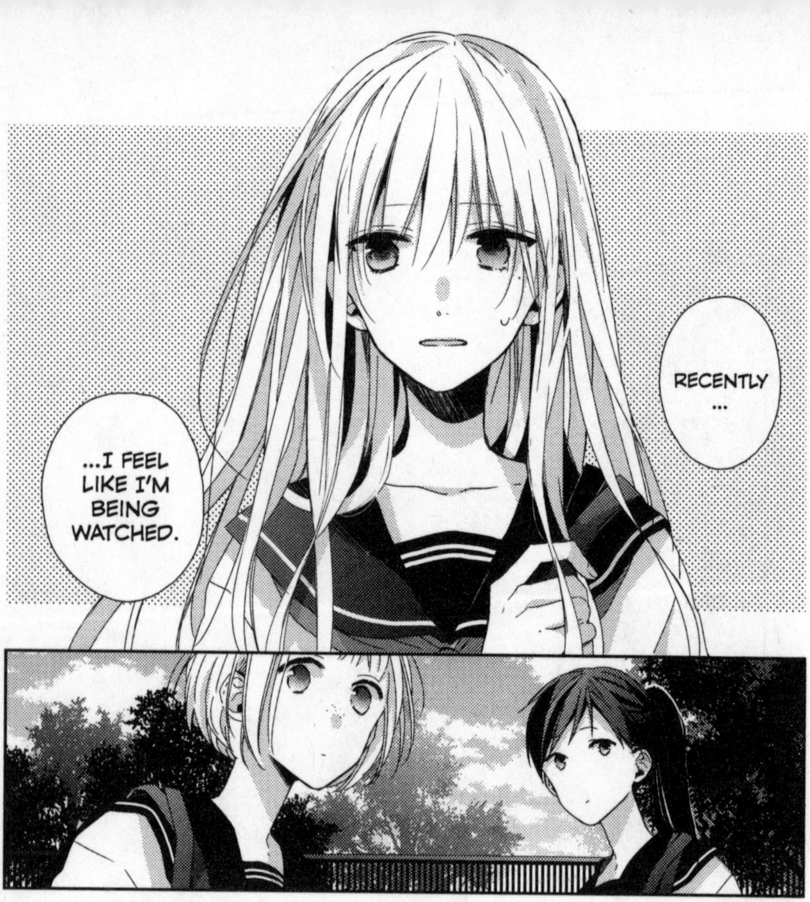
RECENTLY ...
...I FEEL LIKE I'M BEING WATCHED.

That Wolf-Boy is Mine!

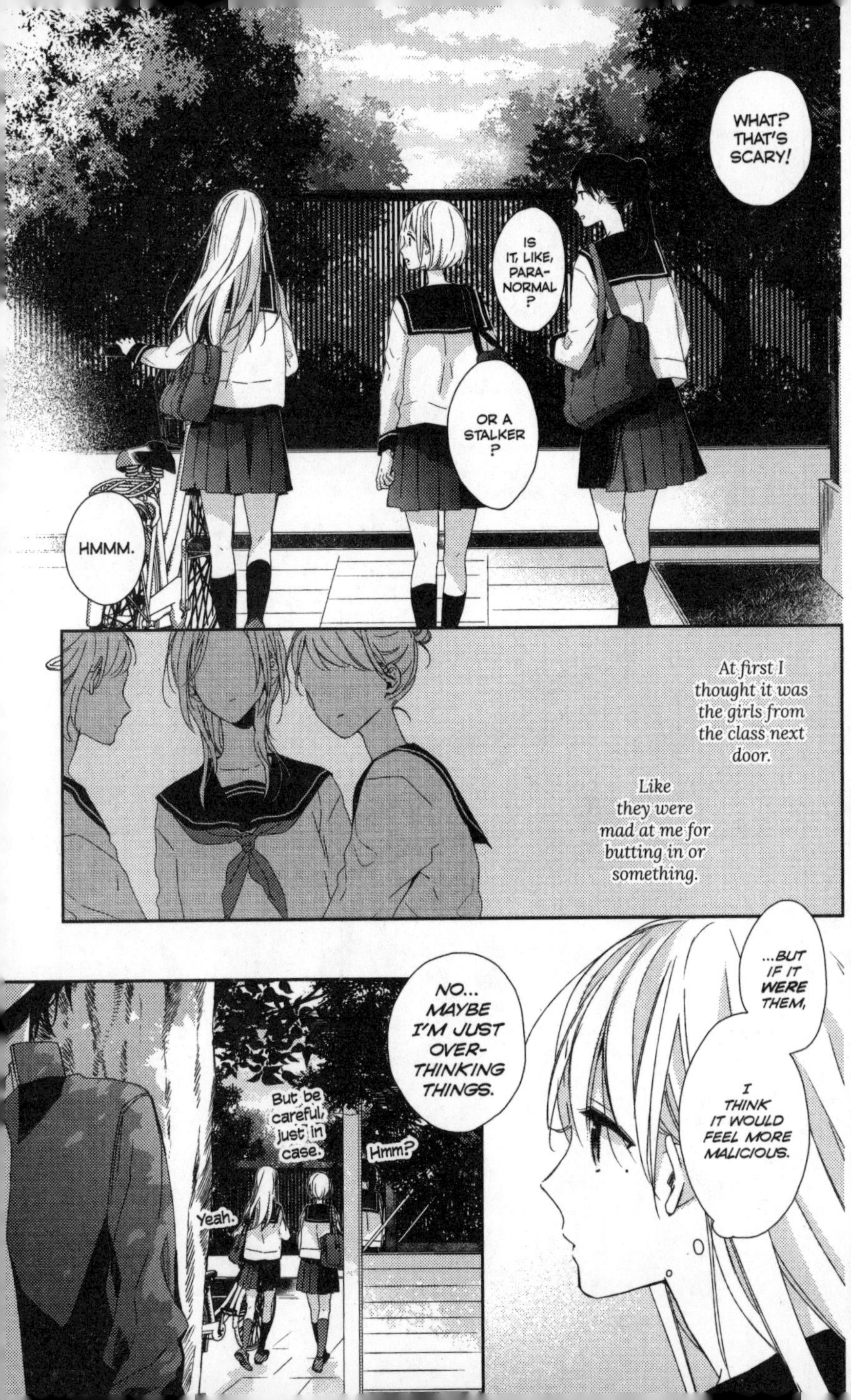
WHAT? THAT'S SCARY!
IS IT, LIKE, PARA-NORMAL?
OR A STALKER?
HMMM.
At first I thought it was the girls from the class next door.
Like they were mad at me for butting in or something.
...BUT IF IT WERE THEM,
I THINK IT WOULD FEEL MORE MALICIOUS.
NO... MAYBE I'M JUST OVER-THINKING THINGS.
Hmm?
But be careful, just in case.
Yeah.

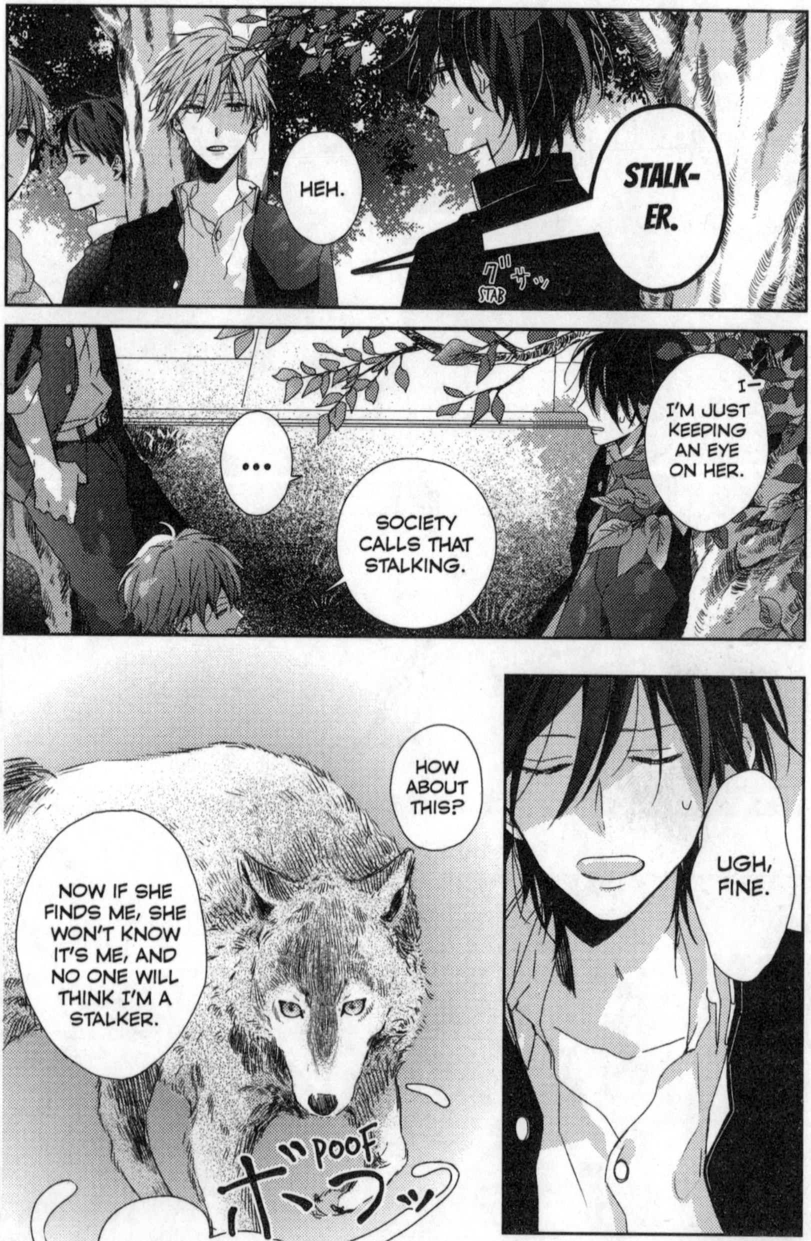
STALK-ER.
STAB
HEH.
I— I'M JUST KEEPING AN EYE ON HER.
SOCIETY CALLS THAT STALKING.
...
UGH, FINE.
HOW ABOUT THIS?
NOW IF SHE FINDS ME, SHE WON'T KNOW IT'S ME, AND NO ONE WILL THINK I'M A STALKER.
POOF

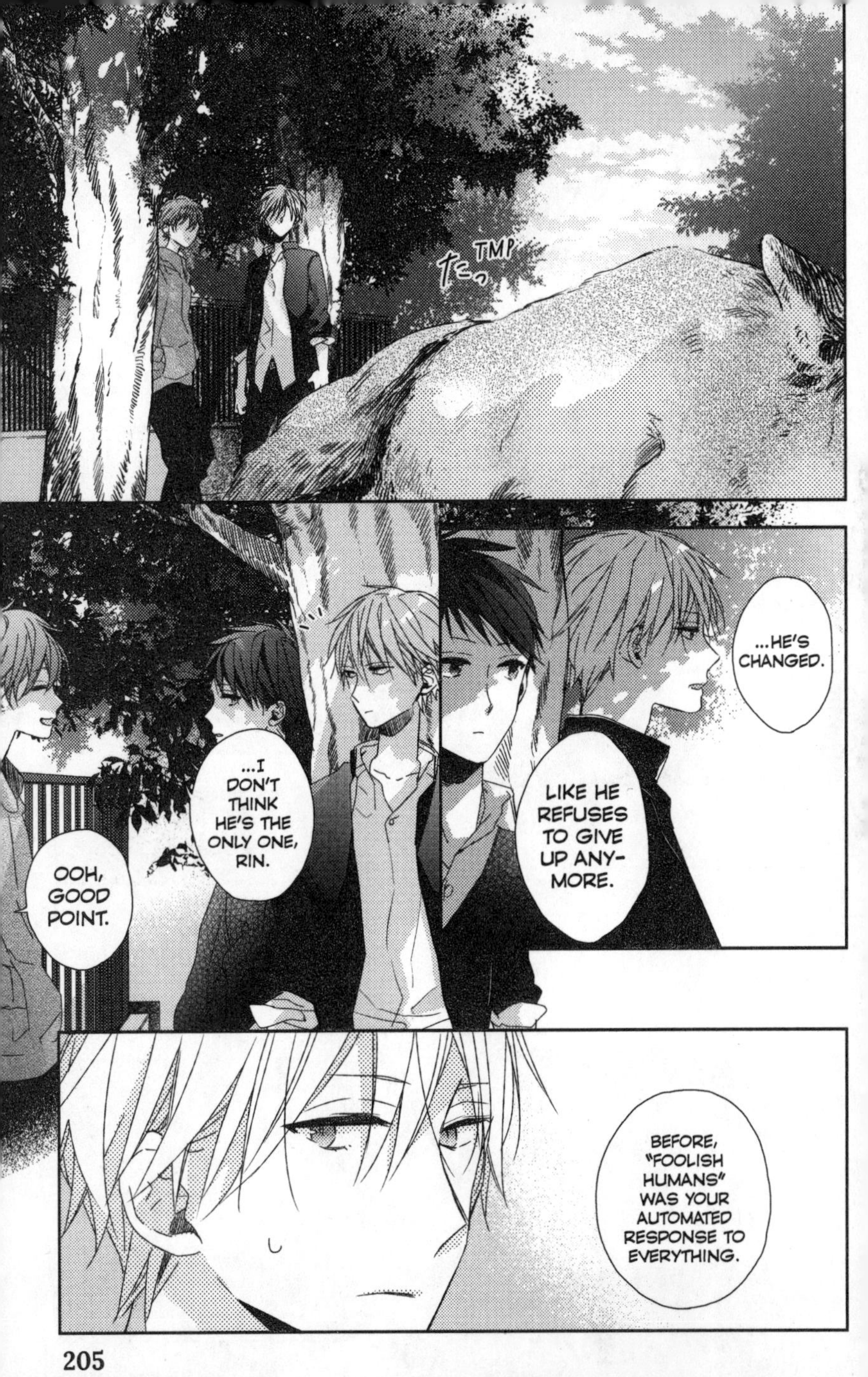
TMP
...HE'S CHANGED.
LIKE HE REFUSES TO GIVE UP ANY-MORE.
...I DON'T THINK HE'S THE ONLY ONE, RIN.
OOH, GOOD POINT.
BEFORE, "FOOLISH HUMANS" WAS YOUR AUTOMATED RESPONSE TO EVERYTHING.

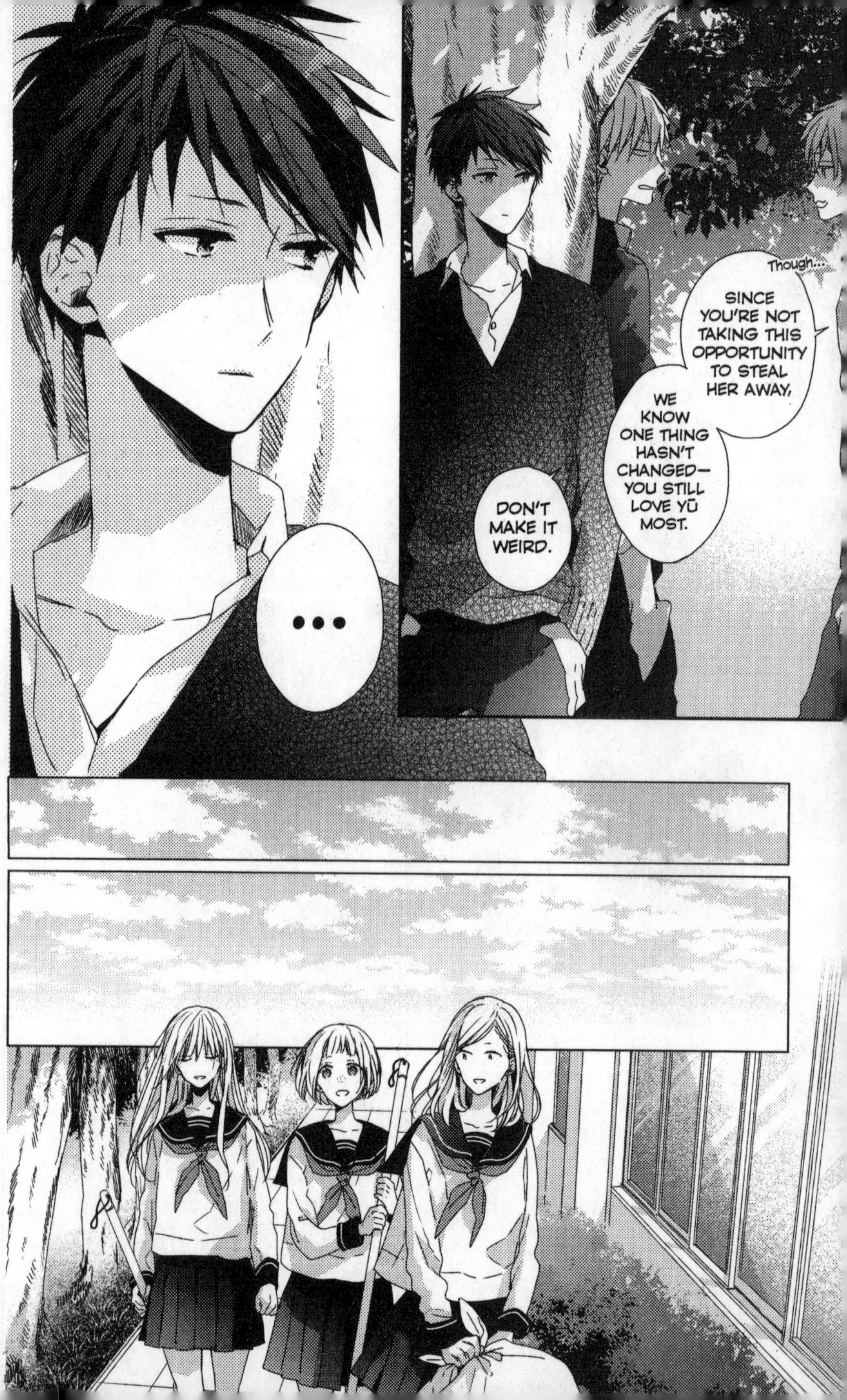
Though...
SINCE YOU'RE NOT TAKING THIS OPPORTUNITY TO STEAL HER AWAY,
WE KNOW ONE THING HASN'T CHANGED—YOU STILL LOVE YŪ MOST.
DON'T MAKE IT WEIRD.
...

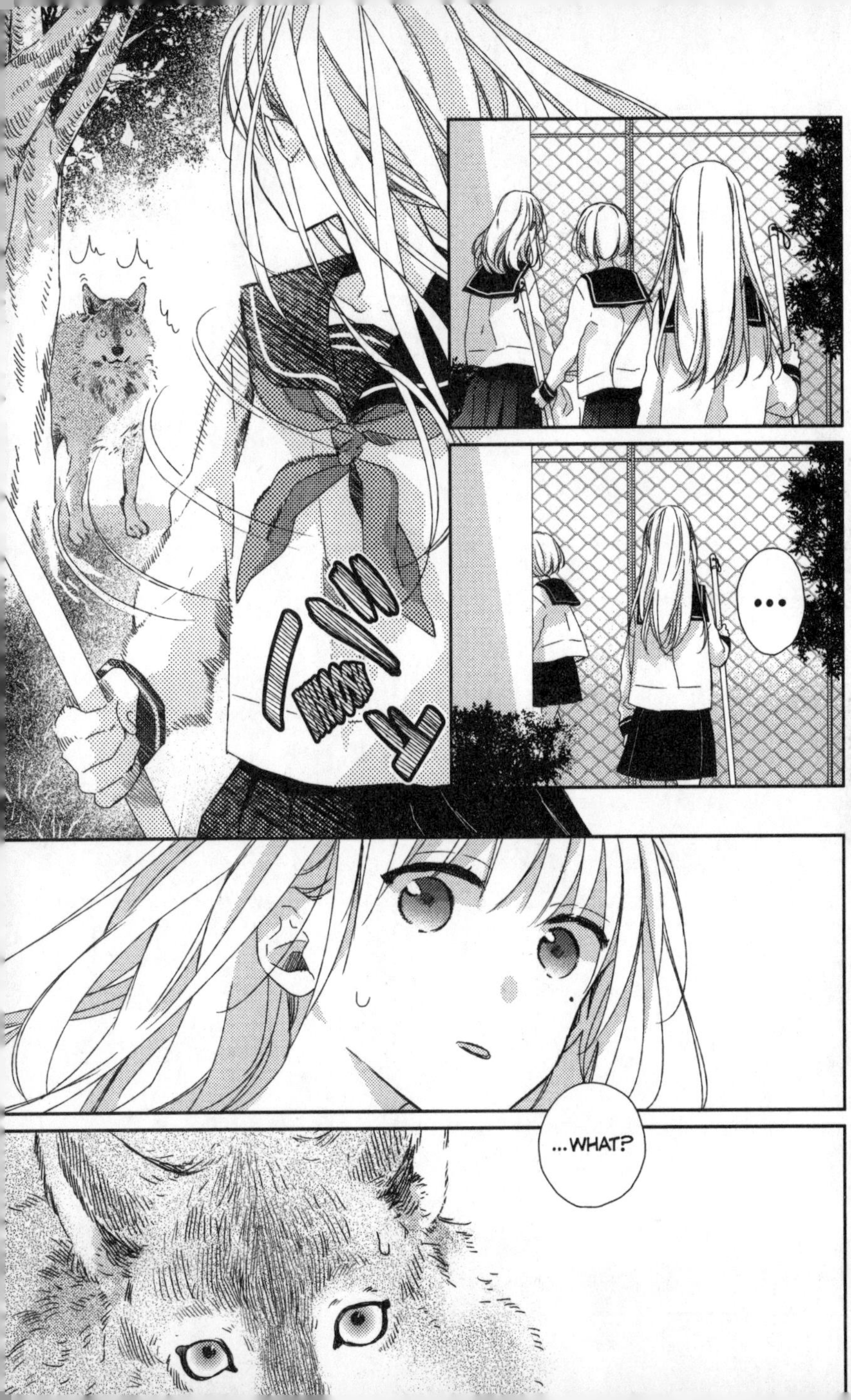
...
...WHAT?

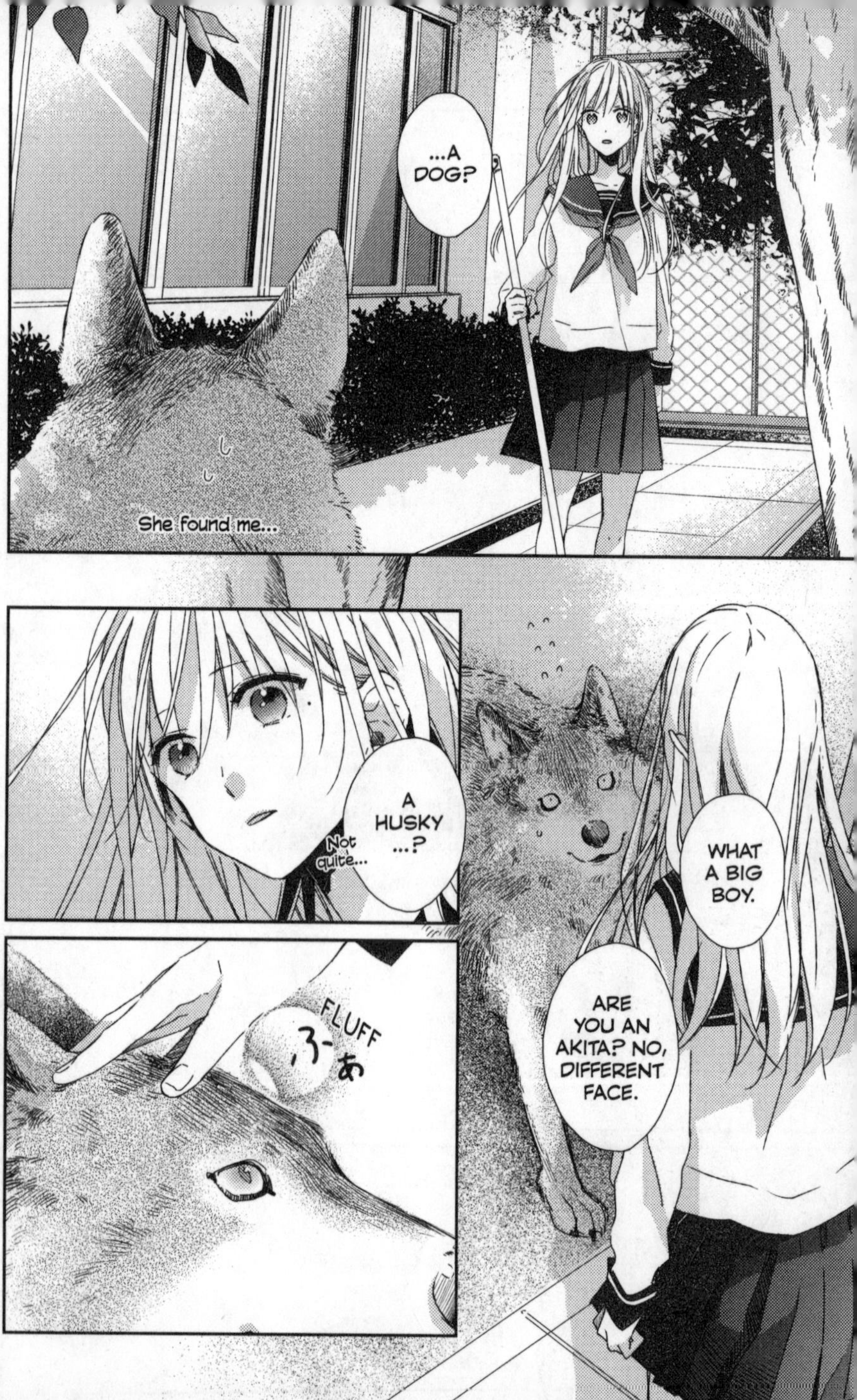
...A DOG?
She found me...
WHAT A BIG BOY.
ARE YOU AN AKITA? NO, DIFFERENT FACE.
A HUSKY ...?
Not quite...
FLUFF
ふーあ

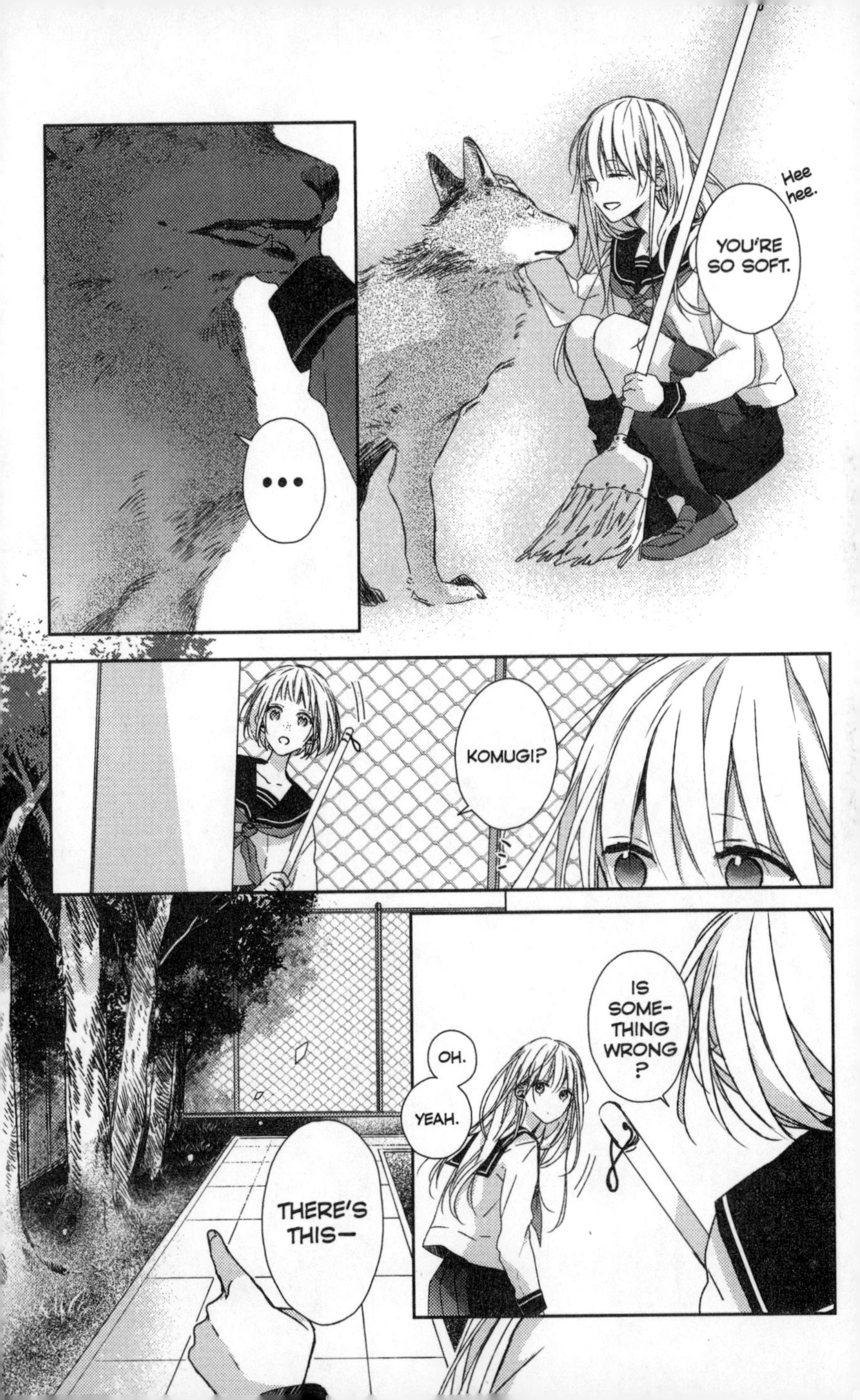
Hee hee.
YOU'RE SO SOFT.
...
KOMUGI?
IS SOME-THING WRONG?
OH.
YEAH.
THERE'S THIS—

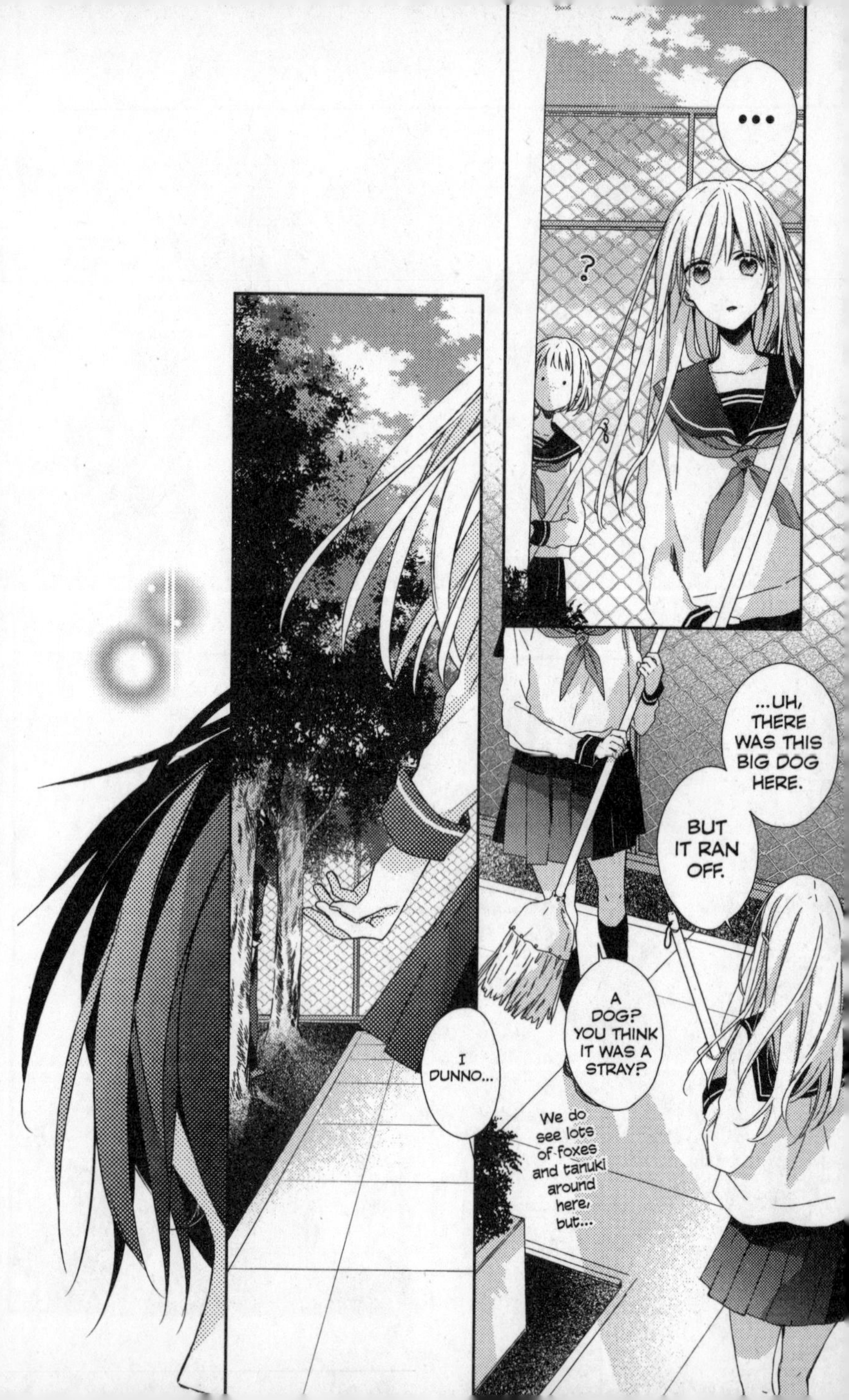
...
?
...UH, THERE WAS THIS BIG DOG HERE.
BUT IT RAN OFF.
A DOG? YOU THINK IT WAS A STRAY?
I DUNNO...
We do see lots of foxes and tanuki around here, but...

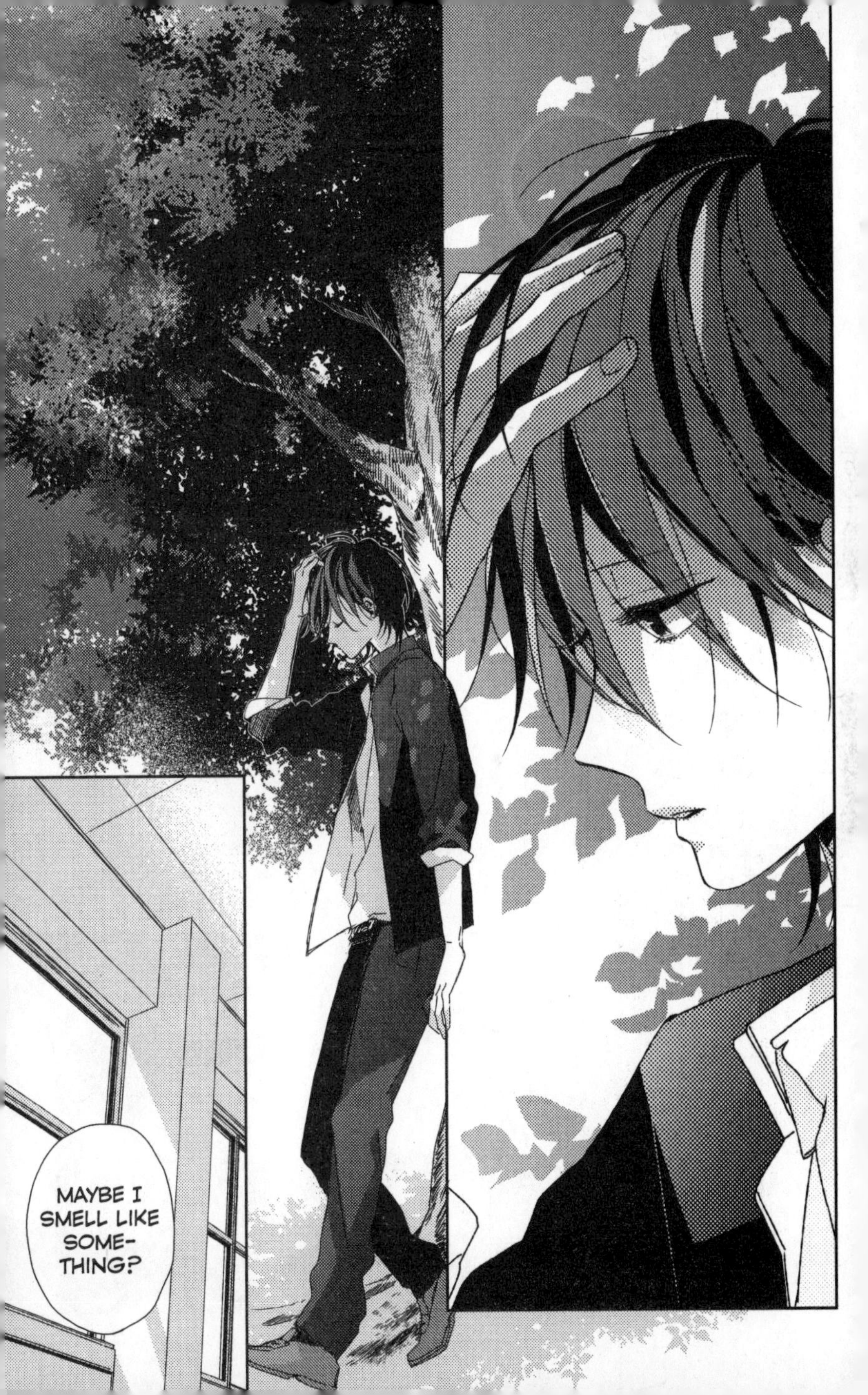
MAYBE I SMELL LIKE SOME-THING?

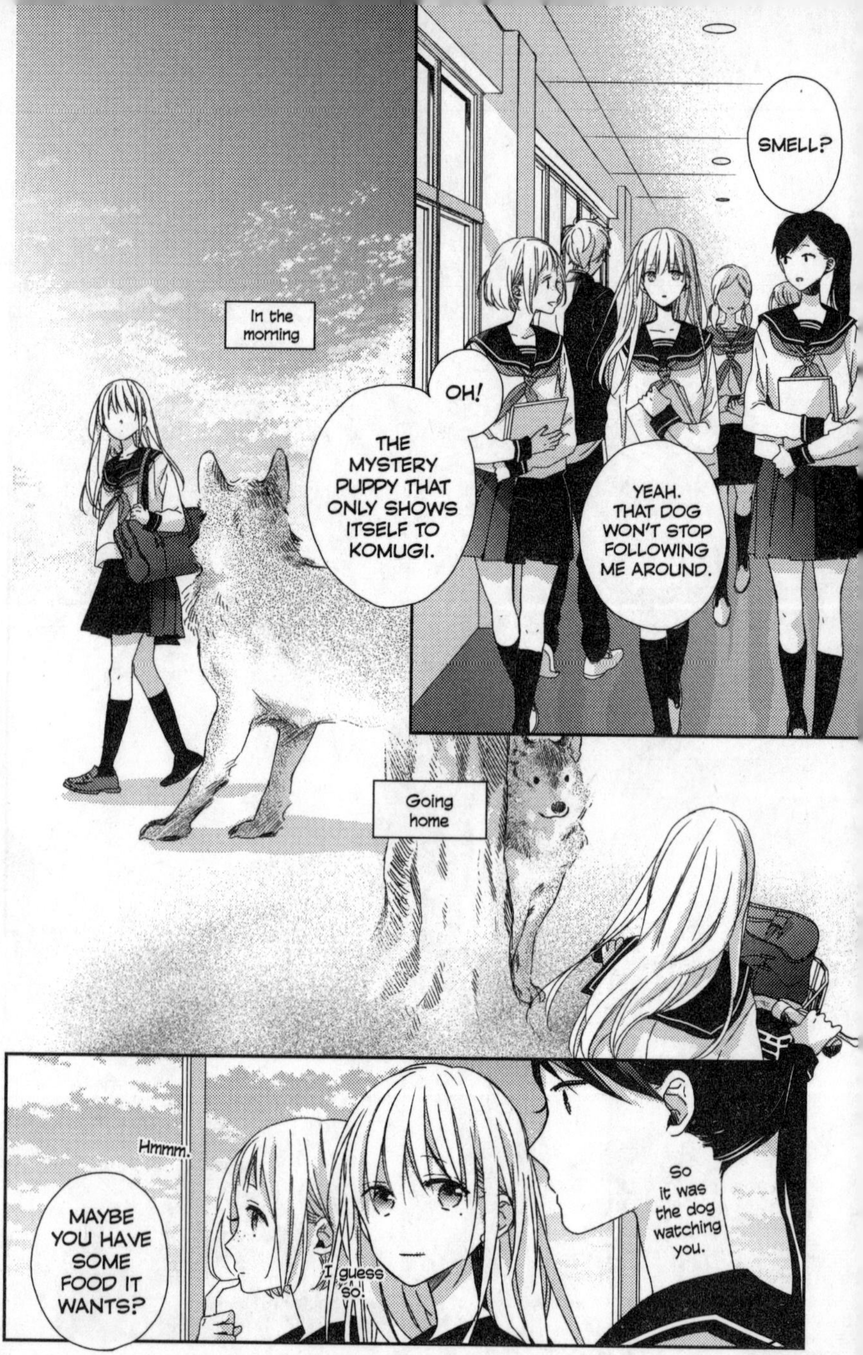
SMELL?
YEAH. THAT DOG WON'T STOP FOLLOWING ME AROUND.
OH!
THE MYSTERY PUPPY THAT ONLY SHOWS ITSELF TO KOMUGI.
In the morning
Going home
So it was the dog watching you.
I guess so.
Hmmm.
MAYBE YOU HAVE SOME FOOD IT WANTS?

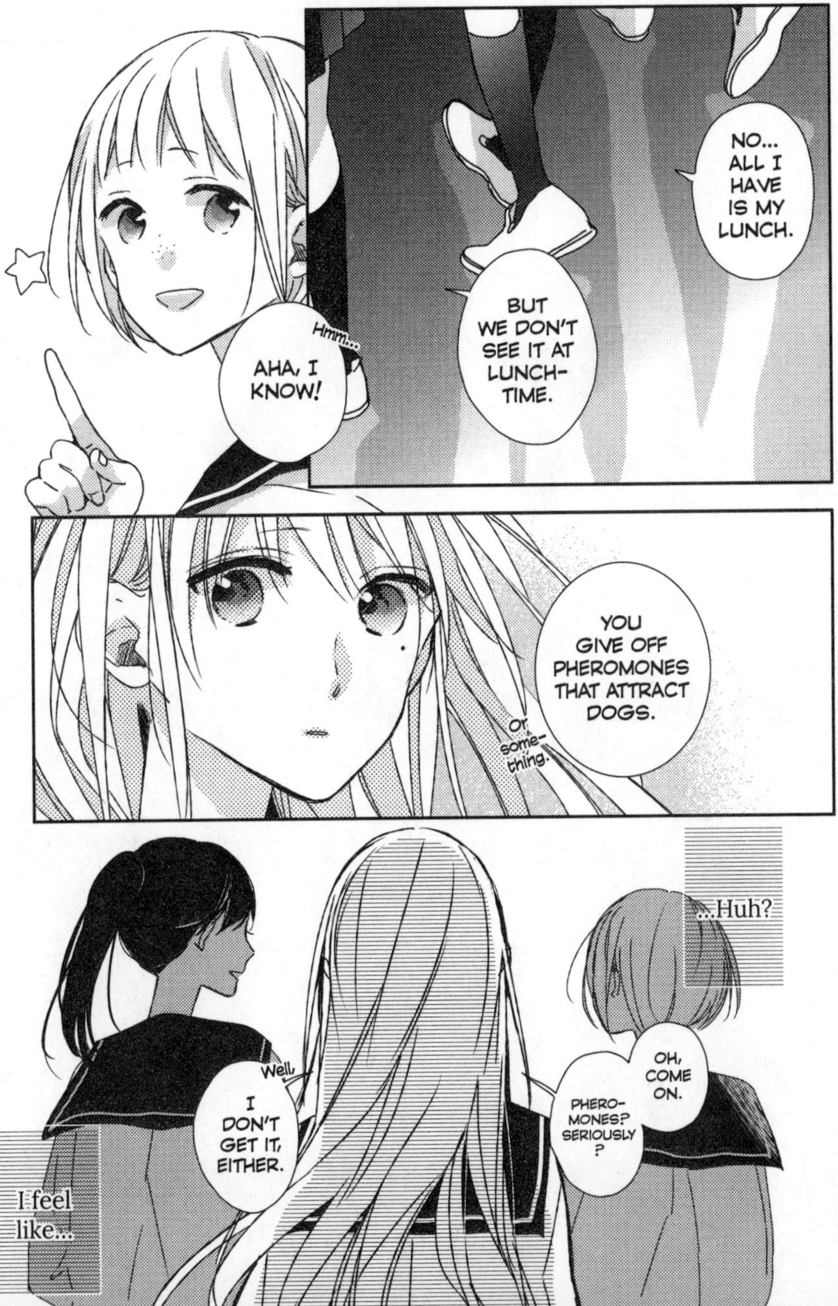
NO... ALL I HAVE IS MY LUNCH.
BUT WE DON'T SEE IT AT LUNCH-TIME.
Hmm...
AHA, I KNOW!
YOU GIVE OFF PHEROMONES THAT ATTRACT DOGS.
Or some-thing.
...Huh?
OH, COME ON.
PHERO-MONES? SERIOUSLY?
Well,
I DON'T GET IT, EITHER.
I feel like...

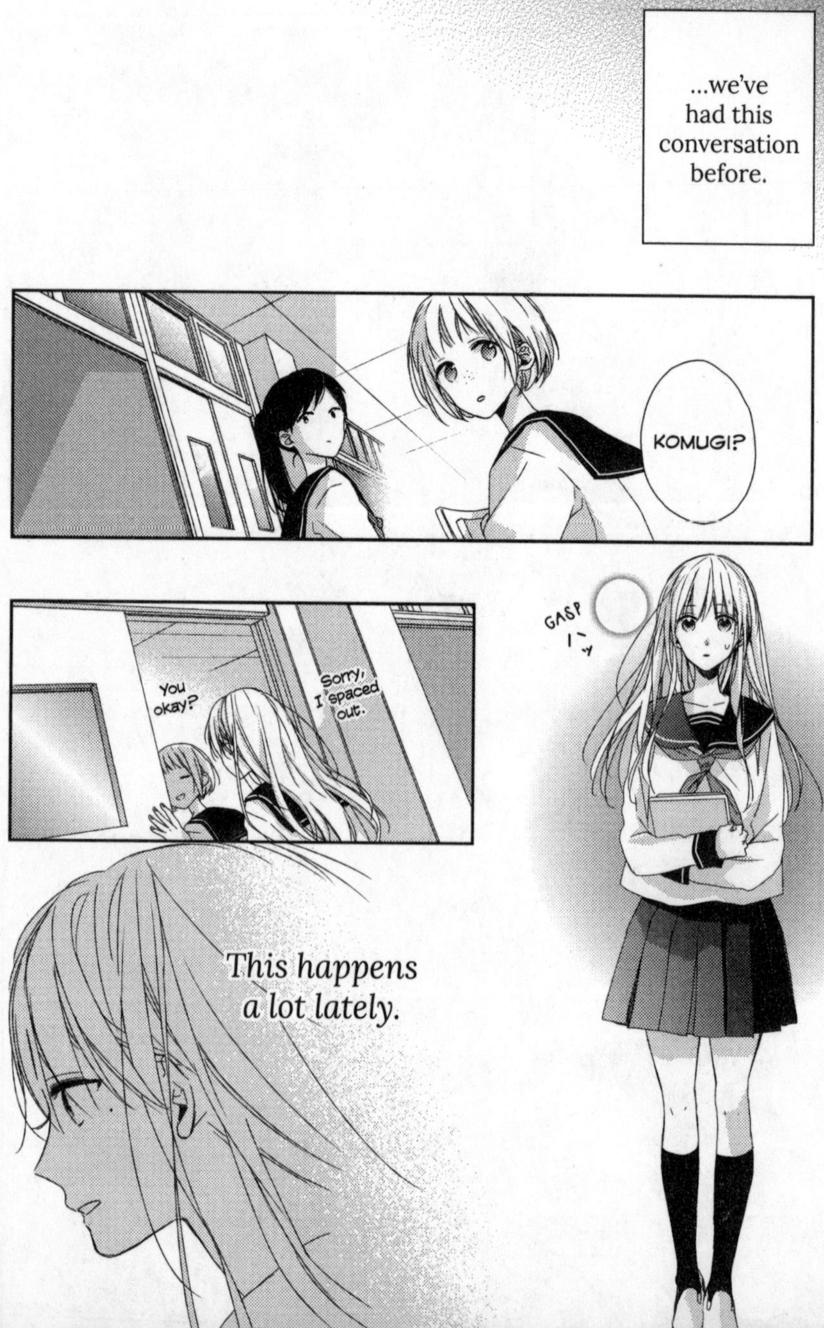
...we've had this conversation before.
KOMUGI?
GASP
You okay?
Sorry, I spaced out.
This happens a lot lately.

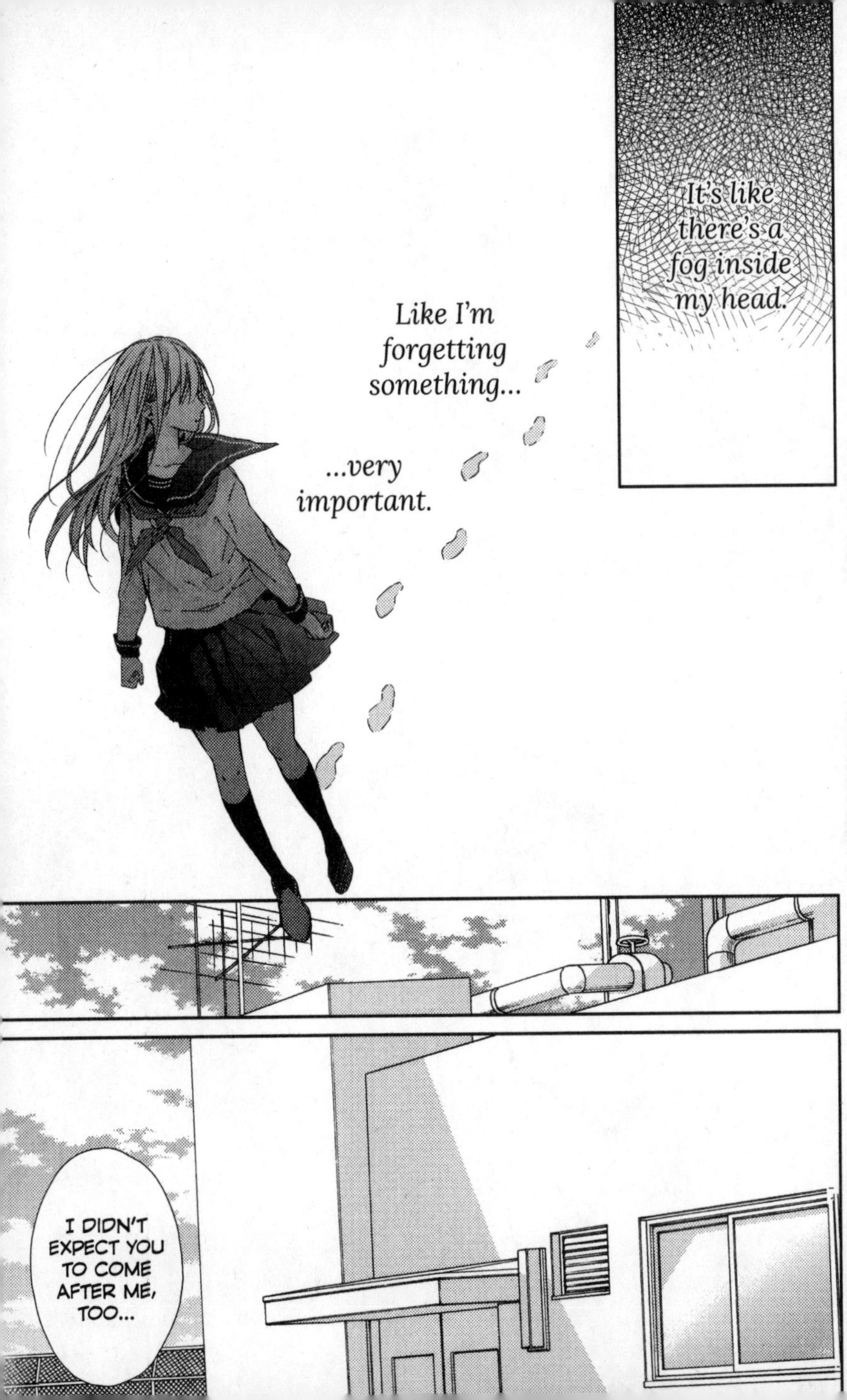
It's like there's a fog inside my head.
Like I'm forgetting something...
...very important.
I DIDN'T EXPECT YOU TO COME AFTER ME, TOO...

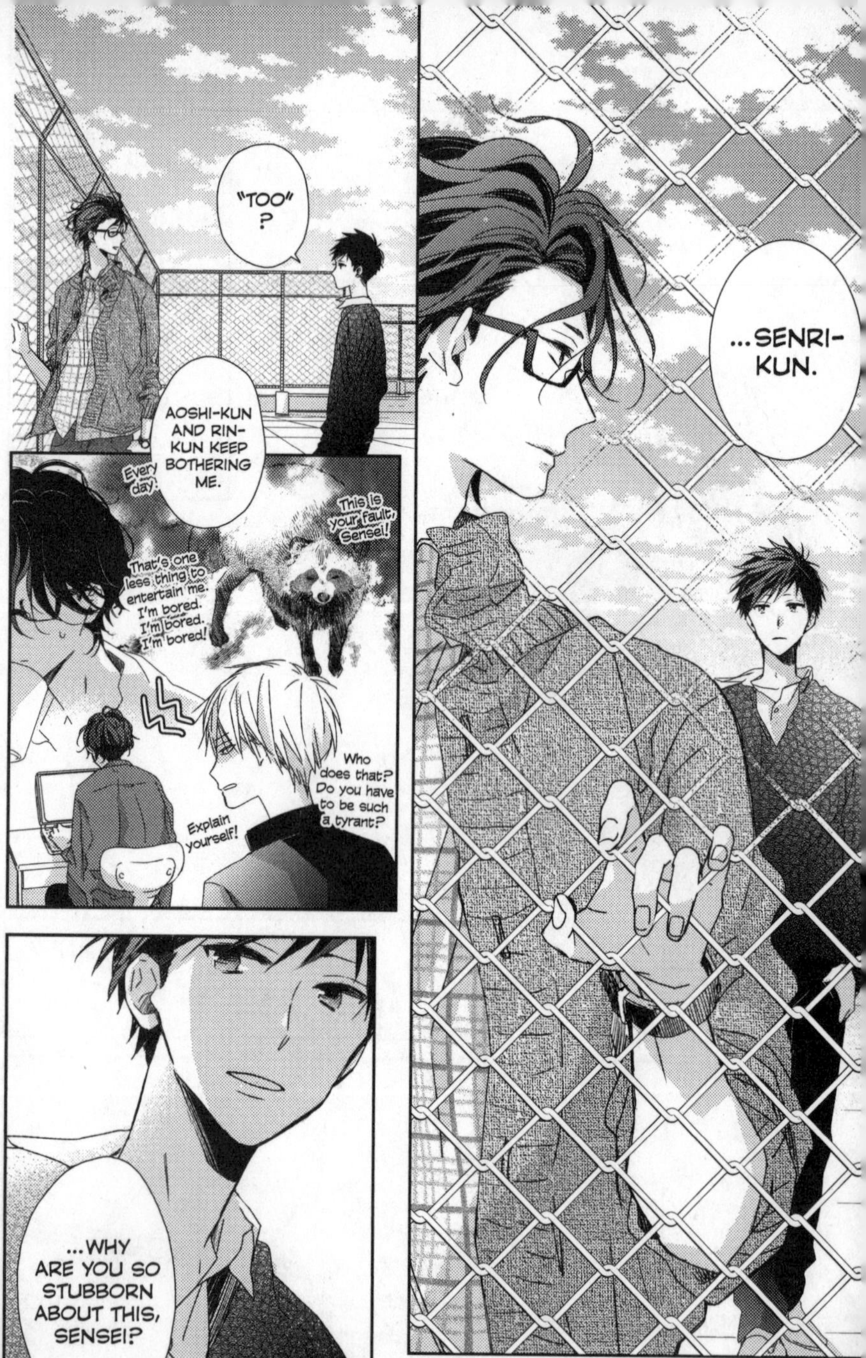
...SENRI-KUN.
"TOO"?
AOSHI-KUN AND RIN-KUN KEEP BOTHERING ME.
Every day.
This is your fault, Sensei!
That's one less thing to entertain me. I'm bored. I'm bored. I'm bored!
Who does that? Do you have to be such a tyrant?
Explain yourself!
...WHY ARE YOU SO STUBBORN ABOUT THIS, SENSEI?

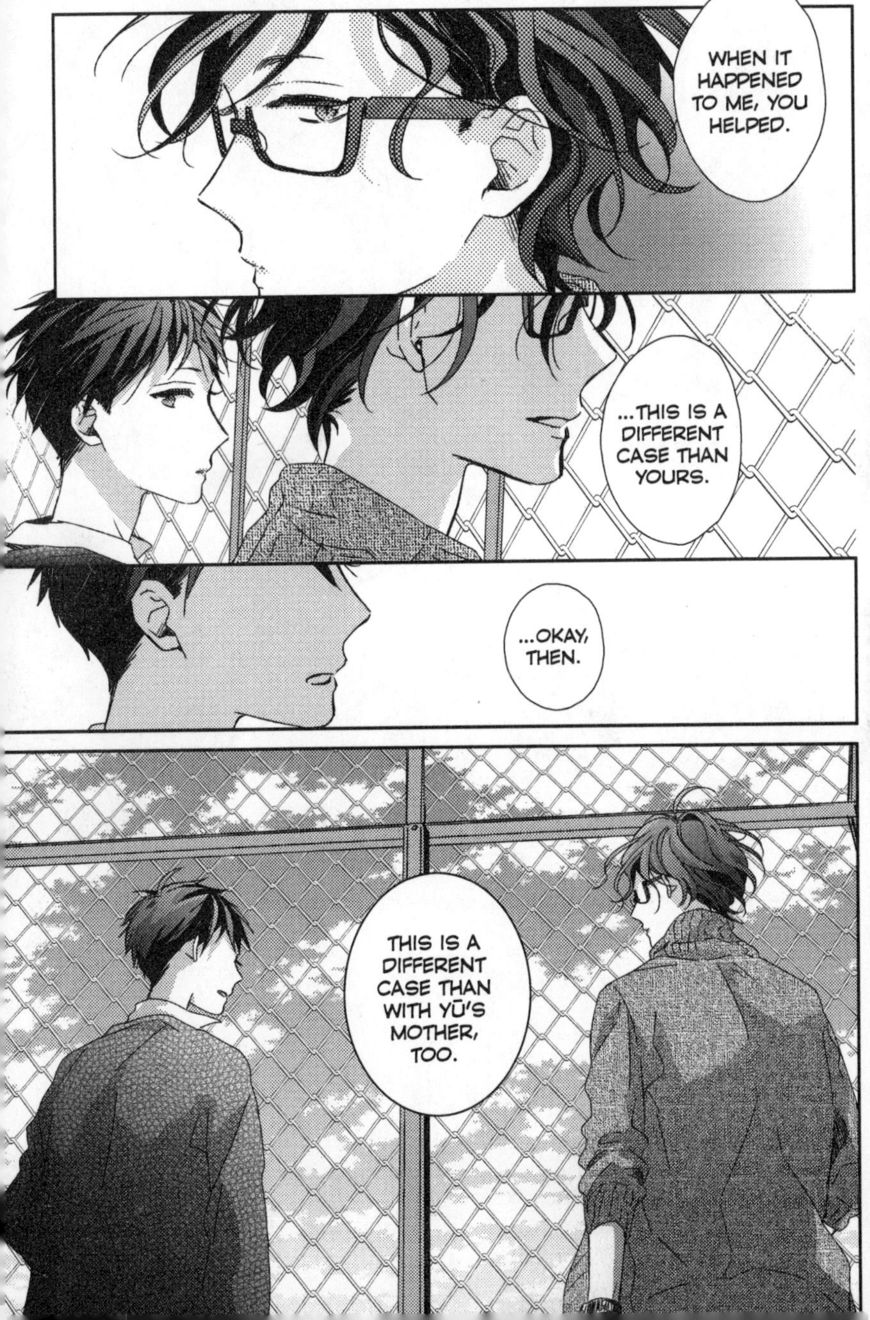
WHEN IT HAPPENED TO ME, YOU HELPED.
...THIS IS A DIFFERENT CASE THAN YOURS.
...OKAY, THEN.
THIS IS A DIFFERENT CASE THAN WITH YŪ'S MOTHER, TOO.

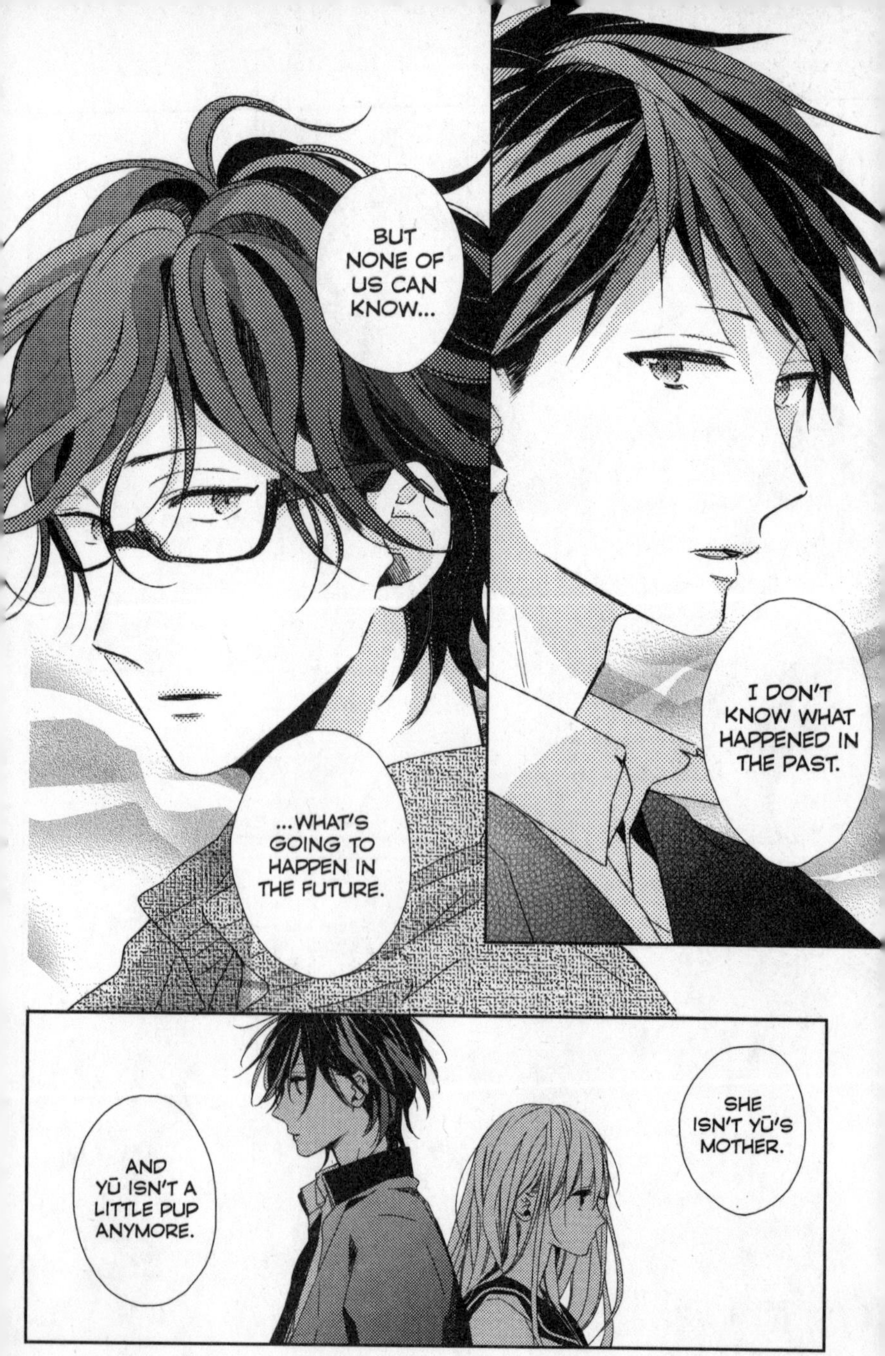
I DON'T KNOW WHAT HAPPENED IN THE PAST.
BUT NONE OF US CAN KNOW...
...WHAT'S GOING TO HAPPEN IN THE FUTURE.
SHE ISN'T YŪ'S MOTHER.
AND YŪ ISN'T A LITTLE PUP ANYMORE.

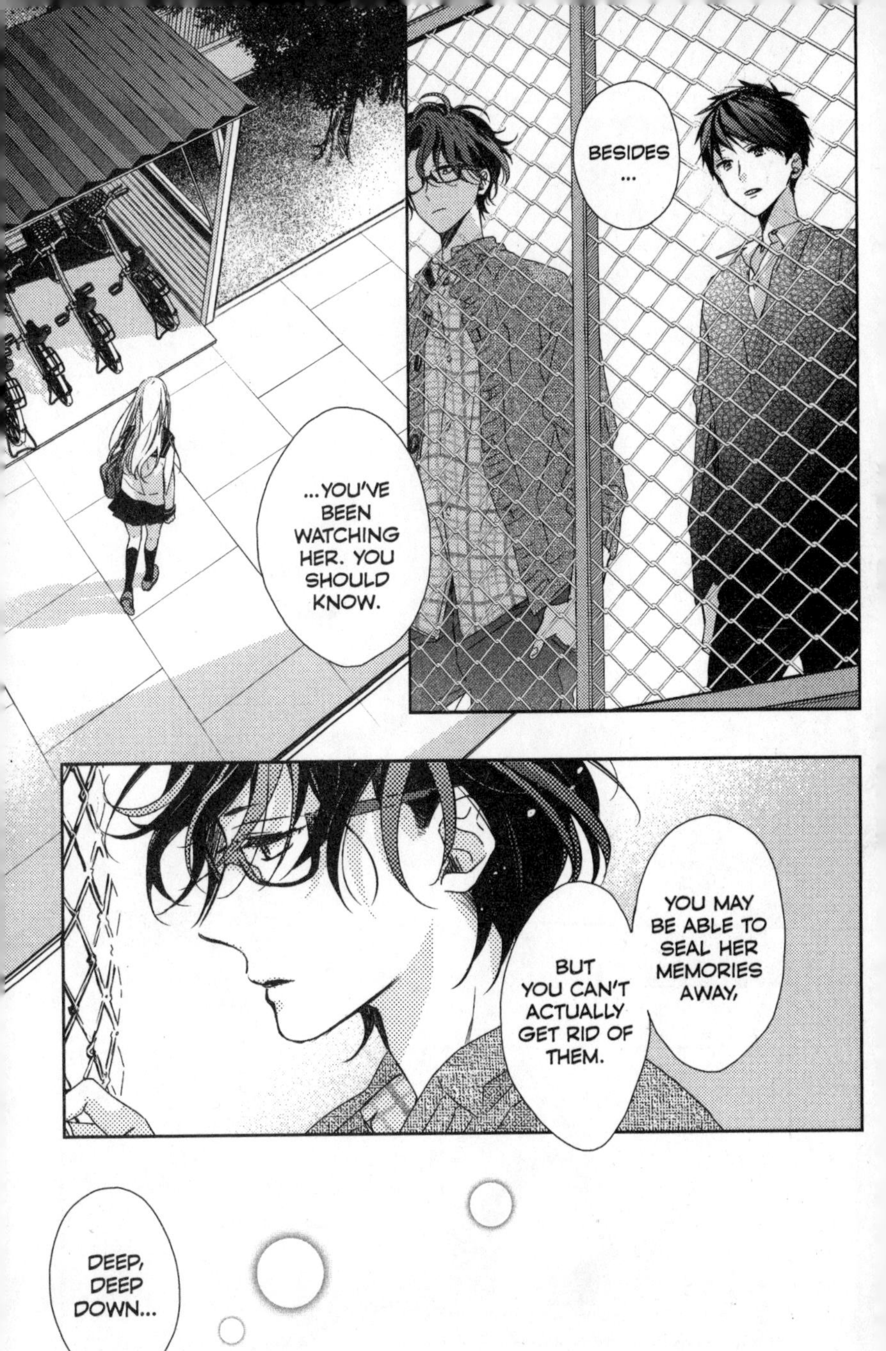
BESIDES...
...YOU'VE BEEN WATCHING HER. YOU SHOULD KNOW.
YOU MAY BE ABLE TO SEAL HER MEMORIES AWAY,
BUT YOU CAN'T ACTUALLY GET RID OF THEM.
DEEP, DEEP DOWN...

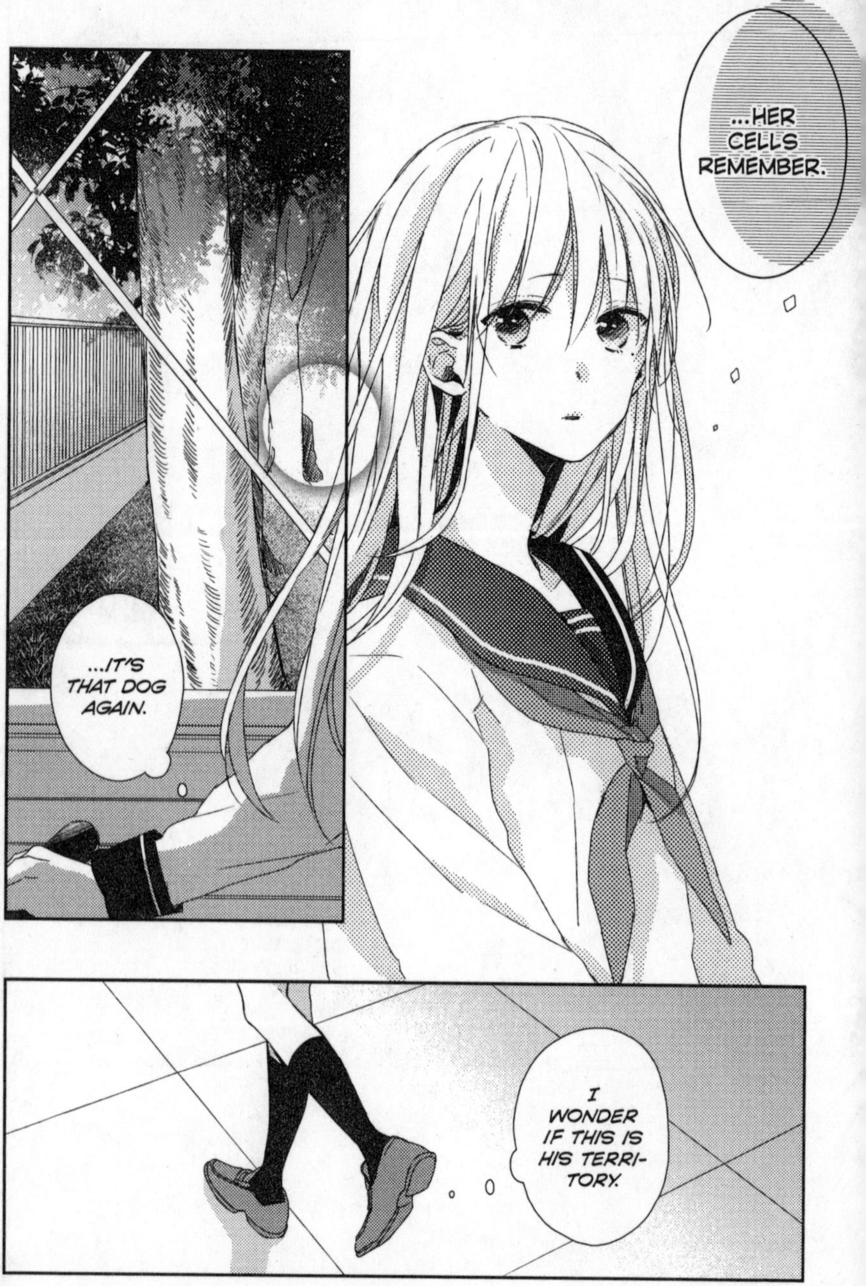
...HER CELLS REMEMBER.
...IT'S THAT DOG AGAIN.
I WONDER IF THIS IS HIS TERRI-TORY.

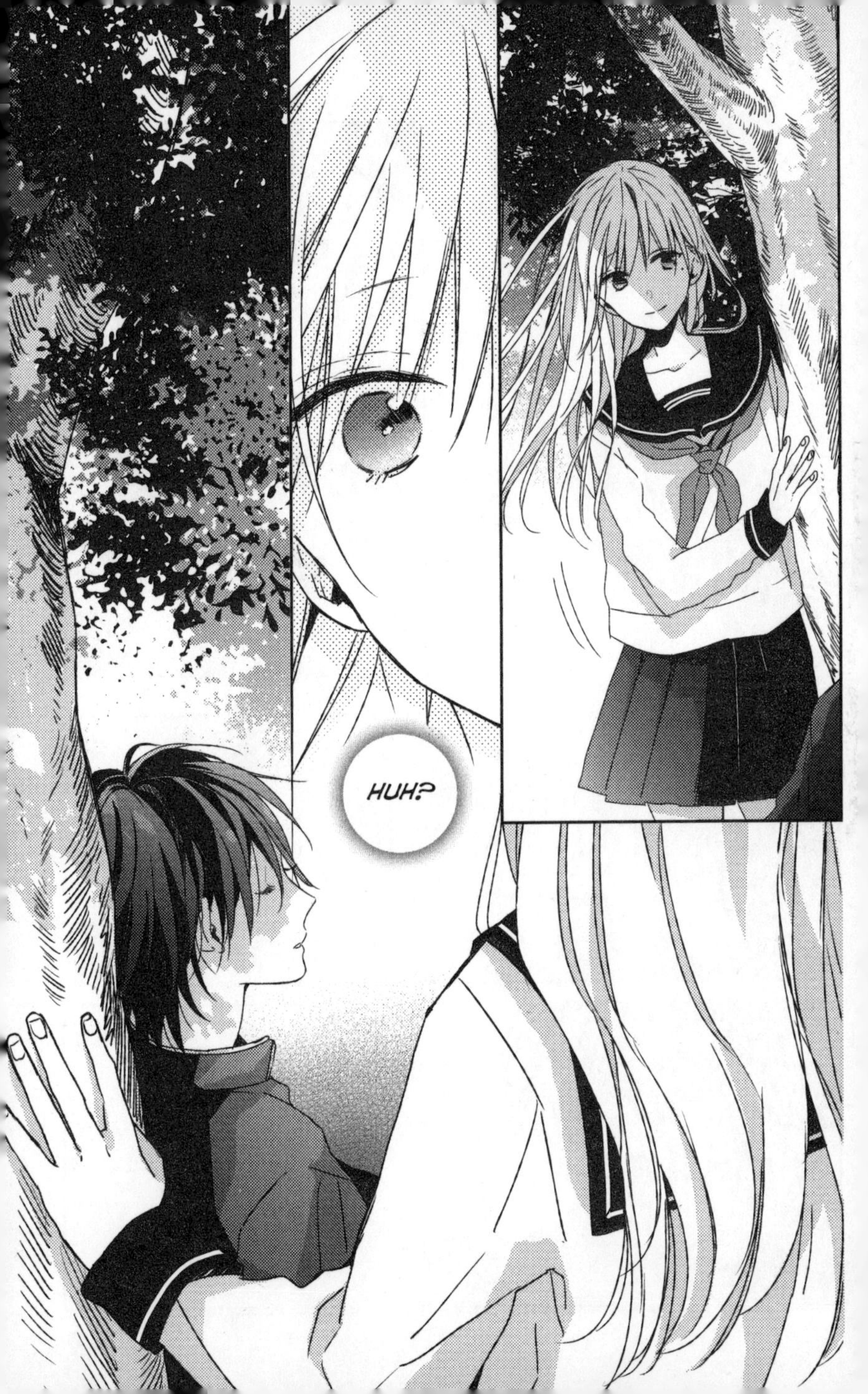
HUH?

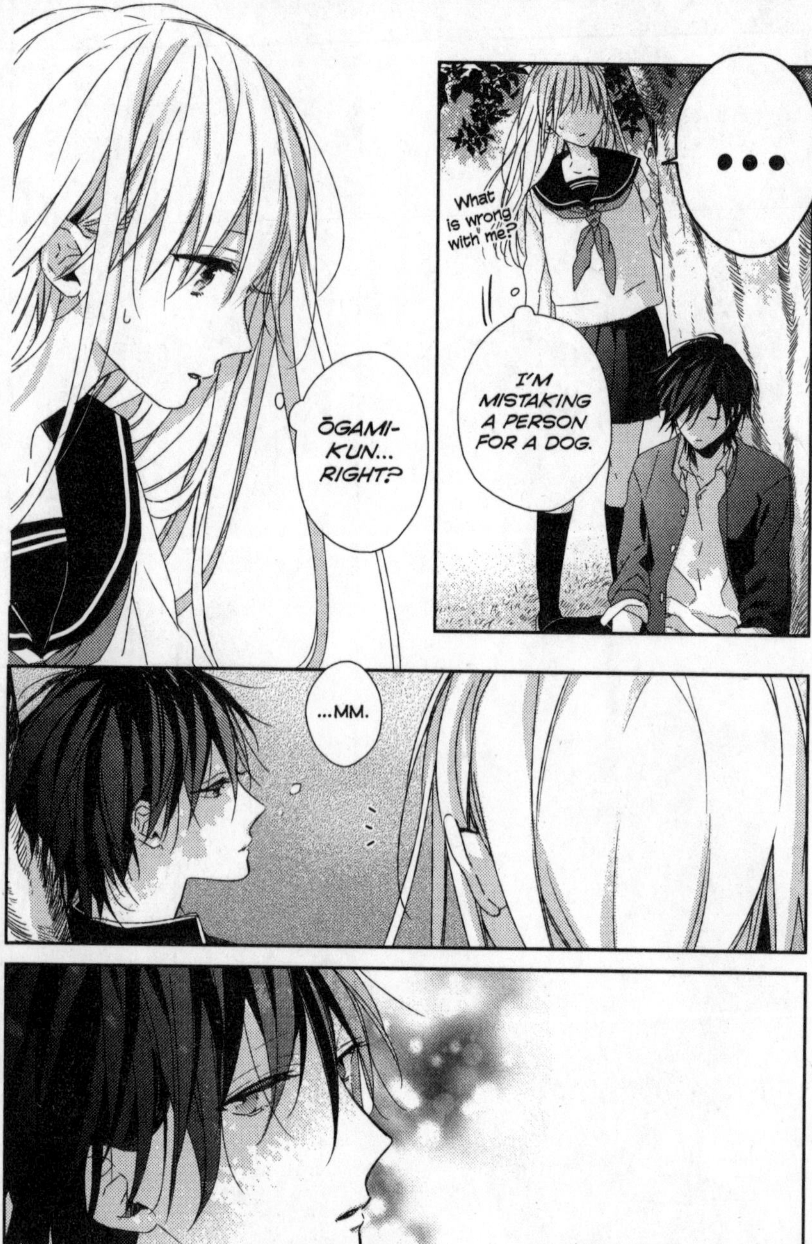
...
What is wrong with me?
I'M MISTAKING A PERSON FOR A DOG.
ŌGAMI-KUN... RIGHT?
...MM.

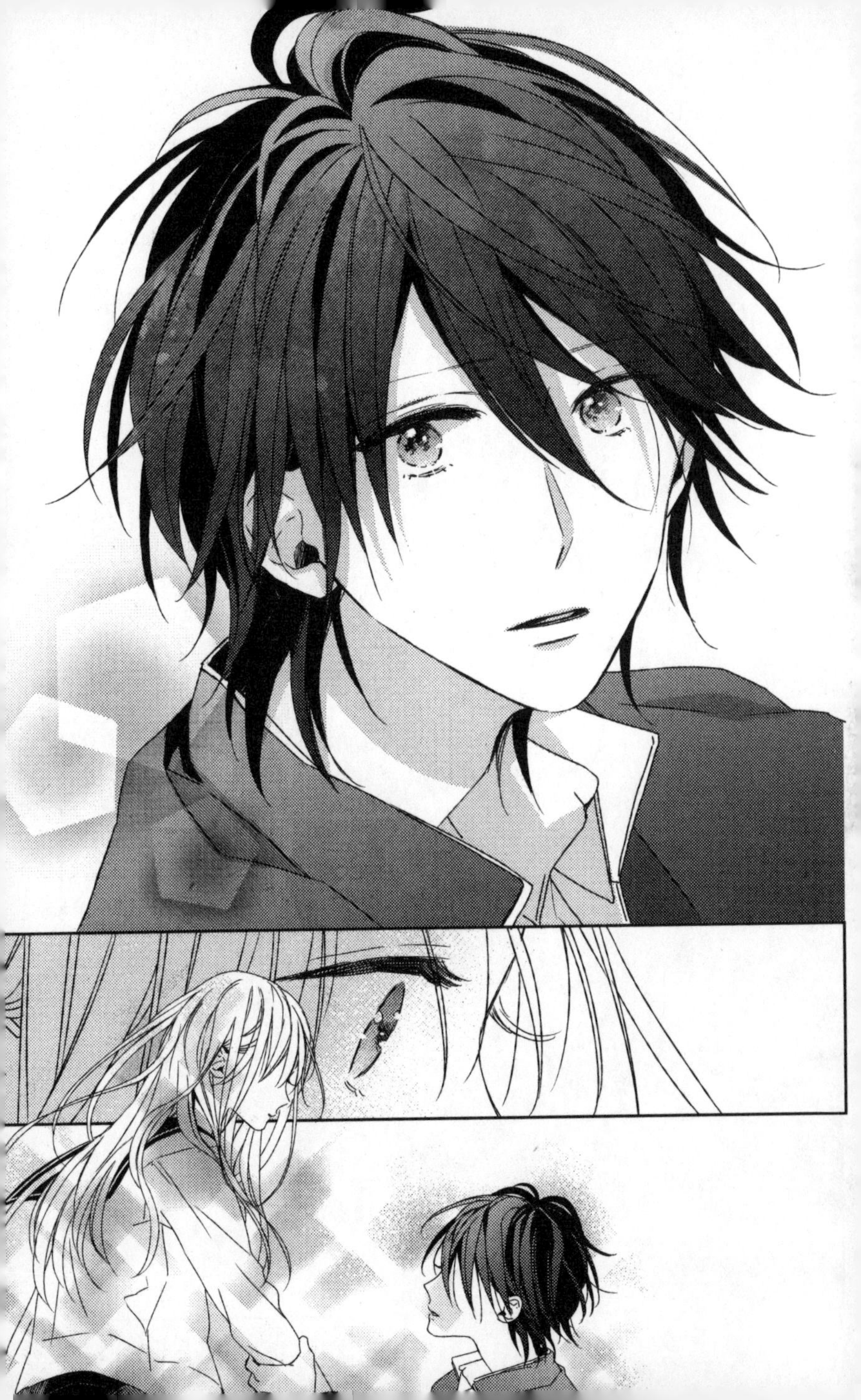

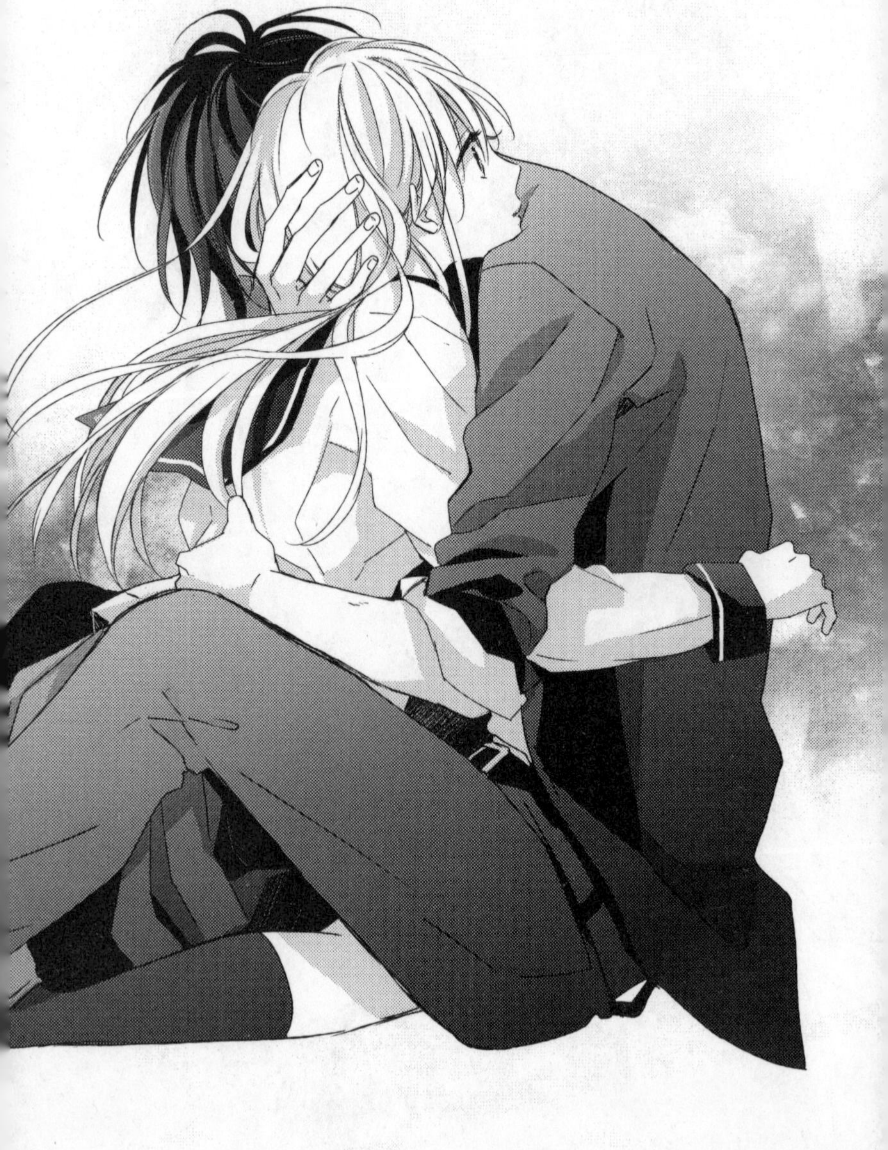

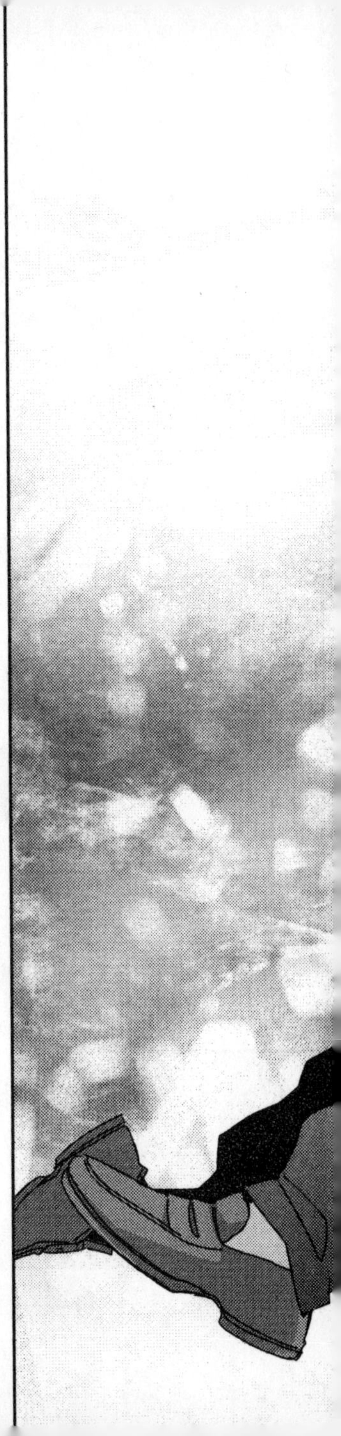

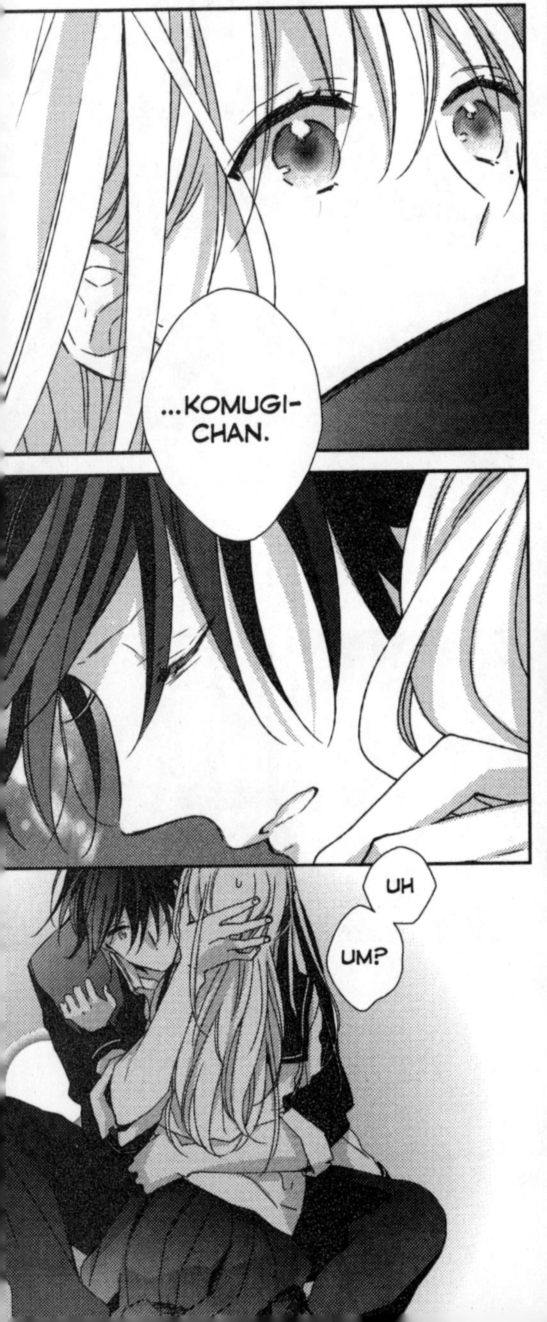
...KOMUGI-CHAN.
UH
UM?

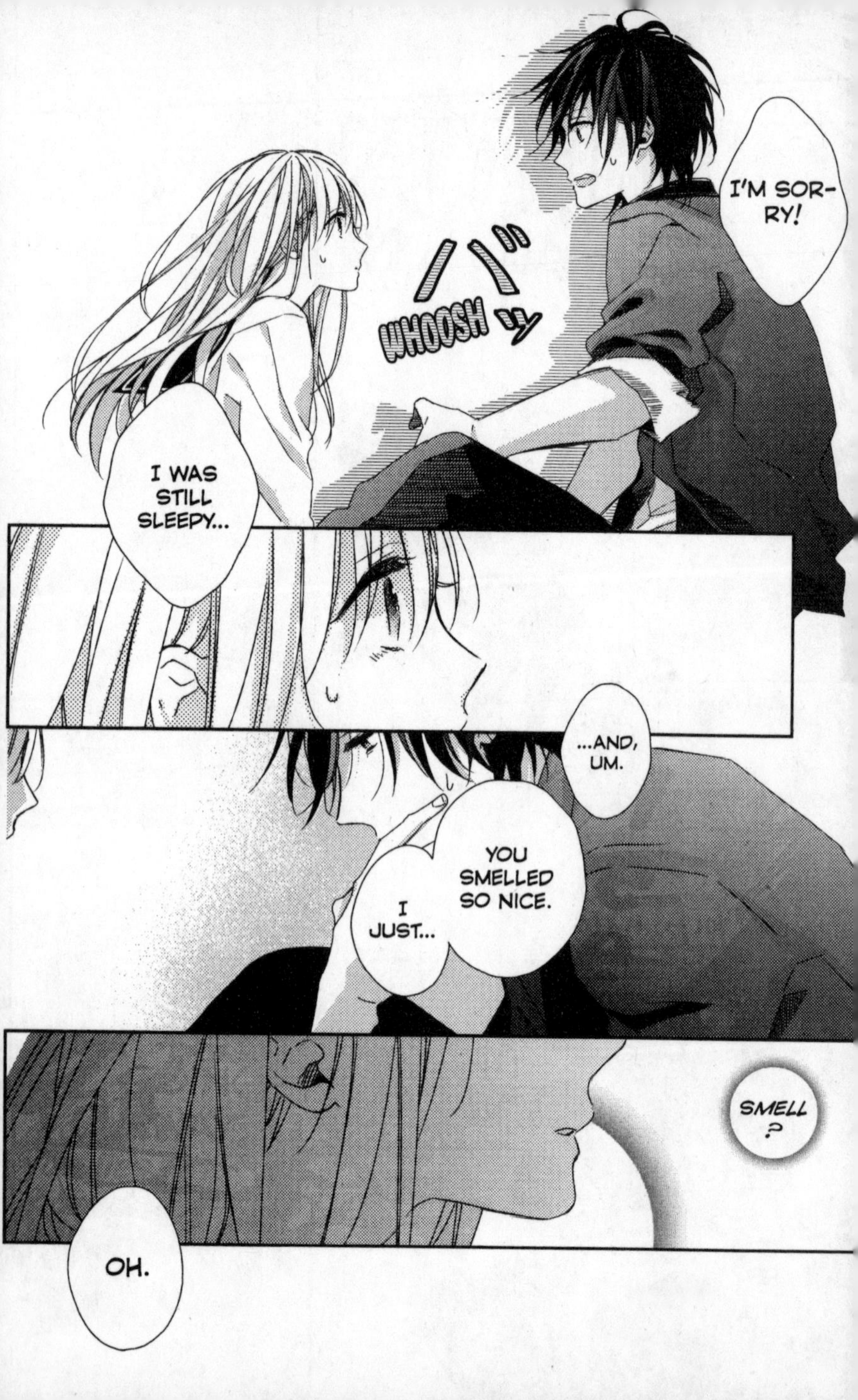
I'M SORRY!
バッ
WHOOSH
I WAS STILL SLEEPY...
...AND, UM.
YOU SMELLED SO NICE.
I JUST...
SMELL?
OH.

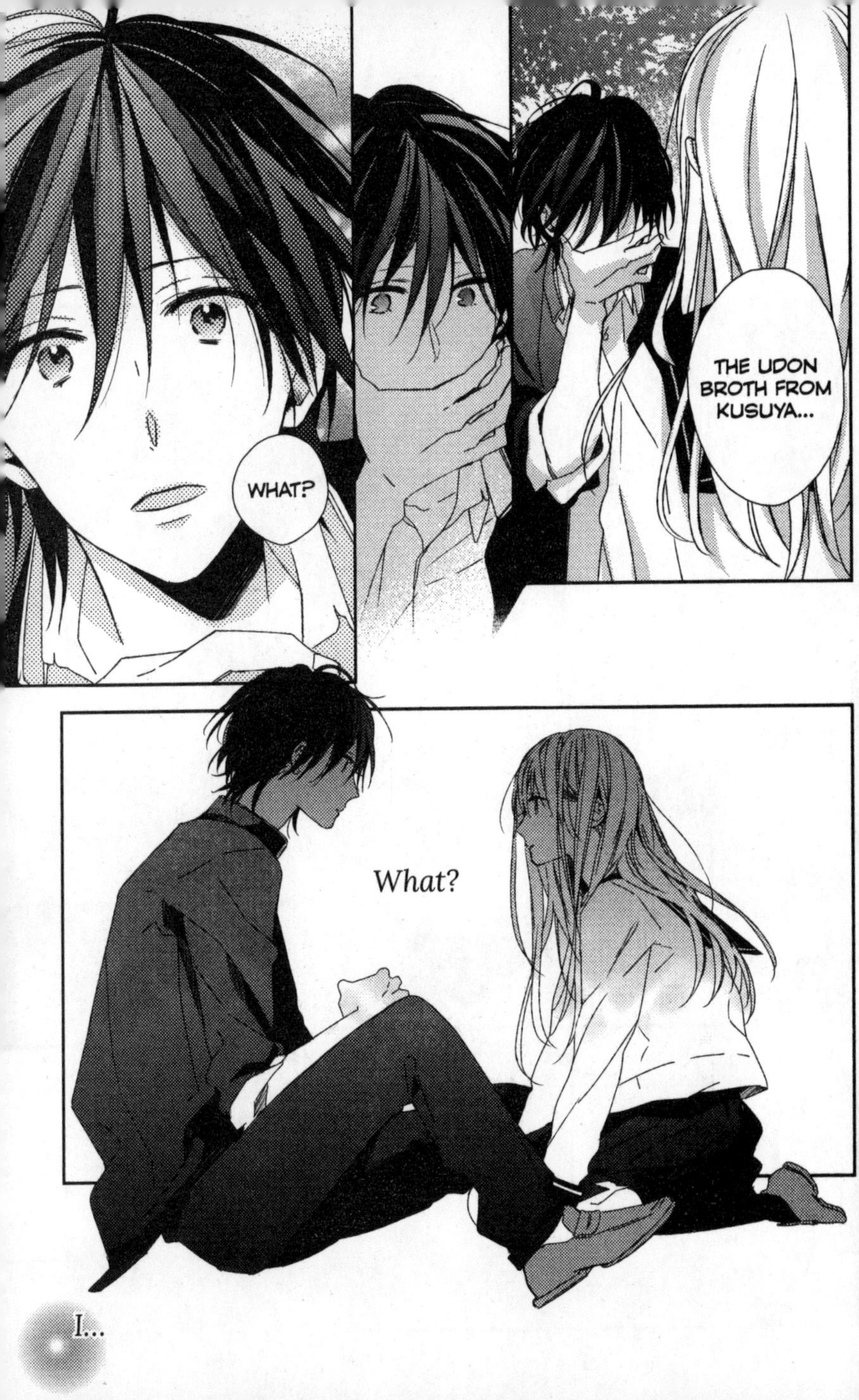
THE UDON BROTH FROM KUSUYA...
WHAT?
What?
I...

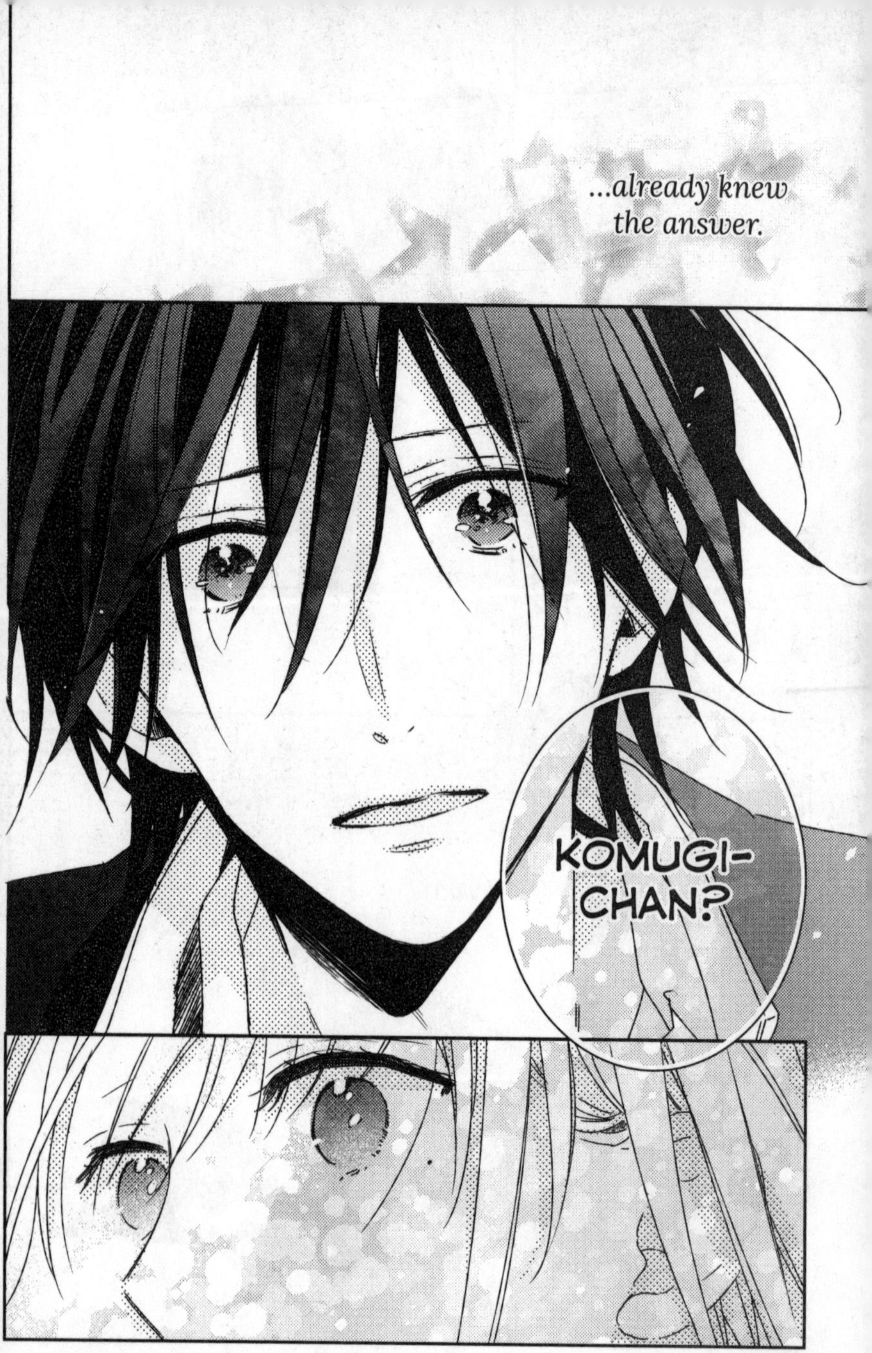
...already knew the answer.
KOMUGI-CHAN?

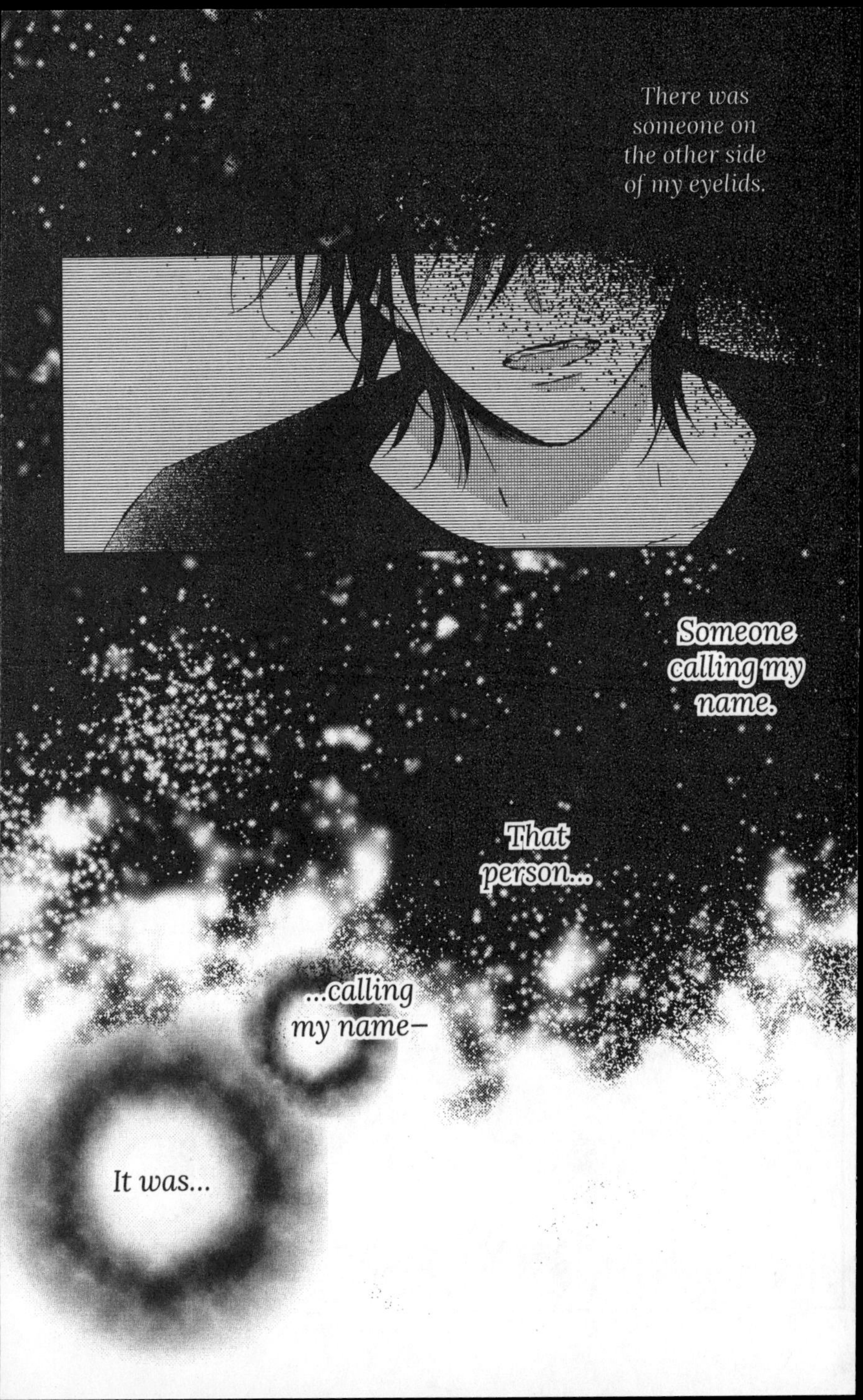
There was someone on the other side of my eyelids.
Someone calling my name.
That person...
...calling my name–
It was...

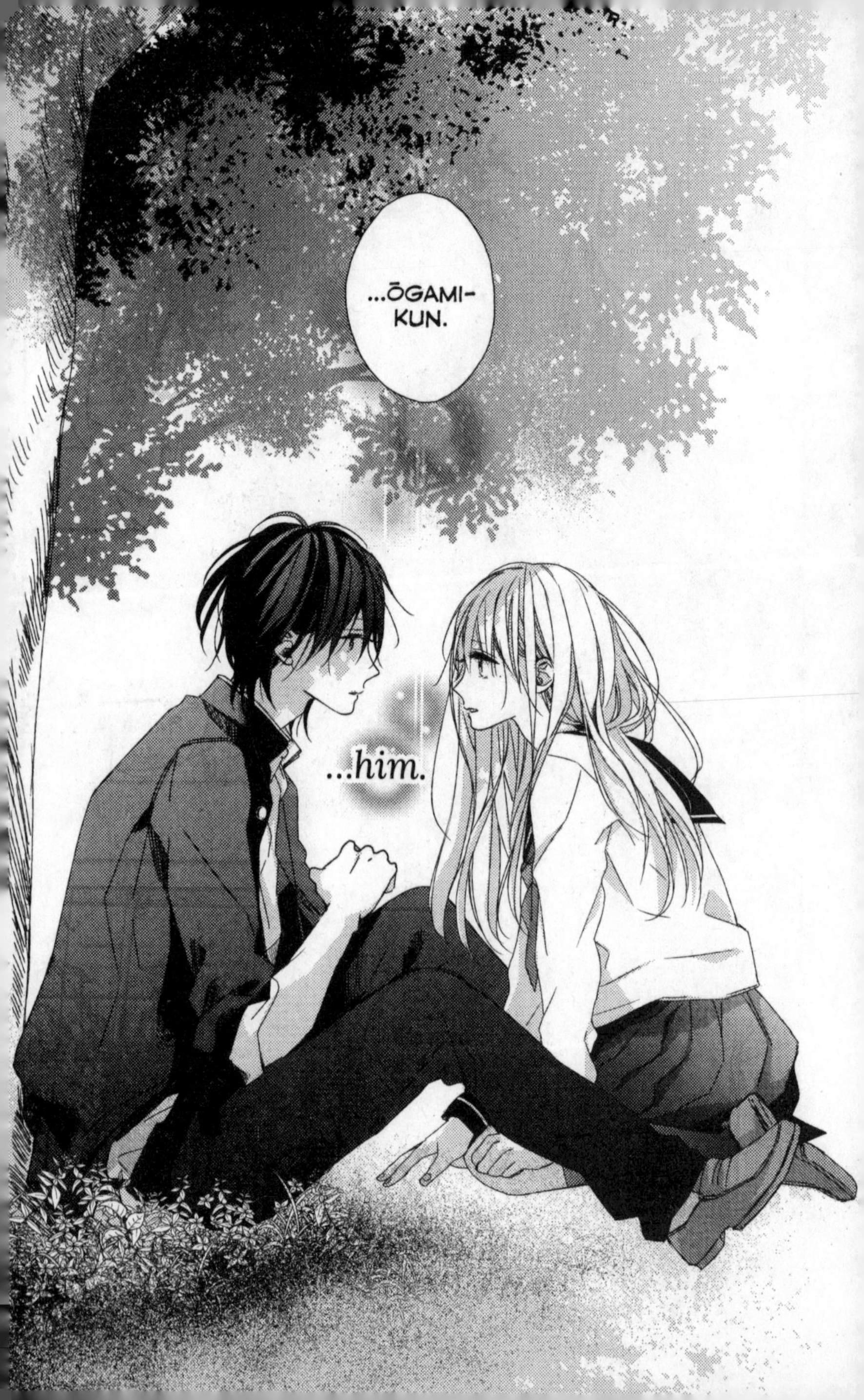
...ŌGAMI-KUN.
...him.

Chapter 16

"Ōgami-kun."

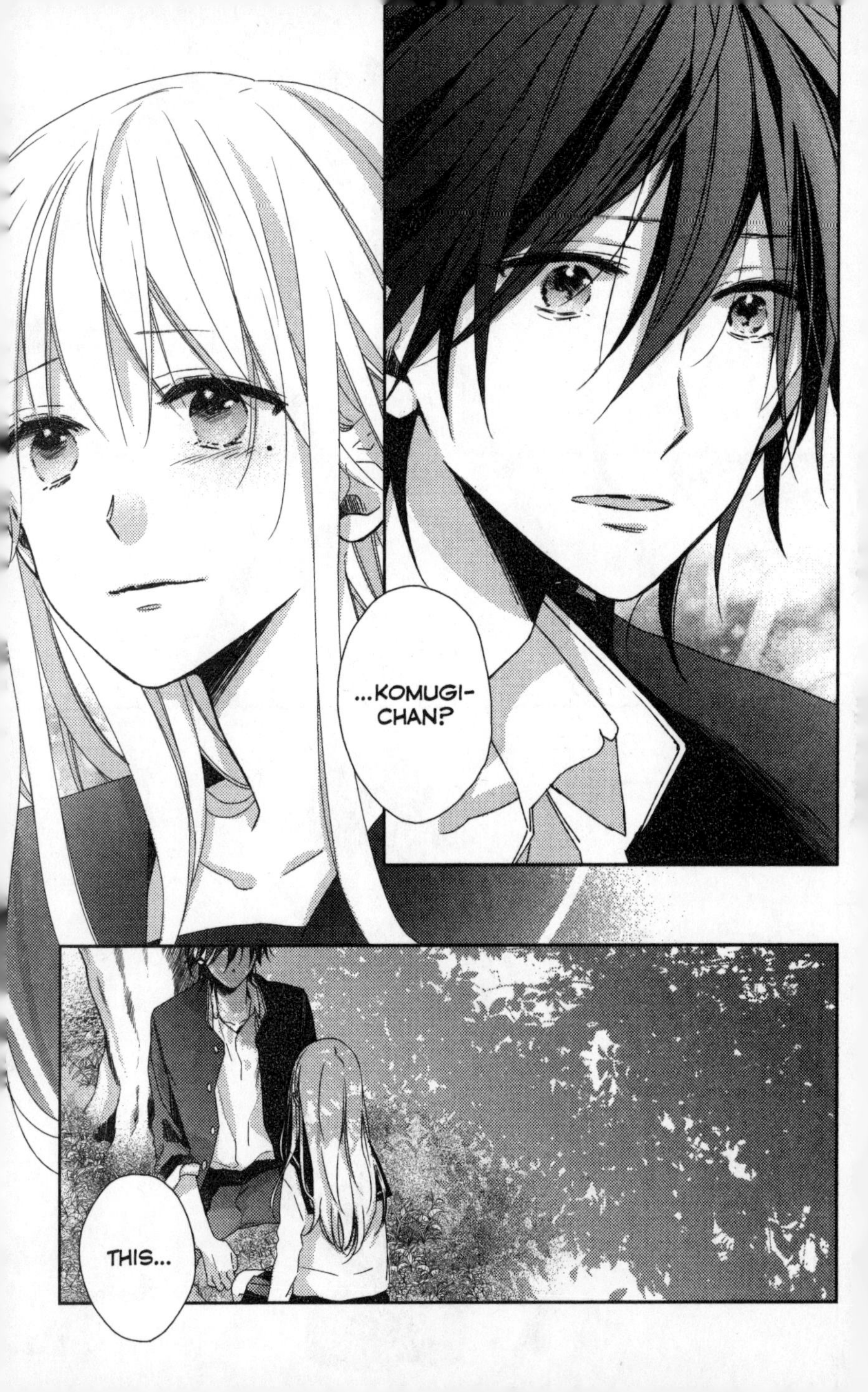
...KOMUGI-CHAN?
THIS...

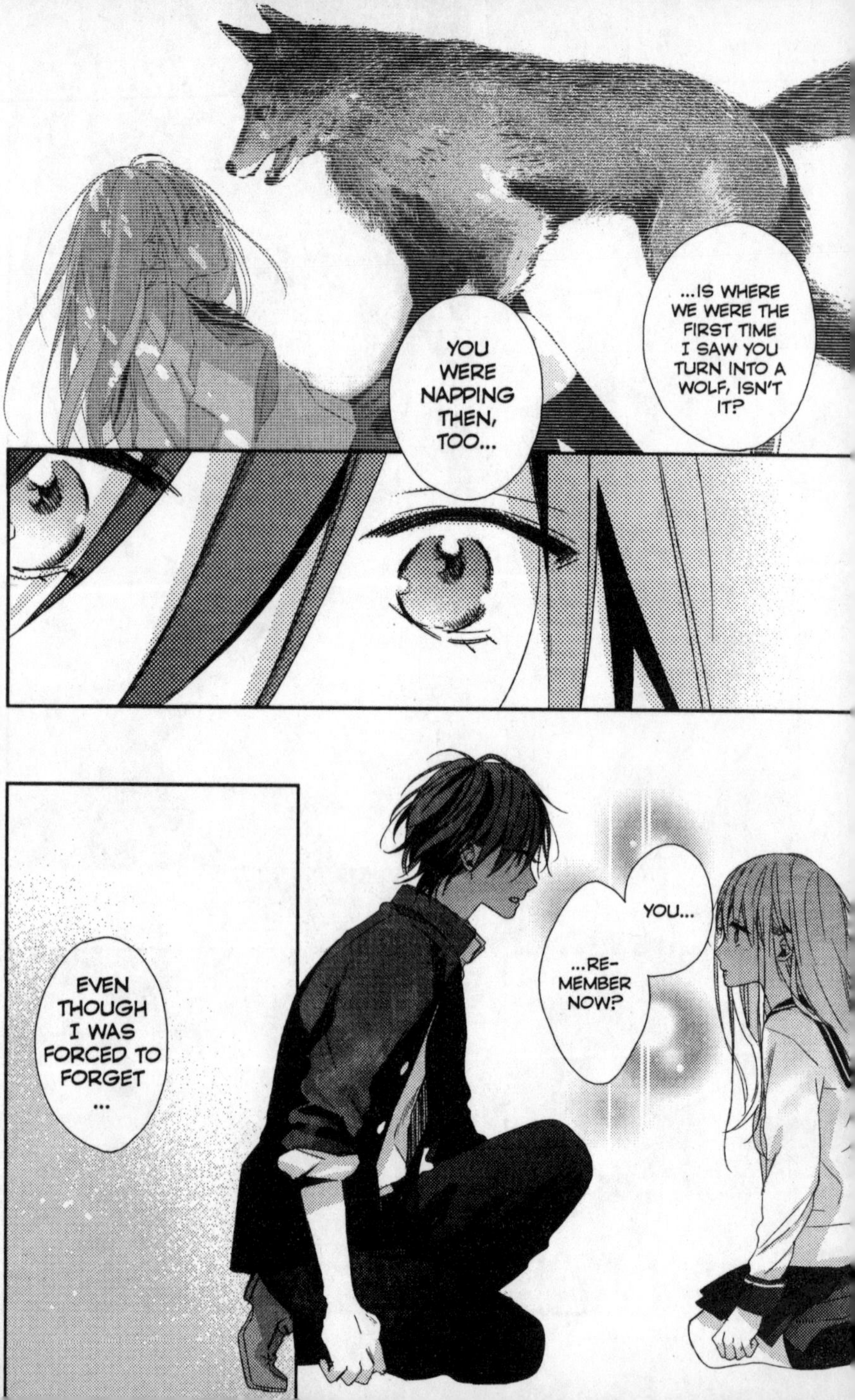
...IS WHERE WE WERE THE FIRST TIME I SAW YOU TURN INTO A WOLF, ISN'T IT?
YOU WERE NAPPING THEN, TOO...
YOU...
...RE-MEMBER NOW?
EVEN THOUGH I WAS FORCED TO FORGET ...

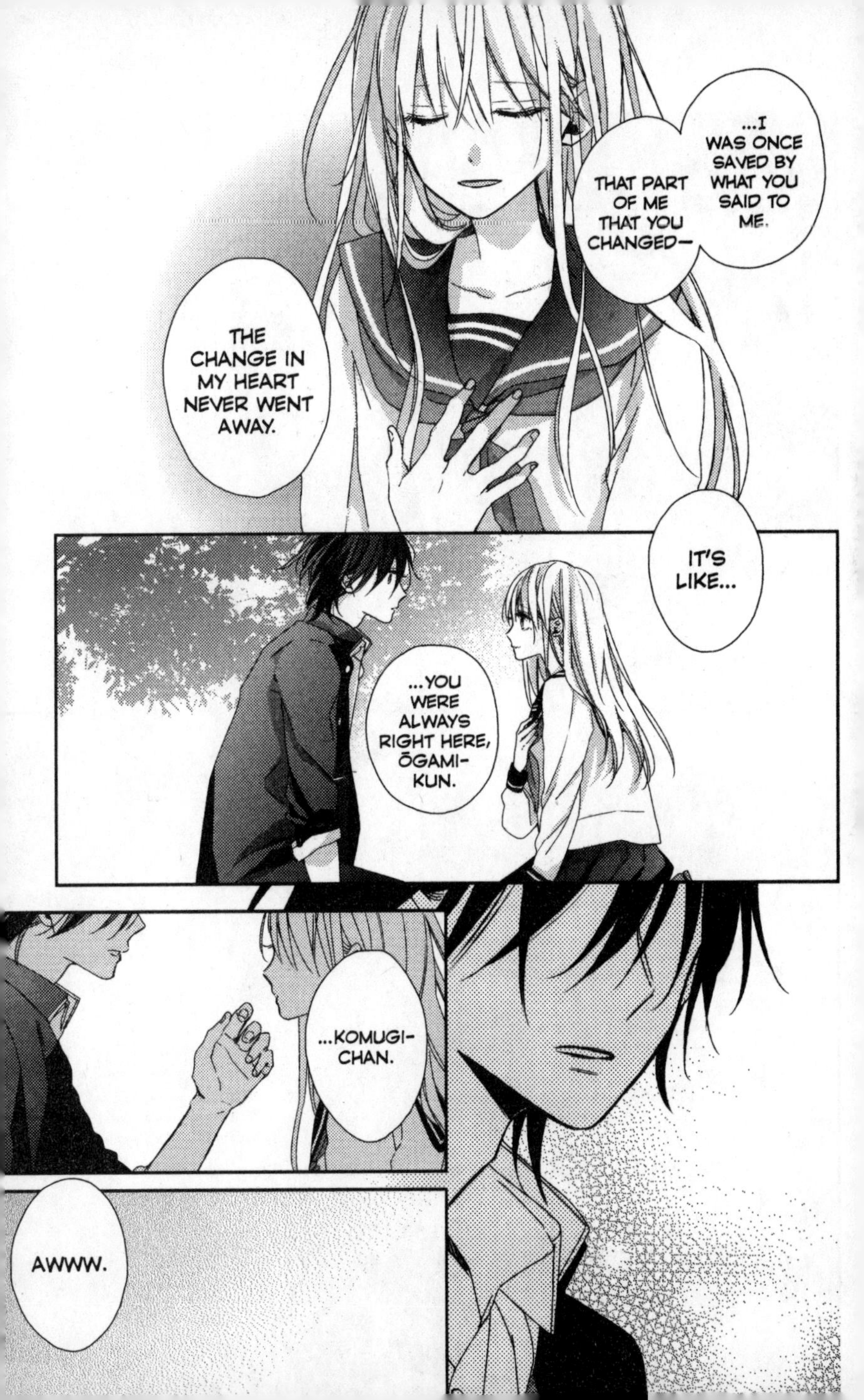
...I WAS ONCE SAVED BY WHAT YOU SAID TO ME.
THAT PART OF ME THAT YOU CHANGED—
THE CHANGE IN MY HEART NEVER WENT AWAY.
IT'S LIKE...
...YOU WERE ALWAYS RIGHT HERE, ŌGAMI-KUN.
...KOMUGI-CHAN.
AWWW.

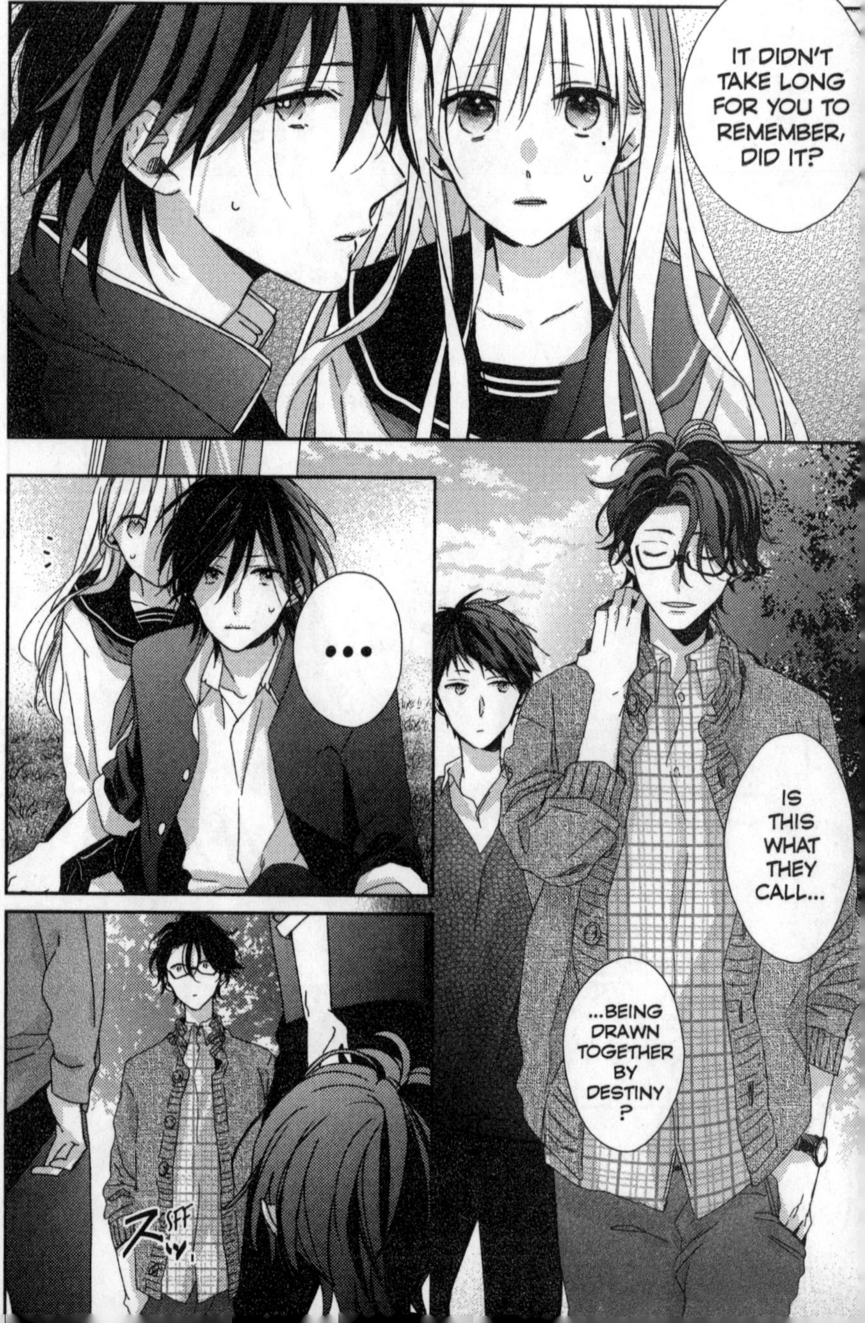
IT DIDN'T TAKE LONG FOR YOU TO REMEMBER, DID IT?
IS THIS WHAT THEY CALL...
...BEING DRAWN TOGETHER BY DESTINY?
...
SFF

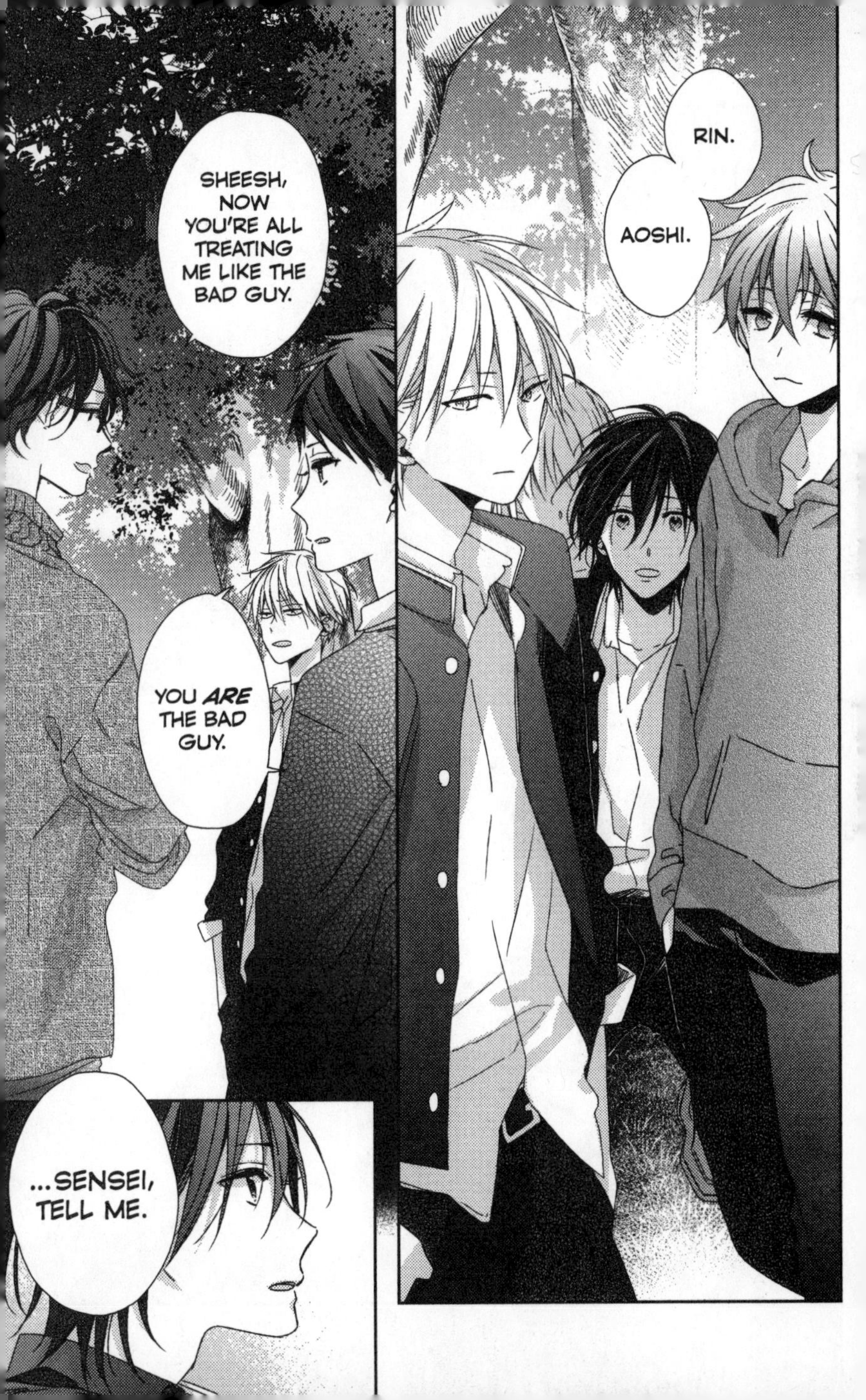
RIN.
AOSHI.
SHEESH, NOW YOU'RE ALL TREATING ME LIKE THE BAD GUY.
YOU *ARE* THE BAD GUY.
...SENSEI, TELL ME.

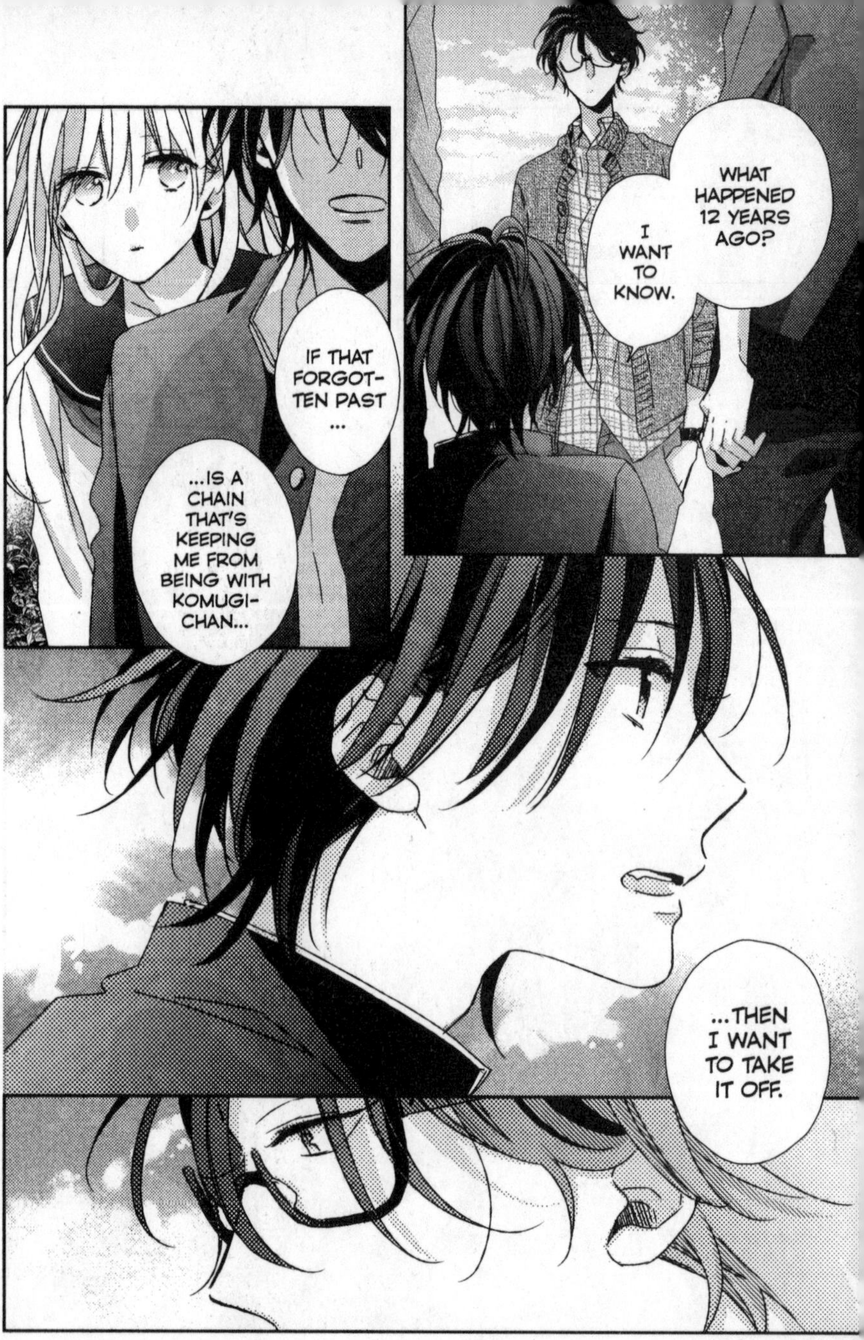
WHAT HAPPENED 12 YEARS AGO?
I WANT TO KNOW.
IF THAT FORGOT-TEN PAST ...
...IS A CHAIN THAT'S KEEPING ME FROM BEING WITH KOMUGI-CHAN...
...THEN I WANT TO TAKE IT OFF.

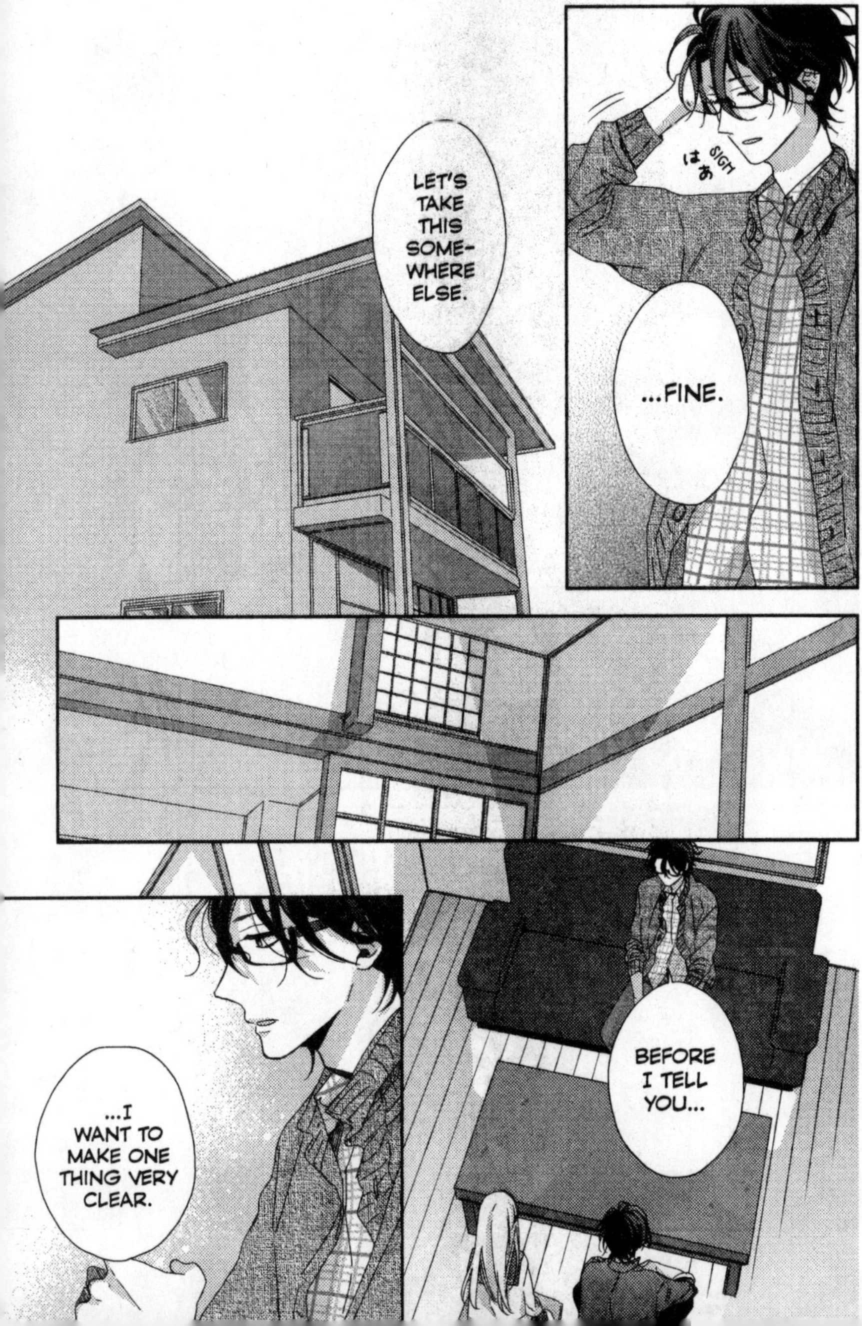
SIGH
はあ
...FINE.
LET'S TAKE THIS SOME-WHERE ELSE.
BEFORE I TELL YOU...
...I WANT TO MAKE ONE THING VERY CLEAR.

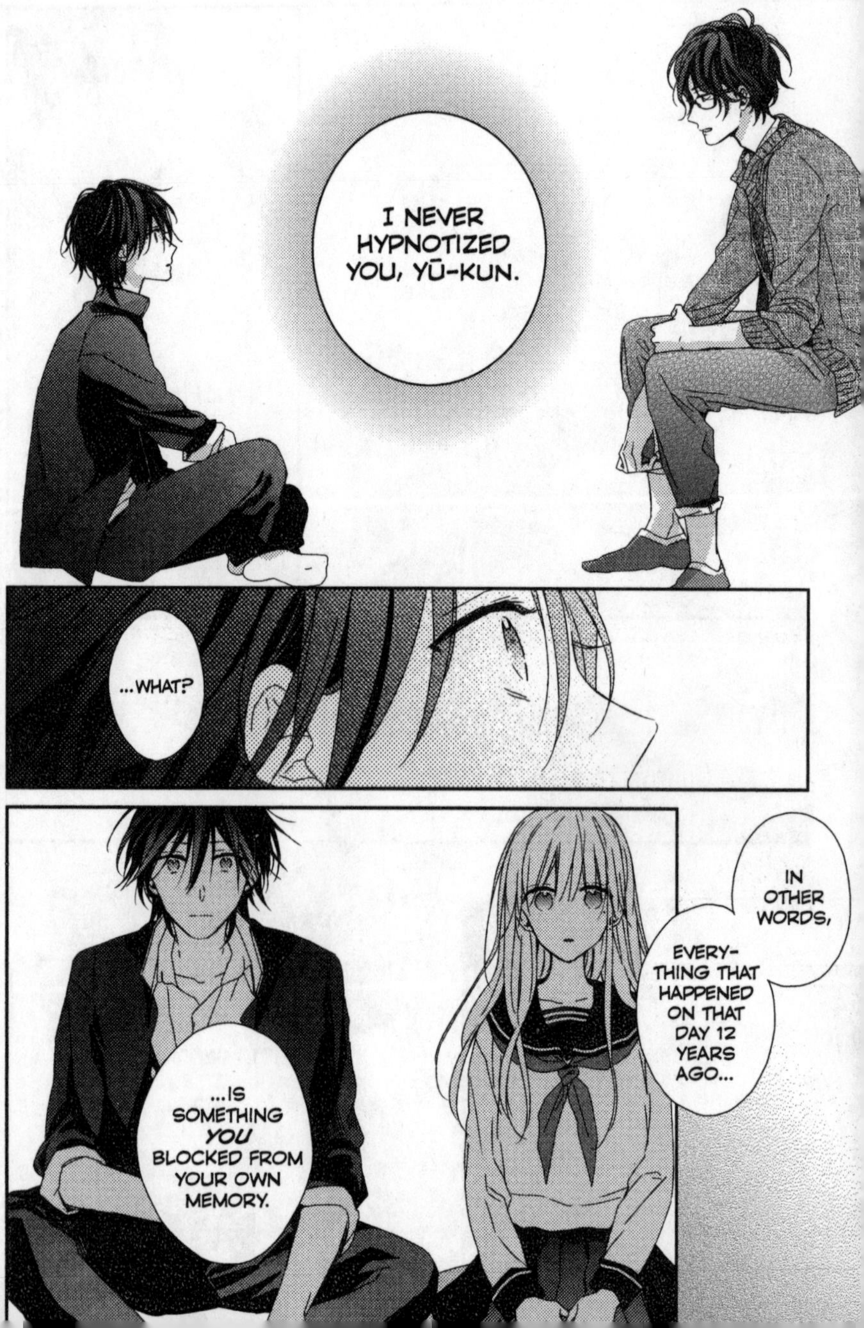
I NEVER HYPNOTIZED YOU, YŪ-KUN.
...WHAT?
IN OTHER WORDS,
EVERY-THING THAT HAPPENED ON THAT DAY 12 YEARS AGO...
...IS SOMETHING *YOU* BLOCKED FROM YOUR OWN MEMORY.

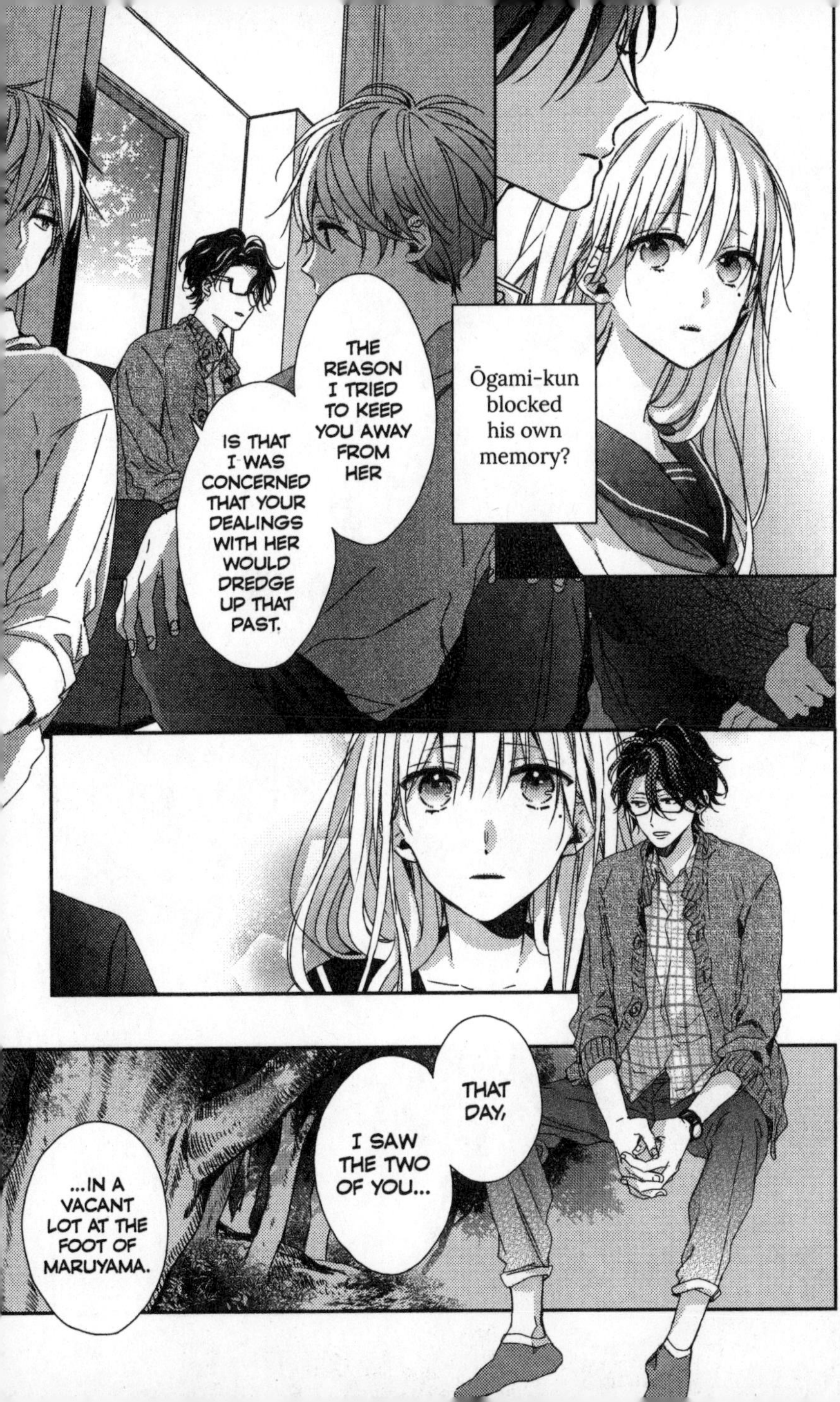
Ōgami-kun blocked his own memory?
THE REASON I TRIED TO KEEP YOU AWAY FROM HER
IS THAT I WAS CONCERNED THAT YOUR DEALINGS WITH HER WOULD DREDGE UP THAT PAST.
THAT DAY,
I SAW THE TWO OF YOU...
...IN A VACANT LOT AT THE FOOT OF MARUYAMA.

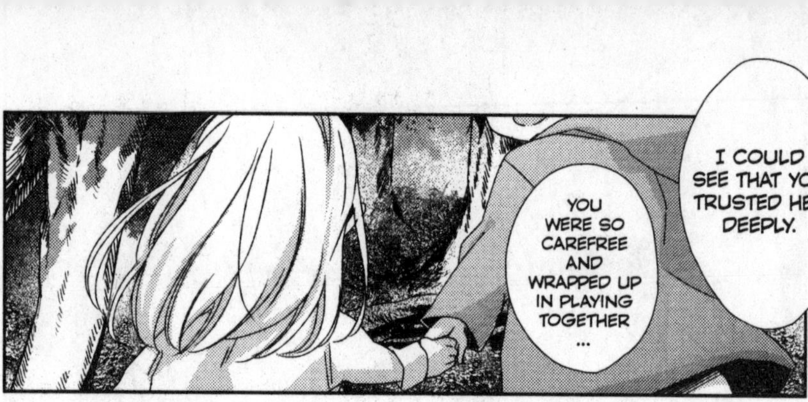
I COULD SEE THAT YOU TRUSTED HER DEEPLY.
YOU WERE SO CAREFREE AND WRAPPED UP IN PLAYING TOGETHER ...
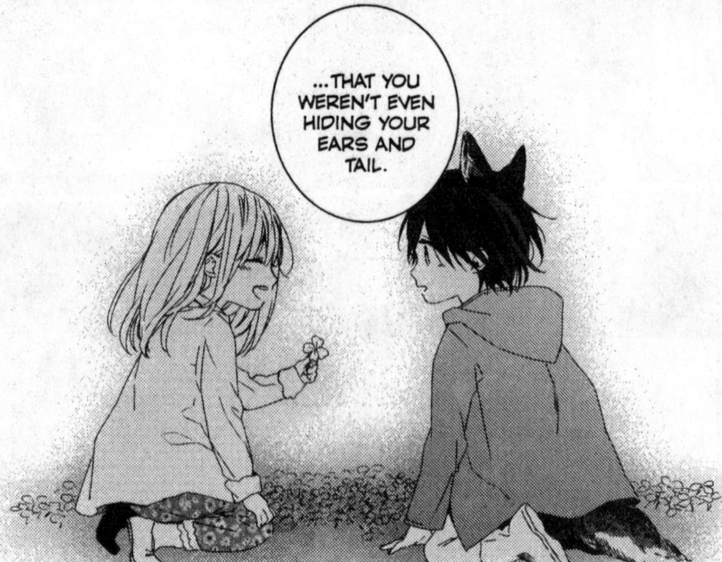
...THAT YOU WEREN'T EVEN HIDING YOUR EARS AND TAIL.
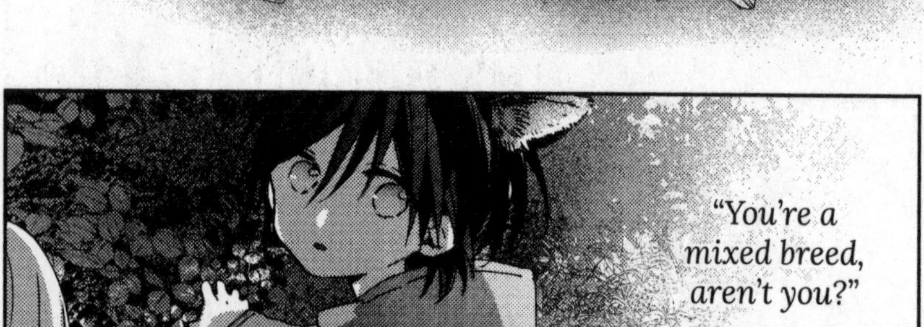
"You're a mixed breed, aren't you?"

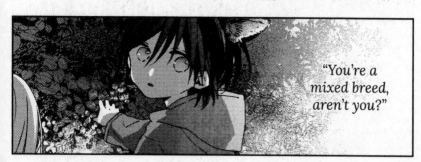

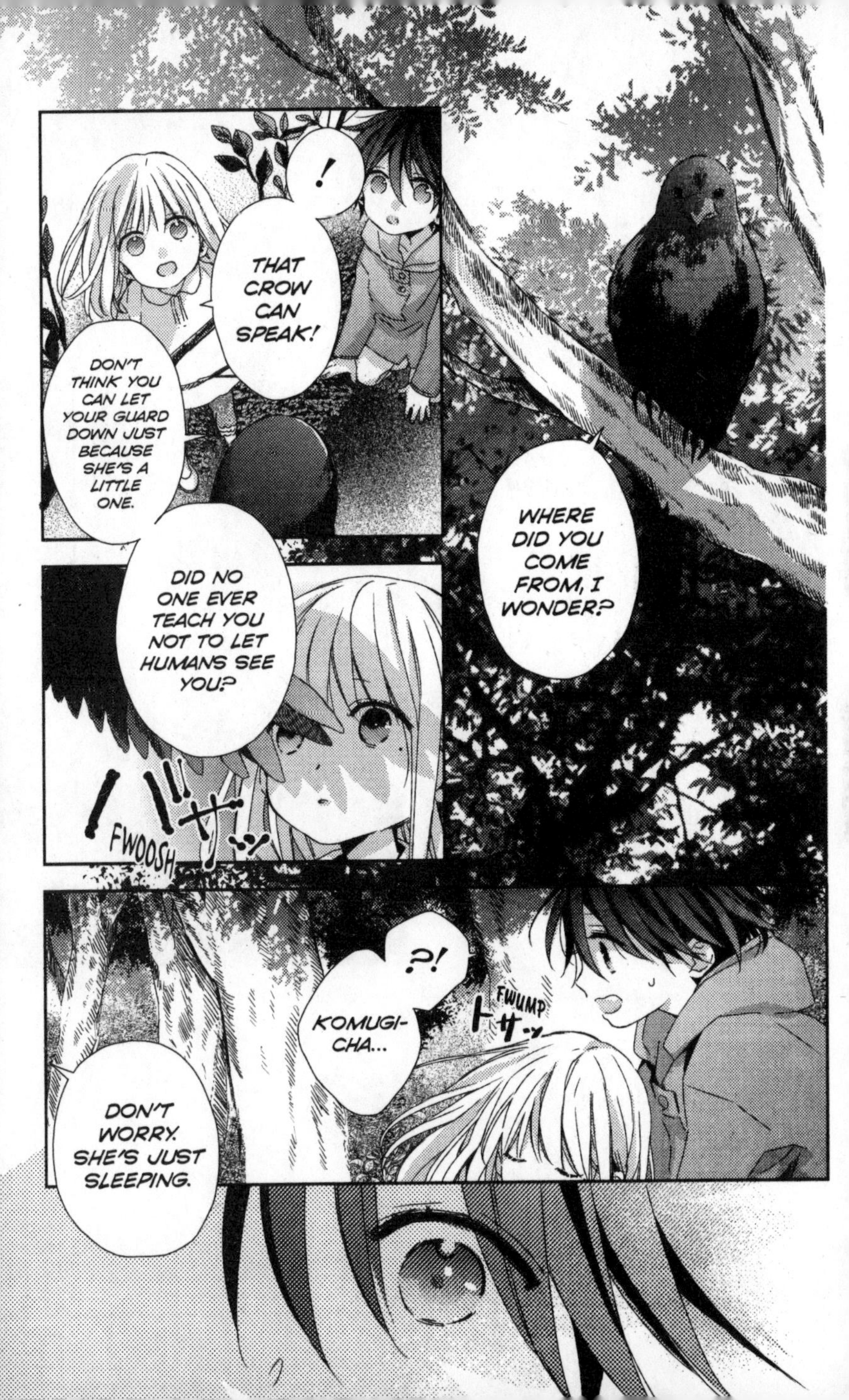
WHERE DID YOU COME FROM, I WONDER?
!
THAT CROW CAN SPEAK!
DON'T THINK YOU CAN LET YOUR GUARD DOWN JUST BECAUSE SHE'S A LITTLE ONE.
DID NO ONE EVER TEACH YOU NOT TO LET HUMANS SEE YOU?
FWOOSH
?!
FWUMP
KOMUGI-CHA...
DON'T WORRY. SHE'S JUST SLEEPING.

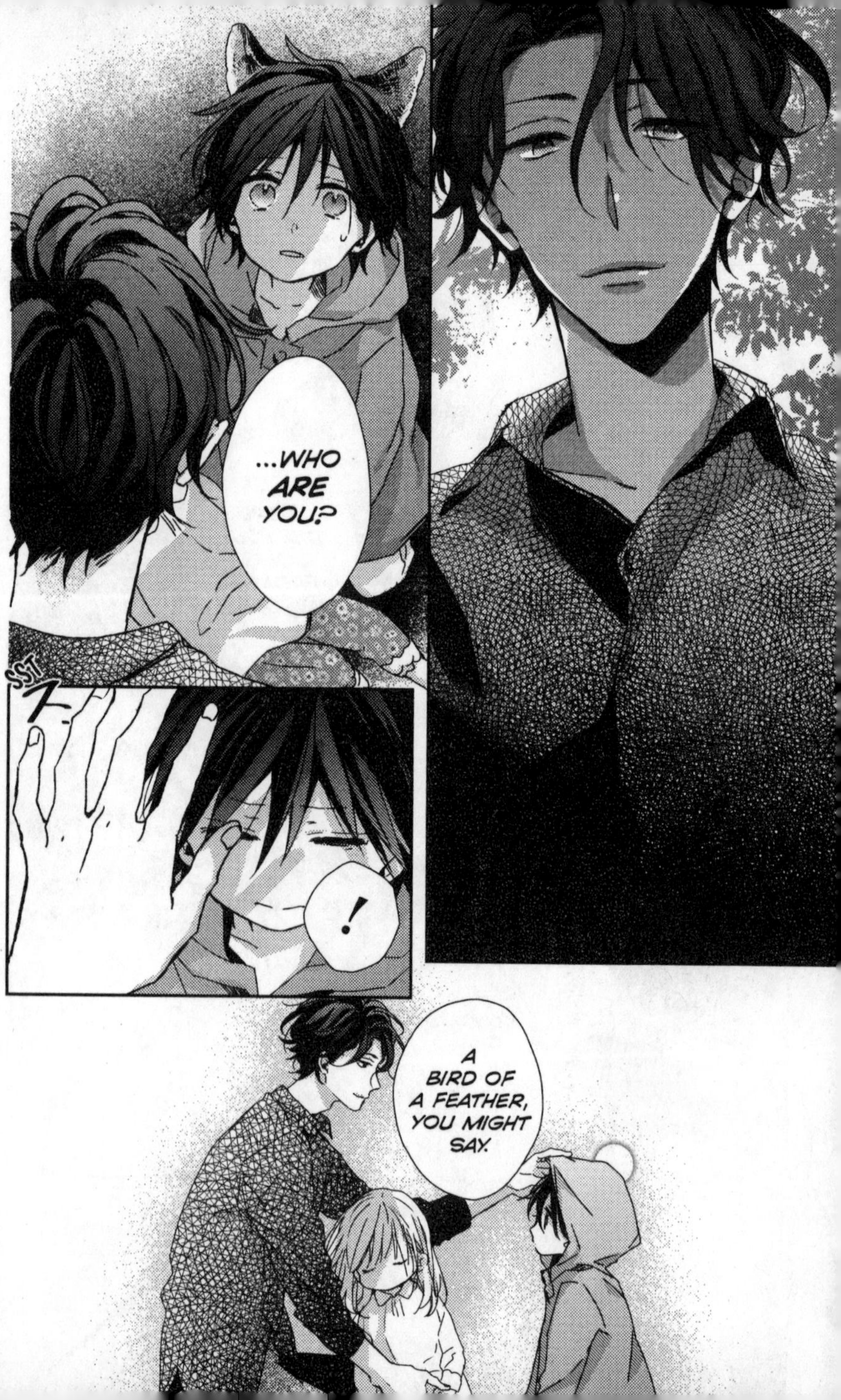
...WHO ARE YOU?
SST
!
A BIRD OF A FEATHER, YOU MIGHT SAY.

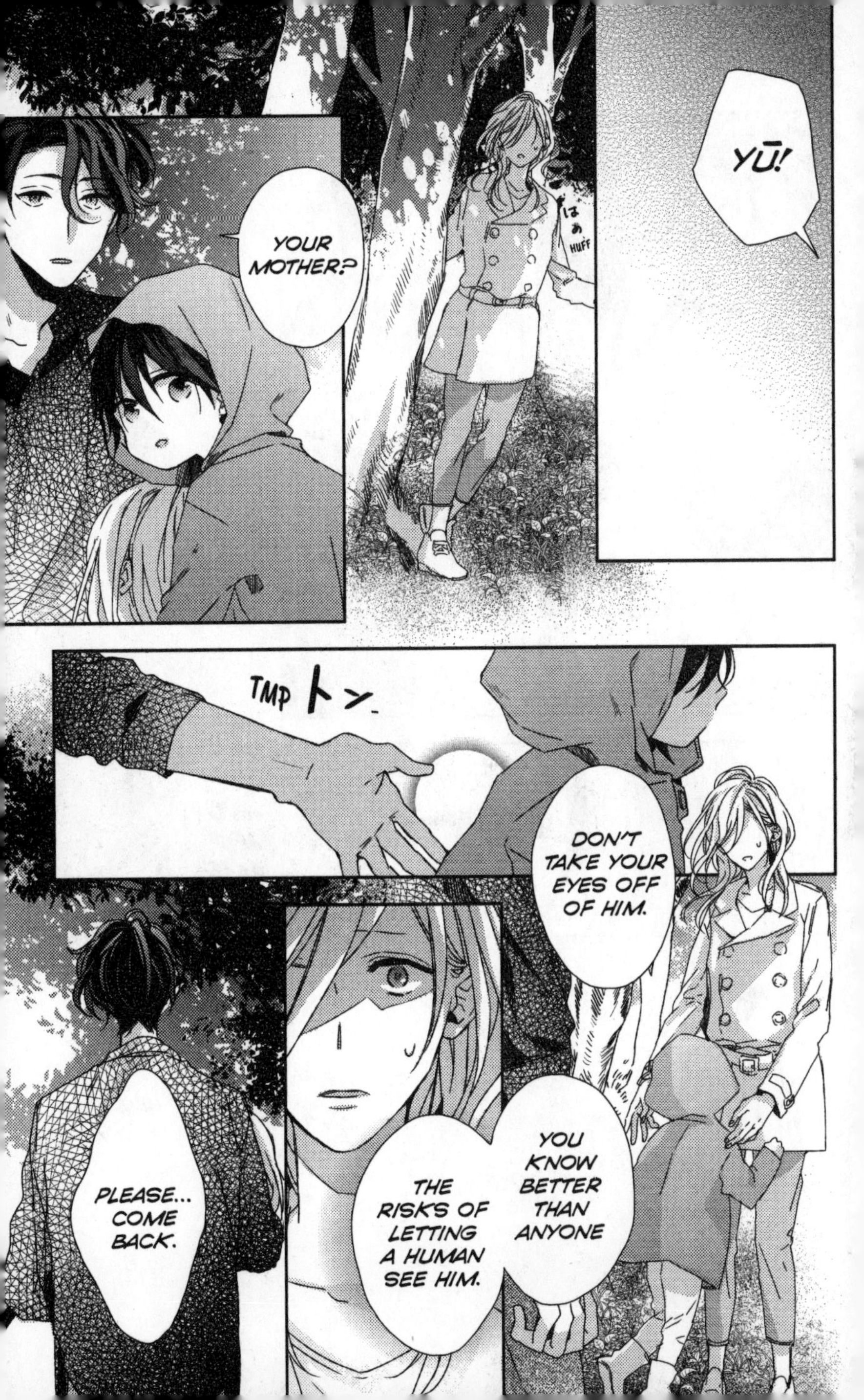
YŪ!
はぁ HUFF
YOUR MOTHER?
TMP トン
DON'T TAKE YOUR EYES OFF OF HIM.
YOU KNOW BETTER THAN ANYONE
THE RISKS OF LETTING A HUMAN SEE HIM.
PLEASE... COME BACK.

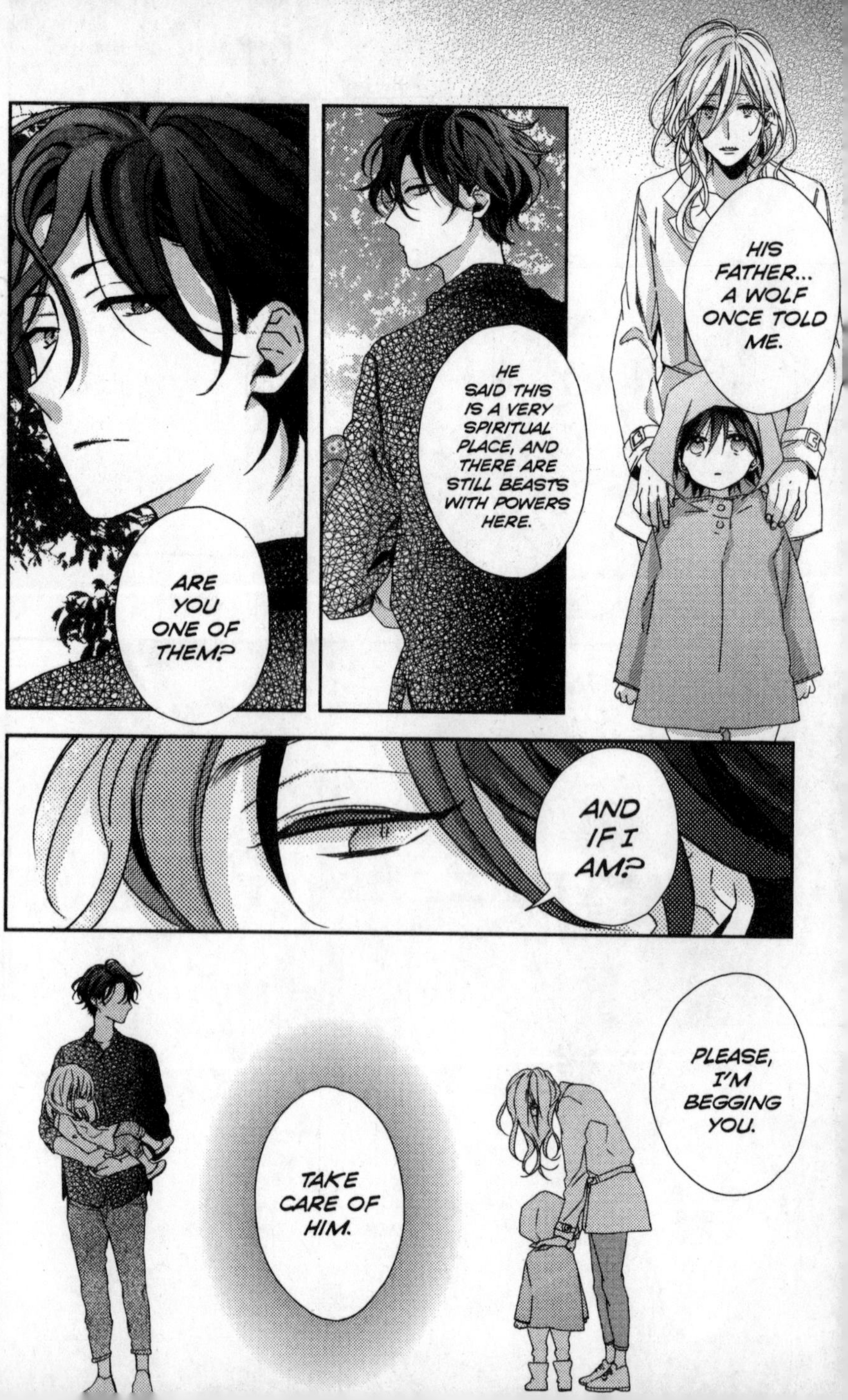
HIS FATHER... A WOLF ONCE TOLD ME.
HE SAID THIS IS A VERY SPIRITUAL PLACE, AND THERE ARE STILL BEASTS WITH POWERS HERE.
ARE YOU ONE OF THEM?
AND IF I AM?
PLEASE, I'M BEGGING YOU.
TAKE CARE OF HIM.

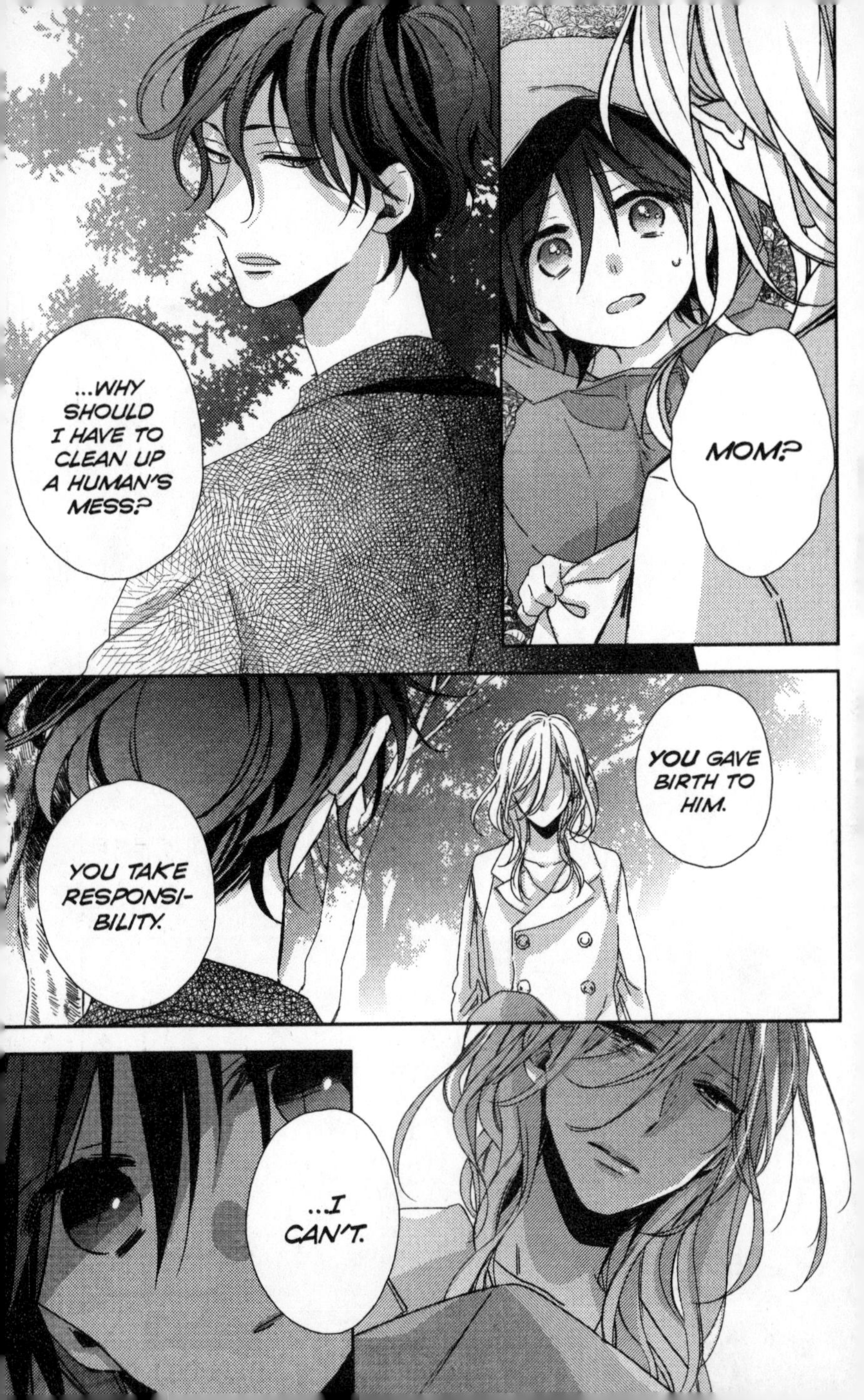
MOM?
...WHY SHOULD I HAVE TO CLEAN UP A HUMAN'S MESS?
YOU GAVE BIRTH TO HIM.
YOU TAKE RESPONSI-BILITY.
...I CAN'T.

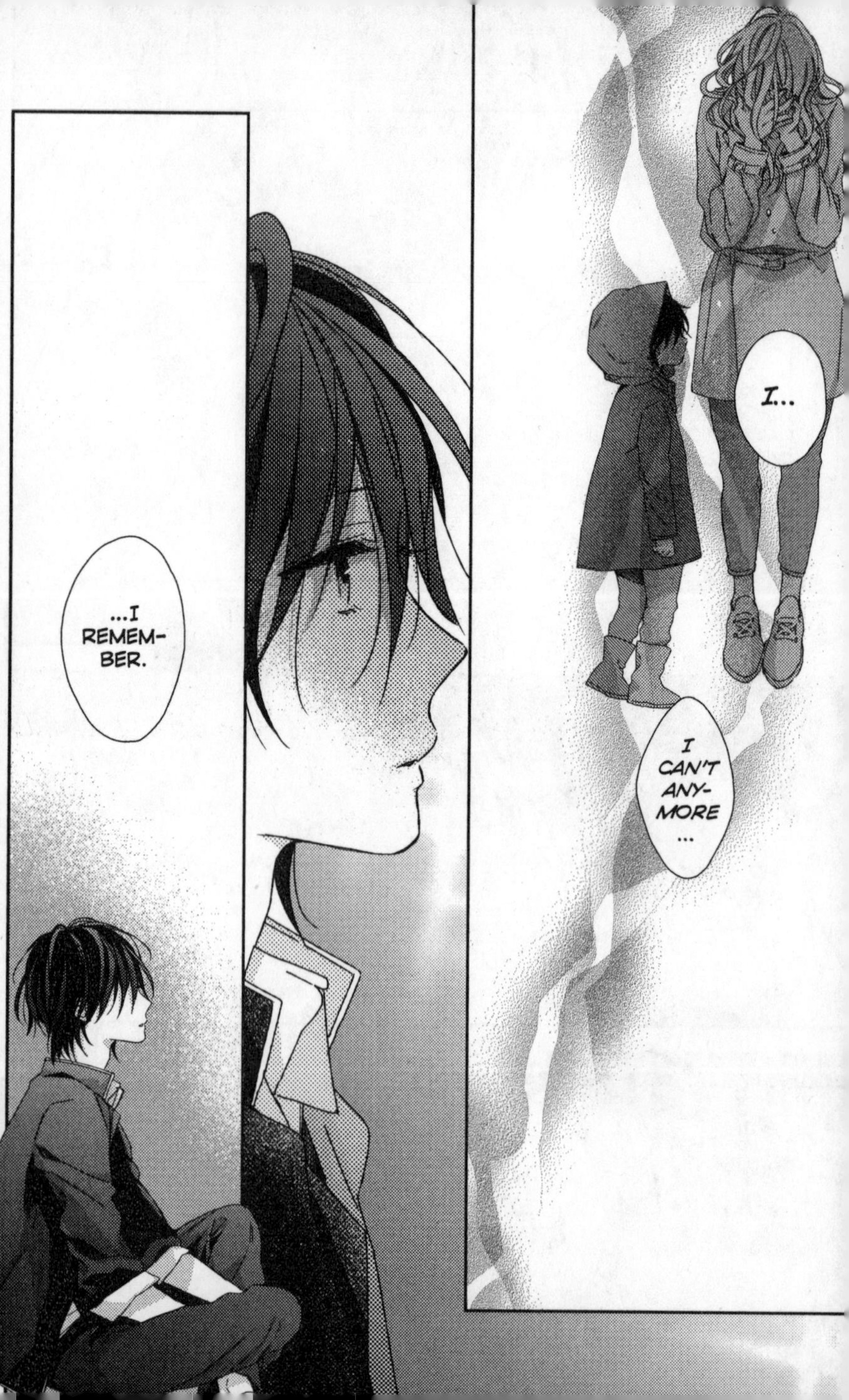
I...
I CAN'T ANY-MORE ...
...I REMEM-BER.

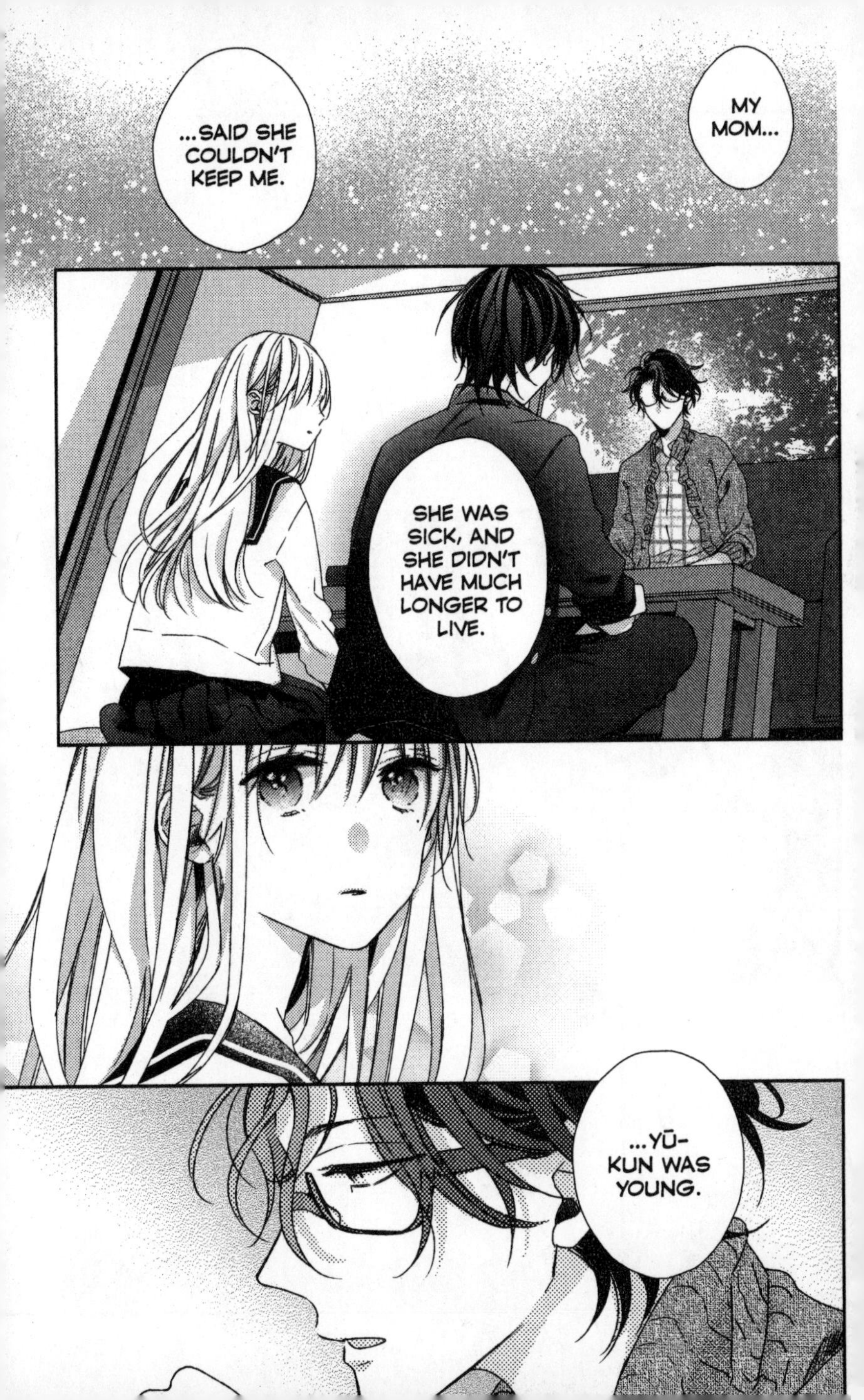
MY MOM...
...SAID SHE COULDN'T KEEP ME.
SHE WAS SICK, AND SHE DIDN'T HAVE MUCH LONGER TO LIVE.
...YŪ-KUN WAS YOUNG.

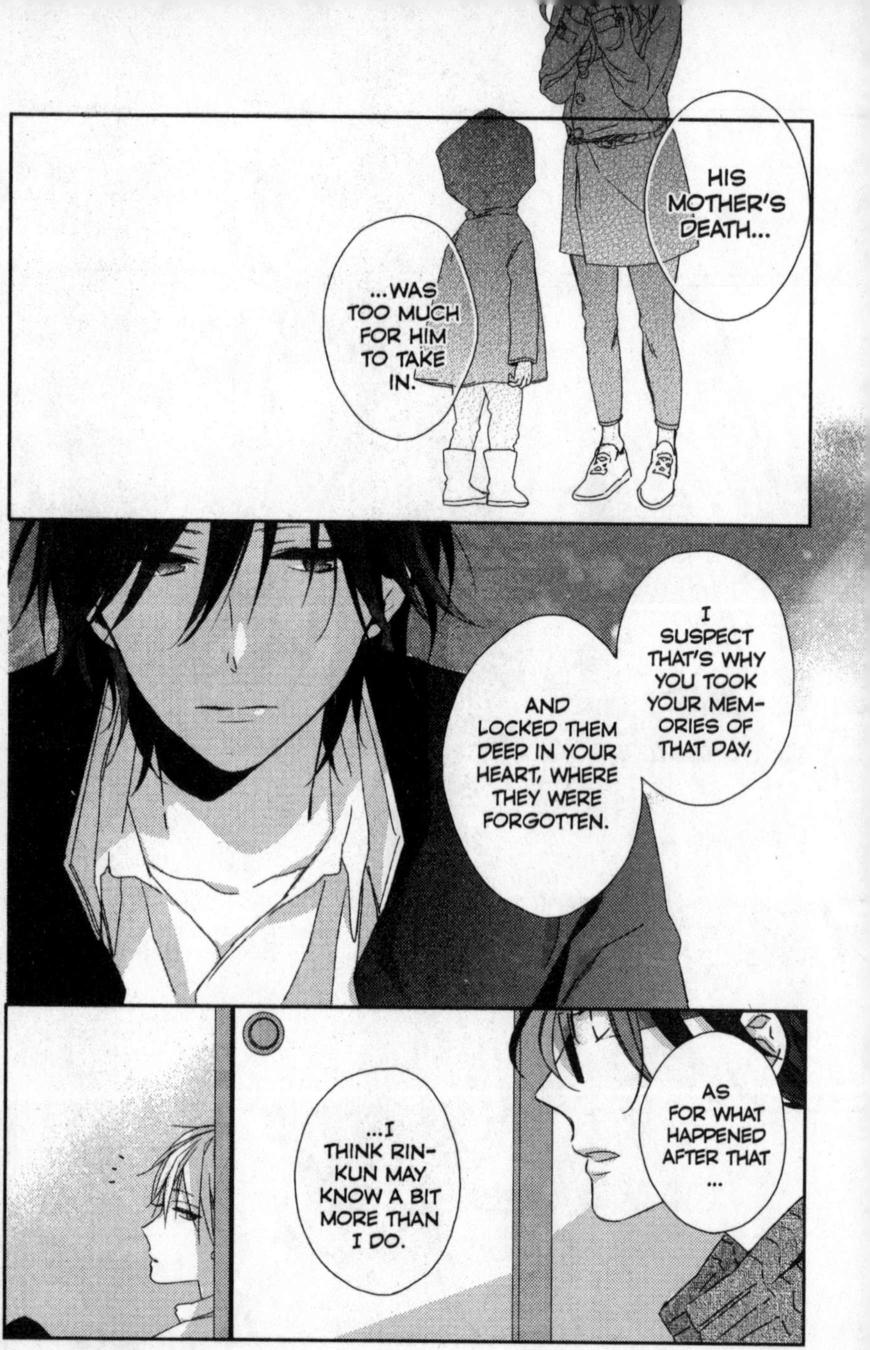
HIS MOTHER'S DEATH...
...WAS TOO MUCH FOR HIM TO TAKE IN.
I SUSPECT THAT'S WHY YOU TOOK YOUR MEMORIES OF THAT DAY,
AND LOCKED THEM DEEP IN YOUR HEART, WHERE THEY WERE FORGOTTEN.
AS FOR WHAT HAPPENED AFTER THAT ...
...I THINK RIN-KUN MAY KNOW A BIT MORE THAN I DO.

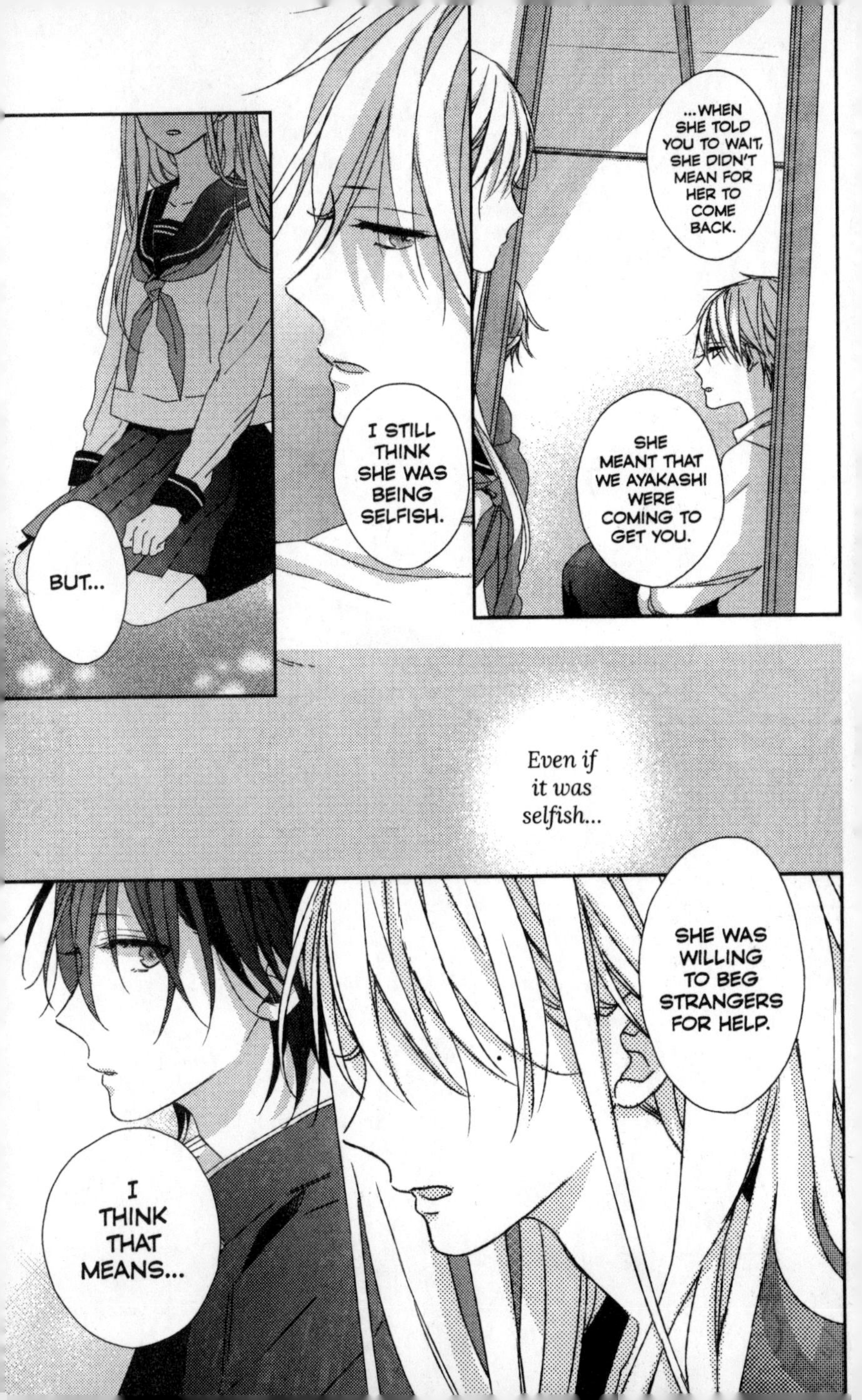
...WHEN SHE TOLD YOU TO WAIT, SHE DIDN'T MEAN FOR HER TO COME BACK.
SHE MEANT THAT WE AYAKASHI WERE COMING TO GET YOU.
I STILL THINK SHE WAS BEING SELFISH.
BUT...
Even if it was selfish...
SHE WAS WILLING TO BEG STRANGERS FOR HELP.
I THINK THAT MEANS...

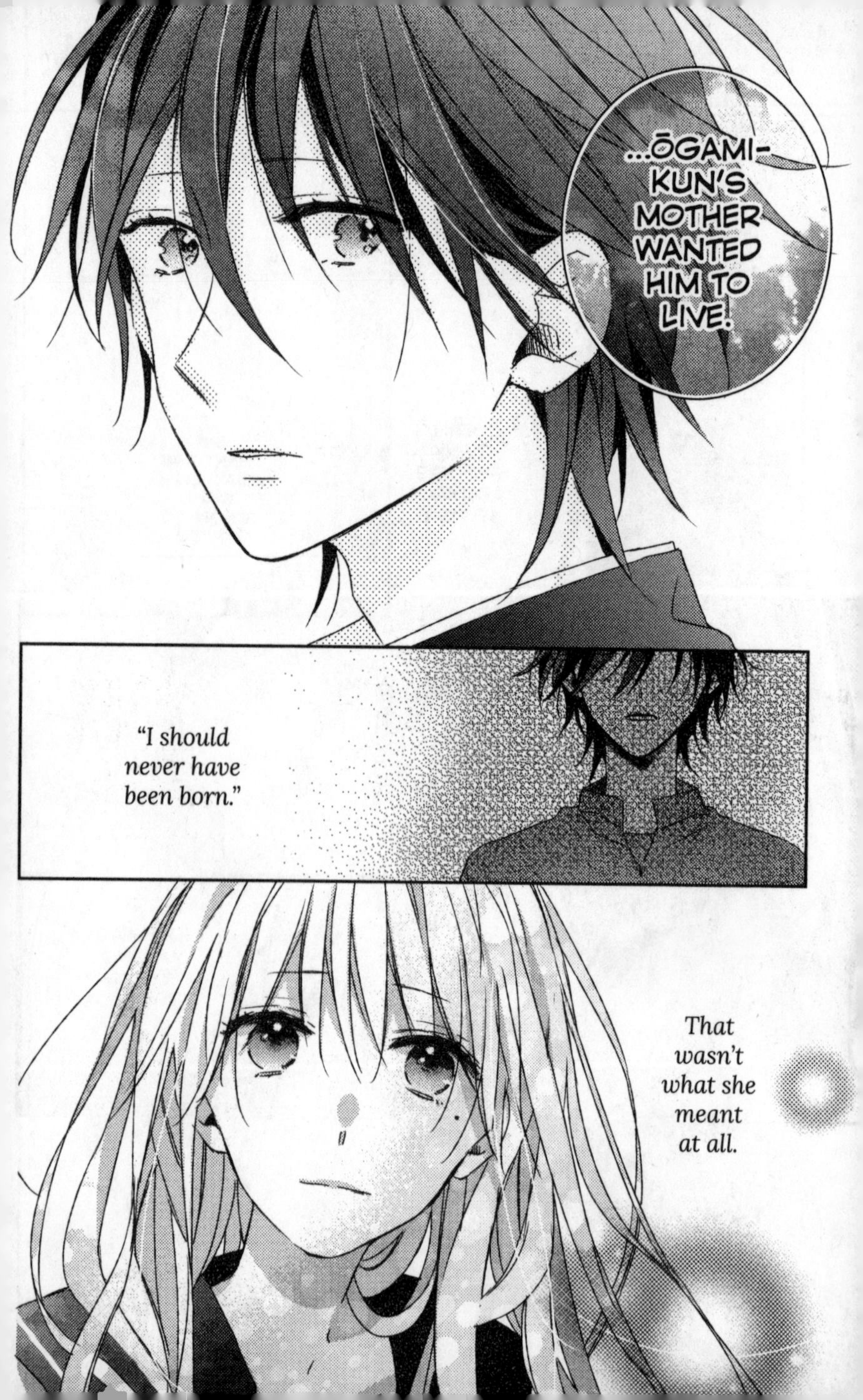
...ŌGAMI-KUN'S MOTHER WANTED HIM TO LIVE.
"I should never have been born."
That wasn't what she meant at all.

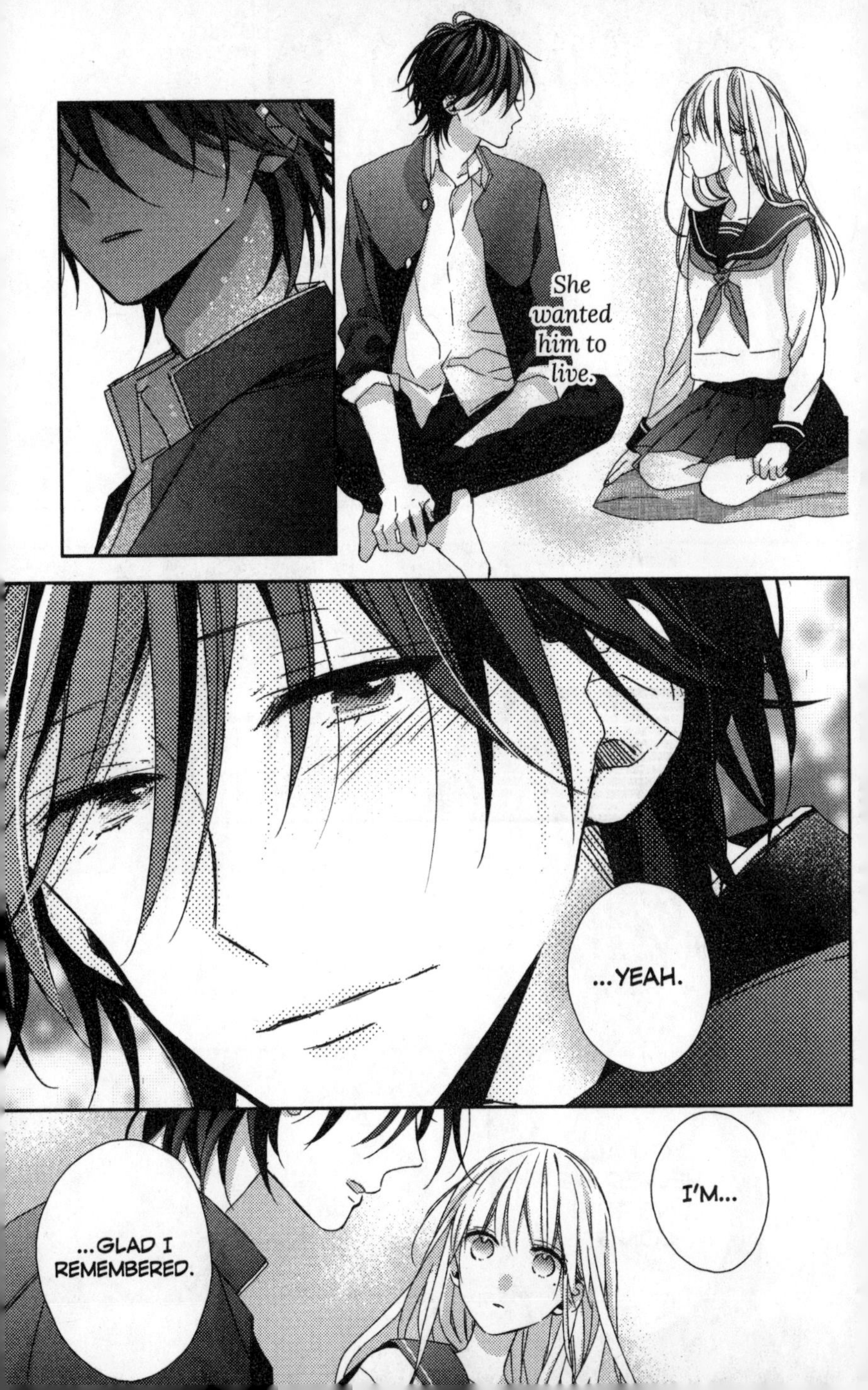
She wanted him to live.
...YEAH.
I'M...
...GLAD I REMEMBERED.

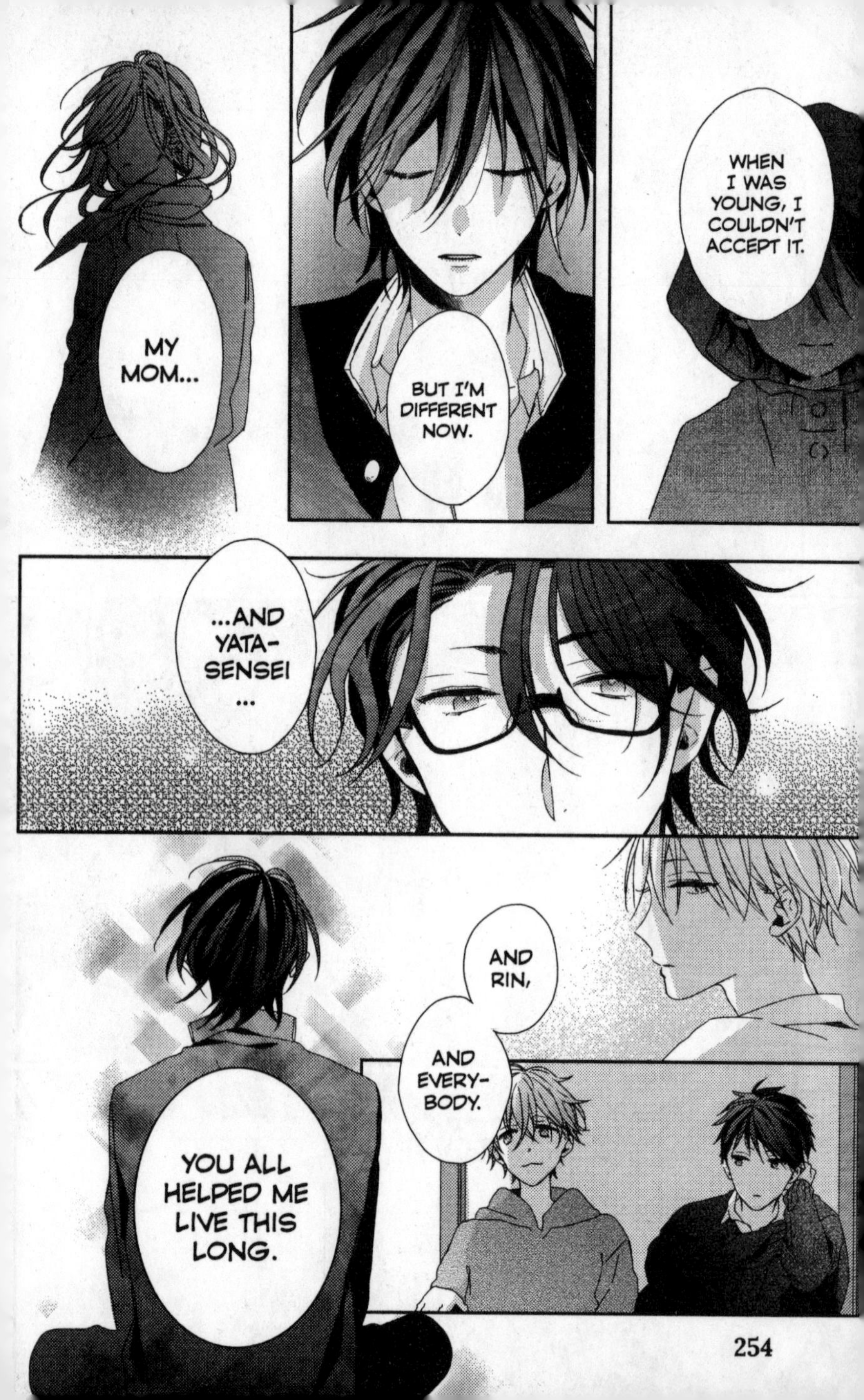
WHEN I WAS YOUNG, I COULDN'T ACCEPT IT.
BUT I'M DIFFERENT NOW.
MY MOM...
...AND YATA-SENSEI ...
AND RIN,
AND EVERY-BODY.
YOU ALL HELPED ME LIVE THIS LONG.

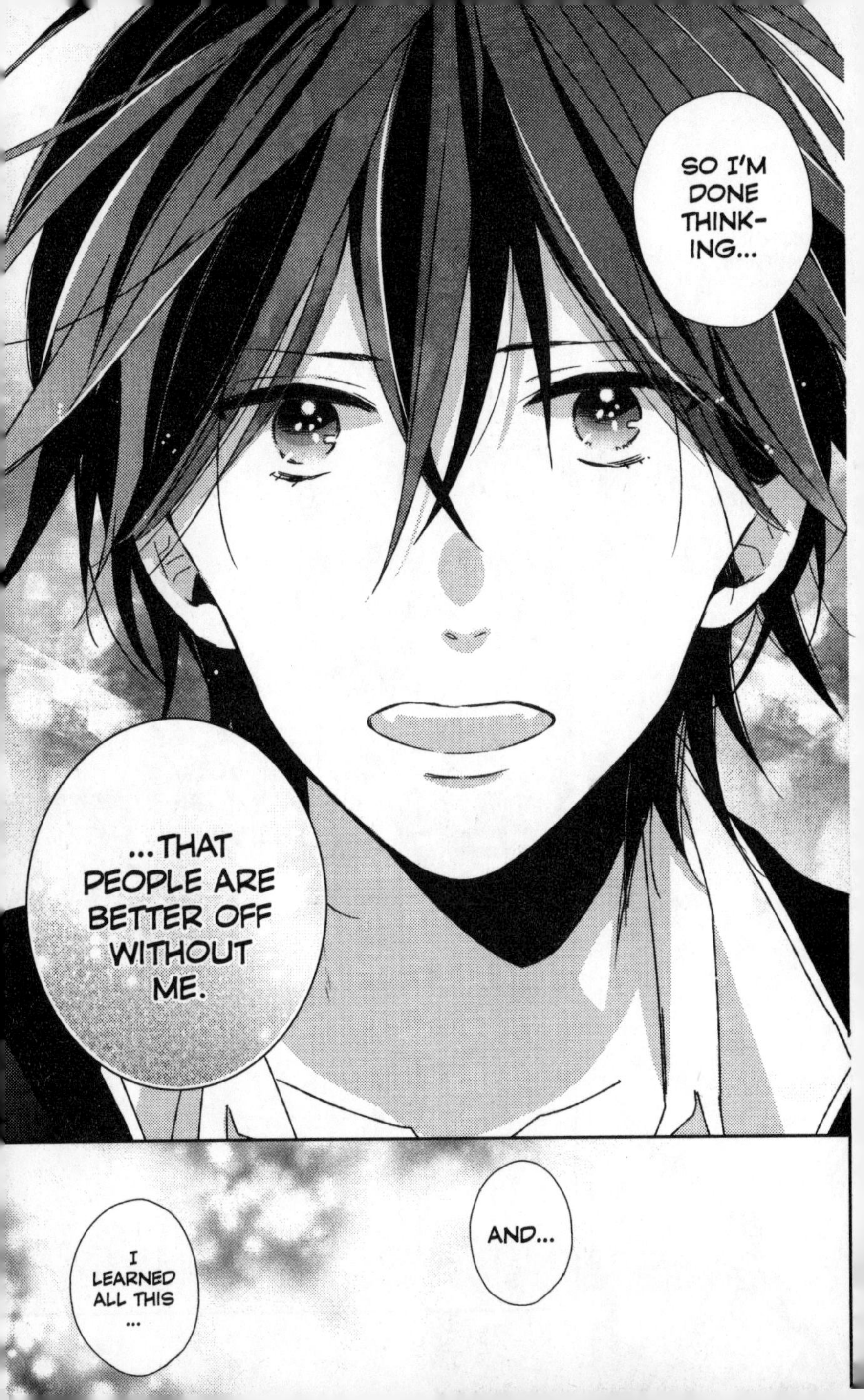
SO I'M DONE THINKING...
...THAT PEOPLE ARE BETTER OFF WITHOUT ME.
AND...
I LEARNED ALL THIS ...

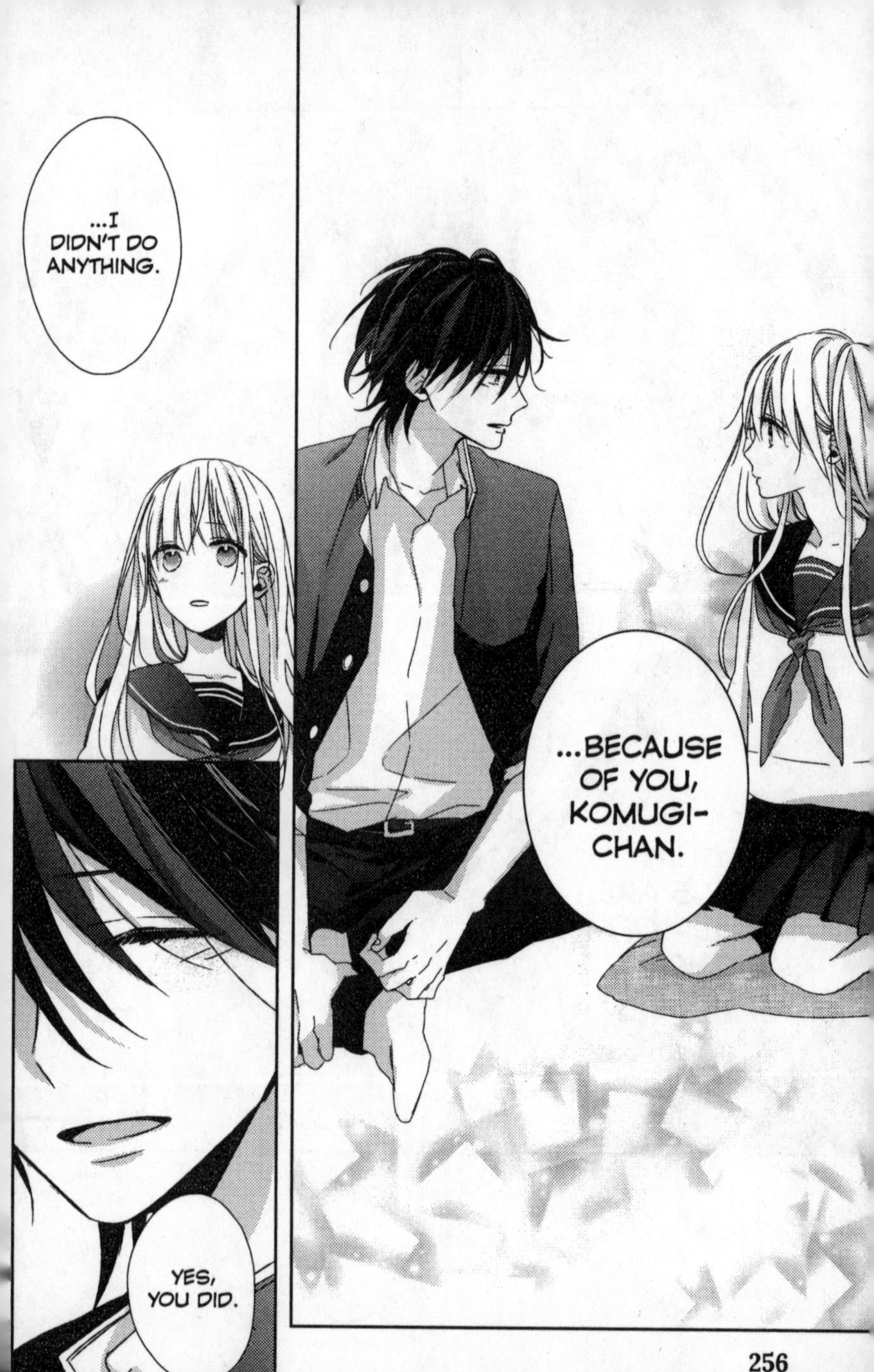
...BECAUSE OF YOU, KOMUGI-CHAN.
...I DIDN'T DO ANYTHING.
YES, YOU DID.

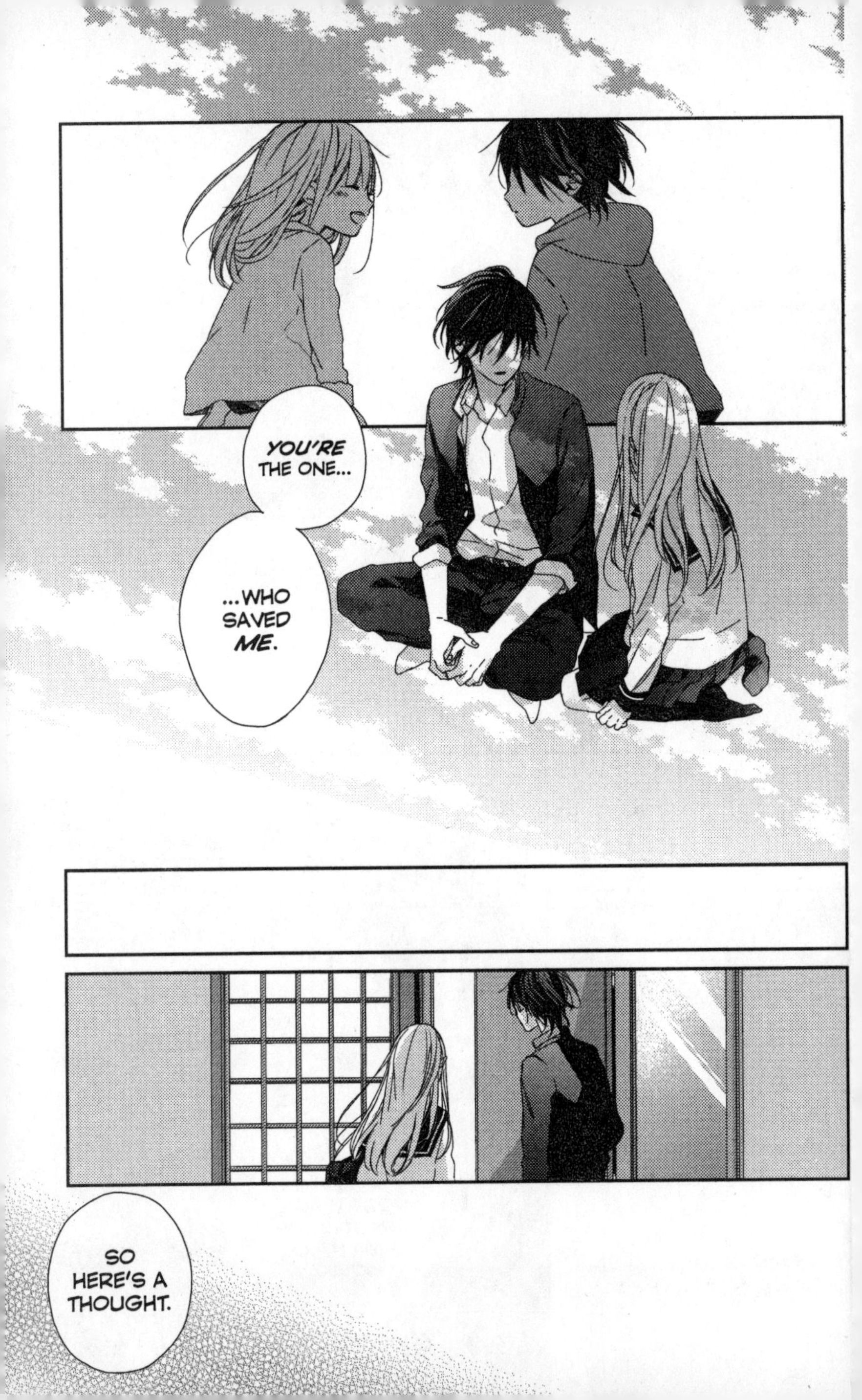
YOU'RE THE ONE...
...WHO SAVED ME.
SO HERE'S A THOUGHT.

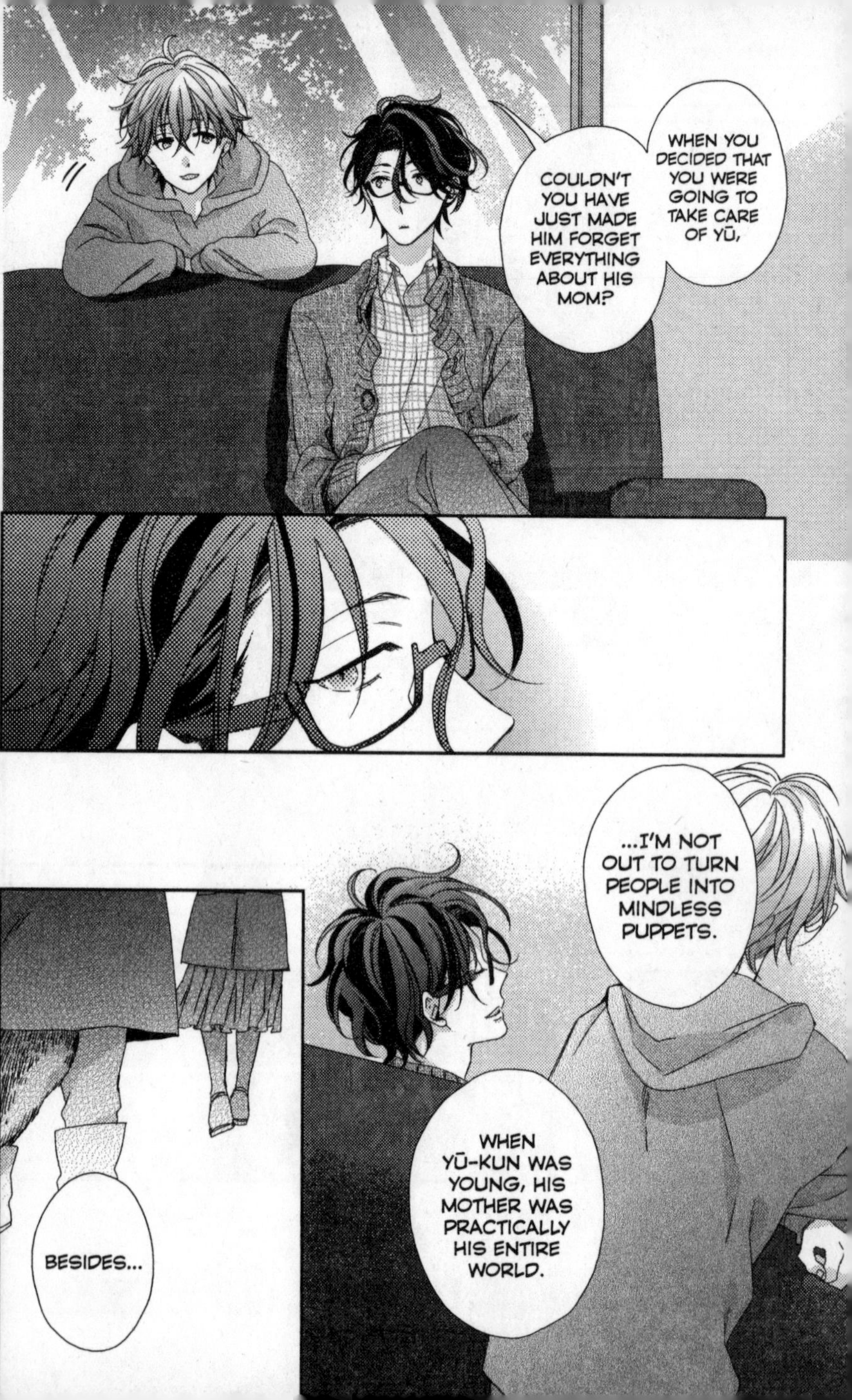
WHEN YOU DECIDED THAT YOU WERE GOING TO TAKE CARE OF YŪ,
COULDN'T YOU HAVE JUST MADE HIM FORGET EVERYTHING ABOUT HIS MOM?
...I'M NOT OUT TO TURN PEOPLE INTO MINDLESS PUPPETS.
WHEN YŪ-KUN WAS YOUNG, HIS MOTHER WAS PRACTICALLY HIS ENTIRE WORLD.
BESIDES...

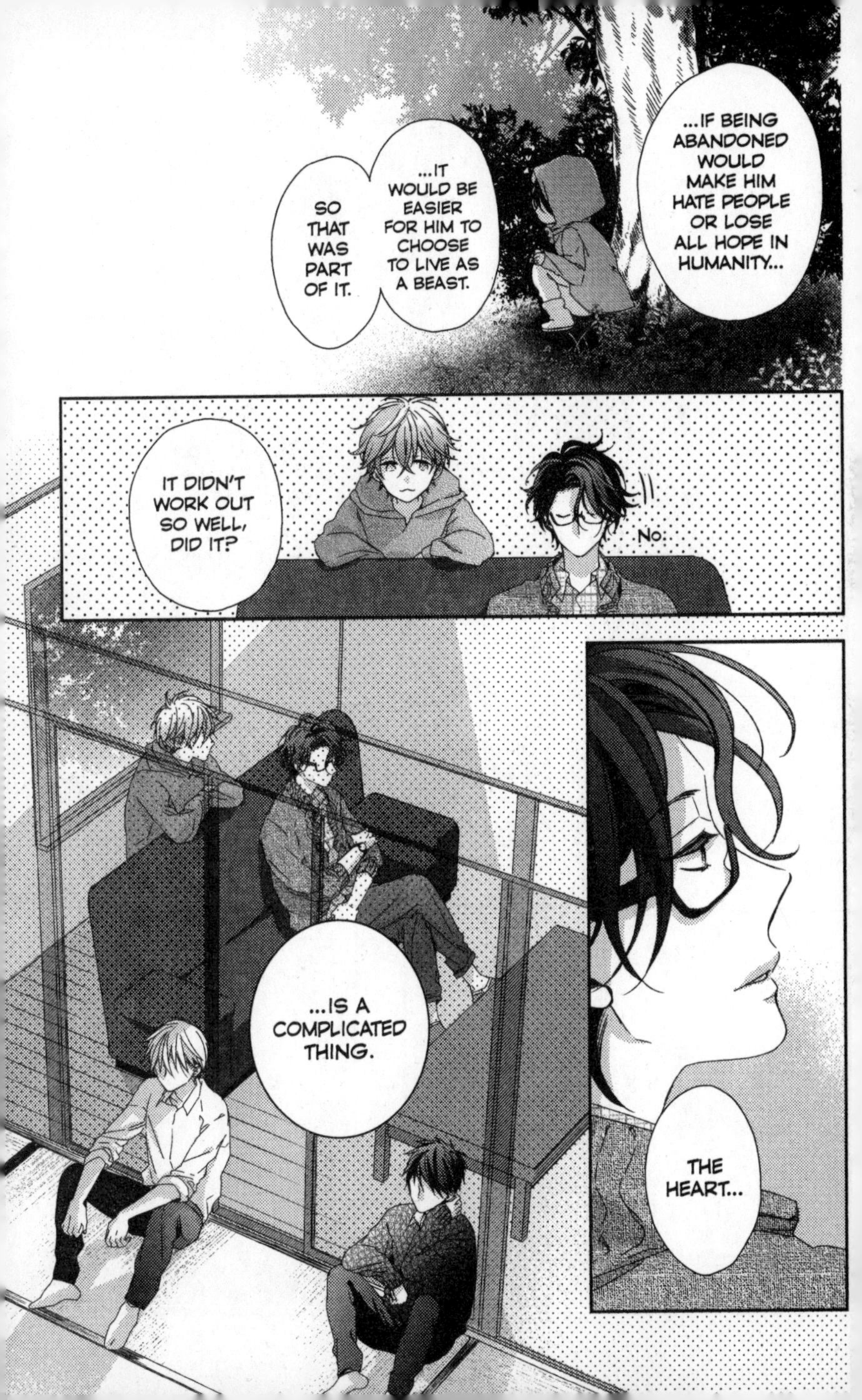
...IF BEING ABANDONED WOULD MAKE HIM HATE PEOPLE OR LOSE ALL HOPE IN HUMANITY...
...IT WOULD BE EASIER FOR HIM TO CHOOSE TO LIVE AS A BEAST.
SO THAT WAS PART OF IT.
IT DIDN'T WORK OUT SO WELL, DID IT?
No.
THE HEART...
...IS A COMPLICATED THING.

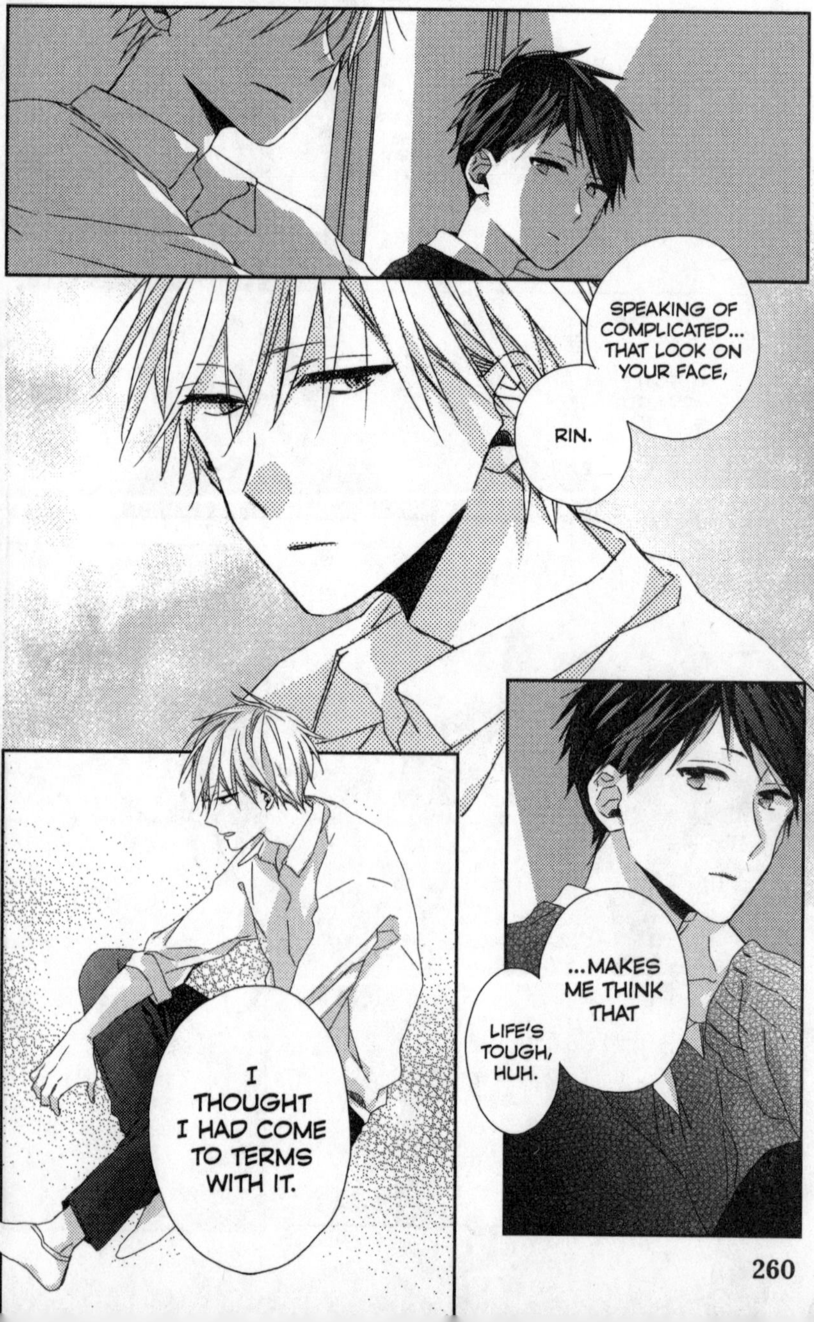
SPEAKING OF COMPLICATED... THAT LOOK ON YOUR FACE,
RIN.
...MAKES ME THINK THAT
LIFE'S TOUGH, HUH.
I THOUGHT I HAD COME TO TERMS WITH IT.

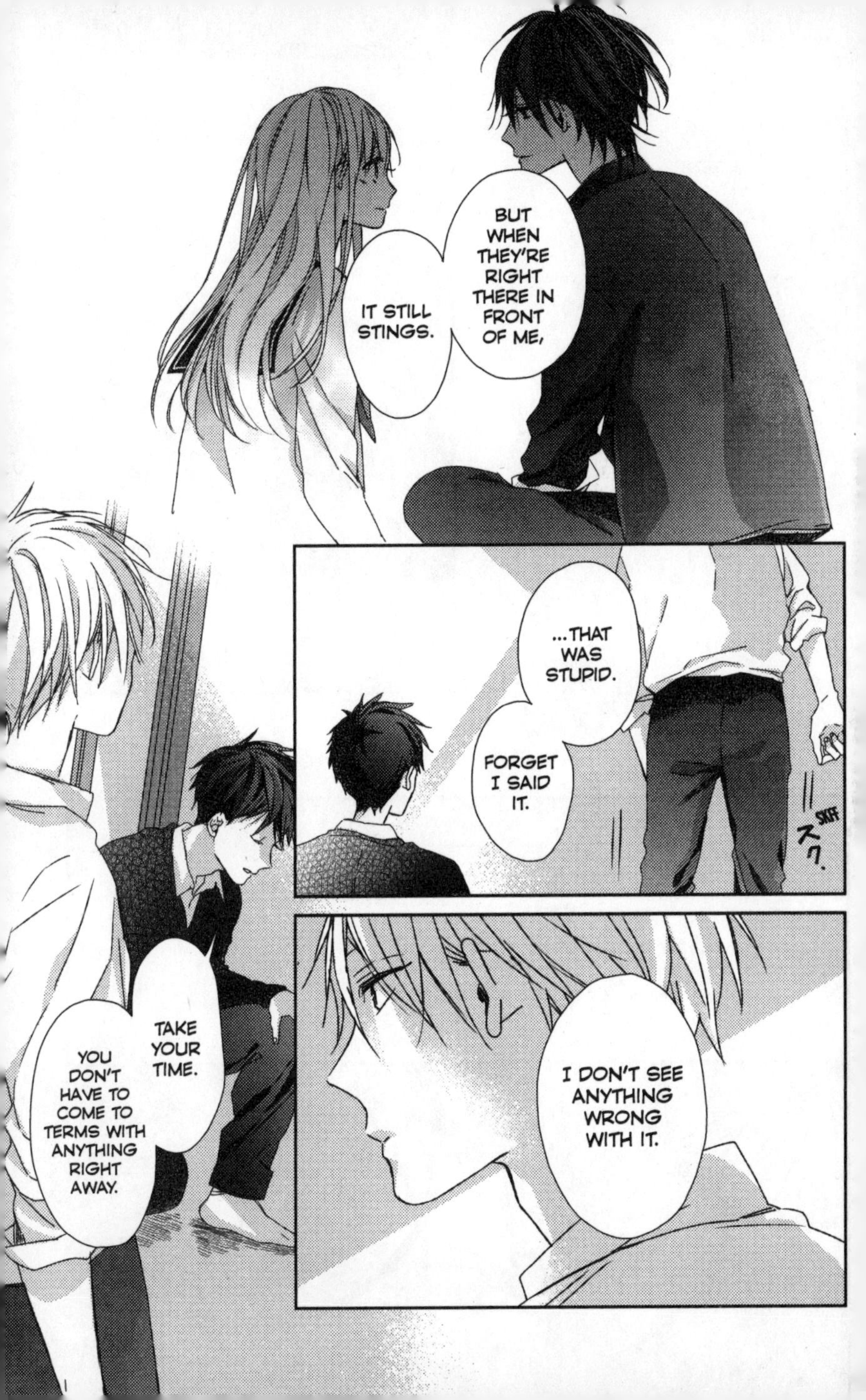
BUT WHEN THEY'RE RIGHT THERE IN FRONT OF ME,
IT STILL STINGS.
...THAT WAS STUPID.
FORGET I SAID IT.
SKFF
I DON'T SEE ANYTHING WRONG WITH IT.
TAKE YOUR TIME.
YOU DON'T HAVE TO COME TO TERMS WITH ANYTHING RIGHT AWAY.

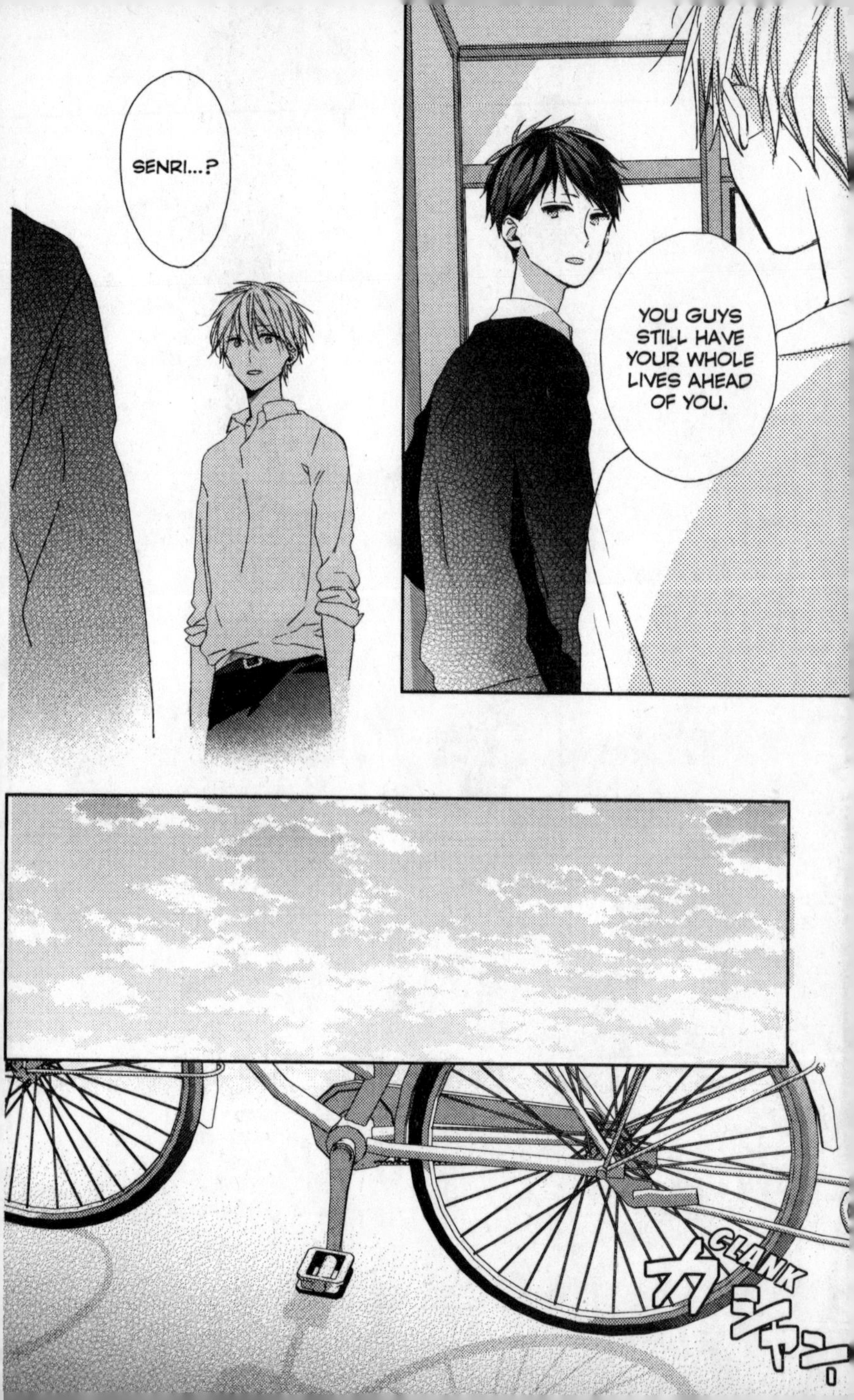
YOU GUYS STILL HAVE YOUR WHOLE LIVES AHEAD OF YOU.
SENRI...?
CLANK
カシャン

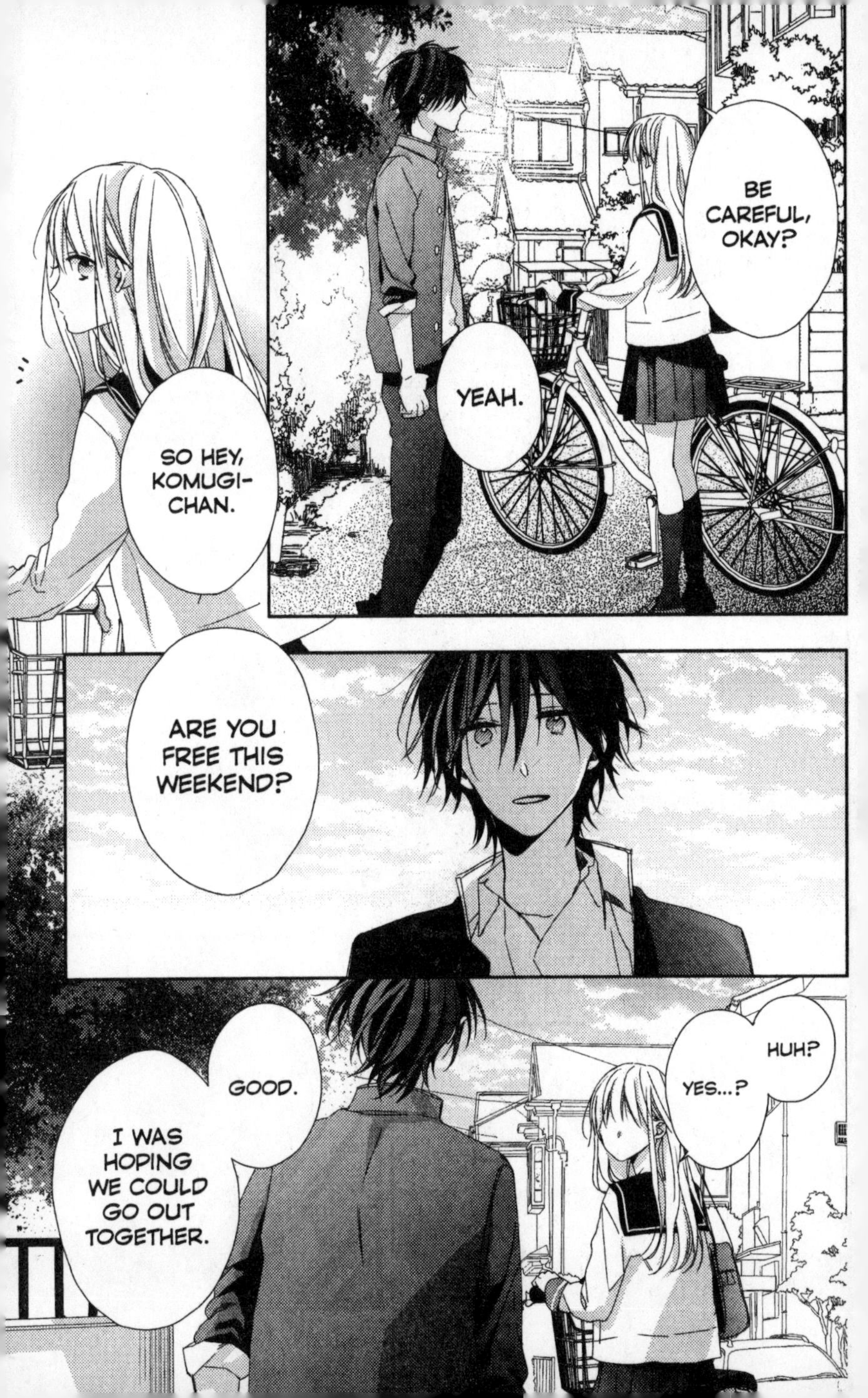
BE CAREFUL, OKAY?
YEAH.
SO HEY, KOMUGI-CHAN.
ARE YOU FREE THIS WEEKEND?
HUH?
YES...?
GOOD.
I WAS HOPING WE COULD GO OUT TOGETHER.

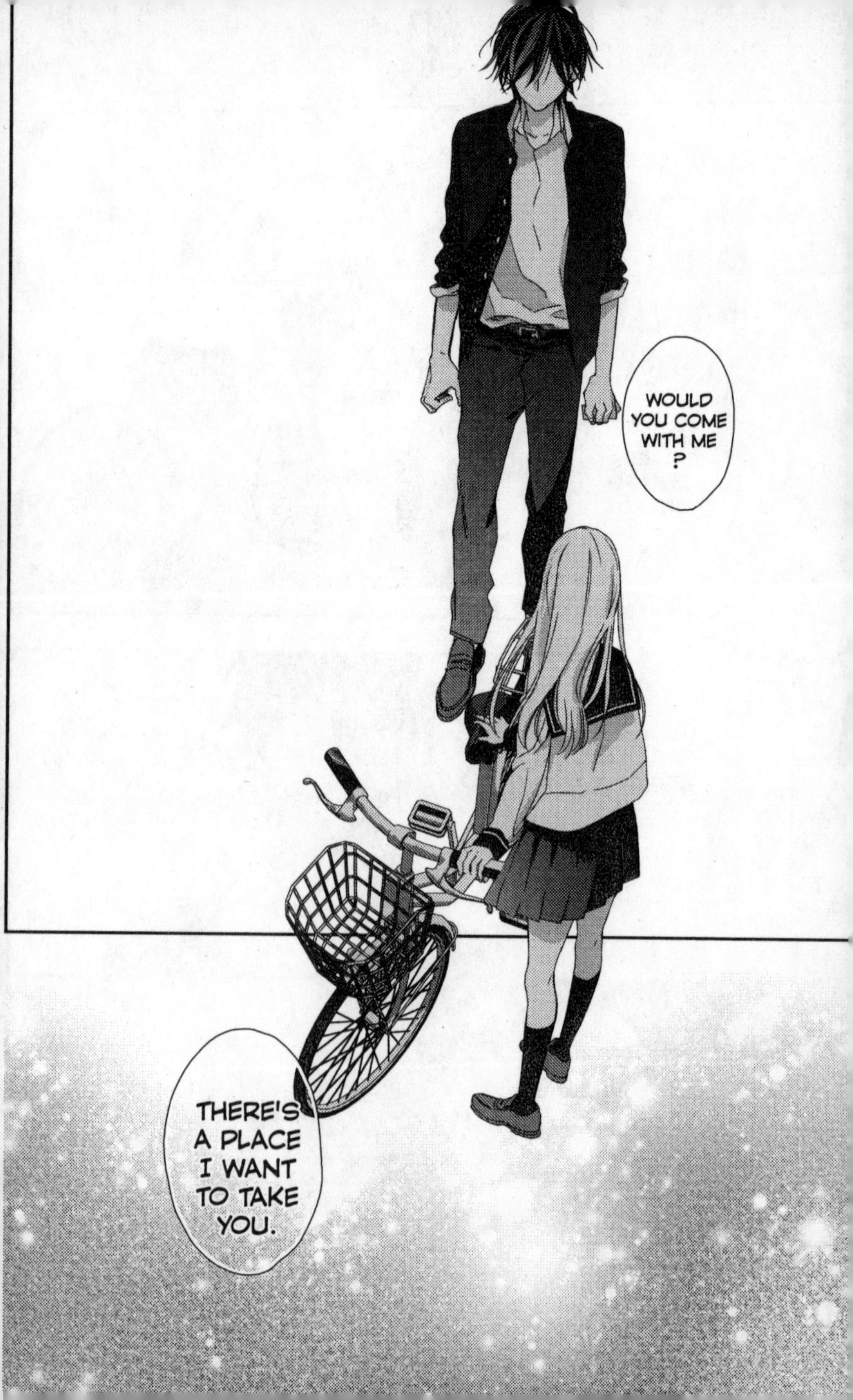
WOULD YOU COME WITH ME ?
THERE'S A PLACE I WANT TO TAKE YOU.

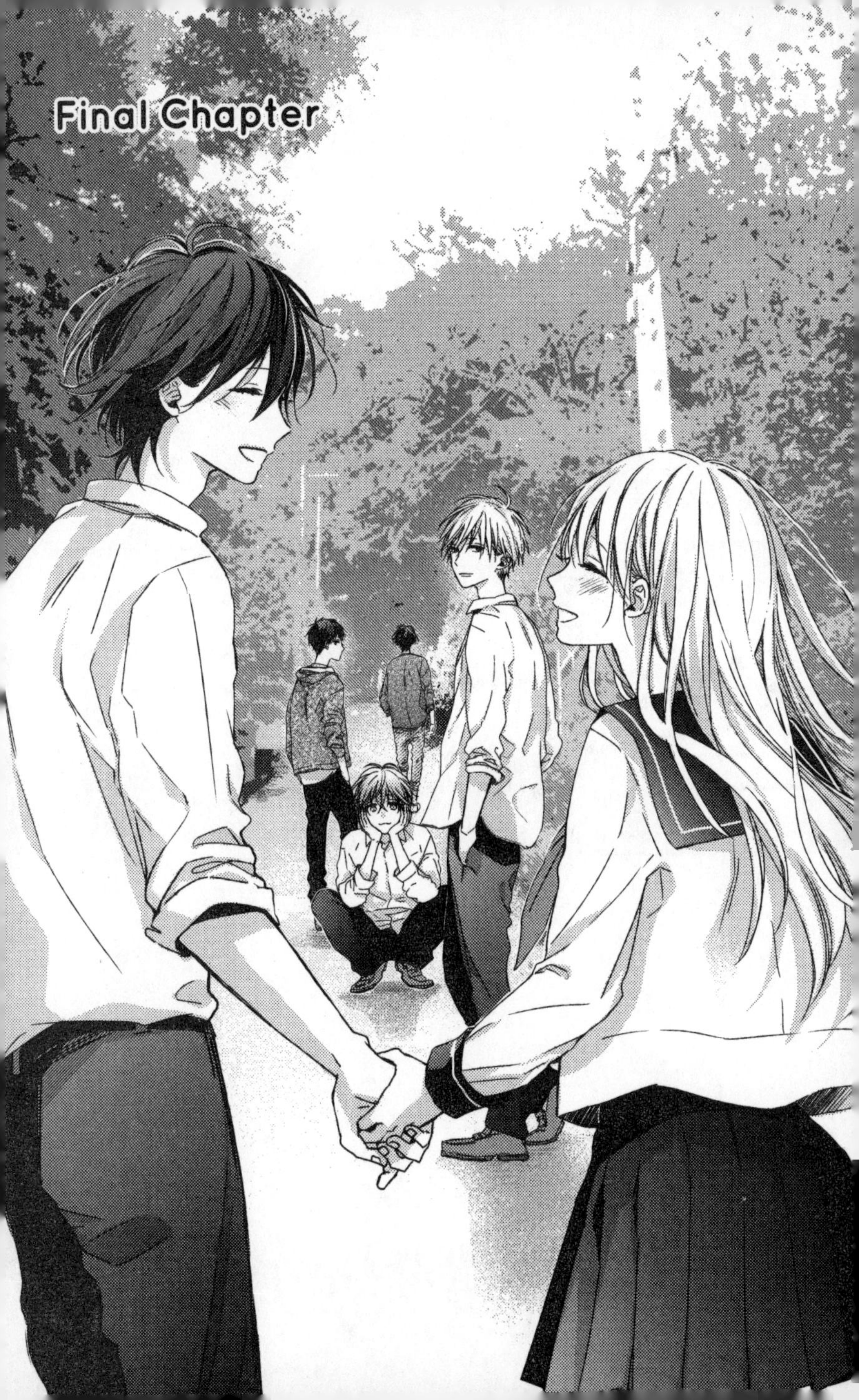
Final Chapter

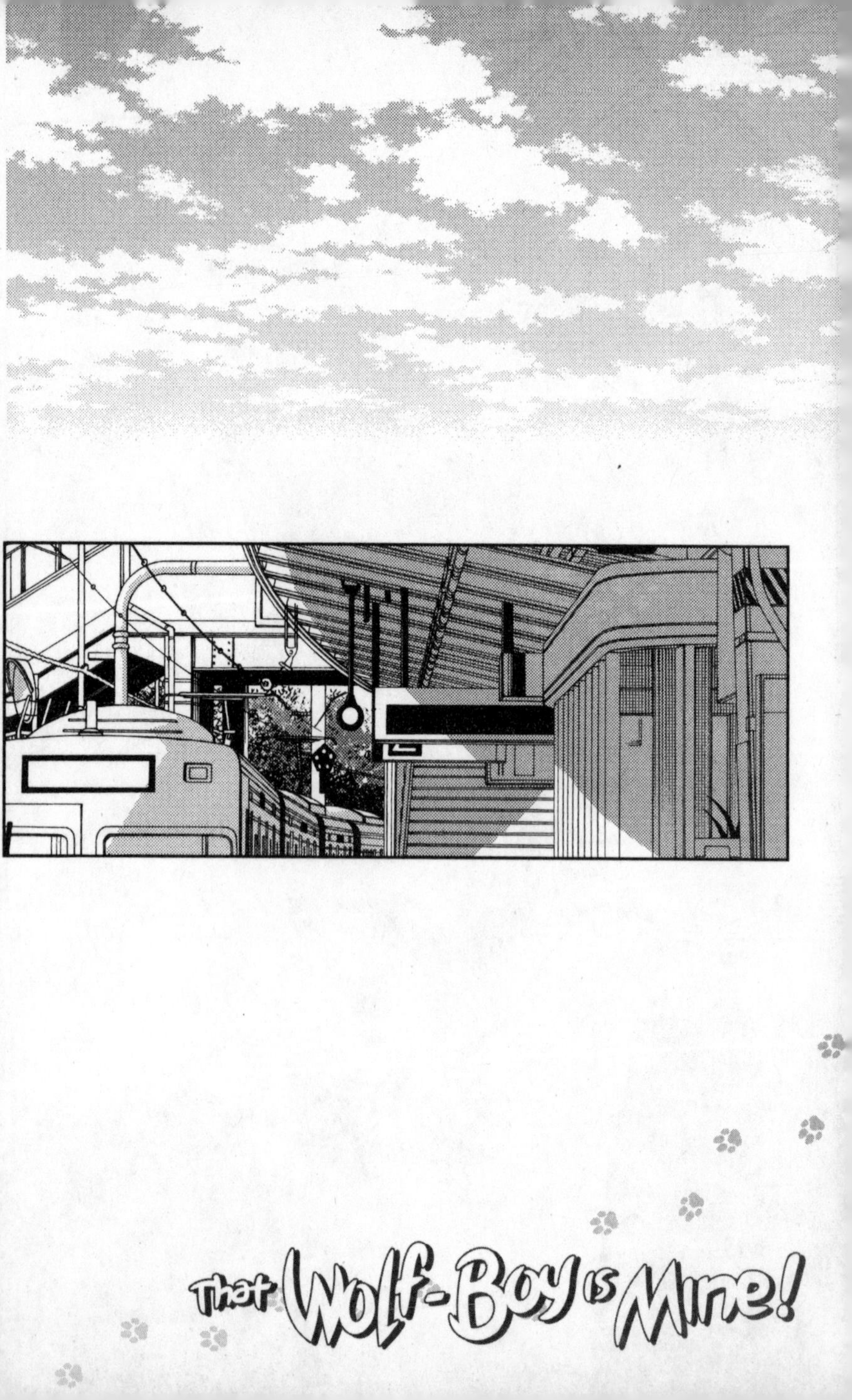
That Wolf-Boy is Mine!

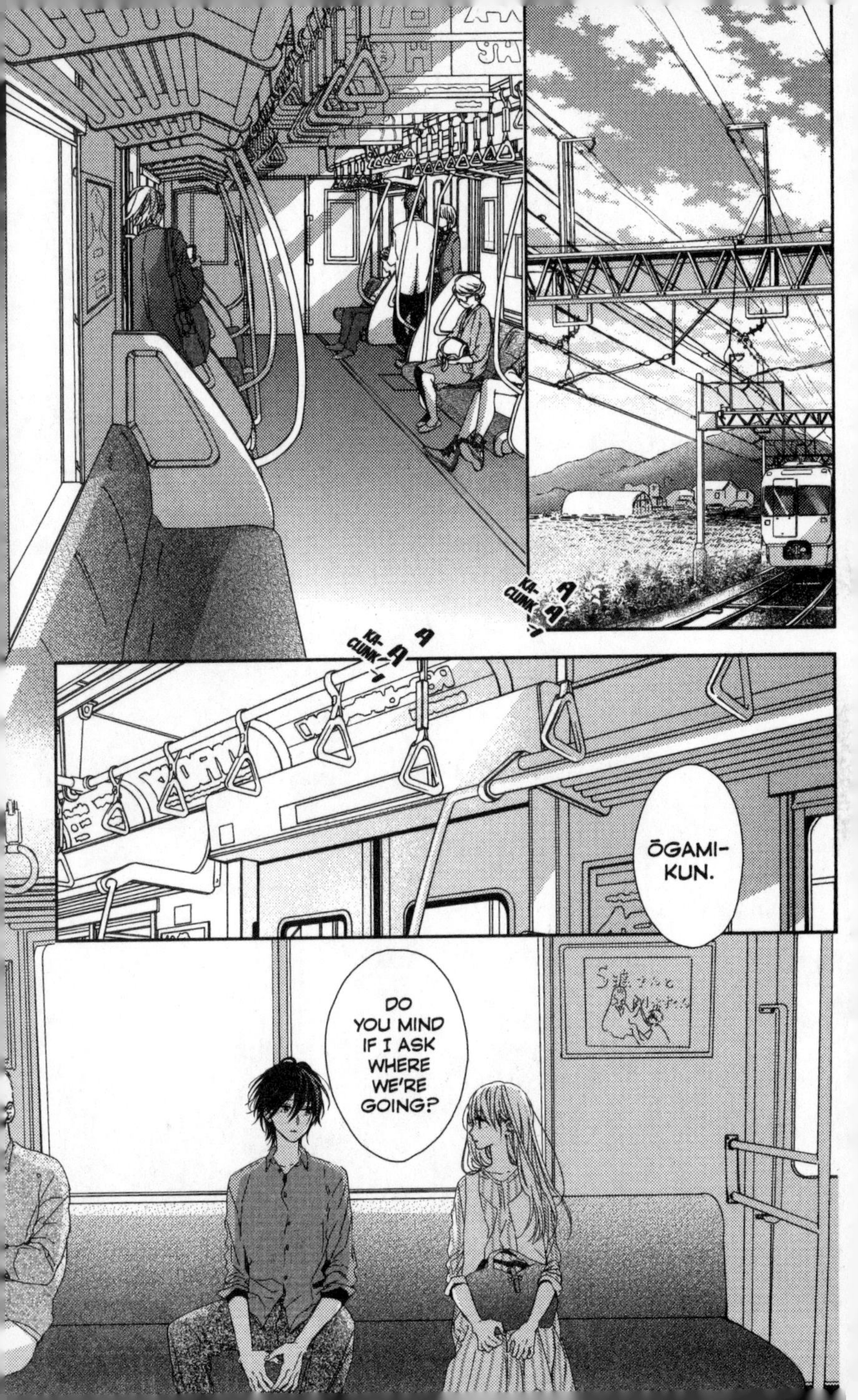
KA-CLUNK
KA-CLUNK
ŌGAMI-KUN.
DO YOU MIND IF I ASK WHERE WE'RE GOING?

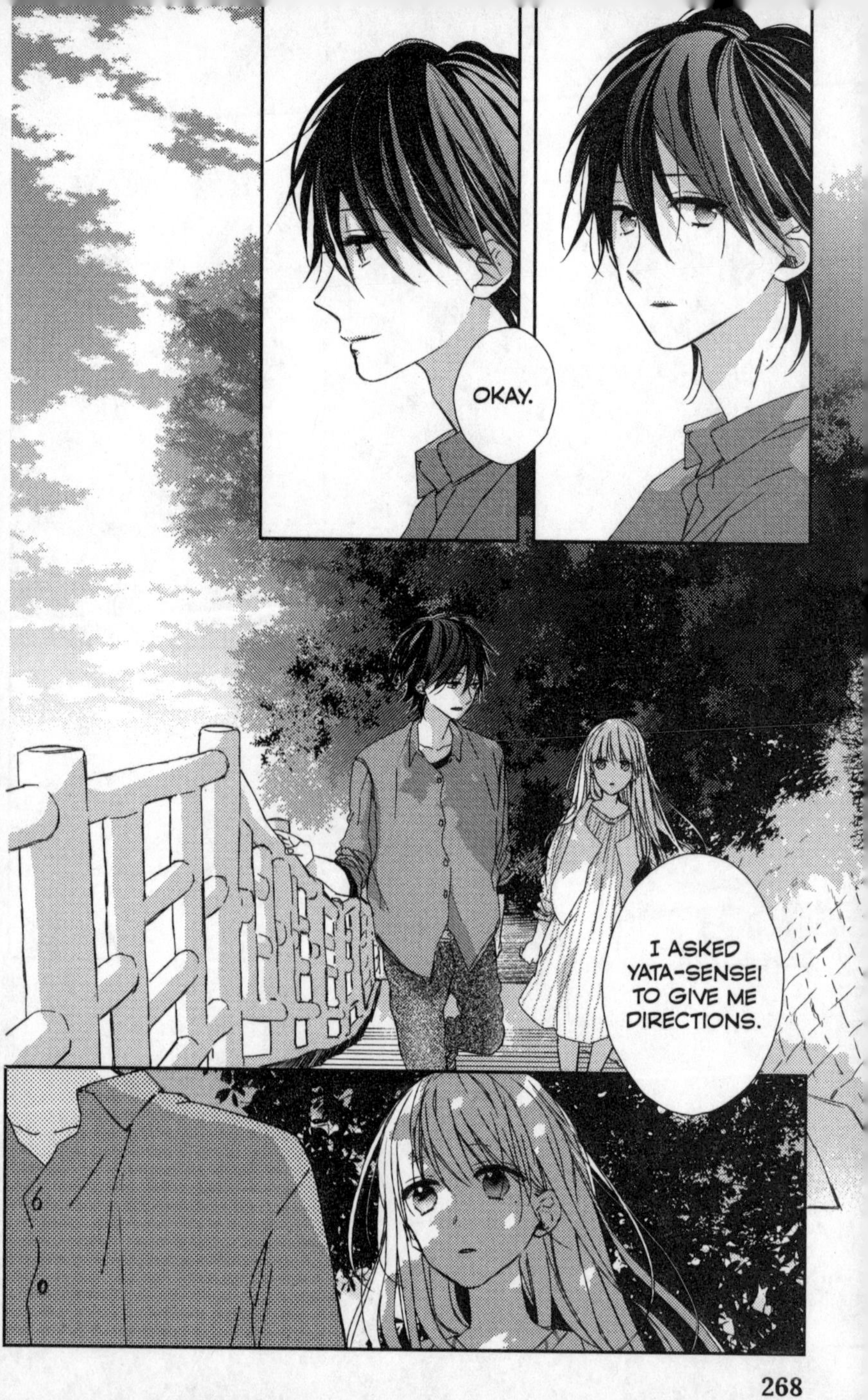
OKAY.
I ASKED YATA-SENSEI TO GIVE ME DIRECTIONS.

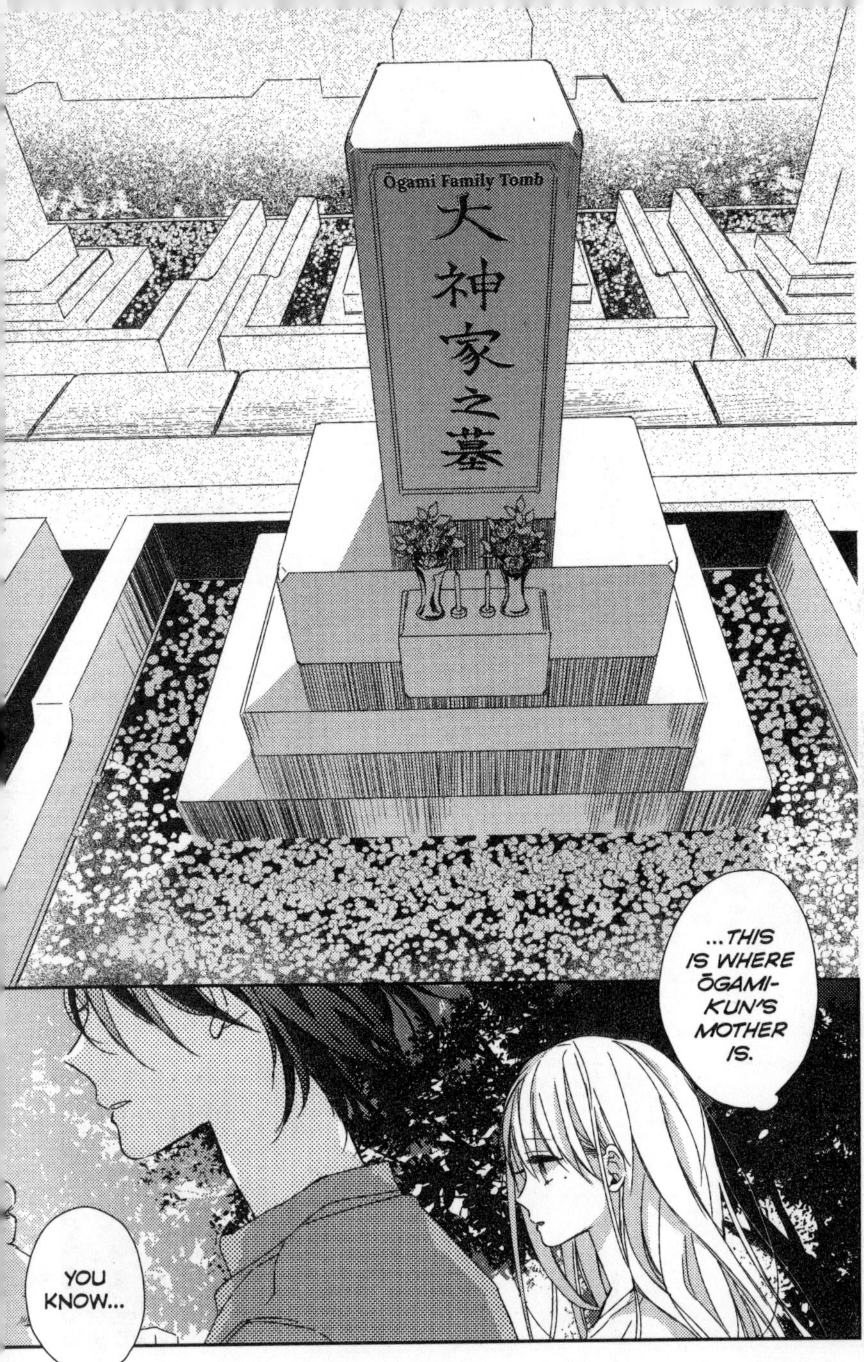
Ōgami Family Tomb
大神家之墓
...THIS IS WHERE ŌGAMI-KUN'S MOTHER IS.
YOU KNOW...

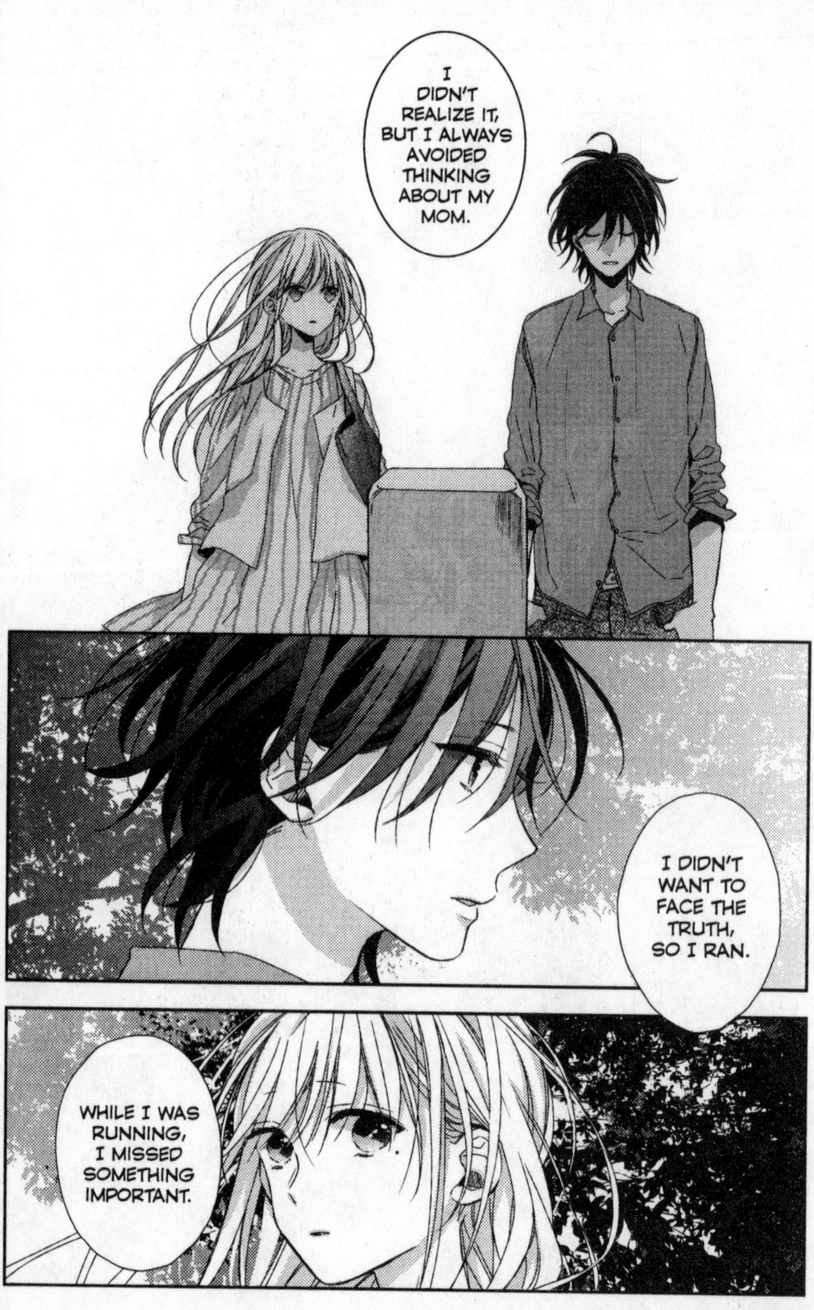
I DIDN'T REALIZE IT, BUT I ALWAYS AVOIDED THINKING ABOUT MY MOM.
I DIDN'T WANT TO FACE THE TRUTH, SO I RAN.
WHILE I WAS RUNNING, I MISSED SOMETHING IMPORTANT.

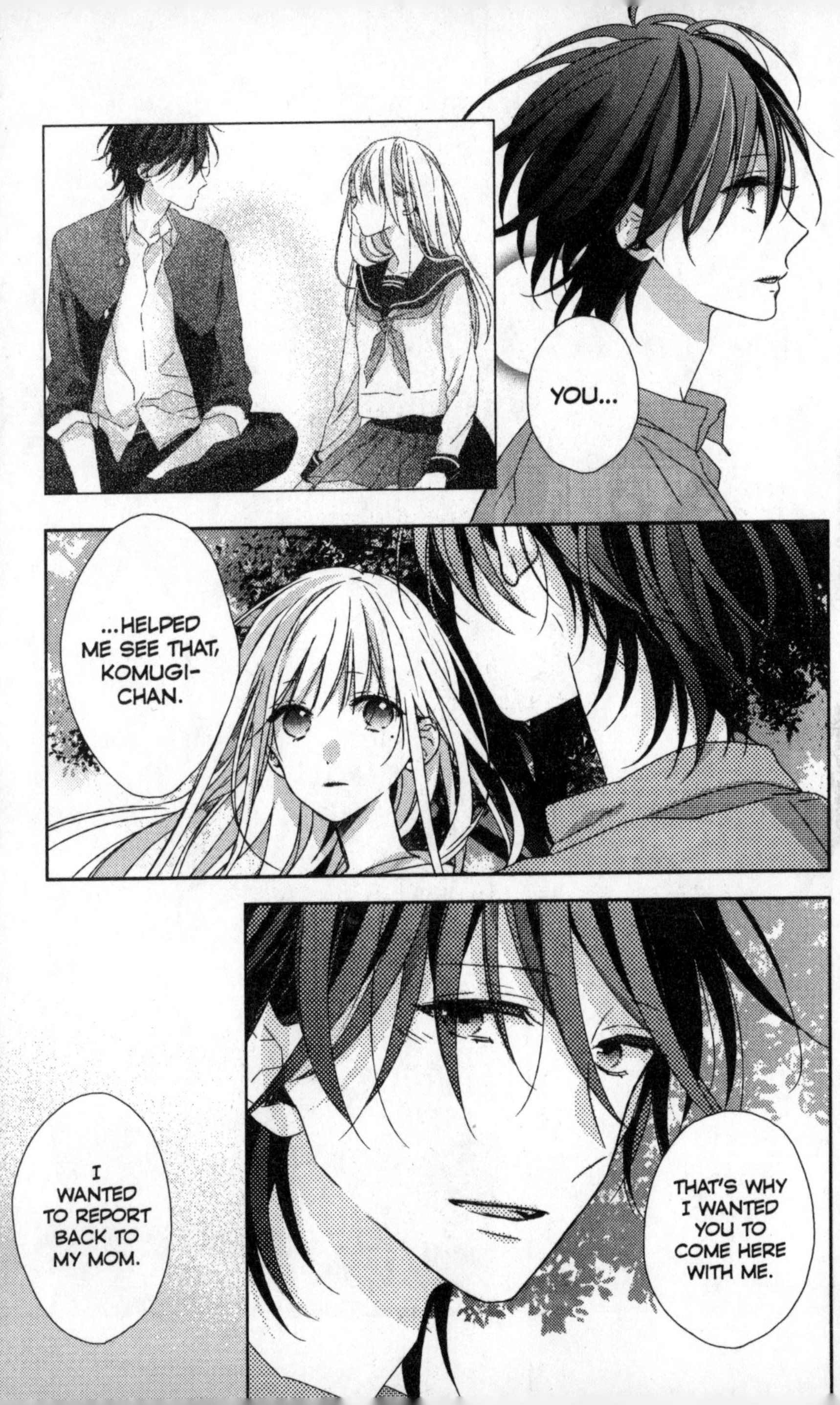
YOU...
...HELPED ME SEE THAT, KOMUGI-CHAN.
THAT'S WHY I WANTED YOU TO COME HERE WITH ME.
I WANTED TO REPORT BACK TO MY MOM.

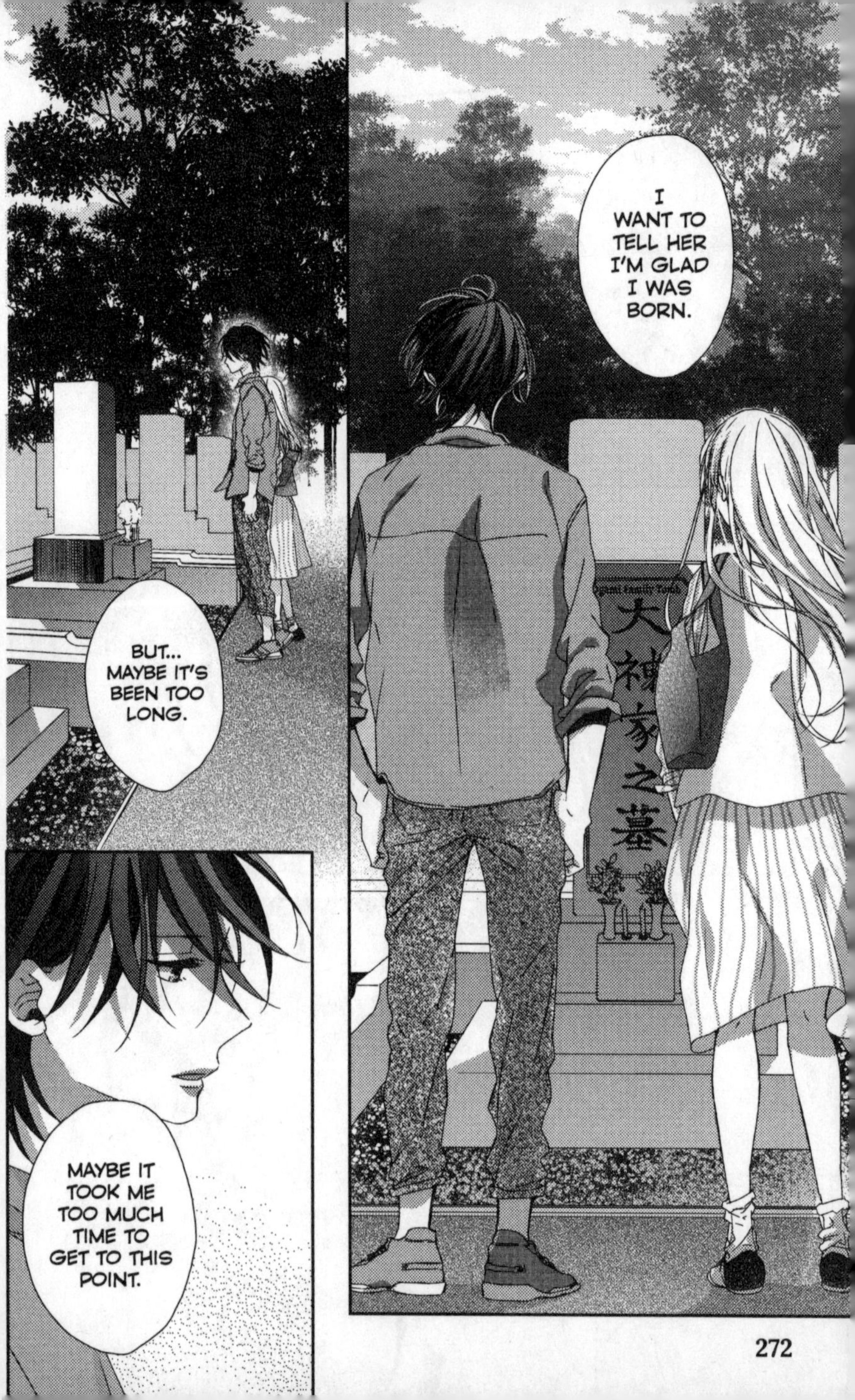
I WANT TO TELL HER I'M GLAD I WAS BORN.
BUT... MAYBE IT'S BEEN TOO LONG.
MAYBE IT TOOK ME TOO MUCH TIME TO GET TO THIS POINT.

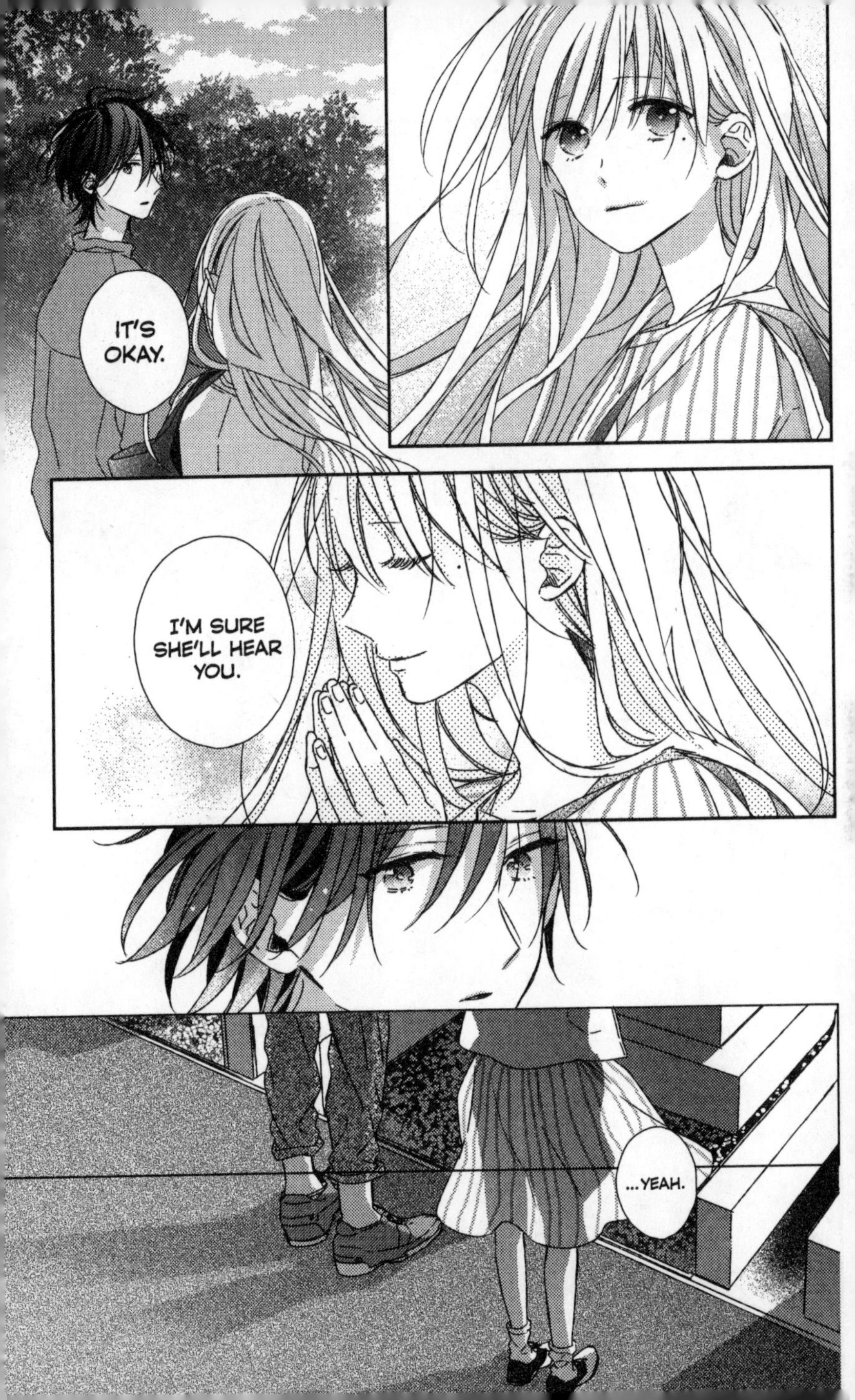
IT'S OKAY.
I'M SURE SHE'LL HEAR YOU.
...YEAH.

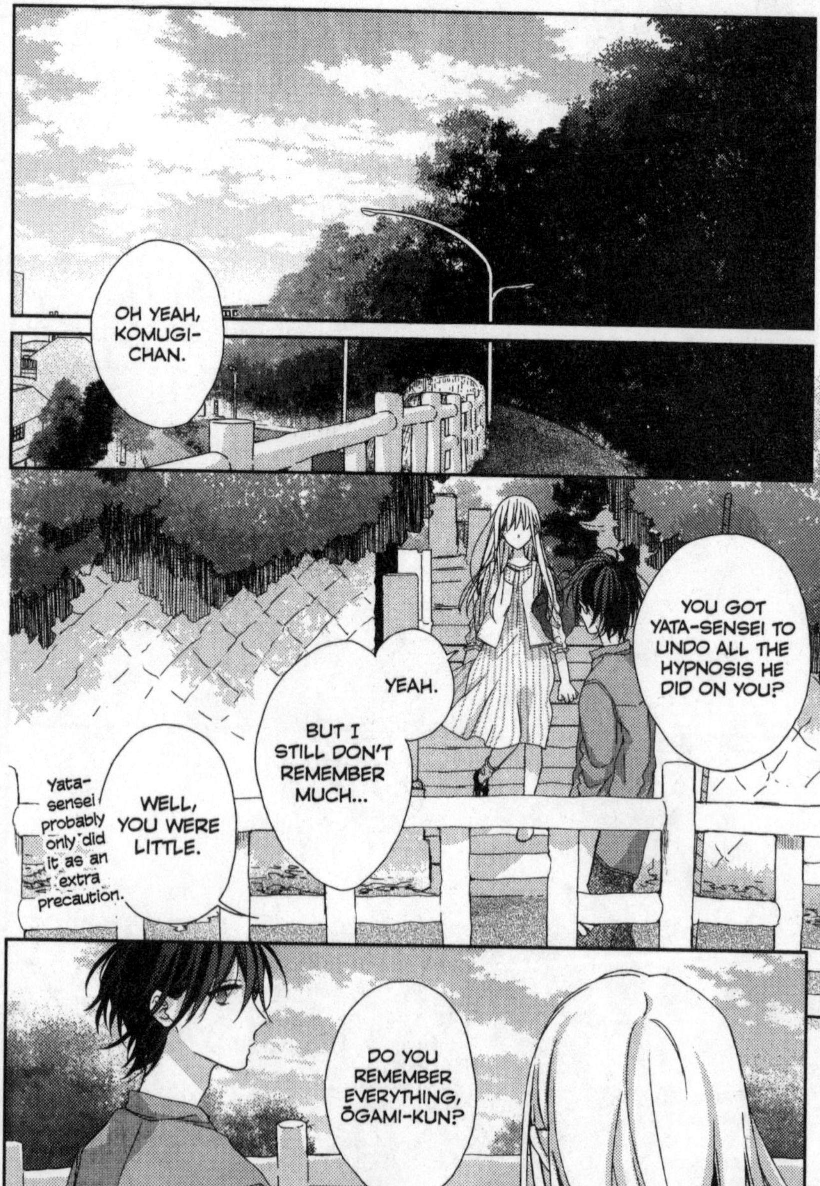
OH YEAH, KOMUGI-CHAN.
YOU GOT YATA-SENSEI TO UNDO ALL THE HYPNOSIS HE DID ON YOU?
YEAH.
BUT I STILL DON'T REMEMBER MUCH...
WELL, YOU WERE LITTLE.
Yata-sensei probably only did it as an extra precaution.
DO YOU REMEMBER EVERYTHING, ŌGAMI-KUN?

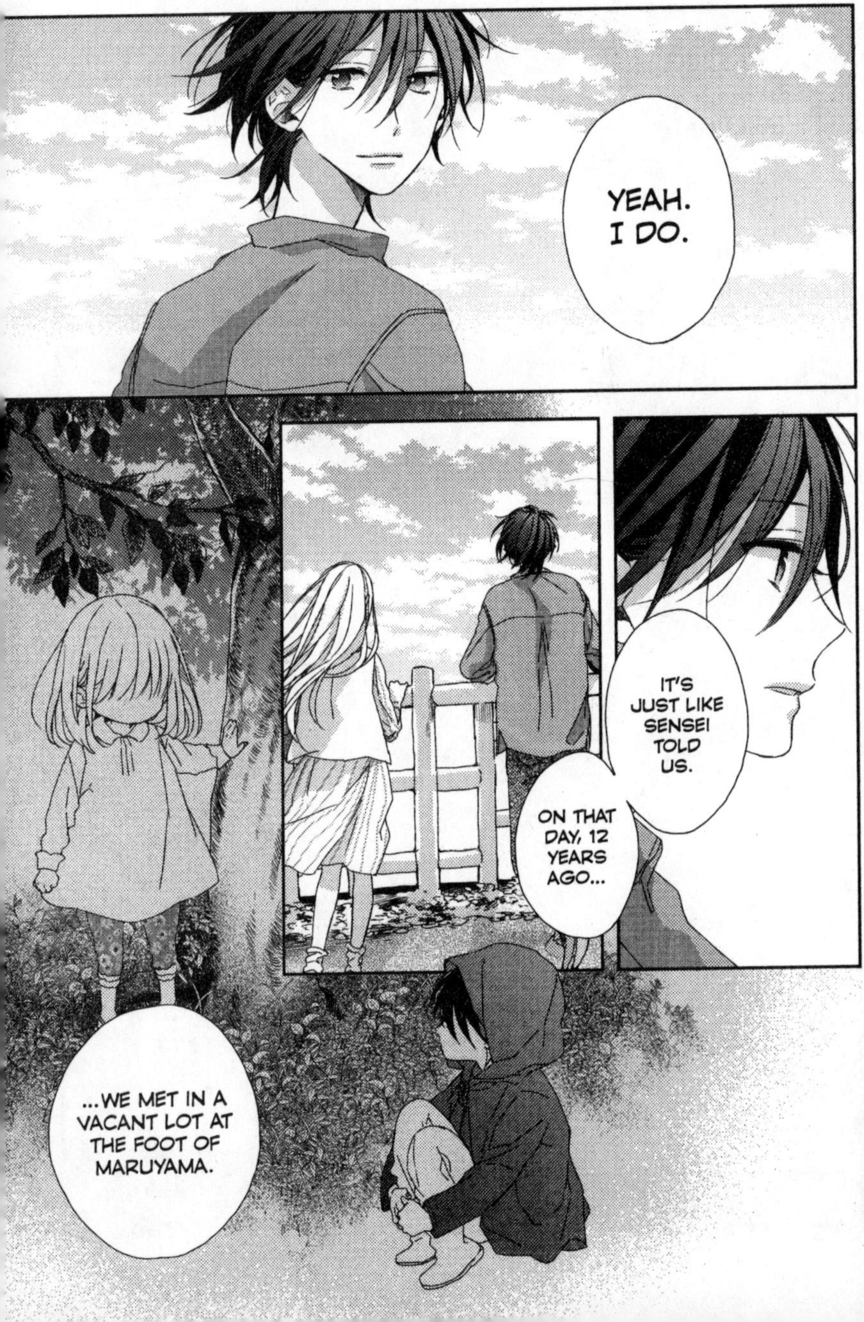
YEAH. I DO.
IT'S JUST LIKE SENSEI TOLD US.
ON THAT DAY, 12 YEARS AGO...
...WE MET IN A VACANT LOT AT THE FOOT OF MARUYAMA.

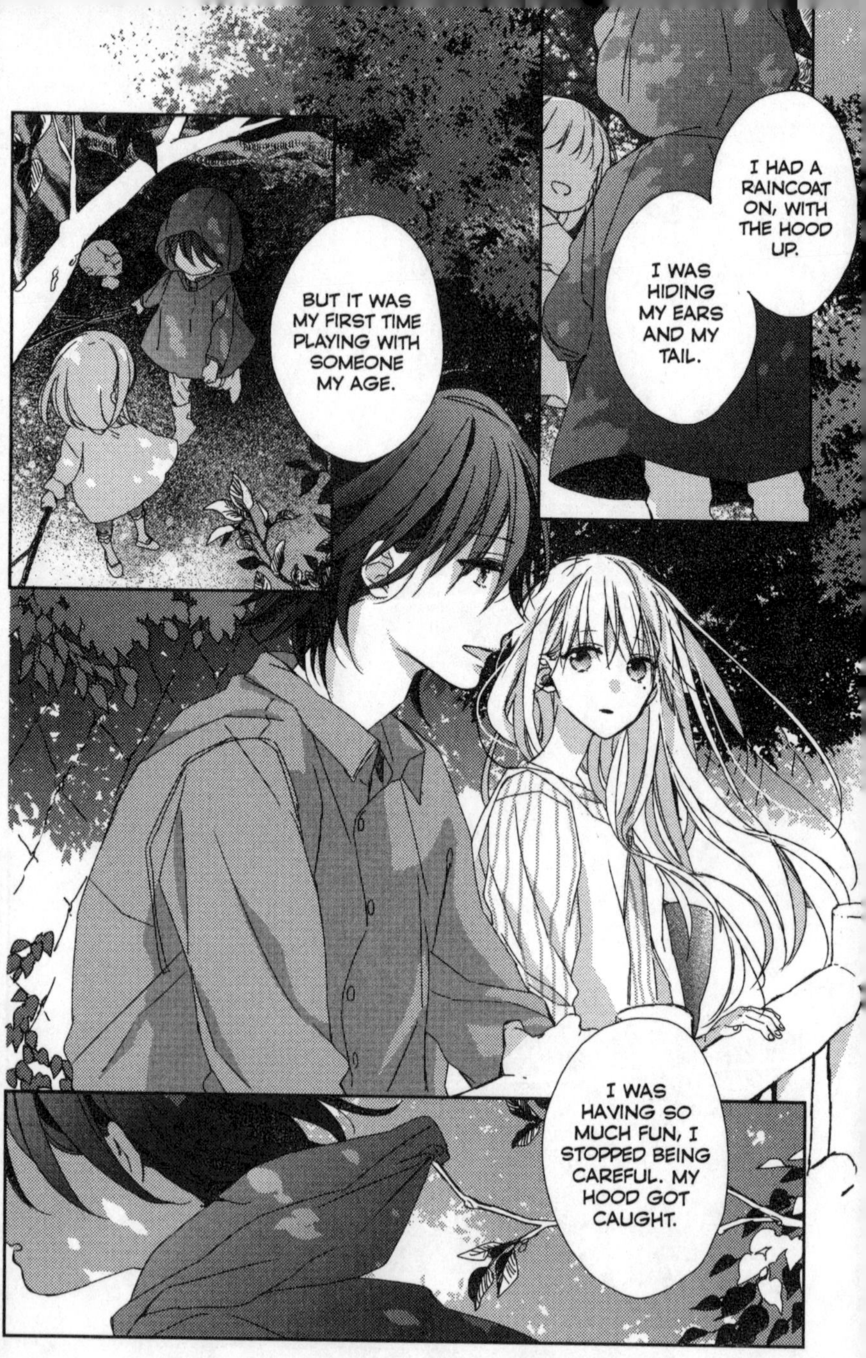
I HAD A RAINCOAT ON, WITH THE HOOD UP.
I WAS HIDING MY EARS AND MY TAIL.
BUT IT WAS MY FIRST TIME PLAYING WITH SOMEONE MY AGE.
I WAS HAVING SO MUCH FUN, I STOPPED BEING CAREFUL. MY HOOD GOT CAUGHT.

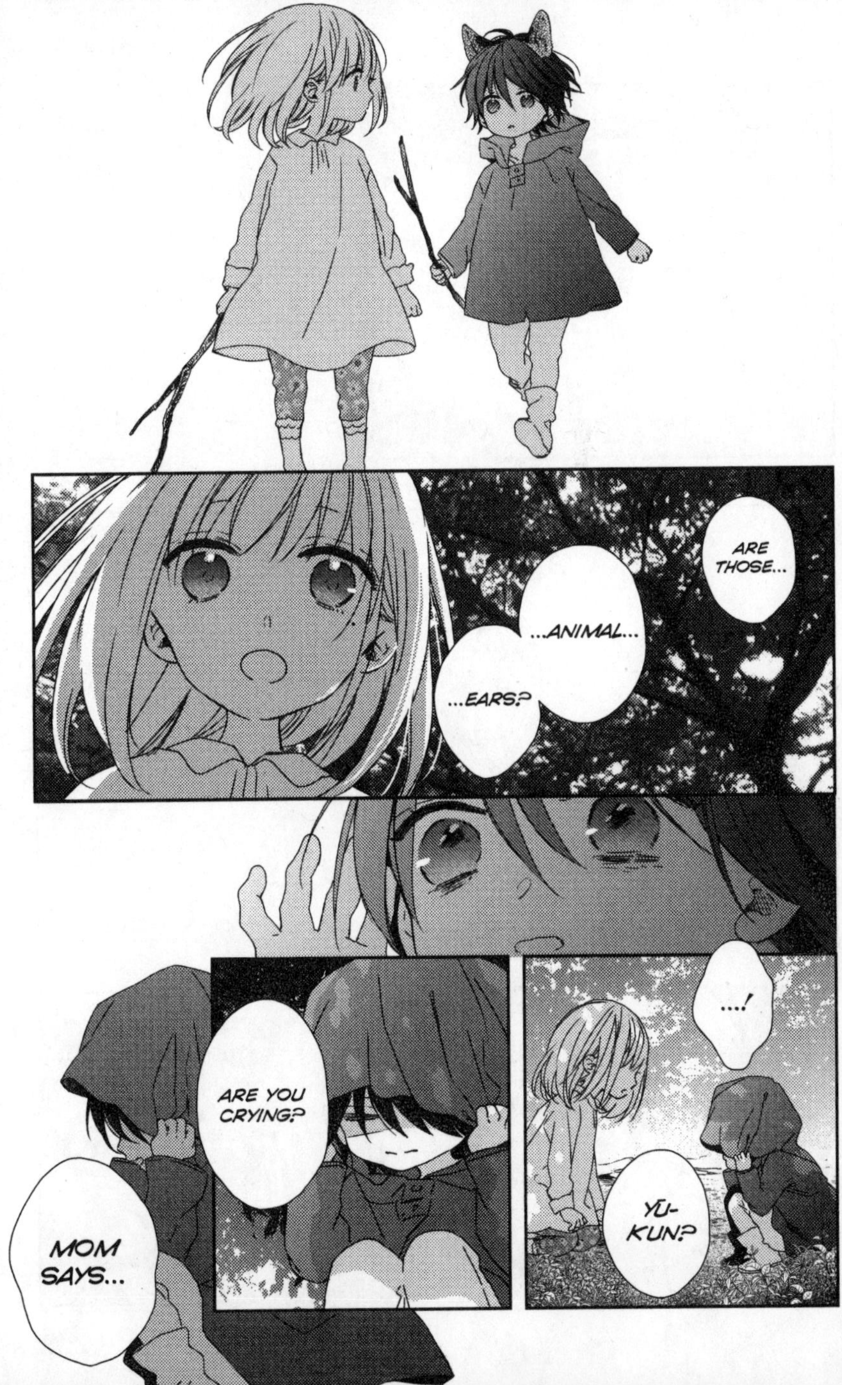
ARE THOSE...
...ANIMAL...
...EARS?
...!
YU-KUN?
ARE YOU CRYING?
MOM SAYS...

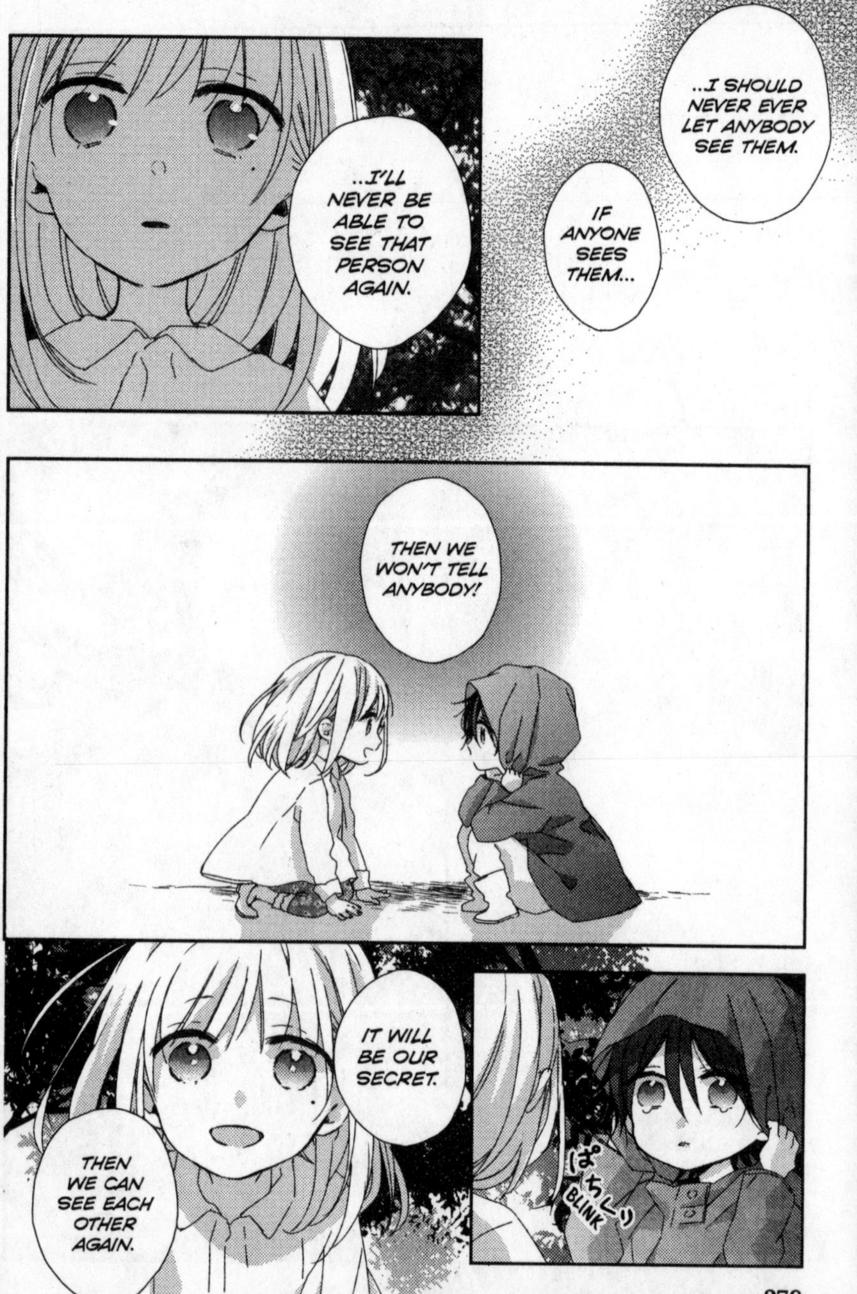
...I SHOULD NEVER EVER LET ANYBODY SEE THEM.
IF ANYONE SEES THEM...
...I'LL NEVER BE ABLE TO SEE THAT PERSON AGAIN.
THEN WE WON'T TELL ANYBODY!
ぱちくり
BLINK
IT WILL BE OUR SECRET.
THEN WE CAN SEE EACH OTHER AGAIN.

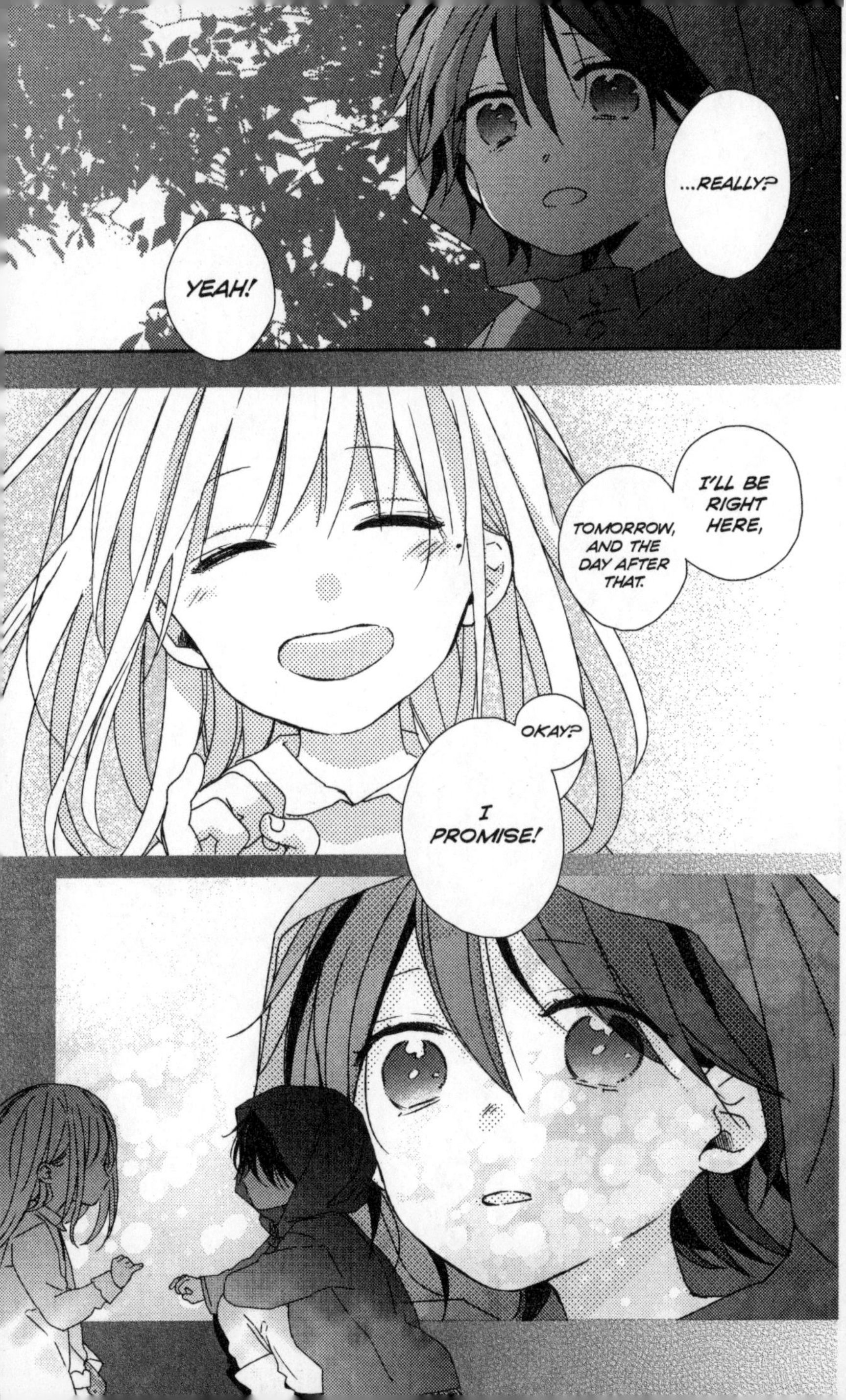
...REALLY?
YEAH!
I'LL BE RIGHT HERE,
TOMORROW, AND THE DAY AFTER THAT.
OKAY?
I PROMISE!

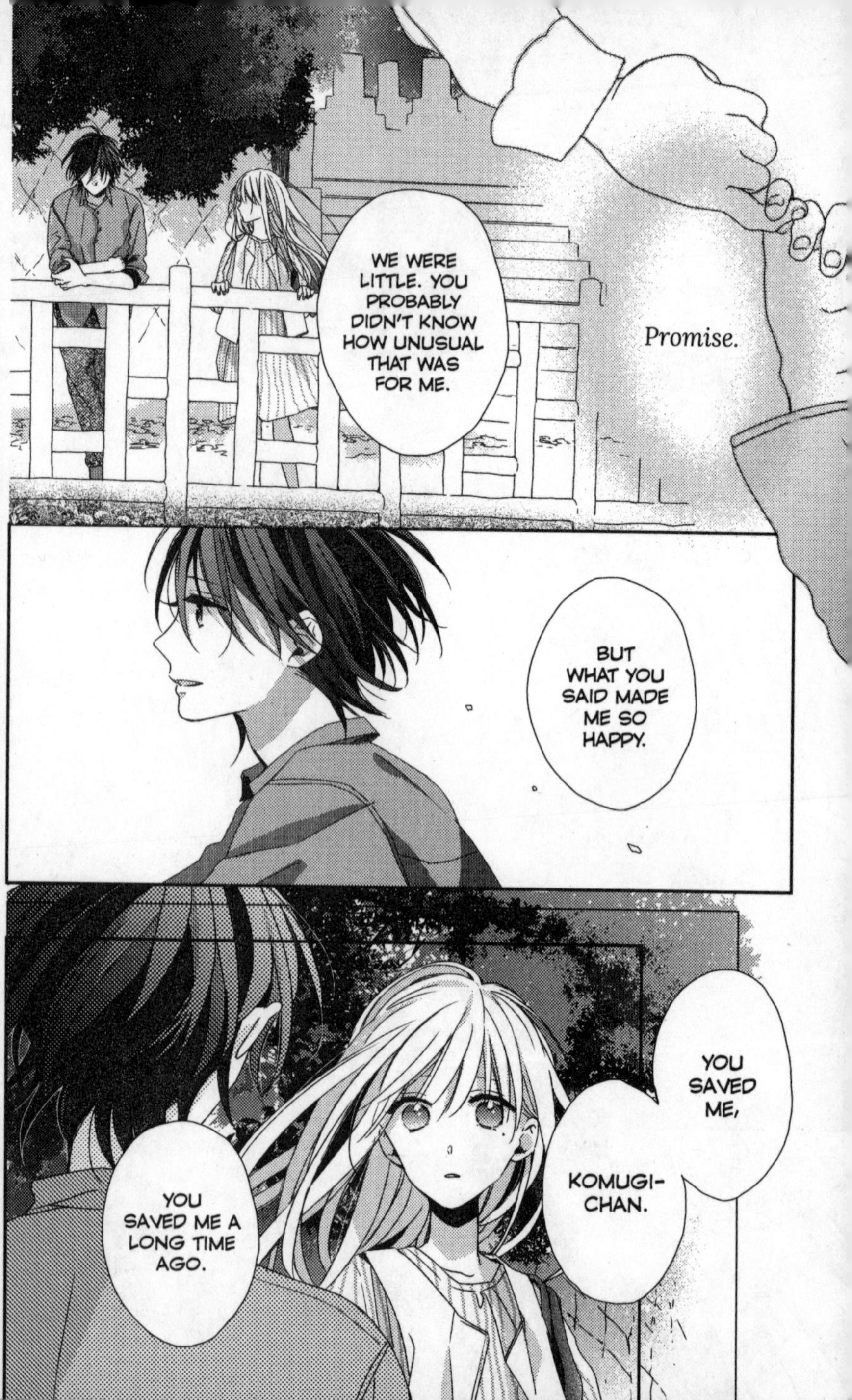
Promise.
WE WERE LITTLE. YOU PROBABLY DIDN'T KNOW HOW UNUSUAL THAT WAS FOR ME.
BUT WHAT YOU SAID MADE ME SO HAPPY.
YOU SAVED ME,
KOMUGI-CHAN.
YOU SAVED ME A LONG TIME AGO.

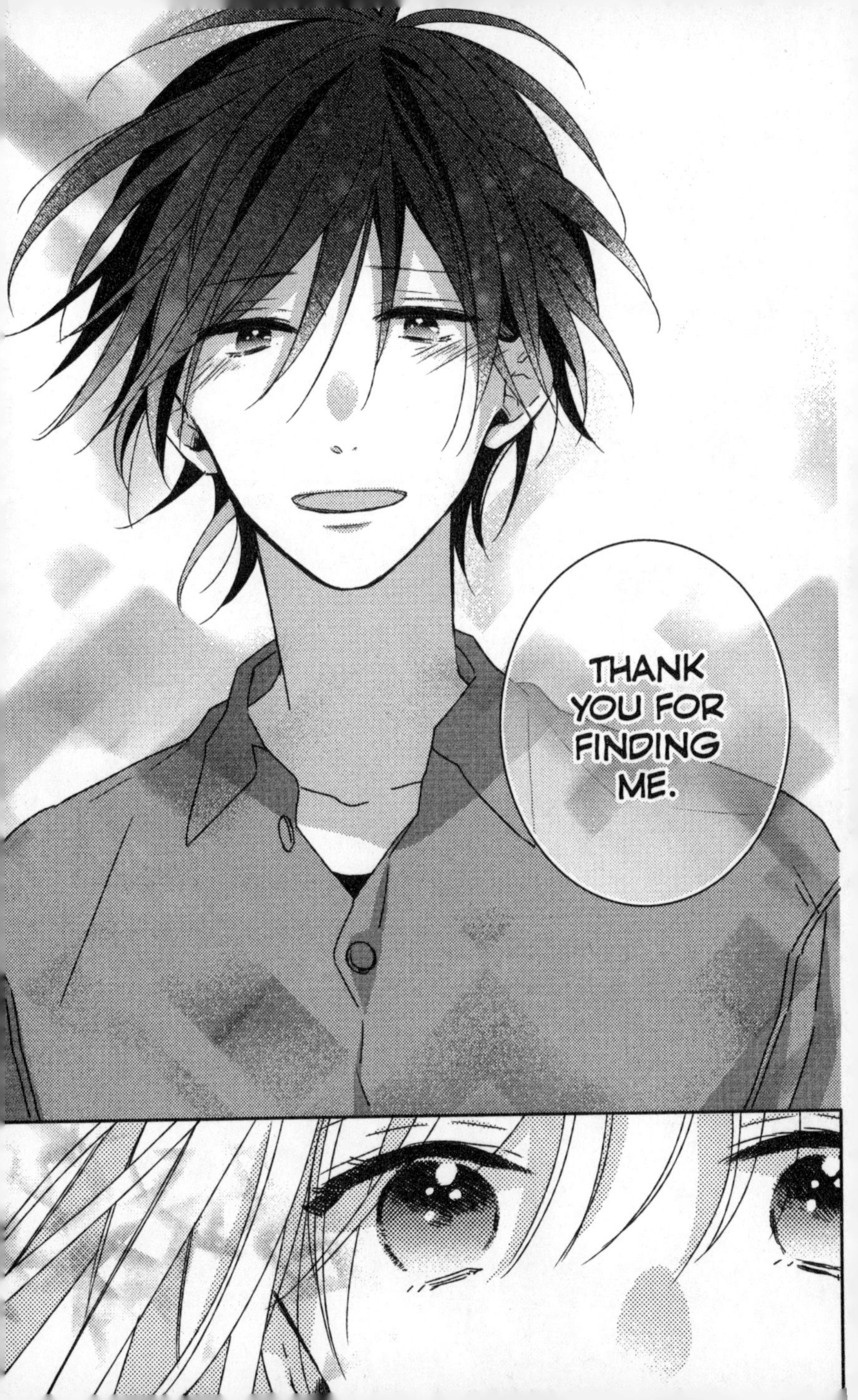
THANK YOU FOR FINDING ME.

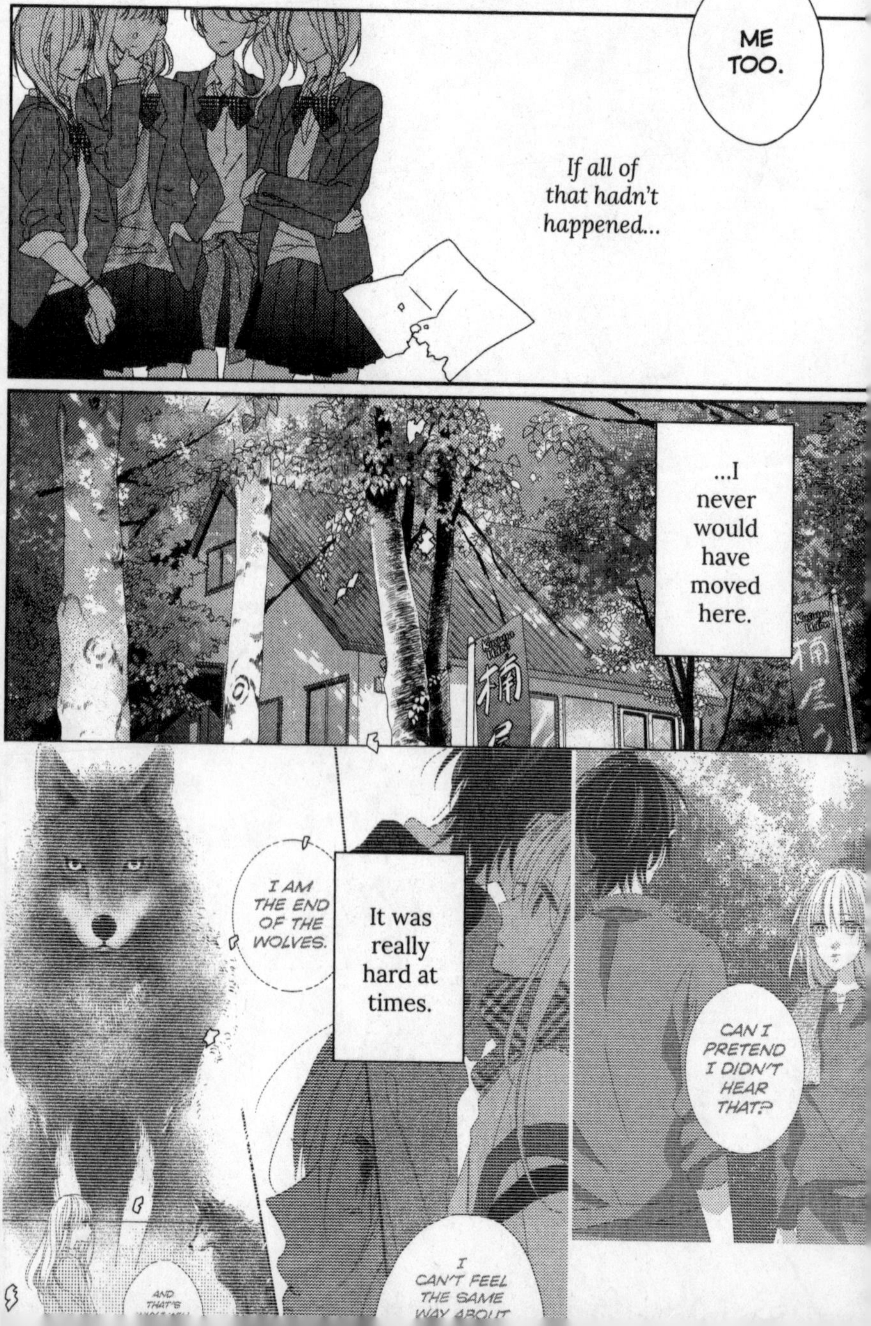
ME TOO.
If all of that hadn't happened...
...I never would have moved here.
CAN I PRETEND I DIDN'T HEAR THAT?
It was really hard at times.
I AM THE END OF THE WOLVES.
I CAN'T FEEL THE SAME WAY ABOUT
AND THAT'S

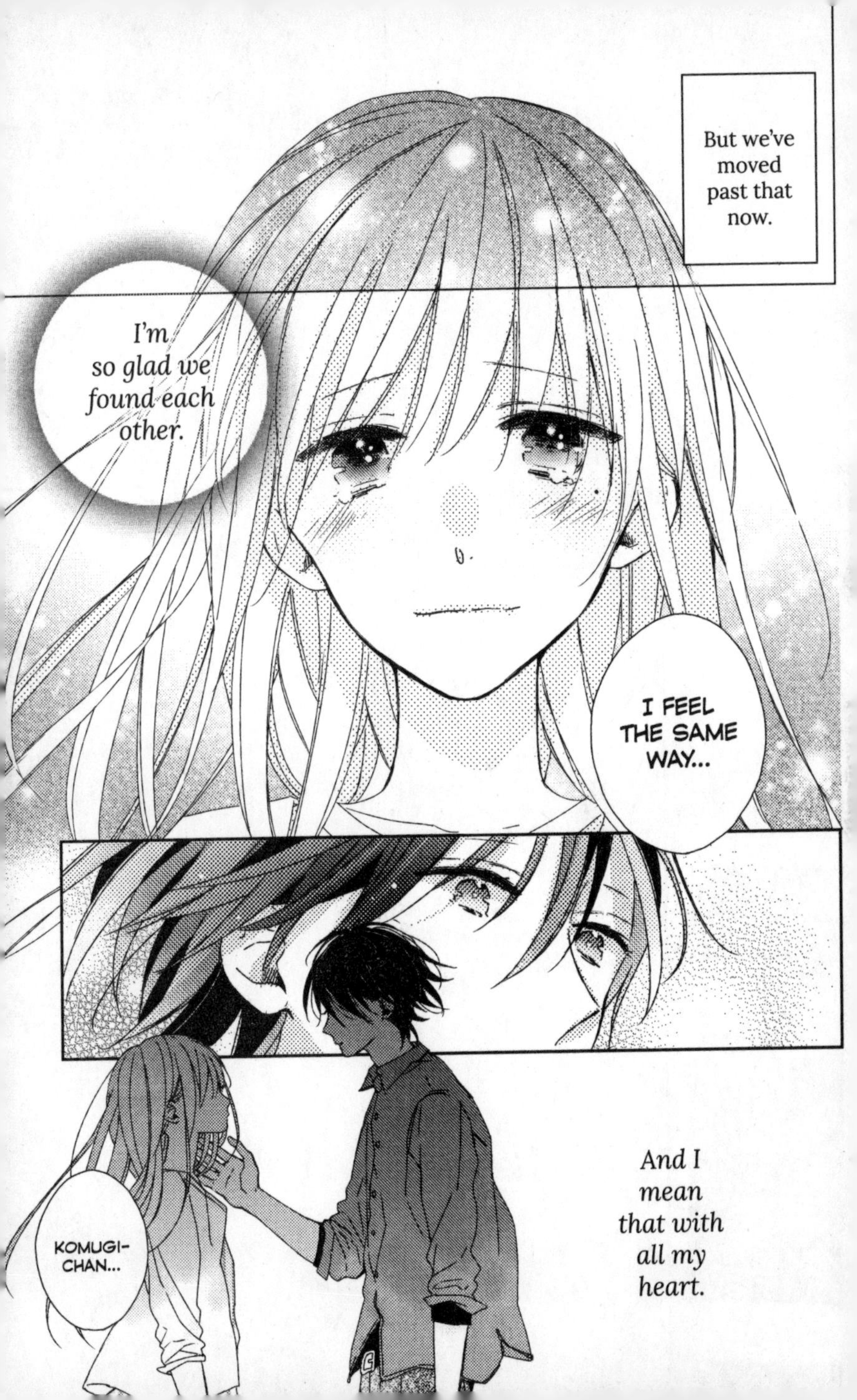
But we've moved past that now.
I'm so glad we found each other.
I FEEL THE SAME WAY...
And I mean that with all my heart.
KOMUGI-CHAN...

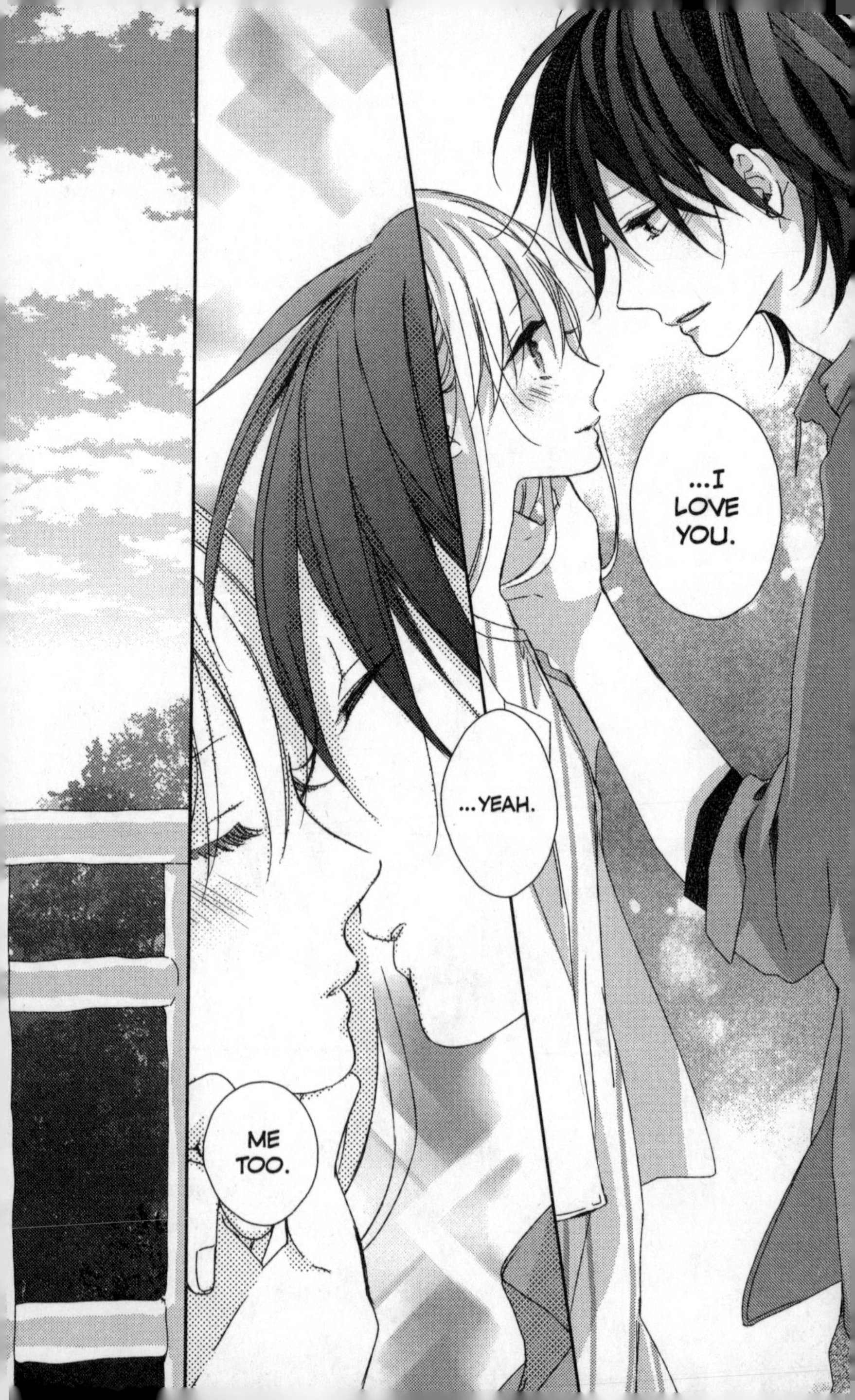
...I LOVE YOU.
...YEAH.
ME TOO.

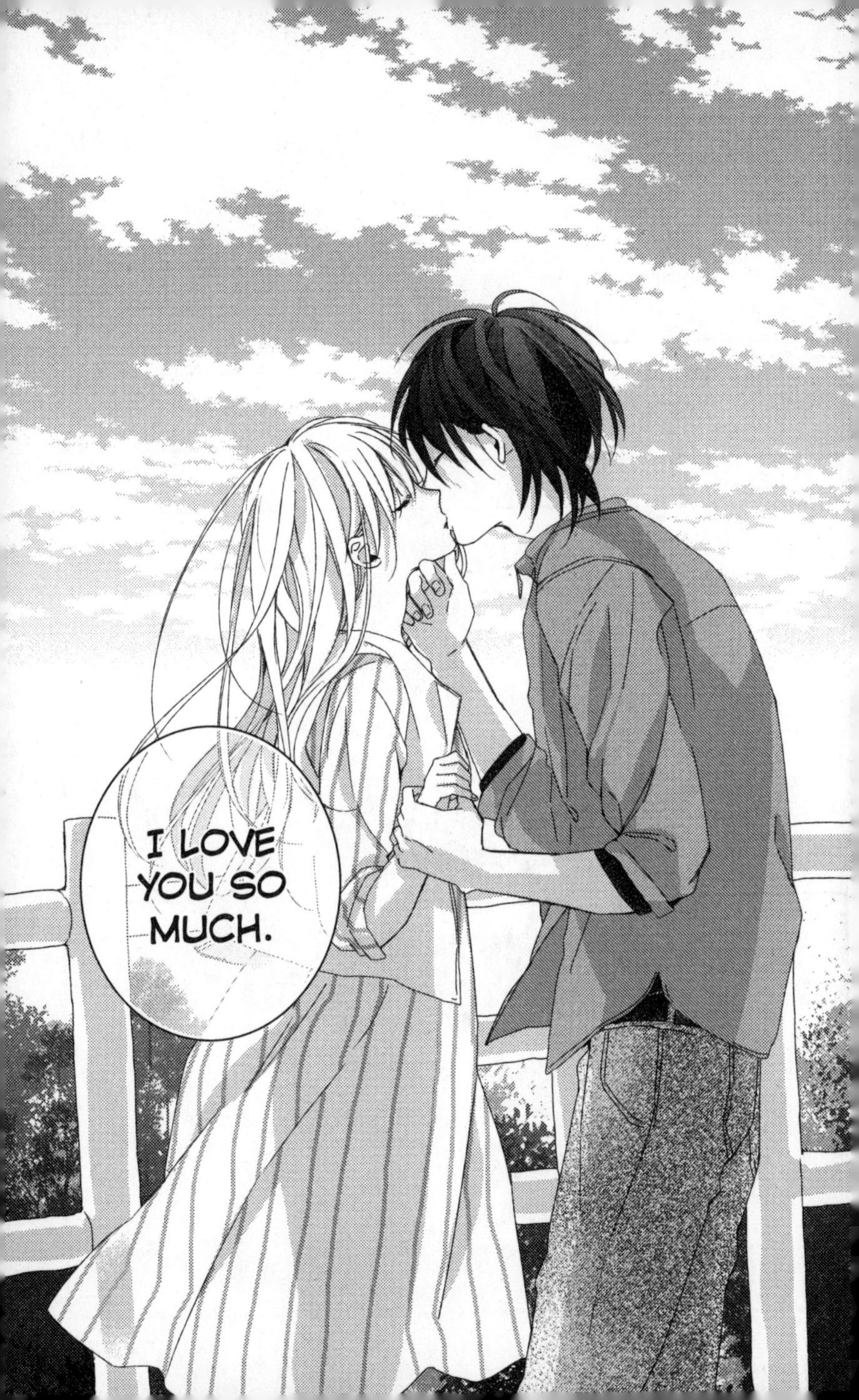
I LOVE YOU SO MUCH.

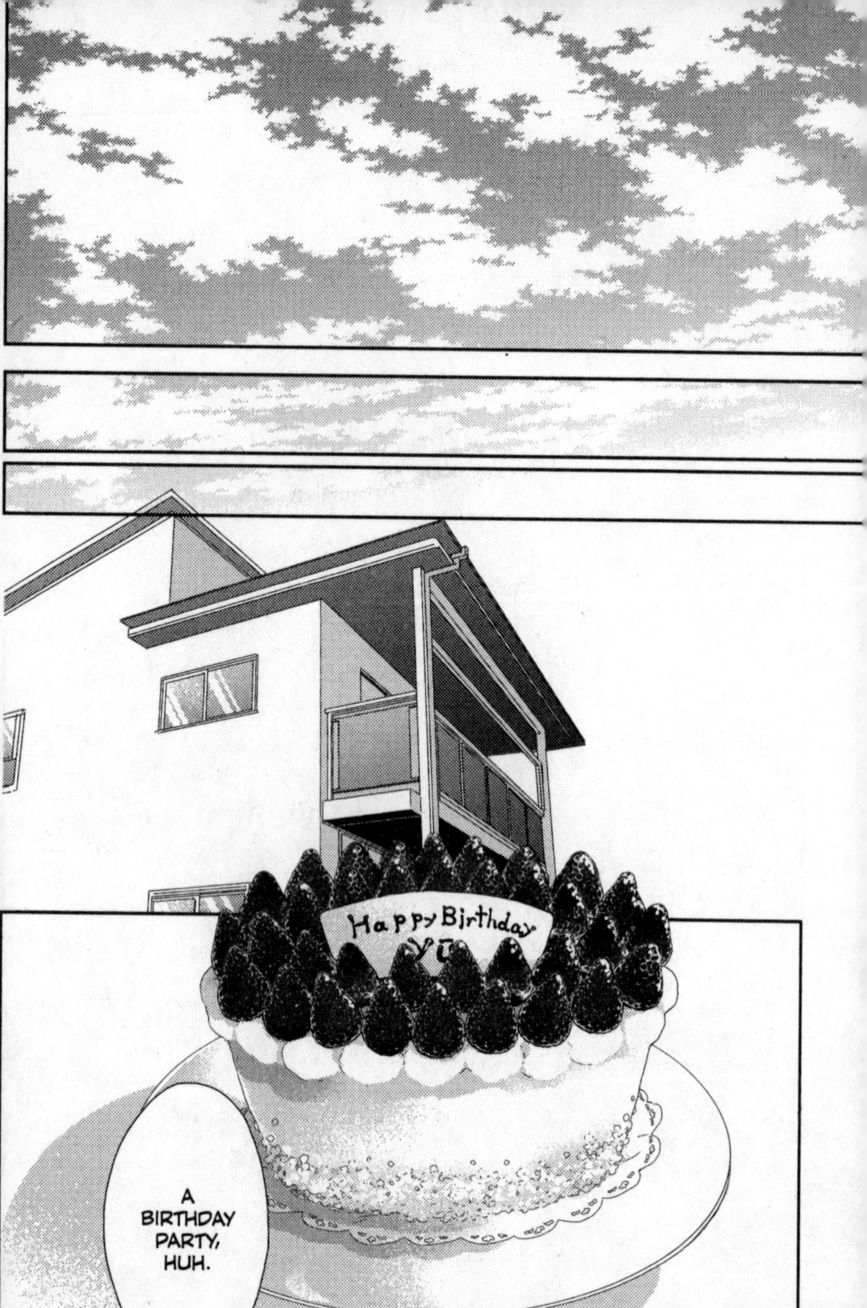
Happy Birthday
A BIRTHDAY PARTY, HUH.

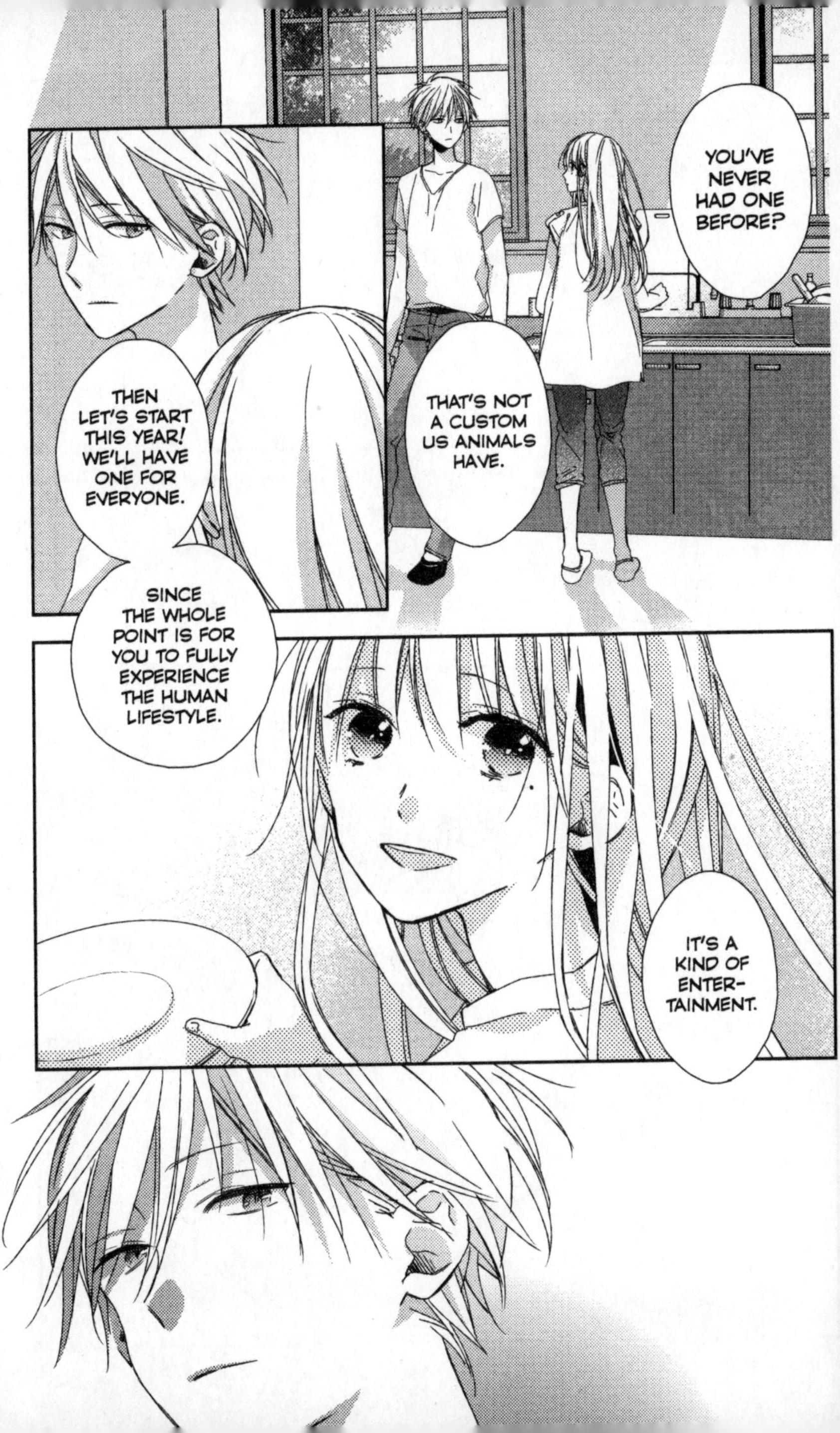
YOU'VE NEVER HAD ONE BEFORE?
THAT'S NOT A CUSTOM US ANIMALS HAVE.
THEN LET'S START THIS YEAR! WE'LL HAVE ONE FOR EVERYONE.
SINCE THE WHOLE POINT IS FOR YOU TO FULLY EXPERIENCE THE HUMAN LIFESTYLE.
IT'S A KIND OF ENTER-TAINMENT.

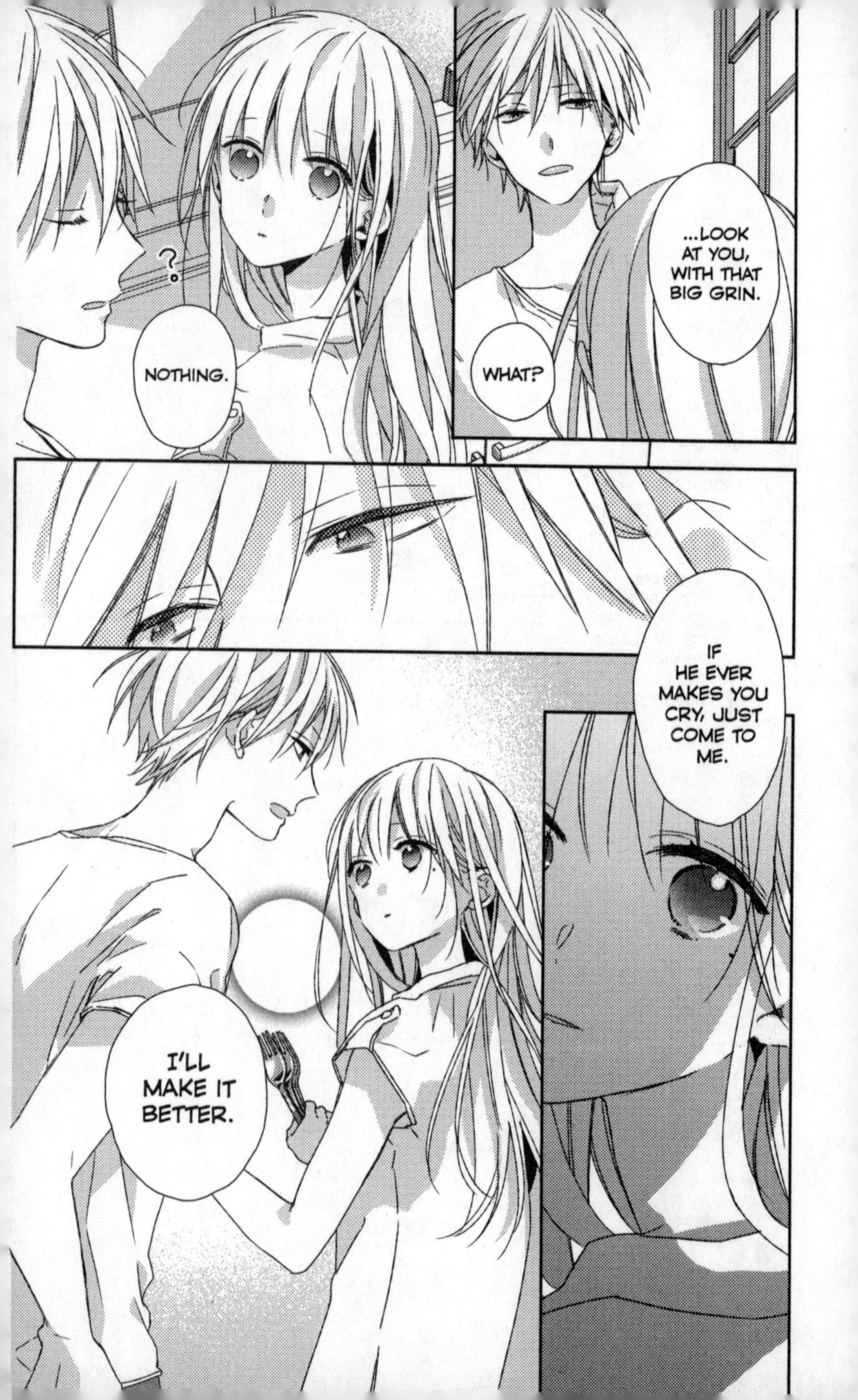
...LOOK AT YOU, WITH THAT BIG GRIN.
WHAT?
?
NOTHING.
IF HE EVER MAKES YOU CRY, JUST COME TO ME.
I'LL MAKE IT BETTER.

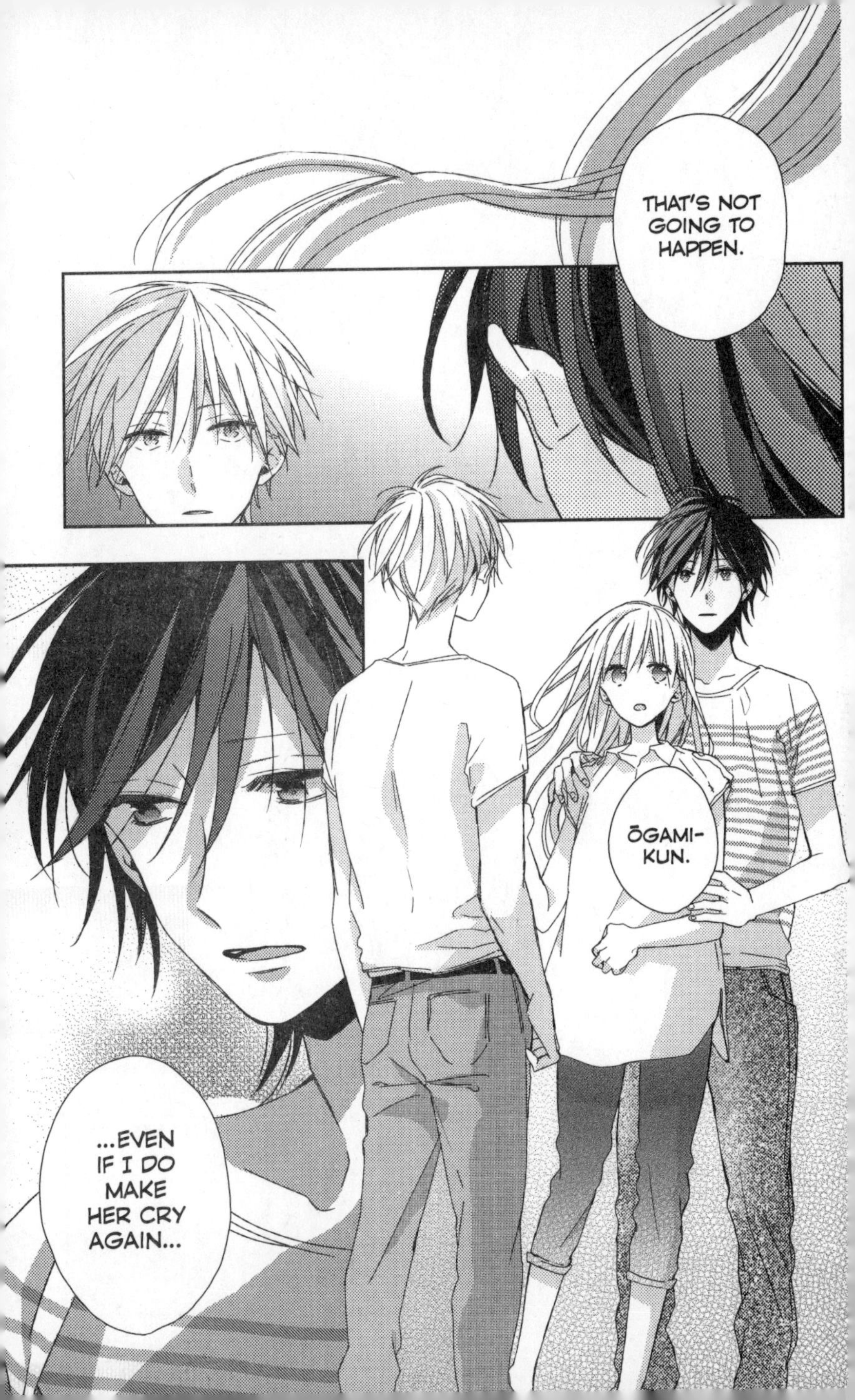
THAT'S NOT GOING TO HAPPEN.
ŌGAMI-KUN.
...EVEN IF I DO MAKE HER CRY AGAIN...

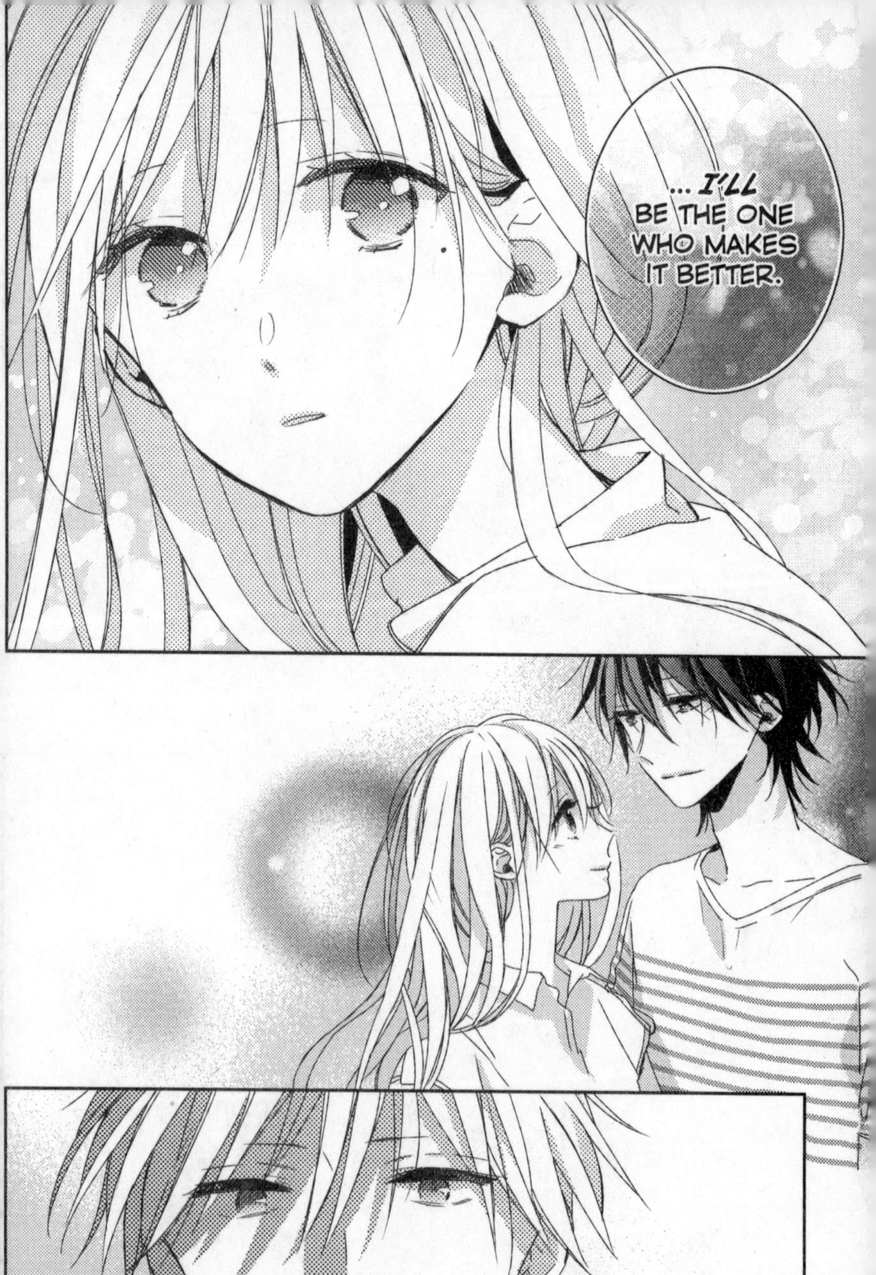
...I'LL BE THE ONE WHO MAKES IT BETTER.

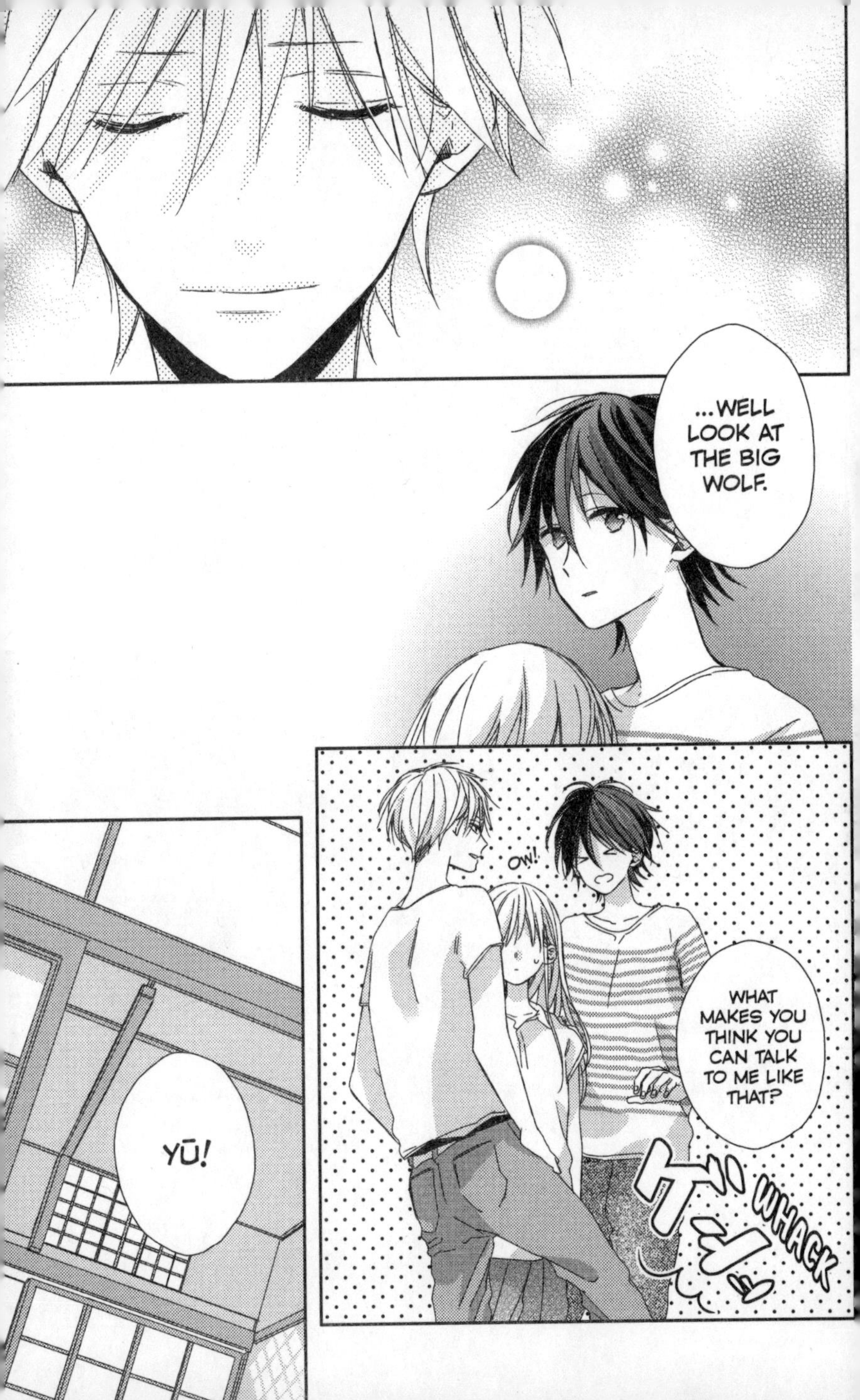
...WELL LOOK AT THE BIG WOLF.
OW!
WHAT MAKES YOU THINK YOU CAN TALK TO ME LIKE THAT?
WHACK
YŪ!

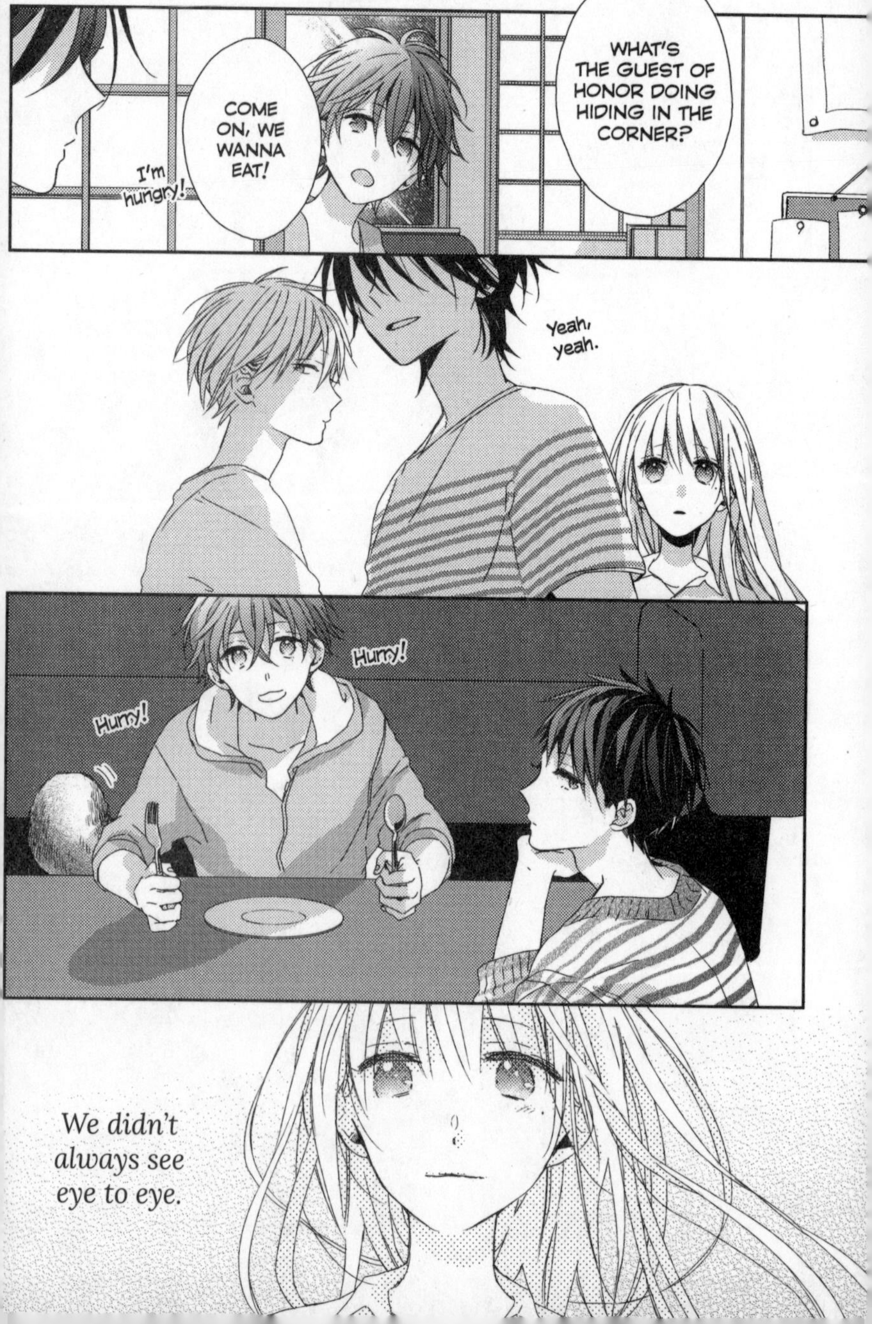
WHAT'S THE GUEST OF HONOR DOING HIDING IN THE CORNER?
COME ON, WE WANNA EAT!
I'm hungry!
Yeah, yeah.
Hurry!
Hurry!
We didn't always see eye to eye.

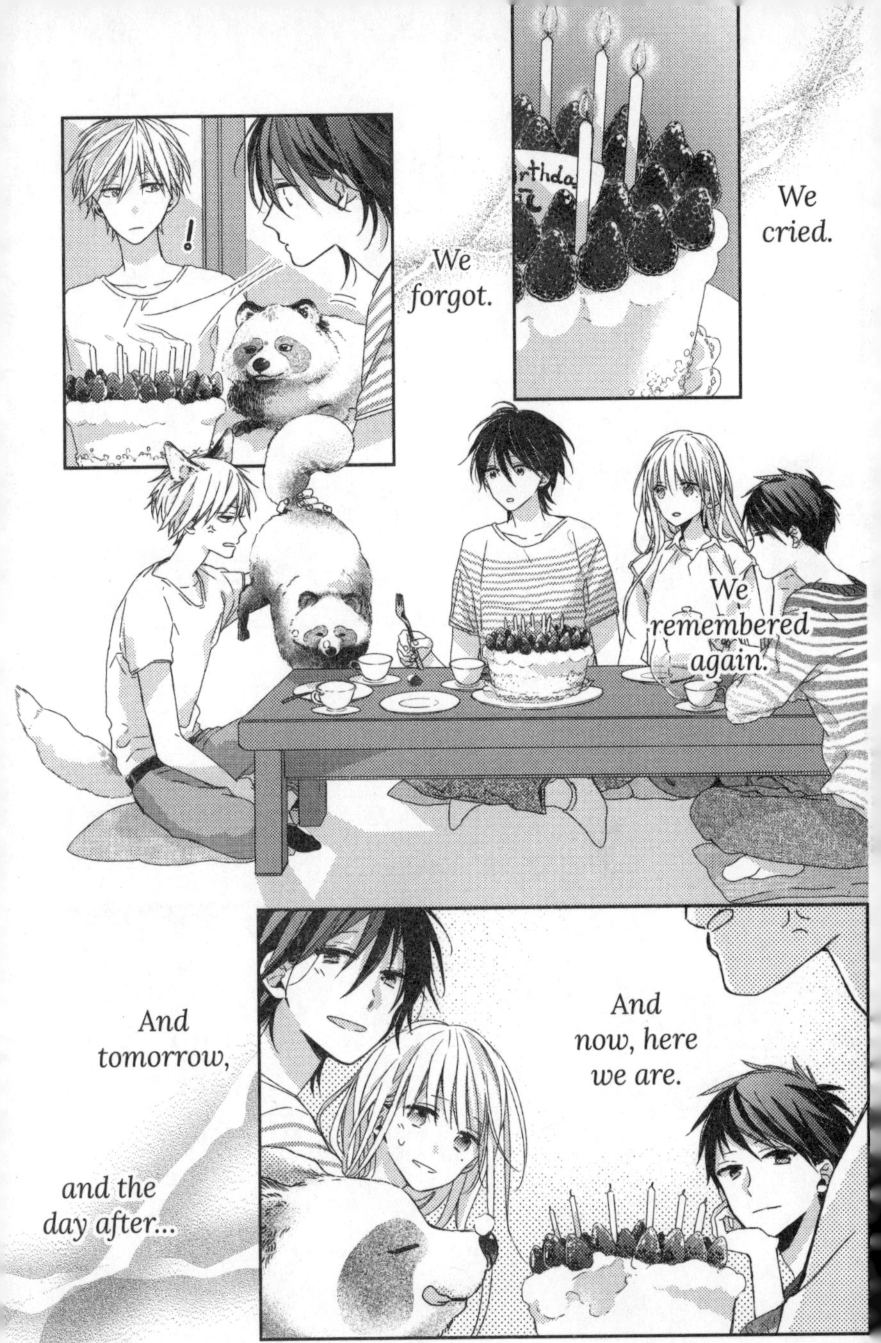
We cried.
rthda
We forgot.
!
We remembered again.
And now, here we are.
And tomorrow,
and the day after...

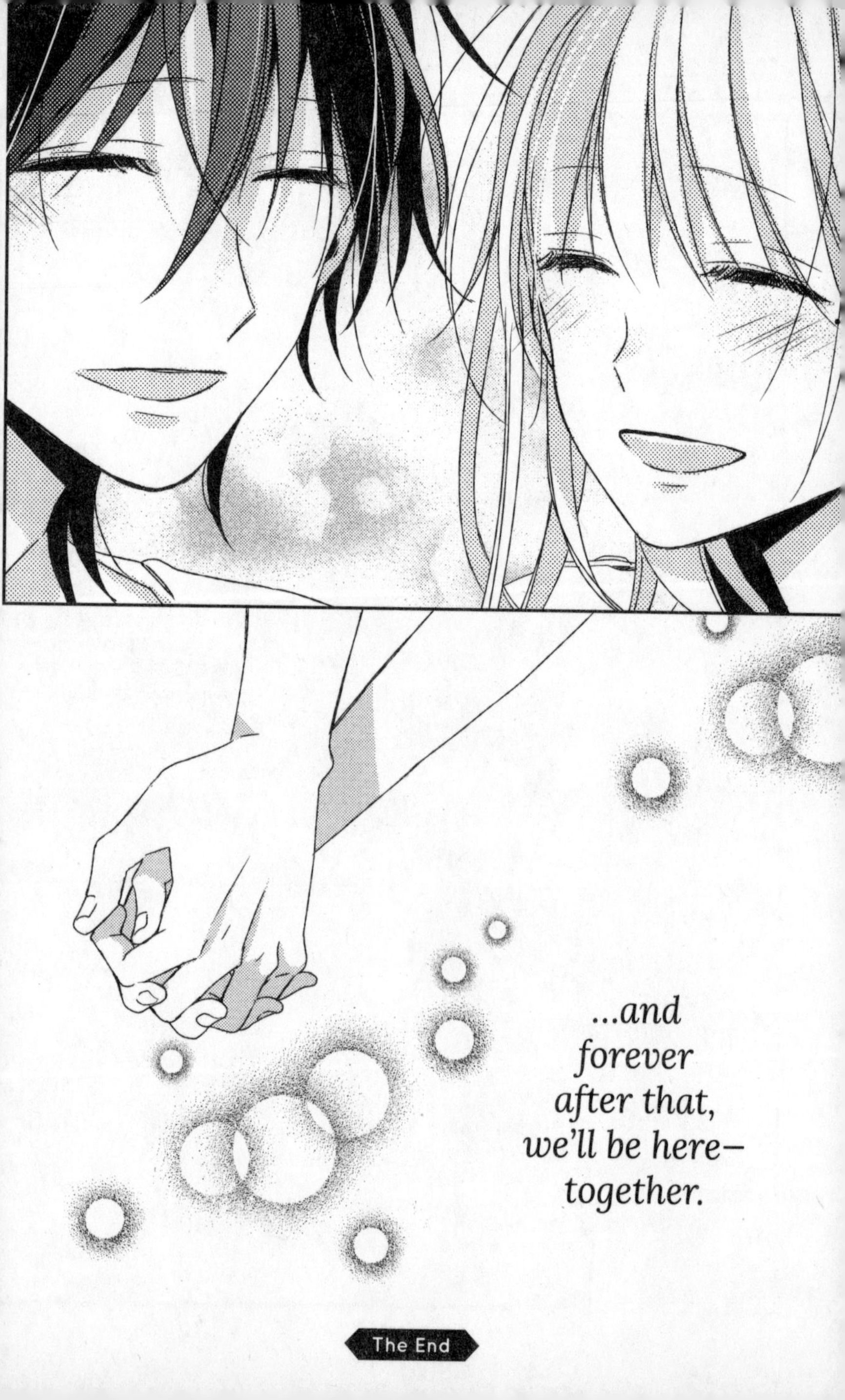
...and forever after that, we'll be here—together.
The End

Bonus Chapter

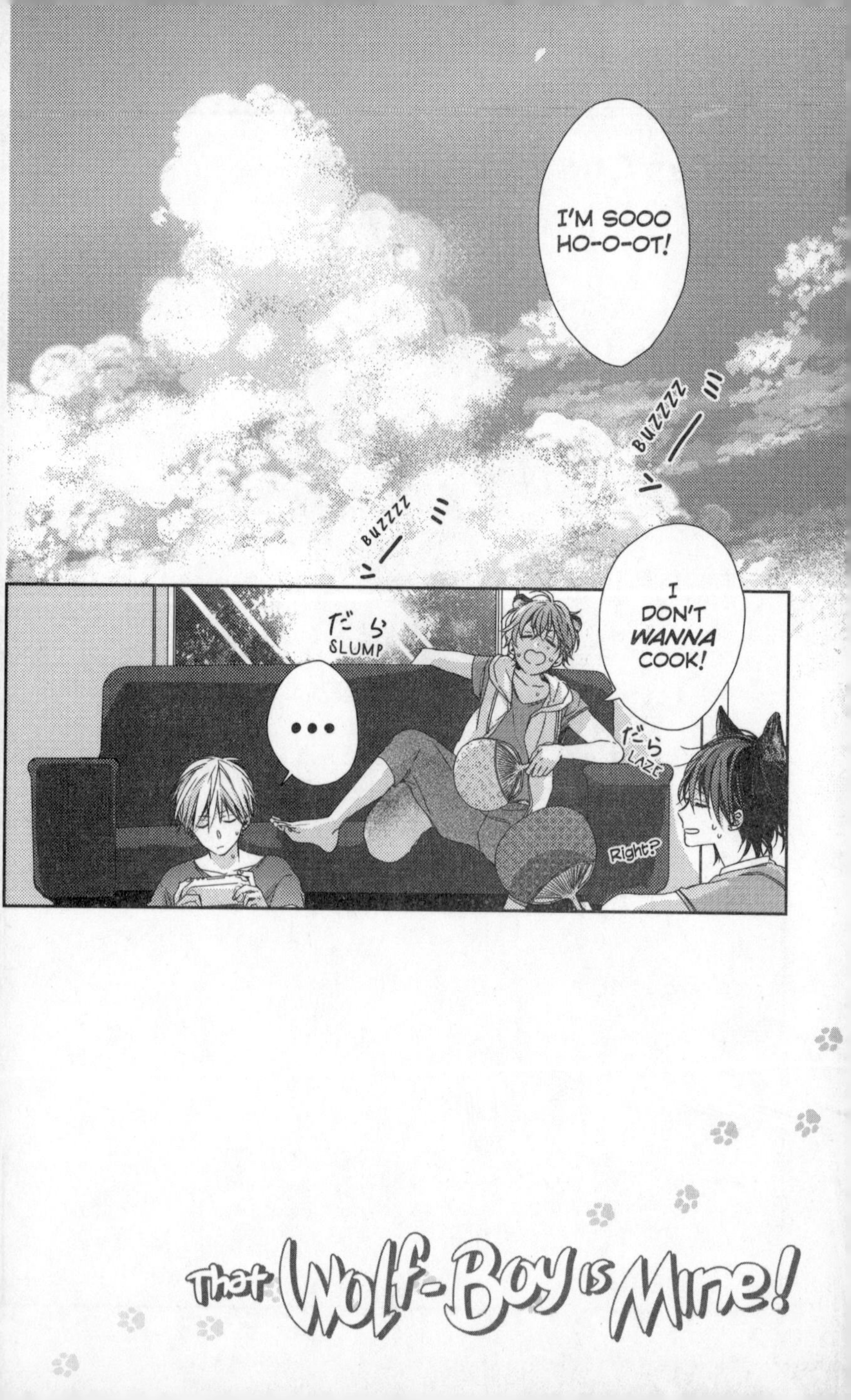
I'M SOOO HO-O-OT!
BUZZZZ
BUZZZZ
I DON'T WANNA COOK!
だら LAZE
Right?
だら SLUMP
...
That Wolf-Boy is Mine!

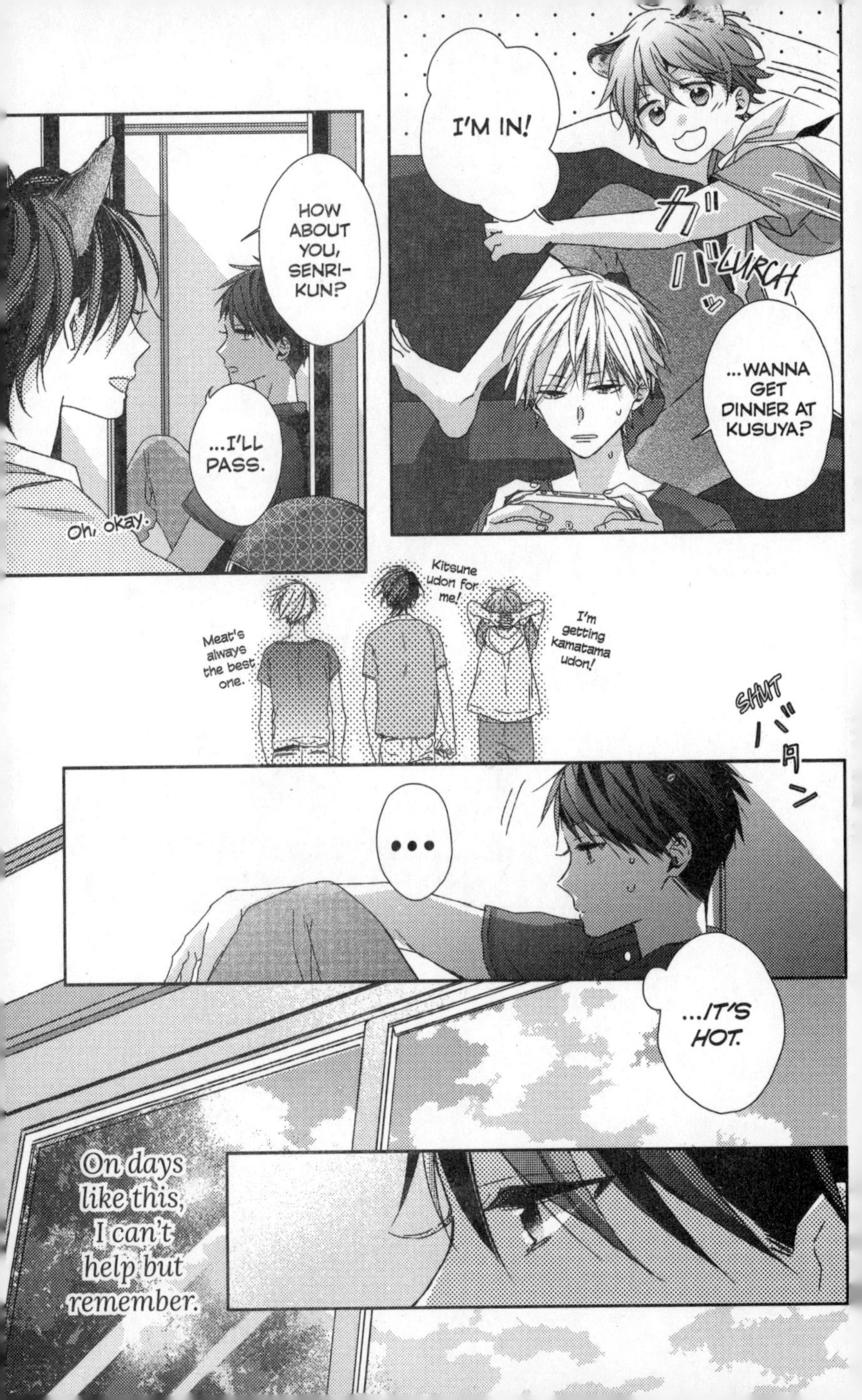
...WANNA GET DINNER AT KUSUYA?
I'M IN!
ガバッ
LURCH
HOW ABOUT YOU, SENRI-KUN?
...I'LL PASS.
Oh, okay.
I'm getting kamatama udon!
Kitsune udon for me!
Meat's always the best one.
SHUT
バタン
...
...IT'S HOT.
On days like this, I can't help but remember.

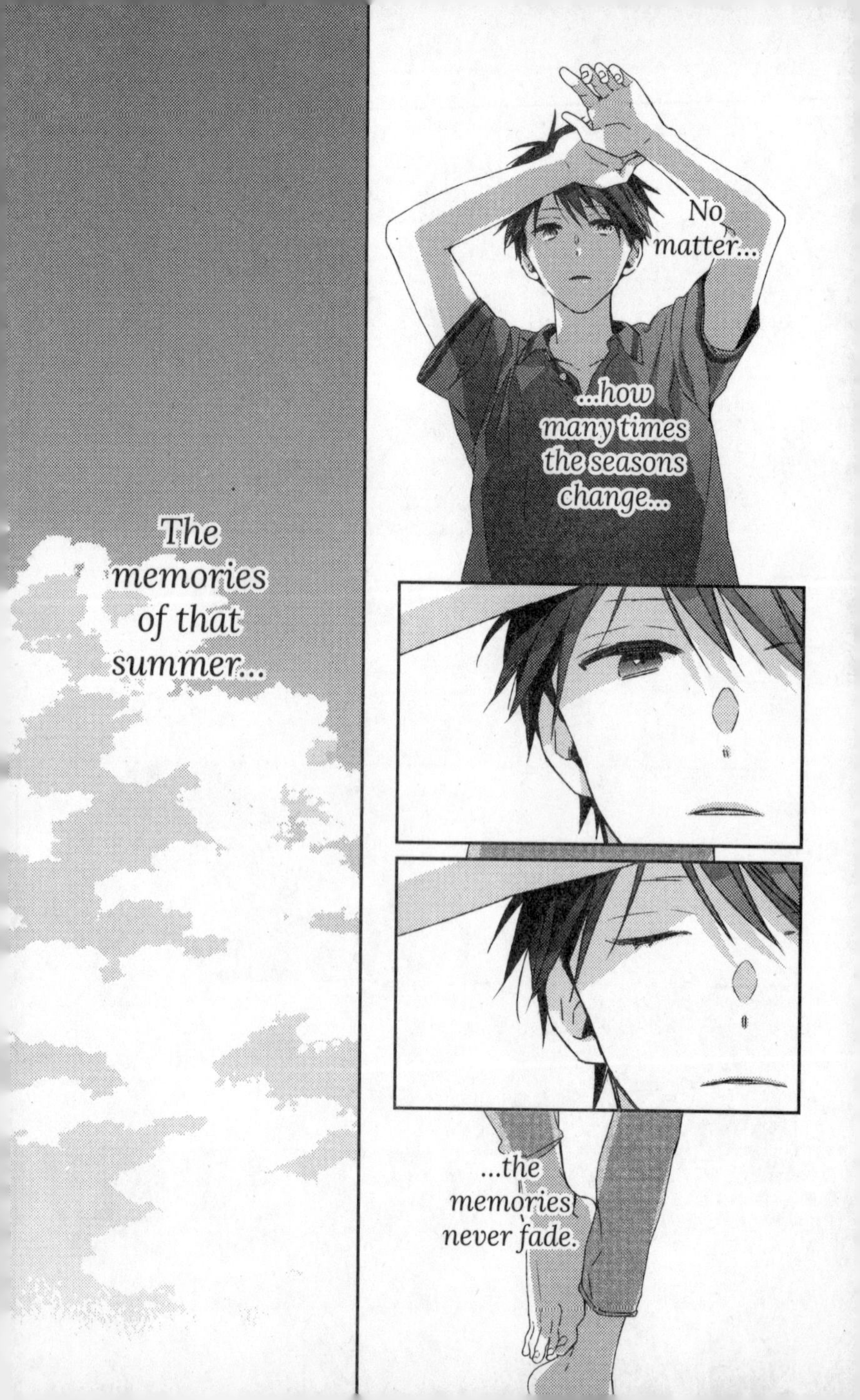
No matter...
...how many times the seasons change...
...the memories never fade.
The memories of that summer...

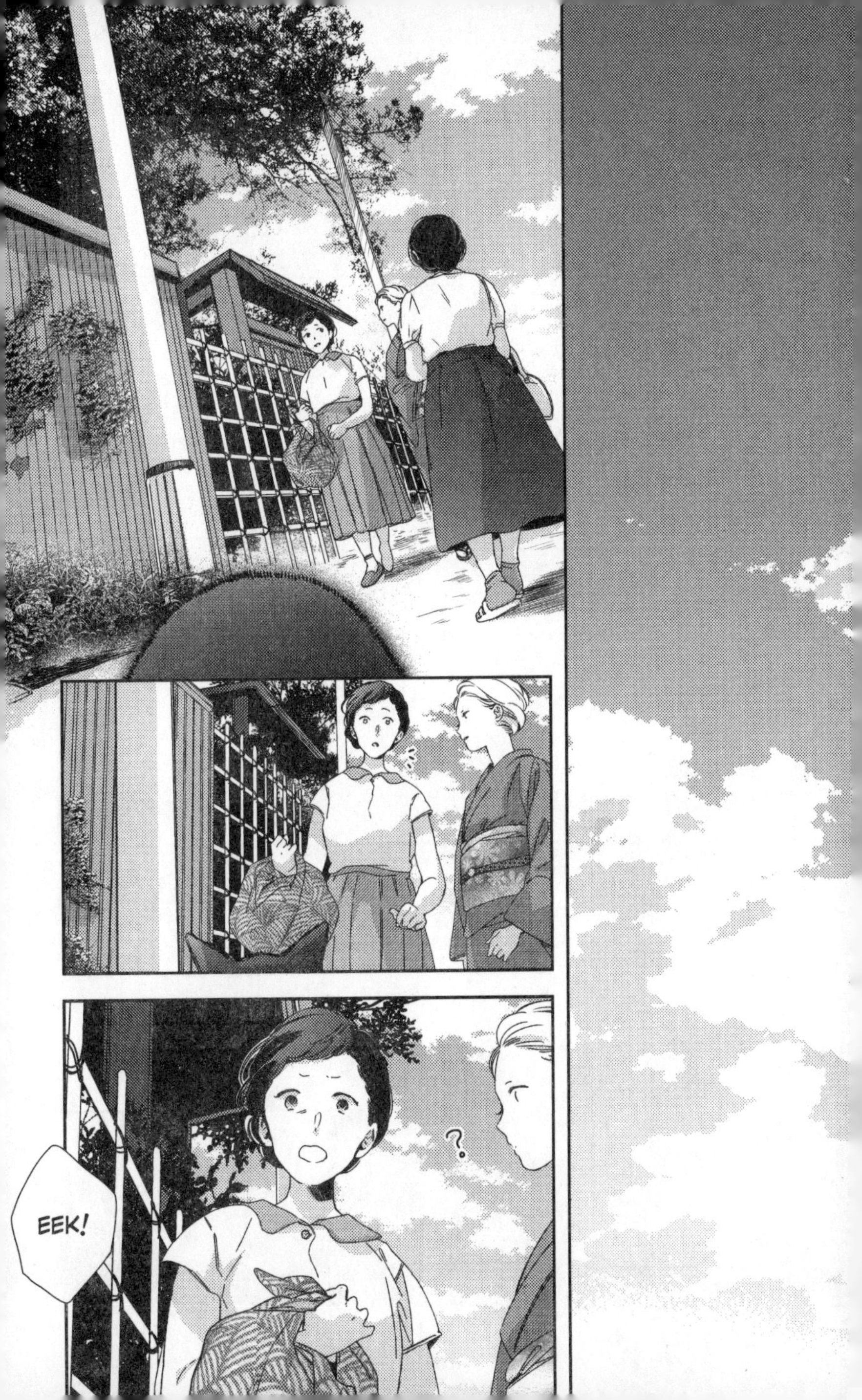
?
EEK!

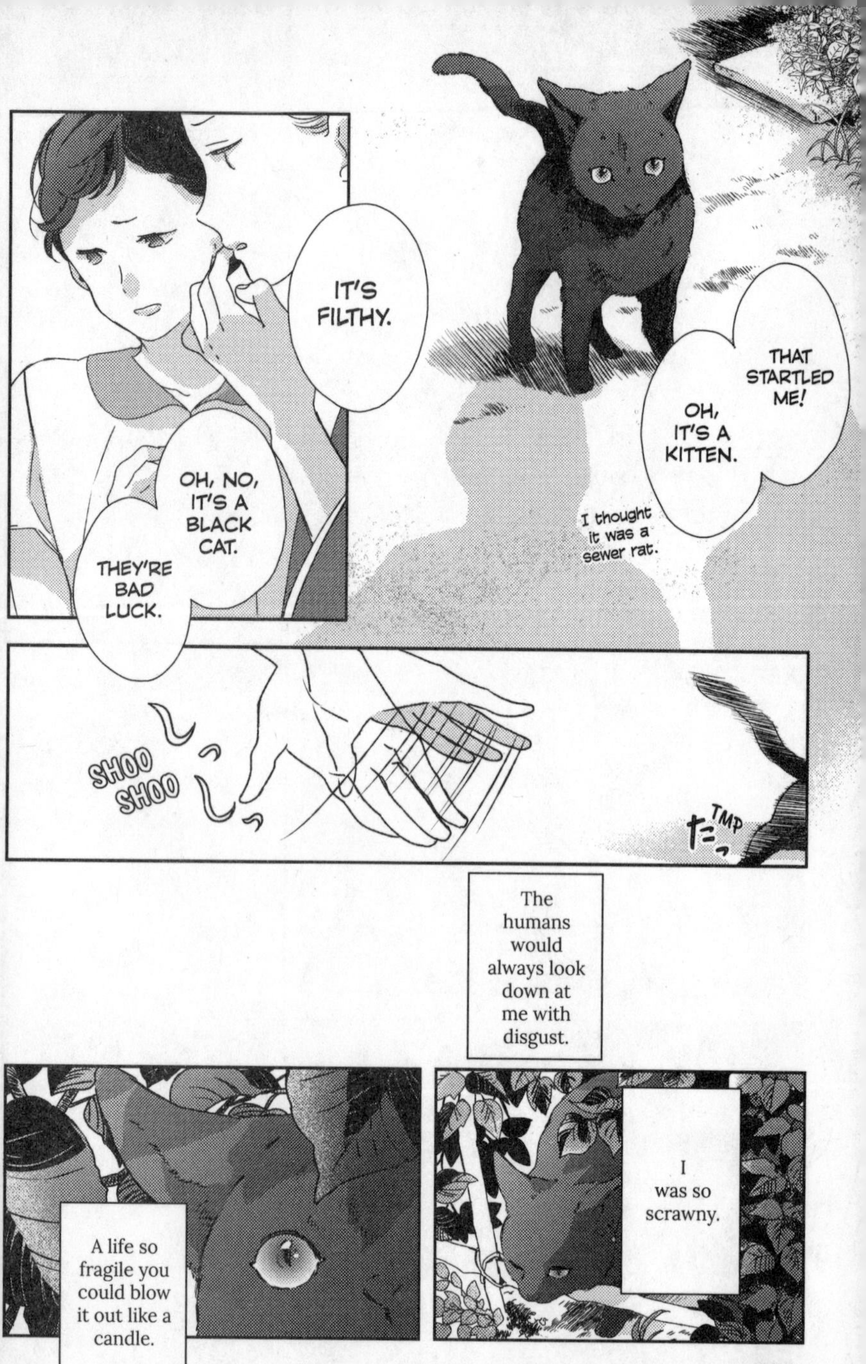

THAT STARTLED ME!
OH, IT'S A KITTEN.
I thought it was a sewer rat.
IT'S FILTHY.
OH, NO, IT'S A BLACK CAT.
THEY'RE BAD LUCK.
TMP
SHOO SHOO
The humans would always look down at me with disgust.
I was so scrawny.
A life so fragile you could blow it out like a candle.

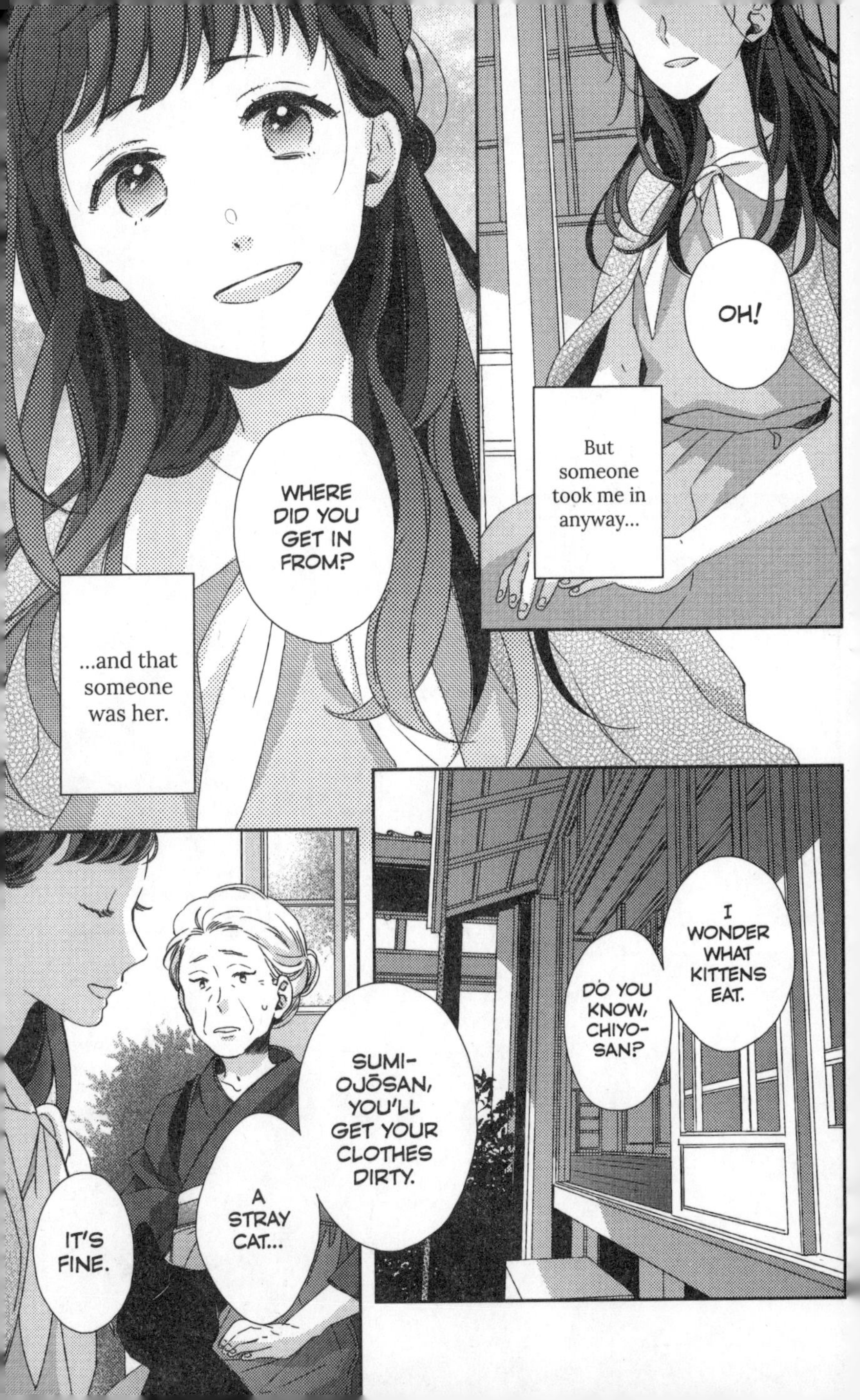
OH!
But someone took me in anyway...
WHERE DID YOU GET IN FROM?
...and that someone was her.
I WONDER WHAT KITTENS EAT.
DO YOU KNOW, CHIYO-SAN?
SUMI-OJŌSAN, YOU'LL GET YOUR CLOTHES DIRTY.
A STRAY CAT...
IT'S FINE.

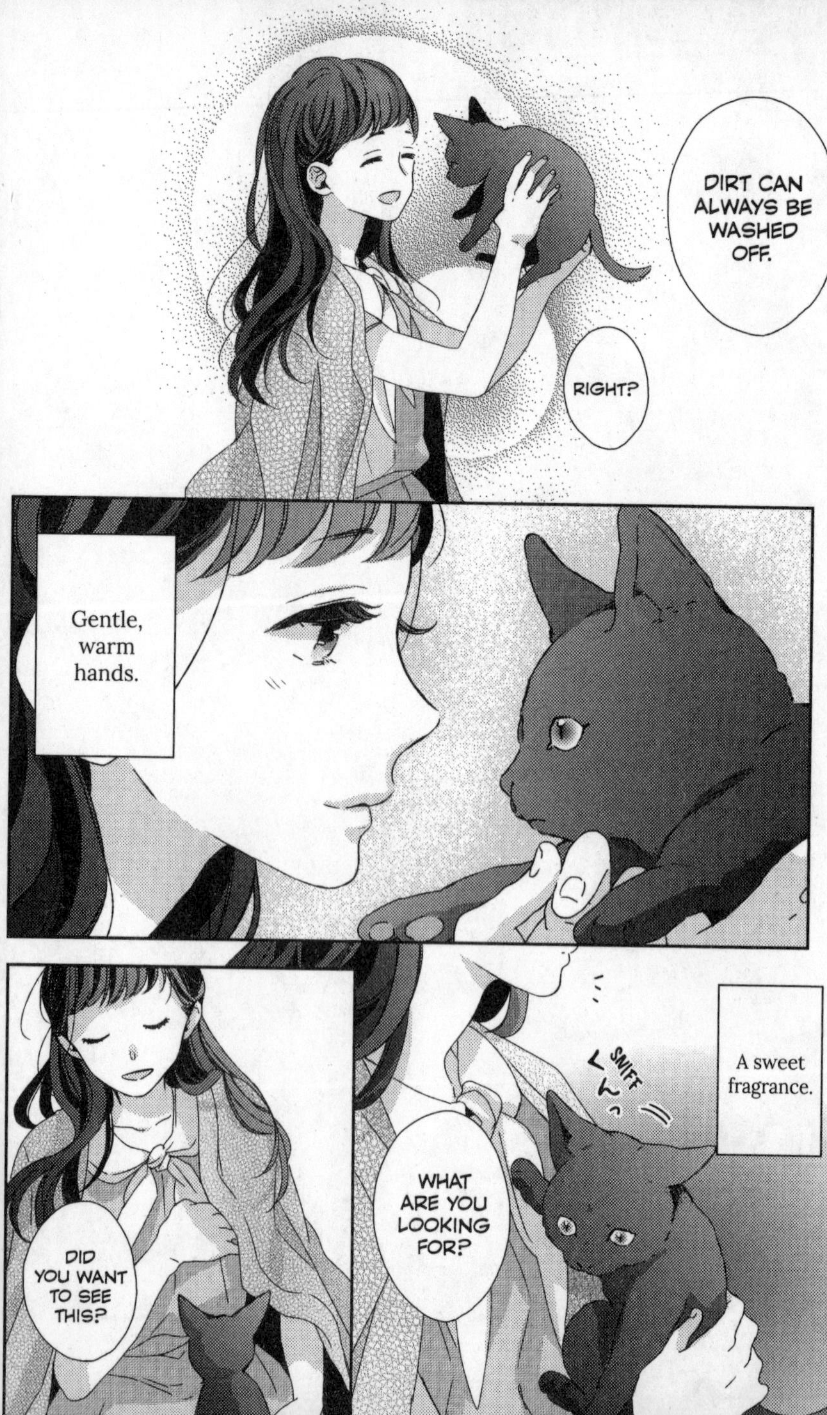
DIRT CAN ALWAYS BE WASHED OFF.
RIGHT?
Gentle, warm hands.
A sweet fragrance.
SNIFF
くん
WHAT ARE YOU LOOKING FOR?
DID YOU WANT TO SEE THIS?

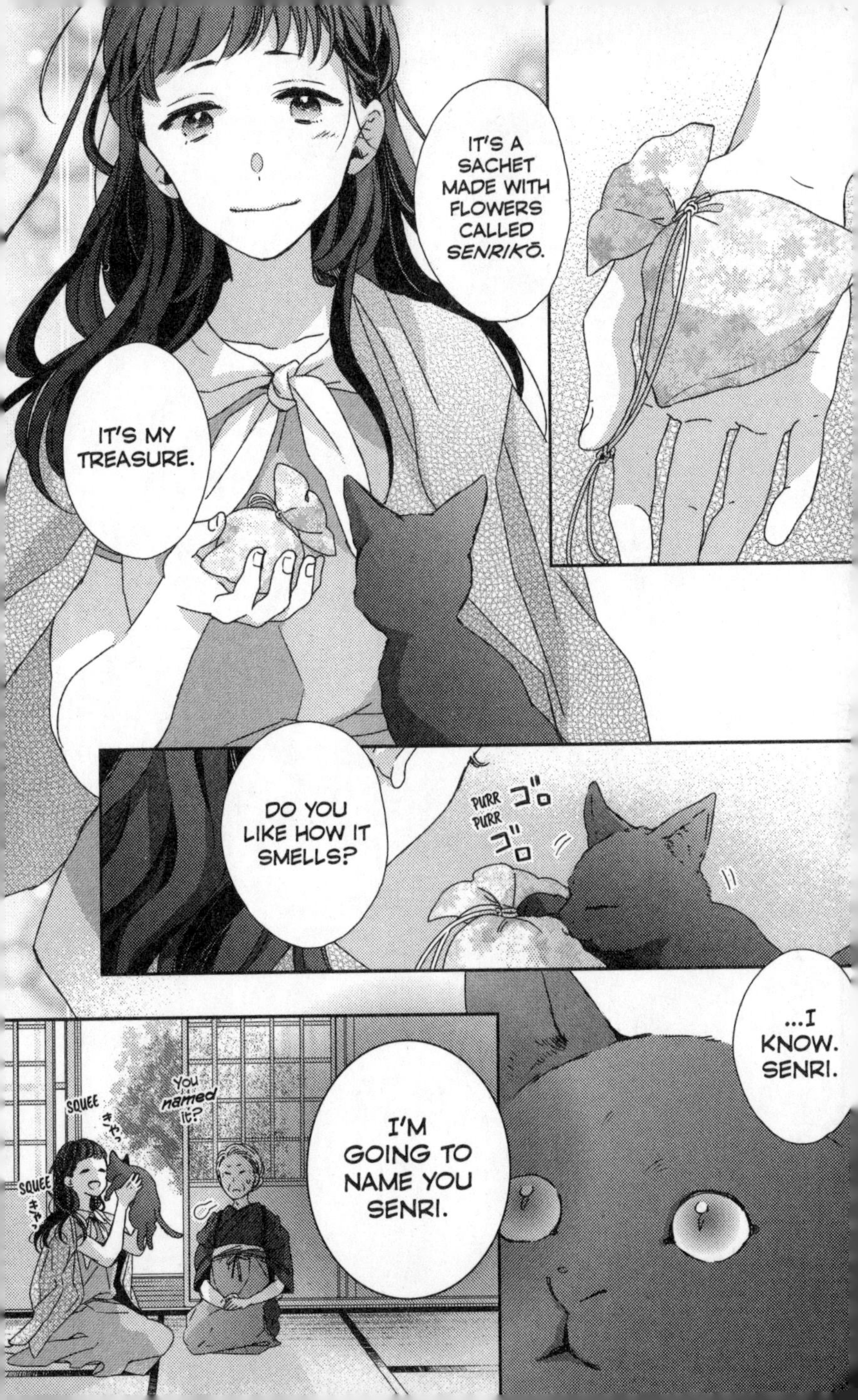
IT'S A SACHET MADE WITH FLOWERS CALLED SENRIKŌ.
IT'S MY TREASURE.
DO YOU LIKE HOW IT SMELLS?
PURR ゴロ
PURR ゴロ
...I KNOW. SENRI.
I'M GOING TO NAME YOU SENRI.
You named it?
SQUEE きゃっ
SQUEE きゃっ

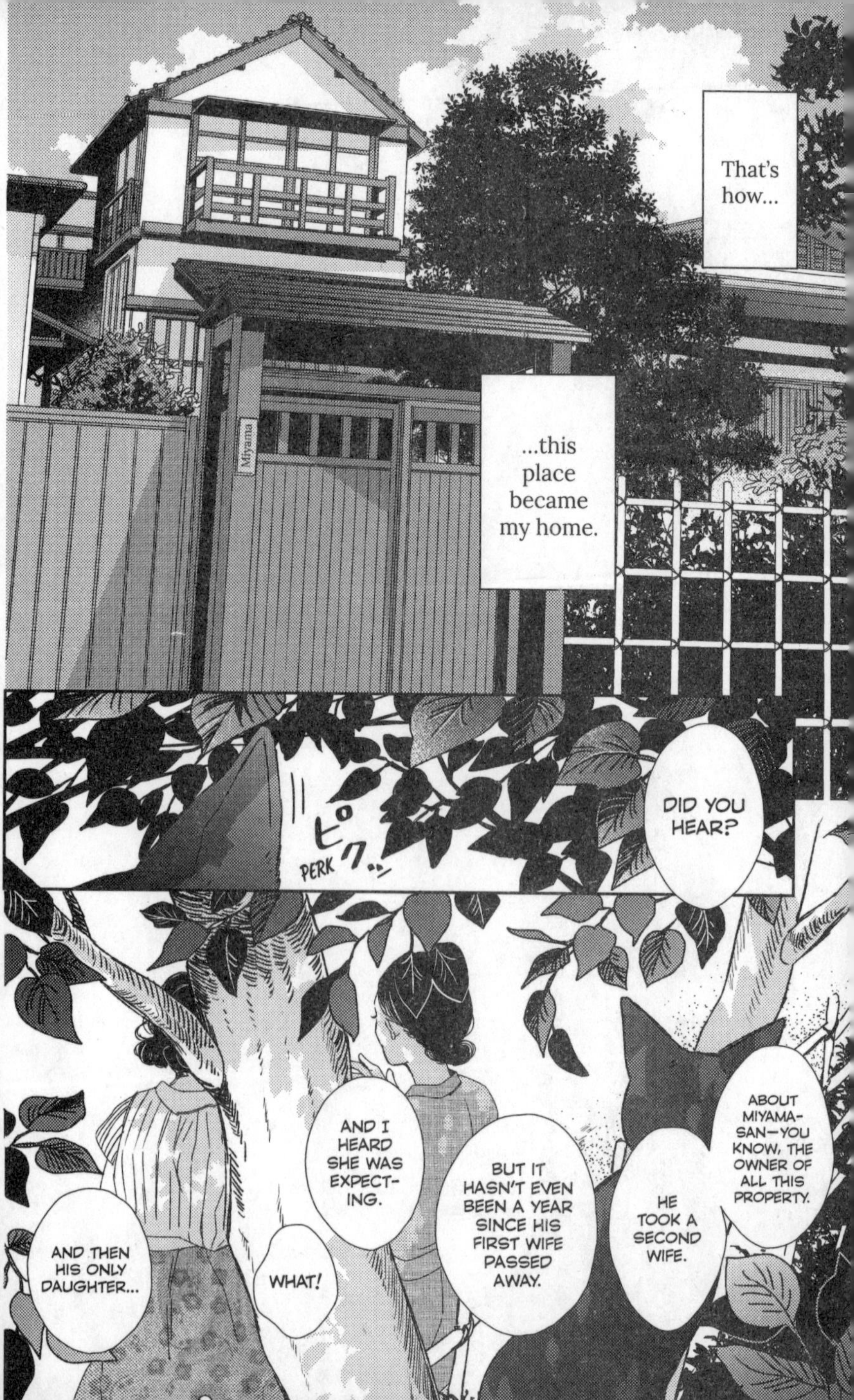
That's how...
...this place became my home.
Miyama
ピク
PERK
DID YOU HEAR?
ABOUT MIYAMA-SAN—YOU KNOW, THE OWNER OF ALL THIS PROPERTY.
HE TOOK A SECOND WIFE.
BUT IT HASN'T EVEN BEEN A YEAR SINCE HIS FIRST WIFE PASSED AWAY.
AND I HEARD SHE WAS EXPECTING.
WHAT!
AND THEN HIS ONLY DAUGHTER...

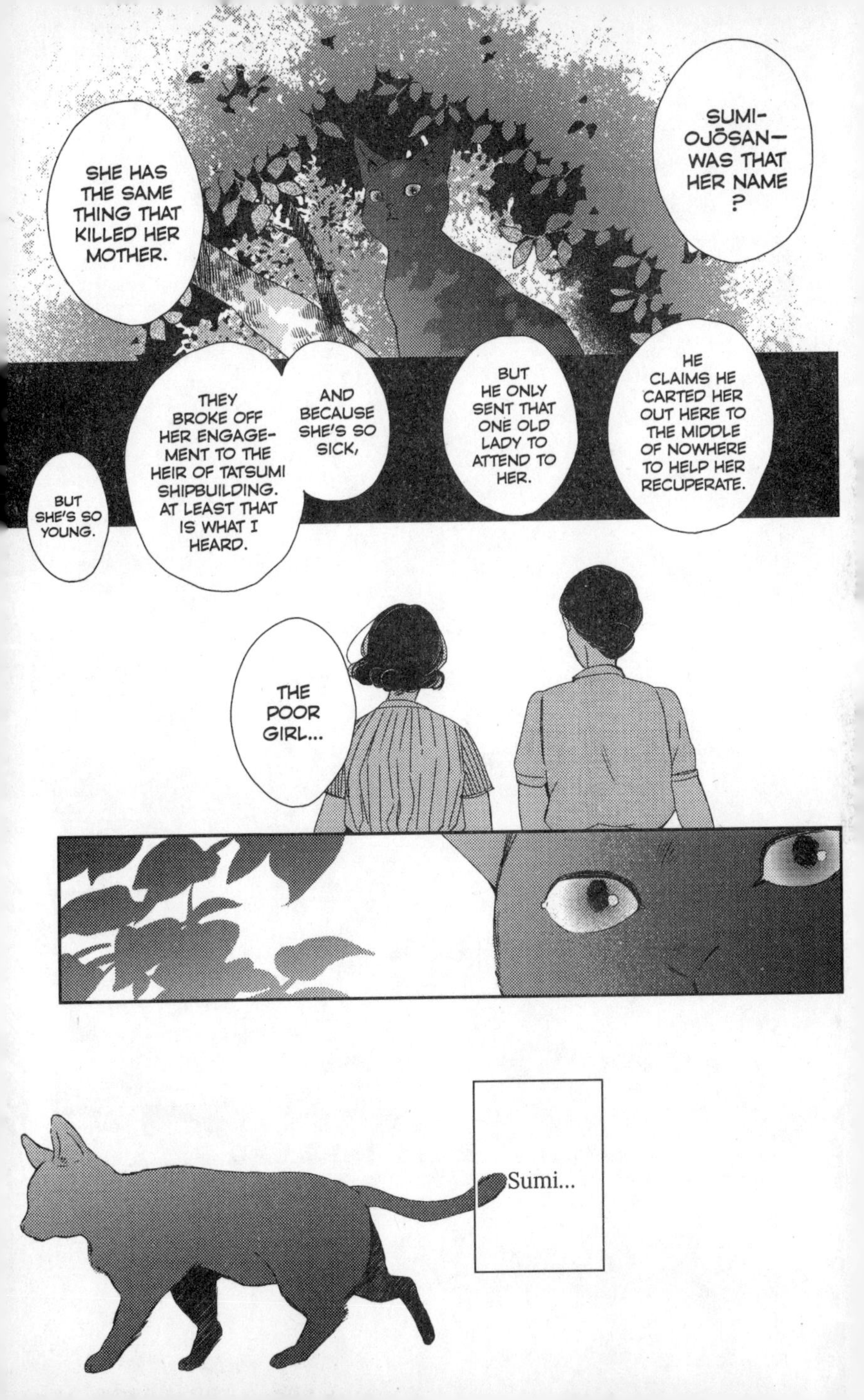
SUMI-OJŌSAN—WAS THAT HER NAME?
SHE HAS THE SAME THING THAT KILLED HER MOTHER.
HE CLAIMS HE CARTED HER OUT HERE TO THE MIDDLE OF NOWHERE TO HELP HER RECUPERATE.
BUT HE ONLY SENT THAT ONE OLD LADY TO ATTEND TO HER.
AND BECAUSE SHE'S SO SICK,
THEY BROKE OFF HER ENGAGE-MENT TO THE HEIR OF TATSUMI SHIPBUILDING. AT LEAST THAT IS WHAT I HEARD.
BUT SHE'S SO YOUNG.
THE POOR GIRL...
Sumi...

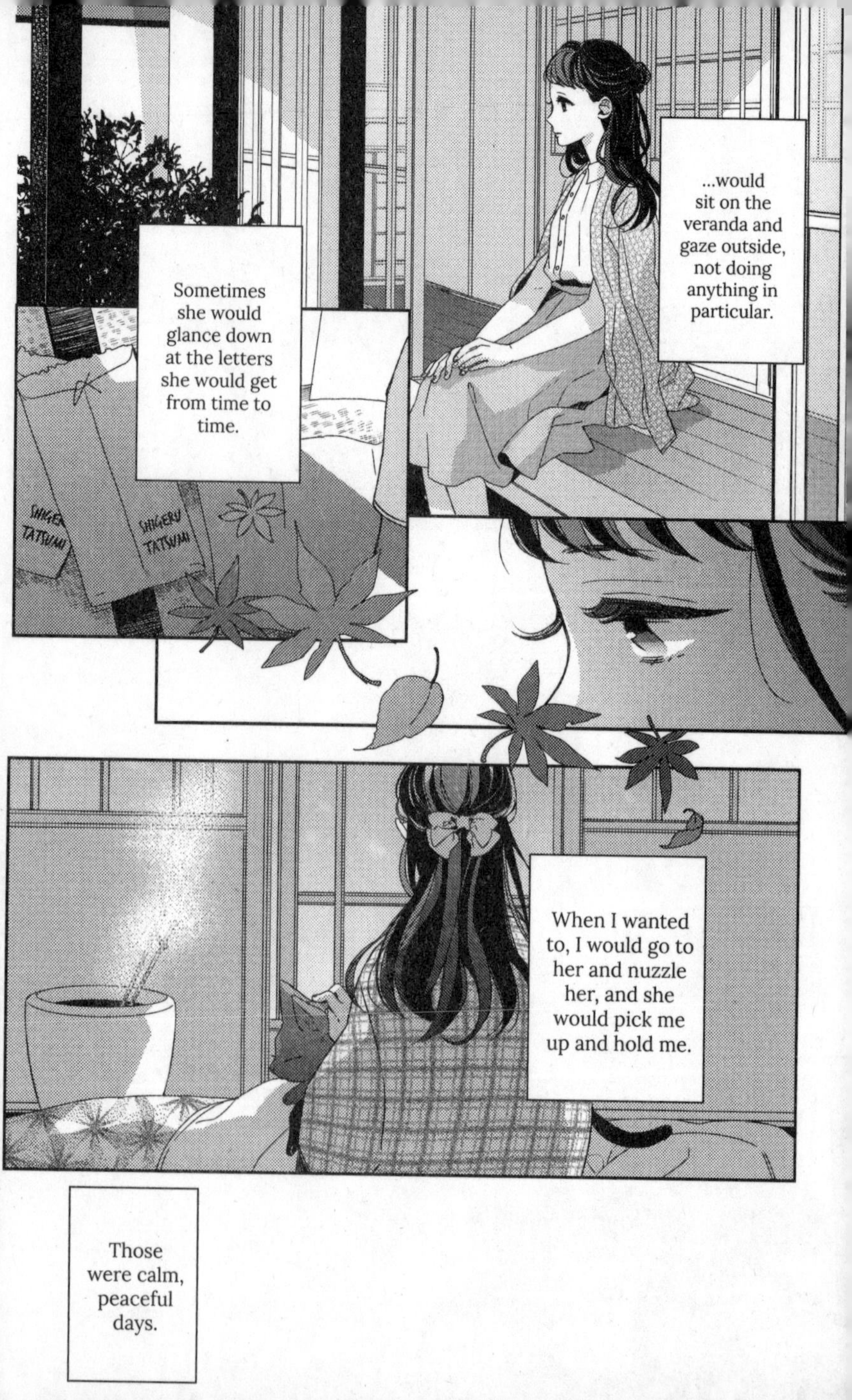
...would sit on the veranda and gaze outside, not doing anything in particular.
Sometimes she would glance down at the letters she would get from time to time.
SHIGERU TATSUMI
SHIGERU TATSUMI
When I wanted to, I would go to her and nuzzle her, and she would pick me up and hold me.
Those were calm, peaceful days.

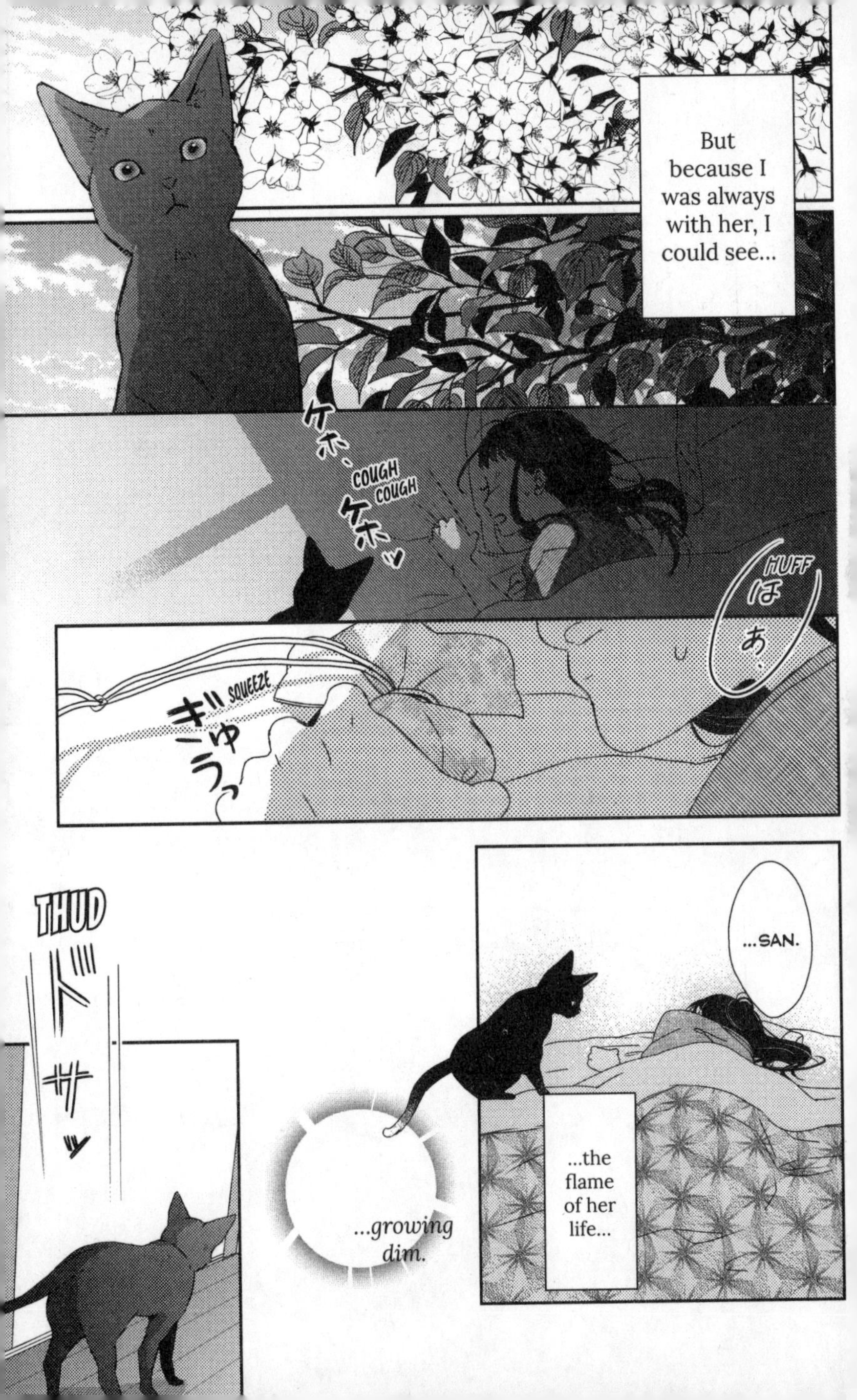

But because I was always with her, I could see...
ケホ、ケホッ
COUGH COUGH
はぁ、
HUFF
ぎゅうっ
SQUEEZE
...SAN.
...the flame of her life...
...growing dim.
ドサッ
THUD

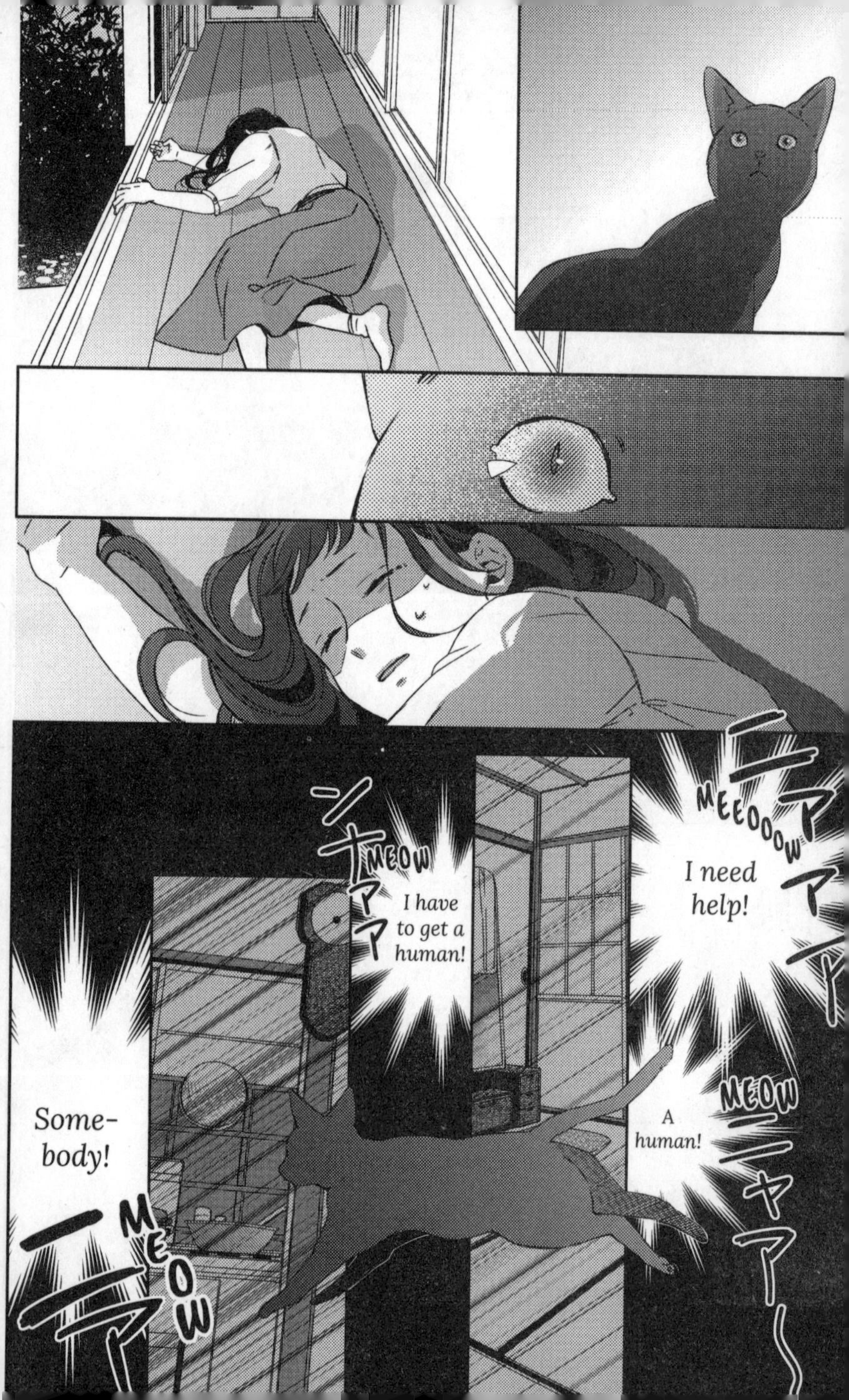
MEEOOOOW
I need help!
MEOW
A human!
MEOW
I have to get a human!
Some-body!
MEOW

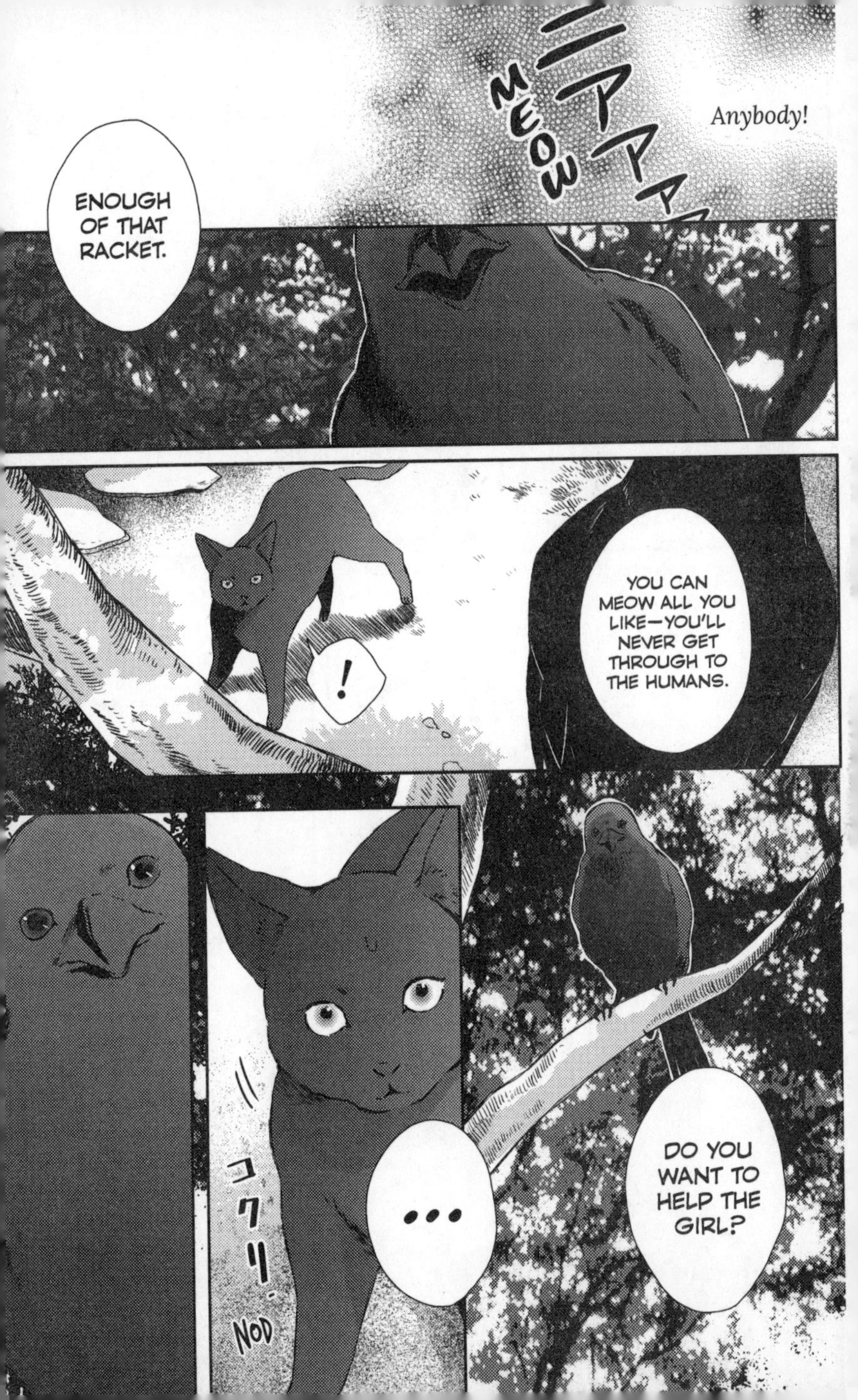
Anybody!
MEOW
ENOUGH OF THAT RACKET.
YOU CAN MEOW ALL YOU LIKE—YOU'LL NEVER GET THROUGH TO THE HUMANS.
!
DO YOU WANT TO HELP THE GIRL?
...
NOD

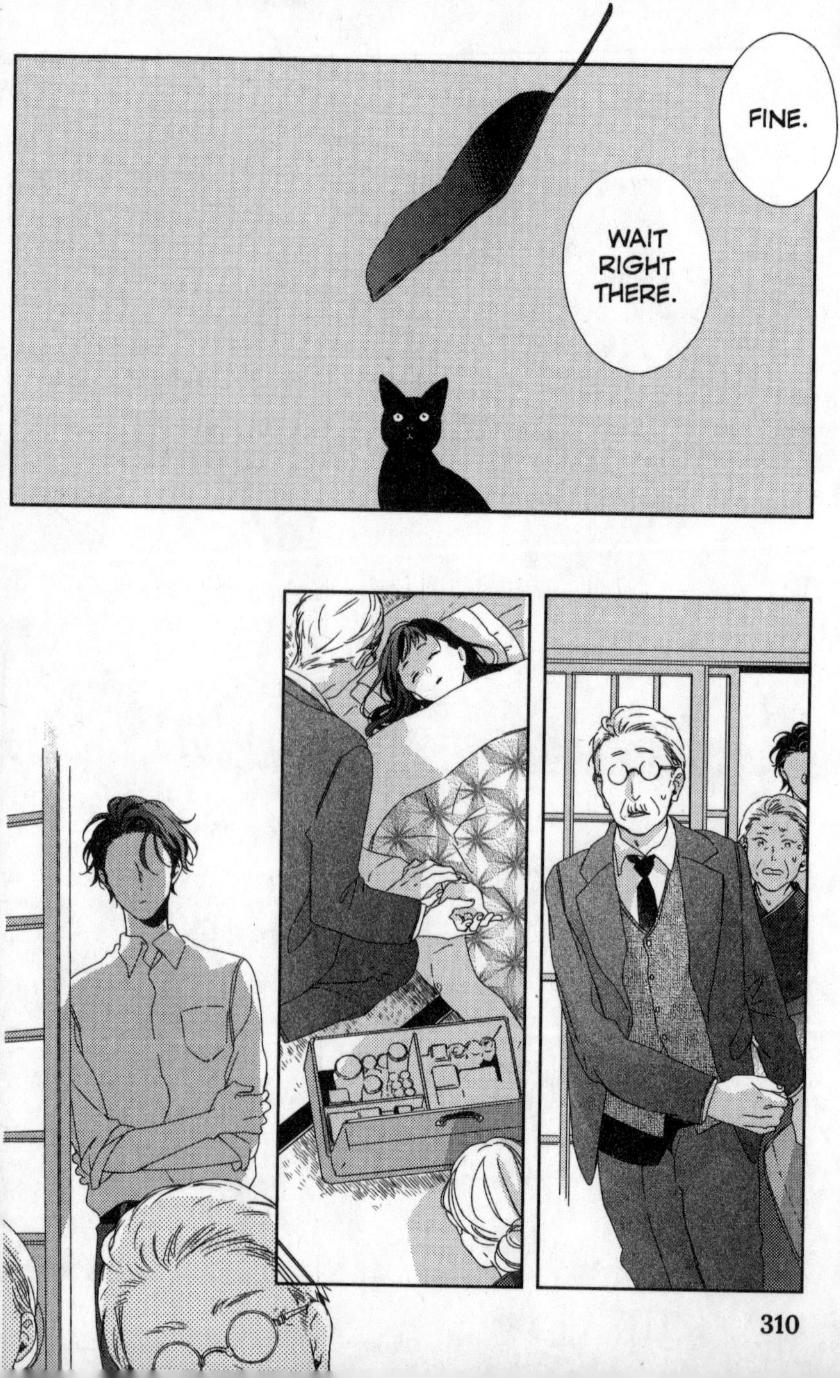
FINE.
WAIT RIGHT THERE.

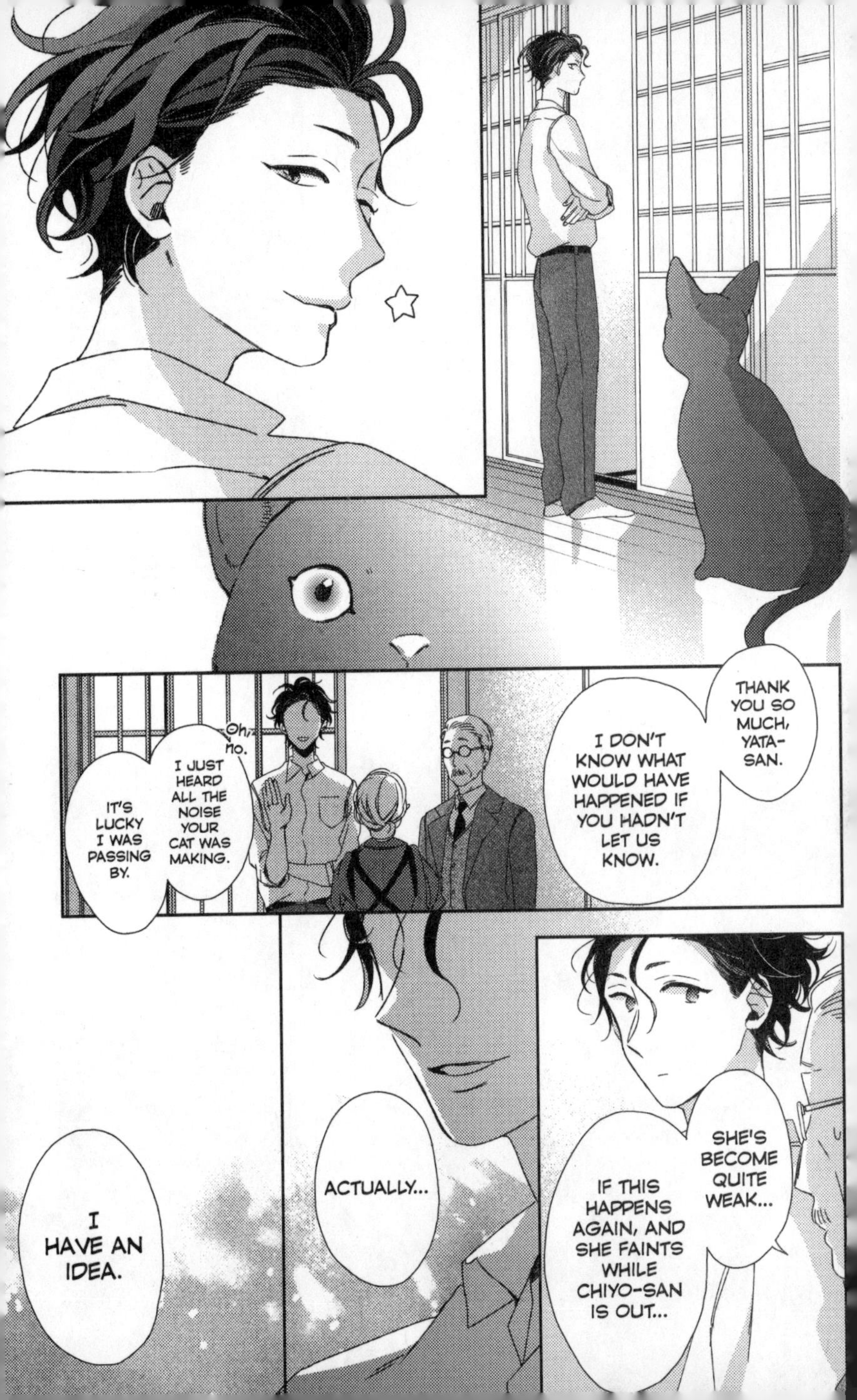
THANK YOU SO MUCH, YATA-SAN.
I DON'T KNOW WHAT WOULD HAVE HAPPENED IF YOU HADN'T LET US KNOW.
Oh, no.
I JUST HEARD ALL THE NOISE YOUR CAT WAS MAKING.
IT'S LUCKY I WAS PASSING BY.
SHE'S BECOME QUITE WEAK...
IF THIS HAPPENS AGAIN, AND SHE FAINTS WHILE CHIYO-SAN IS OUT...
ACTUALLY...
I HAVE AN IDEA.

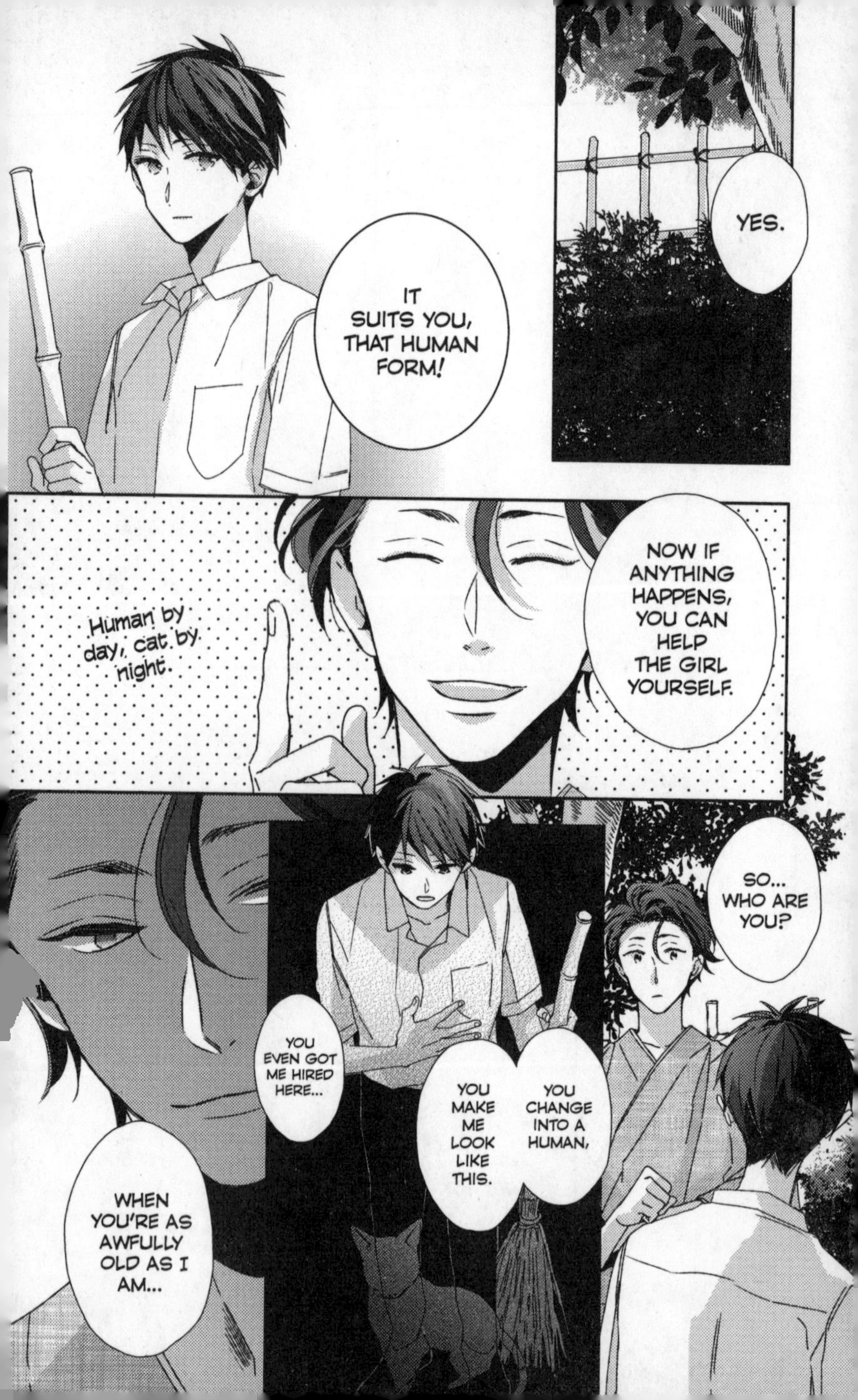
YES.
IT SUITS YOU, THAT HUMAN FORM!
NOW IF ANYTHING HAPPENS, YOU CAN HELP THE GIRL YOURSELF.
Human by day, cat by night.
SO... WHO ARE YOU?
YOU CHANGE INTO A HUMAN,
YOU MAKE ME LOOK LIKE THIS.
YOU EVEN GOT ME HIRED HERE...
WHEN YOU'RE AS AWFULLY OLD AS I AM...

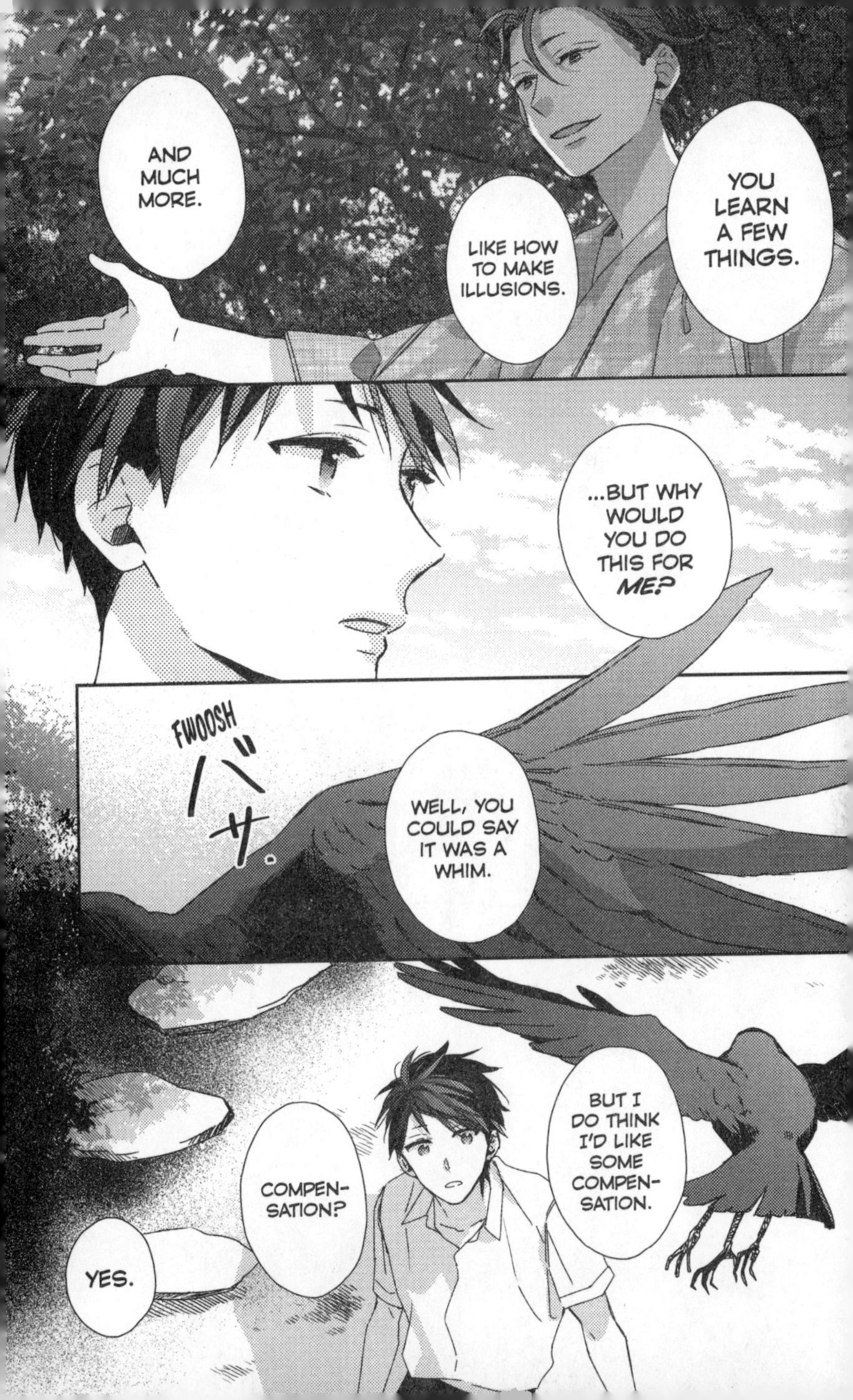
YOU LEARN A FEW THINGS.
LIKE HOW TO MAKE ILLUSIONS.
AND MUCH MORE.
...BUT WHY WOULD YOU DO THIS FOR *ME?*
WELL, YOU COULD SAY IT WAS A WHIM.
FWOOSH
バサ
BUT I DO THINK I'D LIKE SOME COMPEN-SATION.
COMPEN-SATION?
YES.

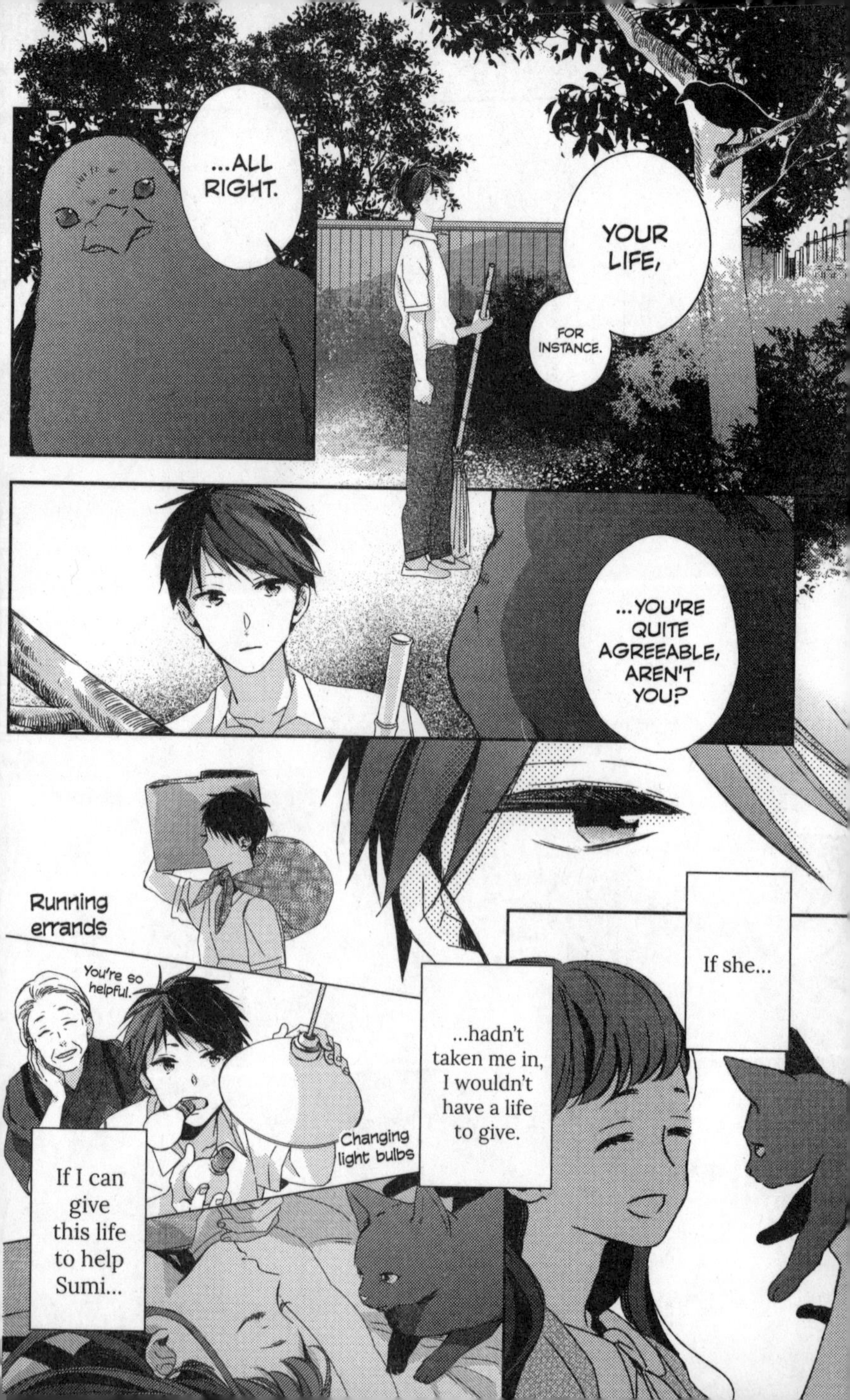
YOUR LIFE,
FOR INSTANCE.
...ALL RIGHT.
...YOU'RE QUITE AGREEABLE, AREN'T YOU?
If she...
...hadn't taken me in, I wouldn't have a life to give.
Running errands
You're so helpful.
Changing light bulbs
If I can give this life to help Sumi...

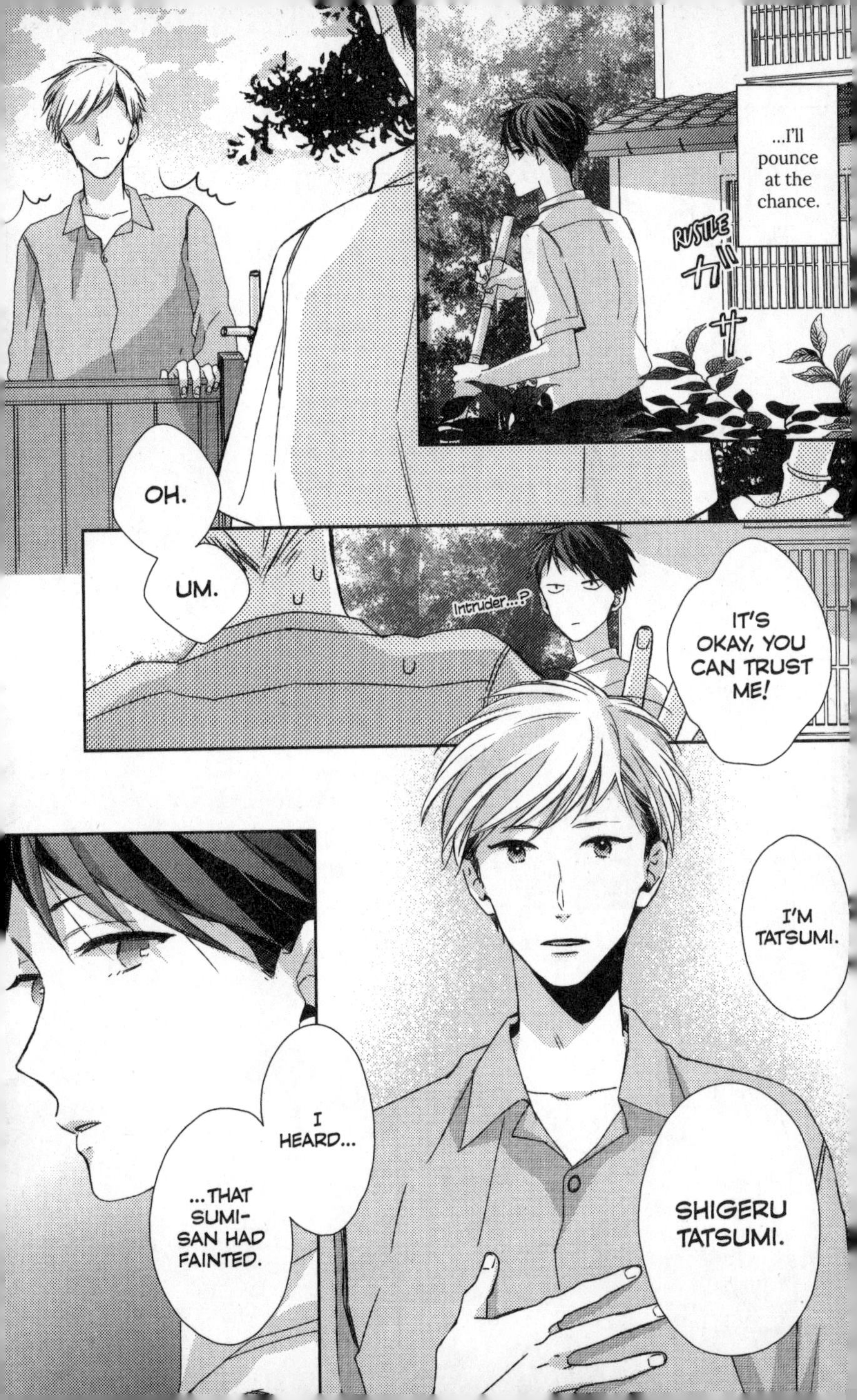
...I'll pounce at the chance.
RUSTLE
OH.
UM.
IT'S OKAY, YOU CAN TRUST ME!
Intruder...?
I'M TATSUMI.
SHIGERU TATSUMI.
I HEARD...
...THAT SUMI-SAN HAD FAINTED.

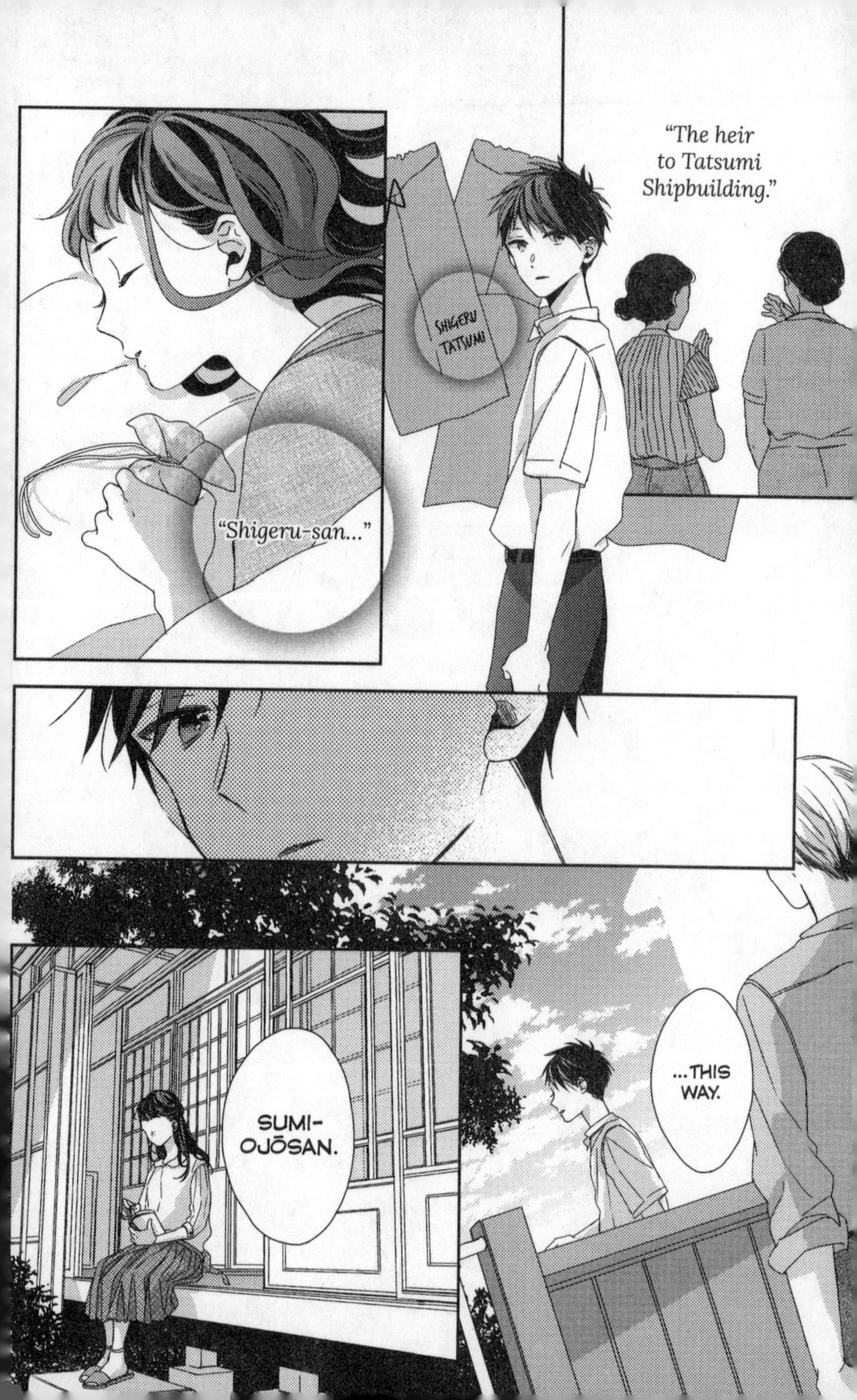
"The heir to Tatsumi Shipbuilding."
SHIGERU TATSUMI
"Shigeru-san..."
...THIS WAY.
SUMI-OJŌSAN.

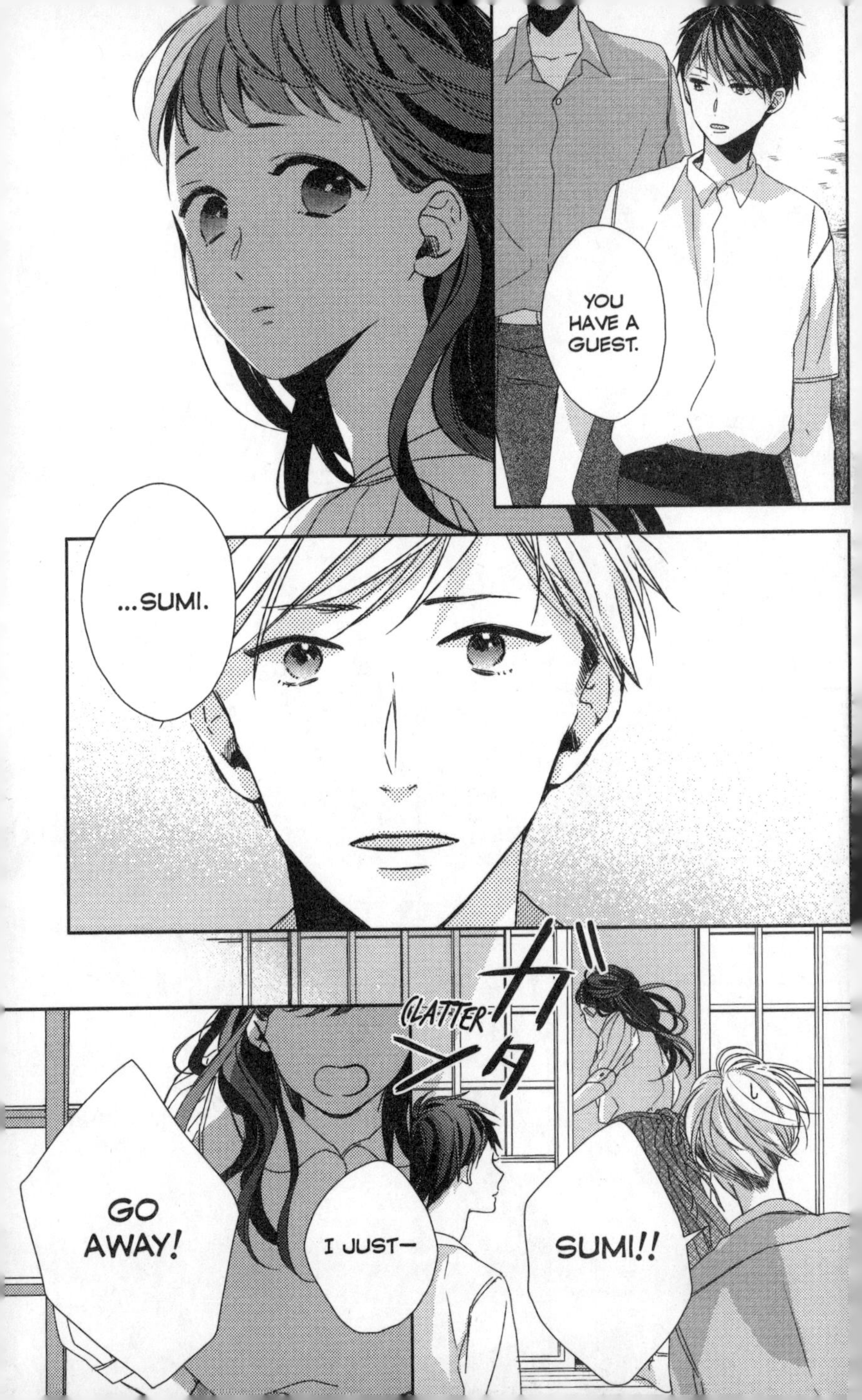
YOU HAVE A GUEST.
...SUMI.
ガタン
CLATTER
SUMI!!
I JUST—
GO AWAY!

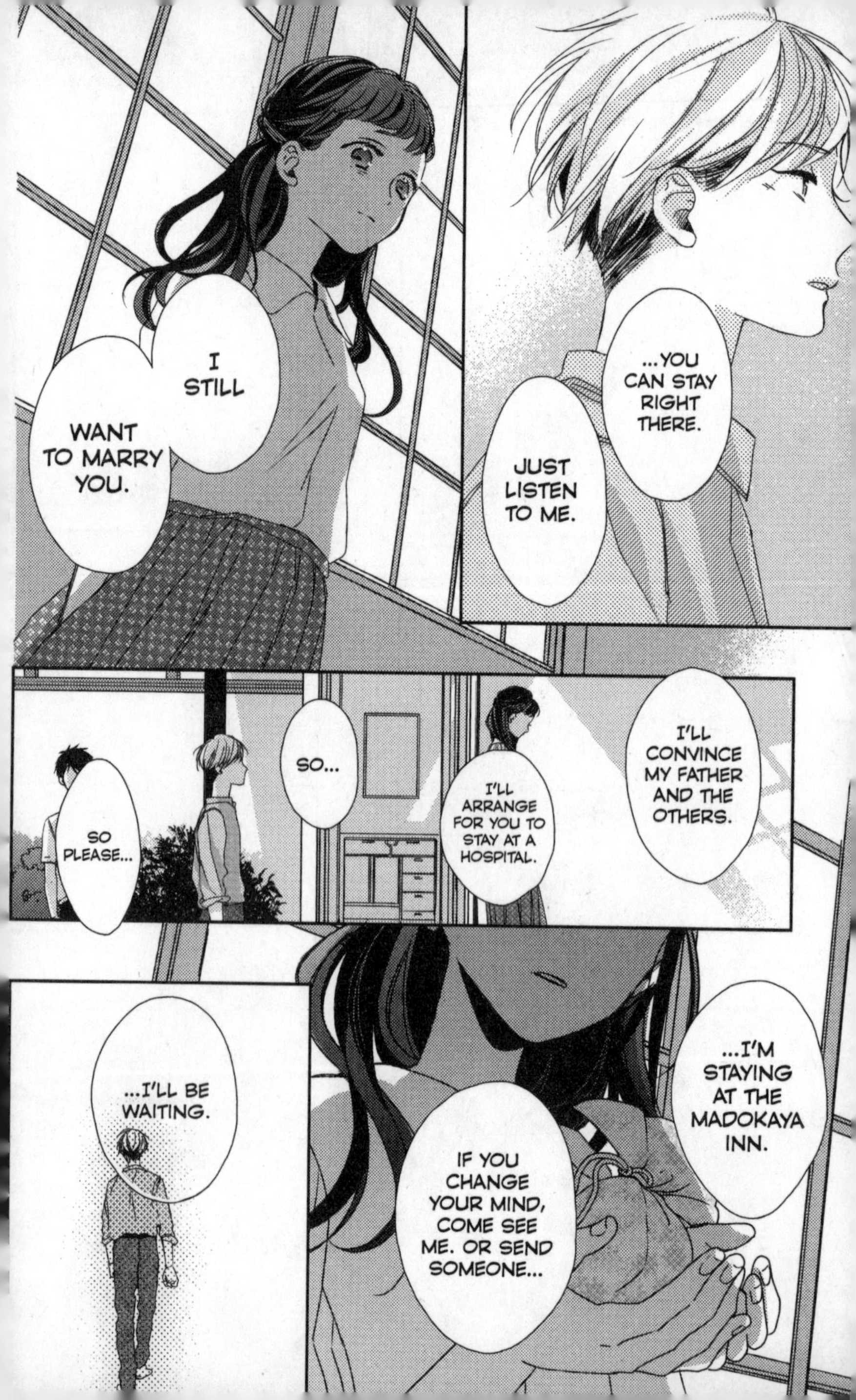
...YOU CAN STAY RIGHT THERE.
JUST LISTEN TO ME.
I STILL
WANT TO MARRY YOU.
I'LL CONVINCE MY FATHER AND THE OTHERS.
I'LL ARRANGE FOR YOU TO STAY AT A HOSPITAL.
SO...
SO PLEASE...
...I'M STAYING AT THE MADOKAYA INN.
IF YOU CHANGE YOUR MIND, COME SEE ME. OR SEND SOMEONE...
...I'LL BE WAITING.

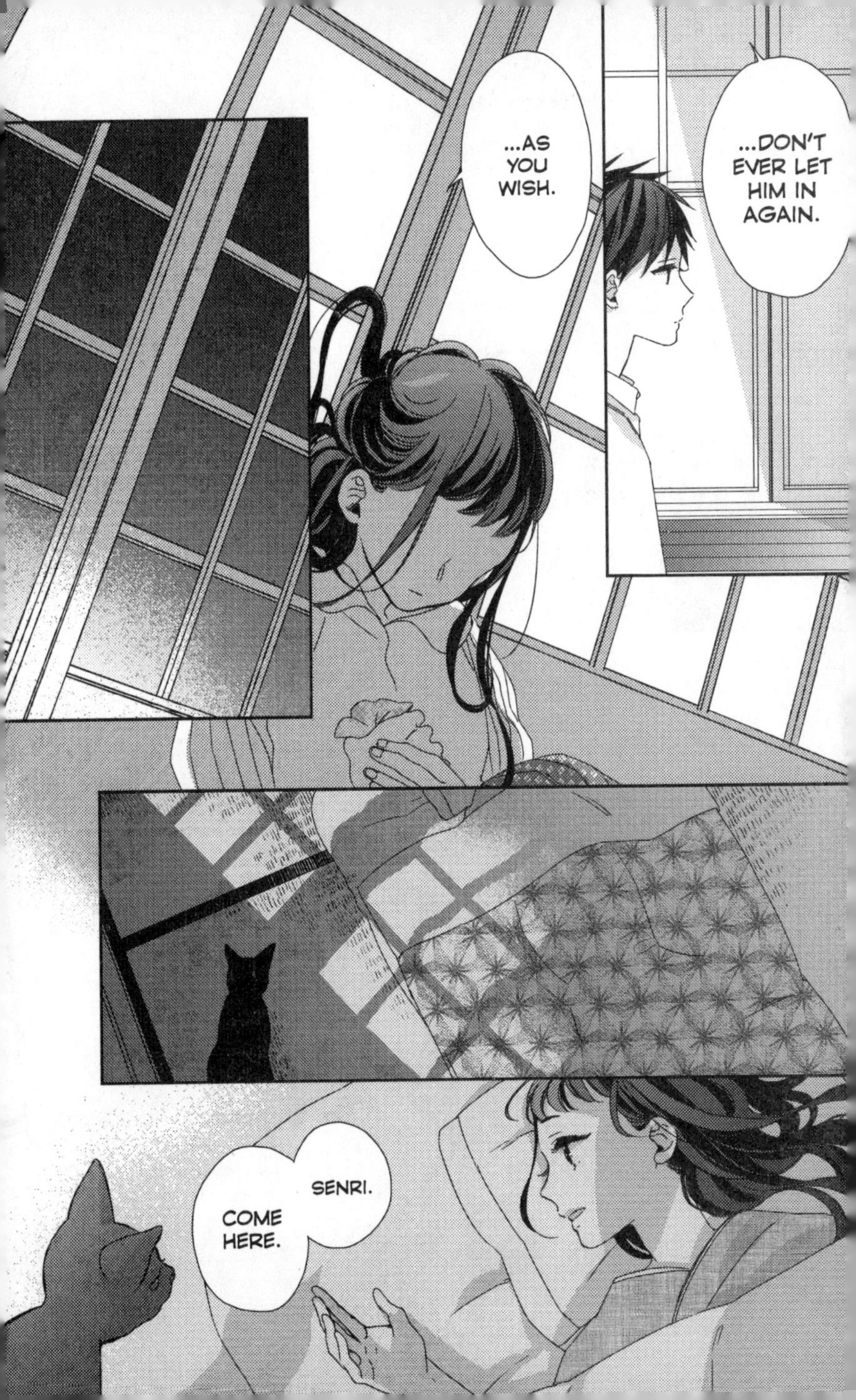
...DON'T EVER LET HIM IN AGAIN.
...AS YOU WISH.
SENRI.
COME HERE.

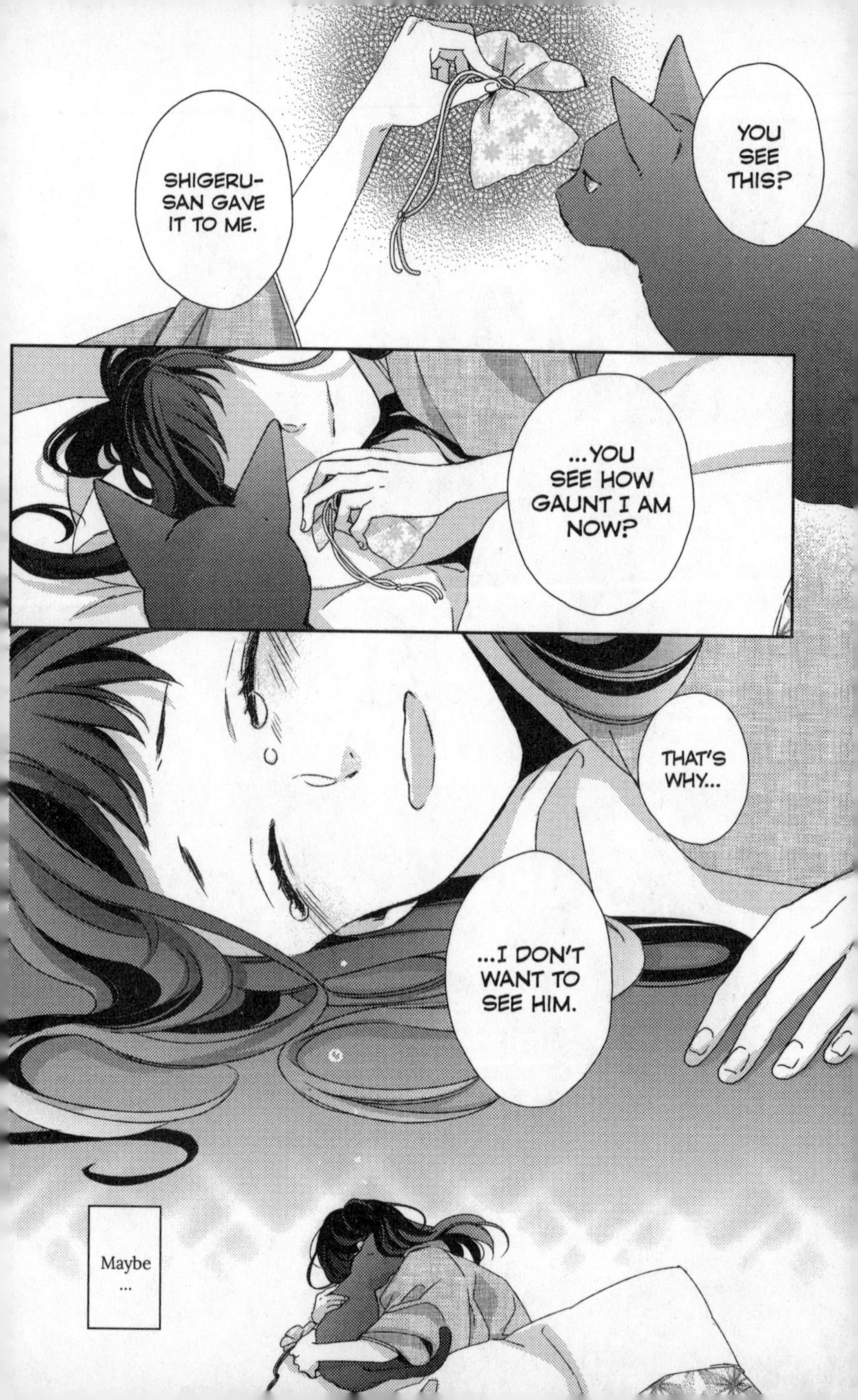
YOU SEE THIS?
SHIGERU-SAN GAVE IT TO ME.
...YOU SEE HOW GAUNT I AM NOW?
THAT'S WHY...
...I DON'T WANT TO SEE HIM.
Maybe ...

"Shigeru-san."

...I was wrong.

But I've heard...

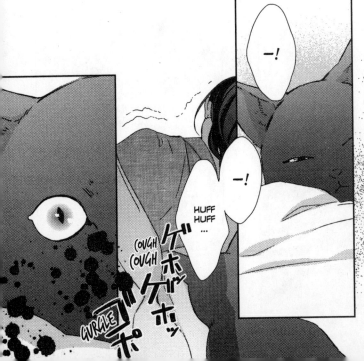

—!

—!

HUFF
HUFF
...

COUGH
COUGH

GURGLE

...the way she calls his name.

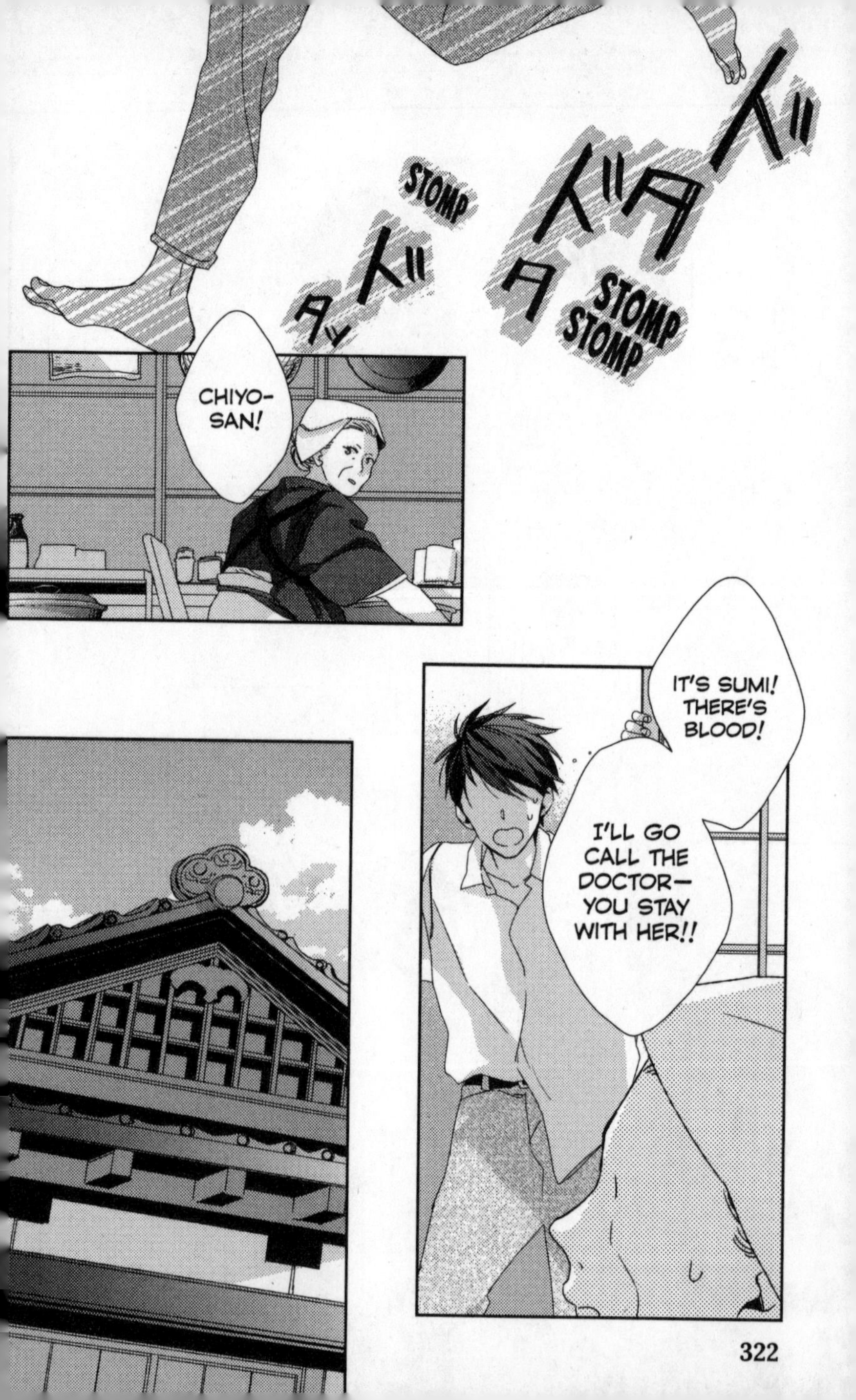
STOMP STOMP
STOMP
CHIYO-SAN!
IT'S SUMI! THERE'S BLOOD!
I'LL GO CALL THE DOCTOR— YOU STAY WITH HER!!

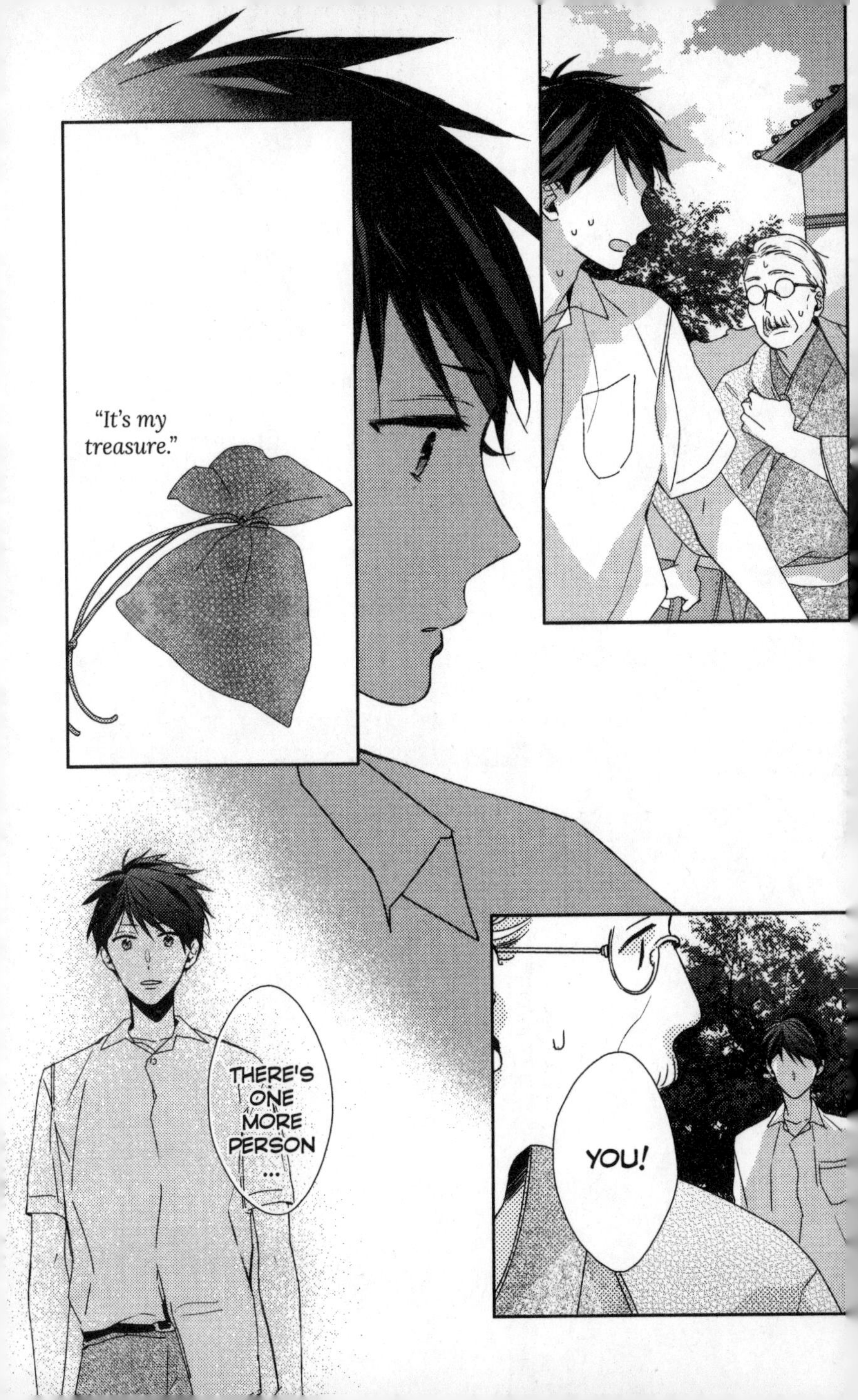
"It's my treasure."
YOU!
THERE'S ONE MORE PERSON ...

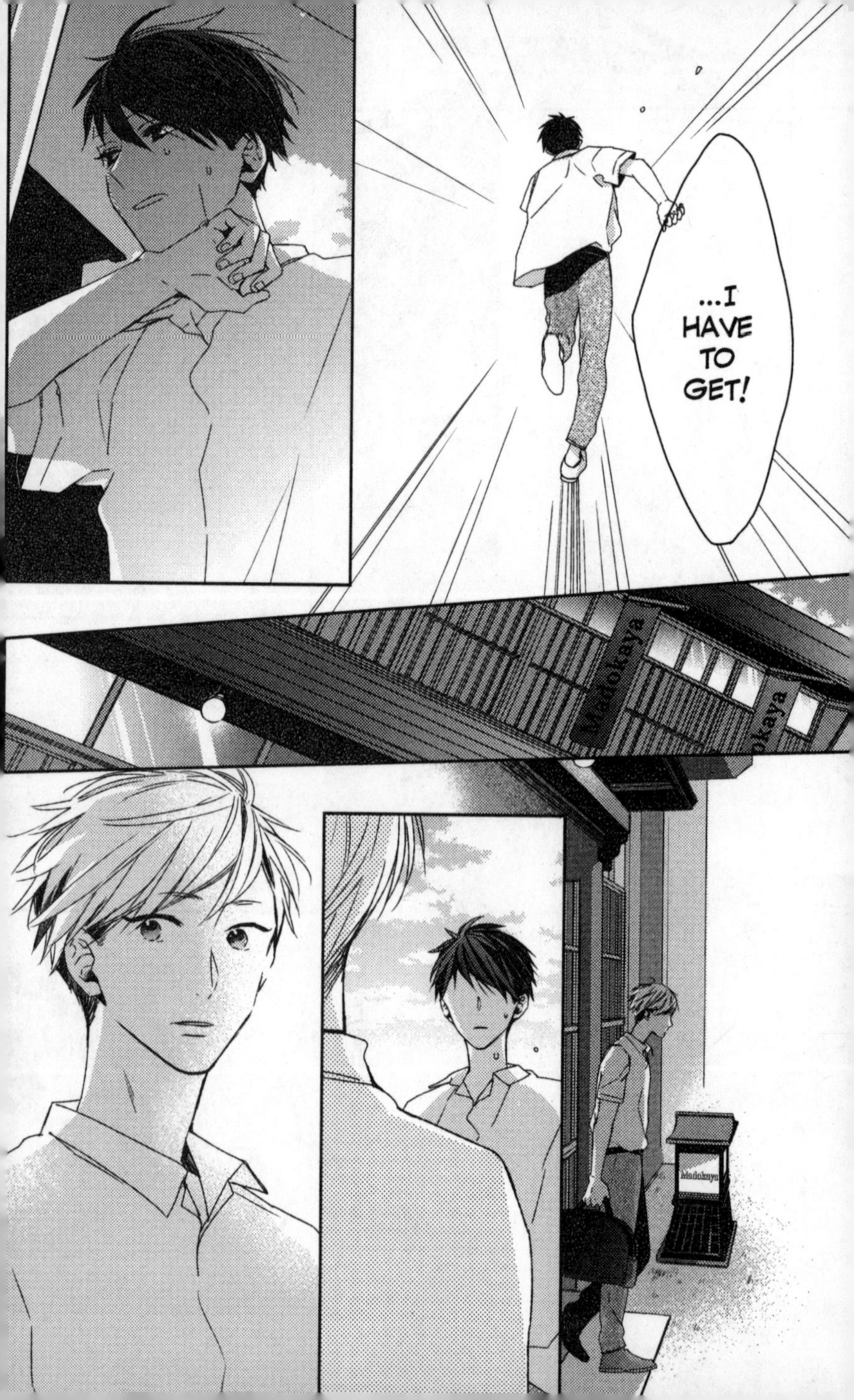
...I HAVE TO GET!
Madokaya
Madokaya

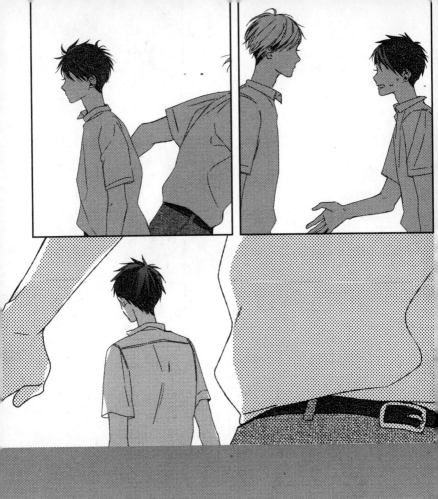

"It's a sachet made with flowers called senrikō."

"I'm going to name you..."

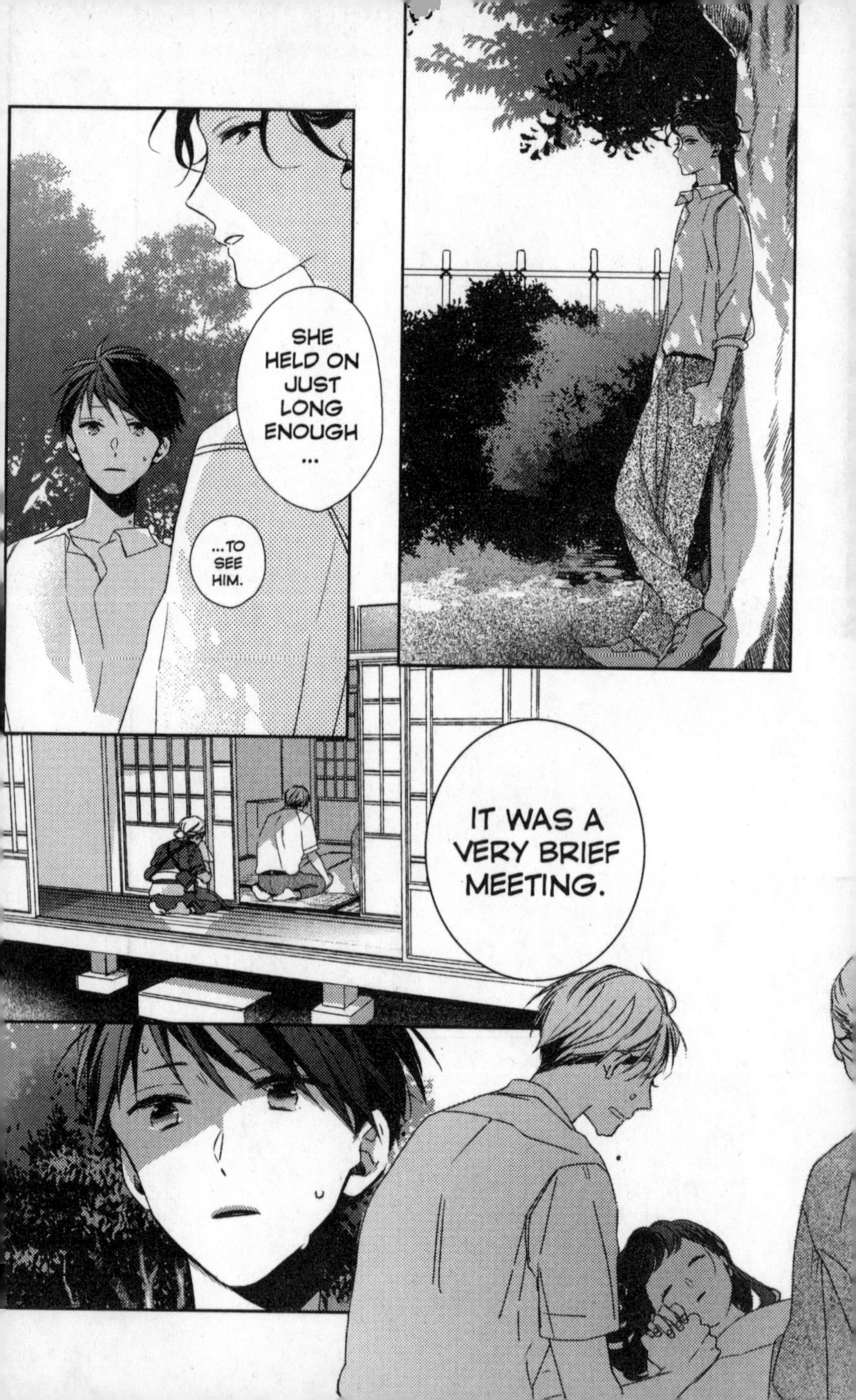
SHE HELD ON JUST LONG ENOUGH ...
...TO SEE HIM.
IT WAS A VERY BRIEF MEETING.

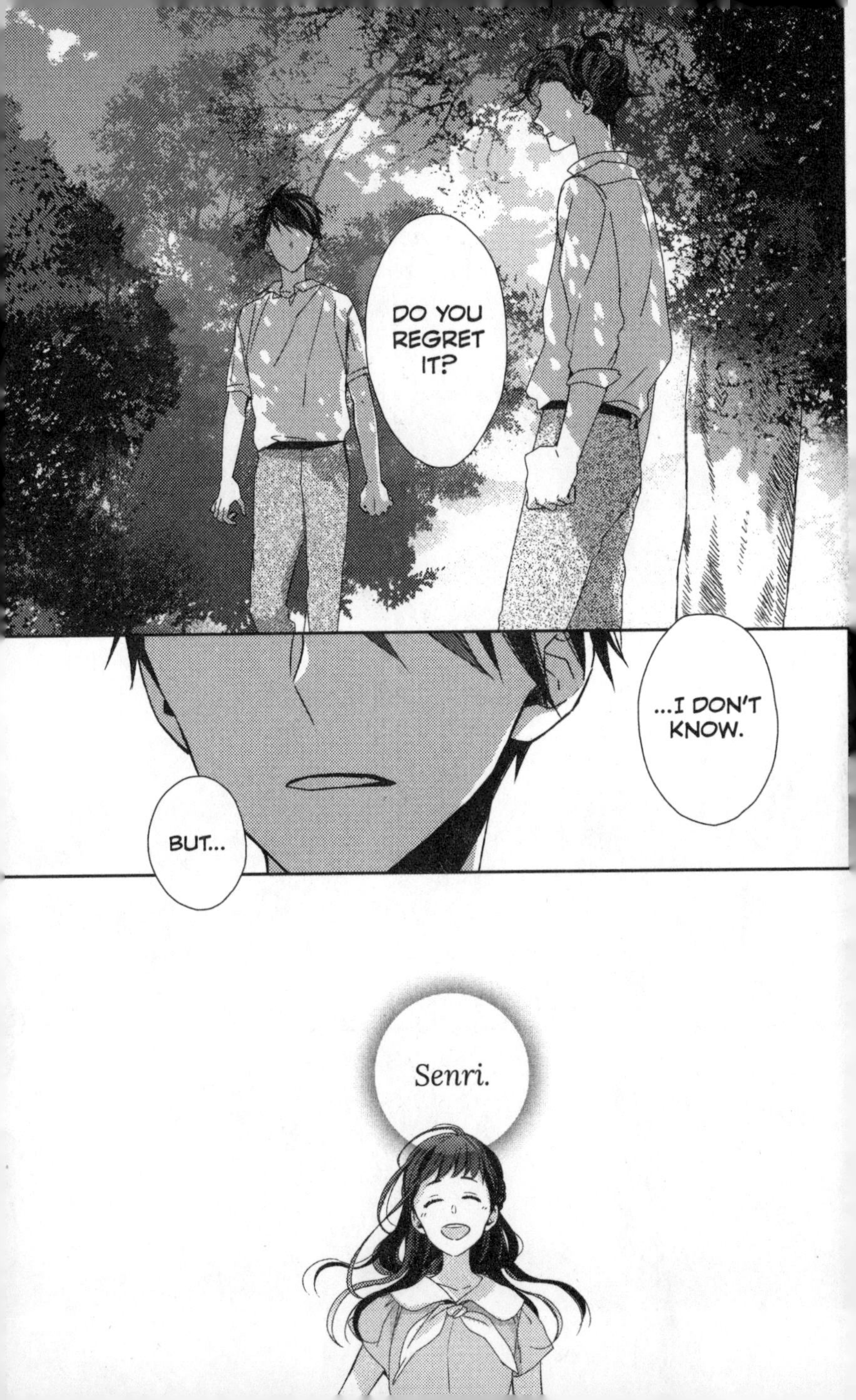
DO YOU REGRET IT?
...I DON'T KNOW.
BUT...
Senri.

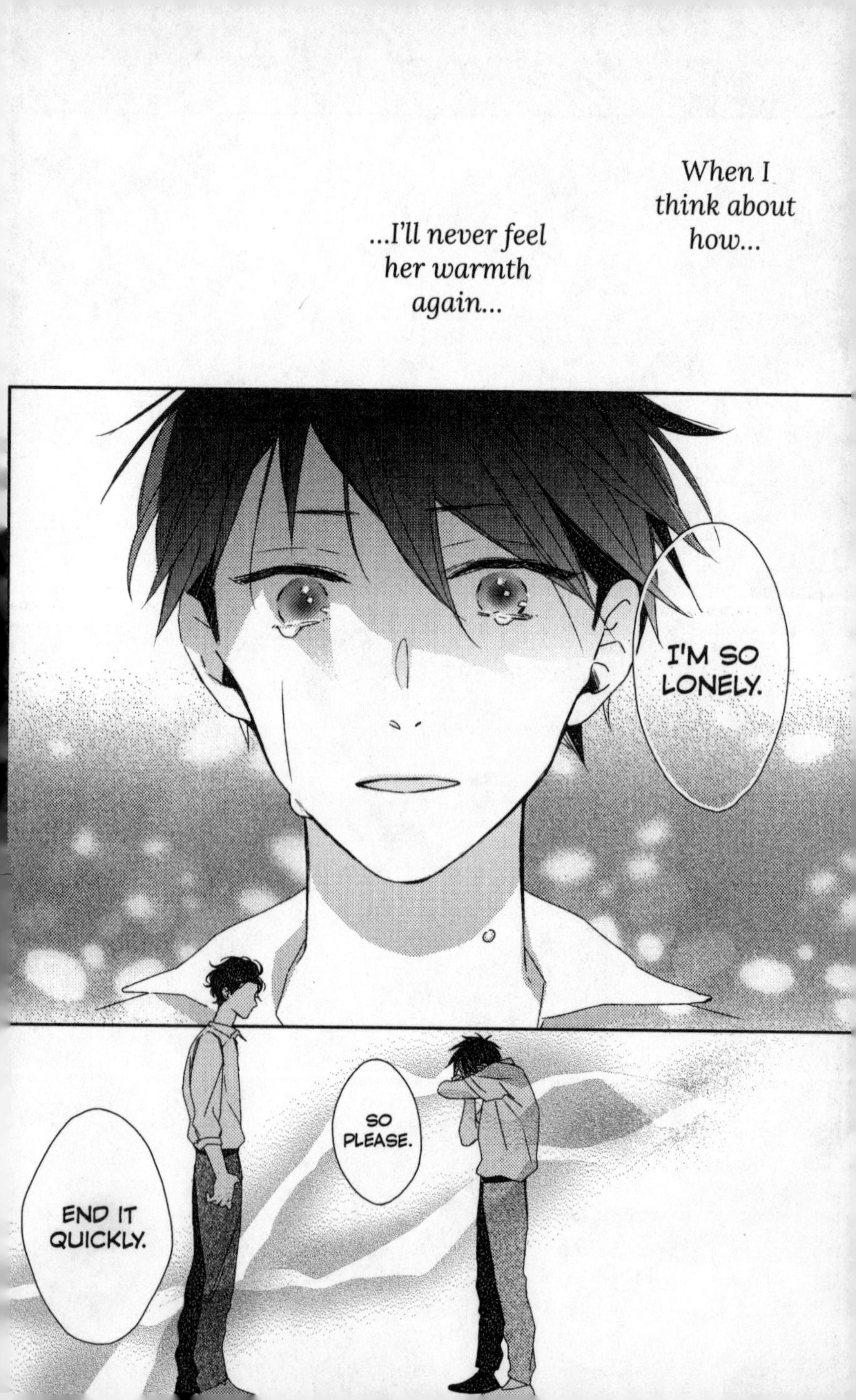
When I think about how...
...I'll never feel her warmth again...
I'M SO LONELY.
SO PLEASE.
END IT QUICKLY.

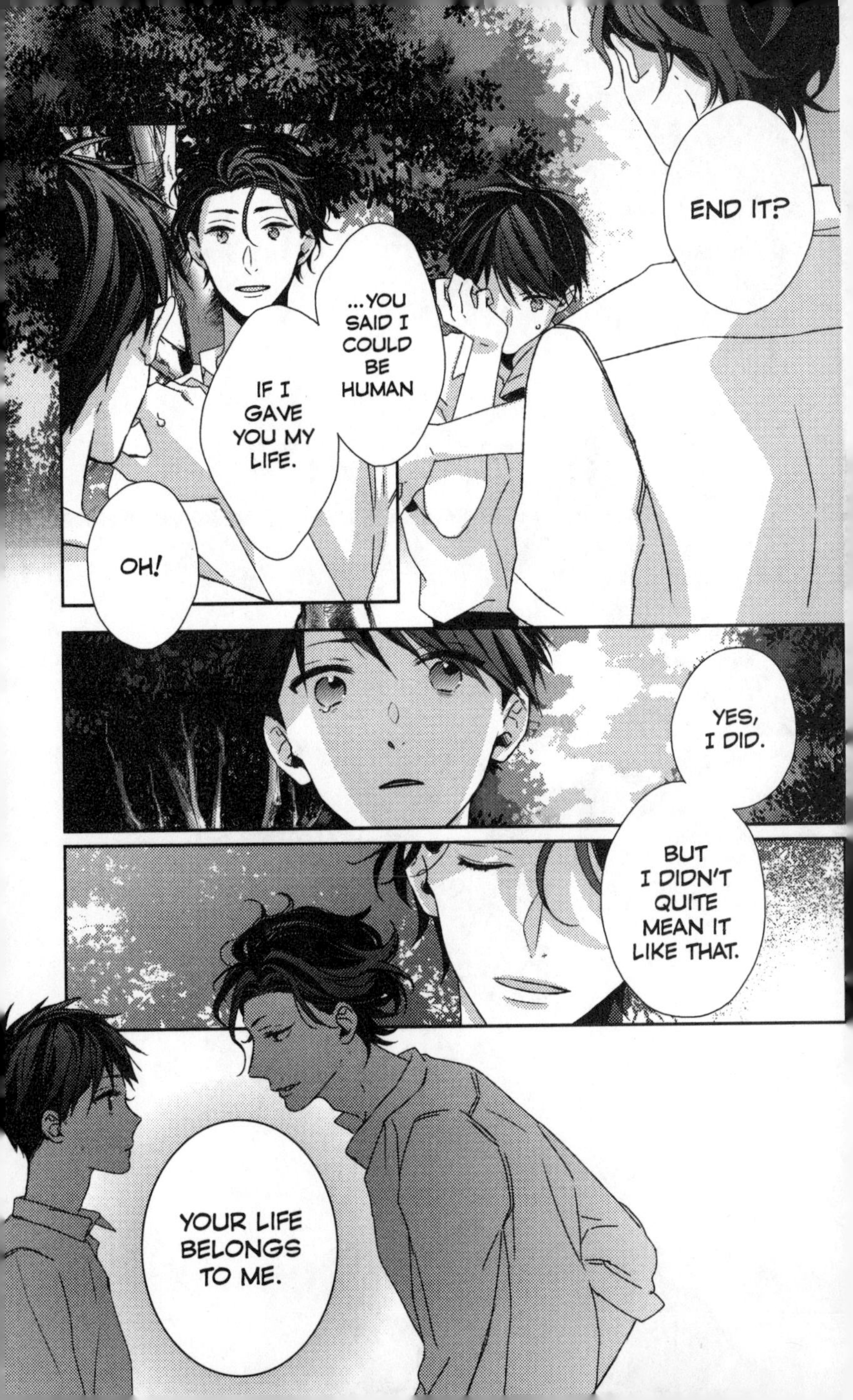
END IT?
...YOU SAID I COULD BE HUMAN
IF I GAVE YOU MY LIFE.
OH!
YES, I DID.
BUT I DIDN'T QUITE MEAN IT LIKE THAT.
YOUR LIFE BELONGS TO ME.

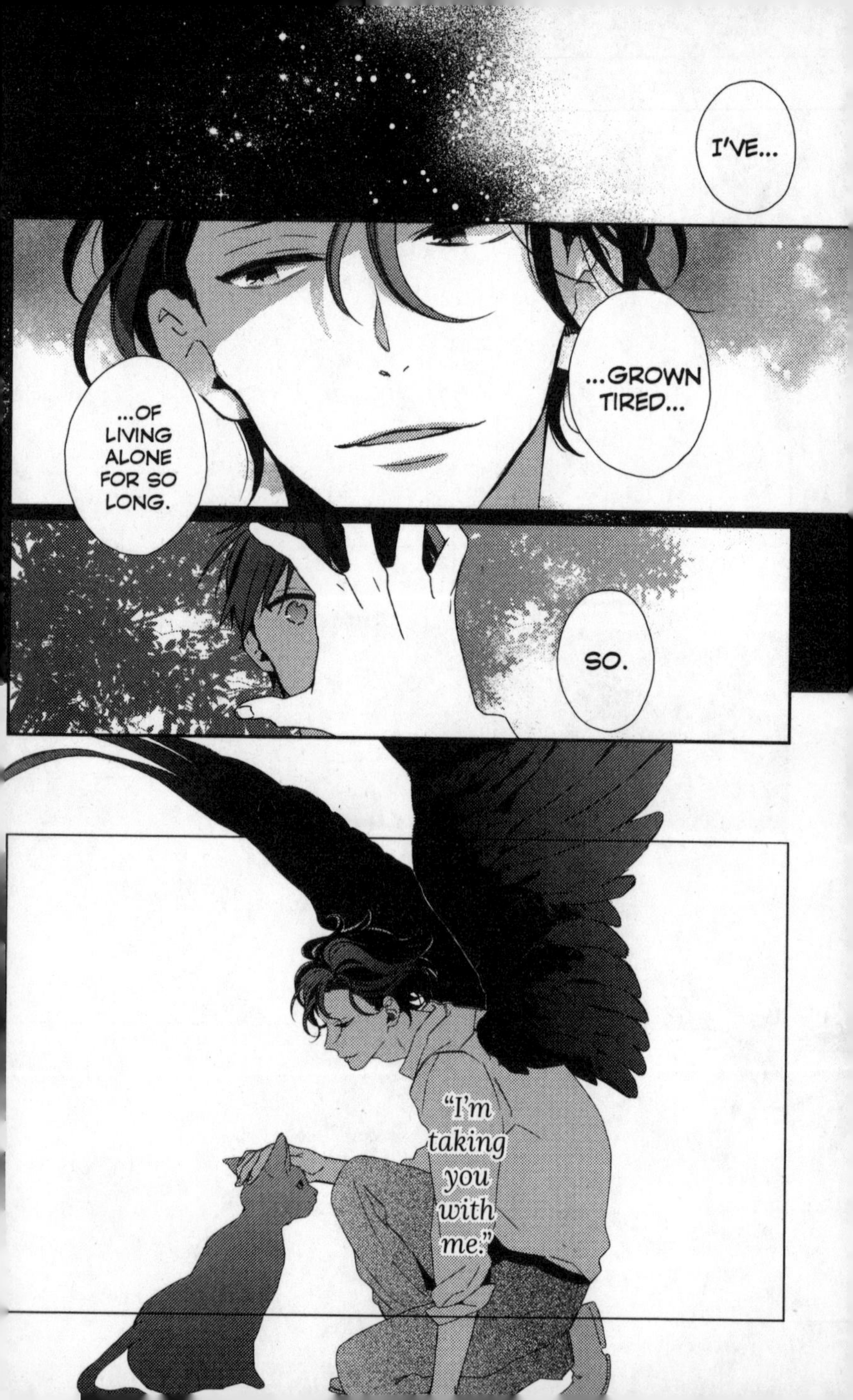
I'VE...
...GROWN TIRED...
...OF LIVING ALONE FOR SO LONG.
SO.
“I'm taking you with me.”

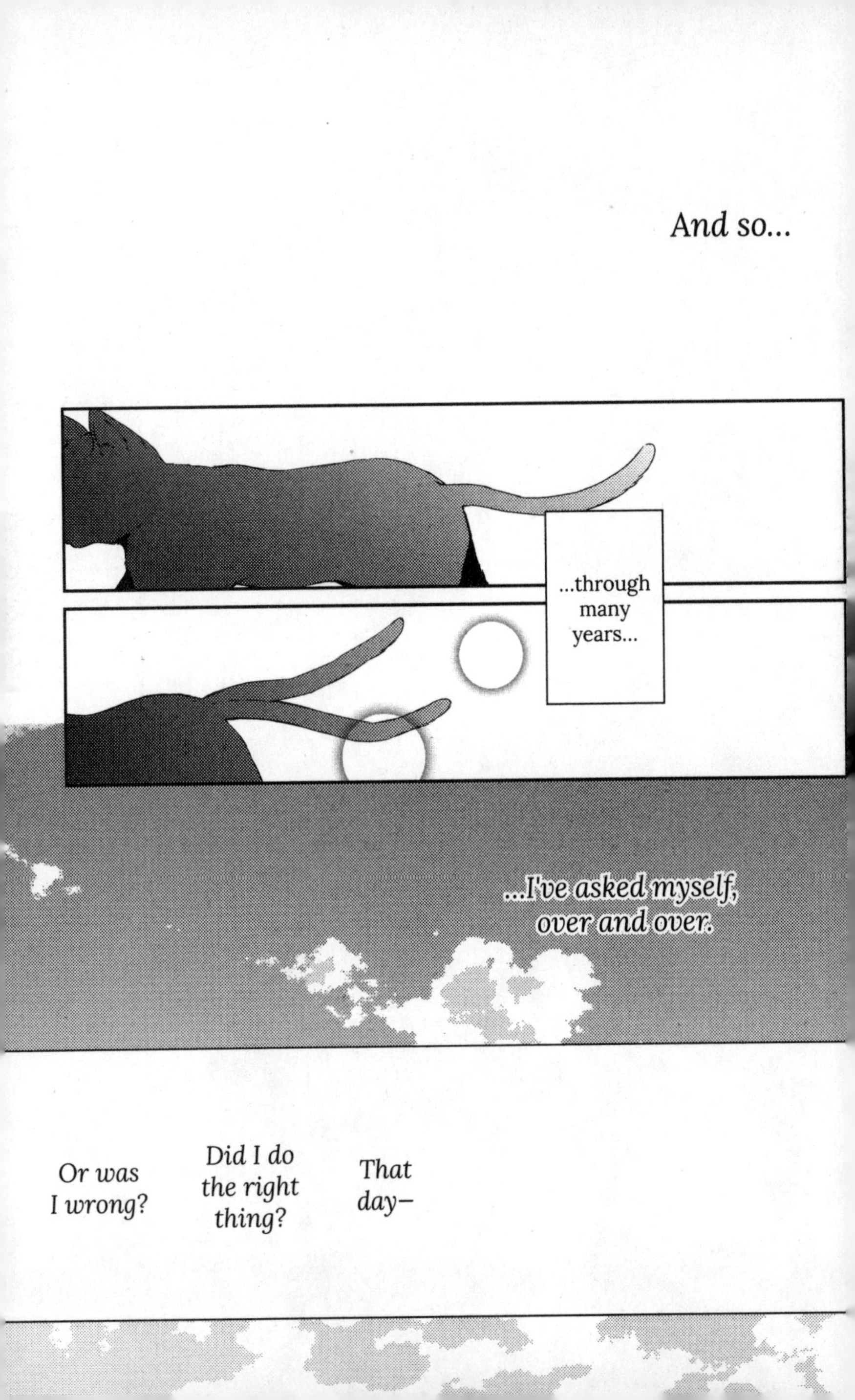

And so...

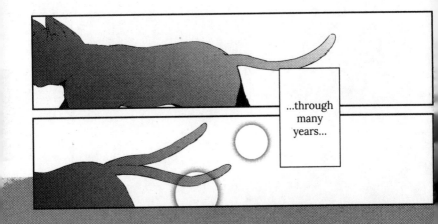

...through
many
years...

...I've asked myself,
over and over.

Or was
I wrong?

Did I do
the right
thing?

That
day—

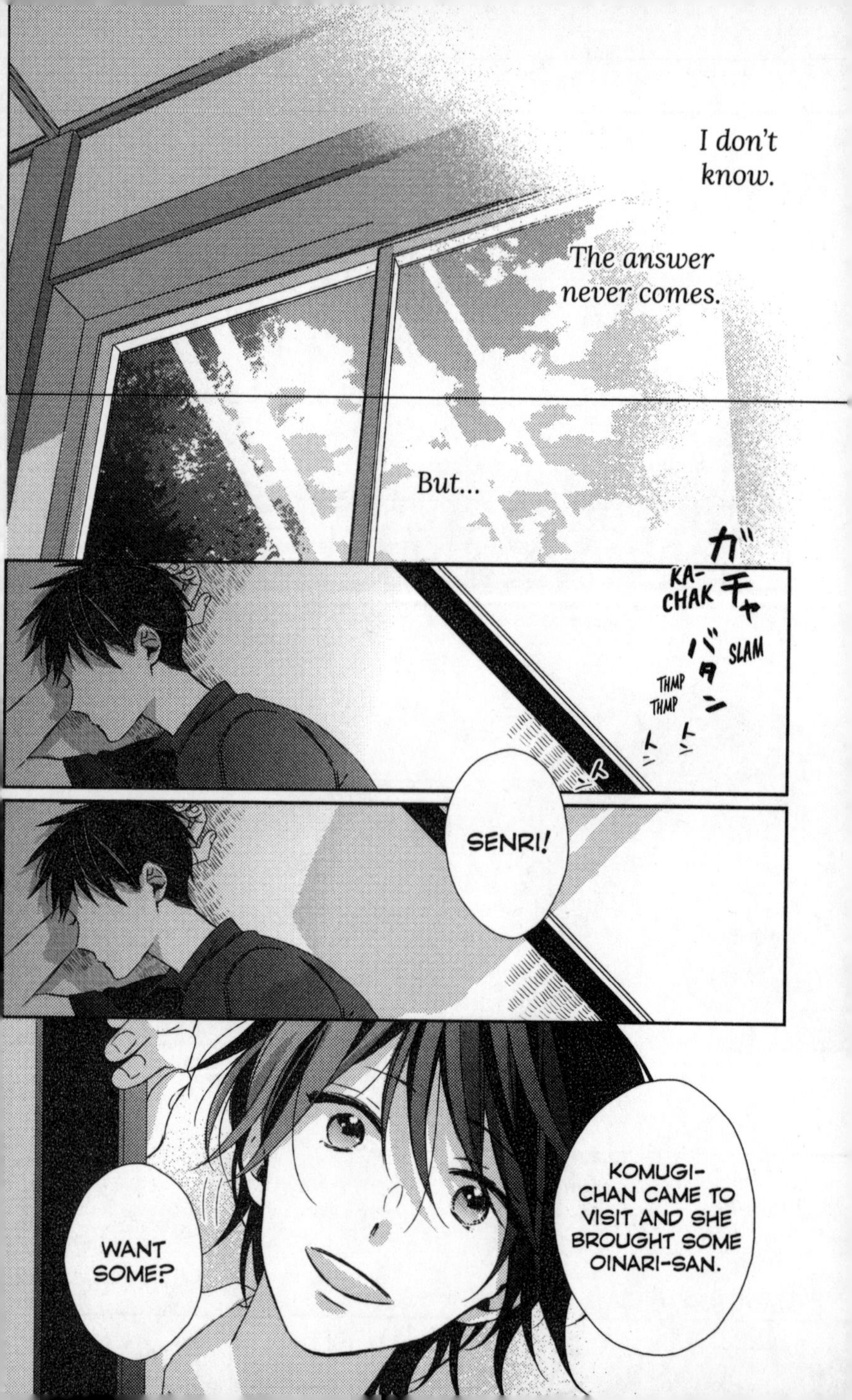
I don't know.
The answer never comes.
But...
ガチャ
KA-CHAK
バタン
SLAM
トントン
THMP THMP
SENRI!
KOMUGI-CHAN CAME TO VISIT AND SHE BROUGHT SOME OINARI-SAN.
WANT SOME?

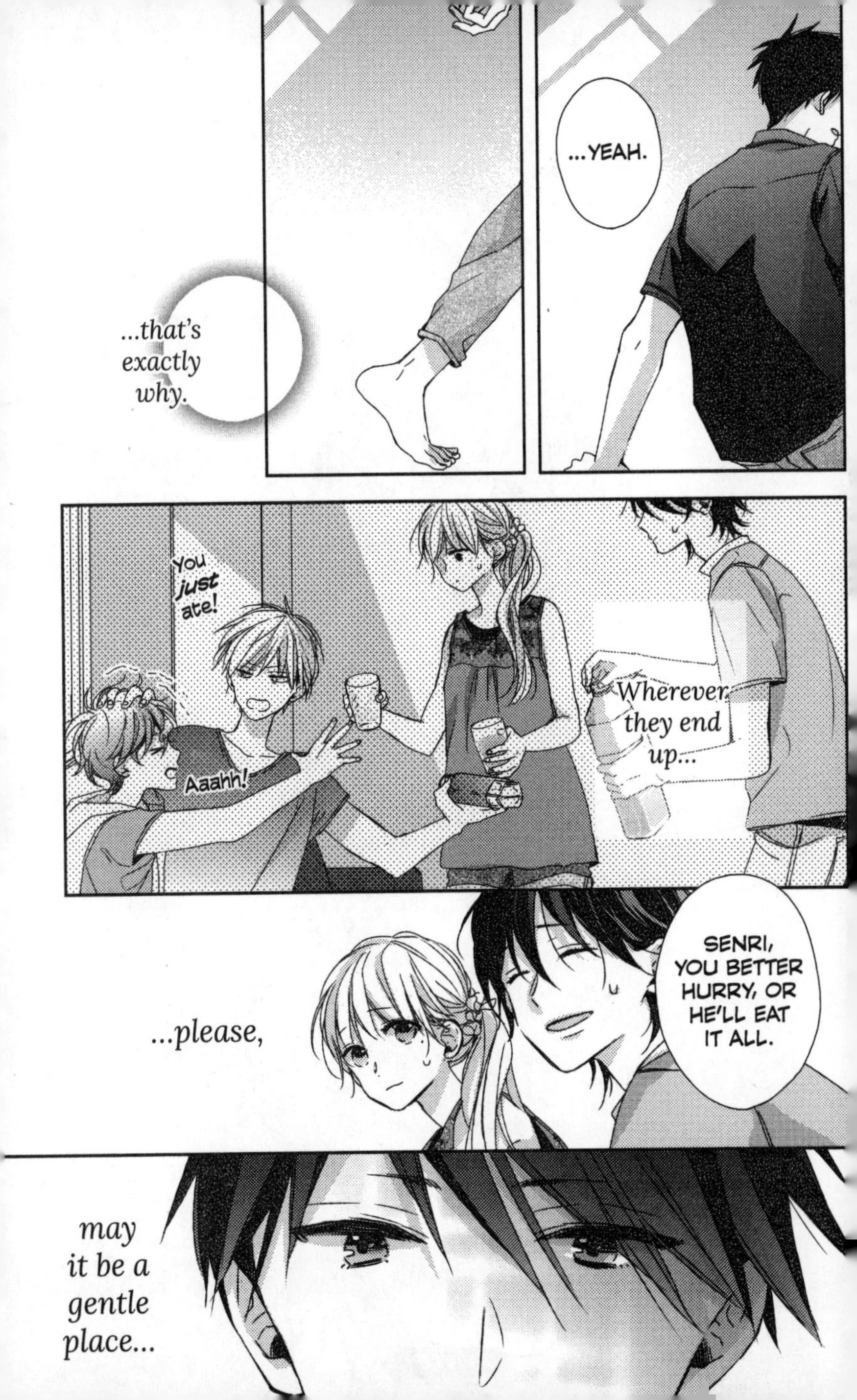
...YEAH.
...that's exactly why.
Wherever they end up...
You just ate!
Aaahh!
SENRI, YOU BETTER HURRY, OR HE'LL EAT IT ALL.
...please,
may it be a gentle place...

I can't help but pray for that.

The End

That Wolf-Boy is Mine!

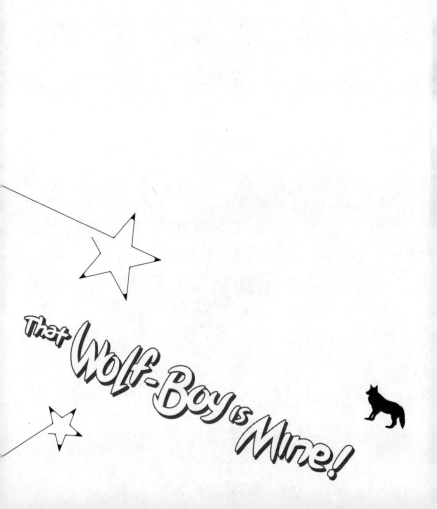

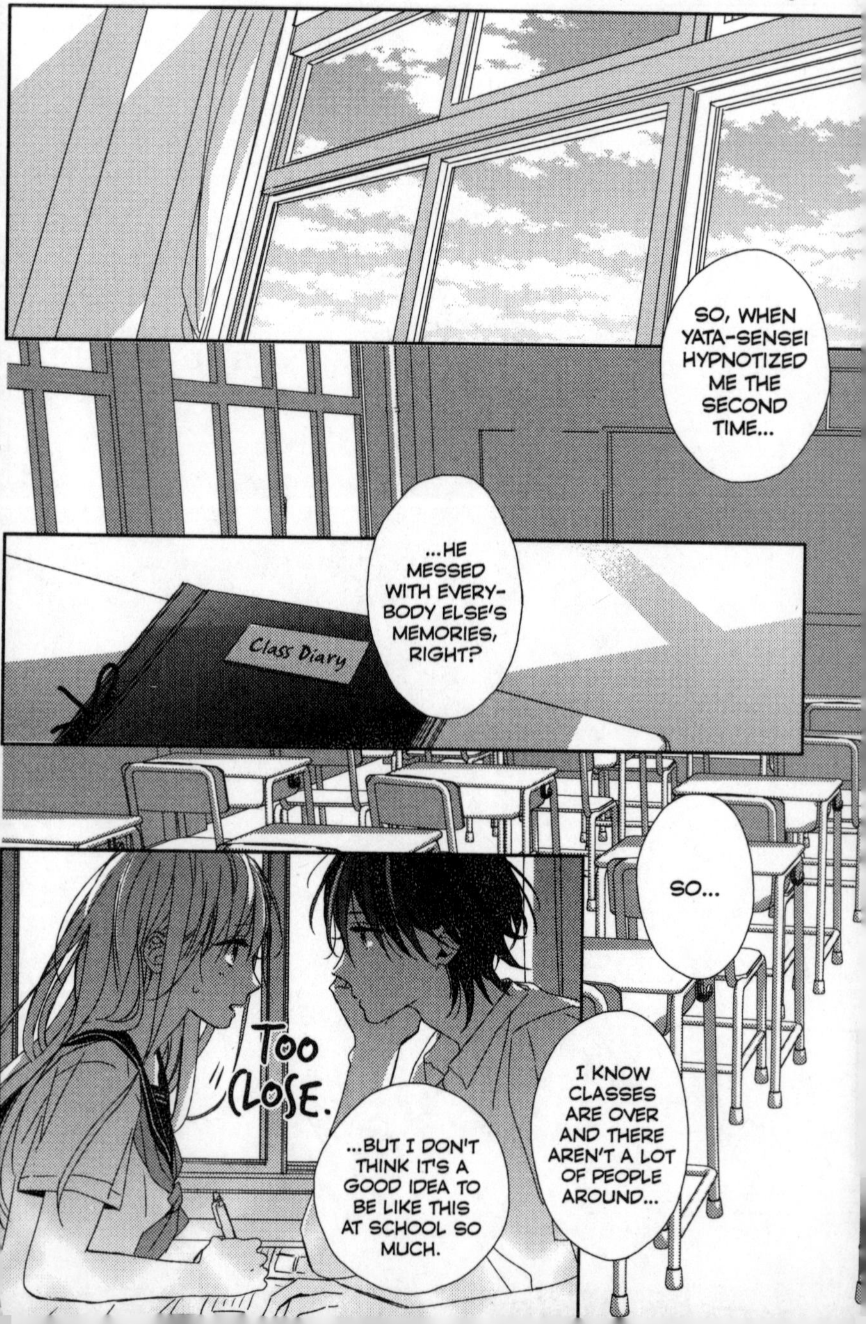
SO, WHEN YATA-SENSEI HYPNOTIZED ME THE SECOND TIME...
...HE MESSED WITH EVERY-BODY ELSE'S MEMORIES, RIGHT?
Class Diary
SO...
I KNOW CLASSES ARE OVER AND THERE AREN'T A LOT OF PEOPLE AROUND...
...BUT I DON'T THINK IT'S A GOOD IDEA TO BE LIKE THIS AT SCHOOL SO MUCH.
TOO CLOSE.

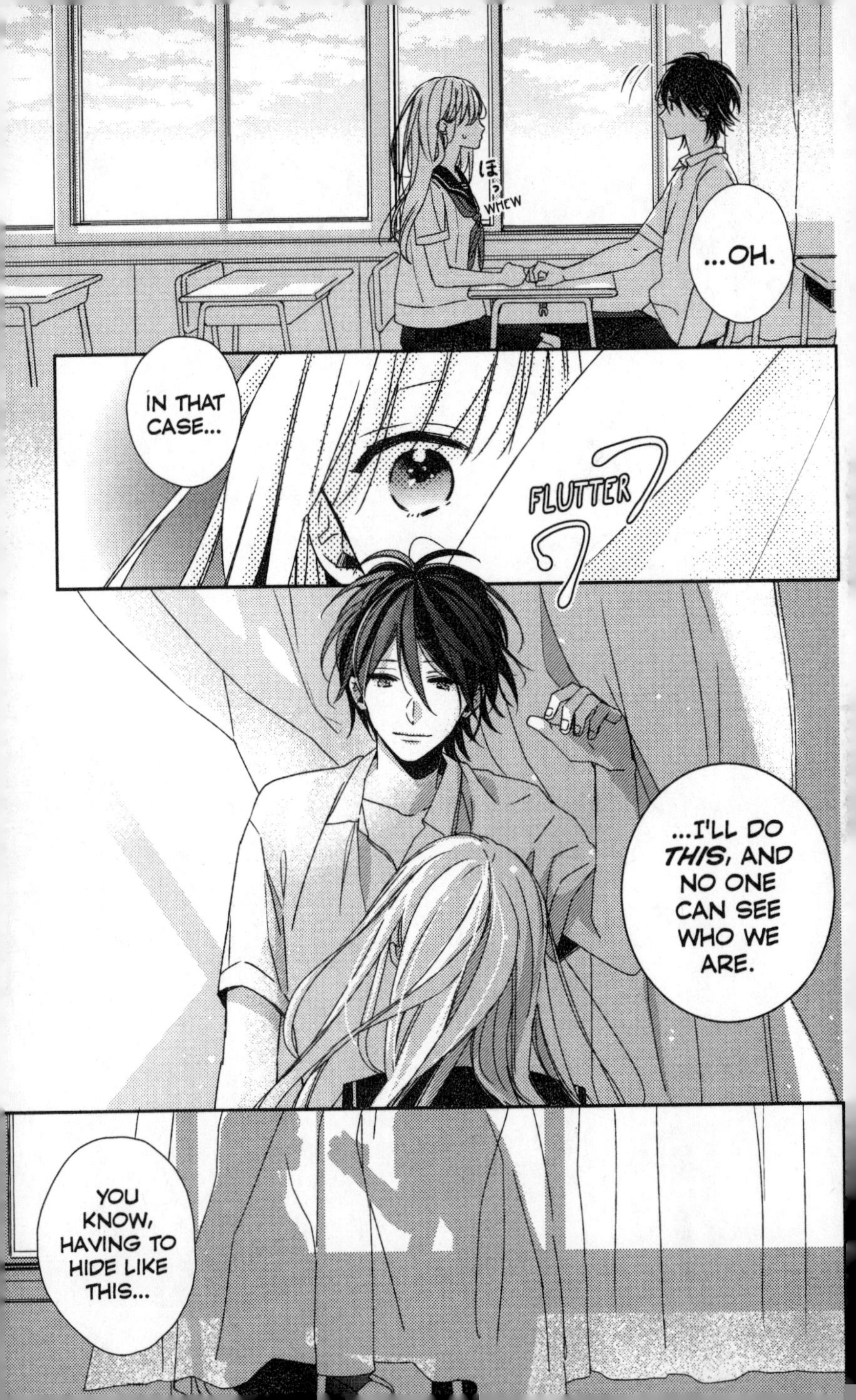
...OH.
ほっ
WHEW
IN THAT CASE...
FLUTTER
...I'LL DO *THIS*, AND NO ONE CAN SEE WHO WE ARE.
YOU KNOW, HAVING TO HIDE LIKE THIS...

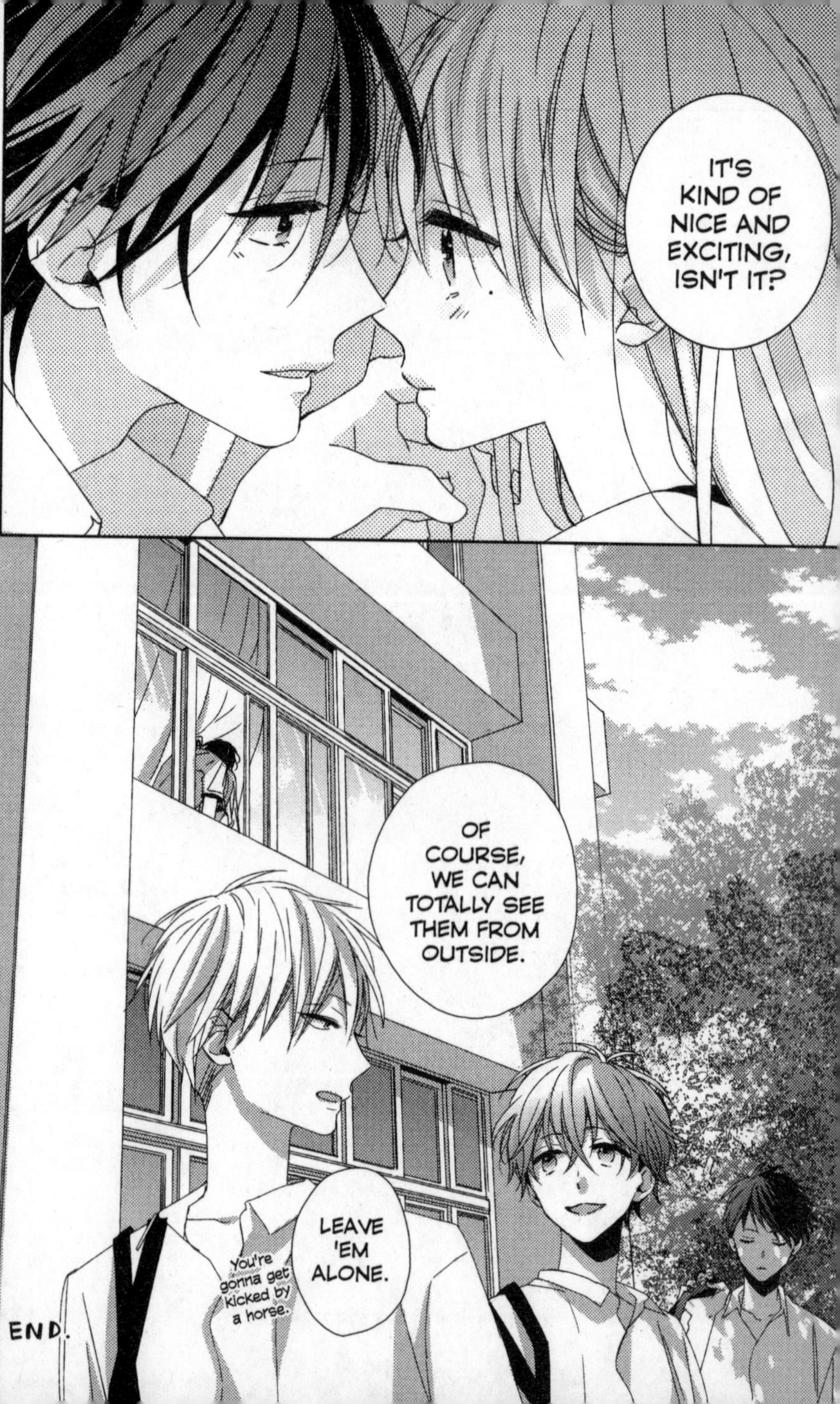
IT'S KIND OF NICE AND EXCITING, ISN'T IT?
OF COURSE, WE CAN TOTALLY SEE THEM FROM OUTSIDE.
LEAVE 'EM ALONE.
You're gonna get kicked by a horse.
END.

Afterword

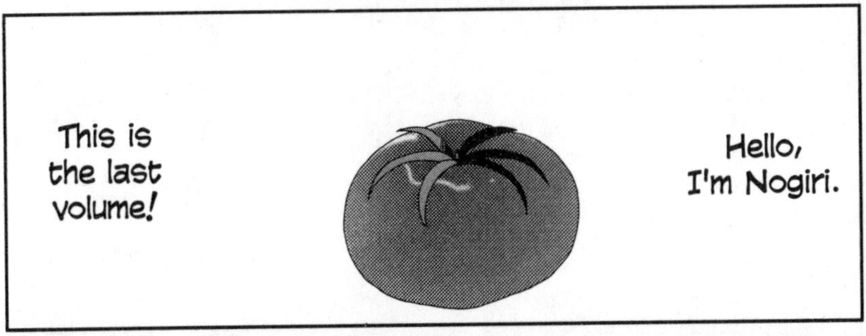
Hello, I'm Nogiri.
This is the last volume!

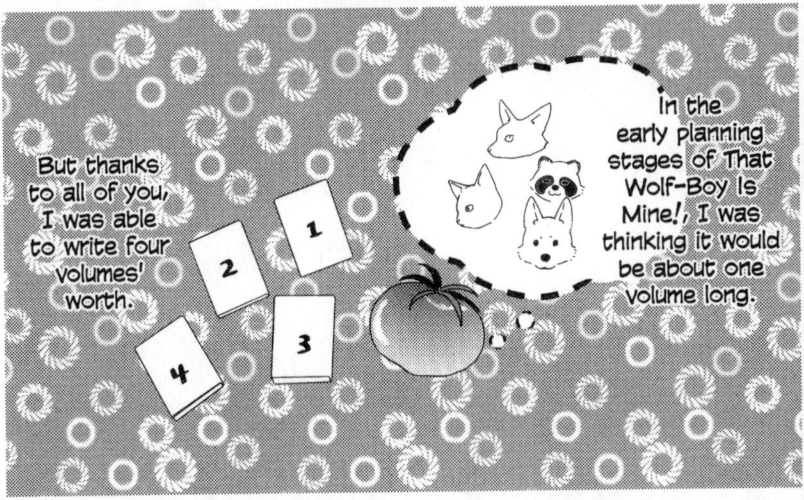
In the early planning stages of That Wolf-Boy Is Mine!, I was thinking it would be about one volume long.
1
2
3
4
But thanks to all of you, I was able to write four volumes' worth.

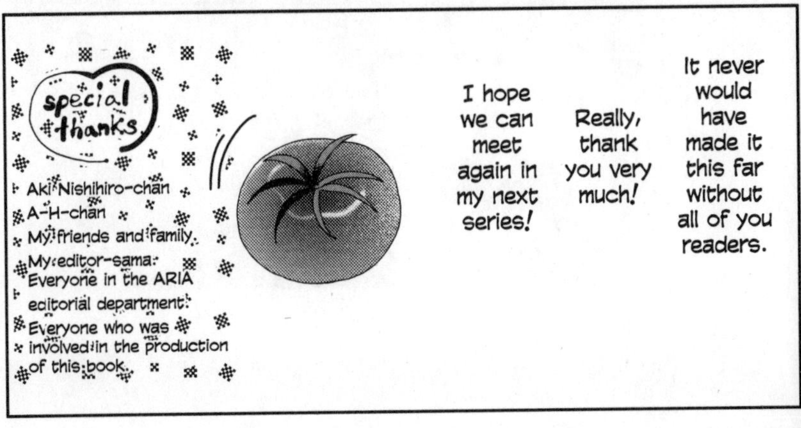
It never would have made it this far without all of you readers.
Really, thank you very much!
I hope we can meet again in my next series!
special thanks
Aki Nishihiro-chan
A-H-chan
My friends and family
My editor-sama
Everyone in the ARIA editorial department
Everyone who was involved in the production of this book

Translation Notes

Sneaky little tanuki, page 63
It might be interesting to note that in the Japanese text, Komugi only calls Aoshi a tanuki, which, as we all know, is what he is. But according to Japanese traditions, tanuki are known for being sneaky and deceptive, so it's not uncommon to call a human with those traits a "tanuki."

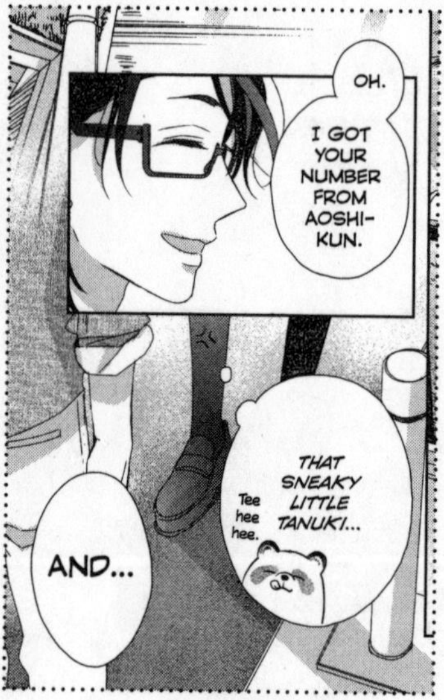
OH.
I GOT YOUR NUMBER FROM AOSHI-KUN.
THAT SNEAKY LITTLE TANUKI...
Tee hee hee.
AND...

Day duty, page 79
In Japanese schools, the students in each class take turns with certain clerical responsibilities, such as keeping the class diary and preparing materials for certain classes.

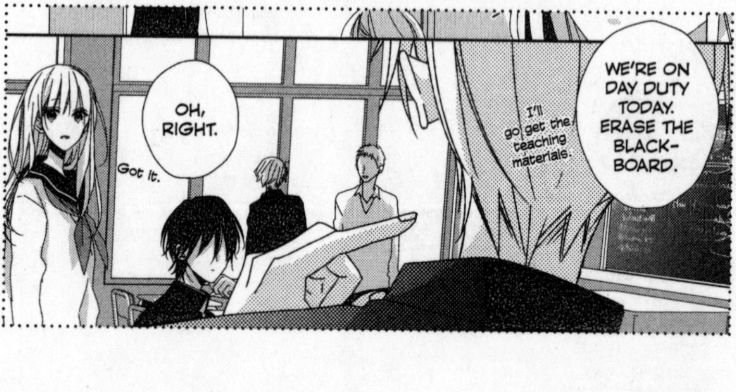
WE'RE ON DAY DUTY TODAY. ERASE THE BLACK-BOARD.
I'll go get the teaching materials.
OH, RIGHT.
Got it.

Manjū, page 103
A *manjū* is Japanese for any type of Asian bun, savory or sweet. Here, the grandparents are talking about a Japanese confection with a doughy outside, filled with something sweet. A common and traditional filling is *anko*, a sweet red bean paste.

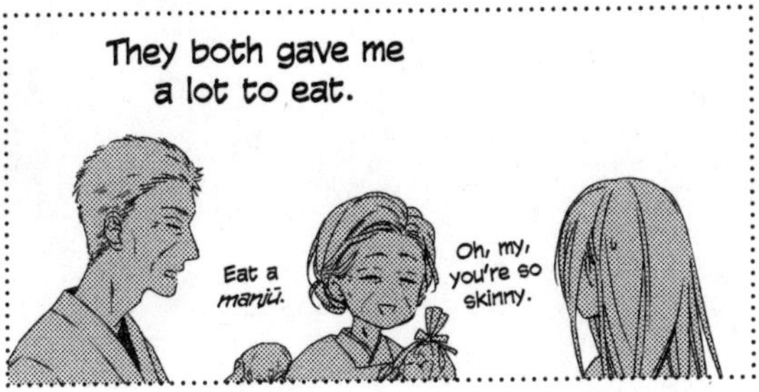
They both gave me a lot to eat.
Oh, my, you're so skinny.
Eat a manjū.

I left my son, page 127
In the original Japanese, this statement doesn't sound quite as heartless. She uses the word *azukeru*, which means "to leave **in the care of [someone],**" indicating that she didn't just abandon him in the woods; she expected that he would be taken care of somehow, or at least that's the impression she wanted to give.

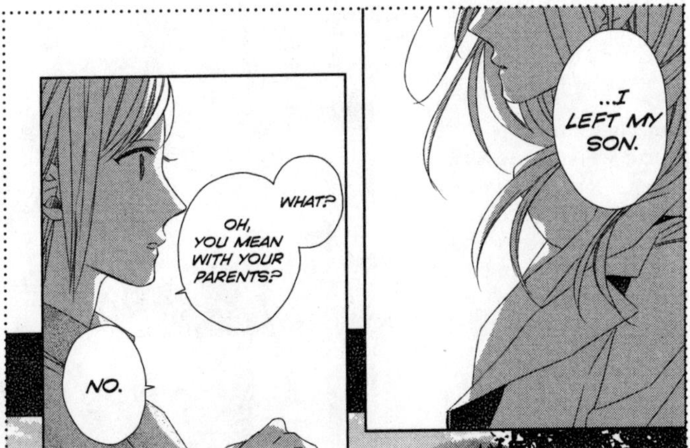
...I LEFT MY SON.
WHAT?
OH, YOU MEAN WITH YOUR PARENTS?
NO.

Translation Notes

Family Tomb, page 269
In Japan, one tombstone is often enough for one family. This is because the bodies of the deceased are usually cremated, and their ashes are placed in urns. These vessels are kept in a chamber under the tombstone.

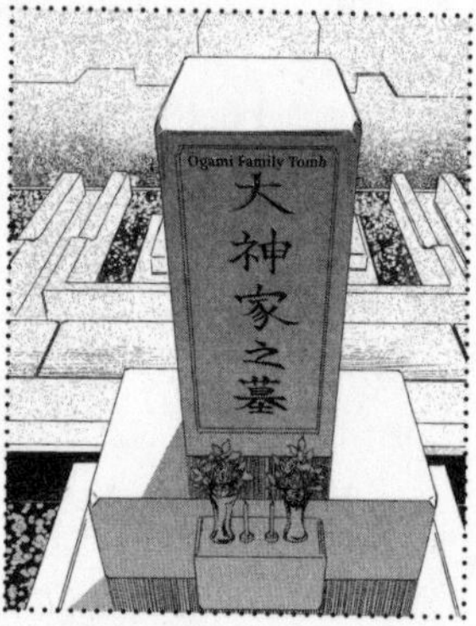
Ogami Family Tomb
大神家之墓

Kamatama udon, page 297
Kamatama udon, also known as Kagawa style, is udon in a raw egg sauce. Although the eggs will definitely offer protein, they're not exactly "meat," so with Aoshi ordering egg udon and Yū ordering udon topped with bean curd, Rin feels the need to remind them both that meat is the superior choice–especially since they're all carnivores.

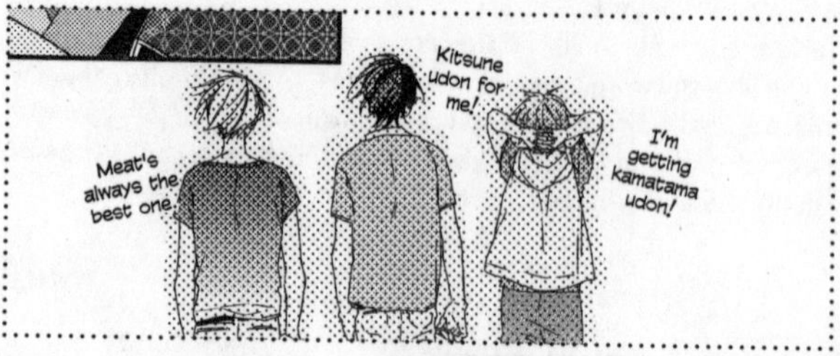
I'm getting kamatama udon!
Kitsune udon for me!
Meat's always the best one.

Ojōsan, page 301
This is a term of respect used when addressing a young woman. It is most frequently used to refer to young women from well-to-do families and implies a certain level of class or social status.

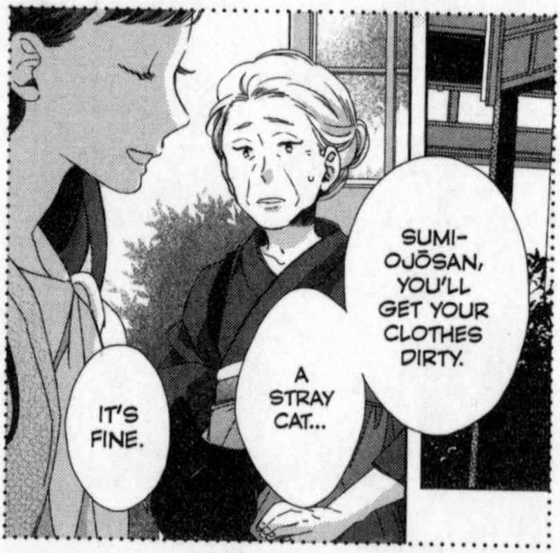
SUMI-OJŌSAN, YOU'LL GET YOUR CLOTHES DIRTY.
A STRAY CAT...
IT'S FINE.

Senrikō, page 303
This is the name of a type of cherry blossom. It means "fragrant over a long distance."

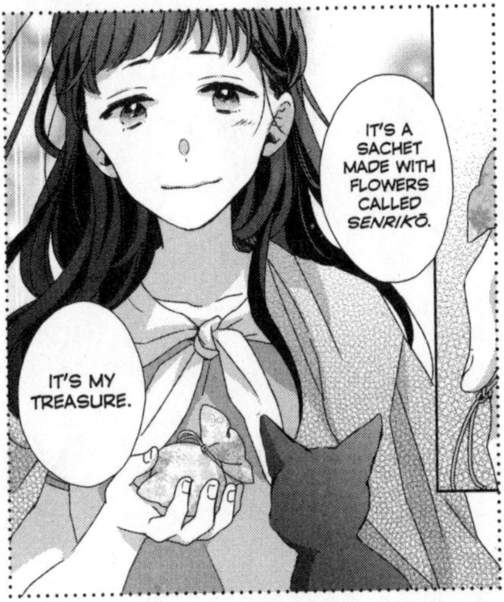
IT'S A SACHET MADE WITH FLOWERS CALLED SENRIKŌ.
IT'S MY TREASURE.

Kicked by a horse, page 338
According to a saying from the Edo era, this is the fate awaiting any who would be so rude as to thwart a couple who are in love.

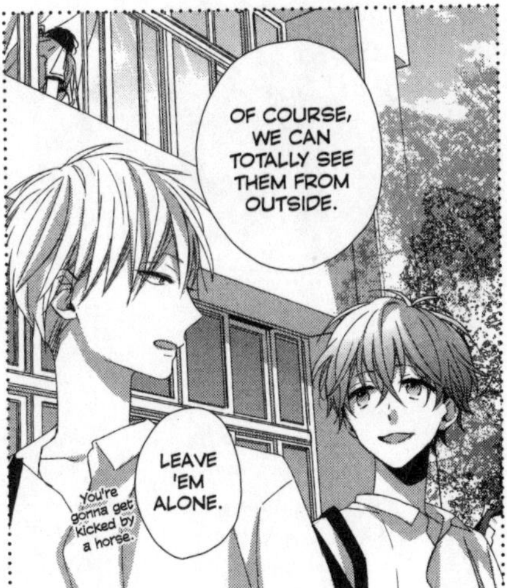
OF COURSE, WE CAN TOTALLY SEE THEM FROM OUTSIDE.
LEAVE 'EM ALONE.
You're gonna get kicked by a horse.

THE WORLD OF CLAMP!

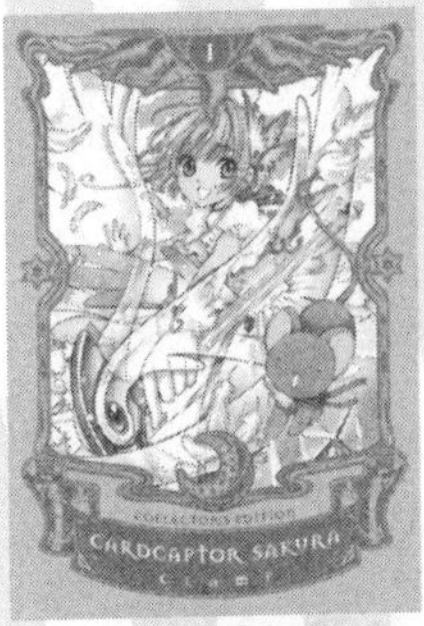
CARDCAPTOR SAKURA

Cardcaptor Sakura Collector's Edition

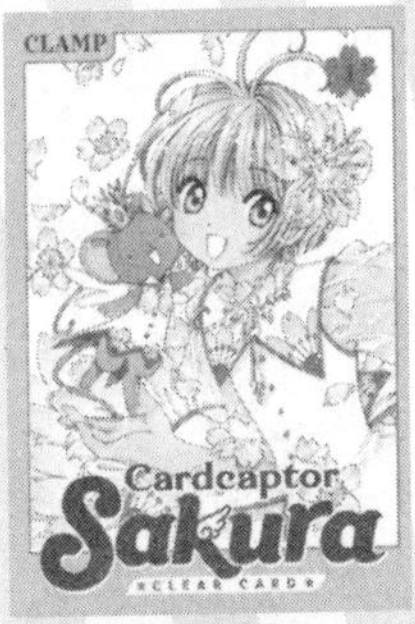
CLAMP
Cardcaptor
Sakura
CLEAR CARD

Cardcaptor Sakura: Clear Card

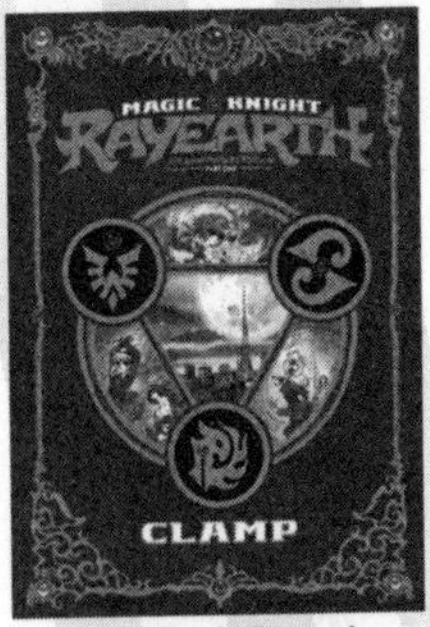
MAGIC KNIGHT
RAYEARTH
CLAMP

Magic Knight Rayearth 25th Anniversary Box Set

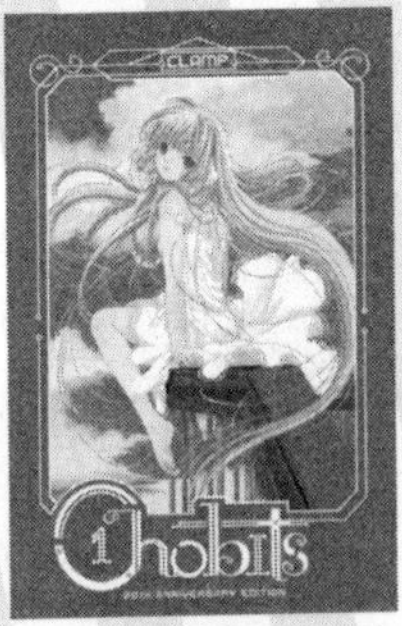
CLAMP
Chobits
1

Chobits

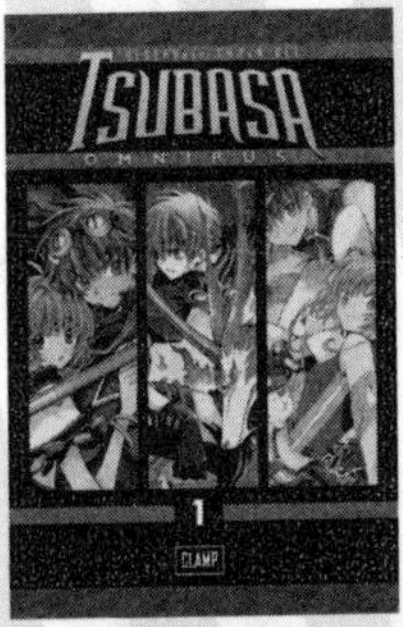
TSUBASA
1
CLAMP

TSUBASA Omnibus

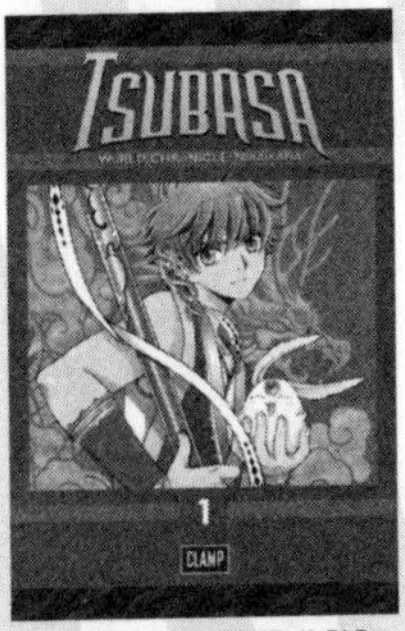
TSUBASA
1
CLAMP

TSUBASA WoRLD CHRoNiCLE

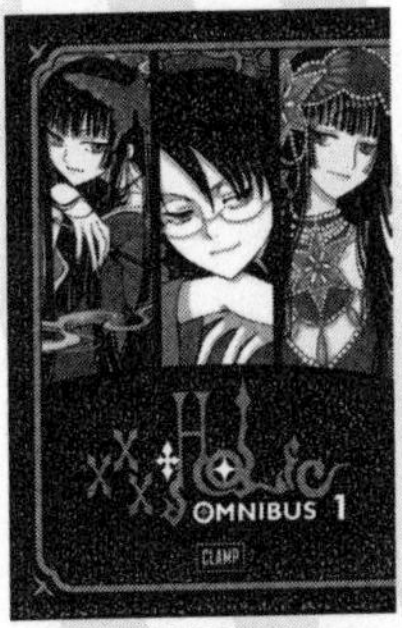
xxxHOLiC
OMNIBUS 1
CLAMP

xxxHOLiC Omnibus

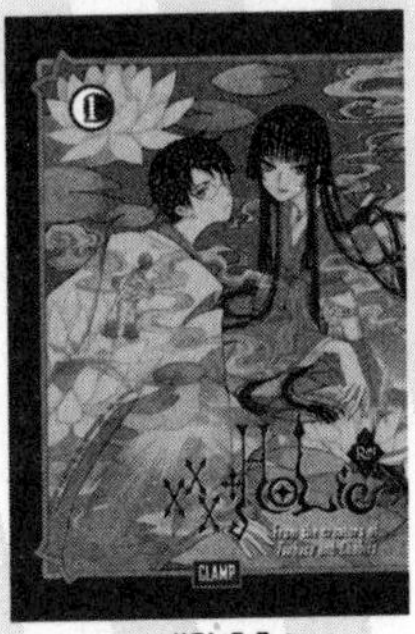
xxxHOLiC
CLAMP

xxxHOLiC Rei

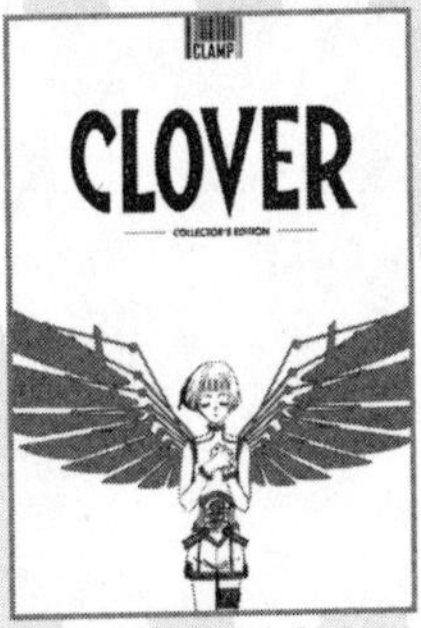
CLAMP
CLOVER
COLLECTOR'S EDITION

CLOVER Collector's Edition

KC KODANSHA COMICS

Kodansha Comics welcomes you to explore the expansive world of CLAMP, the all-female artist collective that has produced some of the most acclaimed manga of the century. Our growing catalog includes icons like *Cardcaptor Sakura* and *Magic Knight Rayearth*, each crafted with CLAMP's one-of-a-kind style and characters!

Young characters and steampunk setting, like *Howl's Moving Castle* and *Battle Angel Alita*

Beyond the Clouds © 2018 Nicke / Ki-oon

A boy with a talent for machines and a mysterious girl whose wings he's fixed will take you beyond the clouds! In the tradition of the high-flying, resonant adventure stories of Studio Ghibli comes a gorgeous tale about the longing of young hearts for adventure and friendship!

The adorable new odd-couple cat comedy manga from the creator of the beloved *Chi's Sweet Home*, in full color!

Praise for Chi's Sweet Home

"Nearly impossible to turn away... a true all-ages title that anyone, young or old, cat lover or not, will enjoy. The stories will bring a smile to your face and warm your heart."

—School Library Journal

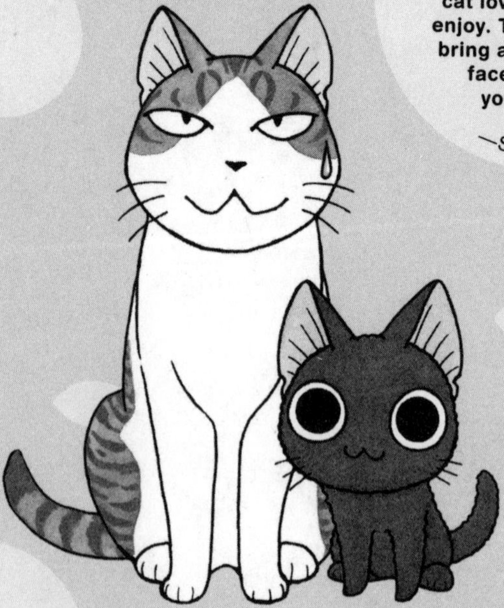

Sue & Tai-chan

Konami Kanata

Sue is an aging housecat who's looking forward to living out her life in peace... but her plans change when the mischievous black tomcat Tai-chan enters the picture! Hey! Sue never signed up to be a catsitter! *Sue & Tai-chan* is the latest from the reigning meow-narch of cute kitty comics, Konami Kanata.

PERFECT WORLD

Rie Aruga

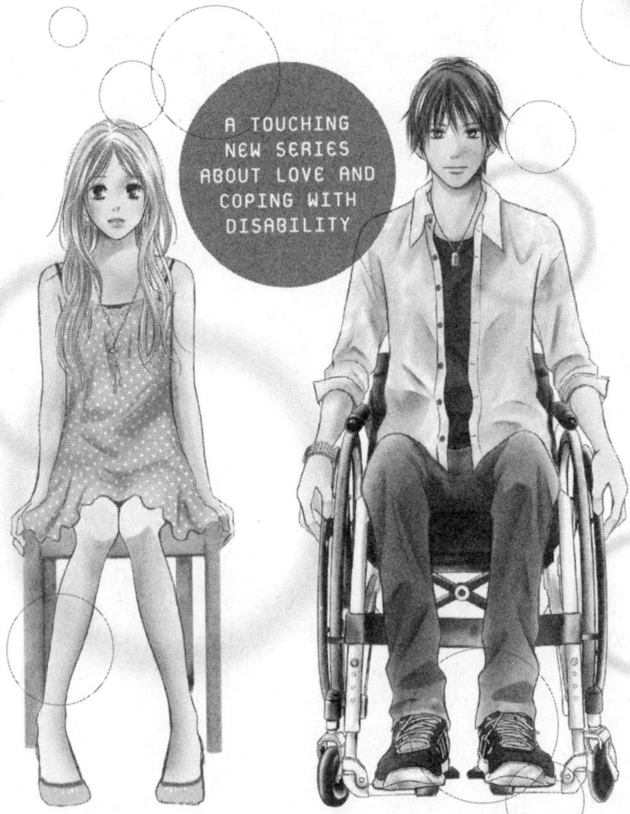
A TOUCHING NEW SERIES ABOUT LOVE AND COPING WITH DISABILITY

An office party reunites Tsugumi with her high school crush Itsuki. He's realized his dream of becoming an architect, but along the way, he experienced a spinal injury that put him in a wheelchair. Now Tsugumi's rekindled feelings will butt up against prejudices she never considered — and Itsuki will have to decide if he's ready to let someone into his heart...

"Depicts with great delicacy and courage the difficulties some with disabilities experience getting involved in romantic relationships... Rie Aruga refuses to romanticize, pushing her heroine to face the reality of disability. She invites her readers to the same tasks of empathy, knowledge and recognition."
—Slate.fr

"An important entry [in manga romance]... The emotional core of both plot and characters indicates thoughtfulness... [Aruga's] research is readily apparent in the text and artwork, making this feel like a real story."
—Anime News Network

KC KODANSHA COMICS

Knight of the Ice ©Yayoi Ogawa

SKATING THRILLS AND ICY CHILLS WITH THIS NEW TINGLY ROMANCE SERIES!

A rom-com on ice, perfect for fans of *Princess Jellyfish* and *Wotakoi*. Kokoro is the talk of the figure-skating world, winning trophies and hearts. But little do they know... he's actually a huge nerd! From the beloved creator of *You're My Pet* (*Tramps Like Us*).

Chitose is a serious young woman, working for the health magazine *SASSO*. Or at least, she would be, if she wasn't constantly getting distracted by her childhood friend, international figure skating star Kokoro Kijinami! In the public eye and on the ice, Kokoro is a gallant, flawless knight, but behind his glittery costumes and breathtaking spins lies a secret: He's actually a hopelessly romantic otaku, who can only land his quad jumps when Chitose is on hand to recite a spell from his favorite magical girl anime!

That Wolf-Boy is Mine!

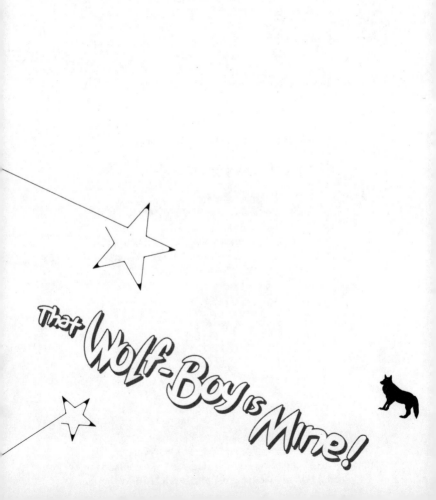

That Wolf-Boy is Mine! Omnibus 2 is a work of fiction. Names, characters, places, and incidents are the products of the author's imagination or are used fictitiously. Any resemblance to actual events, locales, or persons, living or dead, is entirely coincidental.

A Kodansha Comics Trade Paperback Original
That Wolf-Boy is Mine! Omnibus 2 copyright © 2015-2016 Hiro Mashima
English translation copyright © 2021 Hiro Mashima

All rights reserved.

Published in the United States by Kodansha Comics, an imprint of
Kodansha USA Publishing, LLC, New York.

Publication rights for this English edition arranged through
Kodansha Ltd., Tokyo.

First published in Japan in 2015-2016 by Kodansha Ltd., Tokyo.

ISBN 978-1-64651-368-0

Printed in the United States of America.

www.kodansha.us

2nd Printing
Translation: Alethea Nibley & Athena Nibley
Lettering: Sara Linsley
Editing: Haruko Hashimoto, Alejandro Arbona
Kodansha Comics edition cover design by Phil Balsman

Publisher: Kiichiro Sugawara

Director of publishing services: Ben Applegate
Associate director of operations: Stephen Pakula
Publishing services managing editors: Madison Salters, Alanna Ruse
Production managers: Emi Lotto, Angela Zurlo